D1084425

Nickel reads the Quran primarily as a rhetorical text engaged in polemics, mostly against Jews and Christians. His reading is done largely through the lens of – and to some extent in response to – classical Muslim exegesis, though he does not often refer to the classical *occasions of the revelation* as the Quran's exclusive historical setting. This, in my view, is very commendable, for it allows him to adopt a fresh reading of the text. He does, nevertheless, often assume this classical rhetorical reading, and in this sense his commentary is often a response to classical interpretation.

Nickel's reading resists the temptation of being driven by a polemical agenda, and indeed he allows himself to be positively surprised by the Quran's primary meaning, even when he shows awareness of more classical polemical readings. By doing so, Nickel reflects a desire to discern in the Quran a more positive and apologetic stance towards earlier scriptures and their recipients, removing himself from a negative polemic. By doing so, he is, in my view, imminently fair to the text.

The occasional articles on specific issues, interspersed throughout his commentary, such as on the tampering with the scriptures, *jihad*, apocryphal references in the Quran, the death of Jesus, manuscripts of the Quran, or the Quran's language of love, are useful to varying degrees. Some contain a more polemical edge than others, reflecting more or less faithfulness to the spirit of the Quran.

Overall, Nickel's Christian commentary on the Quran is a very helpful work that offers the contemporary English reader a useful entry into a text that can otherwise appear as rather opaque to the uninitiated.

—MARTIN ACCAD, associate professor of Islamic studies,
Arab Baptist Theological Seminary in Lebanon and Fuller
Theological Seminary in Pasadena, California

Dr. Gordon Nickel displays an encyclopedic intimacy with the Quran and the tradition of classical commentary that ambushes its margins. He brings a committed Christian perspective without compromising high standards of detached scholarly engagement. At times combative, always clear and eloquent, and never evasive, this learned commentary on the entire Islamic scripture will both provoke and inform thoughtful Muslim and Christian readers alike. Believers eager to probe and question but not too ready with stereotypical answers shall find in it a treasure of insights.

Dr. Nickel notes and assesses the Quran's high "Quranology," that is, its many self-referential verses about its uniquely miraculous status. He ultimately rejects the book's claims and finds its assessment of its two rival faiths exaggerated and unwarranted. He emphasizes that the Quran, despite appearances,

endorses the scriptural and textual integrity of its two revealed biblical prede-
cessors. However, he concludes that despite its confident claims to the contrary,
the Quran fails to be an adequate sequel to the Bible.

Dr. Nickel has placed both Muslim and Christian scholars in his debt with
this remarkable work of Christian advocacy, offered in the spirit of Christian
humility and courtesy. This is a major contribution to critical quranic scholarship, a discipline not found among the traditional sciences of the Quran
approved by Islamic orthodoxy.

—SHABBIR AKHTAR, faculty of theology, University of
Oxford, author of *The New Testament in Muslim Eyes*

The text of the Quran is reproduced here in the excellent translation of Droge
and supplemented by a substantial introduction, many explanatory notes,
and several focus articles that shed light on various key themes of the Quran.
Gordon Nickel has done very fine work in providing the Christian reader
precious keys for approaching the quranic text and interreligious dialogue
with Muslims.

—GUILLAUME DYE, professor in Islamic
studies, Université libre de Bruxelles

This admirably comprehensive commentary explains the contents of the
Quran to non-Muslim readers. In analyzing and interpreting key verses and
passages that address the "People of the Book," namely Christians and Jews,
Gordon Nickel, along with his team of top-ranking scholars, brilliantly opens
up the varied historical contexts, meanings, and implications of the Quran to
a wider readership. Muslims and non-Muslims alike will benefit immensely
from the erudition and exegesis that this commentary manifests, resulting in
a more accurate understanding of how Islam fundamentally stands apart from
the other Abrahamic faiths.

—GRANT HAVERS, chair, Department of
Philosophy, Trinity Western University

One can hardly think of a more important book for Christians to appear this
year. This translation of the Quran contains commentary by Gordon Nickel,
a foremost scholar of Islam who lived among Muslims for many years. The
commentary is immensely informed, fair, and accessible. Every class on Islam
ought to use this text.

—GERALD R. MCDERMOTT, Anglican chair of divinity, director
of the Institute of Anglican Studies, Beeson Divinity School

In this landmark study, Dr. Nickel carefully explains the meaning of the text of the Quran for non-Muslim readers. Dr. Nickel is a highly respected authority on the Quran, and his knowledge of its content, historical context, and the history of its interpretation by Muslim commentators is astounding. He writes with a gracious respect for the Quran and for Muslims, but he also raises important questions for thoughtful readers to consider. This is a treasure trove of information and insight, and it will undoubtedly become the standard work on the subject for years to come.

—HAROLD NETLAND, professor of philosophy of religion and intercultural studies, Trinity Evangelical Divinity School

Gordon D. Nickel's Christian commentary on the Quran fills a gap in the Christian book market, allowing non-Arabic speakers to get deep insight into the contents and theology of the Quran. All 114 surahs of the Quran are translated and commented on with a focus on quranic statements about Christianity. This much-desired work is the fruit of a life-long study of Islam and interaction with Muslim friends – a must-have for all who aim at obtaining a deeper understanding of Islam and engaging with Muslims.

—CHRISTINE SCHIRRMACHER, professor of Islamic studies and Middle Eastern languages, Department of Oriental and Asian Studies, Universität Bonn

In this commentary on the scripture of Islam, Gordon Nickel has performed a great service for Christians who wish to know about Islam. The Quran presents distinctive accounts of stories familiar from the Bible and directly denies fundamental Christian doctrines. Nickel's unfailingly respectful yet unmistakably Christian responses present the similarities and differences between the quranic and biblical traditions with unflinching directness. He has produced a reliable and accessible resource for both students studying the Quran and general readers.

—DAVID THOMAS, FBA, emeritus professor of Christianity and Islam, University of Birmingham, United Kingdom

THE
QURAN
WITH
CHRISTIAN
COMMENTARY

THE QURAN
WITH
CHRISTIAN
COMMENTARY

A GUIDE TO UNDERSTANDING
THE SCRIPTURE
OF ISLAM

GORDON D. NICKEL

J. DUDLEY WOODBERRY, CONSULTING EDITOR

Quran Translation by A. J. Droge

ZONDERVAN ACADEMIC

The Quran with Christian Commentary
Commentary: Copyright © 2020 by Gordon D. Nickel
Quran translation: Copyright © 2013 by Equinox Publishing Ltd

ISBN 978-0-310-53472-3 (hardcover)

ISBN 978-0-310-53473-0 (ebook)

Requests for information should be addressed to:
Zondervan, *3900 Sparks Dr. SE, Grand Rapids, Michigan 49546*

Quran text taken from *The Qur'ān: A New Annotated Translation* by A. J. Droge. Used by permission of Equinox Publishing Ltd 2013.

Cover design: Studio Gearbox
Cover photo: © Ilona Ignatova / Shutterstock
Interior design: Kait Lamphere

Printed in the United States of America

20 21 22 23 24 25 26 27 28 29 30 /LSC/ 18 17 16 15 14 13 12 11 10 9 8 7 6 5 4 3 2 1

Contents

Acknowledgments

I am very thankful to Zondervan for giving me this opportunity to write what I have learned through academic study and teaching of the Quran and through conversations with Muslims and Christians living in Muslim societies. Zondervan editor Madison Trammel provided helpful guidance throughout the writing of this commentary.

Friends from Mennonite Brethren churches have supported much of my research and work since first giving me the chance to study Islam at the School of Oriental and African Studies in London. These friends continued to support me during the past three years of writing this commentary, during which I also taught at the South Asia Institute of Advanced Christian Studies in Bangalore, India.

I want to thank the students to whom I have taught courses on the Quran in Pakistan, India, Malaysia, Canada, and the United States. I don't know whether my teaching met your expectations, students, but I know that I enjoyed getting to know you and interacting with your written assignments.

Of the many friends who have encouraged and supported me over the years, I would like to acknowledge three in particular: Harold Jantz, Andrew Rippin, and Gwenyth Nickel.

Harold Jantz supervised my first work as a writer for a denominational fortnightly and became a kind of "good uncle" to me for the long term. I have learned from him a great deal about the joy of language and writing for a lively faith community. In recent years he has provided sound advice and helped to raise interest and support for my writing and teaching.

I was very fortunate to do my PhD research and writing under a great scholar of quranic studies, Andrew Rippin. After I completed my degree, Dr. Rippin remained a faithful friend. Dr. Rippin, who passed away in 2016, was a generous man who helped many scholars. I am thankful for the help and friendship he gave to me, and I miss him very much.

My wife, Gwenyth, and I have worked together for more than thirty years. We have shared the adventure of parenting and now also grandparenting. Gwenyth has supplied to our partnership many essential components that I could not. As I wrote this book, I constantly checked ideas and wordings with her. For her friendship and her solid, centered confidence, I thank God.

Gordon Nickel
Eagle Bay, BC
April 2019

INTRODUCTION

The Quran is the scripture of the Muslim community, revered by Muslims around the world and given authority by them to instruct both faith and life. Its 114 chapters, called *sūras*, are arranged approximately in order of length from longest to shortest. The entire collection is introduced by a short prayer known as *al-Fātiḥa*, or "the Opening."

The contents of the Quran come from the Middle East in the seventh century AD, though scholars do not agree on precisely how or where it came together. The Quran that most Muslims use today reflects a decision of Muslim leaders in Egypt in 1924 to adopt one particular "reading" of the text from among many possible and officially accepted readings.

This commentary is an attempt to explain the contents of the Quran to non-Muslim readers alongside the full translated text of the Quran. The Muslim community believes the Quran to be the word of Allah. The Quran addresses the Muslim community as "you who believe" (e.g., 2.104) and assumes that its assertions and commands will be accepted by them.

The Quran also directly addresses a number of other groups, such as the "Sons of Israel" (e.g., 2.40), "the People of the Book" (e.g., 4.171), "you who are Jews" (e.g., 62.6), "Sons of Adam" (e.g., 7.26), or simply "people" (e.g., 2.21) and "human" (e.g., 82.6). It conceives its contents to be not only for those who accept its claims but also for those who reject them. In this sense the Quran makes an open appeal to all of humankind.

Since the Quran addresses itself to non-Muslims, a careful study of its contents and a response to its claims from non-Muslims is clearly appropriate. In addition, the Quran includes many characterizations of Jews and Christians, their beliefs, and their behavior. For example, it makes a number of claims about the Jewish and Christian treatment of their scriptures. At the same time the Quran frequently claims that its contents confirm the Jewish and Christian scriptures. Those who are the custodians of those scriptures would understandably be interested in how they, their beliefs, and their scriptures are portrayed.

Perhaps even more in need of comment are the quranic denials of the beliefs

– or perceived beliefs – of Christians and Jews. For example, the quranic Jesus, called ʿĪsā, is "quoted" in this book written some six hundred years after the Gospel accounts, making statements that contradict the New Testament. Who has more interest to respond to this than those the Quran calls "the people of the Gospel" (5.46)?

Beyond this, the Quran contains frequent commands to the "believers," meaning Muslims, about how they should deal with people outside of their community – variously called "disbelievers," "associators," "the enemies of Allah," and "those who have been given the Book." Again, those who would be affected by such commands have an understandable interest in the actions they stipulate. In the cases of some verses, both the characterizations and the commands live on in the minds of Muslims to the present day.

Focus on the Contents

The first aim of this commentary is to observe and explain the contents of each sūra in general and selected passages and verses in particular. Of course, the meanings of many verses and passages in the Quran have been disputed since the earliest works of Muslim interpretation. Therefore, the commentary will frequently qualify descriptions with *seems* or *appears*.

This commentary treats the text of the Quran as literature and describes its contents largely through literary analysis. The commentary proceeds from the understanding that respect is best shown to Muslims by taking their beliefs seriously and responding authentically. Non-Muslims who do not accept the Muslim claim that the contents of the Quran are revealed by God cannot honestly treat the Quran as divine scripture.

After describing the contents of the Quran, this commentary will often provide further information on traditional Muslim interpretations, the narrative framework offered by the traditional Muslim stories about Muhammad, and critical academic perspectives, as well as analyses and responses to many important themes in the Quran.

Not every passage or verse will be explained, but rather key verses and passages throughout. The criterion of selection will be the importance and interest of the contents to non-Muslim readers, especially Christians. However, many other passages and verses will be explained in terms of their importance to Muslim faith and life.

Different Kinds of Literature

For many non-Muslims, the experience of reading the Quran is confusing and even frustrating because of the text's abrupt changes of topic and tone.

The "voice" of the text also changes frequently from "we" to "you" to "I" to "they," often suddenly and often without providing information about whom these pronouns represent.

Much of this confusion can be avoided by first noting a limited number of types of literature that repeat throughout the Quran.

Much of the Quran is made up of the following two types of literature:

- **Polemic:** Readers of the first hundred pages of the Quran will encounter quite a bit of material that seems to be argument or controversy between the Quran and the "People of the Book" (usually considered to be Jews and Christians). Sometimes the Jews are mentioned, sometimes Christians, but many times the context alone suggests the identity of the unnamed audience. This kind of literature is known as *polemic* – that is, it challenges the foundations of the faith of the audience and makes a case for the new faith.
- **Narrative:** Readers will also notice stories about characters familiar from the Bible, including Adam, Noah, Moses, Abraham, and 'Īsā (the quranic Jesus). This kind of literature can conveniently be called *narrative*.

A number of additional types can also be identified:

- **End times** material about rewards and punishments on the Day of Resurrection
- **Signs** of the Creator's presence and power
- **Laws**, often accompanying commands to obey the messenger
- **Battle scenes**, often with commands to fight, kill, or struggle
- **Messenger** passages, in which the Quran directly addresses an unnamed messenger
- **Self-referential** passages that vouch for the Quran, the messenger, or Islam
- **Personal situation** passages address the domestic details of the messenger

These nine types of literature make up most of the Quran. Readers who learn to recognize the repeating types will enjoy a more meaningful reading experience.

Regarding changes in tone and voice, the reader need not assume consistency in speaker/author or in audience. There is an assumption in traditional Muslim teaching that the Quran has to do with a single person – that is, the book contains the recitations of a single messenger gathered into a book after his death. But the non-Muslim who is not committed to this belief may read the text more openly, without feeling constricted by this traditional understanding.

Muslim Story of Islamic Origins

For most Muslims, the contents of the Quran are accompanied by a tradition of interpretation that reaches back more than a thousand years. This tradition asserts that the historical context of its contents is to be found in a story about Muhammad that first appeared in writing during the second and third centuries of Islam (eighth to ninth centuries AD). Muslim scholars subsequently worked out a chronology for the 114 sūras based on acceptance of the Muslim story of Islamic origins. They therefore identified individual sūras as "Meccan" or "Medinan," according to their concept of when the sūra was first recited in the story. In Western study of the Quran during the past two centuries, many non-Muslim scholars have accepted both the chronology of the sūras taught by Muslim tradition and the rough outlines of the Muslim story.

This commentary, however, does not take the Muslim story of Islamic origins to be the historical context for the contents of the Quran, though several of the focus article scholars make use of this framework. There is no independent historical evidence that the events took place as the story tells. The earliest written narrative accounts about Islamic origins date from around two hundred years after the events they relate (early ninth century AD), and sometimes were written under the patronage of powerful Muslim rulers. The written accounts themselves differ significantly in many details and often contradict one another. The classical collections of sayings attributed to Islam's messenger known as the hadith were written down at an even later stage, around the middle of the third century of Islam (mid-ninth century AD).

This is not to insist that no part of the Muslim story of origins is historically true, but simply to observe that there is no way to be certain of its historicity. Without adequate historical evidence for the story, non-Muslims are free to think broadly on the meanings of the Quran without being bound by the Muslim story.

To aid the understanding of non-Muslim readers, this commentary will sometimes mention how Muslims have linked verses of the Quran to the story of Muhammad in the four best-known early Muslim stories of Islamic origins. These are the *Sīrat al-nabawiyya* of Ibn Isḥāq (d. AD 767), edited by Ibn Hishām (d. 833); the *Kitāb al-maghāzī* of al-Wāqidī (d. 823); the *Kitāb al-ṭabaqāt* of Ibn Saʿd (d. 845); and the *Taʾrīkh al-rusul wa ʾl-mulūk* of al-Ṭabarī (d. 923).

These works are available in English translation, though the translation of the *Kitāb al-ṭabaqāt* is unfortunately hard to find. Many university libraries will have one or more of these translations. When this commentary mentions the traditional Muslim story of Islamic origins, it refers to the English translations by the following abbreviations (see the full references in the bibliography):

Sīra – *The Life of Muhammad*, translated by A. Guillaume
Raids – *The Life of Muhammad*, translated by Rizwi Faizer
History – *The History of al-Ṭabarī*, 40 volumes (All volumes of *History* are accessible at https://archive.org/details/TabariEnglish; volumes 6–9 are about Muhammad.)

Many non-Muslim scholars accept the Muslim story of Islamic origins because they find it plausible, because there is no alternative story that has gained wide acceptance, or because working with the story is convenient for their writing and teaching. People of faith may consider an additional dimension. The Muslim story of Islam's origins mixes incidental details with major theological truth claims in the same narrative. For example, one can easily accept that a messenger in the first part of the seventh century went into the hills of central Arabia to meditate. However, the claim that there the Almighty Creator God began to reveal to that messenger his word in revelations that continued for twenty-two years has implications for the whole world. If this is indeed true, it not only affects Judaism and Christianity but every faith prior to and since the events.

Muslim stories about how the Quran itself came together are also based on writings that first appeared in the third century of Islam (ninth century AD). For example, the famous story about the caliph 'Uthmān organizing an editorial team to produce the standard text of the Quran seems to have first appeared in the hadith collection of al-Bukhārī (d. 870). (See Harald Motzki, "The Collection of the Qur'ān," in bibliography.)

Long Tradition of Interpretation

In addition to accepting the traditional stories of Islamic origins as the historical context of the Quran, many Muslims affirm the interpretations found in an illustrious and extensive series of Muslim commentaries written over a period of more than twelve centuries. For many Muslims, the Quran does not mean what individual Muslims might gather from their own readings today, but it means what the greatest Muslim commentaries interpret it to mean. The meaning, in other words, is traditional rather than individual.

This commentary will sometimes refer to the interpretations in classical Muslim commentaries. For readers who would like to read more of this interesting material, here are some of the translations that are available (full references in the bibliography):

Mahmood Ayoub, *The Qur'an and its Interpreters* (two volumes)
A. F. L. Beeston, *Baiḍāwī's Commentary on Sūra 12 of the Qur'ān*
J. Cooper, *The Commentary on the Qur'ān* (first part of Ṭabarī's commentary)
Helmut Gätje, *The Qur'án and its Exegesis*
D. S. Margoliouth, *The Commentary of el-Baiḍāwī on Sura 3*
Andrew Rippin, *Classical Islam* (seven commentaries on Sūra 98)
Seyyed Hossein Nasr, *The Study Quran* (summaries of classical interpretation)

Classical commentaries report deep disagreement about the interpretation of many – and in some cases most – of the Quran's verses. At several points the commentaries also show that the interpreters were simply unable to make sense of some of the Quran's content. For example, the great exegete Fakhr al-Dīn al-Rāzī (d. 1209) wrote about one of the verses in Sūra 98, "May Allah Most High have mercy on whoever attempts to summarize the nature of the difficulty in the verse."

By presenting traditional Muslim interpretations, therefore, this commentary does not mean to say that these are the definitive meanings of the verses. Rather, they are offered out of high regard for this great Islamic intellectual creation and in order to provide perspective to the reader. Classical Muslim *tafsīr* ("commentary") is the area of my doctoral studies and ongoing research, and I would have liked to include much more than has been possible in this book.

Academic Critical Writing on the Quran

Some scholars attempt to study the Quran through methodologies commonly applied to the study of literature and especially the study of the Bible. Such study of the Quran has a much shorter history than the similar study of the Bible. One key scholar wrote in 1977 that critical study of the Quran had barely begun.

Academic studies range from those that generally accept Muslim beliefs about the Quran's origin and chronology to those that put both Muslim tradition and commentaries to one side in order to discern the meanings of the Quran from a wider linguistic and regional palette. For example, an increasing number of scholars may refer to Syriac vocabulary and writings that they believe illuminate the meanings of the Arabic text.

Critical writing does not mean that scholars want to say something negative about the Quran. Rather, *critical* in the sense intended here means asking common-sense questions about a work of literature and analyzing its merits and faults. Such writing is to be encouraged. Yet the question may be asked: To what extent has academic critical study of the Quran been inhibited by political sensitivities and fear of consequences?

Some comments and sūra introductions in this commentary refer to particular scholarly perspectives that may be relevant or interesting for readers. Full information on brief references is available in the bibliography. Many other comments reflect the general influence of key works of scholarship on the Quran from the last hundred years. See the list of influential scholarly works in the bibliography.

Use of the Name *Allah*

The Quran speaks of *Allah* as the deity more than 2,500 times. The translation of A. J. Droge used in this commentary consistently translates the name *Allah* as "God."

Allah is the word for "God" in Arabic. Arabic translations of the Bible also use *Allah* for the Hebrew *Elohim* and the Greek *Theos*. However, in many instances the Quran does not seem to use *Allah* as a generic word for "God." In Arabic the generic word for (a) god is *ilāh*, and the Quran states that there is no god except Allah (*lā ilāha illa 'llāh*; e.g., 37.35, 47.19).

In many important theological passages, the Quran seems to use the name *Allah* deliberately to distinguish it from other concepts of God. For example, the Quran directly addresses the "People of the Book" in this way: "Do not go beyond the limits in your religion, and do not say about Allah (anything) but the truth" (4.171). The verse goes on to deny Christian beliefs in the deity of Jesus. Other examples are Sūras 112 and 5.17, 72–77. Perhaps for this reason, many English translations by Muslims leave the term as *Allah* (e.g., Marmaduke Pickthall, Yusuf Ali, Shakir, Mohsin Khan, Dr. Ghali, Sahih International).

When the Quran commands people to fight and kill "in the way of Allah," it is appropriate to distinguish this description of deity from the generic *God*. These commands should not be associated with the way of the God of the New Testament. However, when quranic descriptions and biblical descriptions share the same referent, for example "the Creator," both scriptures are referring to the same deity.

The theological questions that the Quran's description of Allah raises are part of the interest and enjoyment of the Quran for the non-Muslim reader. This commentary presents the translation of A. J. Droge as it is, with *God* for

Allah. Writers of thematic focus articles use *God* in some cases, *Allah* in others. My own comments discuss the Allah described in the Arabic text and often substitute *Allah* for Droge's *God*. See also the focus articles on "Allah in the Quran" (p. 90) and on "Creation in the Quran" (p. 224).

Bible in the Background

The Bible stands solidly in the background of much of the material readers encounter in the Quran. Though difficult to picture now, the Middle East in the seventh century AD was home to large and thriving communities of Christians and Jews. These communities had possessed and studied the Bible for hundreds of years in the original languages as well as in a number of important translations, including Aramaic, Syriac, Coptic, Armenian, and Latin. During the seventh century, Jewish scholars in the Middle East were preparing the text of the Hebrew Bible that later became known as the Masoretic Text.

It is therefore reasonable to assume that the Bible is the source of at least the general outlines of the Quran's stories of Moses, Abraham, Noah, Joseph, and other characters. The Quran's stories do not seem to come from an explicit knowledge of the biblical text but mainly through verbal tellings of the stories. These stories also include many details that are not known in the Bible but are familiar from Christian apocryphal and Jewish Rabbinic works.

The Quran itself mentions three scriptures of the People of the Book: the Torah (*tawrāt*), the Gospel (*injīl*), and the Psalms (*zabūr*). Whenever the Quran names these scriptures, it describes them only in the most positive and respectful ways. The Quran also frequently claims to "confirm" the pre-Islamic scriptures, which it says are "with" the Jews and Christians. Further, the Quran tells the stories of biblical characters in a referential style that assumes familiarity with the Bible stories among the audience.

Academics have shown a great deal of interest in the Quran's references to Bible stories, but there is a wide range of opinions about the relationship of the Bible to the Quran. For example, one influential view argues that the Quran has a "biblical subtext" – that the Quran assumes a connection of continuity with biblical literature. Another view makes the case that the Quran "repurposed" biblical materials for use in the establishment of a very different new religion, Islam.

Notes in this commentary on some of the best-known stories about biblical characters highlight details that might be of interest to non-Muslim readers. Many quranic stories appear in several different versions. The commentary indicates details that distinguish each version and often makes comparison convenient through a system of cross-references. As for the earlier biblical accounts of those characters, the notes sometimes invite comparison by giving the biblical references, but they highlight differences only when those differences seem to raise reasonable questions about provenance and theology, among other things.

Many readers may be interested in speculating on the reasons for repetition of certain stories and the differences between the versions. Such discussions appear in comments on versions of stories further along in the Quran, after the observation and straightforward description of those stories in the first part of the book.

Please note the list of recommended books on the relationship of the Bible to the Quran in the bibliography.

Polemic in the Quran

The Quran contains many passages of controversy, in which a messenger seems to be arguing with his audience. The messenger strives to make the best case for his preaching and names the aspects of his audience's faith and life that he considers to be false or wrong. This kind of literature is known as "polemic" – defined by one scholar as "discussion of controversial (religious) matters or allusion to them."

Passages that contain vigorous arguments, as well as refutations of the beliefs of others, figure prominently in the Quran. The target audience is sometimes "the Sons of Israel," sometimes "the People of the Book," sometimes "associators," and sometimes disbelievers in general.

While polemic to "the People of the Book" often addresses Jews alone, or Jews and Christians together, in some cases it clearly calls out to Christians. In 4.171–73, for example, the point of contention is the identity of the Messiah, and the passage denies some key New Testament teachings about Jesus. The passage proposes a different set of beliefs about Jesus, changes his name to 'Īsā, and promises a painful punishment to anyone too "arrogant" not to accept those new beliefs.

For some readers, "polemic" may seem a negative or pejorative term, but this commentary does not intend a negative meaning for the word. It is simply a way to describe a genre of literature. Likely the majority of the Quran's material on Judaism and Christianity is polemical.

Insofar as it requires the refutation of others' beliefs, polemic is not viewed favorably by some in the modern West. However, the idea of dealing seriously with matters of truth – not only defending one's own views but pointing out the weaknesses of other views – is a normal topic of conversation in many cultures.

Readers of the Quran do not need to wait long to encounter controversial material and can decide by themselves how to describe it. Most of the first half of the second sūra is polemic addressed to the "Sons of Israel," from 2.40 up to about verse 162. The third sūra similarly opens with a long passage that Muslim commentators understand to be in tension with the beliefs of Christians (3.1–80). Sūras 4 and 5 also contain major passages addressed to "the People of the Book" that translator A. J. Droge calls "diatribes."

Christian Response

Though the Quran does not provide historical context for its passages of polemic, a famous monument left by the Arab Conquest offers a datable expression of Muslim faith at a very early stage. The Dome of the Rock on the Temple Mount in Jerusalem contains an Arabic inscription that reflects the state of Islam in AD 691.

In the 240-meter line of Kufic Arabic script written in mosaic along the top of the ambulatories inside the Dome, some 175 out of a total of 370 Arabic words are about the identity of Jesus, here called 'Īsā. Jerusalem in the seventh century AD was a city full of Christians. Three of the longest passages in the inscription bear wordings similar to quranic passages about 'Īsā: 4.171, 19.33–36, and Sūra 112. The inscription ends with a passage similar in wording to 3.18–19 that contains polemic about "those who were given the book" and a threat against them.

The statements inscribed in the Dome of the Rock were made by the conquering Arab Empire to the conquered "People of the Book." Among those statements are commands as direct as this denunciation of the Trinity: "Do not say three! Stop!" Significantly, the start of controversy was not Christians attacking a developed Islam but rather Arab rulers attacking a subject population and its developed faith. The north gate of the Dome bears the inscription (also found three times in the Quran): "He it is who has sent his messenger with the guidance and the religion of truth, so that he may cause it to prevail over all religion, however much the associators may hate it."

In the seventh century and for more than a millennium after, Islam was the religion of the conqueror and ruler of the Middle East. Christians and Jews were vanquished peoples who had surrendered or "submitted" to Islam. They lived in the Arab Empire as dhimmis – communities with reduced rights who paid an extra tax known as the *jizya*. The Muslim denials of Christian faith from that era are permanently inscribed in the Dome and can still be read today – but not the Christian response.

Like the inscriptions in the Dome, the Quran addresses the identity of Jesus and denies some of the most important beliefs of Christianity. The Quran contains the denials but provides no space for Christians to clarify their beliefs, to correct misunderstandings, or to make a friendly case for their beliefs in answer to strong denials.

For this reason, this commentary seeks to analyze and respond to passages directly addressed to the "People of the Book," as well as to characterizations of Christians and Jews and their beliefs and practices. In particular, the characterization of Jewish and Christian treatment of their scriptures will be carefully examined, along with the claims that the contents of the Quran confirm the pre-Islamic scriptures.

Denial of the beliefs of Christians and Jews – and sometimes denials of falsely perceived beliefs – also deserve a non-Muslim response. For example, the Quran asserts that the Jews say Ezra is the son of Allah (9.30) and that Christians include Mary in their Trinity (5.116). Beyond false perceptions, however, many denials show a keen sense of some of the implications of the deity and death of Jesus. These quranic denials live on until today in ordinary interfaith conversation. With no answer in the Quran from non-Muslim groups addressed there, and with little knowledge of the contents of the Quran among non-Muslims, many Muslims today assume that Christians live and believe the way the Quran characterized them in the seventh century.

The Quran's instructions and commands to believers about how to treat non-Muslims extend beyond faith and worship practices into politics and daily relationships in multifaith societies. Sometimes the commands specify the target, and sometimes it is more difficult to determine. For example, one of the Quran's commands to fight is applied to "those who have been given the scripture" – generally considered to be Jews and Christians (9.29). One of the key commands to kill is against "associators" (*mushrikūn*) – a term considered by some to mean idolaters but also applied to Christians, who according to the Quran associate a merely human 'Īsā with Allah (9.5; cf. 9.31). Elsewhere the target is simply identified as "disbelievers."

Among the commands to fight and kill, there is also an uncertainty about whether Allah commands fighting because of aggressive actions on the part of the enemy or whether non-Muslims deserve attack merely because they do not accept Muslim claims for the prophethood of the messenger and the source of his recitations. The concept of believers "fighting in the way of Allah" raises important theological questions that undergird human behavior. The Quran also sometimes misrepresents pre-Islamic prophets and messengers as warriors. All who hope for peaceable coexistence will be interested in this material and its interpretations.

Much non-Muslim scholarship on the Quran seems reluctant to engage with its religious claims. Yet it is exactly in the area of religious claims that the Quran seems to make its most emphatic appeals. These appeals deserve careful consideration and a reasonable and amicable response. The author of this commentary claims no special status or appointment to speak for Christians or Christianity. I am a rather uncomplicated Christian: I believe the Bible to be God's Word and the authority for faith and life. My own spiritual heritage is a relatively small Peace Church that emerged out of the Radical Reformation, and I work comfortably and gratefully with committed Christians from many other traditions. Although I cannot speak for all Christians or Christianity, my notes seek to represent the broad stream of orthodox Christian beliefs and teachings accurately.

Principle of Selection

This commentary remarks on verses and passages that are likely to interest non-Muslim readers in general and Christians in particular. Of course, many other parts of the Quran are interesting and very important for Muslims. However, a principle of selection is needed in order that a commentary on 6,236 verses not expand to an unreasonable number of pages.

Though the Quran's content related to the death and deity of Jesus is of central interest, readers will be interested in many other stories and themes as well. The "focus articles" listed in the table of contents, as well the analysis index at the back of the book, give an idea of the range of interests in this commentary beyond comments on individual verses.

The Text of the Quran and Its English Translation

The Quran translation of Arthur Droge is an excellent translation, and I am thankful to Equinox Publishing for their willingness to let us use this scholarly translation. I agree with this translation most of the time, and when I do not, I try to cite the Arabic original between us and explain why I would render it otherwise. By doing so, I do not mean to say that I know better than Dr. Droge. In fact, likely more often than disagreeing, I commend his translation for providing direct translations of wording that many other translations interpret away.

From a scholarly perspective, the Arabic text of the Quran is not completely certain. Most Muslims use a version of the text that was determined in Cairo, Egypt, less than a hundred years ago (1924). The Muslim scholars responsible for this version chose one of fourteen different readings of the Quran permitted by Muslim tradition. This version was not determined after a careful study of the most ancient manuscripts of the Quran, but rather simply from Muslim tradition on the so-called Ḥafṣ ʿan ʿĀṣim reading.

There is no critical edition of the Quran as exists for the Hebrew Bible (Old Testament) and the New Testament. In biblical critical texts, all known manuscript variants are listed at the bottom of the page in a critical apparatus. No such critical edition exists for the Quran. Translators therefore generally use the Cairo standard edition, and some may rarely mention variant readings or variant manuscripts. For expertise on the history of quranic manuscripts, I defer to scholars such as Keith Small, Daniel Brubaker (see his focus article on "Manuscripts of the Quran"), and François Déroche, all of whom I have consulted (see their publications in the bibliography). Sadly, Dr. Small passed away during the preparation of this commentary. He is greatly missed.

Bibliography

Books and articles by the author related to the Quran and its interpretation provide a more extensive discussion of many important verses, passages, and themes touched on in this commentary. Many of the articles are accessible at https://saiacs.academia.edu/GordonNickel.

1. Books

Nickel, Gordon D. *The Gentle Answer to the Muslim Accusation of Biblical Falsification*. Calgary: Bruton Gate, 2015.

———. *Narratives of Tampering in the Earliest Commentaries on the Qur'ān*. Leiden: Brill, 2011.

2. Essays

Nickel, Gordon D. "Aaron (Islam)." "Adam (Islam)." "Adam and Eve, Story of (Islam)." "Adultery (Islam)." In *Encyclopedia of the Bible and Its Reception*, edited by Hans-Josef Klauck et al., vol. 1, 22–23, 322–23, 350–51, 467. Berlin: De Gruyter, 2009.

———. "Abraham." In *Oxford Bibliographies in Islamic Studies*, edited by Tamara Sonn. New York: Oxford University Press, 2012. https://www.oxfordbibliographies.com/obo/page/islamic-studies.

———. "'A Common Word' in Qur'ānic Context and Commentary." *London School of Theology Occasional Papers* 9 (August 2009): 6–19.

———. "Conquest and Controversy: Intertwined Themes in the Islamic Interpretive Tradition." *Numen* 58 (2011): 232–58.

———. "Early Muslim Accusations of *Tahrīf*: Muqātil ibn Sulaymān's Commentary on Key Qur'ānic Verses." In *The Bible and Arab Christianity*, edited by David Thomas, 207–23. Leiden: Brill, 2006.

———. "Jesus." In *The Wiley Blackwell Companion to the Qur'an*, edited by Andrew Rippin and Jawid Mojaddedi, 2nd ed., 288–302. Oxford: Wiley-Blackwell, 2017.

———. "The Language of Love in Qur'ān and Gospel." In *Sacred Text: Explorations in Lexicography*, edited by Juan Pedro Monferrer-Sala and Angel Urban, 223–48. Frankfurt: Peter Lang, 2009.

———. "Muqātil on Zayd and Zaynab: 'The *Sunna* of Allah Concerning Those Who Passed Away Before' (Q 33:38)." In *Islamic Studies Today: Essays in Honor of Andrew Rippin*, edited by Majid Daneshgar and Walid A. Saleh, 43–61. Leiden: Brill, 2016.

———. "Qur'anic and Islamic Interpretation of the Bible." In *The Oxford Encyclopedia of Biblical Interpretation*, edited by Steven L. McKenzie, vol. 2, 167–76. New York: Oxford University Press, 2013.

———. "'Self-Evident Truths of Reason': Challenges to Clear Thinking in the *Tafsīr Al-Kabīr* of Fakhr Al-Dīn Al-Rāzī." *Islam and Christian-Muslim Relations* 22, no. 2 (2011): 161–72.

———. "'They Find Him Written with Them': The Impact of Q 7.157 on Muslim Interaction with Arab Christianity." In *Arab Christians and the Qur'an from the Origins of Islam to the Medieval Period*, edited by Mark Beaumont, 106–30. Leiden: Brill, 2018.

———. "'We Will Make Peace With You': The Christians of Najrān in Muqātil's *Tafsīr*." *Collectanea Christiana Orientalia* 3 (2006): 1–18.

Nickel, Gordon D., and Andrew Rippin. "The Qur'ān." In *The Islamic World*, edited by Andrew Rippin, 145–56. London: Routledge, 2008.

Scholarly Studies on the Quran

Azaiez, Mehdi, Gabriel Said Reynolds, Tommaso Tesei, and Hamza M. Zafer, eds. *The Qur'an Seminar Commentary: A Collaborative Study of 50 Qur'anic Passages*. Berlin: De Gruyter, 2016.

Baker, Colin F. *Qur'ān Manuscripts: Calligraphy, Illumination, Design*. London: The British Library, 2007.

Bannister, Andrew G. *An Oral-Formulaic Study of the Qur'an*. New York: Lexington, 2014.

Brubaker, Daniel A. *Corrections in Early Qur'ān Manuscripts: Twenty Examples*. Lovettsville, VA: Think and Tell, 2019.

Déroche, François. *The Abbasid Tradition*. London: Oxford University Press, 1992.

———. *Qur'ans of the Umayyads: A First Overview*. Leiden: Brill, 2014.

Hawting, G. R. *The Idea of Idolatry and the Emergence of Islam*. Cambridge: Cambridge University Press, 1999.

Hilali, Asma. *The Sanaa Palimpsest: The Transmission of the Qur'an in the First Centuries AH*. London: Oxford University Press, 2017.

Izutsu, Toshihiko. *Ethico-Religious Concepts in the Qur'ān*. Montreal: McGill University Press, 1966.

James, David. *Qur'ans and Bindings from the Chester Beatty Library*. [London]: World of Islam Festival Trust, 1980.

Jeffery, Arthur. *The Foreign Vocabulary of the Qur'ān*. Baroda: Oriental Institute, 1938.

———. *Materials for the History of the Text of the Qur'ān: The Old Codices*. Leiden: Brill, 1937.

———. "The Qur'ān as Scripture." *The Muslim World* 40 (1950): 41–55, 106–34, 185–206, 257–75.

Marshall, David. *God, Muhammad and the Unbelievers: A Qur'anic Study*. London: Routledge, 2013.

———. "Punishment Stories." In *Encyclopaedia of the Qur'an*, edited by Jane Dammen McAuliffe, vol. 4, 318–22. Leiden: Brill, 2004.

McAuliffe, Jane Dammen, ed. *Encyclopaedia of the Qur'ān*. 5 vols. Leiden: Brill, 2001–6.

Motzki, Harald. "The Collection of the Qur'ān: A Reconsideration of Western Views in Light of Recent Methodological Developments." *Der Islam* 78 (2001): 1–34.

Neuwirth, Angelika, and Michael A. Sells, eds. *Qur'ānic Studies Today.* London: Routledge, 2016.

Nöldeke, Theodor, Friedrich Schwally, Gotthelf Bergsträsser, and Otto Pretzl. *The History of the Qur'ān.* Edited and translated by Wolfgang H. Behn. Leiden: Brill, 2013.

Rahbar, Daud. *God of Justice: A Study in the Ethical Doctrine of the Qur'ān.* Leiden: Brill, 1960.

Reynolds, Gabriel Said, ed. *New Perspectives on the Qur'ān: The Qur'ān in Its Historical Context 2.* London: Routledge, 2011.

Reynolds, Gabriel Said, ed. *The Qur'ān in Its Historical Context.* London: Routledge, 2008.

Rippin, Andrew, and Jawid Mojaddedi, eds. *The Wiley Blackwell Companion to the Qur'ān.* 2nd ed. Oxford: Wiley Blackwell, 2017.

Robinson, Neal. *Discovering the Qur'an: A Contemporary Approach to a Veiled Text.* 2nd ed. Washington: Georgetown University Press, 2003.

Sinai, Nicolai. *The Qur'an: A Historical-Critical Introduction.* Edinburgh: Edinburgh University Press, 2017.

Small, Keith E. *Textual Criticism and Qur'ān Manuscripts.* New York: Lexington Books, 2011.

Weitbrecht Stanton, H. U. *The Teaching of the Qur'ān.* London: SPCK, 1919.

Wansbrough, John. *Quranic Studies: Sources and Methods of Scriptural Interpretation.* Oxford: Oxford University Press, 1977.

Muslim Commentary on the Quran

Ahmed, Shahab. *Before Orthodoxy: The Satanic Verses in Early Islam.* Cambridge, MA: Harvard University Press, 2017.

Ayoub, Mahmoud M. *The Qur'an and Its Interpreters.* 2 vols. Albany: State University of New York Press, 1984 and 1992.

Beeston, A. F. L. *Baiḍāwī's Commentary on Sūra 12 of the Qur'ān.* Oxford: Clarendon Press, 1963.

Calder, Norman. "Tafsīr from Ṭabarī to Ibn Kathīr: Problems in the Description of a Genre, Illustrated with Reference to the Story of Abraham." In *Approaches to the Qur'ān,* edited by G. R. Hawting and Abdul-Kadar A. Shareef, 101–40. London: Routledge, 1993.

Cooper, John, trans. *The Commentary on the Qur'ān.* (Abridged translation of the first part of al-Ṭabarī's *Jāmi' al-bayān*) Oxford: Oxford University Press, 1987.

Gätje, Helmut. *The Qur'án and Its Exegesis: Selected Texts with Classical and Modern Muslim Interpretations.* Oxford: Oneworld, 1996.

Goldziher, Ignaz. *Schools of Koranic Commentators.* Edited and translated by Wolfgang H. Behn. Wiesbaden: Harrassowitz, 2006.

Margoliouth, D. S., trans. *Chrestomathia Baidawiana: The Commentary of el-Baiḍāwī on Sura 3.* London: Luzac, 1894.

McAuliffe, Jane Dammen. *Qur'ānic Christians: An Analysis of Classical and Modern Exegesis.* Cambridge: Cambridge University Press, 1991.

Nasr, Seyyed Hossein, ed. *The Study Quran: A New Translation and Commentary*. New York: HarperCollins, 2015.

Powers, David S. "The Exegetical Genre *nāsikh al-Qur'ān wa mansūkhuhu*." In *Approaches to the History of the Interpretation of the Qur'ān*, edited by Andrew Rippin, 117–138. Oxford: Oxford University Press, 1988.

Riddell, Peter. *Malay Court Religion, Culture and Language: Interpreting the Qur'ān in 17th Century Aceh*. Leiden: Brill, 2017.

Rippin, Andrew, ed. *Approaches to the History of the Interpretation of the Qur'ān*. Oxford: Clarendon Press, 1988.

Rippin, Andrew. "Tafsīr." *Encyclopaedia of Islam*. New ed. Edited by P. J. Bearman et al., vol. 10, 83–88. Leiden: Brill, 2000.

Rippin, Andrew, Norman Calder, and Jawid Mojaddedi, eds. and trans. *Classical Islam: A Sourcebook of Religious Literature*. 2nd ed. London: Routledge, 2012.

Resources on the Quran and the Bible

Anderson, Mark Robert. *The Qur'an in Context: A Christian Exploration*. Downers Grove, IL: IVP Academic, 2016.

Bridger, J. Scott. *Christian Exegesis of the Qur'ān*. Cambridge: James Clarke, 2015.

Bristow, George. *Sharing Abraham? Narrative Worldview, Biblical and Qur'anic Interpretation and Comparative Theology in Turkey*. Cambridge, MA: Doorlight Academic, 2017.

Cragg, Kenneth. *Jesus and the Muslim: An Exploration*. London: Allen & Unwin, 1985.

Durie, Mark. *The Qur'an and Its Biblical Reflexes: Investigations into the Genesis of a Religion*. London: Lexington Books, 2018.

Elass, Mateen. *Understanding the Koran: A Quick Christian Guide to the Muslim Holy Book*. Grand Rapids: Zondervan, 2004.

Jomier, Jacques. *The Bible and the Qur'an*. San Francisco: Ignatius, 1964.

Muir, William. *The Testimony Borne by the Coran to the Jewish and Christian Scriptures*. Agra: Agra Religious Tract and Book Society, 1856.

Reynolds, Gabriel Said. *The Qur'ān and Its Biblical Subtext*. London: Routledge, 2010.

Reynolds, Gabriel Said. *The Qur'ān and the Bible: Text and Commentary*. New Haven, CT: Yale University Press, 2018.

Wherry, E. M. *A Comprehensive Commentary on the Qurán: Comprising Sale's Translation and Preliminary Discourse*. 4 vols. London: Trübner, 1882–86.

Woodberry, J. Dudley, ed. *Muslims and Christians on the Emmaus Road*. Monrovia, CA: MARC, 1989.

The Muslim Story of Islamic Origins

Faizer, Rizwi, ed. and trans. *The Life of Muhammad: al-Wāqidī's* Kitāb al-maghāzī. London: Routledge, 2011.

Ibn Sa'd. *Ibn Sa'd's Kitab al-Tabaqat al-Kabir*. 2 vols. Translated by S. Moinul Haq and H. K. Ghazanfar. Karachi: Pakistan Historical Society, 1967.

Ibrahim, Ayman S. *The Stated Motivations for the Early Islamic Expansion (622–641): A Critical Revision of Muslims' Traditional Portrayal of the Arab Raids and Conquests.* Frankfurt: Peter Lang, 2018.

Guillaume, A., trans. *The Life of Muhammad: A Translation of Isḥāq's* Sīrat Rasūl Allāh. Oxford: Oxford University Press, 1955.

Peters, F. E. "The Quest of the Historical Muhammad." *International Journal of Middle East Studies* 23 (1991): 291–315.

Powers, David S. *Muhammad Is Not the Father of Any of Your Men: The Making of the Last Prophet.* Philadelphia: University of Pennsylvania Press, 2011.

Rippin, Andrew. "Muḥammad and the Qur'ān: Reading Scripture in the 21st Century." In *The Biography of Muḥammad*, edited by Harald Motzki, 298–309. Leiden: Brill, 2000.

Shoemaker, Stephen J. "Muḥammad and the Qur'ān." In *The Oxford Handbook of Late Antiquity*, edited by Scott Fitzgerald Johnson, 1078–1108. Oxford: Oxford University Press, 2012.

Al-Ṭabarī. *The History of al-Ṭabarī.* 40 vols. Albany: State University of New York Press, 1985–99.

Wansbrough, John. *The Sectarian Milieu: Content and Composition of Islamic Salvation History.* Oxford: Oxford University Press, 1978.

Other Resources Related to the Commentary

Burton, John. *The Sources of Islamic Law: Islamic Theories of Abrogation.* Edinburgh: Edinburgh University Press, 1990.

Cook, David. *Understanding Jihad.* 2nd ed. Oakland: University of California Press, 2015.

Firestone, Reuven. *Jihad: The Origin of Holy War in Islam.* Oxford: Oxford University Press, 2002.

Hoover, Jon. *Ibn Taymiyya's Theodicy of Perpetual Optimism.* Leiden: Brill, 2007.

———. "Perpetual Creativity in the Perfection of God: Ibn Taymiyya's Hadith Commentary on God's Creation of this World." *Journal of Islamic Studies* 15 (2004): 287–329.

İskenderoğlu, Muammer. *Fakhr al-Dīn al-Rāzī and Thomas Aquinas on the Question of the Eternity of the World.* Leiden: Brill, 2002.

Khadduri, Majid. *Al-Shāfiʿī Risāla: Treatise on the Foundation of Islamic Jurisprudence.* Cambridge: Islamic Texts Society, 1997.

Kuiper, Matthew J. *Daʿwa and Other Religions: Indian Muslims and the Modern Resurgence of Global Islamic Activism.* London: Routledge, 2015.

Muir, William. *The Apology of Al Kindy, Written at the Court of Al Mâmûn, in defense of Christianity against Islam.* London: Smith, Elder, 1882.

Tien, Anton, trans. "The Apology of al-Kindi." In *The Early Christian-Muslim Dialogue*, edited by N. A. Newman, 381–545. Hatfield, PA: Interdisciplinary Biblical Research Institute, 1993.

Padwick, Constance. *Muslim Devotions: A Study of Prayer-Manuals in Common Use.* London: SPCK, 1961.

Provan, Iain. *Seriously Dangerous Religion: What the Old Testament Really Says and Why It Matters*. Waco, TX: Baylor University Press, 2014.

Rippin, Andrew. *Muslims: Their Religious Beliefs and Practices*. 2nd ed. London: Routledge, 2001.

Schacht, Joseph. *The Origins of Muhammadan Jurisprudence*. Oxford: Oxford University Press, 1950.

Shenk, David. *Journeys of the Muslim Nation and the Christian Church: Exploring the Mission of Two Communities*. Scottdale: Herald, 2003.

THE OPENING
AL-FĀTIḤA

1

The name of this first sūra means "opening" or "beginning." The sūra's path of the blessed on the one hand and the path of those who go astray on the other resembles the dichotomy in Psalm 1, and indeed Sūra 1 seems to serve a function similar to Psalm 1 as the introduction to a collection of texts.

¹ In the Name of God, the Merciful, the Compassionate.
² Praise (be) to God, Lord of the worlds, ³ the Merciful, the Compassionate,

---

1.2 – *Praise (be) to God, Lord of the worlds*

The Quran begins with a prayer addressed to Allah. This short prayer is one of the best-known parts of the Quran to Muslims and non-Muslims alike. Its seven verses play a central role in the five daily ritual prayers of the Muslim community.

From this point on, the Quran will mainly speak of God as *Allāh*. The name *Allāh* appears in the Quran more than 2,500 times. The translation of A. J. Droge consistently renders *Allāh* as *God*. The Quran also gives names for God such as "Lord of the worlds" and *al-Raḥmān* (1.3). Perhaps not so well known is the fact that in 33 of the Quran's 114 sūras, the name Allah does not appear.

Allāh is the Arabic word for God. Arabic translations of the Bible also give *Allāh* for the Hebrew *Elohim* (e.g., Genesis 1:1) and the Greek *Theos* (e.g., Matthew 1:23). The fascinating question for readers is what particular concept of deity the Allah of the Quran portrays. See "Allah in the Quran" (p. 572).

The first sūra is not typical of the book it "opens," because direct address to Allah is unusual in the Quran. The Muslim belief about the Quran is that all of its words are dictated by Allah through the angel Gabriel to a human messenger. Many passages in the Quran are introduced with the command, "Say!" However, this first sūra is addressed to Allah from people.

1.3 – *the Merciful, the Compassionate*

"Merciful" and "Compassionate" are the translations that A. J. Droge gives for the Arabic terms *raḥmān* and *raḥīm*. These translations also appear in the basmala that comes at the beginning of every sūra except Sūra 9. Many Muslim translations of the

⁴ Master of the Day of Judgment. ⁵ You we serve and You we seek for help.
⁶ Guide us to the straight path: ⁷ the path of those whom You have blessed, not
(the path) of those on whom (Your) anger falls, nor of those who go astray.

---

basmala render the Arabic terms similar to Marmaduke Pickthall's "Beneficent" and
"Merciful." The word *compassionate* has the sense of "suffering with," and readers
may explore whether "suffering with" is one of the characteristics that the Quran
ascribes to Allah.

1.4 – *Master of the Day of Judgment*

The themes of judgment for humanity and Allah as Judge are very important
in the Quran. Many passages describe the rewards and punishments to be given
out on the Day of Judgment (*yawm al-dīn*), also called the Day of Resurrection.
See "Eschatology in the Quran" (p. 604).

1.6 – *Guide us to the straight path*

Guidance for humanity is another of the Quran's most important themes, and
providing guidance is one of the key activities of Allah.

1.7 – *not (the path) of those on whom (Your) anger falls*

When the Quran translation puts parentheses around words, this means that
the words are not in the Arabic text but rather are added to smooth out the English
translation.

This verse can simply be taken as referring to people in general with whom Allah
is angry. One of the trends in Muslim tradition, however, starting with the earliest
commentaries, was to interpret "those on whom (Your) anger falls" to mean the
Jews. Verses elsewhere in the Quran seem to make this connection (e.g., 2.61; 5.60).

1.7 – *nor of those who go astray*

Like the preceding phrase, this expression can be taken in its plain meaning. In
Muslim tradition, however, most commentators interpreted "those who go astray"
to mean the Christians, sometimes cross-referencing 5.77. In this way, many Muslims
have understood this first sūra to reference the beliefs and behavior of Jews and
Christians. This theme will become more explicit in Sūras 2–5.

THE COW
AL-BAQARA

2

Sūra 2 is the first major sūra that readers encounter – and that Muslims recite or memorize – in the canonical progression of the Quran. It is the longest sūra (286 verses). This sūra touches on many themes that are important throughout the Quran and often sets the tone for those themes. Bible readers may be surprised to see numerous important connections to biblical characters in this opening section of the Quran.

Verses 1–29 – Introduction: belief and unbelief
30–39 – Creation, Adam, and Satan
40–86 – Moses and the "Sons of Israel"
87–121 – Polemic with Jews and Christians
122–41 – Abraham and Ishmael
142–67 – Islamic direction of prayer and pilgrimage
168–245 – Commands to believers
246–51 – Samuel, Saul, David, and Goliath
258–60 – Abraham
261–83 – Commands to believers

As the outline shows, the sūra is almost evenly divided between controversy with Jews and Christians and instructions for the community of believers. Different parts of the sūra explicitly address "people," "Sons of Israel," and "you who believe." The sūra offers stories of Adam, Abraham, and Moses. The sūra's title comes from an episode in its long Moses narrative, namely, a curious discourse about what sort of cow should be sacrificed (vv. 67–71).

Both Muslim commentary and academic scholarship have highlighted the importance of the long central passage, approximately verses 42–162, containing controversy with the Jews (and to some extent Christians). This passage includes the preaching of the messenger, the responses of the audience, controversies between the messenger and his audience, and stories from the past brought in as support for the messenger's preaching.

Muslim commentators have understood the Jews as the subject long before they are named in the sūra, for example at verses 26 and 27 – and even from verse 1! The best-known Muslim story of Islamic origins, the *Sīra* of Ibn Isḥāq, offers an extensive narrative framework for Sūra 2 from verses 1–170 (*Sīra*, 247–59). The main characters in this *Sīra* narrative are Jewish rabbis.

In the Name of God, the Merciful, the Compassionate

[1] Alif Lām Mīm.

[2] That is the Book – (there is) no doubt about it – a guidance for the ones who guard (themselves), [3] who believe in the unseen, and observe the prayer, and contribute from what We have provided them, [4] and who believe in what

---

2.1 – *Alif Lām Mīm.*

Three letters of the Arabic alphabet known as "disconnected" or "opening" letters. Twenty-nine sūras begin with such letters, but the mystery of their meaning and function has never been solved by Muslim commentators or by modern scholars.

For example, the early commentary of Muqātil ibn Sulaymān (d. AD 767) tells a story in which the Jews of Medina who hear Muhammad's recitation take these disconnected letters to represent the number of years of his reign. This is just one of many speculations, and Muslim interpreters have not been able to agree.

2.2 – *That is the Book – (there is) no doubt about it*

The Quran contains many "self-referential" verses in which the Quran makes claims for itself and/or for the messenger, often at the beginning of sūras. See "Different Kinds of Literature" (p. 14).

Because the verse reads "that is the Book" rather than "this," some Muslim commentaries included the opinion that this verse might be referring to the Torah (*tawrāt*), the first part of the Hebrew Bible and first five books of the Old Testament.

2.3 – *who believe*

Faith (*īmān*), believing (*āmana*), and believers (*mu'minūn*) form one of the central concepts in the Quran.

2.4 – *in what has been sent down to you*

The Quran claims that its contents are "sent down" to the messenger. This is the Quran's normal vocabulary of revelation (*nazzala, anzala, tanzīl*). This expression helpfully indicates that frequently in the Quran the "belief" in view is not a general "religious faith" but the particular belief that the messenger is a true prophet and that Allah "sends down" the messenger's recitations.

The Quran frequently addresses personal messages to the messenger. See

has been sent down to you, and what was sent down before you, and they are certain of the Hereafter. ⁵ Those (stand) on guidance from their Lord, and those – they are the ones who prosper. ⁶ Surely those who disbelieve – (it is) the same for them whether you warn them or do not warn them. They will not believe. ⁷ God has set a seal on their hearts and on their hearing, and on their sight (there is) a covering. For them (there is) a great punishment.

⁸ (There are) some people who say, 'We believe in God and in the Last Day,' but they are not believers. ⁹ They try to deceive God and the believers, but they only deceive themselves, though they do not realize (it). ¹⁰ In their hearts is a sickness, so God has increased their sickness, and for them (there is) a painful punishment because they have lied. ¹¹ When it is said to them, 'Do not foment corruption on the earth,' they say, 'We are setting (things) right.' ¹² Is it not a fact that they – they are the ones who foment corruption, though they do not realize (it)? ¹³ When it is said to them, 'Believe as the people believe,' they say, 'Shall we believe as the fools believe?' Is it not a fact that they – they are the fools, but they do not know (it)? ¹⁴ When they meet those who believe, they say, 'We believe,' but when they go privately to their satans, they say, 'Surely we are with you. We were only mocking.' ¹⁵ God will mock them, and increase them in their insolent transgression, wandering blindly. ¹⁶ Those are the ones who have purchased error with the (price of) guidance. Their transaction has not profited (them), and they have not been (rightly) guided. ¹⁷ Their parable is like the parable of the one who kindled a fire.

"Different Kinds of Literature" (p. 14). Muslims believe that the Quran's voice is Allah, that the messenger is Muhammad, and that the recitation "sent down" is the Quran.

2.4 – *and what was sent down before you*

The Quran shows an awareness of revelations prior to Islam. In this way the Quran raises the question of the relationship between the messenger's recitation and the pre-Islamic scriptures.

2.6 – *Surely those who disbelieve*

The opposite to believing, disbelieving (*kafara*), also makes its appearance at the beginning of the book. Throughout the Quran, faith and unbelief (*kufr*) are in opposition and conflict.

In this opening passage of the sūra (v. 1–39), the Quran does not specify who "the disbelievers" are. This is a typical feature of the Quran: various groups of people are referred to by pronouns but not named.

2.17 – *Their parable is like the parable of the one who kindled a fire*

The Quran does not often speak in parables (*amthāl*), though it claims to do so at a number of points (e.g., 13.17; 24.35; 29.43; 59.21). This verse and the following verses (17–20) describe disbelievers through the pictures of a fire and lightning.

When it lit up what was around him, God took away their light, and left them in darkness – they do not see. [18] Without hearing or speech or sight – so they do not return. [19] Or (it is) like a cloudburst from the sky, with darkness and thunder and lightning. They put their fingers in their ears because of the thunderbolts, afraid of death – God surrounds the disbelievers. [20] The lightning almost takes away their sight. Whenever it flashes for them, they walk in it, but when it becomes dark over them, they stand (still). If God (so) pleased, He could indeed take away their hearing and their sight. Surely God is powerful over everything.

[21] People! Serve your Lord, who created you and those who were before you, so that you may guard (yourselves). [22] (He it is) who made the earth as a couch for you, and the sky a dome, and sent down water from the sky, by means of which He produced fruits as a provision for you. So do not set up rivals to God, when you know (better). [23] If you are in doubt about what We have sent down to Our servant, then bring a sūra like it, and call your witnesses, other than God, if you are truthful. [24] If you do not (do this), and you will not (do it), then guard (yourselves) against the Fire – its fuel is people and stones – which is prepared for the disbelievers.

[25] Give good news to those who believe and do righteous deeds, that for them (there are) Gardens through which rivers flow. Whenever they are

---

2.21 – *People! Serve your Lord, who created you*

The need for humans to serve their Lord is a major quranic theme that becomes especially prominent in Sūras 10–46. The Lord has created (*khalaqa*) humankind and the world (vv. 21–22, 28–29) and expects a response of gratefulness, obedience, and worship from the people he has created. The affirmation of God as Creator is familiar to the "People of the Book" and one of the most important beliefs that observant Jews, Christians and Muslims share. See "Creation in the Quran" (p. 224).

Notice that the direct address (i.e., vocative) here is to humankind in general.

2.23 – *If you are in doubt about what We have sent down to Our servant, then bring a sūra like it*

The Quran claims that the recitations of the messenger are "sent down," but the audience seldom accepts this. The Quran's challenge to the audience is to compose a speech or text like the recitation. Similar challenges appear at 10.38; 11.13; 17.88; 28.49; and 52.34. In Muslim tradition these verses became known as the "challenge" (*taḥaddī*) verses. See analysis of these verses at 52.34 (p. 529).

2.25 – *Give good news to those who believe and do righteous deeds*

The "good news" here is the promise of Gardens (*jannāt*), which is a common quranic expression for heaven. Passages about judgment in the end times, describing reward and punishment, occur frequently in the Quran. See "Different Kinds of Literature" (p. 14), and "Eschatology in the Quran" (p. 604).

provided with fruit from there as provision, they will say, 'This is what we were provided with before,' (for) they will be given similar things (to eat). There they will also have pure spouses, and there they will remain.

[26] Surely God is not ashamed to strike a parable even of a gnat or anything above it. As for those who believe, they know that it is the truth from their Lord, but as for those who disbelieve, they will say, 'What does God intend by this parable?' He leads many astray by it and guides many by it, but He does not lead any astray by it except the wicked, [27] who break the covenant of God, after its ratification, and sever what God has commanded to be joined, and foment corruption on the earth. Those – they are the losers. [28] How can you disbelieve in God, when you were (once) dead and He gave you life? Then He causes you to die, then He gives you life (again), (and) then to Him you are returned? [29] He (it is) who created for you what is on the earth – all (of it). Then He mounted (upward) to the sky and fashioned them (as) seven heavens. He has knowledge of everything.

[30] (Remember) when your Lord said to the angels, 'Surely I am placing on the earth a ruler.' They said, 'Will You place on it someone who will foment corruption on it, and shed blood, while we glorify (You) with Your praise and call You holy?' He said, 'Surely I know what you do not know.' [31] And He taught Adam the names – all of them. Then He presented them to the angels, and said, 'Inform Me of the names of these, if you are truthful.' [32] They said, 'Glory to You! We have no knowledge except for what You have taught us. Surely You – You are the Knowing, the Wise.' [33] He said, 'Adam! Inform them of their names.' And when he had informed them of their names, He said, 'Did I not say to you, "Surely I know the unseen (things) of the heavens and the earth"? I know what you reveal and what you have concealed.'

[34] (Remember) when We said to the angels, 'Prostrate yourselves before Adam,' and they prostrated themselves, except Iblīs. He refused and became arrogant,

---

In the Quran, to "believe and do righteous deeds" is the way people achieve entry into the Gardens on the Day of Judgment.

2.30 – *when your Lord said to the angels, "Surely I am placing on the earth a ruler"*

Here is the first story of a character familiar from the Bible, Adam (v. 30–38). The story starts with a conversation between the Lord (*rabb*) and the angels, in which the Lord commands the angels to bow down to Adam (v. 34). In this version of the story, the Lord forbids Adam and his wife (her name is not given in the Quran) to go near to "this tree" (v. 35), but Satan "caused them both to slip from there" (v. 36).

2.34 – *when We said to the angels*

Here the Lord speaks in first-person plural ("We," vv. 34–39) after speaking in first-person singular ("I," vv. 30, 33) and being described in second- and third-person

and was one of the disbelievers. ³⁵ And We said, 'Adam! Inhabit the Garden, you and your wife, and eat freely of it wherever you please, but do not go near this tree, or you will both be among the evildoers.' ³⁶ Then Satan caused them both to slip from there, and to go out from where they were. And We said, 'Go down, some of you an enemy to others! The earth is a dwelling place for you, and enjoyment (of life) for a time.' ³⁷ Then Adam received certain words from his Lord, and He turned to him (in forgiveness). Surely He – He is the One who turns (in forgiveness), the Compassionate. ³⁸ We said, 'Go down from it – all (of you)! If any guidance comes to you from Me, whoever follows My guidance – (there will be) no fear on them, nor will they sorrow. ³⁹ But those who disbelieve and call Our signs a lie – those are the companions of the Fire. There they will remain.'

⁴⁰ Sons of Israel! Remember My blessing which I bestowed on you. Fulfill

---

singular ("You," "He," vv. 31–32). Following the Adam story, the text returns to first-person singular (vv. 40–41). Abrupt changes in voice are common in the Quran.

Muslims understand both plural and singular to be the voice of Allah and explain the "We" to mean not a plural deity but the so-called "royal we," or *pluralis majestatis,* an honorific plural.

The story of Adam repeats in different versions in 7.10–27 and 20.115–23. See the analysis of the Quran's Adam stories at 20.121 (p. 327).

Some of the elements in these stories are not familiar to Bible readers, such as the command to the angels to bow down to Adam. The Quran shows great interest in this aspect, recounting this part in four further sūras (15; 17; 18; 38) – in two cases without mentioning Adam's name. Such extrabiblical details in quranic stories of biblical characters are often also found in Jewish rabbinic and Christian apocryphal versions of the stories. In this case, the details seem to come from the *Life of Adam and Eve* (fourth century AD) and the *Questions of Bartholomew* (third century AD). See "Apocryphal Details in Quranic Stories" (p. 229).

2.34 – *they prostrated themselves, except Iblīs. He refused and became arrogant*
The name *Iblīs* appears a number of times in the Quran where it seems to be the name of the rebel against God. The tempter of humans is Satan (*Shayṭān,* v. 36). *Iblīs* seems to come from the Greek *diabolos,* which translates into English as "accuser" or "devil." On Iblīs's refusal to bow down, see the comments on 38.73–74 (p. 458).

2.38 – *If any guidance comes to you from Me*
According to this verse, Allah looks ahead from the time of Adam to the coming of guidance in the future.

2.40 – *Sons of Israel! Remember My blessing which I bestowed on you*
This passage (v. 40–48) is addressed directly to the Sons of Israel (*Banū Isrā'īl*). This is a good example of a kind of literature known as "polemic," which challenges others'

My covenant (and) I shall fulfill your covenant, and Me – fear Me (alone).
[41] Believe in what I have sent down, confirming what is with you, and do not
be the first to disbelieve in it. Do not sell My signs for a small price, and guard
(yourselves) against Me. [42] Do not mix the truth with falsehood, and do not conceal the truth when you know (better). [43] Observe the prayer and give the alms,
and bow with the ones who bow. [44] Do you command the people to piety and
forget yourselves, though you recite the Book? Will you not understand? [45] Seek
help in patience and the prayer. Surely it is hard indeed, except for the humble,
[46] who think that they will meet their Lord, and that they will return to Him.
[47] Sons of Israel! Remember My blessing which I bestowed on you, and that I
have favored you over the worlds. [48] Guard (yourselves) against a Day when no
one will intercede for another at all, and no intercession will be accepted from
him, and no compensation taken from him, nor will they be helped.

[49] (Remember) when We rescued you from the house of Pharaoh. They were
inflicting on you the evil punishment, slaughtering your sons and sparing your

---

beliefs or practices. Polemic literature appears frequently in the Quran. It brings to
mind a confrontation between a messenger and his audience. See "Different Kinds
of Literature" (p. 14).

2.41 – *Believe in what I have sent down, confirming what is with you*

The Quran claims revelation for itself and asserts that its contents "confirm" (*muṣaddiq*) that which is "with" the audience. Since this verse is addressed to the Children of
Israel, 2.41 seems to claim that the recitations of the messenger confirm the Torah (*tawrāt*,
the Pentateuch or "Books of Moses"). See the analysis of this claim at 46.12 (p. 502).

The Quran appeals to the Children of Israel to believe that the messenger's recitations are "sent down" by Allah.

2.47 – *that I have favored you over the worlds*

The "Sons of Israel" are given a very high position several times in the Quran
(e.g., 2.122, 7.140, 44.32; cf. 3.33, 6.86).

2.48 – *no intercession will be accepted from him*

The question of whether intercession (*shafāʿa*) between humans and Allah is
possible finds a range of answers in the Quran, from this categorical prohibition in
2.48 (cf. 2.123, 254) to indications of Allah's permission for intercession (e.g., 2.255), to
acceptance of one particular intercessor (e.g., 21.28). See the comments on intercession at 39.44 (p. 464).

2.49–74 – *(Remember) when We rescued you from the house of Pharaoh*

Direct address to the "Sons of Israel" moves into a story about Israel in the past
through the simple expression "and when" (*wa idh*). The long narrative that follows
(vv. 49–73) is a series of reminders, starting with God's deliverance of the Children

women. In that was a great test from your Lord. ⁵⁰ And when We parted the sea for you, We rescued you, and We drowned the house of Pharaoh while you were looking on.

⁵¹ (Remember) when We appointed for Moses forty nights. Then you took the calf after he (was gone), and you were evildoers. ⁵² Then We pardoned you after that, so that you might be thankful. ⁵³ And (remember) when We gave Moses the Book and the Deliverance, so that you might be (rightly) guided. ⁵⁴ And when Moses said to his people, 'My people! Surely you have done yourselves evil by taking the calf. So turn to your Creator (in repentance), and kill one another. That will be better for you in the sight of your Creator.' Then He

---

of Israel from Egypt and continuing until their worship of the calf. The text slips into commentary and direct address a number of times (e.g., vv. 61, 72), as if the story is being told to a particular audience. Finally, at verse 74 the passage returns to direct address to accuse that "your hearts became hardened after that, and they (became) like stones or even harder."

There are more stories about Moses in the Quran than about any other character. See the table on the details and distribution of these stories (p. 390). This first canonical appearance of the stories contains a number of narrative elements familiar from the biblical account of Moses. Several details in the Quran's story are not found in the Bible – for example, the elaborate search for the right kind of cow to slaughter (vv. 67–71). An even longer Moses story in Sūra 7 parallels this first story in many details and also fills in some of the gaps (7.103–71).

2.49 – *We rescued you*

The language of salvation in the Quran revolves around two forms of the Arabic verb *najā*, here translated "rescued." This verb occurs most often in stories about characters familiar from the Old Testament. The verb repeats in verse 50. See "Salvation in the Quran" (p. 180).

2.53 – *And (remember) when We gave Moses the Book and the Deliverance*

The Quran acknowledges the pre-Islamic scriptures and always refers to them in the most positive and respectful ways. Often this is with the particular names *tawrāt* (Torah) and *injīl* (Evangel or Gospel), but here the Torah is simply the book that Allah gave to Moses. The affirmation "We gave Moses the book" appears again in verse 87.

"Deliverance" translates the Arabic term *furqān*, which elsewhere is frequently rendered "criterion." See the comments at 25.1 on *furqān*, its seven occurrences in the Quran, and what they refer to (p. 363).

2.54 – *So turn to your Creator (in repentance), and kill one another*

The command in this verse, "kill one another," seems to be an echo of the command of Moses to the Levites in Exodus 32:27.

turned to you (in forgiveness). Surely He – He is the One who turns (in forgiveness), the Compassionate.

[55] (Remember) when you said, 'Moses! We shall not believe you until we see God openly,' and the thunderbolt took you while you were looking on. [56] Then We raised you up after your death, so that you might be thankful. [57] And We overshadowed you (with) the cloud, and We sent down on you the manna and the quails: 'Eat from the good things which We have provided you.' They did not do Us evil, but they did themselves evil.

[58] (Remember) when We said, 'Enter this town and eat freely of it wherever you please, and enter the gate in prostration and say: "Ḥiṭṭa." We shall forgive you your sins and increase the doers of good.' [59] But those who did evil exchanged a word other than that which had been spoken to them. So We sent down on those who did evil wrath from the sky, because they were acting wickedly.

[60] (Remember) when Moses asked for water for his people, and We said, 'Strike the rock with your staff,' and (there) gushed forth from it twelve springs. All the people already knew their drinking place: 'Eat and drink from the provision of God, and do not act wickedly on the earth, fomenting corruption.'

[61] (Remember) when you said, 'Moses! We cannot endure just one kind of food. Call on your Lord for us, that He may bring forth for us some of what the earth grows: its green herbs, its cucumbers, its corn, its lentils, and its onions.' He said, 'Would you exchange what is worse for what is better? Go (back) down

---

2.55 – Moses! We shall not believe you until we see God openly

The demand of the Children of Israel to "see Allah openly" (also at 4.153) seems to be a development from the words of Yahweh to Moses in Exodus 19:21: "Go down and warn the people so they do not force their way through to see the Lᴏʀᴅ and many of them perish."

2.59 – But those who did evil exchanged a word other than that which had been spoken to them

The story in verses 58–59 is unknown outside the Quran. It seems to portray a command to the Sons of Israel to enter a town in a certain posture and to say a particular word, *ḥiṭṭa*. Some instead pronounce a different word while entering, so Allah punishes them.

"Exchanged" translates the Arabic verb *baddala*, from which the expression *tabdīl* ("change") comes. Perhaps for this reason, some Muslim polemicists have claimed that verse 59 accuses the Jews of falsifying the Torah (*tawrāt*). However, most early Muslim commentators understood the verse to refer to a verbal act during the days of Moses. This detail repeats at 7.161–62 and is briefly referred to in 4.154. See "Tampering with the Pre-Islamic Scriptures" (p. 142).

to Egypt! Surely you will have what you ask for.' Humiliation and poverty were stamped upon them, and they incurred the anger of God. That was because they had disbelieved in the signs of God, and killed the prophets without any right. That was because they disobeyed and went on transgressing. [62] Surely those who believe, and those who are Jews, and the Christians, and the Sabians – whoever believes in God and the Last Day, and docs righteousness – they have their reward with their Lord. (There will be) no fear on them, nor will they sorrow.

[63] (Remember) when We took a covenant with you, and raised the mountain above you: 'Hold fast what We have given you, and remember what is in it, so that you may guard (yourselves).' [64] Then you turned away after that, and if (it were) not (for the) favor of God on you, and His mercy, you would indeed

---

2.61 – *they . . . killed the prophets without any right*

This verse seems to switch from a story about the Sons of Israel in the distant past to a general judgment on Jews. It states that the Jews disbelieved in the signs of God, killed the prophets, and disobeyed. The statement that the Jews killed the prophets repeats a number of times in Sūras 2–5, including in this sūra verses 87 and 91.

The Quran claims that because of this judgment, the Jews suffer humiliation and poverty and incur the anger of God. The Arabic word for "anger" here, *ghaḍab*, is the same word used in the short first sūra, "those on whom (Your) anger falls" (1.7). The word also appears at 5.60, "whomever He is angry with," in a passage that gives further reasons for judgment on the Jews. See the comments at 2.65.

2.62 – *Surely those who believe, and those who are Jews, and the Christians, and the Sabians*

This verse appears to say that Jews and Christians (*Naṣārā*) who believe and do righteousness will be rewarded. The identity of the third group, the Sabians, is not clear. Is this a favorable comment about the faith and life of non-Muslims?

The statement should be read in terms of the immediate context, and more generally in comparison with other statements about non-Muslims in the Quran. Muqātil ibn Sulaymān (d. 767), author of the earliest existing complete commentary on the Quran, interpreted *believe* in this verse to mean "believe in Muhammad."

This verse repeats at 5.69 and appears in a quite different version at 22.17.

2.63 – *when We . . . raised the mountain above you*

This detail seems to be a development from the account of Moses in Exodus 19, where the Children of Israel stood at the foot of Mount Sinai and "the whole mountain trembled violently" (19:17–18). This detail repeats in the Quran at 2.93; 4.154; and 7.171.

have been among the losers. [65] Certainly you know those of you who transgressed in (the matter of) the sabbath, and (that) We said to them, 'Become apes, skulking away!' [66] We made it a punishment for their own time and what followed, and an admonition for the ones who guard (themselves).

[67] (Remember) when Moses said to his people, 'Surely God commands you to slaughter a cow.' They said, 'Do you take us in mockery?' He said, 'I take refuge with God from being one of the ignorant.' [68] They said, 'Call on your Lord for us, so that He may make clear to us what it (should be).' He said, 'Surely He says, "Surely it is to be a cow, not old and not young, (but) an age between that." Do what you are commanded!' [69] They said, 'Call on your Lord for us, so that He may make clear to us what color it (should be).' He said, 'Surely He says, "Surely it is to be a yellow cow, its color bright, delighting to the onlookers."' [70] They said, 'Call on your Lord for us, so that He may make clear to us what (kind) it (should be). Surely cows are all alike to us. And surely (then), if God pleases, we shall indeed be (rightly) guided.' [71] He said, 'Surely He says, "Surely it is to be a cow, not broken in to plough the earth or to water the field, (but one that is) sound, without any blemish on it."' They said, 'Now you have brought the truth.' So they slaughtered it, though they nearly did not.

[72] (Remember) when you killed a man, and you argued about it, but God brought forth what you were concealing. [73] So We said, 'Strike him with part of it.' In this way God brings the dead to life, and shows you His signs so that

---

2.65 – *those of you who transgressed in (the matter of) the sabbath, and (that) We said to them, "Become apes, skulking away!"*

For a transgression on the sabbath, Allah changes a group from the Sons of Israel into apes. The story – and the statement about transformation into apes – appears again at 7.163–67 with additional details about the transgression. The Quran connects this story with the concept of a curse on the "People of the Book" at 5.60. There, as an example of people whom Allah has cursed and is angry with, the Quran tells of those whom Allah "made apes, and pigs, and slaves of al-Ṭāghūt."

2.67 – *When Moses said to his people, "Surely God commands you to slaughter a cow"*

The Sons of Israel search for a particular cow to slaughter (*dhabaḥa*). Moses gives them a series of clues so that they can identify the correct animal (vv. 68–71). The name of the sūra comes from this cow (*baqara*).

2.73 – *So We said, "Strike him with part of it"*

Muslim commentaries interpret this to mean that the Sons of Israel should strike the man killed in verse 72 with part of the cow (v. 71) in order to find out who killed him.

you may understand. [74] Then your hearts became hardened after that, and they (became) like stones or even harder. Surely (there are) some stones indeed from which rivers gush forth, and surely (there are) some indeed which have been split open, so that water comes out of them, and surely (there are) some indeed which fall down from fear of God. God is not oblivious of what you do.

[75] Are you eager that they should believe you , even though a group of them has already heard the word of God, (and) then altered it after they had understood it – and they know (they have done this)? [76] When they meet those who believe, they say, 'We believe,' but when some of them meet with others, they say, 'Do you report to them what God has disclosed to you, so that they may dispute with you by means of it in the presence of your Lord? Will you not understand?' [77] Do they not know that God knows what they keep secret and what they speak aloud? [78] Some of them are common people – they do not know the Book, only wishful thinking, and they only conjecture. [79] So woe to those who write the Book with their (own) hands, (and) then say, 'This is from

---

2.75 – *Are you eager that they should believe you*

After the long address to the Sons of Israel and the reminders of their past (vv. 40–74), the Quran addresses the "believers" in order to discuss the Jews (named at vv. 62, 111). This verse introduces a long passage (vv. 75–162) of polemic or controversy between the messenger and his audience. In this passage the Quran switches back and forth between the believers and the Jews, and sometimes addresses the messenger alone. The basic issue seems to be that the "People of the Book" choose not to accept the authority of the messenger or to follow him (see v. 145).

This verse seems to question the behavior of the Jews at the time of the first recitation of these words on the basis of the behavior of the Sons of Israel in the distant past.

2.75 – *a group of them has already heard the word of God, (and) then altered it*

This is the first of four verses in the Quran that contain the Arabic verb *ḥarrafa* – often translated as "change" or "distort" but understood by the earliest Muslim commentators on the Quran to mean "tampering with" or "mishandling" (also 4.46; 5.13; 5.41).

In this case, the object of the verb is the speech (*kalām*) of Allah. The context of the verse – coming just after the long story about Moses – seems to influence its interpretation. Early Muslim commentators understood this verse to mean that some leaders of the Sons of Israel do not faithfully relay the words of God that Moses reports to them. See "Tampering with the Pre-Islamic Scriptures" (p. 142).

2.79 – *woe to those who write the Book with their (own) hands*

A number of verses in the Quran show an attitude of suspicion toward the

God,' in order to sell it for a small price. Woe to them for what their hands have written, and woe to them for what they earn. [80] And they say, 'The Fire will only touch us for a number of days.' Say: 'Have you taken a covenant with God? God will not break His covenant. Or do you say about God what you do not know? [81] Yes indeed! Whoever commits evil and is encompassed by his sin – those are the companions of the Fire. There they will remain. [82] But those who believe and do righteous deeds – those are the companions of the Garden. There they will remain.'

[83] (Remember) when We took a covenant with the Sons of Israel: 'Do not serve (anyone) but God, and (do) good to parents and family, and the orphans, and the poor, and speak well to the people, and observe the prayer and give the alms.' Then you turned away in aversion, except for a few of you. [84] And when We took a covenant with you: 'Do not shed your (own) blood, and do not expel your (own people) from your homes,' then you agreed (to it) and bore witness. [85] Then you became those who were killing yourselves, and expelling some of you from their homes, supporting each other against them in sin and enmity. And if they come to you as captives, you ransom (them), though their expulsion was forbidden to you. Do you believe in part of the Book and disbelieve in part? What is the payment for the one among you who does that, except disgrace in

---

treatment of the pre-Islamic scriptures by the "People of the Book." The expression "those who write the Book with their (own) hands" in 2.79 is one of the best-known of these verses.

The preceding context refers vaguely to acts of conspiracy (v. 76), deception (v. 77), and ignorance (v. 78). This mood of suspicion then seems to continue into verse 79 about the writing of a book (*kitāb*).

Many Muslim commentators and polemicists interpreted this verse to mean that the Jews falsify the text of the Torah (*tawrāt*). In most cases, their accusation was that the Jews of Medina changed or erased the description of Muhammad from the Torah. See "Tampering with the Pre-Islamic Scriptures" (p. 142).

2.83 – *(Remember) when We took a covenant with the Sons of Israel*

The text returns to a couple of "when" statements about the establishment of the covenant, but now the judgments come very quickly: the Sons of Israel turned away from the covenant and transgressed its stipulations (vv. 83–86).

2.85 – *What is the payment for the one among you who does that*

This verse speaks of a reckoning "in this present life" as well as on the Day of Judgment. The Quran offers a range of scenarios of reckoning for unbelievers, from punishment only after this life on the one end, to punishment at the hands of believers in this life on the other.

this present life, and on the Day of Resurrection they will be returned to the harshest punishment? God is not oblivious of what you do. [86] Those are the ones who have purchased this present life with (the price of) the Hereafter. The punishment will not be lightened for them, nor will they be helped.

[87] Certainly We gave Moses the Book, and followed up after him with the messengers, and We gave Jesus, son of Mary, the clear signs, and supported him with the holy spirit. (But) whenever a messenger brought you what you yourselves did not desire, did you become arrogant, and some you called liars and some you killed? [88] And they say, 'Our hearts are covered.' No! God has cursed them for their disbelief, and so little will they believe. [89] When (there) came to them a Book from God, confirming what was with them – though before

---

2.87 – *Certainly We gave Moses the Book*

The Quran again affirms the revelation of the Torah to Moses.

2.87 – *We gave Jesus, son of Mary, the clear signs, and supported him with the holy spirit*

The Quran calls Jesus *'Īsā*. This is not the same as the Arabic word for Jesus, which is *Yasū'a*. Muslim and non-Muslim scholars alike have tried to explain why the Quran uses the name *'Īsā*, but no conclusive answer has been found. In terms of Semitic root letters, the Quran seems to have flipped the consonants of the Hebrew *Yēshūa'* back to front. One consequence of the Quran's renaming Jesus is that the name *'Īsā* carries with it none of the sense of salvation that the angel assumes in Matthew 1:21.

The name *'Īsā* appears here for the first time in the canonical progression. It occurs twenty-four more times, including twice more in this sūra (vv. 136, 253). The Quran offers longer passages on *'Īsā* in the third, fifth, and nineteenth sūras, while the fourth and fifth sūras contain several crucial shorter passages.

The difference in names between the Quran and the Bible alerts non-Muslim readers to the larger question of how the quranic *'Īsā* compares to the biblical Jesus. For this reason, this commentary maintains the name *'Īsā* for the quranic Jesus and carefully observes the characteristics of *'Īsā* in order to facilitate a meaningful interaction with this central question. See an analysis of the *'Īsā* passages at 57.27 (p. 548).

The Arabic for "holy spirit," *rūḥ al-qudus* (lit. "the spirit of the holy") resembles the Hebrew words *ruaḥ ha-ḳodesh* (cf. Psalm 51:11; Isaiah 63:10, 11). But what does the Quran mean by it? See the analysis of "holy spirit" passages at 16.102 (p. 283).

2.89 – *When (there) came to them a Book from God, confirming what was with them*

The Quran claims that this writing (or "book") is from Allah and states that its contents "confirm" (*muṣaddiq*) that which is "with" the audience. This verse starts a series of verses that claim correspondence (2.89, 91, 97, 101). See the analysis of this claim at 46.12 (p. 502).

(this) they had asked for victory against those who disbelieved – when what they recognized came to them, they disbelieved in it. So the curse of God is on the disbelievers. [90] Evil is what they have sold themselves for: they disbelieve in what God has sent down, (because of) envy that God should send down some of His favor on whomever He pleases of His servants. So they have incurred anger upon anger, and for the disbelievers (there is) a humiliating punishment.

[91] When it is said to them, 'Believe in what God has sent down,' they say, 'We believe in what has been sent down on us,' but they disbelieve in anything after that, when it is the truth confirming what is with them. Say: 'Why did you kill the prophets of God before, if you were believers?' [92] Certainly Moses brought you the clear signs, (but) then you took the calf after he (was gone), and you were evildoers. [93] And when We took a covenant with you, and raised the mountain above you: 'Hold fast what We have given you, and hear,' they said, 'We hear and disobey.' And they were made to drink the calf in their hearts because of their disbelief. Say: 'Evil is what your belief commands you, if you are believers.'

[94] Say: 'If the Home of the Hereafter with God is yours alone, to the exclusion of the people, and not for (the rest of) the people, wish for death, if you are truthful.' [95] But they will never wish for it because of what their (own) hands have sent forward. God knows the evildoers. [96] Indeed you will find them the most desirous of people for life – even more so than the idolaters. One of them wishes to live for a thousand years, but (even) such a long life will not spare him from the punishment. God sees what they do.

[97] Say: 'Whoever is an enemy to Gabriel – surely he has brought it down

---

2.91 – *When it is said to them, "Believe in what Allah has sent down"*

Dense discussion continues about a group who will not accept the present recitations to be from God (v. 91) or the authority of the person reciting (v. 101). Though they are not named in this passage (vv. 91–101), the Jews seem to be the target of the discussion, and verses 92 and 93 strongly suggest this. The description of the group is punctuated with references to their past, the speeches of the messenger, and the Quran's claim that the message is coming from Allah (v. 99).

2.91 – *when it is the truth confirming what is with them*

The Quran commands the audience to believe that the messenger's recitations are sent down by Allah on the basis of the claim that his recitations confirm the scriptures they possess. See the analysis of this claim at 46.12 (p. 502).

2.97 – *Say: "Whoever is an enemy to Gabriel"*

The name Gabriel (*jibrīl*) appears three times in the Quran (also 2.98; 66.4). Here the Quran states that Gabriel reveals (*nazzala*) to the heart of the messenger. On the claim that this recitation confirms what "was before it," see the comments at 46.12 (p. 502).

on your heart by the permission of God, confirming what was before it, and as a guidance and good news to the believers. [98] Whoever is an enemy to God, and His angels, and His messengers, and Gabriel and Michael – surely God is an enemy to the disbelievers.' [99] Certainly We have sent down to you clear signs, and no one disbelieves them except the wicked. [100] Whenever they have made a covenant, did a group of them toss it away? No! Most of them do not believe. [101] When a messenger came to them from God, confirming what was with them, a group of those who were given the Book tossed the Book of God behind their backs, as if they did not know (about it). [102] And they followed what the satans used to recite over the kingdom of Solomon. Solomon did not disbelieve, but the satans disbelieved. They taught the people magic, and what had been sent down to the two angels (in) Babylon, Hārūt and Mārūt.

2.99 – *Certainly We have sent down to you clear signs*

The voice of the Quran speaks directly to the messenger to claim that the "clear signs" (*āyāt*) have been "sent down" to him. This kind of apparently self-conscious "messenger" material repeats many times throughout the Quran (e.g., vv. 119–20, 145).

Muslims understand the voice of the Quran to be Allah and the addressee to be Muhammad. Curiously, however, the name Muhammad is never directly addressed in the Quran.

2.101 – *When a messenger came to them from God*

Here the Quran speaks to an audience *about* "a messenger" (*rasūl*) and claims that he comes from Allah to people "who were given the book." This is the first occurrence of this kind of "self-referential" affirmation of a messenger and his recitations, but it repeats many times throughout the Quran (e.g., vv. 108, 151). See "self-referential" and "messenger" passages in the list of "Different Kinds of Literature" (p. 14).

Muslims understand the unnamed messenger in this sūra to be Muhammad. That name does not appear until 3.144, and after that it appears only three more times (33.40; 47.2; 48.29).

2.101 – *confirming what was with them*

The Quran frequently states that its contents confirm that which is "with" the audience. This verse charges "those who were given the Book" with the guilt of rejection, based on the claim that the messenger's recitations confirm what they know from their scriptures. See the analysis of this claim at 46.12 (p. 502).

2.102 – *they followed what the satans used to recite over the kingdom of Solomon*

The details of this verse, including the identities of the angels "Hārūt and Mārūt," are obscure, and the Quran provides no further explanation elsewhere. In the Quran Solomon is often associated with the satans (21.82, 38.37) and the *jinn* (27.17, 39; 34.12, 14).

Neither of them taught anyone, unless they both (first) said, 'We are only a temptation, so do not disbelieve.' And they learned from both of them how to separate a husband from his wife. Yet they did not harm anyone in this way, except by the permission of God. What they learned (only) harmed them and did not benefit them. Certainly they knew that whoever buys it has no share in the Hereafter. Evil indeed is what they have sold themselves for, if (only) they knew. [103] If they had believed and guarded (themselves), a reward from God (would) indeed (have been) better, if (only) they knew.

[104] You who believe! Do not say, 'Observe us,' but say, 'Regard us,' and hear. For the disbelievers (there is) a painful punishment. [105] Those who disbelieve among the People of the Book, and the idolaters, do not like (it) that anything good should be sent down on you from your Lord. But God chooses whomever He pleases for His mercy, and God is full of great favor. [106] Whatever verse We cancel or cause to be forgotten, We bring a better (one) than it, or (one) similar to it. Do you not know that God is powerful over everything? [107] Do you not know that God – to Him (belongs) the kingdom of the heavens and the earth, and you have no ally and no helper other than God. [108] Or do you wish to question your messenger, as Moses was questioned before? Whoever exchanges belief for disbelief has indeed gone astray from the right way. [109] Many of the People of the Book would like (it) if you turned back into disbelievers,

---

2.105 – *Those who disbelieve among the People of the Book*

The expression "People of the Book" appears here for the first time in the Quran's canonical progression. "People of the Book" are usually considered to include Jews and Christians, though the context of 2.105 seems mainly to have Jews in mind. This verse describes the People of the Book as begrudging that "anything good should be sent down" on the "believers." See a discussion of the Quran's approach to the People of the Book at 98.1 (p. 641).

2.106 – *Whatever verse We cancel or cause to be forgotten, We bring a better (one) than it*

This is one of the most important verses for the Islamic theory of abrogation. The Quran contains different kinds of material – both in style and subject. This sets up contradictions of content in such areas as response to conflict, treatment of non-Muslims, and predestination and freewill. Muslim scholars have traditionally dealt with contradiction by citing verses like 2.106, which seems to suggest that what Allah reveals at one time, in one set of circumstances, he may abrogate or replace at a later time.

For a fuller explanation of the Islamic theory of abrogation and the quranic verses used to support it, see the comments on 16.101 (p. 282).

after your believing, (because of) jealousy on their part, after the truth has become clear to them. So pardon and excuse (them), until God brings His command. Surely God is powerful over everything. [110] Observe the prayer and give the alms. Whatever good you send forward for yourselves, you will find it with God. Surely God sees what you do.

[111] They say, 'No one will enter the Garden unless they are Jews or Christians.' That is their wishful thinking. Say: 'Bring your proof, if you are truthful.' [112] Yes indeed! Whoever submits his face to God, and he is a doer of good, has his reward with his Lord. (There will be) no fear on them, nor will they sorrow. [113] The Jews say, 'The Christians have no ground to stand on;' and the Christians say, 'The Jews have no ground to stand on,' though they (both) recite the Book. In this way those who have no knowledge say something similar to their saying. God will judge between them on the Day of Resurrection concerning their differences.

[114] And who is more evil than the one who prevents the mosques of God from having His name remembered in them, and strives for their destruction? Those – it was not for them to enter them except in fear. For them (there is) disgrace in this world, and a great punishment for them in the Hereafter. [115] The East and the West (belong) to God, so wherever you turn, there is the face of God. Surely God is embracing, knowing.

[116] They say, 'God has taken a son.' Glory to Him! No! Whatever is in the heavens and the earth (belongs) to Him. All are obedient before Him

---

2.109 – *So pardon and excuse (them), until God brings His command*

This command to pardon and excuse the People of the Book indicates a positive direction for relationships with non-Muslims. Yet there is a qualifier: "until Allah brings His command." Some Muslim commentaries interpret this to mean that later in the story of Muhammad a harsher treatment of the Jewish tribes in Medina was required, and therefore newer recitations abrogated 2.109. For example, Muqātil ibn Sulaymān (d. 767) wrote that harsher treatment included the killing and captivity of Banū Qurayẓa and the expulsion from Medina of the Banū Naḍīr.

2.111 – *They say, "No one will enter the Garden unless they are Jews or Christians"*

This verse seems to reflect a confrontation between the messenger and his audience that continues at least to verse 121 and perhaps as far as verse 141, or even up to verse 162. In response to the claims of the audience, the Quran tells the messenger what to "say."

2.116 – *They say, "God has taken a son." Glory to him! No!*

Unidentified people are saying that "Allah has taken a son" (*walad*). The verse does not make clear who "they" are. However, Christians are mentioned in the near

[117] – Originator of the heavens and the earth. When He decrees something, He simply says to it, 'Be!' and it is.

[118] Those who have no knowledge say, 'If only God would speak to us, or a sign would come to us.' In this way those who were before them said something similar to their saying. Their hearts are alike. We have already made the signs clear to a people (who) are certain (in their belief). [119] Surely We have sent you with the truth, as a bringer of good news and a warner. You will not be questioned about the companions of the Furnace.

[120] Neither the Jews nor the Christians will ever be pleased with you until you follow their creed. Say: 'Surely the guidance of God – it is the (true) guidance.' If indeed you follow their (vain) desires, after the knowledge which has come to you, you will have no ally and no helper against God. [121] Those to whom We have given the Book recite it as it should be recited. Those (people) believe in it. But whoever disbelieves in it – those (people) – they are the losers.

---

context (vv. 111, 113, 120), so it is reasonable to assume that the Quran has their confession in mind.

This is the first mention of an important theme in the Quran. Its concern from the start is theological. Allah is sovereign over the universe. The Quran seems to claim that saying "Allah has taken a son" threatens Allah's sovereignty. The expression "Allah has taken a son" appears frequently in the Quran, and the response "Glory to him" (*subhānahu*) repeats as well. See "Son of God in the Quran" (p. 352).

2.117 – *When He decrees something, He simply says to it only, "Be!" and it is*

Immediately after denying that "Allah has taken a son," the Quran declares that Allah simply needs to command "Be!" to create anything. The implications of this statement for the identity of 'Īsā become clear in a short set of verses on this theme (3.47, 59; 19.35). See the analysis of denials of Jesus' deity at 43.59 (p. 491).

2.119 – *Surely We have sent you with the truth, as a bringer of good news and a warner*

The voice of the Quran speaks directly to the messenger to claim that Allah has sent him and to prescribe his role.

The following verses mention the Jews and Christians explicitly as groups who will not accept the claims in verse 119. However, verse 121 asserts that those who read their scriptures with the right reading will believe in the truth sent with the messenger.

2.120 – *Neither the Jews nor the Christians will ever be pleased with you until you follow their creed*

This verse clearly indicates a situation of controversy and debate between the messenger and the People of the Book.

[122] Sons of Israel! Remember My blessing which I bestowed on you, and that I have favored you over the worlds. [123] Guard (yourselves) against a Day when no one will intercede for another at all, and no compensation will be accepted from him, and no intercession will benefit him, nor will they be helped.

[124] (Remember) when his Lord tested Abraham with (certain) words, and he fulfilled them. He said, 'Surely I am going to make you a leader for the people.' He said, 'And of my descendants?' He said, 'My covenant does not extend to the evildoers.' [125] And when We made the House a place of meeting and security for the people, and (said), 'Take the standing place of Abraham as a place of prayer,' and We made a covenant with Abraham and Ishmael: 'Both of you purify My House for the ones who go around (it), and the ones who are devoted to it, and the ones who bow, (and) the ones who prostrate themselves.' [126] And when Abraham said, 'My Lord, make this land secure, and provide its people with fruits – whoever of them who believes in God and the Last Day,' He said, 'And whoever

---

2.123 – *no intercession will benefit him, nor with they be helped*

This repetition of verse 48 again seems to prohibit intercession to the Children of Israel. See an analysis of verses about intercession at 39.44 (p. 464).

2.124 – *(Remember) when his Lord tested Abraham with (certain) words, and he fulfilled them*

This verse begins an extended passage on Abraham (vv. 124–41), the first of many passages about this important character. The first part of the passage (vv. 125–27) associates Abraham with "the House" (*al-bayt*) and a set of rituals to perform there (also 3.96–97).

Though this sūra does not further identify the "House," 14.37 uses the expression "the Sacred House" in relation to Abraham. The Quran also associates "the Sacred House" with the *Ka'ba* at 5.97, though Abraham is not mentioned in the context. Muslims have traditionally interpreted the *Ka'ba* to mean a cube-like structure located in Mecca.

This is one of several passages that suggest that Abraham traveled deep into the Arabian Peninsula (also 3.96–97; 14.37; 22.26–31). See a discussion of Abraham in Arabia at 22.26 (p. 341).

However, only here is Abraham accompanied by Ishmael (vv. 125, 127). The name of Ishmael appears in the Quran mostly in lists of figures familiar from the Bible (e.g., 4.163). In other verses Ishmael is named together with Isaac (2.133, 136, 140; 3.84; 4.163; 14.39).

There is more about Abraham in the Quran than about any figure except Moses – more than 240 verses in 25 of the Quran's 114 sūras. See "Abraham in the Quran" (p. 90).

disbelieves – I shall give him enjoyment (of life) for a little (while), (and) then I shall force him to the punishment of the Fire – and it is an evil destination!' ¹²⁷ And when Abraham raised up the foundations of the House, and Ishmael (with him): 'Our Lord, accept (this) from us. Surely You – You are the Hearing, the Knowing. ¹²⁸ Our Lord, make us both submitted to You, and (make) from our descendants a community submitted to You. And show us our rituals, and turn to us (in forgiveness). Surely You – You are the One who turns (in forgiveness), the Compassionate. ¹²⁹ Our Lord, raise up among them a messenger from among them, to recite Your signs to them, and to teach them the Book and the wisdom, and to purify them. Surely You – You are the Mighty, the Wise.'

¹³⁰ Who prefers (another creed) to the creed of Abraham except the one who makes a fool of himself? Certainly We have chosen him in this world, and surely in the Hereafter he will indeed be among the righteous. ¹³¹ When his Lord said to him, 'Submit!,' he said, 'I have submitted to the Lord of the worlds.' ¹³² And Abraham charged his sons with this, and Jacob (did too): 'My sons! Surely God has chosen the (true) religion for you, so do not die without submitting.' ¹³³ Or were you witnesses when death approached Jacob, when he said to his sons, 'What will you serve after me?' They said, 'We will serve your God, and the God of your fathers, Abraham, and Ishmael, and Isaac: one God – to Him we submit.' ¹³⁴ That community has passed away. To it what it has earned, and to you what you have earned. You will not be questioned about what they have done.

¹³⁵ They say, 'Be Jews or Christians, (and then) you will be (rightly) guided.' Say: 'No! The creed of Abraham the Ḥanīf. He was not one of the idolaters.'

2.129 – *Our Lord, raise up among them a messenger from among them*

Abraham's prayer (vv. 127–29) includes a request to raise up from among his descendants a messenger. The concept of "a messenger from among them" appears again at 2.151; 3.164; 50.2; and 62.2. Muslims sometimes cite 2.129 when they claim that Muhammad's name and/or description would be found in the Bible.

2.130 – *Who prefers (another creed) to the creed of Abraham except the one who makes a fool of himself?*

With this question, the text shifts from narrative about Abraham to controversy and polemic concerning the identity of Abraham (vv. 130–41). The Quran claims that Abraham is a *muslim* (vv. 131–33, "one who submits") rather than a Jew or Christian (vv. 135, 140; cf. 3.67).

2.135 – *The creed of Abraham the Ḥanīf*

This is the first appearance of *Ḥanīf*, a word that appears ten times in the Quran, mostly in association with Abraham. Both Muslim confessional and non-Muslim

[136] Say: 'We believe in God, and what has been sent down to us, and what has been sent down to Abraham, and Ishmael, and Isaac, and Jacob, and the tribes, and what was given to Moses and Jesus, and what was given to the prophets from their Lord. We make no distinction between any of them, and to Him we submit.' [137] If they believe in something like what you believe in, they have been (rightly) guided, but if they turn away, they are only in defiance. God will be sufficient for you against them. He is the Hearing, the Knowing.

[138] The dye(ing) of God, and who is better than God at dye(ing)? We serve Him. [139] Say: 'Do you dispute with us about God, when He is our Lord and your Lord? To us our deeds and to you your deeds. We are devoted to Him. [140] Or do you say, "Abraham, and Ishmael, and Isaac, and Jacob, and the tribes were Jews or Christians"?' Say: 'Do you know better, or God? Who is more evil than the one who conceals a testimony which he has from God? God is not oblivious of what you do.' [141] That community has passed away. To it what it has earned, and to you what you have earned. You will not be questioned about what they have done.

---

scholars have made great efforts to understand this word, but all are limited by the lack of Arabic literature contemporary with the Quran and the lack of non-quranic support for the story of Abraham's presence in Arabia. English translations render *Ḥanīf* as "upright" or "a man of pure faith," and some scholars suggest the word indicates a kind of ancient monotheism unconnected with either Jewish or Christian faith.

Enquiring into the origin of *Ḥanīf* in *Foreign Vocabulary of the Qur'ān*, Arthur Jeffery suggested that the term came from the Syriac word *ḥanpā*, meaning "heathen" (see bibliography). For more on *Ḥanīf*, see "Abraham in the Quran" (p. 90).

2.136 – *We believe in God, and what has been sent down to us, and what has been sent down to Abraham*

This statement of faith seems to put the present recitation of the messenger on the same level as God's revelations to prophets prior to Islam. The verse also claims that the speakers make no distinction among the prophets (cf. v. 285). To what extent does the remainder of the Quran bear this out?

2.140 – *Who is more evil than the one who conceals a testimony which he has from God?*

The idea that someone is hiding important information – already seen at 2.42 and 77 – now repeats in a tight series of claims (vv. 140, 146, 159, 174). This verse seems to accuse someone of hiding a testimony (*shahāda*) about the identity of Abraham and his descendants.

[142] The fools among the people will say, 'What has turned them from the direction (of prayer) which they were (facing) toward?' Say: 'The East and the West (belong) to God. He guides whomever He pleases to a straight path.' [143] In this way We have made you a community (in the) middle, so that you may be witnesses over the people, and that the messenger may be a witness over you. And We established the direction (of prayer) which you were (facing) toward only so that We might know the one who would follow the messenger from the one who would turn back on his heels. Surely it was hard indeed, except for those whom God guided. But God was not one to let your belief go to waste. Surely God is indeed kind (and) compassionate with the people.

[144] We do see you turning your face about in the sky, and We shall indeed turn you in a direction which you will be pleased with. Turn your face in the direction of the Sacred Mosque, and wherever you are, turn your faces in its direction. Surely those who have been given the Book know indeed that it is the truth from their Lord. God is not oblivious of what they do. [145] Yet even if you bring every sign to those who have been given the Book, they will not follow your direction. You are not a follower of their direction, nor are they followers of each other's direction. If indeed you follow their (vain) desires, after the knowledge which has come to you, surely then you will indeed be among the evildoers. [146] Those to whom We have given the Book recognize it, as they recognize their (own) sons, yet surely a group of them indeed conceals the truth – and they know (it). [147] The truth is from your Lord, so do not be one of the doubters. [148] Each has a direction to which he turns. So race (toward doing)

2.142 – *What has turned them from the direction (of prayer) which they were (facing) toward?*

The direction of Muslim ritual prayer is known as the *qibla*. This passage (vv. 142–50) seems to refer to a dispute about the correct direction. According to Muslim tradition, the Muslims in Medina prayed in the direction of Jerusalem until Muhammad recited that they should instead turn around and pray in the direction of Mecca (understood from "the Sacred Mosque" in vv. 144, 149–50).

2.144 – *We do see you turning your face about in the sky*

The Quran directly addresses the messenger to approve his preference for the direction of prayer.

2.145 – *they will not follow your direction*

In all of the long preceding passage from verse 75 and continuing till verse 162, the main issue seems to be that the People of the Book choose not to accept the authority of the messenger.

good deeds. Wherever you may be, God will bring you all together. Surely God is powerful over everything.

¹⁴⁹ From wherever you go forth, turn your face toward the Sacred Mosque. Surely it is the truth indeed from your Lord. God is not oblivious of what you do. ¹⁵⁰ From wherever you go forth, turn your face toward the Sacred Mosque. And wherever you are, turn your faces toward it, so that the people will not have any argument against you – except for the evildoers among them; do not fear them, but fear Me – and so that I may complete My blessing on you, and that you may be (rightly) guided, ¹⁵¹ even as We have sent among you a messenger from among you. He recites to you Our signs, and purifies you, and teaches you the Book and the wisdom, and teaches you what you did not know. ¹⁵² So remember Me (and) I shall remember you. Be thankful to Me and do not be ungrateful to Me.

¹⁵³ You who believe! Seek help in patience and prayer. Surely God is with the patient. ¹⁵⁴ Do not say of anyone who is killed in the way of God, '(They are) dead.' No! (They are) alive, but you do not realize (it). ¹⁵⁵ We shall indeed test you with some (experience) of fear and hunger, and loss of wealth and lives and fruits. But give good news to the patient, ¹⁵⁶ who say, when a smiting smites them, 'Surely we (belong) to God, and surely to Him we return.' ¹⁵⁷ Those – on them (there are) blessings from their Lord, and mercy. Those – they are the (rightly) guided ones.

2.151 – *We have sent among you a messenger from among you. He recites to you Our signs*

The Quran speaks to an audience about "a messenger" among them and claims that both the messenger and his recitations are sent from Allah. See this "self-referential" kind of literature in "Different Kinds of Literature" (p. 14).

2.153 – *You who believe!*

After a long passage that began in verse 40 discussing the People of the Book and frequently addressing them directly, the content of the sūra shifts at this point largely to the concerns of "believers." The second half of the sūra takes up many areas of Muslim practice, such as dietary rules, fasting, pilgrimage, prayer, marriage, and fighting.

2.154 – *Do not say of anyone who is killed in the way of God, "(They are) dead." No! (They are) alive*

The idea that believers who die fighting are martyrs who go straight to heaven has its quranic basis in a series of verses, of which this is the first. Other verses like this are 3.157–58, 169–72, 195; 22.58–59; and 47.4–6. See an analysis of these verses at 47.4 (p. 509).

For the concept of fighting "in the way of Allah," see the analysis at 73.20 (p. 597).

¹⁵⁸ Surely al-Ṣafā and al-Marwa are among the symbols of God. Whoever performs pilgrimage to the House or performs visitation – (there is) no blame on him if he goes around both of them. And whoever does good voluntarily – surely God is thankful, knowing.

¹⁵⁹ Surely those who conceal what We have sent down of the clear signs and the guidance, after We have made it clear to the people in the Book, those – God will curse them, and the cursers will curse them, ¹⁶⁰ except for those who turn (in repentance), and set (things) right, and make (it) clear. Those – I shall turn to them (in forgiveness). I am the One who turns (in forgiveness), the Compassionate. ¹⁶¹ Surely those who disbelieve, and die while they are disbelievers, those – on them is the curse of God, and the angels, and the people all together. ¹⁶² There (they will) remain – the punishment will not be lightened for them, nor will they be spared.

¹⁶³ Your God is one God – (there is) no god but Him, the Merciful, the Compassionate. ¹⁶⁴ Surely in the creation of the heavens and the earth, and the alternation of the night and the day, and the ship which runs on the sea with what benefits the people, and the water which God sends down from the sky, and by means of it gives the earth life after its death, and He scatters on it all (kinds of) creatures, and (in the) changing of the winds, and the clouds controlled between the sky and the earth – (all these are) signs indeed for a people who understand. ¹⁶⁵ But (there are) some of the people who set up rivals to God. They love them with a love like (that given to) God. Yet those who believe are stronger in love for God. If (only) those who do evil could see (the Day), when they will see the punishment, that the power (belongs) to God altogether,

---

2.158 – *Surely al-Ṣafā and al-Marwa are among the symbols of God*
Al-Ṣafā and al-Marwa are the names of two hills near Mecca that remain important today in the rituals of the pilgrimage.

2.163 – *Your God is one God – (there is) no god but Him*
This verse states clearly both the concept of one (*wāḥid*) god (*ilāha*) and the belief that there is no god except him.

2.164 – *Surely in the creation of the heavens and the earth . . . signs*
The "signs" of a merciful Creator, expressed beautifully here, are a major theme in many sūras.

2.165 – *those who believe are stronger in love for God*
This verse is one of just a handful of verses that mention human love for Allah (also 3.31; 5.54; perhaps 2.177 and 76.8). There is no command in the Quran to love either Allah or other humans. See the summary of human love for Allah at 5.54 (p. 146), as well as the essay "The Language of Love in the Quran" (p. 560).

and that God is harsh in punishment. [166] When those who were followed disown those who followed them, and they see the punishment, and the ties with them are cut, [167] and those who followed say, 'If (only) we had (another) turn, so that we might disown them as they have disowned us.' In this way God will show them their deeds as regrets for them. They will never escape from the Fire.

[168] People! Eat from what is permitted (and) good on the earth, and do not follow the footsteps of Satan. Surely he is clear enemy to you. [169] He only commands you to evil and immorality, and that you should say about God what you do not know. [170] When it is said to them, 'Follow what God has sent down,' they say, 'No! We shall follow what we found our fathers doing' – even though their fathers did not understand anything and were not (rightly) guided? [171] The parable of those who disbelieve is like the parable of the one who calls out to what hears nothing but a shout and a cry. Without hearing or speech or sight – they do not understand.

[172] You who believe! Eat from the good things which We have provided you, and be thankful to God, if it is Him you serve. [173] He has only forbidden to you: the dead (animal), and the blood, and swine's flesh, and what has been dedicated to (a god) other than God. But whoever is forced (by necessity), not desiring or (deliberately) transgressing – no sin (rests) on him. Surely God is forgiving, compassionate.

[174] Surely those who conceal what God has sent down of the Book, and sell it for a small price, those – they will not eat (anything) but the Fire in their bellies. God will not speak to them on the Day of Resurrection, nor will He purify them. For them (there is) a painful punishment. [175] Those are the ones who have purchased error with the (price of) guidance, and punishment with the price of forgiveness. How determined they are to (reach) the Fire! [176] That is because God has sent down the Book with the truth. Surely those who differ about the Book are indeed in extreme defiance.

[177] Piety is not turning your faces toward the East and the West, but (true) piety (belongs to) the one who believes in God and the Last Day, and the angels,

---

2.168 – *People! Eat from what is permitted (and) good on the earth*

This verse begins an extended passage primarily concerned with law. Many of the verbs, like "eat," now appear in the form of commands. Between this verse and verse 245, the Quran stipulates dietary rules (vv. 168–73), retaliation (vv. 178–79), bequests (vv. 180–82, 240–42), fasting (vv. 183–87), pilgrimage (vv. 189, 196–203), fighting and killing (vv. 190–94, 216–18, 244), and marriage and divorce (vv. 221, 226–37).

These laws use the language of "permitted" (*ḥalāl*) and "prescribed" (*kutib*, lit. "written").

and the Book, and the prophets, and (who) gives his wealth, despite his love for it, to family, and the orphans, and the poor, and the traveler, and beggars, and for the (freeing of) slaves, and (who) observes the prayer and gives the alms, and those who fulfill their covenant when they have made it, and those who are patient under violence and hardship, and in times of peril. Those are the ones who are truthful, and those – they are the ones who guard (themselves).

[178] You who believe! The (law of) retaliation is prescribed for you in (the case of) those who have been killed: the free man for the free man, the slave for the slave, and the female for the female. But whoever is granted any pardon for it by his brother, it should be (done) rightfully, and payment should be rendered with kindness. That is a concession from your Lord, and a mercy. Whoever transgresses after that – for him (there is) a painful punishment. [179] In the (law of) retaliation (there is) life for you – those (of you) with understanding! – so that you may guard (yourselves).

[180] It is prescribed for you, when death approaches one of you, if he leaves behind any goods, (to make) bequests for parents and family rightfully. (It is) an obligation on the ones who guard (themselves). [181] And whoever changes it after hearing (it) – the sin (rests) only on those who change it. Surely God is hearing, knowing. [182] But whoever suspects any injustice or sin from the one making the bequest, and resolves (the matter) between them – no sin (rests) on him. Surely God is forgiving, compassionate.

[183] You who believe! Fasting is prescribed for you, as it was prescribed for those who were before you, so that you may guard (yourselves). [184] (Fast for) a number of days. Whoever of you is sick or on a journey, (let him fast) a certain number of other days. And for those who can afford it, (there is) a ransom: feeding a poor person. Whoever does good voluntarily – it is better for him. But to fast is better for you, if (only) you knew.

[185] The month of Ramaḍān, in which the Qur'ān was sent down as a guidance for the people, and as clear signs of the guidance and the Deliverance: so whoever

---

2.178 – *You who believe! The (law of) retaliation is prescribed for you*

Retaliation is not only permitted but is also prescribed (lit. "written"). This brings to mind the Quran's verse on "the life for the life," referring to the Torah (5.45).

2.183 – *You who believe! Fasting is prescribed for you*

This verse begins a passage of instructions for fasting (vv. 183–85).

2.185 – *The month of Ramaḍān, in which the Qur'ān was sent down*

The word *qur'ān*, which means "recitation," need not mean the completed Muslim scripture in a book form. According to Muslim tradition, the Quran did not yet exist as a book at the time of the recitation of this sūra. Even so, the month of Ramadan has

of you is present during the month, let him fast in it, but whoever of you is sick or on a journey, (let him fast) a certain number of other days. God wishes to make it easy for you, and does not wish any hardship for you. And (He wishes) that you should fulfill the number (of days), and that you should magnify God for having guided you, and that you should be thankful. [186] When My servants ask you about Me, surely I am near. I respond to the call of the caller when he calls on Me. So let them respond to Me, and believe in Me, so that they may be led aright.

[187] It is permitted to you on the night of the fast to have sexual relations with your wives. They are a covering for you, and you are a covering for them. God knows that you have been betraying yourselves (in this regard), and has turned to you (in forgiveness) and pardoned you. So now have relations with them, and seek what God has prescribed for you. And eat and drink, until a white thread may be discerned from a black thread at the dawn. Then keep the fast completely until night, and do not have relations with them while you are devoted to the mosques. Those are the limits (set by) God, so do not go near them. In this way God makes clear His signs to the people, so that they may guard (themselves).

[188] Do not consume your wealth among yourselves by means of falsehood, nor offer it to the judges, so that you may consume some of the property of the people sinfully, when you know (better).

[189] They ask you about the new moons. Say: 'They are appointed times for the people, and for the pilgrimage.'

It is not piety to come to (your) houses from their backs, but (true) piety (belongs to) the one who guards (himself). Come to (your) houses by their doors, and guard (yourselves) against God, so that you may prosper.

[190] Fight in the way of God against those who fight against you, but do

---

a special status in the Islamic doctrine of scripture. In Sūra 97, the "night of power" is considered to be one of the last nights of Ramadan. For a discussion of the Quran's doctrine of scripture, see the comments at 85.21–22 (p. 624).

2.186 – *When my servants ask you about Me, surely I am near*

The Quran addresses the messenger directly to assure him of Allah's presence. The idea of Allah's nearness does not appear often, but see also 50.15.

2.190 – *Fight in the way of God against those who fight against you*

Suddenly, and without warning in the Quran to this point, the theme of conflict appears.

This verse commands the reader or listener to fight, using the Arabic verb *qātala*. The three following verses contain another command to fight and two commands to kill – using the verb *qatala*. Commands to fight and kill using these forms appear mainly in Sūras 8 and 9, but several such commands also come in Sūras 2, 4, and 49.

not commit aggression. Surely God does not love the aggressors. [191] And kill them wherever you come upon them, and expel them from where they expelled you. Persecution is worse than killing. But do not fight them near the Sacred

---

In all, there are twelve commands to fight and five commands to kill in the Quran. See "Fighting and Killing in the Quran" (p. 220).

These commands often come with conditions regarding who is to fight, the identity of the enemy, the purpose of the fighting, and the extent of hostilities. For example, 2.190 commands those who "believe" (v. 183) to fight against those who are fighting them but not to commit aggression.

Muslim tradition generally relates the quranic commands to fight and kill to partic-ular situations in the story of Muḥammad and his followers. Muslim biographies and commentaries match 2.190–94 with "the truce of Ḥudaybiyya" during the sixth year of Muḥammad's reign in Medina, when the Muslims were preparing to enter Mecca.

2.190 – *in the way of God*

When the Quran commands listeners or readers to fight "in the way (*sabīl*) of Allah," it makes a theological claim by associating Allah with human fighting. See the analysis of these expressions at 73.20 (p. 597).

Of its forty-nine occurrences in the Quran, the phrase "in the way of Allah" follows the verb *qātala* ("fight") fifteen times and *jāhada* ("struggle") fourteen times. In Muslim tradition, "in the way of Allah" became inseparable from the concept of holy war.

2.190 – *God does not love the aggressors*

The Quran contains twenty-four statements about the kinds of people whom Allah does not love and twenty-two statements about the people whom Allah loves (see v. 195). These statements are relevant to the theology of the Quran and its teaching on Allah's relationship with humans. For this reason the commentary briefly notes the "love" verses throughout.

The "aggressors" (*mu'tadūn*) are among the groups most frequently denied the love of Allah (also 5.87; 7.55). For a summary of such verses, see "The Language of Love in the Quran" (p. 560).

2.191 – *And kill them wherever you come upon them. . . . If they fight you, kill them*

This verse commands the reader or listener to kill, using the Arabic verb *qatala*. It contains two of the Quran's five commands to kill. The verse seems to command those who "believe" (v. 183) to kill the group from verse 190, "those who fight against you." The reasons for the killing seem to include both "persecution" and "such is the payment for the disbelievers" (*kāfirūn*). The limitations put on killing include not fighting if the enemy is near the "sacred mosque" or if the enemy stops (v. 192).

2.191 – *Persecution is worse than killing*

What is worse than killing? The word translated as "persecution" is *fitna*, a difficult

Mosque until they fight you there. If they fight you, kill them – such is the payment for the disbelievers. [192] But if they stop (fighting) – surely God is forgiving, compassionate. [193] Fight them until (there) is no persecution and the religion is God's. But if they stop, (let there be) no aggression, except against the evildoers. [194] The sacred month for the sacred month; sacred things are (subject to the law of) retaliation. Whoever commits aggression against you, commit aggression against him in the same manner (as) he committed aggression against you. Guard (yourselves) against God, and know that God is with the ones who guard (themselves).

[195] Contribute in the way of God. Do not cast (yourselves) to destruction with your own hands, but do good. Surely God loves the doers of good.

[196] Complete the pilgrimage and the visitation for God. But if you are prevented, (make) whatever offering is easy to obtain. Do not shave your heads until the offering has reached its lawful place. Whoever of you is sick or has an injury to his head, (there is) a ransom of fasting or a freewill offering or a

---

word that is also rendered "trial," "temptation," "deviation," or "strife." The concept seems to be that it is worse to turn people away from religion than to kill the person who turns people away. The same idea repeats in verses 193 and 217 in this sūra.

2.193 – *Fight them until (there) is no persecution and the religion is God's*

This verse commands the reader or listener to fight, similar to verse 190. The fighters and enemies seem to be the same as in verses 190 to 192 (those who "believe" and those who fight against them), but the scope of fighting is now extended "until (there) is no persecution and the religion is Allah's." This reaches well beyond defensive fighting to fighting to remove all obstacles to the messenger's religion.

Commands to fight and kill in the Quran are relevant to non-Muslims for a number of important reasons. First of all, some Muslims may understand non-Muslims to be the target of the commands. Second, the commands affect the possibility of peaceful coexistence in today's world. Third, if the commands are followed by the expression "in the way of Allah," they make claims about God that non-Muslims might dispute. For these reasons, each remaining command to fight or kill will be carefully observed in these notes for justifications, identity of fighters and enemies, and extent of hostilities.

2.195 – *Surely God loves the doers of good*

The statement that Allah loves the doers of good (*muḥsinūn*) is the most frequent affirmation of Allah's love in the Quran. The statement repeats at 3.134, 148; 5.13, 93. See "The Language of Love in the Quran" (p. 560).

2.196 – *Complete the pilgrimage and the visitation for Allah*

This verse begins a passage on pilgrimage (vv. 196–203).

sacrifice. When you are secure, whoever makes use of (the time from) the visitation until the pilgrimage, (let him make) whatever offering is easy to obtain. Whoever cannot find (an offering), (let him perform) a fast of three days during the pilgrimage, and seven (days) when you return. That is ten (days) in all. That is for the one whose family is not present at the Sacred Mosque. Guard (yourselves) against God, and know that God is harsh in retribution.

¹⁹⁷ The pilgrimage (falls in certain) specified months. Whoever undertakes the pilgrimage in them – (there should be) no sexual relations or wickedness or quarreling during the pilgrimage. Whatever good you do, God knows it. And take provision (for the journey), but surely the best provision is the guarding (of oneself). So guard (yourselves) against Me, those (of you) with understanding!

¹⁹⁸ There is no blame on you in seeking favor from your Lord. When you press on from 'Arafāt, remember God at the Sacred Monument, and remember Him as He has guided you, though before you were indeed among those who had gone astray. ¹⁹⁹ Then press on from where the people press on, and ask forgiveness from God. Surely God is forgiving, compassionate. ²⁰⁰ When you have performed your rituals, remember God, as you remember your fathers, or (even with) greater remembrance. (There are) some of the people who say, 'Our Lord, give us (good) in this world.' For them (there will be) no share in the Hereafter. ²⁰¹ But (there are others) of them who say, 'Our Lord, give us good in this world and good in the Hereafter, and guard us against the punishment of the Fire.' ²⁰² Those – for them (there will be) a portion of what they have earned, and God is quick at the reckoning.

²⁰³ Remember God during a (certain) number of days. Whoever hurries (through it) in two days – no sin (rests) on him, and whoever delays – no sin (rests) on him, (at least) for the one who guards (himself). Guard (yourselves) against God, and know that you will be gathered to Him.

²⁰⁴ Among the people (there is) one who impresses you (with) his speech in this present life, and who calls God to witness about what is in his heart, though he is the most contentious of opponents. ²⁰⁵ And when he turns away, he strives to foment corruption on the earth, and to destroy the crops and livestock. God does not love the (fomenting of) corruption. ²⁰⁶ When it is said to him, 'Guard (yourself) against God,' false pride carries him away to more sin. Gehenna will be enough for him – it is an evil bed indeed! ²⁰⁷ But among the people (there is) one who sells himself, seeking the approval of God. God is kind with (His) servants.

²⁰⁸ You who believe! Enter into the unity all together, and do not follow the footsteps of Satan. Surely he is a clear enemy to you. ²⁰⁹ But if you slip, after the clear signs have come to you, know that God is mighty, wise.

²¹⁰ Do they expect (anything) but God to come to them in the shadow of the cloud with the angels? The affair has been decided, and to God (all) affairs return. ²¹¹ Ask the Sons of Israel how many of the clear signs We gave them. Whoever changes the blessing of God after it has come to him – surely God is harsh in retribution. ²¹² This present life is made to appear enticing to those who disbelieve, and they ridicule those who believe. But the ones who guard (themselves) will be above them on the Day of Resurrection. God provides for whomever He pleases without reckoning.

²¹³ The people were (once) one community. Then God raised up the prophets as bringers of good news and warners, and with them He sent down the Book with the truth to judge among the people concerning their differences. Only those who had been given it differed concerning it, after the clear signs had come to them, (because of) envy among themselves. And God guided those who believed to the truth concerning which they differed, by His permission. God guides whomever He pleases to a straight path.

²¹⁴ Or did you think that you would enter the Garden before you had experienced what those who passed away before you experienced? Violence and hardship touched them, and they were (so) shaken that the messenger, and those who believed with him, said, 'When will the help of God come?' Is it not a fact that the help of God is near?

²¹⁵ They ask you (about) what they should contribute. Say: 'Whatever good you have contributed is for parents and family, and the orphans, and the poor, and the traveler. Whatever good you do, surely God knows about it.'

²¹⁶ Fighting is prescribed for you, though it is hateful to you. You may happen to hate a thing though it is good for you, and you may happen to love a thing though it is bad for you. God knows and you do not know. ²¹⁷ They ask you about the sacred month – (about) fighting during it. Say: 'Fighting during it is a serious (matter), but keeping (people) from the way of God – and disbelief

---

2.213 – *The people were (once) one community. . . . Only those who had been given it differed concerning it*

The Quran often says that peoples of the past "differed." Here those who were given the book disagree about it. See the comments on this theme at 98.4 (p. 642).

2.216 – *Fighting is prescribed for you, though it is hateful to you*

This verse seems to refer to a battle situation in which the messenger is urging the "believers" to fight (*al-qitāl*) but they do not want to fight.

In other quranic passages, "permission is given" to fight and kill (22.39, 3.152). Here, however, "fighting is prescribed" (also 4.77), and the verse seems to imply that this would be good for the believers. See "Fighting and Killing in the Quran" (p. 220).

in Him – and the Sacred Mosque, and expelling its people from it, (are even) more serious in the sight of God. Persecution is more serious than killing.' They will not stop fighting you until they turn you back from your religion, if they can. Whoever of you turns away from his religion and dies while he is a disbeliever, those – their deeds have come to nothing in this world and the Hereafter. Those are the companions of the Fire. There they will remain. [218] Surely those who believe, and those who have emigrated and struggled in the way of God, those – they hope for the mercy of God. God is forgiving, compassionate.

[219] They ask you about wine and games of chance. Say: 'In both of them (there is) great sin, but (also some) benefits for the people, yet their sin is greater than their benefit.'

They ask you about what they should contribute. Say: 'The excess.' In this way God makes clear to you the signs, so that you may reflect [220] in this world and the Hereafter.

They ask you about the orphans. Say: 'Setting right (their affairs) for them

---

2.217 – *Persecution is more serious than killing*
This expression, which also appears at verse 191, is further explained in this verse. Here "persecution" (*fitna*) seems to include turning people away from the way of Allah, disbelieving in Allah and the "sacred mosque," and expelling people from the mosque. Muslim commentators often explained *fitna* in such verses as *shirk* – that is, "associating" anything or anyone with Allah.

2.217 – *Whoever of you turns away from his religion and dies while he is a disbeliever*
What is the consequence for Muslims who turn away from Islam? This verse seems to say that they go to hell when they die. A further question is whether the Quran prescribes punishment in this world for whoever turns away from Islam. See a list of other verses related to the topic of apostasy at 16.106.

2.218 – *those who have emigrated and struggled in the way of God*
Struggled is a translation of the Arabic verb *jāhada*, from which the word *jihād* comes. The context helps determine what sense of struggling the Quran intends in each appearance of the verb. When it closely follows verses about fighting (e.g., 2.216–17), *struggling* tends to adopt the sense of fighting. See "Jihad in the Quran" (p. 368).

2.219 – *They ask you about wine and games of chance*
The Quran shows an inconsistent – perhaps ambivalent – attitude toward wine (*khamr*). Here wine (and gambling) are said to have more sin than benefits for humankind (also 5.90). This contrasts with 16.67, where wine is a benefit, and 47.15, where among the delights in the heavenly Garden are the rivers of wine (also 83.25).

is good. And if you become partners with them, (they are) your brothers. God knows the one who foments corruption from the one who sets (things) right. If God (so) pleased, He could indeed cause you to suffer. Surely God is mighty, wise.'

²²¹ Do not marry idolatrous women until they believe. A believing slave girl is better than a (free) idolatrous woman, even if she pleases you. And do not marry idolatrous men until they believe. A believing slave is better than a (free) idolatrous man, even if he pleases you. Those (people) – they call (you) to the Fire, but God calls (you) to the Garden and forgiveness, by His permission. He makes clear His signs to the people, so that they may take heed.

²²² They ask you about menstruation. Say: 'It is harmful. Withdraw from women in menstruation, and do not go near them until they are clean. When they have cleansed themselves, come to them as God has commanded you.' Surely God loves those who turn (in repentance), and He loves those who purify themselves. ²²³ Your women are (like) a field for you, so come to your field when you wish, and send forward (something) for yourselves. Guard (yourselves) against God, and know that you will meet Him. And give good news to the believers.

²²⁴ Do not, on account of your oaths, make God an obstacle to doing good, and guarding (yourselves), and setting (things) right among the people. Surely God is hearing, knowing. ²²⁵ God will not take you to task for a slip in your oaths, but He will take you to task for what your hearts have earned. God is forgiving, forbearing.

²²⁶ For those who renounce their wives, (there is) a waiting period of four months. If they return – surely God is forgiving, compassionate. ²²⁷ But if they are determined to divorce – surely God is hearing, knowing. ²²⁸ (Let) the

---

2.221 – *Do not marry idolatrous women until they believe*

This verse begins a substantial passage of laws on marriage, divorce, and family (vv. 221–41).

2.222 – *Surely God loves those who turn (in repentance)*

The Quran contains twenty-two statements about the kinds of people whom Allah loves. This verse offers two such objects: those who turn and those who purify themselves. See "The Language of Love in the Quran" (p. 560).

2.223 – *Your women are (like) a field for you, so come to your field when you wish*

Here the Quran tells men that their women are a "tillage" or "plowing" (*ḥarth*) for them.

2.226 – *For those who renounce their wives, (there is) a waiting period of four months*

This verse begins an extended passage of laws concerning divorce (vv. 226–41).

divorced women wait by themselves for three periods. It is not permitted to them to conceal what God has created in their wombs, if they believe in God and the Last Day. Their husbands have a better right to take them back in that (period), if they wish to set (things) right. Women rightfully have the same privilege (as is exercised) over them, but men have a rank above them. God is mighty, wise.

²²⁹ Divorce (may take place) twice, (with the option of) retaining (them) rightfully, or sending (them) away with kindness. It is not permitted to you to take (back) anything of what you have given them, unless the two of them fear that they cannot maintain the limits (set by) God. But if you fear that they cannot maintain the limits (set by) God, (there is) no blame on either of them in what she ransoms (herself) with. Those are the limits (set by) God, so do not transgress them. Whoever transgresses the limits (set by) God, those – they are the evildoers. ²³⁰ If he divorces her, she is not permitted to him (to marry) after that, until she marries another husband. And then if he divorces her, (there is) no blame on (either of) them to return to each other, if they think that they can maintain the limits (set by) God. Those are the limits (set by) God. He makes them clear to a people who know.

²³¹ When you divorce women, and they have reached (the end of) their term, either retain them rightfully, or send them away rightfully. Do not retain them harmfully, so that you transgress. Whoever does that has done himself evil. Do not take the signs of God in mockery, but remember the blessing of God on you, and what he has sent down to you of the Book and the wisdom. He admonishes you by means of it. Guard (yourselves) against God, and know that God has knowledge of everything. ²³² When you divorce women, and they have reached (the end of) their term, do not prevent them from marrying their (new) husbands, when they make an agreement together rightfully. That is what anyone who believes in God and the Last Day is admonished. That is purer for you, and cleaner. God knows and you do not know.

²³³ Mothers shall nurse their children for two full years, for those who wish to complete the nursing (period). (It is an obligation) on the father for him (to supply) their provision and their clothing rightfully. No one is to be burdened beyond their capacity. A mother is not to suffer on account of her child, nor a father on account of his child. The (father's) heir has a similar (obligation) to that. If the two of them wish, by mutual consent and consultation, to wean (the child earlier), (there is) no blame on (either of) them. And if you wish to seek nursing for your children, (there is) no blame on you, provided you pay what you have rightfully promised. Guard (yourselves) against God, and know that God sees what you do.

²³⁴ Those of you who are taken, and leave behind wives – (let the widows) wait by themselves for four months and ten (days). When they have reached (the end) of their waiting period, (there is) no blame on you for what they may rightfully do with themselves. God is aware of what you do. ²³⁵ (There is) no blame on you concerning the proposals you offer to women, or (the proposals) you conceal within yourselves. God knows that you will be thinking about them. But do not make a proposal to them in secret, unless you speak rightful words. And do not tie the knot of marriage until the prescribed (term) has reached its end. Know that God knows what is within you. So beware of Him, and know that God is forgiving, forbearing.

²³⁶ (There is) no blame on you if you divorce women whom you have not touched, nor promised any bridal gift to them. Yet provide for them rightfully – the wealthy according to his means, and the poor according to his means – (it is) an obligation on the doers of good. ²³⁷ If you divorce them before you have touched them, but you have already promised them a bridal gift, (give them) half of what you have promised, unless they relinquish (it), or he relinquishes (it) in whose hand is the knot of marriage. To relinquish (it) is nearer to the guarding (of oneself), and do not forget generosity among you. Surely God sees what you do.

²³⁸ Watch over the prayers, and the middle prayer. And stand before God obedient. ²³⁹ If you fear (danger), (pray) on foot or (while) riding. But when you are secure, remember God, since He has taught you what you did not know.

²⁴⁰ Those of you who (are about to be) taken, and (are going to) leave behind wives, (let them make) a bequest for their wives: provision for the year without evicting (them from their homes). But if they do leave, (there is) no blame on you for what they may rightfully do with themselves. God is mighty, wise. ²⁴¹ For divorced women (there is) a rightful provision – (it is) an obligation on the ones who guard (themselves). ²⁴² In this way God makes clear to you His signs, so that you may understand.

²⁴³ Have you not considered those who went forth from their homes – and they were thousands – afraid of death? And God said to them, 'Die!' (But) then He brought them to life. Surely God is indeed full of favor to the people, but most of the people are not thankful (for it). ²⁴⁴ So fight in the way of God,

---

2.242 – *In this way God makes clear His signs*

The Quran claims that the preceding commandments on divorce and other areas of human behavior are from Allah, calling them signs.

2.244 – *So fight in the way of God*

This verse commands the reader or listener to fight, using the Arabic verb *qātala*. The command to fight seems to be addressed to those who "believe" (see vv. 208,

and know that God is hearing, knowing. ²⁴⁵ Who is the one who will lend to God a good loan, and He will double it for him many times? God withdraws and extends, and to Him you will be returned.

²⁴⁶ Have you not considered the assembly of the Sons of Israel after (the time of) Moses? They said to a prophet of theirs, 'Raise up a king for us, (and) we shall fight in the way of God.' He said, 'Is it possible that, if fighting is prescribed for you, you will not fight?' They said, 'Why should we not fight in the way of God, when we have been expelled from our homes and our children?' Yet when fighting was prescribed for them, they (all) turned away, except for a few of them. God has knowledge of the evildoers.

²⁴⁷ And their prophet said to them, 'Surely God has raised up for you Ṭālūt as king.' They said, 'How can he possess the kingship over us, when we are more deserving of the kingship than him, and he has not been given abundant wealth?' He said, 'Surely God has chosen him (to be) over you, and has increased him abundantly in knowledge and stature. God gives His kingdom to whomever He pleases. God is embracing, knowing.'

²⁴⁸ And their prophet said to them, 'Surely the sign of his kingship is that the ark will come to you. In it is a Sakīna from your Lord, and a remnant of what the house of Moses and the house of Aaron left behind. The angels (will) carry it. Surely in that is a sign indeed for you, if you are believers.'

---

254), but their enemy and purpose are not clear. In the following story about the Sons of Israel, the people fight because they have been expelled from their homes and children (v. 246). See "Fighting and Killing in the Quran" (p. 220).

When the Quran gives commands to fight "in the way (*sabīl*) of Allah," it makes a theological claim by associating Allah with human fighting. This association continues in verse 246 in a story of a prophet from the "Sons of Israel." See the analysis of these expressions at 73.20 (p. 597).

2.247 – *their prophet said to them, "Surely God has raised up for you Ṭālūt as king"*

Readers of the Bible will hear an echo of 1 Samuel in this passage (2.246–48). Though the name of Samuel is not given, and the name of Saul here is *Ṭālūt*, the story of the Sons of Israel asking for a king has a familiar ring (1 Sam. 8).

Note how the Quran uses this biblical story. When the elders of Israel asked Samuel to appoint a king in 1 Samuel 8, what was the response of Samuel – and Yahweh? According to the wider context of the *Ṭālūt* story (Q 2.243–53), how does the Quran use the story?

2.248 – *the ark will come to you. In it is a Sakīna from your Lord*

The Arabic word *Sakīna* may bring to mind the late Hebrew *shekhīnā* (found in the Jewish Talmud, not the Bible). The Hebrew term refers to the presence of God

[249] When Ṭālūt set out with his forces, he said, 'Surely God is going to test you by means of a river. Whoever drinks from it is not on my side, but whoever does not taste it is surely on my side, except for whoever scoops (it) up with his hand.' But they (all) drank from it, except for a few. So when he crossed it, he and those who believed with him, they said, 'We have no strength today against Jālūt and his forces.' But those who thought that they would meet God said, 'How many a small cohort has overcome a large cohort by the permission of God? God is with the patient.' [250] So when they went forth to (battle) Jālūt and his forces, they said, 'Our Lord, pour out on us patience, and make firm our feet, and help us against the people who are disbelievers.' [251] And they routed them by the permission of God, and David killed Jālūt, and God gave him the kingdom and the wisdom, and taught him about whatever He pleased. If God had not repelled some of the people by means of others, the earth would indeed have been corrupted. But God is full of favor to the worlds.

[252] Those are the signs of God. We recite them to you in truth. Surely you are indeed one of the envoys. [253] Those are the messengers – We have favored some of them over others. (There were) some of them to whom God spoke, and some of them He raised in rank. And We gave Jesus, son of Mary, the clear signs, and supported him with the holy spirit. If God had (so) pleased, those who (came) after them would not have fought each other, after the clear signs had come to them. But they differed, and (there were) some of them who believed and some of them who disbelieved. If God had (so) pleased, they would not have fought each other. But God does whatever He wills.

---

in the tabernacle and is thought by some scholars to express the concept of "glory" (Heb. *kabōd*) in Exodus 40:34–5. In the Quran, all six occurrences of *Sakīna* appear in battle contexts (also 9.26, 40; 48.4, 18, 26).

2.249 – *Surely God is going to test you by means of a river*

An episode in the biblical account of the judge Gideon (Judges 7:4–7) is here placed in the story of *Ṭālūt* (Saul).

2.252 – *These are the signs of God. We recite them to you in truth*

The Quran addresses the messenger directly to claim that the preceding recitations are signs (*āyāt*) from Allah and that he is one of the messengers (*mursalūn*).

2.253 – *And We gave Jesus, son of Mary, the clear signs, and supported him with the holy spirit.*

For the second time in this sūra, the Quran describes 'Īsā as supported by the holy spirit. See the comments on the name 'Īsā at 2.87 (p. 48) and on the holy spirit at 16.102 (p. 283).

On the disagreement and in-fighting of those who "followed after them," see the comments at 98.4 (p. 642).

[254] You who believe! Contribute from what We have provided you, before a Day comes when (there will be) no bargaining, and no friendship, and no intercession. The disbelievers – they are the evildoers.

[255] God – (there is) no god but Him, the Living, the Everlasting. Slumber does not overtake Him, nor sleep. To Him (belongs) whatever is in the heavens and whatever is on the earth. Who is the one who will intercede with Him, except by His permission? He knows whatever is before them and whatever is behind them, but they cannot encompass any of His knowledge, except whatever He pleases. His throne comprehends the heavens and the earth. Watching over both of them does not weary him. He is the Most High, the Almighty.

[256] (There is) no compulsion in religion. The right (course) has become clearly distinguished from error. Whoever disbelieves in al-Ṭāghūt, and believes in God, has grasped the firmest handle, (which) does not break. God is hearing, knowing. [257] God is the ally of those who believe. He brings them out of the darkness into the light. But those who disbelieve – their allies are al-Ṭāghūt, who bring them out of the light into the darkness. Those are the companions of the Fire. There they will remain.

2.255 – *His throne comprehends the heavens and the earth*

Known as the first of the "throne verses," this verse packs a lot of theology into a small space. It begins with a statement very similar to the first part of the Muslim confession of faith ("no god except Allah") and includes the anthropomorphic image of Allah seated on a heavenly throne.

This verse suggests the possibility of intercession through one who has Allah's permission. See the analysis of verses on intercession at 39.44 (p. 464).

2.256 – *(There is) no compulsion in religion*

This famous expression seems to say that force may be used neither to compel a non-Muslim into Islam, nor to prevent a Muslim from leaving Islam. Understood in this way, the verse is a very welcome affirmation of freedom of religion.

In the history of Muslim interpretation, the meaning of the verse has not been so straightforward. Early Muslim commentators tended to say that the first recitation of the verse applied to a particular situation in Medina, and thus they did not envision a universal application. Translations of early Muslim interpretations are available in Mahmoud Ayoub's *The Qur'an and its Interpreters* (see bibliography).

In recent years, Muslims have often cited this verse to support the claim that Islam is a religion of peace. If the verse indeed calls for peace, it needs to be read in the context of this sūra, including the commands to fight and kill (vv. 190–94, 216–17, 244).

²⁵⁸ Have you not considered the one who disputed (with) Abraham concerning his Lord, because God had given him the kingdom? When Abraham said, 'My Lord is the One who gives life and causes death,' he said, 'I give life and cause death.' Abraham said, 'Surely God brings the sun from the East, so you bring it from the West.' And then the one who disbelieved was confounded. God does not guide the people who are evildoers.

²⁵⁹ Or (have you not considered) the example of the one who passed by a town that had collapsed in ruins? He said, 'How will God give this (town) life after its death?' So God caused him to die for a hundred years, (and) then raised him up. He said, 'How long have you remained (dead)?' He said, 'I have remained (dead) for a day or part of a day.' He said, 'No! You have remained (dead) for a hundred years. Look at your food and drink, it has not spoiled, and look at your donkey – and (this happened) so that We might make you a sign to the people – and look at the bones, how We raise them up, (and) then clothe them with flesh.' So when it became clear to him, he said, 'I know that God is powerful over everything.'

²⁶⁰ (Remember) when Abraham said, 'My Lord, show me how You give the dead life.' He said, 'Have you not believed?' He said, 'Yes indeed! But (show me) to satisfy my heart.' He said, 'Take four birds, and take them close to you, then place a piece of them on each hill, (and) then call them. They will come rushing to you. Know that God is mighty, wise.'

²⁶¹ The parable of those who contribute their wealth in the way of God is like the parable of a grain of corn that grows seven ears: in each ear (there are) a hundred grains. (So) God doubles for whomever He pleases. God is embracing, knowing. ²⁶² Those who contribute their wealth in the way of God, (and) then do not follow up what they have contributed (with) insult and injury, for them – their reward is with their Lord. (There will be) no fear on them, nor will they sorrow. ²⁶³ Rightful words and forgiveness are better than a freewill offering followed by injury. God is wealthy, forbearing.

²⁶⁴ You who believe! Do not invalidate your freewill offerings by insult

---

2.258 – *Have you not considered the one who disputed (with) Abraham concerning his Lord*

Two episodes in the life of Abraham are referred to in verses 158 and 160. The first is an encounter with an unbeliever, and the second a conversation with his Lord. See "Abraham in the Quran" (p. 90).

2.263 – *Rightful words and forgiveness are better*

This verse and several other verses in this sūra indicate a sense of perspective on ritual practices in comparison to behavior with others (also vv. 177, 264, 271).

and injury, like the one who contributes his wealth in order to be seen by the people, but who does not believe in God and the Last Day. His parable is like the parable of a smooth rock with dirt on top of it. A heavy rain smites it (and) leaves it bare. They have no power over anything they have earned. God does not guide the people who are disbelievers. [265] But the parable of those who contribute their wealth, seeking the approval of God and confirmation for themselves, is like the parable of a garden on a hill. A heavy rain smites it, and it yields its produce twofold. And if a heavy rain does not smite it, a shower (does). God sees what you do.

[266] Would any of you like to have a garden of date palms and grapes, (with) rivers flowing through it, and in it (there is) every (kind of) fruit for him? (Then) old age smites him, and he has (only) weak children. Then a whirlwind, with a fire in it, smites it. Then it was burned. In this way God makes clear to you the signs, so that you will reflect.

[267] You who believe! Contribute from the good things you have earned, and from what We have produced for you from the earth. And do not designate for contributions bad things, when you would never take them (yourselves), except with disdain. Know that God is wealthy, praiseworthy.

[268] Satan promises you poverty, and commands you to immorality, but God promises you forgiveness from Him, and favor. God is embracing, knowing. [269] He gives wisdom to whomever He pleases, and whoever is given wisdom has been given much good. Yet no one takes heed except those with understanding.

[270] Whatever contribution you make, and whatever vow you vow, surely God knows it. But the evildoers have no helper.

[271] If you make freewill offerings publicly, that is excellent, but if you hide it and give it to the poor, that is better for you, and will absolve you of some of your evil deeds. God is aware of what you do.

[272] Their guidance is not (dependent) on you, but God guides whomever He pleases. Whatever good you contribute is for yourselves, even though you contribute (as a result of) seeking the face of God. And whatever good you contribute will be repaid to you in full, and you will not be done evil. [273] (Freewill offerings are) for the poor who are constrained in the way of God, and are unable to strike forth on the earth. The ignorant suppose them to be rich because of (their) self-restraint, but you know them by their mark – they do not constantly beg from people. Whatever good you contribute, surely God knows it. [274] Those who contribute their wealth in the night and in the day, in secret and in open, for them – their reward is with their Lord. (There will be) no fear on them, nor will they sorrow.

[275] Those who devour usury will not stand, except as one stands whom Satan

has overthrown by (his) touch. That is because they have said, 'Trade is just like usury,' though God has permitted trade and forbidden usury. Whoever receives an admonition from his Lord, and stops (practicing usury), will have whatever is past, and his case is in the hands of God, but whoever returns (to usury) – those are the companions of the Fire. There they will remain. [276] God destroys usury but causes freewill offerings to bear interest. God does not love any ungrateful one (or) sinner. [277] Surely those who believe and do righteous deeds, and observe the prayer and give the alms, for them – their reward is with their Lord. (There will be) no fear on them, nor will they sorrow.

[278] You who believe! Guard (yourselves) against God, and give up the usury that is (still) outstanding, if you are believers. [279] If you do not, be on notice of war from God and His messenger. But if you turn (in repentance), you will have your principal. You will not have committed evil or been done evil. [280] If he should be in hardship, (let there be) a postponement until (there is) some relief (of his situation). But that you remit (it as) a freewill offering is better for you, if (only) you knew. [281] Guard (yourselves) against a Day on which you will be returned to God. Then everyone will be paid in full what they have earned – and they will not be done evil.

[282] You who believe! When you contract a debt with one another for a fixed term, write it down. Let a scribe write it down fairly between you, and let the scribe not refuse to write it down, seeing that God has taught him. So let him write, and let the one who owes the debt dictate, and let him guard (himself) against God his Lord, and not diminish anything from it. If the one who owes the debt is weak of mind or body, or unable to dictate himself, let his ally dictate fairly. And call in two of your men as witnesses, or, if there are not two men, then one man and two women, from those present whom you approve of as witnesses, so that if one of the two women goes astray, the other will remind her. And let the witnesses not refuse when they are called on. Do not disdain to write it down, (however) small or large, with its due date. That is more upright in the sight of God, more reliable for witnessing (it), and (makes it) more likely that you will not be in doubt (afterwards) – unless it is an actual transaction

---

2.276 – *God does not love any ungrateful one (or) sinner*

The Quran contains twenty-four statements about the kinds of people whom Allah does not love. Here Allah withholds his love from the unbeliever (*kaffār*) and the sinner (*athīm*). See "The Language of Love in the Quran" (p. 560).

2.279 – *be on notice of war from Allah and His messenger*

The practice of usury (taking interest for loans) is forbidden in verse 278, but this verse backs up the prohibition with the threat of war.

you exchange among yourselves, and then there is no blame on you if you do not write it down. But take witnesses when you do business with each other. Only let the scribe or the witness not injure either party, or, if you do, that is wickedness on your part. So guard (yourselves) against God. God teaches you, and God has knowledge of everything.

²⁸³ And if you are on a journey, and do not find a scribe, (let) a security be taken. But if one of you trusts another, let him who is trusted pay back what is entrusted, and let him guard (himself) against God his Lord. Do not conceal the testimony. Whoever conceals it, surely he is sinful – (that is) his heart. God knows what you do.

²⁸⁴ To God (belongs) whatever is in the heavens and whatever is on the earth. Whether you reveal what is within you or hide it, God will call you to account for it. He forgives whomever He pleases and He punishes whomever He pleases. God is powerful over everything.

²⁸⁵ The messenger believes in what has been sent down to him from his Lord, and (so do) the believers. Each one believes in God, and His angels, and His Books, and His messengers. We make no distinction between any of His messengers. And they say, 'We hear and obey. (Grant us) Your forgiveness, our Lord. To You is the (final) destination.'

²⁸⁶ God does not burden any person beyond his capacity. What they have earned is either to their credit or against their account.

'Our Lord, do not take us to task if we forget or make a mistake. Our Lord, do not lay on us a burden such as You laid on those before us. Our Lord, do not burden us beyond what we have the strength (to bear). Pardon us, and forgive us, and have compassion on us. You are our Protector. Help us against the people who are disbelievers.'

2.285 – *The messenger believes in what has been sent down to him from his Lord*
Once more at the end of this long and lively sūra the Quran commends the messenger and claims that his recitations have a divine origin.

2.286 – *Our Lord, do not take us to task if we forget or make a mistake*
A short prayer ends the sūra.

HOUSE OF 'IMRĀN
ĀL-'IMRĀN

3

The third sūra is justly famous for offering the first substantial passage on 'Īsā – the quranic Jesus. Just as the second sūra opens with a long passage that takes issue with the Jews, so here fundamental Christian beliefs about Jesus are challenged.

The tone of this passage is also polemical. It frequently speaks about, or directly addresses, the "People of the Book." In several verses we learn that the audience is disputing the preaching of the messenger (vv. 20, 61, 65–66, 73). According to Muslim tradition, the first eighty or so verses of the sūra were first recited to (or about) a delegation of Christians from Najrān who came to Medina to make terms with the messenger (*Sīra*, 270–77).

The second half of the sūra turns its focus to "you who believe," with commands to obey both Allah and the messenger. An extended passage (vv. 121–80) calls to mind a battle scene. Muslim tradition has associated many verses with two battles in its story of Islamic origins. In fact, the name given to one of the battles, *Badr*, appears only here (v. 123).

For Christians, the claims made in this sūra are very serious. The claims confuse or deny the biblical witness to the deity and death of Jesus. They also seem to give God a partisan role in human battle. The Quran similarly takes its claims very seriously. According to Muslim tradition, after making claims about Jesus the Quran calls for an Elijah-like confrontation: call down the curse of Allah on whoever is lying about Jesus (v. 61).

In the Name of God, the Merciful, the Compassionate
[1] Alif Lām Mīm.

[2] God – (there is) no god but Him, the Living, the Everlasting. [3] He has sent

---

3.2 – *God – (there is) no god but Him*

The Quran distinguishes Allah from other "gods" or concepts of God. This expression, which repeats in many parts of the Quran (e.g., vv. 18, 61), is similar to the first part of the Islamic confession of faith, "No god except Allah."

down on you the Book with the truth, confirming what was before it, and He sent down the Torah and the Gospel [4] before (this) as guidance for the people, and (now) He has sent down the Deliverance. Surely those who disbelieve in the signs of God – for them (there is) a harsh punishment. God is mighty, a taker of vengeance.

[5] Surely God – nothing is hidden from Him on the earth or in the sky. [6] He (it is) who fashions you in the wombs as He pleases. (There is) no god but Him, the Mighty, the Wise.

[7] He (it is) who has sent down on you the Book, of which some verses are clearly composed – they are the mother of the Book – but others are ambiguous.

3.3 – *He has sent down on you the Book with the truth*

The Quran directly addresses the messenger to affirm him and to make a claim for the divine origin of "the Book" (*al-kitāb*). This kind of self-referential speech to the "messenger" appears in many parts of the Quran (including vv. 7, 44, 58, 60–61, 108, 138, 184). See "Different Kinds of Literature" (p. 14).

3.3–4 – *confirming what was before it, and He sent down the Torah and the Gospel before (this) as guidance for the people*

Here the Quran names two pre-Islamic scriptures that it recognizes as "sent down" – the *tawrāt* and the *injīl*. One can see the similarities between these Arabic words and their English counterparts, *Torah* and *Evangel* (or *Gospel*). Here, as in all other occurrences of these terms in the Quran, the Quran describes these two scriptures in a positive and respectful way ("guidance," v. 4). Most of the verses that name the Torah and Gospel come in Sūras 3 and 5. See the analysis of the Quran's "Gospel" verses at 57.27 (p. 549).

The Quran frequently claims that its contents confirm (*muṣaddiq*) what is "with" the audience or "what was before it" (*mā bayna yadayhi*, lit. "what is between his two hands"). See the analysis of the Quran's claim of confirmation at 46.12 (p. 502).

3.4 – *He has sent down the Deliverance*

"Deliverance" translates the Arabic term *furqān*, which is often translated as "criterion." See the comment at 25.1 on *furqān* (p. 363), its seven occurrences in the Quran, and what they refer to.

3.7 – *some verses are clearly composed . . . but others are ambiguous*

The Quran seems to say that one part of "the book" is ambiguous, causing some to seek interpretation for the ambiguous verses. This verse says that no one knows the interpretation of the ambiguous part except Allah.

The expression "mother of the Book" appears here and at 13.39 and 43.4. It seems to refer to a concept of an original book in heaven from which all revelation comes. See the discussion of the "doctrine of scripture" within the Quran at 85.21–22 (p. 624).

As for those in whose hearts (there is) a turning aside, they follow the ambiguous part of it, seeking (to cause) trouble and seeking its interpretation. No one knows its interpretation except God. And (as for) the ones firmly grounded in knowledge, they say, 'We believe in it. All (of it) is from our Lord.' Yet no one takes heed except those with understanding. [8] 'Our Lord, do not cause our hearts to turn aside after You have guided us, and grant us mercy from Yourself. Surely You – You are the Giver. [9] Our Lord, surely You will gather the people for a Day – (there is) no doubt about it. Surely God will not break the appointment.'

[10] Surely those who disbelieve – neither their wealth nor their children will be of any use against God. And those – they will be fuel for the Fire, [11] like the case of the house of Pharaoh, and those who were before them, who called Our signs a lie. God seized them because of their sins, and God is harsh in retribution. [12] Say to those who disbelieve: 'You will be conquered and gathered into Gehenna – it is an evil bed!' [13] There was a sign for you in the two cohorts which met: one cohort fighting in the way of God, and another disbelieving. They saw them twice as many (as themselves) with (their own) eyesight. God supports with His help whomever He pleases. Surely in that is a lesson indeed for those have sight.

[14] Enticing to the people is love of desires: women and sons, qinṭārs upon qinṭārs of gold and silver, and the finest horses, cattle, and fields. That is the provision of this present life. But God – with Him is the best place of return. [15] Say: 'Shall I inform you of (something) better than that? For the ones who guard (themselves), (there are) Gardens with their Lord, through which rivers flow, there to remain, and (there are) pure spouses and approval from God.' God sees (His) servants [16] who say, 'Our Lord, surely we believe. Forgive us our sins and guard us against the punishment of the Fire.' [17] (They are) the patient, the truthful, the obedient, those who contribute, the askers of forgiveness in the mornings.

[18] God has borne witness that (there is) no god but Him – and (so have) the angels, and the people of knowledge, (who) uphold justice. (There is) no god but Him, the Mighty, the Wise. [19] Surely the religion with God is Islam. Those who

---

3.13 – *one cohort fighting in the way of Allah, and another disbelieving*

When the Quran describes the "believers" as "fighting in the way (*sabīl*) of Allah," it makes a theological claim by associating Allah with human fighting. See an analysis of such expressions at 73.20 (p. 597).

According to Muslim tradition, this verse refers to a battle in which the Muslims of Medina fought against the people of Mecca, known as the battle of Badr.

3.18 – *God has borne witness that (there is) no god but Him*

The words of verses 18 and 19 are also found in the mosaic inscriptions in the Dome of the Rock in Jerusalem, which was built in AD 691. The reason is not hard

were given the Book did not differ until after the knowledge had come to them, (because of) envy among themselves. Whoever disbelieves in the signs of God – surely God is quick at the reckoning. [20] If they dispute with you, say: 'I have submitted to God, and (so have) those who follow me.' And say to those who have been given the Book, and to the common people: 'Have you submitted?' If they submit, they have been (rightly) guided, but if they turn away – only (dependent) on you is the delivery (of the message). God sees (His) servants.

[21] Surely those who disbelieve in the signs of God, and kill the prophets without any right, and kill those of the people who command justice – give them news of a painful punishment. [22] Those are the ones whose deeds come to nothing in this world and the Hereafter. They will have no helpers.

[23] Have you not seen those who were given a portion of the Book? They were called to the Book of God in order that it might judge between them.

---

to discern. The words make exclusive claims for Allah and for Islam and also comment on "those who were given the book" – that is, the then conquered communities of Christians and Jews in the Arab Empire.

3.19 – *Surely the religion with God is Islam*

Several verses in this sūra make exclusive claims for Islam. This verse declares that Allah's religion (*dīn*) is Islam. Further claims for Islam come at verses 67 and 85 (see also v. 110). In Arabic, *islām* simply means "submission" or "surrender," so the Quran does not necessarily have the religion in mind every time it uses this word (see v. 20). *Islām* by itself also does not necessarily mean "surrender to Allah," because the very same word is used for political surrender or submission.

3.19 – *Those who were given the Book did not differ*

The Quran contains a number of statements that the People of the Book differed (*ikhtalafa*). The "knowledge" in the verse is not explained, but Muslim commentators have tended to identify this knowledge with the recitations of the messenger. See the comments on this theme at 98.4 (p. 642).

3.23 – *They were called to the Book of God in order that it might judge between them*

This verse draws attention to "those who were given a portion of the Book." These are not further identified, and neither is the "Book of God" specified nor the one who did the calling. This lack of context and identification is typical of many passages in the Quran.

The Islamic interpretive tradition identified the caller as Muhammad, the audience as the Jews of Medina, and the "Book of God" as the Torah. Muslim commentators have differed about the issue that needed judgment, but all seem to have agreed that the messenger of Islam appealed to the authority of the Torah.

If by "the Book of God" the Quran indeed means the Torah, this verse seems to

Then a group of them turned away in aversion. [24] That is because they said, 'The Fire will only touch us for a number of days.' What they forged has deceived them in their religion. [25] How (will it be) when We gather them for a Day – (there is) no doubt about it – and everyone will be paid in full what he has earned, and they will not be done evil? [26] Say: 'God! Master of the kingdom, You give the kingdom to whomever You please and You take away the kingdom from whomever You please. You exalt whomever You please and You humble whomever You please. In Your hand is the good. Surely You are powerful over everything. [27] You cause the night to pass into the day, and cause the day to pass into the night. You bring forth the living from the dead, and bring forth the dead from the living. You provide for whomever You please without reckoning.'

[28] Let not the believers take the disbelievers as allies, rather than the believers – whoever does that, he has nothing from God – unless you guard (yourselves) against them as a precaution. God warns you to beware of Him. To God is the (final) destination. [29] Say: 'Whether you hide what is in your hearts or reveal it, God knows it. He knows whatever is in the heavens and whatever is on the earth. God is powerful over everything.' [30] On the Day when everyone will find the good he has done brought forward, and (also) the evil he has done, he will wish that there were a great distance between himself and it. God warns you to beware of Him. God is kind with (His) servants. [31] Say: 'If you love God, follow me. God will love you and will forgive you your sins.

---

be a remarkable, unqualified nod to the authority of the pre-Islamic scriptures. The same kind of recommendation of the Torah – without caveats – seems to come later in this sūra at verse 93 and also at 10.94. See the comment on such verses at 10.94 (p. 234).

3.26 – *Master of the kingdom, You give the kingdom to whomever You please and You take away the kingdom from whomever You please*

These words are also found on a plaque that was posted in AD 691 above the eastern door of the Dome of the Rock in Jerusalem, where they refer to the Arab Conquest.

3.28 – *Let not the believers take the disbelievers as allies, rather than the believers*

The behavior of "believers" toward "unbelievers" is in focus here (see also v. 118). The Arabic word translated as "allies" (*walīy*) can also simply mean "friends."

3.31 – *If you love God, follow me. God will love you and will forgive you your sins*

This verse refers to human love for Allah, and a reciprocal love from Allah – on the condition that the reader or listener obeys the command to "follow me."

Muslims understand the word *me* to refer to Muhammad, so the condition here for the love of Allah is to follow Muhammad.

God is forgiving, compassionate.' [32] Say: 'Obey God and the messenger.' If they turn away – surely God does not love the disbelievers.

[33] Surely God has chosen Adam and Noah, and the house of Abraham and the house of 'Imrān over the worlds, [34] some of them descendents of others. God is hearing, knowing.

[35] (Remember) when the wife of 'Imrān said, 'My Lord, surely I vow to You what is in my belly, (to be) dedicated (to Your service). Accept (it) from me.

This verse is one of just a handful of verses that mention human love for Allah (also 2.165; 5.54; perhaps 2.177 and 76.8). There is no command in the Quran to love either Allah or other humans. See the response to these verses at 5.54 (p. 146). See also "The Language of Love in the Quran" (p. 560).

As for the condition for Allah's love for humans (that humans follow the messenger), this verse brings to mind the words of Jesus in John 14:23: "If anyone loves me, he will obey my teaching. My Father will love him, and we will come to him and make our home with him." Does Q 3.31 possibly set up a rivalry for the love and obedience of humans?

3.32 – *Obey God and the messenger*

After telling the reader or listener to follow the messenger in verse 31, the Quran now commands obedience to him. This is the first time in its canonical progression that the Quran associates "the messenger" with Allah, but the two are linked at least eighty-four more times. The command to obey Allah and the messenger also appears here for the first time and will repeat in this sūra at verse 132. The Quran associates the messenger with Allah for obedience or disobedience a total of twenty-eight times, most frequently in Sūras 4, 8, 24, and 33.

Quranic commands to obey the messenger became very important in the writings of the influential Muslim jurist al-Shāfiʿī (d. 820), who insisted they gave divine authority to traditional sayings (known as "hadith") that Muslims attribute to Muhammad. See an analysis of these commands at 64.12 (p. 574).

3.32 – *surely God does not love the disbelievers*

The Quran contains twenty-four statements about the kinds of people whom Allah does not love. Here the object is disbelievers (*kāfirūn*, also 30.45). See "The Language of Love in the Quran" (p. 560).

3.35 – *when the wife of 'Imrān said*

Verse 35 begins the first extended passage (vv. 35–62) about 'Īsā, the quranic Jesus. The story in this passage includes the characters Zachariah, John (*Yaḥyā*), Mary, and 'Īsā.

The Quran here identifies the father of Mary as 'Imrān (also 66.12). In the Old Testament, the father of Moses, Aaron, and Miriam is 'Amrām (Exodus 6:20, cf.

Surely You – You are the Hearing, the Knowing.' [36] And when she had delivered her, she said, 'My Lord, surely I have delivered her, a female' – God knew
very well what she had delivered, (since) the male is not like the female – 'and
I have named her Mary, and I seek refuge for her with You, and for her descendants, from the accursed Satan.' [37] So her Lord accepted her fully and caused
her to grow up well, and Zachariah took charge of her. Whenever Zachariah
entered upon her (in) the place of prayer, he found a provision (of food) with
her. He said, 'Mary! Where does this (food) come to you from?' She said, 'It is
from God. Surely God provides for whomever He pleases without reckoning.'
[38] There Zachariah called on his Lord. He said, 'My Lord, grant me a good
descendant from Yourself. Surely You are the Hearer of the call.' [39] And the
angels called him while he was standing, praying in the place of prayer: 'God
gives you good news of John, confirming a word from God. (He will be) a man
of honor, and an ascetic, and a prophet from among the righteous.' [40] He said,
'My Lord, how shall I have a boy, when old age has already come upon me and
my wife cannot conceive?' He said, 'So (it will be)! God does whatever He
pleases.' [41] He said, 'My Lord, make a sign for me.' He said, 'Your sign is that
you will not speak to the people for three days, except by gestures. Remember
your Lord often, and glorify (Him) in the evening and the morning.'

[42] And (remember) when the angels said, 'Mary! Surely God has chosen you

---

15:20–21). Together with Q 19.28, where Mary is called the "sister of Aaron," 3.35
seems to suggest confusion between the New Testament Mary and the Miriam of
the Hebrew Bible.

According to Muslim tradition, this passage (vv. 1–64) was first recited in the
middle of a conversation between Muhammad and a group of Christians from
Najrān, a town in the southwest corner of the Arabian Peninsula (*Sīra*, 272–77).

Two other extended passages about 'Īsā are found at 5.110–20 and 19.2–36.

3.39 – *God gives you good news of John, confirming a word from God*
Here the Quran refers to John the Baptist, using the name *Yaḥyā*, and describes
him in a positive way for "confirming a word from God" (see v. 45).

3.42 – *when the angels said, "Mary! Surely God has chosen you . . . over all other
women."*
The story of Mary's encounter with angels, her pregnancy, and her question,
"How shall I have a child?" (v. 47) bring to mind some of the details in the first chapter
of the Gospel according to Luke. The story also seems to have an affirmative tone.
The message of the angels here about the one to be born (vv. 42–46) is worth careful
comparison to Gabriel's words about the child in Luke 1:31–35.

The Quran uses a reverent expression to describe Mary, who was chosen literally

and purified you, and He has chosen you over all other women. [43] Mary! Be obedient to your Lord, and prostrate yourself and bow with the ones who bow.' [44] – That is one of the stories of the unseen. We inspired you (with) it. You were not with them when they cast their pens (as lots to see) which of them would take charge of Mary. Nor were you with them when they were disputing. – [45] When the angels said, 'Mary! Surely God gives you good news of a word from Him: his name is the Messiah, Jesus, son of Mary, eminent in this world and the Hereafter, and one of those brought near. [46] He will speak to the people (while he is still) in the cradle and in adulthood, and (he will be) one of the

---

"over the women of the worlds." This view of Mary brings to mind Luke 1:28, 30, and 42. Another story of the birth of 'Īsā appears in Sūra 19, and several other individual verses comment on how Mary came to be pregnant (Q 21.91; cf. 66.12).

3.44 – *You were not with them when they cast their pens*

In the middle of the speech of the angels to Mary, this verse takes a break to directly address the messenger in a kind of "aside." The messenger was "not with them" at the time of the story, which seems to imply that he would not have known this story if Allah had not revealed it to him. Instead, "We inspired you (with) it." Similar expressions appear at 11.49; 12.102; and 28.44. See the response to these expressions at 28.44 (p. 395).

The detail about those who "cast their pens" is not found in the Gospel accounts but resembles a detail from a Christian apocryphal work known as the *Proto-Gospel of James*. In addition, the angels' speech omits a very important affirmation related to the identity of Jesus that Gabriel was careful to announce twice in the Gospel (Luke 1:32, 35). See the discussion of this omission at Q 19.21 (p. 312).

3.45 – *Mary! Surely God gives you good news of a word from him*

This verse describes 'Īsā as the Messiah and a word from Allah. For the quranic name 'Īsā, see the explanation at 2.87 (p. 48).

The Quran gives the title "Messiah" (*al-Masīḥ*) to 'Īsā in a number of other passages (4.157, 171, 172; 5.17, 72, 75; 9.30, 31) but seems to understand the term as simply part of 'Īsā's name. It is a good example of the crucial significance in a biblical term that did not make it through to the Quran. The original meaning of Messiah as one who is "anointed" is never explained. The Quran seems to strip "Messiah" of its biblical meaning and use the term in a unique way.

As for describing 'Īsā as "a word" (*kalima*) from Allah, many Christians have wondered whether there is a link from this to the "Word" who was in the beginning with God in the Gospel according to John (1:1). 'Īsā is also referred to as "a word from God" in Q 3.39, as the word of God ("his word") in 4.171, and possibly as "a statement of the truth" in 19.34. For the Quran's response to this question, see verse 47.

righteous.' [47] She said, 'My Lord, how shall I have a child, when no man has touched me?' He said, 'So (it will be)! God creates whatever He pleases. When He decrees something, He simply says to it, "Be!" and it is.'

[48] And He will teach him the Book and the wisdom, and the Torah and the Gospel. [49] And (He will make him) a messenger to the Sons of Israel. 'Surely I have brought you a sign from your Lord: I shall create for you the form of a bird from clay. Then I will breathe into it and it will become a bird by the permission of God. And I shall heal the blind and the leper, and give the dead life by the permission of God. And I shall inform you of what you may eat, and what you may store up in your houses. Surely in that is a sign indeed for you, if you are believers. [50] And (I come) confirming what was before me of the Torah, and

---

3.47 – *God creates whatever He pleases. When He decrees something, He simply says to it, 'Be!' and it is*

In answer to Mary's question about how she could have a child without contact with a man, the angel answers that Allah simply creates what he pleases. This answer took on a lively significance in Muslim commentaries on the Quran and in Muslim thought generally. It represents a concept of an 'Īsā simply created in the womb, not the eternal divine Word who became a human (John 1:14; Philippians 2:6–7).

The quranic claim that 'Īsā is a created being repeats in this sūra at verse 59 and also at 2.117 and 19.35. See the analysis of the Quran's denials of the deity of 'Īsā at 43.59 (p. 491).

3.48 – *And He will teach him the . . . Torah and the Gospel*

For this concept that Allah teaches 'Īsā the Gospel, see the analysis and response at 57.27 (p. 549).

3.49 – *I shall create for you the form of a bird from clay*

'Īsā says that he will perform a number of miracles like those that Jesus performed in the Gospel accounts: he heals the blind and the leper and gives life to the dead. Here 'Īsā also informs the Sons of Israel about what they eat. But the most curious miracle described here is that 'Īsā creates a bird from clay and blows his breath into it, making it come to life. There is no mention of this episode in the canonical Gospel accounts, but a similar story appears in a Christian apocryphal writing known as the *Infancy Gospel of Thomas*. Also worth noting is that the Arabic verb translated "create" (*khalaqa*, also in 5.110) is elsewhere only used with Allah as subject in the Quran.

The miracles of 'Īsā are also given at Q 5.110. There, as here, the Quran seems concerned to specify that 'Īsā performed these miracles only "by the permission of Allah." See the analysis of these miracle verses at 5.110 (p. 153).

3.50 – *And (I come) confirming what was before me of the Torah*

The idea that 'Īsā "confirmed" the Torah (also at 5.46 and 61.6, cf. 5.110) raises the

to make permitted to you some things which were forbidden to you (before). I have brought you a sign from your Lord, so guard (yourselves) against God, and obey me. ⁵¹ Surely God is my Lord and your Lord, so serve Him! This is a straight path.'

⁵² When Jesus perceived disbelief from them, he said, 'Who will be my helpers to God?' The disciples said, 'We will be the helpers of God. We believe in God. Bear witness that we submit. ⁵³ Our Lord, we believe in what You have sent down, and we follow the messenger. So write us down among the witnesses.'

⁵⁴ They schemed, but God schemed (too), and God is the best of schemers. ⁵⁵ (Remember) when God said, 'Jesus! Surely I am going to take you and raise you to Myself, and purify you from those who disbelieve. And I am going to place those who follow you above those who disbelieve until the Day of Resurrection. Then to Me is your return, and I shall judge between you

---

interesting question of Jesus' relationship to the Old Testament. See the discussion of this concept at 61.6 (p. 563).

3.51 – *Surely God is my Lord and your Lord, so serve Him!*

'Īsā's statement and command here match several other verses in which the Quran quotes 'Īsā as denying his own deity (also 5.72, 116–17; 19.36; 43.64; cf. 3.79, 4.172). See an analysis of these statements at 43.64 (p. 492).

3.54 – *God is the best of schemers.*

The Arabic verb translated here as "to scheme" is *makara*, which is commonly defined as to deceive, delude, or cheat. The same description of Allah repeats at 8.30.

Perhaps because of its proximity to the next verse, 3.55, Muslim commentators have tended to interpret this verse to mean that Allah "deceived the deceivers" by causing the appearance of 'Īsā to fall on someone else at the time of his arrest.

3.55 – *Jesus! Surely I am going to take you and raise you to Myself*

This verse is one of just a few verses that touch on the death of 'Īsā in the Quran and the first in its canonical progression. Its Arabic wording has given trouble to both commentators and translators.

A. J. Droge translates the key Arabic phrase *mutawaffīka* as "I am going to take you," adding "in death" in a footnote. A number of translators have rendered the same phrase, "I will cause you to die" (George Sale, Edward Palmer, Muhammad Ali, Sher Ali, Muhammad Asad). Other translators have used expressions like "I will take you" (Arberry, Yusuf Ali, Alan Jones, Sahih International).

The source of confusion is the Arabic verb *tawaffā*. When it is not used in relation to 'Īsā in the Quran, this word is almost always translated as having to do with death (e.g., 10.46; 10.104; 12.101; 13.40; 16.28; 40.77). When the word is used in relation to

concerning your differences. [56] As for those who disbelieve, I shall punish them (with) a harsh punishment in this world and the Hereafter. They will have no helpers.' [57] As for those who believe and do righteous deeds, He will pay them their rewards in full. God does not love the evildoers. [58] That – We recite it to you from the signs and the wise Reminder.

[59] Surely the likeness of Jesus is, with God, as the likeness of Adam. He created him from dust, (and) then He said to him, 'Be!' and he was. [60] The truth (is) from your Lord, so do not be one of the doubters. [61] Whoever disputes with you about him, after what has come to you of the knowledge, say: 'Come, let us call our sons and your sons, our wives and your wives, ourselves and yourselves. Then let us pray earnestly and place the curse of God upon the liars.' [62] Surely this – it indeed is the true account. (There is) nothing of (the nature of) a god but God. Surely God – He indeed is the Mighty, the Wise. [63] If they turn away – surely God knows the fomenters of corruption.

ʿĪsā, however (in 3.55 and 5.117), it is usually translated as "taking." Because the translation of 3.55 raises such an important truth question for Christians, this commentary will highlight the translation of several verses containing the verb *tawaffā* further along in the Quran. See also "The Death of Jesus in the Quran" (p. 314).

3.57 – *God does not love the evildoers*

The Quran contains twenty-four statements about the kinds of people whom Allah does not love. "Evildoers" (*ẓālimūn*) are among the most frequent objects (also 3.140; 42.40). See "The Language of Love in the Quran" (p. 560).

3.59 – *Surely the likeness of Jesus is, with God, as the likeness of Adam*

This verse makes an important statement about the nature of ʿĪsā. According to this verse, ʿĪsā is a created being like Adam. That comes in stark contrast with New Testament teaching on this theme. The Gospel says that all things were made through Jesus (John 1:3, 10), and other passages affirm that the universe was created through him (1 Corinthians 8:6, Hebrews 1:2), by him, and for him (Colossians 1:16).

See the analysis of the Quran's denials of the deity of ʿĪsā at Q 43.59 (p. 491).

3.62 – *Surely this – it indeed is the true account*

The Quran's first extended passage about ʿĪsā ends with an ultimatum (vv. 60–63): this "is the true account" about ʿĪsā (v. 62). Verse 61 seems to command the messenger – if the audience persists in disputing his recitations about the nature of ʿĪsā – to initiate a cursing ceremony in which the punishment of Allah would fall upon those who state falsehood about ʿĪsā. The Quran also seems to insist on the truth of its portrayal of ʿĪsā at 4.174 and 19.34.

Immediately after a denial of the deity of ʿĪsā, the Quran makes a claim that resembles the first part of the Islamic confession of faith: "There is no god except

⁶⁴ Say: 'People of the Book! Come to a word (which is) common between us and you: "We do not serve (anyone) but God, and do not associate (anything) with Him, and do not take each other as Lords instead of God."' If they turn away, say: 'Bear witness that we are Muslims.'

⁶⁵ People of the Book! Why do you dispute about Abraham, when the Torah

---

Allah" (*mā min ilāhin illā 'llāh*). This raises the question of what "god" (*ilāha*) Muslims have in mind when they recite their *shahāda*.

Like many Muslim Quran commentaries, the early commentary of Muqātil ibn Sulaymān (d. 767) included the story of the visit of Christians from Najrān to the messenger of Islam (see the comment at v. 35). In Muqātil's version, the first question the Christians ask Islam's messenger is, "Why do you abuse and dishonor our master?"

3.64 – *People of the Book! Come to a word (which is) common between us and you*

Here the Quran directly addresses the "People of the Book" for the first time in its canonical progression. In this and the following fifty verses, the expression "People of the Book" appears eleven times, including half of the direct appeals in the Quran. Many readers will understand this expression in the positive sense of communities that have the scriptures. But the majority of the thirty plus occurrences of "People of the Book" in the Quran appear in polemical passages. See a discussion of the Quran's approach to the People of the Book at 98.1 (p. 641).

Verse 64 became quite famous in 2007 when a group of Muslims posted a statement on the internet proposing dialog with Christians on the basis of "a common word." Many Christians greatly appreciated the initiative.

In the long history of Muslim interpretation of the Quran, however, this verse was understood rather as a call to Christians to worship no other than Allah, to ascribe no partner to Allah, and to take no other as Lord beside Allah. Many commentaries charge Christians with failing in all three areas because of Christian belief in the deity and Lordship of Jesus. See the analysis of the Quran's denials of the deity of 'Īsā at 43.59 (p. 491). See also my article, "'A Common Word' in Qur'ānic Context and Commentary," listed in the bibliography.

Though this verse is explicitly addressed to the "People of the Book," it uses the language of associating ("do not associate [anything] with him"). This indicates that the Quran's accusation of "associating" includes a broader range of meaning than merely "idolatry," as A. J. Droge translates it.

3.65 – *People of the Book! Why do you dispute about Abraham*

The messenger and his audience are debating Abraham. The contention in this passage is that since Abraham lived before the Torah and Gospel were "sent down," he can be neither a Jew nor a Christian (v. 67).

Abraham is portrayed here not as a link between the "monotheistic religions"

and the Gospel were not sent down until after him. Will you not understand? [66] There you are! Those who have disputed about what you know. Why do you dispute about what you do not know? God knows, but you do not know. [67] Abraham was not a Jew, nor a Christian, but he was a Ḥanīf, a Muslim. He was not one of the idolaters. [68] Surely the people nearest to Abraham are those indeed who followed him, and this prophet, and those who believe. God is the ally of the believers.

Abraham in the Quran
George Bristow

Despite widespread usage of the term "Abrahamic religions" for Judaism, Christianity and Islam, Abraham occupies far less common ground in the Quran and the Bible than might be expected. According to the Quran, the only "religion of Abraham" is Islam (2.130–35). Abraham is neither Jewish nor Christian (3.65–67; 42.13–14) but a prophet of pure monotheism, an ideal Muslim, and the founder of the pilgrimage rituals.

Abraham is found faithful in every test and is called the friend of God – *khalīl* (4.125). As a man of pure faith, a *Ḥanīf*, he rejects all idolatry and recognizes the primacy of the hereafter (2.135; 3.67, 95; 4.125; 6.79, 161; 16.120, 123; 19.41). He bears bold, confrontational witness to the one Creator. Like other prophets, he receives revelation (2.136; 3.84; 4.163; 19.41; 33.7; 53.36–37; 57.26; 87.19). He is an example of fervent prayer and intercession, pleading not to be ashamed on the dreadful Day of Reckoning (2.126–29, 260; 9.114; 11.74–76; 14.35–41; 26.83–102; 29.32; 37.100; 60.4). Muslims repeat a version of his petition at the end of each daily prayer (*Salat*).

The Quran nowhere presents a complete Abraham narrative, but we can

---

but as exclusively a *Ḥanīf* and a *muslim* ("one who submits"). Similar to 2.135 and 140, this passage seems to present Abraham as a bone of contention and a source of religious claim and counterclaim. On *Ḥanīf*, see the comment at 2.135 (p. 55).

3.68 – *Surely the people nearest to Abraham are those indeed who followed him, and this prophet*

References to "the prophet" do not occur frequently in the Quran, and most of the occurrences come in Sūras 8; 9; 33; and 66. The expression "this prophet" – implying the speaker of this polemic against the People of the Book – appears only here in the Quran. See an analysis of "the prophet" at 66.9 (p. 579).

reconstruct the general shape of an understood story from the twenty-five sūras where he is mentioned. Below I piece together four distinct episodes from fragments, which in context function like sermon illustrations drawn from familiar tales to support the Quran's message.

Episode 1: Disputation with idolaters (6.74–87; 19.41–50; 21.51–73; 26.69–102; 29.16–27; 37.83–100; 43.26–28; 60.4–7). Early in life Abraham observes the setting astral bodies and, reasoning from creation to the unchanging creator, turns his face as a true believer toward "Him who created the heavens and the earth" (6.75–79). He rejects the idolatry of his kinsfolk and derides their foolishness. In some accounts, they cast Abraham into a fire from which God rescues him. Although this story and its heroic portrait is absent from Genesis, it is found in later Jewish parabiblical writings (e.g., *Jubilees*). Abraham's active opposition to idolatry and his message of "tawhid" (divine unity) fits the quranic pattern for all prophets.

Episode 2: Hosting angelic visitors (11.69–83; 15.51–77; 29.31–32; 37.99–113; 51.24–37). Abraham welcomes messengers with a meal, which they do not eat. Whereas in Genesis the Lord comes as one of three guests who eat at Abraham's table, here they are all angels sent to announce the impending birth of Isaac and to bring judgment on the people of Lot while delivering his family. In two sūras, the story of Lot's people's destruction follows directly (as in Genesis 18–19), warning listeners of the certain doom of all who persist in defying God's messenger.

Episode 3: Constructing the House (2.124–141; 3.95–97; 14.35–41; 22.26–33). In this story, which has no parallels with Genesis or later Jewish writings, God appoints "the House" (traditionally understood as the *Ka'ba*) as a "holy place and a guidance," commanding Abraham and Ishmael to purify it for pilgrimage. While raising the foundations, they pray for the land to be fruitful and for their offspring to be preserved from idolatry and to keep the "holy rites." Abraham also prays for God to send a messenger to the people of this region (traditionally Mecca) and seeks forgiveness on the Day of Judgment. Strikingly, other than the Prophet of Islam, only Abraham (with Ishmael) among the many quranic prophets has any explicit relation to this house of worship.

Episode 4: The near-offering of his son (37.83–113). When Abraham prays for a son, he receives good news of the birth of an unnamed "patient son" (37.100–101). While most Muslims have traditionally understood this son to be Ishmael (Isaac's birth is in fact mentioned separately in 37.112), many early Muslim commentators identified him as Isaac. When the boy grows up, Abraham recounts a dream in which he is sacrificing his son. The boy states his willingness to obey God, and both are found "surrendered." As in Genesis 22, at the last moment God intervenes, "ransoms" the boy with a "mighty sacrifice," and rewards Abraham with a posterity who will "bless" him. This story illustrates obedient submission to God (2.131–32) and explains the annual sacrifice festival, *Eid al-Adha*.

As with all quranic prophet stories, these episodes from Abraham's life reflect a worldview where heeding the prophetic message of divine unity and judgment is the preeminent virtue. In this pattern, Abraham and the "Prophet" addressed throughout the Quran (understood as Muhammad by Muslims) are inseparably connected. In fact, this quranic connection is nearly as clear as that between Abraham and Jesus traced by the New Testament. Christians will find that the Quran's *prophet-centered* view of Abraham includes very little of the familiar biblical narrative (only Genesis 18–19; 22) and shares almost nothing with the New Testament's *Christ-centered* view of Abraham.

[69] A contingent of the People of the Book would like to lead you astray, but they only lead themselves astray, though they do not realize (it). [70] People of the Book! Why do you disbelieve in the signs of God, when you are witnesses (to them)? [71] People of the Book! Why do you mix the truth with falsehood, and conceal the truth, when you know (better)? [72] A contingent of the People of the Book has said, 'Believe in what has been sent down on those who believe at the beginning of the day, and disbelieve at the end of it, perhaps (then) they may return.' [73] And: 'Do not believe (anyone) except the one who follows your religion.' Say: 'Surely the (true) guidance is the guidance of God – that anyone should be given what you have been given, or (that) they should dispute with you before your Lord!' Say: 'Surely favor is in the hand of God. He gives it to whomever He pleases. God is embracing, knowing. [74] He chooses whomever He pleases for His mercy, and God is full of great favor.'

[75] Among the People of the Book (there is) one who, if you entrust him with a qinṭār, will pay it back to you, but among them there is one who, if you entrust him with a dīnār, will not pay it back to you unless you stand over him. That is because they say, 'There is no way (of obligation) on us concerning the common people.' They speak lies against God, and they know (it). [76] Yes indeed!

Whoever fulfills his covenant and guards (himself) – surely God loves the ones who guard (themselves). [77] Surely those who sell the covenant of God and their oaths for a small price will have no share in the Hereafter. God will not speak to them or look at them on the Day of Resurrection, nor will He purify them. For them (there is) a painful punishment.

[78] Surely (there is) indeed a group of them who twist their tongues with the Book, so that you will think it is from the Book, when it is not from the Book. And they say, 'It is from God,' when it is not from God. They speak lies against God, and they know (it). [79] It is not (possible) for a human being that God should give him the Book, and the judgment, and the prophetic office, (and) then he should say to the people, 'Be my servants instead of God's.' Rather (he would say), 'Be rabbis by what you have been teaching of the Book and by what you have been studying (of it).' [80] He would not command you to take the angels and the prophets as Lords. Would he command you to disbelief after you have submitted?

[81] (Remember) when God took a covenant with the prophets: 'Whatever indeed I have given you of the Book and wisdom, when a messenger comes to you confirming what is with you, you are to believe in him and you are to help him.' He said, 'Do you agree and accept My burden on that (condition)?' They said, 'We agree.' He said, 'Bear witness, and I shall be with you among the witnesses.' [82] Whoever turns away after that, those – they are the wicked.

3.76 – *God loves the ones who guard (themselves)*

Here Allah loves the God-fearing or pious. See "The Language of Love in the Quran" (p. 560).

3.78 – *a group of them who twist their tongues with the Book*

Verse 78 is another important verse in the series of quranic verses that seem to show suspicion about the treatment of the pre-Islamic scriptures. Here the action in view is "twisting their tongues with the book" – perhaps mispronouncing or changing the words. The preceding context addresses "People of the Book," so they may be assumed to be the subject here; however, if a scripture is meant, it is not named. See "Tampering with the Pre-Islamic Scriptures" (p. 142).

3.81 – *when a messenger comes to you confirming what is with you*

This verse says that Allah made a covenant with the prophets in the past to believe in and help a messenger to come in the future, and that the prophets agreed. Muslims understand the unnamed messenger to be Muhammad.

The Quran frequently claims that the recitations of the messenger confirm (*muṣaddiq*) that which is "with" the People of the Book. See the analysis of this claim, and a response, at 46.12 (p. 502).

⁸³ Do they desire a religion other than God's, when whoever is in the heavens and the earth has submitted to Him, willingly or unwillingly, and to Him they will be returned? ⁸⁴ Say: 'We believe in God, and what has been sent down on us, and what has been sent down on Abraham, and Ishmael, and Isaac, and Jacob, and the tribes, and what was given to Moses, and Jesus, and the prophets from their Lord. We make no distinction between any of them, and to Him we submit.' ⁸⁵ Whoever desires a religion other than Islam, it will not be accepted from him, and in the Hereafter he will be one of the losers.

⁸⁶ How will God guide a people who have disbelieved after having believed, and (after) they have borne witness that the messenger is true, and the clear signs have come to them? God does not guide the people who are evildoers. ⁸⁷ Those – their payment is that on them (rests) the curse of God, and the angels, and the people all together. ⁸⁸ There (they will) remain – the punishment will not be lightened for them, nor will they be spared ⁸⁹ – except for those who turn (in repentance) after that and set (things) right. Surely God is forgiving, compassionate. ⁹⁰ Surely those who disbelieve after their believing, (and) then increase in disbelief – their repentance will not be accepted. And those – they are the ones who go astray. ⁹¹ Surely those who disbelieve, and die while they are disbelievers – not all the world's gold would be accepted from (any) one of them, even if he (tried to) ransom (himself) with it. Those – for them (there is) a painful punishment. They will have no helpers.

⁹² You will not attain piety until you contribute from what you love, and whatever you contribute, surely God knows it.

⁹³ All food was permitted to the Sons of Israel, except for what Israel forbade himself before the Torah was sent down. Say: 'Bring the Torah and read it, if you are truthful.' ⁹⁴ Whoever forges lies against God after that, those – they are

---

3.84 – *We believe in . . . what has been sent down on . . . Moses, and Jesus, and the prophets from their Lord. We make no distinction between any of them*

This verse seems to place what is "sent down upon us" on the same level with the pre-Islamic revelations. To what extent has the Muslim community demonstrated faith in pre-Islamic revelations? Has it indeed made "no distinction" between what is "sent down upon us" and the pre-Islamic revelations?

3.85 – *Whoever desires a religion other than Islam, it will not be accepted from him*

This is another verse in this sūra that seems to make exclusive claims for Islam (also vv. 19, 67; cf. 110).

3.93 – *Bring the Torah and read it, if you are truthful*

This verse contains one of several quranic expressions that seem to show an unqualified acceptance of the authority of the Torah (*tawrāt*). The same attitude can

the evildoers. [95] Say: 'God has spoken the truth, so follow the creed of Abraham the Ḥanīf. He was not one of the idolaters.'

[96] Surely the first House laid down for the people was indeed that at Becca, a blessed (House) and a guidance for the worlds. [97] In it are clear signs: the standing place of Abraham. Whoever enters it is secure. Pilgrimage to the House is (an obligation) on the people to God – (for) anyone who is able (to make) a way to it. Whoever disbelieves – surely God is wealthy beyond the worlds.

[98] Say: 'People of the Book! Why do you disbelieve in the signs of God, when God is a witness of what you do?' [99] Say: 'People of the Book! Why do you keep those who believe from the way of God, desiring (to make) it crooked, when you are witnesses? God is not oblivious of what you do.'

[100] You who believe! If you obey a group of those who have been given the Book, they will turn you back (into) disbelievers after having believed. [101] Yet how can you disbelieve, when the signs of God are recited to you, and His messenger is among you? Whoever holds fast to God has been guided to a straight path.

[102] You who believe! Guard (yourselves) against God – guarding (yourselves) against Him is an obligation – and (see to it that) you do not die unless you have submitted. [103] And hold fast to the rope of God – all (of you) – and do not become divided. Remember the blessing of God on you: when you were

---

be found at 3.23; 5.43–44; and 10.94. See a summary and response at 10.94 (p. 234), and "Tampering with the Pre-Islamic Scriptures" (p. 142).

3.96 – *Surely the first House laid down for the people was indeed that at Becca*

To what does the Arabic word *bakka* (Becca) refer? A number of Muslim translations of this verse make it another name for Mecca. But the word *makka* only appears once in the Quran, at 48.24. In Arabic script, the letter *bā'* is quite a different shape from the *mīm*.

As for "the House" where Abraham stood up to pray (v. 97), see the comments at 2.124 (p. 54).

3.100 – *You who believe!*

After much discussion of the "People of the Book" and many speeches directed toward them (e.g., vv. 98, 99), the sūra shifts its focus to the quranic "believers." Most of the rest of the sūra concerns that "community" (*umma*, vv. 104, 110), though the People of the Book are mentioned at a number of points (e.g., vv. 113, 181, 199).

3.101 – *the signs of God are recited to you, and His messenger is among you*

The Quran claims that the messenger and his recitations are from Allah. This kind of "self-referential" language repeats many times in the Quran, including in this sūra at verses 138 and 164 (cf. 81, 144). See "Different Kinds of Literature" (p. 14).

enemies and He united your hearts, so that by His blessing you became brothers. You were on the brink of a pit of the Fire, and He saved you from it. In this way God makes clear to you His signs, so that you may be (rightly) guided.

[104] Let there be (one) community of you, calling (people) to good, and commanding right and forbidding wrong. Those – they are the ones who prosper. [105] Do not be like those who became divided and differed, after the clear signs had come to them. Those – for them (there is) a great punishment, [106] on the Day when (some) faces will become white and (other) faces will become black. As for those whose faces are blackened: 'Did you disbelieve after having believed? Taste the punishment for what you were disbelieving!' [107] As for those whose faces are whitened, (they will be) in the mercy of God. There they will remain. [108] Those are the signs of God. We recite them to you in truth. God does not intend any evil to the worlds.

[109] To God (belongs) whatever is in the heavens and whatever is on the earth. To God all affairs are returned.

[110] You are the best community (ever) brought forth for humankind, commanding right and forbidding wrong, and believing in God. If the People of the Book had believed, it would indeed have been better for them. Some of them are believers, but most of them are wicked. [111] They will not cause you any harm, except for a (little) hurt. And if they fight you, they will turn their backs to you, (and) then they will not be helped. [112] Humiliation will be stamped upon them wherever they are found, unless (they grasp) a rope from God and a

---

3.105 – *Do not be like those who became divided and differed*

On division and disagreement, see the comments at 98.4 (p. 642).

3.106 – *on the Day when (some) faces will become white and (other) faces will become black*

The Day of Judgment and what will take place afterward is a very important topic in the Quran. References to the "day" or the "hour" become especially frequent in Sūras 11–47. See "Eschatology in the Quran" (p. 604).

3.110 – *You are the best community (ever) brought forth for humankind*

The Arabic term translated "community" is *umma*. This is the key term for the Islamic worldwide nation. To command right behavior and forbid indecency is certainly a great accomplishment for any community.

3.110 – *If the People of the Book had believed, it would indeed have been better for them*

The unbelief of the People of the Book is mentioned here in the past tense, which suggests that the "belief" wished for in this verse is the belief that the messenger is a true prophet and that his recitations are from Allah.

rope from the people. They have incurred the anger of God, and poverty will be stamped upon them. That is because they have disbelieved in the signs of God and killed the prophets without any right. That is because they have disobeyed and transgressed.

[113] (Yet) they are not (all) alike. Among the People of the Book (there is) a community (which is) upstanding. They recite the signs of God during the hours of the night and prostrate themselves. [114] They believe in God and the Last Day, and command right and forbid wrong, and are quick in the (doing of) good deeds. Those are among the righteous. [115] Whatever good they do, they will not be denied (the reward of) it. God knows the ones who guard (themselves). [116] Surely those who disbelieve – neither their wealth nor their children will be of any use against God – those are the companions of the Fire. There they will remain. [117] The parable of what they contribute in this present life is like the parable of a freezing wind, which smites the field of a people who have done themselves evil, and destroys it. God did not do them evil, but they did themselves evil.

[118] You who believe! Do not take outsiders as intimate friends. They will not fail to cause you ruin. They desire what you are distressed at. (Their) hatred is already apparent from their mouths, but what their hearts hide is (even) greater. We have already made clear to you the signs, if you are understanding. [119] There you are! You are those who love them, but they do not love you. You believe in the Book – all of it. And when they meet you they say, 'We believe,' but when they are alone, they bite their fingers at you out of rage. Say: 'Die in your rage! Surely God knows what is in the hearts.' [120] If some good touches you, it distresses them, but if some evil smites you, they gloat over it. Yet if you are

---

3.113 – *Among the People of the Book (there is) a community (which is) upstanding*

Here the Quran describes a group (also *umma*) from the People of the Book who are upstanding (*qā'ima*) in Muslim terms. See a similar description in verse 199, where there is also a response.

3.119 – *You are those who love them, but they do not love you*

This verse pictures Muslims loving non-Muslims but non-Muslims not loving back. These non-Muslims are also hateful (v. 118), deceptive, and full of *Schadenfreude* (v. 120). In this case the Muslims are doing what is right, and the non-Muslims are in the wrong.

For Christians this is a great failure. Whatever the disagreements may be, whatever the political situation, Jesus commands his followers not only to love their neighbors as themselves (Matthew 19:19) but also to love whoever may consider Christians their enemy (Matthew 5:44). When they hate others, Christians disobey their Lord. See "The Language of Love in the Quran" (p. 560).

patient and guard (yourselves), their plot will not harm you at all. Surely God encompasses what they do.

[121] (Remember) when you went out early from your family to post the believers (in their) positions for the battle – God is hearing, knowing – [122] when two contingents of you were inclined to lose courage, though God was their ally – in God let the believers put their trust. [123] Certainly God helped you at Badr, when you were an utterly insignificant (force). So guard (yourselves) against God, that you may be thankful.

[124] (Remember) when you said to the believers, 'Is it not sufficient for you that your Lord increases you with three thousand angels (specially) sent down? [125] Yes indeed! If you are patient and guard (yourselves), and they come against you suddenly, your Lord will increase you with five thousand angels (specially) designated.' [126] God only intended that as good news for you, and to satisfy your hearts by means of it. Help (comes) only from God, the Mighty, the Wise, [127] so that He might cut off a part of those who disbelieve, or disgrace them, so that they would turn back disappointed. [128] You have nothing to do with the matter, whether He turns to them (in forgiveness) or punishes them. Surely they are evildoers. [129] To God (belongs) whatever is in the heavens and whatever is on the earth. He forgives whomever He pleases and He punishes whomever He pleases. God is forgiving, compassionate.

[130] You who believe! Do not devour usury, (making it) double and redouble, but guard (yourselves) against God, so that you may prosper. [131] And guard (yourselves) against the Fire which is prepared for the disbelievers.

[132] Obey God and the messenger, so that you may receive compassion. [133] And

---

3.121 – *when you went out early from your family to post the believers (in their) positions for the battle*

This verse begins a long passage that brings to mind a military conflict (vv. 121–80). Though in much of the passage it seems difficult to get one's bearings, some orientation is offered by the language of "battle" (v. 121), "wound" (vv. 140, 172), "enemy" (v. 140), "struggle" (v. 142), killing and being killed (*qatala/qutila*, vv. 144, 152, 154, 156–58, 168–69), and fighting (v. 146, 156, 167).

The earliest Muslim stories of Islamic origins linked this passage of sixty verses with the "battle of Uḥud" (*Sīra*, 392–401 [3.121–79]; *Raids* 154–60 [3.121–200]). This passage also mentions "Badr" (v. 123), an earlier battle according to Muslim tradition. See "Muslim Story of Islamic Origins" (p. 16).

3.132 – *Obey God and the messenger*

Once more the sūra associates the messenger with Allah for obedience, with a promise of mercy. See the analysis of such commands at 64.12 (p. 574).

be quick to (obtain) forgiveness from your Lord, and a Garden – its width (is like) the heavens and the earth – prepared for the ones who guard (themselves), [134] who contribute (alms) in prosperity and adversity, and who choke back their anger and pardon the people. God loves the doers of good, [135] and those who, when they commit immorality or do themselves evil, remember God and ask forgiveness for their sins – and who forgives sins but God? – and do not persist in (doing) what they did, when they know (better). [136] Those – their payment is forgiveness from their Lord, and Gardens through which rivers flow, there to remain. Excellent is the reward of the doers!

[137] Customary practices have passed away before you. Travel the earth and see how the end was for the ones who called (it) a lie. [138] This is an explanation for the people, and a guidance and admonition for the ones who guard (themselves).

[139] Do not grow weak and do not sorrow, when you are the prevailing (force), if you are believers. [140] If a wound has touched you, a similar wound has already touched the enemy. We cause days like this to alternate among the people, so that God may know those who believe, and that He may take martyrs from you – God does not love the evildoers – [141] and so that God may purge those who believe, and destroy the disbelievers. [142] Or did you think that you would enter the Garden, when God did not yet know those of you who would struggle, and know the (ones who would be) patient? [143] Certainly you were desiring death before you met it. Now you have seen it, and you are staring (at it).

[144] Muḥammad is only a messenger. Messengers have already passed away

3.134 – God loves the doers of good

The statement that Allah loves the doers of good is the most frequent affirmation of Allah's love in the Quran. The statement repeats at 3.148; 5.13, 93. See "The Language of Love in the Quran" (p. 560).

3.137 – Travel the earth and see how the end was for the ones who called (it) a lie

This frequent refrain reminds the reader or listener to consider what happened to peoples who denied Allah's messages and messengers in the past.

3.140 – Allah does not love the evildoers

See the comment on this expression earlier in this sūra at verse 57.

3.144 – Muhammad is only a messenger. Messengers have already passed away before him

This is the first appearance of the name *Muḥammad* in the canonical progression of the Quran. Here Muhammad is "nothing but a messenger" who could die or be killed.

The context surrounding the verse calls to mind a military scene. There are battle wounds and "struggle" (vv. 120, 140, 143). The Quran mentions fighting and killing

before him. If he dies or is killed, will you turn back on your heels? Whoever turns back on his heels will not harm God at all. God will repay the thankful. [145] It is not (given) to anyone to die, except by the permission of God – (it is) determined (in) writing. Whoever desires the reward of this world, We shall give him (a share) of it, and whoever desires the reward of the Hereafter, We shall give him (a share) of it. We shall repay the thankful.

[146] How many a prophet has fought, (and along) with him (fought) many thousands? Yet they did not weaken at what smote them in the way of God. They were not weak nor did they humiliate themselves. God loves the patient. [147] All that they said was, 'Our Lord, forgive us our sins and our wantonness

---

(vv. 146, 152). Muslim stories of Islamic origins associate 3.144 with the defeat of the Muslims in the battle of Uḥud.

The name *Muḥammad* appears only three other times in the Quran. This is striking, given that Muslims believe the Quran was revealed to Muhammad. All four occurrences are in the third person, declaring something about Muhammad, and never in the second person or direct address ("O Muhammad"). See the discussion of the four appearances of the name at 48.29 (p. 516).

3.146 – *How many a prophet has fought, (and along) with him (fought) many thousands?*

This question seems to represent a concept of prophets that is quite different from the portrait painted in most other parts of the Quran, where Allah rescues the prophet and his supporters from those who oppose them. Here the prophet and his supporters pray for "victory over the people who are disbelievers" (v. 147). The context is a long passage in which the believers seem to be involved in battle in the present (3.121–86), and verses 146–48 seem to be an attempt to validate the fighting.

The concept of prophets who fight also appears in relation to the quranic Saul and David (2.246–51) and 'Īsā (61.14, cf. 3.52); quranic prophets also show hatred of their enemies (Abraham, 60.4–6) and curse them ('Īsā and David, 5.78). See a response to this concept at 61.14 (p. 566).

3.146 – *God loves the patient*

From the context of this verse, the "patient" seem to be those who fought "in the way of Allah." See "The Language of Love in the Quran" (p. 560).

3.147 – *Our Lord, forgive us our sins and our wantonness in our affair*

This verse characterizes prophets as asking forgiveness for their sins (*dhunūb*, sing. *dhanb*). Indeed, many quranic prophets ask for forgiveness: Adam (7.23), Noah (11.47), Abraham (26.82), Moses (28.16), and David (38.24).

The messenger addressed by the Quran is also commanded to ask forgiveness for his sin (40.55, 47.19, cf. 48.2). See an analysis of this theme at 48.2 (p. 513).

in our affair, and make firm our feet, and give us victory over the people who are disbelievers.' [148] So God gave them the reward of this world and the good reward of the Hereafter. God loves the doers of good.

[149] You who believe! If you obey those who disbelieve, they will turn you back on your heels, and you will return as losers. [150] No! God is your Protector. He is the best of helpers. [151] We shall cast dread into the hearts of those who disbelieve, because they have associated with God what He has not sent down any authority for. Their refuge is the Fire. Evil is the dwelling place of the evildoers!

[152] Certainly God fulfilled His promise to you when you were killing them by His permission, until you lost courage and argued about the matter, and disobeyed after He had shown you what you love. (There are) some of you who desire this world, and some of you who desire the Hereafter. Then He turned you away from them, so that He might test you. Certainly He has pardoned you. God is full of favor to the believers.

[153] (Remember) when you were going up, and not turning aside for anyone, and the messenger was calling to you from behind: He repaid you (with) distress upon distress, so that you might not sorrow over what eluded you or what smote you. God is aware of what you do. [154] Then, after the distress, He sent down on you security: a slumber covering a contingent of you, but (another) contingent (of you) was obsessed about themselves, thinking about God (something) other than the truth – thought(s) of the (time of) ignorance. They were

---

3.148 – *God loves the doers of good*

See the comment on this expression at verse 134. In this verse, the "doers of good" seem to be those who gain victory over the "disbelievers" (v. 147).

3.151 – *We shall cast dread into the hearts of those who disbelieve*

In the midst of a battle scene, the Quran states that Allah casts terror or "dread" (ru'b) into the hearts of unbelievers. This expression repeats at 8.12; 33.26; and 59.2. According to this verse, Allah acts in this way because those who "disbelieve" associate partners with Allah. See the discussion of terror and terrorizing at 59.2 (p. 554).

3.152 – *Certainly God fulfilled His promise to you when you were killing them by His permission*

This idea, that one group of humans kills another group by the permission of Allah and according to his promise, needs to be carefully examined for both its theology and its morality. The goal of peaceful coexistence in a multifaith world would seem to counter it.

This verse joins 22.39 in claiming that Allah gives permission for fighting and 9.14 in asserting that Allah punishes people at the hands of "believers." See "Allah in the Quran" (p. 572).

saying, 'Do we have any part at all in the affair?' Say: 'Surely the affair – all of it – (belongs) to God.' They hide within themselves what they do not reveal to you. They were saying, 'If we had any part in the affair, we would not have been killed here.' Say: '(Even) if you had been in your houses, those for whom death was written would (still) indeed have gone forth to the places where they lie (dead).' (That happened) in order that God might test what was in your hearts, and that He might purge what was in your hearts. God knows what is in the hearts. [155] Surely those of you who turned back on the day the two forces met – (it was) only Satan (who) caused them to slip because of something they had earned. Certainly God has pardoned them. Surely God is forgiving, forbearing.

[156] You who believe! Do not be like those who disbelieve, and say of their brothers when they strike forth on the earth or are on a raid, 'If they had been with us, they would not have died or been killed' – so that God may make that a (cause of) regret in their hearts. (It is) God (who) gives life and causes death. God sees what you do. [157] If indeed you are killed in the way of God, or die – forgiveness from God, and mercy, are indeed better than what they accumulate. [158] If indeed you die or are killed, you will indeed be gathered to God. [159] (It was) by a mercy from God (that) you have been soft on them. If you had been harsh (and) stern of heart, they would indeed have deserted from your ranks. So pardon them, and ask forgiveness for them, and consult with them about the affair. When you have made up your mind, put your trust in God. Surely God loves the ones who put their trust (in Him). [160] If God helps you, (there is) no one to overcome you, but if He forsakes you, who (is there) who (will) help you after Him? In God let the believers put their trust.

[161] It is not for a prophet to defraud. Whoever defrauds will bring what he has defrauded on the Day of Resurrection. Then everyone will be paid in full what they have earned – and they will not be done evil. [162] Is the one who follows after the approval of God like the one who incurs the anger of God? His refuge

---

3.157 – *If indeed you are killed in the way of God, or die – forgiveness from God*

The idea that believers who die fighting are martyrs who go straight to heaven has its quranic basis in verses like this, one of three such passages in this sūra. Here fighters are promised forgiveness, mercy, and being gathered to Allah (v. 158). Other verses like this are 2.154; 3.169–72, 195; 22.58–59; and 47.4–6. See an analysis of these verses at 47.4 (p. 509).

3.159 – *Surely Allah loves the ones who put their trust (in Him)*

The Quran contains twenty-four statements about the kinds of people whom Allah loves, here those who trust (*mutawakkilūn*) in him. See "The Language of Love in the Quran" (p. 560).

will be Gehenna – and it is an evil destination! [163] They (have different) ranks with God, and God sees what they do. [164] Certainly God bestowed favor on the believers when He raised up among them a messenger from among them, to recite His signs to them, and to purify them, and to teach them the Book and the wisdom, though before (this) they were indeed clearly astray. [165] Why, when a smiting smote you – you had already smitten twice (as many in comparison to) it – did you say, 'How is this?' Say: 'You yourselves are to blame. Surely God is powerful over everything.'

[166] What smote you on the day when the two forces met (happened) by the permission of God, so that He might know the (true) believers, [167] and that He might know those who played the hypocrite. It was said to them, 'Come, fight in the way of God, or defend!' But they said, 'If we knew (how) to fight, we would indeed follow you.' They were nearer to disbelief that day than to belief. They were saying with their mouths what was not in their hearts. But God knows what they were concealing – [168] those who said of their brothers, when they (themselves) sat (at home), 'If they had obeyed us, they would not have been killed.' Say: 'Avert death from yourselves, if you are truthful.'

[169] Do not think of those who have been killed in the way of God as dead.

3.164 – *Certainly God bestowed favor on the believers when He raised up among them a messenger from among them*

In the midst of the battle scene comes this "self-referential" verse claiming that Allah sends both the messenger and his recitations. Who is the speaker of verses in which both Allah and messenger are in third person and in which there is no command to the messenger to "say" the recitations that Allah dictates? See "Different Kinds of Literature" (p. 14).

3.167 – *It was said to them, "Come, fight in the way of Allah, or defend!"*

The command to "fight! (*qātilū*)" gives the reader an indication of what is going on in this long and context-less passage (vv. 121–80). The hypocrites are commanded to fight but make the excuse that they do not know how. This command joins twelve direct commands to fight in the Quran. Here the enemy and the limits of the hostilities are unclear, but verse 166 gives a reason for the fighting: that Allah might test them and reveal the true believers. See "Fighting and Killing in the Quran" (p. 220).

Commanding the people to fight "in the way (*sabīl*) of Allah" makes a theological claim by associating Allah with human fighting. See the analysis of these expressions at 73.20 (p. 597).

3.169 – *Do not think of those who have been killed in the way of God as dead. No! (They are) alive with their Lord (and) provided for*

Here the Quran explains what happens to those who "are killed in the way

No! (They are) alive with their Lord (and) provided for, [170] gloating over what God has given them of his favor, and welcoming the good news about those who have not (yet) joined them of those who stayed behind – that (there will be) no fear on them, nor will they sorrow. [171] They welcome the good news of blessing from God, and favor, and that God does not let the reward of the believers go to waste. [172] Those who responded (to the call of) God and the messenger after the wound had smitten them – for those of them who have done good and guarded (themselves), (there is) a great reward. [173] (They are) those to whom the people said, 'Surely the enemy has gathered against you, so fear them!' But it increased them in belief, and they said, 'God is enough for us. Excellent is the Guardian.' [174] So they turned back by the blessing and favor of God, without any evil touching them. They followed after the approval of God, and God is full of great favor. [175] That is only Satan (who) frightens his allies. Do not fear them, but fear Me, if you are believers.

[176] Do not let those who are quick to disbelieve cause you sorrow. Surely they will not harm God at all. God does not wish to assign to them any share in the Hereafter. For them (there is) a great punishment. [177] Surely those who have purchased disbelief with the (price of) belief will not harm God at all. For them (there is) a painful punishment. [178] And let not those who disbelieve think that We spare them for their own good. We only spare them so that they will increase in sin! For them (there is) a humiliating punishment. [179] God is not one to leave the believers in (the situation) you are in until He separates the bad from the good. Nor is God one to inform you of the unseen, but God chooses from His messengers whomever He pleases. So believe in God and His messengers. If you believe and guard (yourselves), for you (there is) a great reward. [180] And let not those who are stingy with what God has given them of His favor think that it is good for them. No! It is bad for them. What they are stingy with will be hung about their necks on the Day of Resurrection. To God (belongs) the inheritance of the heavens and the earth. God is aware of what you do.

[181] Certainly God has heard the words of those who said, 'Surely God is poor and we are rich.' We shall write down what they have said, along with their killing the prophets without any right, and We shall say, 'Taste the punishment of the burning (Fire)! [182] That is for what your (own) hands have sent forward, and (know) that God is not an evildoer to (His) servants.'

---

of Allah" – in other words, who die while fighting. This verse claims that these warriors immediately become alive in the next life and that Allah provides for them. Description of the rewards continues in verses 170–72. Other verses that make this claim in Sūra 3 are 157–58 and 195. See an analysis of these verses at 47.4 (p. 509).

[183] Those (are the same people) who said, 'Surely God has made us promise not to believe in any messenger until he brings a sacrifice which fire devours.' Say: 'Messengers have come to you before me with the clear signs, and with that which you spoke of. So why did you kill·them, if you are truthful?' [184] If they call you a liar, (know that) messengers have been called liars before you, who brought the clear signs, and the scriptures, and the illuminating Book.

[185] Every person will taste death, and you will only be paid your rewards in full on the Day of Resurrection. Whoever is removed from the Fire and admitted to the Garden has triumphed. This present life is nothing but a deceptive enjoyment. [186] You will indeed be tested concerning your wealth and your own lives, and you will indeed hear from those who were given the Book before you, and from those who are idolaters, much hurt. But if you are patient and guard (yourselves) – surely that is one of the determining factors in (all) affairs.

[187] (Remember) when God took a covenant with those who had been given the Book: 'You shall indeed make it clear to the people, and shall not conceal it.' But they tossed it behind their backs, and sold it for a small price. Evil is what they purchased! [188] Do not think (that) those who gloat over what they have brought, and like to be praised for what they have not done – do not think that they are in (a place of) safety from the punishment. For them (there is) a painful punishment. [189] To God (belongs) the kingdom of the heavens and the earth. God is powerful over everything.

[190] Surely in the creation of the heavens and earth, and (in) the alternation of the night and the day, (there are) signs indeed for those with understanding, [191] who remember God, whether standing or sitting or (lying) on their sides, and reflect on the creation of the heavens and the earth: 'Our Lord, You have not created this in vain. Glory to You! Guard us against the punishment of the Fire. [192] Our Lord, surely You – whomever You cause to enter the Fire, You have disgraced him. The evildoers will have no helpers. [193] Our Lord, surely we have heard a caller calling (us) to belief (saying): "Believe in your Lord!" So we have believed. Our Lord, forgive us our sins, and absolve us of our evil deeds,

---

3.183 – *Surely God has made us promise not to believe in any messenger until he brings a sacrifice which fire devours*

The audience says that it will not accept the authority of the messenger unless he brings them a sign like that of the biblical Elijah (1 Kings 18:16–40). The Quran reassures the messenger that the audience denies him just as it denied messengers who brought signs in the past – and indeed killed many of them.

3.191 – *Our Lord! You have not created this in vain*

Near the end of this sūra the Quran offers a prayer (vv. 191b–94).

and take us with the pious. ¹⁹⁴ Our Lord, give us what You have promised us on (the assurance of) Your messengers, and do not disgrace us on the Day of Resurrection. Surely You will not break the appointment.' ¹⁹⁵ And their Lord responded to them: 'Surely I do not let a deed of anyone of you go to waste – whether male or female – you are all alike. Those who have emigrated, and were expelled from their homes, and suffered harm in My way, and have fought and been killed – I shall indeed absolve them of their evil deeds, and I shall indeed cause them to enter Gardens through which rivers flow. A reward from God! God – with Him is the best reward.'

¹⁹⁶ Do not let the disbelievers' comings and goings in the lands deceive you. ¹⁹⁷ A little enjoyment (of life), then their refuge is Gehenna – it is an evil resting place! ¹⁹⁸ But the ones who guard (themselves) against their Lord – for them (there are) Gardens through which rivers flow, there to remain. A reception from God! And what is with God is better for the pious.

¹⁹⁹ Surely (there are) some of the People of the Book who indeed believe in God, and what has been sent down to you, and what has been sent down to them, humbling themselves before God. They do not sell the signs of God for a small price. Those – for them their reward is with their Lord. Surely God is quick at the reckoning.

²⁰⁰ You who believe! Be patient and strive in patience, and be steadfast, and guard (yourselves) against God, so that you may prosper.

3.195 – *Those who have emigrated . . . and have fought and been killed*

This is third of three passages in the sūra that specify rewards for martyrs, and this verse makes explicit the circumstances of their death: they die while fighting. Here the Quran promises such fighters absolution of their evil deeds and entry into "Gardens" – the quranic concept of heaven or paradise. Similar verses in this sūra are 157–58 and 169–72. See an analysis of these verses at 47.4 (p. 509).

WOMEN
AL-NISĀ'

4

The title of this sūra, "The Women," points to the extended opening passage of laws largely concerning women (vv. 1–35). Near the end of this passage is a verse that has been one of the most passionately debated quranic verses in the twenty-first century.

This recent fame should not distract from the fact that this sūra continues the polemical approach toward the "People of the Book" from Sūras 2 and 3 and includes two of the most important verses for Christians in the entire Quran.

Also continuing from the previous two sūras is substantial material that brings to mind a battle scene. The sūra contains two of the Quran's twelve commands to fight, and two of five commands to kill, using the Arabic verb *qatala*. Muslim tradition connects the military passage with a battle in the Muslim story of Islamic origins, the "battle of Uḥud."

Intertwined with the battle scene is a remarkable series of verses that claim authority for the "messenger." Here the Quran not only commands the reader to obey Allah and his messenger but also claims that whoever obeys the messenger obeys Allah. This partly accounts for the importance of this sūra in the development of Islamic Law.

In the Name of God, the Merciful, the Compassionate

¹ People! Guard (yourselves) against your Lord, who created you from one person, and from him created his wife, and scattered from the two of them many men and women. And guard (yourselves) against God, whom you ask each other questions about, and (guard yourselves against) the wombs. Surely God is watching over you.

² Give the orphans their property, and do not exchange the bad for the

---

4.2 – *Give the orphans their property, and do not exchange the bad for the good*

This entire opening passage (vv. 2–43) contains laws for those "who believe" (e.g., vv. 19, 29), including laws about the treatment of orphans and women and rules for marriage, immorality, and ritual purity.

good, and do not consume their property along with your own. Surely it is a great crime. ³ If you fear that you will not act fairly toward the orphan girls, marry what seems good to you of the women: two, or three, or four. But if you fear that you will not be fair, (marry only) one, or what your right (hands) own. That (will make it) more likely that you will not be biased. ⁴ Give the women their dowries as a gift. If they remit to you any part of it on their own, consume it with satisfaction (and) pleasure. ⁵ Do not give the foolish your property which God has assigned to you to maintain, but provide for them by means of it and clothe them, and speak to them rightful words. ⁶ Test the orphan girls until they reach (the age of) marriage. If you perceive right judgment in them, hand over their property to them. Do not consume it wantonly or hastily before they are grown up. Whoever is wealthy should refrain (from using it), and whoever is poor should use (it) rightfully. And when you do hand over their property to them, take witnesses over them. God is sufficient as a reckoner.

⁷ To the men (belongs) a portion of what parents and family leave, and to the women (belongs) a portion of what parents and family leave, (whether there is) a little of it or a lot, an obligatory portion. ⁸ When the family, the orphans, and the poor are present at the distribution (of the estate), provide for them from it, and speak to them rightful words. ⁹ Let those fear who, if they left behind them weak descendants, would fear for them. Let them guard (themselves) against God, and speak a direct word. ¹⁰ Surely those who consume the property of the orphans in an evil manner, they only consume fire in their bellies, and they will burn in a blazing (Fire).

¹¹ God charges you concerning your children: to the male, a share equal to two females. But if they be (only) women, more than two, then to them two-thirds of what he leaves. But if there be (only) one, then to her a half. And to his parents, to each of them, a sixth of what he leaves, if he has children. But if he has no children, and his heirs are his parents, then to his mother a third. And if he has brothers, then to his mother the sixth, after any bequest he may have made or any debt (has been paid). Whether your fathers or your sons are of most benefit to you, you do not know. (This is) an obligation from God. Surely God is knowing, wise.

¹² And to you a half of what your wives leave, if they have no children. But if they have children, then to you the fourth of what they leave, after any bequest they may have made or any debt (has been paid). And to them the fourth of

---

4.3 – *marry what seems good to you of the women: two, or three, or four*

The famous permission for Muslim men to have up to four wives is based on this verse. The surrounding context seems to concern the treatment of orphan girls.

what you leave, if you have no children. But if you have children, then to them the eighth of what you leave, after any bequest you may have made or any debt (has been paid). If a man or a woman has no direct heir, but has a brother or a sister, then to each of them the sixth. But if they are more (numerous) than that, then they share in the third, after any bequest he may have made or any debt (has been paid), without prejudice (to anyone). (This is) a directive from God. God is knowing, forbearing.

¹³ Those are the limits (set by) God. Whoever obeys God and His messenger – He will cause him to enter Gardens through which rivers flow, there to remain. That is the great triumph! ¹⁴ But whoever disobeys God and His messenger, and transgresses His limits – He will cause him to enter the Fire, there to remain. For him (there is) a humiliating punishment.

¹⁵ (As for) those of your women who commit immorality, call witnesses

---

4.13 – *Those are the limits (set by) God. Whoever obeys Allah and His messenger*

The Quran describes the commandments in this extended passage as the statutes, boundaries, or "limits" (*ḥudūd*, also v. 14) of Allah. The expression "limits of Allah" appears twelve times in the Quran and always relates to legislation about marital and family relations.

In this sūra, the messenger is more than a preacher or warner. He is associated with Allah as deserving of obedience (also vv. 59, 69, 80); disobedience to the messenger receives the same punishments as disobedience to Allah (v. 14; cf. 42). Together with Allah, the messenger will be the arbiter of any disagreements (vv. 59, 65; cf. 58), the destination of migration (v. 100), and the object of faith (v. 136).

4.14 – *But whoever disobeys God and His messenger, and transgresses His limits*

This was one of the verses that the brilliant jurist al-Shāfiʿī (d. 820) cited to support the authority of the *sunna* (the life example and sayings attributed to Muhammad). Al-Shāfiʿī's influential arguments guaranteed the importance of Muhammad as a source of Islamic Law.

4.15 – *(As for) those of your women who commit immorality, . . . confine them in their houses until death takes them*

This verse prescribes a punishment for women who are guilty of lewdness. The Arabic word translated "immorality" is *fāḥisha*, meaning "uncleanness" (not the word for "adultery," which is *zinā*). The punishment for this immorality is confinement until death, though the verse seems to suggest another unspecified possibility. The Quran prescribes a punishment for adultery at 24.2.

The expression "until death takes them" uses the Arabic verb *tawaffā*, which causes confusion related to the death of ʿĪsā at 3.55. In this verse, the meaning is clear because the subject of the verb is "death" (*al-mawt*).

against them, four of you. If they bear witness (to the truth of the allegation), confine them in their houses until death takes them, or God makes a way for (dealing with) them. ¹⁶ And (if) two of you commit it, harm both of them. But if they turn (in repentance) and set (things) right, let them be. Surely God turns (in forgiveness), compassionate. ¹⁷ But God only turns (in forgiveness) to those who do evil in ignorance, (and) then turn (in repentance) soon after. Then God will turn to them (in forgiveness). God is knowing, wise. ¹⁸ But (His) turning (in forgiveness) is not for those who continue to do evil deeds, and only when death approaches say, 'Surely I turn (in repentance) now.' Nor (does He turn in forgiveness) to those who die while they are still disbelievers. Those – for them We have prepared a painful punishment.

¹⁹ You who believe! It is not permitted to you to inherit women against their will. And do not prevent them, so that you may take part of what you have given them, unless they commit clear immorality. Associate with them rightfully. If you dislike them, it may be that you dislike something in which God has placed much good. ²⁰ And if you wish to exchange a wife for (another) wife, and you have given one of them a qinṭār, take (back) none of it. Would you take it (back by) slander and clear sin? ²¹ How can you take it (back), seeing that one of you has gone into the other, and they have taken a firm pledge from you?

²² Do not marry women whom your fathers have married, unless it is a thing of the past. Surely it is an immorality, an abhorrent thing, and an evil way. ²³ Forbidden to you are: your mothers, your daughters, your sisters, your paternal aunts, your maternal aunts, (your) brothers' daughters, (your) sisters' daughters, the mothers who have nursed you, (those who are) your sisters by nursing, your wives' mothers, and your stepdaughters who are in your care, (born) of wives you have gone into – but if you have not gone into them, (there is) no blame on you – and wives of your sons, those of your own loins, and that you should have two sisters at the same time, unless it is a thing of the past. Surely God is forgiving, compassionate. ²⁴ And (also forbidden to you are) married women, except what your right (hands) own. (This is) a written decree of God for you. (All women) beyond that are permitted to you to seek (to obtain) by means of your wealth, taking (them) in marriage, not in immorality. So (because of) what you enjoy from them in this way, give them their marriage gifts as an obligation. (There is) no blame on you in anything you may give them by mutual agreement beyond this obligation. Surely God is knowing, wise.

²⁵ Whoever among you cannot wait to marry believing, free women, (let them take) believing young women from what your right (hands) own. God knows your belief, (for) you are all alike. Marry them with the permission of their families, and give them their rightful marriage gifts, (as) married women,

not (as) women who commit immorality or take secret lovers. But if they commit immorality after they are married, they will be liable to half the punishment (inflicted) on free women. That (provision) is for those of you who fear sin. Yet to be patient (would be) better for you. God is forgiving, compassionate. [26] God wishes to make (things) clear to you, and to guide you in the customary ways of those who were before you, and to turn toward you (in forgiveness). God is knowing, wise. [27] God wishes to turn toward you (in forgiveness), but those who follow (their) lusts wish you to swerve far away. [28] God wishes to lighten (your burdens) for you, (for) the human was created weak.

[29] You who believe! Do not consume your property among yourselves by means of falsehood, but (let there) be a transaction among you by mutual agreement. And do not kill one another. Surely God is compassionate with you. [30] Whoever does that in enmity and evil – We shall burn him in a Fire. That is easy for God. [31] If you avoid the gross (sins) of what you are forbidden (to commit), We shall absolve you of your (other) evil deeds, and We shall cause you to enter (through) an entrance of honor.

[32] Do not long for what God has bestowed in favor on some of you over others. To the men (belongs) a portion of what they have earned, and to the women (belongs) a portion of what they have earned. Ask God for some of His favor. Surely God has knowledge of everything. [33] To everyone We have appointed heirs of what parents and family leave; and those with whom your right (hands) have made a pledge, give them their portion. Surely God is a witness over everything.

[34] Men are supervisors of women because God has favored some of them over others, and because they have contributed from their wealth. Righteous women are obedient, watching over (affairs) in the absence (of their husbands) because

---

4.28 – *the human was created weak*

The Quran contains several statements about the condition in which humans were created (also 21.37; 70.19). See the analysis of verses about human nature at 79.40 (p. 612).

4.34 – *(As for) those women whom you fear may be rebellious*

The Quran prescribes for men a way of dealing with wives who show rebellion (*nushūz*). The three stages are first admonishing them, then sleeping separately from them, and finally striking them. The Arabic original of the word translated here as "strike" is the plural imperative form of *ḍaraba*, a verb that is commonly defined as "to beat, strike, or hit."

Discussion of a modern Muslim feminist interpretation of this verse is included in "Women in the Quran" (p. 429).

God has watched over (them). (As for) those women whom you fear may be rebellious: admonish them, avoid them in bed, and (finally) strike them. If they obey you, do not seek (any further) way against them. Surely God is most high, great. ³⁵ If you fear a breach between the two, raise up an arbiter from his family and an arbiter from her family. If they both wish to set (things) right, God will effect a reconciliation between the two. Surely God is knowing, aware.

³⁶ Serve God, and do not associate anything with Him, and (do) good to parents and to family, and the orphans and the poor, and the neighbor who is related and the neighbor who is a stranger, and the companion at your side, and the traveler, and what your right (hands) own.

Surely God does not love anyone who is arrogant (and) boastful, ³⁷ (nor) those who are stingy, and (who) command the people to be stingy, and conceal what God has given them of his favor. We have prepared for the disbelievers a humiliating punishment. ³⁸ (Nor does God love) those who contribute their wealth to show off (before) the people, and who do not believe in God and the Last Day. Whoever has Satan for his comrade – he is an evil comrade! ³⁹ What (harm would it do) them if they believed in God and the Last Day, and contributed from what God has provided them? But God knows about them. ⁴⁰ Surely God does not do (even) a speck's weight of evil. If it is a good (deed), He doubles it, and gives from Himself a great reward. ⁴¹ How (will it be) when We bring from each community a witness, and bring you as a witness against them (all)? ⁴² On that Day those who have disbelieved and disobeyed the messenger will wish that the earth were leveled with them. But they will not (be able to) conceal (any) account from God.

⁴³ You who believe! Do not go near the prayer when you are drunk, until you know what you are saying, or (when you are) defiled, unless (you are) travelers (on the) way, until you wash yourselves. If you are sick or on a journey, or if one

---

4.36 – *Surely God does not love anyone who is arrogant (and) boastful*

The Quran contains twenty-four statements about the kinds of people whom Allah does not love (understanding vv. 37–38 to be a continuation of the last statement in v. 36). The "arrogant (and) boastful" are among the most frequent groups denied the love of Allah (also 31.18; 57.23).

Sūra 4 contains five statements about Allah withholding love but none of the twenty-two quranic statements that say whom Allah loves. See "The Language of Love in the Quran" (p. 560).

4.42 – *On that Day those who have disbelieved and disobeyed the messenger*

Many other verses associate the messenger with Allah for belief and obedience, but this verse makes claims for the messenger alone (also v. 115).

of you has come from the toilet, or if you have touched women, and you do not find any water, take clean soil and wipe your faces and your hands. Surely God is pardoning, forgiving.

⁴⁴ Do you not see those who have been given a portion of the Book? They purchase error and wish that you would go astray from the way. ⁴⁵ God knows about your enemies. God is sufficient as an ally, and God is sufficient as a helper. ⁴⁶ Some of those who are Jews alter words from their positions, and they say, 'We hear and disobey,' and 'Hear, and do not hear,' and 'Observe us,' twisting with their tongues and vilifying the religion. If they had said, 'We hear and obey,' and 'Hear,' and 'Regard us,' it would indeed have been better for them, and more just. But God has cursed them for their disbelief, and so they do not believe, except for a few.

⁴⁷ You who have been given the Book! Believe in what We have sent down, confirming what is with you, before We obliterate faces, and turn them on their backs, or curse them as We cursed the men of the sabbath, and God's command is done. ⁴⁸ Surely God does not forgive (anything) being associated with Him,

---

4.46 – *Some of those who are Jews alter words from their positions*

This is the second of four verses in the Quran that contain the Arabic verb *ḥar-rafa* – often translated as "distort" or (as here) "alter" but understood by the earliest Muslim commentators on the Quran to mean "tampering with" or "mishandling" (also 2.75; 5.13; 5.41).

In this case, the subject is "some who are Jews." Though some Muslim polemicists have used this verse to accuse the Bible of corruption, the verse itself seems to picture a kind of wordplay by the Jews between Hebrew and Arabic that shows disrespect to the messenger. This is how many Muslim commentators understood the expression "twisting with their tongues." See "Tampering with the Pre-Islamic Scriptures" (p. 142).

4.47 – *You who have been given the Book! Believe in what We have sent down, confirming what is with you*

The Quran commands the People of the Book (Jews and Christians) to believe in the messenger's recitations, claiming correspondence, with a threat attached. On the Quran's approach to the People of the Book, see the comments at 98.1 (p. 641).

The Quran frequently states that its contents confirm (*muṣaddiq*) that which is "with" the audience. Since this verse is addressed to the People of the Book, the reader could reasonably assume that it has the Torah and/or Gospel in mind (see 3.3). For an analysis of this claim of confirmation, and a response, see the comments at 46.12 (p. 502).

4.48 – *Surely God does not forgive (anything) being associated with Him.... Whoever associates (anything) with God has forged a great sin*

Here "associating" (*shirk*) is singled out as the one unforgivable sin. This has

but He forgives what is other than that for whomever He pleases. Whoever associates (anything) with God has forged a great sin. [49] Do you not see those who claim purity for themselves? No! (It is) God (who) purifies whomever He pleases – and they will not be done evil in the slightest. [50] See how they forge lies against God. That suffices as a clear sin.

[51] Do you not see those who have been given a portion of the Book? They believe in al-Jibt and al-Ṭāghūt, and they say to those who disbelieve, 'These are better guided (as to the) way than those who believe.' [52] Those are the ones whom God has cursed, and whomever God has cursed – for him you will not find any helper. [53] Or do they have a portion of the kingdom? If that were so, they do not give the people the slightest thing. [54] Or are they jealous of the people for what God has given them of His favor? Yet We gave the house of Abraham the Book and the wisdom, and We gave them a great kingdom. [55] (There are) some of them who believe in it, and some of them who keep (people) from it. Gehenna is sufficient as a blazing (Fire). [56] Surely those who disbelieve in Our signs – We shall burn them in a Fire. Whenever their skins are completely burned, We shall exchange their skins for others, so that they may (continue to) feel the punishment. Surely God is mighty, wise. [57] But those who believe and do righteous deeds – We shall cause them to enter Gardens through which rivers flow, there to remain forever. There they will have pure spouses, and We shall cause them to enter sheltering shade.

[58] Surely God commands you to pay back deposits to their (rightful) owners, and when you judge between the people, to judge with justice. Surely God gives you admonition which is excellent. Surely God is hearing, seeing.

[59] You who believe! Obey God, and obey the messenger and those (who

---

implications for the way that Muslims view Christians, if Muslims believe that Christians "associate" Jesus – whom Muslims consider a mere human prophet – with God. See the summary of verses that accuse the People of the Book of "associating" at 61.9 (p. 565).

4.51 – *They believe in al-Jibt and al-Ṭāghūt*

Who are these figures that this verse says "those who have been given a portion of the Book" believe in? The term *al-Jibt* appears only here in the Quran, *al-Ṭāghūt* occurs again in verses 60 and 76 in this sūra, and also in 2.256; 5.60; 16.36; and 39.17. Some scholars have suggested that al-Jibt and al-Ṭāghūt were the names of gods or idols and that the use of al-Ṭāghūt in 4.60, 76 gives the impression that it was another name for Satan.

4.59 – *You who believe! Obey God, and obey the messenger*

Commands to obey "the messenger" appear several times in Sūra 4 (also vv. 13,

have) the command among you. If you argue about anything, refer it to God and the messenger, if you believe in God and the Last Day. That is better and fairer in interpretation. [60] Do you not see those who claim that they believe in what has been sent down to you, and what was sent down before you? They wish to go (with their disputes) to al-Ṭāghūt for judgment. Yet they have been commanded to disbelieve in him. Satan wishes to lead them very far astray. [61] When it is said to them, 'Come to what God has sent down, and to the messenger,' you see the hypocrites keeping (people) from you. [62] How (will it be) when a smiting smites them for what their (own) hands have sent forward? Then they will come to you swearing, 'By God! We wanted nothing but good and reconciliation.' [63] Those are the ones who – God knows what is in their hearts. So turn away from them, and admonish them, and speak to them effective words about themselves.

[64] We have not sent any messenger, except that he should be obeyed, by the permission of God. If, when they did themselves evil, they had come to you and asked forgiveness from God, and the messenger had asked forgiveness for them, they would indeed have found God turning (in forgiveness), compassionate. [65] But no! By your Lord! They will not believe until they make you judge concerning their disputes. Then they would have no difficulty with what you decided, and would submit (in full) submission. [66] If We had prescribed for them: 'Kill one another' or 'Go forth from your homes,' they would not have

---

69; cf. vv. 14, 42). Such verses became very important in the writings of the influential Muslim jurist al-Shāfiʿī (d. 820), who insisted they gave divine authority to the sayings ("hadith") attributed to Muhammad. See the summary of commands to obey the messenger at 64.12 (p. 574).

Shiʿite Muslims, on the other hand, believe that the phrase "and those (who have) command among you" refers to the line of twelve "Imams" who lead the Shiʿa community. See "Shiʿite Interpretation of the Quran" (p. 538).

4.64 – *We have not sent any messenger, except that he should be obeyed*

This statement appears in the middle of a passage that is making a case for the authority of the Quran's messenger (vv. 59–69), just prior to a longer passage that pictures a battle scene (vv. 71–104).

The statement in this verse does not actually match most of the information given about messengers in the Quran. In most other passages messengers preach and warn and suffer resistance but do not command or enforce. This verse seems to contradict that pattern. From another angle, does this verse match the biblical profile of a prophet? See 25.20 for an analysis of categorical statements about messengers and prophets (p. 365).

done it, except for a few of them. Yet if they had done what they were admonished (to do), it would indeed have been better for them, and a firmer foundation (for them). [67] And then We would indeed have given them a great reward from Us, [68] and indeed guided them to a straight path. [69] Whoever obeys God and the messenger are with those whom God has blessed: the prophets, and the truthful, and the martyrs, and the righteous. Those are good companions! [70] That is the favor of God. God is sufficient as a knower.

[71] You who believe! Take your precautions. Go forth in detachments or go forth all together. [72] Surely among you (there is) the one indeed who lags behind, and if a smiting smites you, he says, 'God has blessed me because I was not a martyr with them.' [73] But if indeed some favor from God smites you, he will indeed say – as if there had not been any friendship between you and him – 'Would that I had been with them and attained a great triumph!' [74] So let those who sell this present life for (the price of) the Hereafter fight in the way of God. Whoever fights in the way of God – whether he is killed or conquers – We shall give him a great reward. [75] What is with you (that) you do you not fight in the way of God, and (on behalf of) the weak among the men, women, and children,

---

4.69 – *Whoever obeys Allah and the messenger*

The Quran associates the messenger with Allah for obedience and commends those who obey.

4.71 – *You who believe! Take your precautions. Go forth in detachments or go forth all together*

These commands begin an extended passage that seems to picture a battle scene. The passage continues till verse 104. This is now the third in sequence of the Quran's long opening sūras that includes a significant battle passage. In the interests of global peaceable coexistence, readers should consider carefully the material in these passages.

The impression that these passages describe battles is not an attempt by non-Muslims to portray Islam in a negative way. Rather, Muslim tradition has linked each of these passages to a particular battle in the story of Islamic origins. In the case of the following verses, Muslim commentaries and narratives have linked them with the "battle of Uḥud."

4.74 – *Whoever fights in the way of God – whether he is killed or conquers – We shall give him a great reward*

This passage (vv. 74–76) is one of the most important of the Quran's statements that Allah rewards fighting. A similar claim comes at 9.119–21. See "Fighting and Killing in the Quran" (p. 220).

Verses 74–76 mention fighting "in the way (*sabīl*) of Allah" four times, using the Arabic verb *qātala*. When the Quran promises a reward to "whoever fights in the way

who say, 'Our Lord, bring us out of this town of the evildoers, and make for us an ally from Yourself, and make for us a helper from Yourself'? [76] Those who believe fight in the way of God, and those who disbelieve fight in the way of al-Ṭāghūt. So fight the allies of Satan! Surely the plot of Satan is weak.

[77] Do you not see those to whom it was said, 'Restrain your hands, and observe the prayer and give the alms'? Then, when fighting is prescribed for them, suddenly (there is) a group of them who fear the people as (much as) they fear God, or even more. And they say, 'Our Lord, why have you prescribed fighting for us? Why not spare us for a time near (at hand)?' Say: 'The enjoyment of this world is a small thing, but the Hereafter is better for the one who guards (himself). You will not be done evil in the slightest.' [78] Wherever you are, death will overtake you, even though you are in well-built towers. And if some good smites them, they say, 'This is from God,' but if some evil smites them, they say, 'This is from you.' Say: 'Everything is from God.' What is (the matter) with these people? They hardly understand any report.

[79] Whatever good smites you is from God, and whatever evil smites you is from yourself. We have sent you as a messenger to the people. God is sufficient as a witness. [80] Whoever obeys the messenger has obeyed God, but whoever turns away

---

of Allah," it also makes a theological statement by claiming that human fighting is Allah's way. See the analysis of these expressions at 73.20 (p. 597).

Verse 74 is also one of a series of verses that claim that Allah rewards those who die fighting. See the analysis of this quranic idea at 47.4 (p. 509).

4.76 – *Those who believe fight in the way of God*

This astonishing assertion raises at least two important questions. The first is what the Quran actually means by "those who believe." The second is whether it is possible – in the heat of battle – to distinguish between those who fight "in the way of Allah" and "the allies of Satan."

This verse also commands the reader or listener to fight using the Arabic verb *qātala*. The preceding verse suggests that the reason for the fighting is to defend vulnerable women, children, and feeble men.

4.77 – *when fighting is prescribed for them*

Some who are commanded to fight resist the command and ask Allah why he has stipulated fighting. See "Fighting and Killing in the Quran" (p. 220).

4.79 – *We have sent you as a messenger to the people*

Amid the battle scene, the Quran addresses the "messenger" directly to claim that Allah has sent him.

4.80 – *Whoever obeys the messenger has obeyed God*

Along with the assertion of verse 79 comes a statement that equates the commands

– We have not sent you as a watcher over them. [81] They say, '(We pledge) obedience (to you).' But when they go forth from your presence, a contingent of them plans by night (to do) other than what you say. God is writing down what they plan. So turn away from them and put your trust in God. God is sufficient as a guardian.

[82] Do they not contemplate the Qur'ān? If it were from any other than God, they would indeed have found in it much contradiction.

[83] When any matter comes to them concerning security or fear, they divulge it. But if they were to refer it to the messenger and to those (who have) the command among them, those who investigate (such things) would indeed have known (about) it. If (it were) not (for the) favor of God on you, and His mercy, you would indeed have followed Satan, except for a few (of you).

[84] Fight in the way of God! You are only responsible for yourself, but urge

---

of "the messenger" with the commands of Allah. This seems to be the logical conclusion to the remarkable series of verses in this sūra that associate the messenger with Allah for obedience and disobedience (see v. 13).

How clearly can human leaders know the will of Allah in the heat of battle? Who actually is speaking in this verse that sets both the messenger and Allah in third person? Does the almighty God, the Creator of the universe, declare that the commands of a messenger in battle are the same as his?

This was another of the verses that the jurist al-Shāfiʿī (d. 820) cited to support his case for the authority of the *sunna* – the life example and sayings attributed to Muhammad (see also 3.32, 4.14, 4.59, 8.1, 24.54, 33.36, 64.12).

4.82 – *If it were from any other than God, they would indeed have found in it much contradiction*

This verse seems to show a confidence that the reader/hearer would not find much discrepancy or "contradiction" (*ikhtilāf*) in the recitations of the messenger. The Quran seems to advance this as if it is a proof of divine origin. If so, such a claim is at least open to discussion.

A number of legitimate questions arise from even the near contexts of this verse. First is the question of whether the Quran confirms the pre-Islamic scriptures, as it claims (v. 47). Second, do the characteristics of the messenger (e.g., vv. 64, 80) match his traits in other parts of the Quran, not to mention the original accounts of prophets in the Bible? Third, why is obedience to the messenger obligatory in Sūra 4 and a few other sūras but not even mentioned in the vast majority of them? Fourth, how do the commands to fight (vv. 76, 84) and kill (vv. 89, 91), which are said to be from Allah and the messenger (v. 59), compare with the message of the storytelling "warner" in so many other sūras?

4.84 – *Fight in the way of God!*

This verse commands the messenger in particular to fight (sing.), using the Arabic

on the believers. It may be that God will restrain the violence of those who disbelieve. God is harsher in violence, and harsher in punishing.

⁸⁵ Whoever intercedes with a good intercession will have a portion of it for himself, but whoever intercedes with an evil intercession will have a portion of it for himself. God is powerful over everything.

⁸⁶ When you receive a greeting, reply with a better greeting, or return it. Surely God is a reckoner of everything.

⁸⁷ God – (there is) no god but Him. He will indeed gather you to the Day of Resurrection – (there is) no doubt about it. Who is more truthful than God in report?

⁸⁸ What is (the matter) with you? (Are there) two cohorts (of you) concerning the hypocrites, when God has overthrown them for what they have earned? Do you wish to guide the one whom God has led astray? Whomever God has led astray – you will not find a way for him. ⁸⁹ They want you to disbelieve as they have disbelieved, and then you would be alike. Do not take any allies from them, until they emigrate in the way of God. If they turn back, seize them and kill them wherever you find them. Do not take any ally or helper from them, ⁹⁰ except those who join a people with whom you have a treaty, or who come to you with their hearts restrained from fighting you or fighting their own people. If God had (so) pleased, He would indeed have given them power over you, and they would indeed have fought you. If they withdraw from you, and do not fight

---

verb *qātala*. The reason seems to be to restrain the violence of those who "disbelieve." See "Fighting and Killing in the Quran" (p. 220).

When the Quran commands the messenger to fight "in the way (*sabīl*) of Allah," it makes a theological claim by associating Allah with human fighting. See the analysis of these expressions at 73.20 (p. 597).

4.89 – *seize them and kill them wherever you find them*

The Quran uses the Arabic verb *qatala* five times to command killing. Two of those occurrences are in this sūra (vv. 89, 91). The reason for the commands seems to be that the "hypocrites" (v. 88) want the "believers" to reject faith. The Quran therefore calls the "believers" to kill the "hypocrites." See "Fighting and Killing in the Quran" (p. 220).

"Wherever you find them" seems to suggest a wide-open attack (also in 9.5), but there are limits to the killing. Here the Quran says that if the "hypocrites" withdraw from the fighting and instead offer peace, the "believers" should stop fighting them (v. 90). The expression "their hearts restrained from fighting" (v. 90) suggests that not all those who heard the command to fight (vv. 74–77, 84) were convinced that this was the way of God.

you but offer you peace, God has not made a way for you against them. [91] You will find others wishing that they were safe from you, and safe from their (own) people. Whenever they are returned to temptation, they are overwhelmed by it. If they do not withdraw from you alone, and offer you peace, and restrain their hands, seize them and kill them wherever you come upon them. Those (people) – We give you clear authority against them.

[92] It is not for a believer to kill a believer, except by mistake. Whoever kills a believer by mistake, (the penalty is) the setting free of a believing slave, and compensation (is to be) paid to his family, unless they remit (it as) a freewill offering. If he is from a people (who are) an enemy to you, and he is a believer, (the penalty is) the setting free of a believing slave. If he is from a people with whom you have a treaty, compensation (is to be) paid to his family and the setting free of a believing slave. Whoever does not find (the means to do that), (the penalty is) a fast for two months consecutively – a repentance (prescribed) by God. God is knowing, wise. [93] Whoever kills a believer intentionally, his payment is Gehenna – there to remain. God will be angry with him, and curse him, and prepare a great punishment for him.

[94] You who believe! When you strike forth in the way of God, be discerning, and do not say to the one who offers you peace, 'You are not a believer,' seeking (the fleeting) goods of this present life. For (there are) many spoils with God. You (too) were like that before, but God bestowed favor on you. So be discerning. Surely God is aware of what you do.

[95] Those of the believers who sit (at home) – other than the injured – are not equal with the ones who struggle in the way of God with their wealth and their lives. God favors in rank the ones who struggle with their wealth and their lives over the ones who sit (at home). To each God has promised the good (reward), but God favors (with) a great reward the ones who struggle over the ones who

---

4.91 – *seize them and kill them wherever you come upon them*

If the "hypocrites" do not offer peace (v. 90), the Quran commands the "believers" to kill them. See "Fighting and Killing in the Quran" (p. 220).

4.95 – *Those of the believers who sit . . . are not equal with the ones who struggle in the way of God*

"The ones who struggle" translates the Arabic *mujāhidūn*, participle of the verb from which the word *jihad* comes. In this verse the participle appears three times. The sense of *struggle* that the Quran intends with this word may be partly determined by context. If the context is a battle scene, or if *struggle* appears close to commands to fight and kill (e.g., 4.84, 89, 91), *struggle* tends to pick up the sense of fighting. See "Jihad in the Quran" (p. 368).

sit (at home): ⁹⁶ (higher) ranks from Him, and forgiveness and mercy. Surely God is forgiving, compassionate.

⁹⁷ Surely those who – (when) the angels take them (while they are doing) themselves evil – they will say, 'What (condition) were you in?' They will say, 'We were weak on the earth.' They will say, 'Was God's earth not wide (enough), so that you might have emigrated in it?' And those – their refuge is Gehenna – and it is an evil destination! – ⁹⁸ except for the (truly) weak among the men, women, and hildren, (who) were not able (to devise) a plan and were not guided to a way (of escape). ⁹⁹ Those – God may pardon them, (for) God is pardoning, forgiving. ¹⁰⁰ Whoever emigrates in the way of God will find on the earth many places of refuge and abundance (of provisions). And whoever goes forth from his house, emigrating to God and His messenger, (and) then death overtakes him – his reward falls on God (to pay). Surely God is forgiving, compassionate.

¹⁰¹ When you strike forth on the earth, there is no blame on you to shorten the prayer, if you fear that those who disbelieve may attack you. Surely the disbelievers are your clear enemies. ¹⁰² When you are among them, and establish the prayer for them, let a contingent of them stand with you, and let them take their weapons. When they have prostrated themselves, let them be behind you, and let another contingent (which has) not prayed come (forward) and pray with you. Let them take their precautions and their weapons. Those who disbelieve want you to be oblivious of your weapons and your baggage. Then they would launch an attack on you (all at) once. (There is) no blame on you if you lay down your weapons because of the harmful effect of rain on you or (because) you are sick. But take your precautions. Surely God has prepared for the disbelievers a humiliating punishment. ¹⁰³ When you have finished the prayer, remember God, whether standing or sitting or (lying) on your sides. Then, when you are secure, observe the prayer. Surely the prayer is a written decree for the believers at appointed times. ¹⁰⁴ But do not grow weak in seeking out the enemy. If you are suffering, surely they (too) are suffering as you are suffering, while what you hope for from God they do not hope for. God is knowing, wise.

4.102 – *let a contingent of them stand with you, and let them take their weapons*

Verses 101–5 give instructions for how fighters should observe ritual prayer in the midst of a battle situation. A contingent should stand guard, holding their weapons (*asliḥa*), while the others pray. Adjustments in prayer are possible during battle, but the Quran encourages the fighters to "not grow weak in seeking out the enemy" (v. 104).

[105] Surely We have sent down to you the Book with the truth, so that you may judge between the people by what God has shown you. Do not be an advocate on behalf of the treacherous. [106] Ask forgiveness from God. Surely God is forgiving, compassionate. [107] Do not dispute on behalf of those who betray themselves. Surely God does not love anyone who is a traitor (or) sinner. [108] They hide themselves from the people, but they do not hide themselves from God. For He is with them when they plan by night (with) the words He finds displeasing. God encompasses what they do. [109] There you are! Those who have disputed on their behalf in this present life, but who will dispute with God on their behalf on the Day of Resurrection? Or who will be a guardian over them? [110] Whoever does evil or does himself evil, (and) then asks forgiveness from God, he will find God is forgiving, compassionate. [111] Whoever earns sin, only earns it against himself. God is knowing, wise. [112] Whoever earns a mistake or sin, (and) then hurls it against an innocent person, will bear (the burden of) slander and clear sin. [113] If (it were) not (for the) favor of God on you, and His mercy, a contingent of them was indeed determined to lead you astray. But they only lead themselves astray; they will not harm you at all. God has sent down on you the Book and the wisdom, and He has taught you what you did not know. The favor of God on you is great. [114] (There is) no good in much of their secret talk, except for the one who commands voluntary giving, or what is right, or setting (things) right among the people. Whoever does that, seeking the approval of God – We shall give him a great reward. [115] But whoever breaks with the messenger after the guidance has become clear to him, and follows a

---

4.105 – *Surely We have sent down to you the Book with the truth*

Immediately after the many commands from the midst of battle (vv. 71–104), the Quran claims to "send down" the book (*kitāb*) to the messenger and give to him authority to judge human behavior. This is another example of the seemingly self-conscious "messenger" passages. See "Different Kinds of Literature" (p. 14).

4.107 – *Surely God does not love anyone who is a traitor (or) sinner*

Here Allah withholds his love from the treacherous and sinful (*athīm*). See "The Language of Love in the Quran" (p. 560).

4.113 – *God has sent down on you the Book and the wisdom*

The Quran directly addresses the messenger to claim that Allah sends down to him "the Book." Who is the speaker of verses in which Allah is in the third person and the messenger in the second person? See "Different Kinds of Literature" (p. 14).

4.115 – *whoever breaks with the messenger after the guidance has become clear to him*

This is the final verse in a remarkable series of verses in this sūra claiming authority for the messenger (see the comments on vv. 13, 42).

way other (than that) of the believers – We shall turn him (over) to what he has turned to, and burn him in Gehenna – and it is an evil destination! [116] Surely God does not forgive (anything) being associated with Him, but He forgives what is other than that for whomever He pleases. Whoever associates (anything) with God has gone very far astray. [117] They only call on females instead of Him. They only call on a rebellious Satan. [118] God cursed him, and he said, 'I shall indeed take an obligatory portion of Your servants, [119] and I shall indeed lead them astray and fill them with longings, and I shall indeed command them and they will cut off the ears of the cattle. I shall indeed command them and they will alter the creation of God.' Whoever takes Satan as an ally, instead of God, has lost utterly (and) clearly. [120] He makes promises to them and fills them with longings. Yet Satan does not promise them (anything) but deception. [121] Those – their refuge is Gehenna, and they will not find any place of escape from it. [122] But those who have believed and done righteous deeds, We shall cause them to enter Gardens through which rivers flow, there to remain forever – the promise of God in truth! Who is more truthful than God in speaking?

[123] (This) is not (in accord) with your wishful thinking, nor (in accord with the) wishful thinking of the People of the Book. Whoever does evil will be repaid with it, and he will not find for himself any ally or helper other than God. [124] But whoever does righteous deeds – whether male or female – and he is a believer, those will enter the Garden – and they will not be done evil in the slightest.

[125] Who is better in religion than one who submits his face to God, and is a doer of good, and follows the creed of Abraham the Ḥanīf? God took Abraham as a friend. [126] To God (belongs) whatever is in the heavens and whatever is on the earth. God encompasses everything.

[127] They ask you for a pronouncement about women. Say: 'God makes a pronouncement to you about them, and what is recited to you in the Book (gives instruction) about female orphans to whom you do not give what is prescribed for them, though you wish to marry them, and (about) the weak among the

---

4.125 – the creed of Abraham the Ḥanīf? God took Abraham as a friend

The sūra briefly mentions Abraham and describes him as an "upright" (*Ḥanīf*) man and a "friend" (*khalīl*). On *Ḥanīf*, see the comment at 2.135 (p. 55) and "Abraham in the Quran" (p. 90).

4.127 – They ask you for a pronouncement about women

This verse returns to the theme that opened the sūra (vv. 3–35) , which again continues for several verses.

children, and that you secure justice for the orphans. Whatever good you do, surely God knows about it.'

[128] If a woman fears rebelliousness from her husband, or desertion, (there is) no blame on the two of them if they set (things) right between themselves. Setting (things) right is better, but people are prone to greed. If you do good and guard (yourselves) – surely God is aware of what you do.

[129] You will not be able to act fairly among the women, even though you are eager (to do so). But do not turn completely away (from one of them) so that you leave her, as it were, in suspense. If you set (things) right and guard (yourselves) – surely God is forgiving, compassionate. [130] But if the two of them separate, God will enrich each (of them) from His abundance. God is embracing, wise.

[131] To God (belongs) whatever is in the heavens and whatever is on the earth. Certainly We have charged those who were given the Book before you, and you (as well), 'Guard (yourselves) against God!' But if you disbelieve – surely to God (belongs) whatever is in the heavens and whatever is on the earth. God is wealthy, praiseworthy.

[132] To God (belongs) whatever is in the heavens and whatever is on the earth. God is sufficient as a guardian. [133] If He (so) pleases, He will do away with you, people, and bring others (in your place). God is powerful over that.

[134] Whoever desires the reward of this world – with God is the reward of this world and the Hereafter. God is hearing, seeing.

[135] You who believe! Be supervisors in justice, witnesses for God, even if it is against yourselves or your parents and family. Whether he be rich or poor, God (stands) closer to both of them. Do not follow (your vain) desire or you will (not) act fairly. If you turn aside or turn away – surely God is aware of what you do.

[136] You who believe! Believe in God and His messenger, and the Book He has sent down on His messenger, and the Book which He sent down before (this). Whoever disbelieves in God and His angels, and His Books and His messengers, and the Last Day, has gone very far astray. [137] Surely those who have believed, then disbelieved, then believed (again), then disbelieved (again), (and) then increased in disbelief – God will not forgive them or guide them (to the) way.

4.136 – *Believe in . . . the Book which He sent down before*

Whereas earlier in this sūra (v. 47) the Quran commands the People of the Book to believe in the messenger's recitations in addition to their own scriptures, this verse commands the "believers" to believe in the scriptures that Allah sent down before Islam in addition to the messenger's recitations.

¹³⁸ Give the hypocrites the news that for them (there is) a painful punishment ¹³⁹ – those who take the disbelievers as allies instead of the believers. Do they seek honor with them? Surely honor (belongs) to God altogether. ¹⁴⁰ He has already sent down on you in the Book: 'When you hear the signs of God being disbelieved and mocked, do not sit with them until they banter about some other topic. Otherwise you will surely be like them.' Surely God is going to gather the hypocrites and the disbelievers into Gehenna – all (of them). ¹⁴¹ (The hypocrites are) those who wait (to see what happens) with you. If a victory comes to you from God, they say, 'Were we not with you?' But if a portion (of good fortune) falls to the disbelievers, they say, 'Did we not prevail over you, and protect you from the believers?' God will judge between you on the Day of Resurrection. God will not make a way for the disbelievers over the believers.

¹⁴² The hypocrites (try to) deceive God, but He deceives them. When they stand up for the prayer, they stand up in a lazy fashion, showing off (before) the people, but they do not remember God, except a little, ¹⁴³ wavering between (this and) that, (belonging) neither to these nor to those. Whomever God leads astray – you will not find a way for him.

¹⁴⁴ You who believe! Do not take disbelievers as allies instead of the believers. Do you wish to give God clear authority against you?

¹⁴⁵ Surely the hypocrites will be in the lowest level of the Fire, and you will not find for them any helper, ¹⁴⁶ except those who turn (in repentance), and set (things) right, and hold fast to God, and devote their religion to God. Those are with the believers, and God will give the believers a great reward. ¹⁴⁷ Why would God punish you, if you are thankful and believe? God is thankful, knowing.

¹⁴⁸ God does not love the public utterance of evil words, except (by one) who has suffered evil. God is hearing, knowing. ¹⁴⁹ If you do good openly or you hide it, or you pardon an evil – surely God is pardoning, powerful.

¹⁵⁰ Surely those who disbelieve in God and His messengers, and wish to make a distinction between God and His messengers, and say, 'We believe in part, but disbelieve in part,' and wish to take a way between (this and) that, ¹⁵¹ those – they in truth are the disbelievers. And We have prepared for the disbelievers a humiliating punishment. ¹⁵² But those who believe in God and His messengers, and make no distinction between any of them, those – He will give them their rewards. God is forgiving, compassionate.

¹⁵³ The People of the Book ask you to bring down on them a Book from the

4.153 – *The People of the Book ask you to bring down on them a Book from the sky*
The sūra returns to the subject of the People of the Book to offer influential diatribes against the Jews (vv. 153–62) and the Christians (vv. 171–73).

sky. They had already asked Moses for (something) greater than that, for they said, 'Show us God openly!' So the thunderbolt took them for their evildoing. Then they took the calf, after the clear signs had come to them. But We pardoned them for that, and We gave Moses clear authority. [154] And We raised the mountain above them, with their covenant, and We said to them, 'Enter the gate in prostration.' And We said to them, 'Do not transgress the sabbath.' And We made a firm covenant with them. [155] So for their breaking their covenant, and their disbelief in the signs of God, and their killing the prophets without any right, and their saying, 'Our hearts are covered' – No! God set a seal on them for their disbelief, so they do not believe, except for a few – [156] and for their disbelief, and their saying against Mary a great slander, [157] and for their saying, 'Surely we killed the Messiah, Jesus, son of Mary, the messenger of God' – yet they did not kill him, nor did they crucify him, but it (only) seemed like (that) to them. Surely those who differ about him are indeed in doubt about him. They have no knowledge about him, only the following of conjecture.

This verse indicates a controversy between the messenger and the Jews. They ask the messenger to bring his book down from heaven. This seems to spark a polemical passage against the Jews that lasts up to verse 162. The passage connects the present behavior of the Jews with their behavior at the time of Moses (vv. 153–55) and also at the time of Mary and 'Īsā (vv. 156–59).

4.154 – *And We raised the mountain above them*

In a very concise way this verse refers to raising the mountain (see the comment at 2.63), entering the gate prostrate (see 2.58), and transgressing the Sabbath (see 2.65).

4.155 – *their killing the prophets*

The Quran frequently ascribes "killing the prophets" to the People of the Book, but in this verse the Quran makes the accusation immediately prior to quite a different claim: the People of the Book said they killed the Messiah but did not.

4.157 – *they did not kill him, nor did they crucify him, but it (only) seemed like (that) to them*

This verse clearly claims that the Jews did not kill or crucify 'Īsā. The preceding context focuses the behavior of the Jews in the past (vv. 153–56). The speech of the Jews that verse 157 opposes is their saying, "Surely we killed the Messiah."

For an explanation of the quranic name 'Īsā, see the comments at 2.87 (p. 48), and for "Messiah," see 3.45 (p. 85). Of the three references to the death of 'Īsā in the Quran, this verse has been by far the most influential. "Certainly they did not kill him." Much less certain is the meaning of the Arabic phrase translated here by Droge as "it (only) seemed like (that) to them." The Arabic phrase *shubbiha lahum* has challenged commentators and translators alike. Translators have offered a great variety of renditions,

Certainly they did not kill him. [158] No! God raised him to Himself. God is mighty, wise. [159] Yet (there is) not one of the People of the Book except that he will indeed believe in it before his death, and on the Day of Resurrection he will be a witness against them.

[160] So for the evildoing of those who are Jews, We have made (certain) good things forbidden to them which were permitted to them (before), and (also) for their keeping many (people) from the way of God. [161] And (for) their taking usury, when they were forbidden (to take) it, and (for) their consuming the wealth of the people by means of falsehood, We have prepared for the disbelievers among them a painful punishment. [162] But the ones who are firm in knowledge among them – and the believers – believe in what has been sent down to you, and what has been sent down before you. And the ones who observe the prayer, and who give the alms, and who believe in God and the Last Day, those – We shall give them a great reward.

[163] Surely We have inspired you as We inspired Noah and the prophets after him, and as We inspired Abraham, and Ishmael, and Isaac, and Jacob, and the tribes, and Jesus, and Job, and Jonah, and Aaron, and Solomon, and We gave David (the) Psalms, [164] and messengers We have already recounted to

---

from "Only a likeness of that was shown to them" (Arberry) to "They thought they did" (N. J. Dawood).

In order to explain the enigmatic expression *shubbiha lahum*, Muslim commentators developed the elaborate story of a change of appearance and confusion on the part of the witnesses. Commentators wrote that Allah causes the appearance of ʿĪsā to fall on another person. In this scenario, the person now appearing like ʿĪsā is seized and crucified, while ʿĪsā is saved and taken up to heaven. See "The Death of Jesus in the Quran" (p. 314).

4.158 – *No! God raised him to Himself*

The Quran says that the Jews did not crucify ʿĪsā but that Allah raised ʿĪsā to himself. Most Muslims believe in an ascension of ʿĪsā without a resurrection from the dead because they take the previous verse to mean that ʿĪsā did not die.

4.163 – *Surely We have inspired you as We inspired Noah and the prophets after him*

The Quran directly addresses the messenger to claim that Allah inspires (*awḥā*) him and that he belongs with the following list of biblical characters. It is surely significant that this bold claim and the assertion of verse 170 should appear between two of the most controversial statements about Jesus in the Quran (vv. 157, 171).

4.163 – *We gave David (the) Psalms*

This is the Quran's first mention of the Psalms (*Zabūr*), here associated with David (see also 17.55; 21.105).

you before, and messengers We have not recounted to you – but God spoke to Moses directly – [165] (and) messengers bringing good news and warning, so that the people might have no argument against God after (the coming of) the messengers. God is mighty, wise.

[166] But God bears witness to what He has sent down to you – He sent it down with His knowledge – and the angels (also) bear witness. Yet God is sufficient as a witness. [167] Surely those who disbelieve and keep (people) from the way of God – they have gone very far astray. [168] Surely those who disbelieve and do evil – God will not forgive them, nor will He guide them (to any) road, [169] except the road to Gehenna, there to remain forever. That is easy for God. [170] People! The messenger has brought you the truth from your Lord, so believe! (It will be) better for you. But if you disbelieve – surely to God (belongs) whatever is in the heavens and the earth. God is knowing, wise.

[171] People of the Book! Do not go beyond the limits in your religion, and do not say about God (anything) but the truth. The Messiah, Jesus, son of Mary, was only a messenger of God, and His word, which He cast into Mary, and a spirit from Him. So believe in God and His messengers, but do not say, 'Three.' Stop!

4.170 – *People! The messenger has brought you the truth from your Lord, so believe!*
The Quran claims authority for the messenger in this "self-referential" statement. "People!" calls out to Muslim and non-Muslim alike immediately prior to the serious theological denials of verse 171.

4.171 – *People of the Book! ... The Messiah, Jesus, son of Mary*
This verse directly addresses the People of the Book, commanding them not to go beyond "the limits in your religion." On the Quran's approach to the People of the Book, see the comments at 98.1 (p. 641).

What follows is a list of affirmations and denials about the identity of ʿĪsā, the quranic Jesus. Here ʿĪsā is the Messiah, son of Mary, a messenger of Allah and his word (*kalima*), which he gave to Mary, and a spirit (*rūḥ*) from him. At the same time, this ʿĪsā is not the son (*walad*) of Allah, nor is he one of three persons in the divine Trinity. On the name ʿĪsā, see the explanation at 2.87 (p. 48), and on "Messiah," see 3.45 (p. 85).

The concern in this verse is explicitly theological. The verse commands the People of the Book to tell the truth about Allah. See "Allah in the Quran" (p. 572). For the Quran, the issue is the perception that Christians confess the deity of Jesus. This is the verse's reason for prohibiting the saying of "Three," and the exclamation of horror at the thought that Allah should have a son. See "Son of God in the Quran" (p. 352).

Two affirmations in the verse that have attracted a lot of discussion are that ʿĪsā is the word of Allah and "a spirit from Him." This has led many readers to think of the opening verse of the Gospel according to John, "In the beginning was the Word, and

(It will be) better for you. God is only one God. Glory to Him! (Far be it) that He should have a son! To Him (belongs) whatever is in the heavens and whatever is on the earth. God is sufficient as a guardian. [172] The Messiah does not disdain to be a servant of God, nor will the angels, the ones brought near. Whoever disdains His service and becomes arrogant – He will gather them to Himself – all (of them). [173] As for those who believe and do righteous deeds, He will pay them their rewards in full and increase them from His favor. But as for those who have become disdainful and arrogant, He will punish them with a painful punishment. They will not find for themselves any ally or helper other than God.

Early Christian Exegesis of the Quran
J. Scott Bridger

The earliest Christian responses to the distinct ideas that would eventually be inscripturated in the Quran began to appear in the later part of the seventh century. By this time Muslim forces had conquered half of the world's Christian population. Initially, leaders from the various ecclesiastical communities responded by offering theological interpretations of the historical and

the Word was with God, and the Word was God." In fact, the translation on John 1:1 in the Arabic Bible uses exactly the same term for "word," *kalima*. From the earliest available Christian responses to Islam, Christian writers used these quranic affirmations to make a case for the Trinity as Allah, his Word, and his Spirit. Whatever the intention of *kalima* in 4.171, however, readers need to take this verse together with other quranic passages about the deity of 'Īsā. See an analysis of the Quran's denials of the deity of 'Īsā at 43.59 (p. 491).

Interestingly, the words of 4.171–72 are found in the inscription in the Dome of the Rock in Jerusalem, considered by some scholars to be the earliest record we have of the developing Islamic beliefs (AD 691). This suggests that these details of the identity of 'Īsā were issues of great theological concern from the earliest years of the emergence of Islam. For readers who would like to get a taste of Muslim interpretation, a translation of the commentary of Zamakhsharī (d. 1144) on this verse is provided in the helpful collection *The Qur'ān and its Exegesis* by Helmut Gätje (see bibliography).

4.172 – *The Messiah does not disdain to be a servant of God*

"Servant" translates the same Arabic word that also means "slave." This verse may connect to the series of verses in the Quran in which 'Īsā denies his own deity. See the analysis of these verses at 43.64 (p. 492).

political events surrounding the conquests, which they generally interpreted as a sign of God's judgment. Subsequently, as they learned more, they began responding to the religious message carried by their conquerors.

Notably, the earliest works that preserve Christian-Muslim encounters rarely contain explicit references to Muḥammad, Islam, or the Quran. Some scholars regard this as evidence that the text had yet to be fixed or canonized. There is, nonetheless, ample evidence of a burgeoning religious dispute between Christians and early adherents of "Islam." For instance, the Chalcedonian monk, Anastasios of Sinai (d. ca. 700), writing in the late seventh century, instructs Greek-speaking Christians to repudiate the accusation by "Arabs" that Christians have taken Jesus and Mary to be "two gods" in place of the one true God (cf. 5.116) and the accusation that Christians believe God has procreated a son (cf. 2.116; 112.3). Additionally, writing in Syriac during the last decade of the seventh century, the Syrian Orthodox (i.e., Jacobite) Bishop Jacob of Edessa (d. 708) evidences awareness of the Muslim affirmation that Jesus is God's "Word" and "a Spirit from Him" (cf. 4.171). Later, these two quranic statements would prove useful for Christian apologists, particularly those writing in Arabic, who sought to interpret them in a manner that comported with their own teachings.

By the time of John of Damascus (d. ca. 749), explicit references to Muslim "writings" and a "book" are more widespread. In *Heresy of the Ishmaelites*, John considers Muḥammad a false prophet and the Muslim "scripture" a preposterous imitation of the Bible; nonetheless, he couches his emphasis on the uniqueness and unity of God in a fashion similar to the Quran.

Throughout the course of the eighth and ninth centuries, Arabic began to replace Greek and Aramaic/Syriac as both a daily and an ecclesiastical language of many Christian communities. But adopting Arabic as a language of Christian theological discourse posed certain challenges. By this time the language had largely been infused with religious meaning derived from the Quran. Thus the Christian theologians who authored works in Arabic were compelled to do so with Islamic and quranic frames of reference in mind, even when Christians were their primary audience.

One of the earliest examples dates from about 755 (or 788). It is the anonymous Melkite (i.e., Chalcedonian) text, "On the Triune Nature of God." The treatise is replete with quranic allusions and echoes, particularly in the opening prayer, which is reminiscent of the rhymed prose style we encounter in parts of the Quran. Throughout the text the author uses quranic points of contact in order to draw his readers into the Bible's world of discourse and the message of salvation centered on Christ's death, burial, and resurrection. The work offers a unique example of a contextualized articulation of the Christian faith authored within the world of Islam. It also demonstrates the emergence of a spectrum of Christian approaches to the Quran.

On the polemical side of this spectrum is the ninth-century Arabic treatise, *The Apology of al-Kindī*. Likely authored by a Jacobite or Nestorian Christian, this work was highly influential among those writing about Islam both inside and outside the Muslim world, particularly after it was translated into Latin in 1141. The author of the *Apology* attributes the Quran to a Nestorian monk who purportedly taught Muḥammad in accord with the gospel. Subsequently, Muḥammad's followers, according to the *Apology*, are thought to have corrupted the book and its teachings.

On the more irenic, if not ambiguous, side of the spectrum is the eight- or ninth-century anonymous Melkite text, "Answers to the Shaykh." Interestingly, the author defends his belief in the Trinity and incarnation on the basis of *kutub Allah* (i.e., "Books of God"), most likely a reference to both the Bible and the Quran.

Another Melkite theologian, Theodore Abū Qurra (d. ca. 830), made both positive and negative uses of the Quran. Positively, in a text depicting a debate in the court of the 'Abbāsid Caliph al-Ma'mūn (d. 833), Abū Qurra uses the Quran to defend the integrity of the Bible. He also makes positive use of the quranic reference to Jesus as God's "Word" to construct a defense of Christ's eternality. Negatively, Abū Qurra points to the Muslim story in which Allah sanctions Muḥammad's marriage to his adopted son's former wife (cf. 33.37) and the reference to celestial virgins (cf. 44.54; 52.20; 56.22) as proof of the Quran's profane origins. Abū Qurra and his contemporaries, namely, the Jacobite theologian Abū Ra'iṭa al-Takrītī (d. 835) and the Nestorian theologian 'Ammār al-Baṣrī (d. 850), are among the first named Christians to author original treatises in Arabic utilizing distinctive interpretations of the Quran in their defenses of Christianity.

---

[174] People! A proof has come to you from your Lord: We have sent down to you a clear light. [175] As for those who believe in God and hold fast to Him,

---

4.174 – *People! A proof has come to you from your Lord*

For the second time, the Quran makes a high claim for its version of the identity

He will cause them to enter into mercy from Himself, and favor, and He will guide them to Himself (on) a straight path.

[176] They ask you for a pronouncement. Say: 'God makes a pronouncement to you about the person who leaves no direct heirs. If a man perishes without children, but has a sister, then to her a half of what he leaves, and he is her heir if she has no children. If there are two (sisters), then to them two-thirds of what he leaves. If there are brothers and sisters, then to the male a share equal to two females. God makes (this) clear to you, so that you do not go astray. God has knowledge of everything.

---

of ʿĪsā (see also 3.60–62). If this verse refers to the Christology of verses 157–58 and 171–72, the Quran now claims to have provided a "proof." Taken together with verses 162–63, 170, this represents a rather dense concentration of self-referential claims for the "revelation" of the recitation and the "inspiration" of its messenger. If so, the reader may ask whether simply stating a claim – even frequently and forcefully – amounts to a proof of its truth.

THE TABLE
AL-MĀ'IDA

5

It is surely remarkable – and for many readers perhaps surprising – that the first four long sūras of the Quran should devote so much material to and about the "People of the Book." Sūra 2 opens with a long passage concerned with the beliefs and practices of Jews; Sūra 3 does the same for Christians. Sūra 4 offers several influential diatribes against both Jews and Christians. And Sūra 5 brings this polemic to a rhetorical climax, making some very sharp judgments against Christian beliefs and drawing some famous conclusions about Muslim relationships with non-Muslims.

These four long sūras make up about one fifth of the total contents of the Quran – six evenings of recitation for Muslims who seek to recite the entire Quran during Ramadan. Classical Muslim commentaries on the Quran dedicate up to one third of their total interpretations to these four sūras.

According to Muslim tradition, Sūra 5 was one of the final sūras to be recited. The first part of Sūra 5 offers legal rulings to those "who believe," and a largely legal passage also comes later in the sūra (vv. 87–108). However, starting with the expression "certainly God took a covenant with the Sons of Israel" (v. 12), the heart of the sūra is about Jews and Christians. The sūra closes with one of the Quran's three extended passages about 'Īsā, the quranic Jesus.

In the Name of God, the Merciful, the Compassionate

¹ You who believe! Fulfill (your) pledges.

Permitted to you (to eat) is (any) animal of the livestock, except for what is recited to you. The hunting (of wild game) is not permitted when you are (in a state of) sanctity. Surely God decrees whatever He wills.

5.1 – *Permitted to you (to eat) is (any) animal of the livestock*

The sūra begins with a series of commands addressed to those "who believe" (v. 2), including laws concerning ritual, diet, marriage, and prayer (vv. 1–11). Legislative material picks up again on commands to "believers" in verses 87–108.

² You who believe! Do not profane the symbols of God, nor the sacred month, nor the offering, nor the ornaments, nor (those) going to the Sacred House seeking favor from their Lord and approval. But when you are free (from your state of sanctity), hunt (wild game). Do not let hatred of the people who kept you from (going to) the Sacred Mosque provoke you to commit aggression. Help one another to piety and the guarding (of yourselves), and do not help each other to sin and enmity. Guard (yourselves) against God. Surely God is harsh in retribution.

³ Forbidden to you (to eat) are: the dead (animal), and the blood, and swine's flesh, and what has been dedicated to (a god) other than God, and the strangled (to death), and the beaten (to death), and the fallen (to death), and the gored (to death), and what a wild animal has devoured – except what you have slaughtered – and what has been sacrificed on stones. And (it is forbidden) that you should divide by divination arrows – that is wickedness for you.

Today those who disbelieve have no hope of (ever destroying) your religion. So do not fear them, but fear Me. Today I have perfected your religion for you, and I have completed My blessing on you, and I have approved Islam for you as a religion.

But if anyone is forced by hunger, without intending to sin – surely God is forgiving, compassionate.

⁴ They ask you what is permitted to them (to eat). Say: 'The good things are permitted to you, and what you have taught some of (your) hunting animals (to catch), training (them), (and) teaching them some of what God has taught you. So eat from what they catch for you, and mention the name of God over it, and guard (yourselves) against God. Surely God is quick at the reckoning.'
⁵ Today the good things are permitted to you, and the food of those who have been given the Book is permitted to you, and your food is permitted to them.

(Permitted to you are) the chaste women among the believers, and the chaste women among those who have been given the Book before you, once you have given them their marriage gifts, taking (them) in marriage, not in immorality, nor taking (them) as secret lovers. Whoever disbelieves in the faith, his deed has come to nothing, and in the Hereafter he will be one of the losers.

⁶ You who believe! When you stand up for the prayer, wash your faces and your hands up to the elbows, and wipe your heads and your feet up to the

---

5.3 – *Today I have perfected your religion for you . . . and I have approved Islam for you as a religion*

This verse brings to mind the confident and exclusive verses of Sūra 3 (see 3.19). Because of the sense of finality in its wording, this verse is considered by some Muslims to be the final verse of the Quran to be recited.

ankles. If you are defiled, purify yourselves. If you are sick or on a journey, or if one of you has come from the toilet, or if you have touched women, and you do not find any water, take clean earth and wipe your faces and your hands with it. God does not wish to place any difficulty on you, but He wishes to purify you and to complete His blessing on you, so that you may be thankful.

[7] Remember the blessing of God on you, and His covenant with which He bound you, when you said, 'We hear and obey.' Guard (yourselves) against God. Surely God knows what is in the hearts.

[8] You who believe! Be supervisors for God, witnesses in justice, and do not let hatred of a people provoke you to act unfairly. Act fairly! It is nearer to guarding (yourselves). Guard (yourselves) against God. Surely God is aware of what you do. [9] God has promised those who believe and do righteous deeds (that there is) forgiveness for them and a great reward. [10] But those who disbelieve and call Our signs a lie – those are the companions of the Furnace.

[11] You who believe! Remember the blessing of God on you. When a people were determined to stretch out their hands against you, He restrained their hands from you. Guard (yourselves) against God, and in God let the believers put their trust.

[12] Certainly God took a covenant with the Sons of Israel, and We raised up among them twelve chieftains, and God said, 'Surely I am with you. If indeed you observe the prayer and give the alms, and believe in My messengers and support them, and lend to God a good loan, I shall indeed absolve you of your evil deeds, and cause you to enter Gardens through which rivers flow. But whoever of you disbelieves after that has gone astray from the right way.'

5.12 – *Certainly God took a covenant with the Sons of Israel . . . believe in My messengers and support them*

Sūra 5 is one of the most important sūras for understanding the Quran's concept of the relationship between Judaism and Christianity on the one hand and the newly developing religion (*dīn*, v. 3) on the other. It contains a number of references to the earlier scriptures, the Torah (*tawrāt*, v. 43) and the Gospel (*injīl*, v. 46), as well as explicit references to Christians (*naṣārā*, v. 14) and Jews (*yahūd*, v. 18). It also contains one of the Quran's three most extensive passages on ʿĪsā, the quranic Jesus.

With "God took a covenant with the Sons of Israel," the sūra begins a series of claims that may or may not match what Jews and Christians believe. Verse 12 says that Allah included in his covenant the stipulation that the Children of Israel would believe in and support Allah's messengers. Muslim commentators interpreted this to mean that "the messengers" included and culminated in – and, for some, primarily referred to – Muhammad.

¹³ For their breaking their covenant, We cursed them and made their hearts hard. They alter words from their positions, and have forgotten part of what they were reminded of. You will continue to see treachery from them, except for a few of them. Yet pardon them and excuse (them). Surely God loves the doers of good.

¹⁴ And with those who say, 'Surely we are Christians,' We took a covenant, but they have forgotten part of what they were reminded of. So We stirred up enmity and hatred among them, until the Day of Resurrection, and (then) God will inform them about what they have done.

¹⁵ People of the Book! Our messenger has come to you, making clear to you much of what you have been hiding of the Book, and overlooking much. Now a light and a clear Book from God has come to you. ¹⁶ By means of it God guides those who follow after His approval (in the) ways of peace, and He brings them out of the darkness to the light, by His permission, and guides them to a straight path.

5.13 – *They alter words from their positions, and have forgotten part of what they were reminded of*

This is the third of four verses in the Quran that contain the Arabic verb *ḥarrafa* – often translated as "distort" or "alter" (as here) but understood by the earliest Muslim commentators to mean "tampering with" or "mishandling" (also 2.75; 4.46; 5.41). See "Tampering with the Pre-Islamic Scriptures" (p. 142).

5.13 – *Surely God loves the doers of good*

The Quran contains twenty-two statements about the kinds of people whom Allah loves. "Doers of good" are among the most common objects of Allah's love (also v. 93; 2.195; 3.134, 148). See "The Language of Love in the Quran" (p. 560).

5.14 – *they have forgotten part of what they were reminded of*

In addition to the Children of Israel, the Christians (*naṣārā*) are explicitly included in the Quran's polemic against the "People of the Book." This verse claims that Allah "stirred up enmity and hatred" among the Christians.

5.15 – *People of the Book! Our messenger has come to you*

In this verse the Quran claims that a new messenger has come to the People of the Book (also v. 19) along with a "clear Book" from Allah. Notice that the claims for the messenger and book in verses 15 and 19 bracket a key denial of the deity of the Messiah (v. 17).

The Quran directly addresses the People of the Book in this verse and four other verses in this sūra (vv. 19, 59, 68, 77), presenting a number of important truth claims. The tone of these appeals is polemical: they censure the beliefs of Jews and Christians in favor of the messenger of Allah. For a discussion of the Quran's attitude to the People of the Book, see the comments at 98.1 (p. 641).

[17] Certainly they disbelieve who say, 'Surely God – He is the Messiah, son of Mary.' Say: 'Who could do anything against God if He wished to destroy the Messiah, son of Mary, and his mother, and whoever is on the earth – all (of them) together? To God (belongs) the kingdom of the heavens and the earth, and whatever is between them. He creates whatever He pleases. God is powerful over everything.'

[18] The Jews and the Christians say, 'We are the sons of God, and His beloved.' Say: 'Then why does He punish you for your sins? No! You are human beings, (part) of what He created. He forgives whomever He pleases and He punishes whomever He pleases. To God (belongs) the kingdom of the heavens and the earth, and whatever is between them. To Him is the (final) destination.'

[19] People of the Book! Our messenger has come to you, making (things) clear to you after an interval between the messengers, in case you should say, 'No bringer of good news has come to us, nor any warner.' Now a bringer of good news and a warner has come to you. God is powerful over everything.

[20] (Remember) when Moses said to his people, 'My people! Remember the

---

5.17 – *Certainly they disbelieve who say, "Surely God – He is the Messiah, son of Mary."*

This is one of the Quran's most important verses about the identity of the Messiah. At issue is the Christian confession of the deity of Jesus (the preceding context mentions "Christians" at v. 14). The Quran judges the Christian confession to be unbelief (*kufr*). The tone of these verses is polemical – they attack the foundations of another faith. And there is a surprising depth of feeling in the idea that Allah could destroy the Messiah, Mary, and "whoever is on the earth." On the name "Messiah," see the comment at 3.45 (p. 85).

In such verses "Allah" represents more than a generic concept of "God." Here the Quran distinguishes Allah from a concept of God that understands the Messiah to be divine and indignantly insists that sovereignty belongs to Allah alone. See "Allah in the Quran" (p. 572).

The judgment in 5.17 on the confession of the deity of the Messiah repeats in 5.72. See the analysis of the quranic denial of the deity of 'Īsā at 43.59 (p. 491).

5.19 – *People of the Book! Our messenger has come to you, making (things) clear to you*

Verses 15 and 19 flank the passage about the Messiah like a pair of parentheses. While verse 17 takes the Messiah down from his divine status in the Gospel, verses 15 and 19 raise up another – a messenger who will expound the hidden and make things plain.

5.20 – *when Moses said to his people, . . . "Remember the blessing of God on you . . ."*

This short passage about Moses (vv. 20–26) features the episode in the story of

blessing of God on you, when He made prophets among you, and made you kings, and gave you what He had not given to anyone of the worlds. [21] My people! Enter the Holy Land which God has prescribed for you, and do not turn your backs, or you will turn out (to be) losers.' [22] They said, 'Moses! Surely (there is) an oppressive people in it, and we shall not (be able to) enter it until they depart from it. If they depart from it, we shall enter (it).' [23] Two men among those who feared (God), whom God had blessed, said, 'Enter (through) the gate against them. When you have entered it, you will be victorious. Put your trust in God, if you are believers.' [24] They said, 'Moses! Surely we shall never enter it as long as they remain in it. So you and your Lord go, and both of you fight. Surely we shall be sitting here.' [25] He said, 'My Lord, surely I have no control over (anyone) but myself and my brother. Make a separation between us and this wicked people.' [26] He said, 'Surely it is forbidden to them for forty years, while they wander on the earth. So do not grieve over this wicked people.'

[27] Recite to them the story of Adam's two sons in truth: when they both offered a sacrifice, and it was accepted from one of them, but was not accepted from the other. (One) said, 'I shall indeed kill you.' (The other) said, 'God only accepts (offerings) from the ones who guard (themselves). [28] If indeed you stretch out your hand against me, to kill me, (still) I shall not stretch out my hand against you, to kill you. Surely I fear God, Lord of the worlds. [29] Surely I wish that you would incur my sin and your sin, so that you may be one of the companions of the Fire. That is the reward of the evildoers.' [30] Then his (own) self compelled him to the killing of his brother. So he killed him and became

---

the Children of Israel when they refused to enter the "Holy Land" (v. 21). Two men encourage the people to trust God and enter "through the gate."

5.27 – *Recite to them the story of Adam's two sons in truth*

The lack of the names of Adam's sons in this short homily on a story familiar from the Bible (vv. 27–31; Genesis 4) is typical of the quranic style and raises interesting questions about the audience of this recitation – and indeed about the reciter. Are the names not given because the reciter did not know them or because the reciter assumed that his audience knew the names? If the audience indeed already knew the names, is this a clue about the audience?

The "raven" in this story is a good example of a detail not present in the Bible but found in Jewish rabbinic writings (*Midrash Tanḥuma*, Jerusalem Targum on Genesis 4:8; *Pirqē de-Rabbī Elī'ēzer*). See "Apocryphal Details in Quranic Stories" (p. 299).

5.30 – *Then his (own) self compelled him to the killing of his brother.*

This verse says that the self or soul (*nafs*) of Cain prompted or "compelled" him to

one of the losers. [31] Then God raised up a raven, scratching in the earth, to show him how to hide the shame of his brother. He said, 'Woe is me! Am I unable to be like this raven, and hide the shame of my brother?' And then he became one of the regretful.

[32] From that time We prescribed for the Sons of Israel that whoever kills a person, except (in retaliation) for another, or (for) fomenting corruption on the earth, (it is) as if he had killed all the people. And whoever gives (a person) life, (it is) as if he had given all the people life. Certainly Our messengers have brought them the clear signs, yet even after that many of them act wantonly on the earth.

[33] The penalty (for) those who wage war (against) God and His messenger, and who strive in fomenting corruption on the earth, is that they be killed or crucified, or their hands and feet on opposite sides be cut off, or they be banished from the earth. That is a disgrace for them in this world, and in the Hereafter (there will be) a great punishment for them, [34] except those who turn (in repentance) before you have them in your power. Know that God is forgiving, compassionate.

---

kill his brother Abel. This expression fits into a series of verses that hint at a deeper diagnosis of human nature. See the analysis of this idea at 79.40.

5.32 – *whoever kills a person, . . . (it is) as if he had killed all the people*

The phrase that begins "whoever kills a person" is one of the most frequently quoted Quran passages in the twenty-first century. The Quran describes this expression as decreed for the "Sons of Israel." Though not found in the Torah, the expression appears in the so-called "oral Torah" of Judaism (*Mishnah Sanhedrin* 4.5).

It is interesting that though the Quran says Allah prescribed (lit. "wrote") this expression, it is in fact not from the Bible. See "Apocryphal Details in Quranic Stories" (p. 299).

The following verse is a good illustration of the diversity among the Quran's teachings on violence and killing.

5.33 – *The penalty (for) those who wage war (against) God and His messenger*

Given that in the previous verses Abel says that he will not kill Cain even if Cain stretches out his hand to kill Abel and that verse 32 seems an encouragement not to kill, it is certainly striking that the very next verse prescribes killing or crucifixion. This verse associates the messenger with Allah in response to conflict.

Al-Wāqidī (d. 823) suggested a particular occasion for the recitation of this verse in his *Kitāb al-maghāzī*. He wrote that the messenger of Islam prescribes this punishment for a group of men from ʿUrayna who steal the messenger's camels and kill his patron (*Raids*, 280).

³⁵ You who believe! Guard (yourselves) against God, and seek access to Him, and struggle in His way, so that you may prosper. ³⁶ Surely those who disbelieve, even if they had whatever is on the earth – all (of it) and as much again – to ransom (themselves) with it from punishment on the Day of Resurrection, it would not be accepted from them. For them (there is) a painful punishment. ³⁷ They will wish to get out of the Fire, but they will not get out of it. For them (there is) a lasting punishment.

³⁸ (As for) the male thief and the female thief: cut off their hands as a penalty for what they have done – a punishment from God. God is mighty, wise. ³⁹ Whoever turns (in repentance) after his evildoing and sets (things) right – surely God will turn to him (in forgiveness). Surely God is forgiving, compassionate. ⁴⁰ Do you not know that God – to Him (belongs) the kingdom of the heavens and the earth – He punishes whomever He pleases and He forgives whomever He pleases. God is powerful over everything.

⁴¹ Messenger! Do not let those who are quick to disbelief cause you sorrow. (They are) among those who say with their mouths, 'We believe,' but their

---

5.35 – *You who believe! . . . struggle in His way*

The Quran contains seven commands to "struggle" using the Arabic verb *jāhada*, from which the word *jihad* comes. Verse 35 is the first occurrence of this imperative in the canonical sequence. The sense of *struggle* that the Quran intends in each command may be partly determined from the context. If the context is a battle scene, or if *struggle* appears close to commands to fight or kill (*qatala*, e.g., 5.33), *struggle* tends to pick up the sense of fighting.

See the analysis of these commands at 66.9 (p. 579) and "Jihad in the Quran" (p. 368).

5.38 – *(As for) the male thief and the female thief: cut off their hands as a penalty for what they have done*

This is one of a number of verses that Muslim jurists decided must be the basis of punishments in law, because in their minds these are the limits or boundaries of Allah (*ḥudūd Allāh*) and therefore the punishment is the "right" of Allah.

5.41 – *Messenger! Do not let those who are quick to disbelief cause you sorrow*

The Quran directly addresses the messenger here, as well as at verses 48–49, 67, and 82. Such verses seem worded as if to comfort the messenger and to claim that his recitations have been "sent down" by Allah.

This verse begins a remarkable extended passage much concerned with the "People of the Book," particularly Jews (vv. 41, 44, 51, 64, 69, 82) and Christians (vv. 47, 69, 82). One of the key issues is acceptance of the authority of the messenger (vv. 41–43).

5.41 – *They alter words from their positions*

This is the last of four verses in the Quran that contain the Arabic verb *ḥarrafa*

hearts do not believe. Among those who are Jews (there are) those who listen to lies, (and who) listen to (other) people who have not come to you. They alter words from their positions, (and) say, 'If you are given this, take it, but if you are not given it, beware.' If God wishes to test anyone, you will not have any power for him against God. Those are the ones whose hearts God does not wish to purify. For them (there is) disgrace in this world, and in the Hereafter (there will be) a great punishment for them. [42] (They are) listeners to lies (and) consumers of what is forbidden. If they come to you, judge between them or turn away from them. If you turn away from them, they will not harm you at all. But if you judge, judge between them in justice. Surely God loves the ones who act fairly. [43] Yet how will they make you (their) judge, when they have

----

– often translated as "distort" or "alter" (as here) but understood by the earliest Muslim commentators on the Quran to mean "tampering with" or "mishandling" (also 2.75; 4.46; 5.13). See "Tampering with the Pre-Islamic Scriptures" (p. 142).

Though some Muslim polemicists have cited this verse to accuse the Bible of corruption, the Islamic interpretive tradition for a thousand years associated this verse with a curious story of Jewish concealment (e.g., *Sīra*, 266–67). According to this story, a group of Jews brings an adulterous couple to Muhammad for a judgment, hoping that he would not know the Torah punishment and would therefore give a more lenient ruling. Islam's messenger asks the Jews to bring a copy of the Torah. The Jews do so, but a rabbi holds his hand over the "verse of stoning" until a Jewish convert to Islam strikes the rabbi's hand away from the verse. With the Torah "verse of stoning" now exposed, the messenger commands the stoning of the adulterous couple.

See the comments on the Quran's punishment for adultery at 24.2.

5.42 – *Surely God loves the ones who act fairly*

People who act fairly (*muqsiṭūn*) are among the most frequent objects of Allah's love (also 49.9; 60.8). See "The Language of Love in the Quran" (p. 560).

5.43 – *they have the Torah, containing the judgment of God*

In contrast to the Muslim polemical use of verses 13 and 41 to accuse the People of the Book of having falsified their scriptures, this verse and the following verses describe those scriptures in a purely positive and respectful way. The Jews possess the Torah; the Torah contains the judgment (*ḥukm*) of Allah, as well as guidance and light (v. 44); God revealed or "sent down" the Torah (v. 44), and 'Īsā confirmed the Torah (v. 46; also v. 110).

The prophets made their judgments according to the Torah; Jewish rabbis and teachers were entrusted with the "Book of Allah" (v. 44), which many Muslim commentators understand to mean the Torah; and verse 48 seems to say that the new recitations confirm and preserve the Torah. Further along in this sūra, the Quran urges the People of the Book to observe the Torah and the Gospel (vv. 66, 68).

the Torah, containing the judgment of God, (and) then turn away after that? Those (people) are not with the believers.

Tampering with the Pre-Islamic Scriptures
Gordon Nickel

The Quran contains numerous verses that show suspicion about the treatment of the pre-Islamic scriptures by the communities who possessed these scriptures. The meanings of the verses are not clear because important details are missing, and the actions referred to are often obscure. However, this has not prevented Muslim polemicists from using these verses to accuse the Bible of being corrupt and falsified.

The Quran refers to the pre-Islamic scriptures by the names *tawrāt* (Torah, eighteen times), *injīl* (Gospel, twelve times), and *zabūr* (Psalms, three times). Wherever the Quran actually names these scriptures, it speaks of them only in the most positive and respectful terms. In several verses the Quran describes the Torah as "complete," "detailed," "guidance," and "a mercy" (e.g., 6.154) and the Gospel as "guidance," "light," and "admonition" (5.46). The Quran also frequently characterizes its relationship to the earlier scriptures as "confirming" what came before (*muṣaddiqan*; e.g., 3.3).

Suggestions of doubtful treatment of these earlier scriptures come in verses that use a series of important Arabic verbs and expressions of action. The most common verbs in this group mean "to conceal" (*katama*, *asarra*, and *akhfā'*). For example, already in the first part of the second sūra, the Quran commands the Children of Israel not to "conceal (*katama*) the truth knowingly" (2.42). By the end of the sixth sūra, the Quran has used these verbs an additional ten times, apparently with reference to treatment of the earlier scriptures.

More difficult to interpret are the verses using the Arabic verbs *ḥarrafa* (2.75; 4.46; 5.13, 41) and *baddala* (2.59; 7.162), or expressions like "twist tongues" (3.78) and "write the book with hands" (2.79). These verses generally lack information as to the precise nature of the action, who is doing the action, and what text, if any, is being acted upon.

Muslim commentaries on the Quran have interpreted most of these verses to mean a range of actions of resistance to the messenger of Islam. The earliest commentaries explain the verb *ḥarrafa* in line with the elastic English concept of "tampering." The commentaries also contain accusations of falsification of the Torah, especially in comments on 2.79 and 3.78. Interpreting these verses, the commentaries often claimed that the People of the Book were changing or removing references to Muhammad from their scriptures.

Between the early commentaries and the later harsh Muslim accusations against the Bible often heard today, the development of the doctrine of tampering with pre-Islamic scriptures is something of a curiosity. None of the early Muslim stories of the life of Islam's messenger include an episode of falsification, nor does the messenger make any such accusation. In the six authoritative collections of hadith (sayings attributed to the messenger), only a single tradition in a single collection accuses Jews and Christians of falsi-fication, and this is attributed not to Muhammad but to a Muslim of a later generation. By contrast, many stories and traditions mentioning the earlier scriptures seem to assume intact texts in the hands of Jews and Christians.

It has been therefore works of Muslim polemic that have given this accusation its great currency and popularity. Many scholars locate the first major development of the accusation in the writings of Ibn Ḥazm (d. 1064) of Cordoba. Ibn Ḥazm's *Kitāb al-fiṣal fī 'l-milal* set up the main lines of the accu-sation. He presented examples from the Hebrew Bible of what he considered to be chronological and geographical inaccuracies, theological impossibil-ities, and behavior of prophets that did not match the Islamic doctrine of the infallibility ('*iṣma*) of prophets. Ibn Ḥazm's critique provided the main inspiration for the accusation until Rahmat Allah Kayranwi added material from European works of "higher criticism" in his 1864 polemic, *Iẓhār al-ḥaqq*.

As far as the Quran is concerned, if the Quran does indeed make an accu-sation of falsification against the Bible, it is a bare claim, not supported in the Quran with anything like material evidence. The accusation therefore needs to be evaluated academically in light of the history of biblical manuscripts – from the earliest Qumran evidence (third century BC), through the origins of the Quran (seventh century AD), and up to the famous manuscripts dated to the first centuries of Islam (e.g., Masoretic Text, tenth century AD). Academic studies have revealed a few inconsistencies in this manuscript history, but none has indicated that any possible material about Muhammad was altered or erased.

⁴⁴ Surely We sent down the Torah, containing guidance and light. By means of it the prophets who had submitted rendered judgment for those who were Jews, and (so did) the rabbis and the teachers, with what they were entrusted

of the Book of God, and they were witnesses to it. So do not fear the people, but fear Me, and do not sell My signs for a small price. Whoever does not judge by what God has sent down, those – they are the disbelievers. [45] We prescribed for them in it: 'The life for the life, and the eye for the eye, and the nose for the nose, and the ear for the ear, and the tooth for the tooth, and (for) the wounds retaliation.' But whoever remits it as a freewill offering, it will be an atonement for him. Whoever does not judge by what God has sent down, those – they are the evildoers.

[46] And in their footsteps We followed up with Jesus, son of Mary, confirming what was with him of the Torah, and We gave him the Gospel, containing guidance and light, and confirming what was with him of the Torah, and as guidance and admonition to the ones who guard (themselves). [47] So let the People of the Gospel judge by what God has sent down in it. Whoever does not judge by what God has sent down, those – they are the wicked.

5.45 – *We prescribed for them in it: "The life for the life, the eye for the eye . . ."*

The first part of this verse seems to be as close as the Quran comes to quoting from the Torah. Even so, the quotation is not exact (Exodus 21:23–25), which suggests that the reciter/writer did not read the passage in the Torah but rather heard a verbal expression of the verse.

5.46 – *And in their footsteps We followed up with Jesus*

This verse makes a number of affirmative statements about ʿĪsā and the Gospel. First of all, ʿĪsā does ministry in continuity with the Torah, confirming the contents to which verses 43–45 refer. The idea that ʿĪsā "confirms" (*muṣaddiq*) the Torah (also at 3.50; 61.6; cf. 5.110) raises the interesting question of Jesus' relationship to the Old Testament. See the discussion of this concept at Q 61.6 (p. 563). For an explanation of the name ʿĪsā, see the comment at 2.87 (p. 48).

5.46 – *We gave him the Gospel, containing guidance and light*

The Quran consistently describes the Gospel (*injīl*) in positive and respectful ways. This verse calls the Gospel guidance, light, and an admonition. The following verse seems to tell the "People of the Gospel" to judge according to its criteria.

Here the Quran says that ʿĪsā is given the Gospel (also 57.27). Elsewhere the Quran says the Gospel is "sent down" on ʿĪsā (3.3; cf. 3.65; 5.66; 5.68), and that Allah "teaches" ʿĪsā the Gospel (3.48; 5.110). These expressions raise a question about the Quran's conception of the Gospel. See the analysis of the Quran's verses about the Gospel at 57.27 (p. 549).

5.47 – *So let the People of the Gospel judge by what God has sent down in it*

The straightforward meaning of this verse is to urge Christians to make their judgments of truth and falsehood according to the criteria of the Gospel.

⁴⁸ And We have sent down to you the Book with the truth, confirming what was with him of the Book, and as a preserver of it. So judge between them by what God has sent down, and do not follow their (vain) desires (away) from what has come to you of the truth. For each of you We have made a pathway and an open road. If God had (so) pleased, He would indeed have made you one community, but (He did not do so) in order to test you by what He has given you. So race (toward doing) good deeds. To God is your return – all (of you) – and then He will inform you about your differences. ⁴⁹ (So) judge between them by what God has sent down, and do not follow their (vain) desires, and beware of them in case they tempt you (to turn away) from any part of what God has sent down to you. If they turn away, know that God intends to smite them for some of their sins. Surely many of the people are wicked indeed. ⁵⁰ Is it the judgment of the (time of) ignorance they seek? Yet who is better in judgment than God, for a people who are certain (in their belief)?

⁵¹ You who believe! Do not take the Jews and the Christians as allies. They are allies of each other. Whoever of you takes them as allies is already one of them. Surely God does not guide the people who are evildoers. ⁵² Yet you see those in whose hearts is a sickness – they are quick (to turn) to them, (and) they say, 'We fear that disaster may smite us.' But it may be that God will bring the victory, or some command from Himself, and they will be full of regret for what

---

5.48 – *And We have sent down to you the Book with the truth, confirming what was with him of the Book*

After mentioning the Torah (vv. 43–44) and the Gospel (vv. 46–47), the Quran claims that "the Book with the truth" has now been "sent down" to the messenger. This verse says that the new book confirms the pre-Islamic scriptures. On the one hand, this claims a relationship of correspondence with the earlier scriptures. On the other hand, this verse raises the messenger's recitation above all earlier scriptures as their judge (see also v. 49).

For an analysis of the Quran's claim of confirmation, and a response, see 46.12 (p. 502). This verse also provides a positive parallel expression to "confirming": "as a preserver of it (*muhayminan 'alayhi*)." At the same time, the messenger is instructed to judge not by the earlier scriptures but by that which the Quran claims Allah "sent down" to him (also v. 49).

5.51 – *You who believe! Do not take the Jews and the Christians as allies*

The seemingly friendly tone in the preceding verses toward the Torah and the Gospel (vv. 43–47) does not carry over to the description of the custodians of those scriptures (see also v. 57; cf. vv. 55–56). Instead, a passage of polemic against the People of the Book seems to develop in verses 48–50 and to continue up to verse 86.

they kept secret within themselves. ⁵³ But those who believe will say, 'Are these those who swore by God the most solemn of their oaths: (that) surely they were indeed with you? Their deeds have come to nothing, and they are the losers.'

⁵⁴ You who believe! Whoever of you turns back from his religion, God will bring (another) people whom He loves, and who love Him, (who are) humble toward the believers, mighty toward the disbelievers, (who) struggle in the way of God, and do not fear the blame of anyone. That is the favor of God. He gives it to whomever He pleases. God is embracing, knowing. ⁵⁵ Your only ally is God, and His messenger, and the believers who observe the prayer and give the alms, and who bow. ⁵⁶ Whoever takes God as an ally, and His messenger, and those who believe – surely the faction of God, they are the victors.

⁵⁷ You who believe! Do not take those who take your religion in mockery and jest as allies, (either) from those who were given the Book before you, or (from) the disbelievers. Guard (yourselves) against God, if you are believers. ⁵⁸ When you make the call to prayer, they take it in mockery and jest. That is because they are a people who do not understand. ⁵⁹ Say: 'People of the Book! Do you take vengeance on us (for any other reason) than that we believe in God and what has been sent down to us, and what was sent down before (this), and because most of you are wicked?' ⁶⁰ Say: 'Shall I inform you of (something) worse than that? Retribution with God! Whomever God has cursed, and

---

5.54 – *Whoever of you turns back from his religion*

This verse uses the verb *irtadda* ("turn back"), which is the most common verb for apostasy. Here the consequence of apostasy seems to be that Allah will replace those who turn back from their religion with other people who love him.

This verse is also one of a handful of verses that mention the possibility of human love for Allah (also 2.165; 3.31; perhaps 2.177 and 76.8). There is no command in the Quran to love either Allah or other humans.

Both the few expressions about human love for Allah and the absence of any command to love Allah provide a rather stark contrast to the importance of love for God in both the Hebrew Bible and the New Testament. That the famous Shema of the Torah should not find an echo in the Quran is especially curious. Any comparison of the human relationship to God between the Bible and the Quran would certainly need to include this difference.

See also "The Language of Love in the Quran" (p. 560).

5.60 – *Whomever God has cursed, and whomever He is angry with – some of whom He made apes, and pigs, and slaves of al-Ṭāghūt*

Who are the people whom Allah has cursed? With whom is Allah angry? This verse is addressed to the People of the Book (v. 59) and refers to people whom Allah

whomever He is angry with – some of whom He made apes, and pigs, and slaves of al-Ṭāghūt – those are in a worse situation and farther astray from the right way.'

⁶¹ When they come to you, they say, 'We believe,' but they have already entered in disbelief and will depart in it. God knows what they are concealing. ⁶² You see many of them being quick to sin and enmity, and consuming what is forbidden. Evil indeed is what they have done! ⁶³ Why do the rabbis and the teachers not forbid them from their saying what is a sin and (from) their consuming what is forbidden? Evil indeed is what they have done!

⁶⁴ The Jews say, 'The hand of God is chained.' (May) their hands (be) chained, and (may) they (be) cursed for what they say! No! Both His hands are outstretched: He gives as He pleases. What has been sent down to you from your Lord will indeed increase many of them in insolent transgression and disbelief. We have cast enmity and hatred among them until the Day of Resurrection. Whenever they light the fire of war, God extinguishes it. But they strive (at) fomenting corruption on the earth, and God does not love the fomenters of corruption. ⁶⁵ Had the People of the Book believed and guarded (themselves), We would indeed have absolved them of their evil deeds, and caused them to enter Gardens of Bliss. ⁶⁶ Had they observed the Torah and the Gospel, and what was sent down to them from their Lord, they would indeed have eaten from (what was) above them and from (what was) beneath their feet. Some of them are a moderate community, but most of them – evil is what they do.

"made apes." A story about Allah transforming disobedient people from among the Children of Israel into apes appears at 2.65 and 7.163–67. Partly for this reason, most Muslim commentators interpreted the phrase in 1.7, "those on whom anger falls," to mean the Jews.

Readers who would like a taste of Muslim interpretation of 1.7 and 2.65 and many other verses will find these accessible in Mahmoud Ayoub's *The Qurʾan and Its Interpreters* and J. Cooper's *The Commentary on the Qurʾān* (see bibliography).

5.64 – *God does not love the fomenters of corruption*

The Quran contains twenty-four statements about the kinds of people whom Allah does not love. The object here is the corrupters (*mufsidūn*, also 28.77). See "The Language of Love in the Quran" (p. 560).

5.66 – *Had they observed the Torah and the Gospel, and what was sent down to them from their Lord*

The Quran's challenge to the People of the Book to observe the Torah and Gospel is well taken (also v. 68). However, if "what was sent down to them from their Lord" means the recitations of the Quran's messenger (as it seems in vv. 67–68), this is a

[67] Messenger! Deliver what has been sent down to you from your Lord. If you do not, you have not delivered His message. God will protect you from the people. Surely God does not guide the people who are disbelievers. [68] Say: 'People of the Book! You are (standing) on nothing until you observe the Torah and the Gospel, and what has been sent down to you from your Lord.' But what has been sent down to you from your Lord will indeed increase many of them in insolent transgression and disbelief. So do not grieve over the people who are disbelievers. [69] Surely those who believe, and those who are Jews, and the Sabians, and the Christians – whoever believes in God and the Last Day, and does righteousness – (there will be) no fear on them, nor will they sorrow.

[70] Certainly We took a covenant with the Sons of Israel, and We sent messengers to them. Whenever a messenger brought them what they themselves did not desire, some they called liars and some they killed. [71] They thought that there would be no trouble (for them), so they became blind and deaf. Then God turned to them (in forgiveness), (and) then many of them became blind and deaf (again). Yet God sees what they do.

[72] Certainly they have disbelieved who say, 'Surely God – He is the Messiah, son of Mary,' when the Messiah said, 'Sons of Israel! Serve God, my Lord and your Lord. Surely he who associates (anything) with God, God has forbidden

---

matter for free discernment and response. Many Jews and Christians will deny the truth of the recitations, and the prophethood of the messenger, by the criteria of the Torah and the Gospel themselves – not least when evaluating the passage of polemic just ahead (vv. 72–77).

5.72 – *Certainly they have disbelieved who say, "Surely God – He is the Messiah, son of Mary"*

This verse repeats the Quran's striking judgment on the Christian confession of the deity of the Messiah at 5.17. Here, as there, those who make this confession are said to "disbelieve." In addition, this verse connects the act of "associating" (*shirk*) with the Christian confession, accusing Christians of associating a mere human prophet with Allah. On the name "Messiah," see the comment at 3.45 (p. 85), and on accusations of "associating" against Christians see the summary at 61.9 (p. 565).

In this verse, the Quran also claims that the Messiah himself commanded people to worship Allah alone (similar to verses 116–17 in this sūra; 3.51; 19.36; 43.64; cf. 4.172). See the analysis of such verses at 43.64 (p. 492).

The passage surrounding this verse is highly polemical – it attacks the beliefs of another faith and promises punishments for those it accuses of "disbelief." The following verse speaks against belief in the Trinity, and verse 75 continues the denial of the deity of ʿĪsā. There the Messiah is described as nothing but a messenger who

him (from) the Garden, and his refuge is the Fire. The evildoers have no helpers.' [73] Certainly they have disbelieved who say, 'Surely God is the third of three,' when (there is) no god but one God. If they do not stop what they are saying, a painful punishment will indeed strike those of them who disbelieve. [74] Will they not turn to God (in repentance) and ask forgiveness from Him? God is forgiving, compassionate. [75] The Messiah, son of Mary, was only a messenger. Messengers have passed away before him. His mother was a truthful woman. They both ate food. See how We make clear the signs to them, then see how deluded they are. [76] Say: 'Do you serve what has no power to (cause) you harm or benefit, instead of God (alone)? God – He is the Hearing, the Knowing.' [77] Say: 'People of the Book! Do not go beyond the limits in your religion, (saying anything) other than the truth, and do not follow (the vain) desires of a people who went astray before (you). They have led many astray, and they have gone astray from the right way.'

[78] Those of the Sons of Israel who disbelieved were cursed by the tongue of David and Jesus, son of Mary – that was because they disobeyed and were

---

proves his human identity by eating. In verse 77 the Quran claims to determine the "limits" of Christianity.

The rhetorical emphasis and apparent confidence of these statements should not distract from the fact that they are merely denials of Christian beliefs. There is no new evidence after the New Testament – written some six hundred years earlier – that would support the quranic denials, nor did anyone hear the speeches that the Quran attributes to ʿĪsā. It is simply a disagreement about the identity of Jesus. See the analysis of the Quran's denials of the deity of ʿĪsā at 43.59 (p. 491).

5.78 – *Those of the Sons of Israel who disbelieved were cursed by the tongue of David and Jesus*

Some verses in the Quran make the reader wonder how the reciter/writer could have gotten Jesus so different from the Gospel accounts. It is not just that Jesus made no such curse in the New Testament, but that Jesus' life went in the opposite direction. One of Jesus' best-known sayings from the Gospel accounts is "bless those who curse you, pray for those who mistreat you" (Luke 6:28). The apostle Paul, evidently writing from his knowledge of Jesus' teachings, wrote, "Bless those who persecute you; bless and do not curse" (Romans 12:14). Paul also wrote, "Christ redeemed us from the curse of the law by becoming a curse for us, for it is written: 'Cursed is everyone who is hung on a tree'" (Galatians 3:13). And at the end of the New Testament, the parting vision is of a city in which "no longer will there be any curse" (Revelation 22:3).

When Jesus looked out over Jerusalem, not long before his crucifixion, he spoke

transgressing. [79] They did not forbid each other any evildoing. Evil indeed is what they have done! [80] You see many of them taking those who disbelieve as allies. Evil indeed is what they have sent forward for themselves! That (is why) God became angry with them, and in the punishment they will remain. [81] If they had believed in God and the prophet, and what has been sent down to him, they would not have taken them as friends. But many of them are wicked.

[82] Certainly you will find that the most violent of people in enmity to the believers are the Jews and the idolaters. Certainly you will find that the closest of them in affection to the believers are those who say, 'We are Christians.' That is because (there are) priests and monks among them, and because they are not arrogant. [83] When they hear what has been sent down to the messenger, you see their eyes overflowing with tears because of what they recognize of the truth. They say, 'Our Lord, we believe, so write us down among those who bear witness. [84] Why should we not believe in God and (in) what has come to us of

---

in the most tender way, using a striking simile: "How often I have longed to gather your children together, as a hen gathers her chicks under her wings" (Matthew 23:37–39; Luke 13:34–35).

5.81 – *If they had believed in God and the prophet*

The Quran often seems to refer to "believing" in general, without providing an object. In this passage, however, the required belief is "in Allah and the prophet." The characterization of Jews in the following verse – and indeed elsewhere in the Quran – may well be because they do not believe that the messenger of Islam is a true prophet of God.

The expression "the prophet" does not occur frequently in the Quran, and most of the occurrences come in Sūras 8; 9; 33; and 66. Here the Quran associates the prophet with Allah and declares that something "has been sent down to him." See the analysis of verses containing "the prophet" at 66.9 (p. 579).

5.82 – *Certainly you will find that the most violent of people in enmity to the believers are the Jews and the idolaters*

The Quran characterizes the Jews as the greatest enemies of the "believers," while the Christians are "the closest of them in affection." The following verses say that some Christians agree with the recitations of the messenger (v. 83) and for that are rewarded (v. 85).

Quranic passages like this that portray the Jews in the most negative ways have the potential to fuel antipathy and even violence against Jews. The Muslim story of Islamic origins seems to support both negative thoughts and deadly actions with its episodes of the treatment of three Jewish tribes in Medina (*Sīra*, 363–64, 437–45, 461–69) and its extensive portrayal of the Jewish rabbis (*Sīra*, 247–72).

the truth, when we are eager for our Lord to cause us to enter with the people who are righteous?' [85] So God has rewarded them for what they said (with) Gardens through which rivers flow, there to remain. That is the reward for the doers of good. [86] But those who disbelieve and call Our signs a lie, those are the companions of the Furnace.

[87] You who believe! Do not forbid the good things which God has permitted to you, and do not transgress. Surely God does not love the transgressors. [88] Eat from what God has provided you as permitted (and) good, and guard (yourselves) against God – the One in whom you are believers.

[89] God will not take you to task for a slip in your oaths, but He will take you to task for what you have pledged by oath. Atonement for it is the feeding of ten poor persons with the average (amount of food) which you feed your households, or clothing them, or the setting free of a slave. Whoever does not find (the means to do that), (the penalty is) a fast for three days. That is the atonement for your oaths when you have sworn (them, and broken them). But guard your oaths! In this way God makes clear to you His signs, so that you may be thankful.

[90] You who believe! Wine, games of chance, stones, and divination arrows are an abomination, part of the work of Satan. So avoid it in order that you may prosper. [91] Satan only wishes to cause enmity and hatred among you with wine and games of chance, and to keep you from the remembrance of God and from the prayer. Will you refrain? [92] Obey God, and obey the messenger, and beware! If you do turn away, know that only (dependent) on Our messenger is the clear delivery (of the message).

5.87 – *You who believe! Do not forbid the good things which God has permitted to you*

Here the sūra returns to commandments addressed to "you who believe," regulating such matters as diet, ritual practice, oaths, wills, wine, and "games of chance" (vv. 87–109).

5.87 – *Surely God does not love the transgressors*

The "transgressors" (*muʿtadūn*) are among the groups most frequently denied the love of Allah (also 2.190; 7.55). See "The Language of Love in the Quran" (p. 560).

5.89 – *Atonement for it is the feeding of ten poor persons*

The sense of atonement or "expiation" (*kaffāra*) in this verse seems to be making up for unintentional failings to keep oaths.

5.90 – *You who believe! Wine, . . . avoid it in order that you may prosper*

Here wine is declared an abomination. See the comment on wine in the Quran at 2.219.

⁹³ There is no blame on those who believe and do righteous deeds for what they may have eaten, so long as they guard (themselves) and believe and do righteous deeds, (and) then (again) guard (themselves) and believe, (and) then (again) guard (themselves) and do good. God loves the doers of good.

⁹⁴ You who believe! God will indeed test you with some of the wild game which your hands and spears obtain, so that God may know who fears Him in the unseen. Whoever transgresses after that, for him (there is) a painful punishment.

⁹⁵ You who believe! Do not kill wild game when you are (in a state of) sanctity. Whoever of you kills it intentionally, (there is) a penalty equivalent (to) what he has killed from the livestock – as two just men among you will determine it – as an offering to reach the Ka'ba. Or (there is) a penalty of the feeding of poor persons, or the equivalent of that in fasting, so that he may taste the consequence of his action. God pardons whatever is past, but whoever returns (to repeat his offense) – God will take vengeance on him. God is mighty, a taker of vengeance.

⁹⁶ Permitted to you is the wild game of the sea and its food, as a provision for you and for the travelers. But forbidden to you is the wild game on the shore, as long as you are (in a state of) sanctity. Guard (yourselves) against God, the One to whom you will be gathered.

⁹⁷ God has made the Ka'ba – the Sacred House – an establishment for the people, and (also) the sacred month, the offering, and the ornaments. That is so that you may know that God knows whatever is in the heavens and whatever is on the earth, and that God has knowledge of everything. ⁹⁸ Know that God is harsh in retribution, and that God is forgiving, compassionate. ⁹⁹ Nothing (depends) on the messenger except the delivery (of the message). God knows what you reveal and what you conceal.

¹⁰⁰ Say: 'The bad and the good are not equal, even though the abundance of bad may cause you to wonder.' Guard (yourselves) against God – those (of you) with understanding! – so that you may prosper.

¹⁰¹ You who believe! Do not ask about anything which, if it were disclosed

---

5.93 – *God loves the doers of good*

On "the doers of good" as the objects of Allah's love, see the comment at verse 13.

5.97 – *God has made the Ka'ba – the Sacred House – an establishment for the people*

The *Ka'ba* is only mentioned twice in the Quran, both times in this sūra (also in v. 95). However, this verse seems to associate the *Ka'ba* explicitly with "the Sacred House" (*al-bayta 'l-ḥarām*), an expression that also appears in a slightly different form at 14.37. See the comment on "the House" at 2.124 (p. 54).

to you, would distress you. But if you do ask about it, when the Qur'ān is being sent down, it will be disclosed to you. God pardons it, (for) God is forgiving, forbearing. [102] A people before you asked about it, (and) then became disbelievers in it.

[103] God has not appointed any baḥīra or sā'iba or waṣīla or ḥāmi, but those who disbelieve forge lies against God. Most of them do not understand. [104] When it is said to them, 'Come to what God has sent down, and to the messenger,' they say, 'What we found our fathers doing is (good) enough for us.' Even if their fathers had no knowledge and were not (rightly) guided? [105] You who believe! Look to yourselves. No one who goes astray can harm you, if you are (rightly) guided. To God is your return – all (of you) – and then He will inform you about what you have done.

[106] You who believe! When death approaches one of you, the testimony among you at the time (of making) bequests will be (that of) two just men of you, or two others of (a people) other than you, if you strike forth on the earth and the smiting of death smites you. Detain them both after the prayer, and let them both swear by God, if you have your doubts (about them): 'We will not sell it for a price, even if he happens to be a family member, and we will not conceal the testimony of God. Surely then we would indeed be among the sinners.' [107] If it is discovered that they both (were guilty of) sin, let two others take their place, from those who have a rightful claim against the two former (false witnesses), and let them both swear by God: 'Certainly our testimony is truer than the testimony of the other two, and we have not transgressed. Surely then we would indeed be among the evildoers.' [108] That will make it more likely that they will give testimony directly, or (else) they will be afraid that (their) oaths will be turned back after they have sworn them. Guard (yourselves) against God and hear! God does not guide the people who are wicked.

[109] On the Day when God gathers the messengers, He will say, 'What response were you given?' They will say, 'We have no knowledge. Surely You – You are the Knower of the unseen.'

[110] (Remember) when God said, 'Jesus, son of Mary! Remember My blessing

---

5.110 – *when God said, "Jesus, son of Mary! Remember My blessing on you and on your mother..."*

This second of three longer passages about the identity of 'Īsā appears rather abruptly at the end of the sūra (vv. 110–19). The passage makes a number of affirmations along with an influential denial. First of all, Allah says that he strengthened 'Īsā by the holy spirit (*ruḥ al-qudus*, lit. "the spirit of the holy"; see the comments at 16.102, p. 283). 'Īsā speaks from the cradle (also in 19.30). Allah says he teaches 'Īsā

on you and on your mother, when I supported you with the holy spirit, (and) you spoke to the people (while you were still) in the cradle, and in adulthood. And when I taught you the Book and the wisdom, and the Torah and the Gospel. And when you created the form of a bird from clay by My permission, and you breathed into it, and it became a bird by My permission, and you healed the blind and the leper by My permission. And when you brought forth the dead by My permission, and when I restrained the Sons of Israel from (violence against) you. When you brought them the clear signs, those among them who had disbelieved said, "This is nothing but clear magic."'

[111] (Remember) when I inspired the disciples: 'Believe in Me and in My messenger.' They said, 'We believe. Bear witness that we submit.' [112] And when the disciples said, 'Jesus, son of Mary! Is your Lord able to send down on us a table

---

the Torah and the Gospel. See the analysis of the Quran's verses about the Gospel at 57.27 (p. 549).

Here four miracles of ʿĪsā are mentioned for the second time (see 3.49) – creating a bird out of clay, healing the blind and the leper, and raising the dead – alongside a fifth: Allah brings down a table from heaven loaded with food for the disciples (vv. 112–15).

One detail of verse 110 that many Muslim commentators have highlighted is the expression "by My permission" (*bi-idhnī*), which appears four times. A similar expression comes twice in 3.49, "by the permission of Allah." Muslim tradition interprets this to mean that ʿĪsā did not work these miracles by his own power but only by the power of Allah. Some Muslim commentaries specified that without this quranic caveat the listener or reader might conclude that these miracles are evidence of ʿĪsā's deity.

Many Christians have been grateful that the Quran mentions some of the miracles of ʿĪsā, and the apparently formulaic listing of the miracles in the Quran bears some similarities to Jesus' own description of his miracles in the Gospel (e.g., Luke 7:22). However, the repetition of "by My permission" in Q 5.110 and "by the permission of Allah" in 3.49 goes against the spirit of the New Testament. The Gospel accounts are more likely to describe the miracles as "signs" (Gk. *sēmeia*) of Jesus' glory (John 2:11; cf. John 1:14; 4.54; 6:2, 14; 9:16; 20:30–31). In most of the miracle reports in the Gospel accounts, Jesus simply responded to human need with divine power.

A second detail in the verse that has attracted a great deal of interesting commentary is the statement that ʿĪsā "created" (*khalaqa*). Elsewhere in the Quran, this verb is used only to describe the creative activity of God himself, including at 3.47 in the immediate context of 3.49.

The other two longer passages about ʿĪsā in the Quran are 3:35–64 and 19:2–35. See the summary of the Quran's material about ʿĪsā at 57.27 (p. 548).

from the sky?,' he said, 'Guard (yourselves) against God, if you are believers.'
[113] They said, 'We wish to eat from it and satisfy our hearts, so that we may
know with certainty that you have spoken truthfully to us, and that we may
be among the witnesses to it.' [114] Jesus, son of Mary, said, 'God! Our Lord, send
down on us a table from the sky, to be a festival for us – for the first of us and
last of us – and a sign from You. Provide for us, (for) You are the best of providers.' [115] God said, 'Surely I am going to send it down on you. Whoever of you
disbelieves after that – surely I shall punish him (with) a punishment (as) I have
not punished anyone among the worlds.'

[116] (Remember) when God said, 'Jesus, son of Mary! Did you say to the
people, "Take me and my mother as two gods instead of God (alone)"?' He said,
'Glory to You! It is not for me to say what I have no right (to say). If I had said
it, You would have known it. You know what is within me, but I do not know
what is within You. Surely You – You are the Knower of the unseen. [117] I only
said to them what You commanded me: "Serve God, my Lord and your Lord!"

5.113 – *so that we may know with certainty that you have spoken truthfully to us*

The disciples ask 'Īsā whether his Lord is able to send down a table from the sky
(v. 112). They say that they are asking for a miracle so they may be certain about the
truth of 'Īsā's message. This detail is interesting because in the early years of the
Arab Empire, when conquered Christians first heard the preaching of Islam, they
asked whether the messenger of Islam had any miracles to his credit to support the
truth claims of Islam. The messenger of the Quran is asked for a "sign" several times,
including at 6.109. See a discussion of verses that question whether the messenger
performs miracles at 43.40 (p. 490).

The word *table* in verses 112 and 114, occurring only here, gives this sūra its name,
al-Mā'ida.

5.116 – *when God said, "Jesus, son of Mary! Did you say to the people . . . ?"*

These three verses (116–18) imagine a conversation in which Allah asks 'Īsā
whether 'Īsā told the people to take him and his mother as two gods besides or
"instead of" Allah. 'Īsā denies saying this and declares that instead he only instructed
the people to serve Allah "my Lord and your Lord" (v. 117).

'Īsā's statement and command here match several other verses in which 'Īsā himself is "quoted" as denying his own deity (3.51; 5.72; 19.36; 43.64; cf. 4.172). See an
analysis of these statements at 43.64 (p. 492).

The second question that these verses raise is the concept of the Trinity in the
mind of the reciter/writer. Verse 116 seems to suggest a Trinity of Allah, 'Īsā, and Mary
– a possible confusion concerning the Trinity. In any case, other references to the
Trinity appear at 4.171 and 5.73.

And I was a witness over them as long as I was among them. But when You took me, You became the Watcher over them. You are a Witness over everything. [118] If You punish them – surely they are Your servants. If You forgive them – surely You are the Mighty, the Wise.' [119] God said, 'This is the Day when their truthfulness will benefit the truthful. For them (there are) Gardens through which rivers flow, there to remain forever. God is pleased with them, and they are pleased with Him. That is the great triumph!' [120] To God (belongs) the kingdom of the heavens and the earth, and whatever is in them. He is powerful over everything.

5.117 – *But when You took me*

The Arabic verb here, *tawaffā*, is the same verb that causes the confusion at 3.55. In all occurrences not related to ʿĪsā, *tawaffā* is commonly translated "cause to die," and some translations render the verb this way here as well (e.g., Shakir; Droge adds "in death" in a footnote). Perhaps in an effort to be consistent with Muslim beliefs about ʿĪsā, most translations render 5.117 with expressions like "when you took me." See a discussion of these *tawaffā* verses at 3.55 (p. 87), and "The Death of Jesus in the Quran" (p. 314).

LIVESTOCK
AL-ANʿĀM

6

After the dense and intense content of sūras 2–5, Sūra 6 seems positively peaceful. Instead of a militant leader who must be obeyed, here the messenger is only a warner. Instead of being a community of "believers" that dominates other faith communities, here the messenger and his followers seem themselves to be embattled, and the messenger needs reassurance.

In fact, this sūra seems to be a completely different kind of literature than the four preceding sūras. From this point on, the reader will notice a number of abrupt shifts from peaceful material to battle scenes and back again. This simple observation of change has been acknowledged by Muslims since the earliest commentaries. Muslim scholars accounted for the differences – especially with regard to violence – by asserting that the two kinds of literature were recited by the same person in different phases of his career.

The sūra begins with verses that draw attention to the "signs" of the Creator's presence and power. This kind of material takes up a significant proportion of the sūra, and it is also an important component of a long series of sūras starting with Sūra 10. However, this positive proclamation is evidently not readily received. Instead, the listeners ignore the signs and call the recitations a lie. Frequently the sūra seems to present the actual objections and questions of the audience and then specifies the words that the messenger should say in reply. Furthermore, the sūra encourages the messenger at a number of points, including when he is mocked.

In the Name of God, the Merciful, the Compassionate

[1] Praise (be) to God, who created the heavens and the earth, and made the darkness and the light! Then (despite that) those who disbelieve equate (others) with their Lord. [2] He (it is) who created you from clay, then decreed a time – and a

---

6.1 – *Praise (be) to God, who created the heavens and the earth*

Allah's creation of the world is one of the most important "signs" (*āyāt*) of his presence and power, according to this passage (vv. 1–3). The Quran contains many

time appointed by Him – then (despite that) you are in doubt. ³ He is God in the heavens and on the earth. He knows your secret and your public utterance, and He knows what you earn. ⁴ Yet not a sign comes to them from the signs of their Lord without their turning away from it. ⁵ They called the truth a lie when it came to them, but the story of what they were mocking will come to them.

⁶ Do they not see how many a generation We have destroyed before them? We established them on the earth in a way in which We have not established you, and We sent the sky (down) on them in abundance (of rain), and made rivers to flow beneath them, and then We destroyed them because of their sins, and produced another generation after them. ⁷ Even if We had sent down on you a Book (written) on papyrus, and they touched it with their hands, those who disbelieve would indeed have said, 'This is nothing but clear magic.' ⁸ They say, 'If only an angel were sent down on him.' Even if We had sent down an angel, the matter would indeed have been decided, (and) then they would not be spared. ⁹ Even if We had made him an angel, We would indeed have made him a man, and have confused for them what they are confusing. ¹⁰ Certainly messengers have been mocked before you, but those of them who ridiculed (were) overwhelmed (by) what they were mocking. ¹¹ Say: 'Travel the earth and see how the end was for the ones who called (it) a lie.'

¹² Say: 'To whom (belongs) whatever is in the heavens and the earth?' Say: 'To God. He has prescribed mercy for Himself. He will indeed gather you to the Day of Resurrection – (there is) no doubt about it. Those who have lost their (own) selves, they do not believe. ¹³ To Him (belongs) whatever dwells in the night and the day. He is the Hearing, the Knowing.'

---

similar passages about the Creator, often beautifully expressed. See "Creation in the Quran" (p. 224).

6.5 – *They called the truth a lie when it came to them*

Throughout this sūra, the main response of the audience is resistance to the messenger's message. Many passages seem to reflect what the listeners say, along with the answers the messenger gives or is commanded to give.

The messenger warns the audience to observe what happened to earlier communities who ignored Allah's signs and resisted the preaching of their messengers (vv. 6, 11).

6.10 – *Certainly messengers have been mocked before you*

The Quran directly addresses the messenger and seems to encourage him by citing the experiences of messengers in the past. See "Different Kinds of Literature" (p. 14).

6.12 – *He will indeed gather you to the Day of Resurrection*

This verse contains the striking expression "[Allah] has prescribed mercy for Himself." In this case, the mercy may be delaying judgment until the Day of Resurrection.

¹⁴ Say: 'Shall I take any other ally than God, Creator of the heavens and the earth, when He feeds (others) and is not fed?' Say: 'Surely I have been commanded to be the first of those who have submitted,' and: 'Do not be one of the idolaters!' ¹⁵ Say: 'Surely I fear, if I disobey my Lord, the punishment of a great Day.' ¹⁶ Whoever is turned from it on that Day – He has had compassion on him. That is the clear triumph! ¹⁷ If God touches you with any harm, (there is) no one to remove it but Him, and if He touches you with any good – He is powerful over everything. ¹⁸ He is the Supreme One above His servants. He is the Wise, the Aware.

¹⁹ Say: 'What thing (is) greater as a witness?' Say: 'God is witness between me and you, and I have been inspired (with) this Qurʾān so that I may warn you by means of it, and whomever it reaches. Do you indeed bear witness that (there are) other gods with God?' Say: 'I do not bear witness.' Say: 'He is only one God. Surely I am free of what you associate.' ²⁰ Those to whom We have given the Book recognize it, as they recognize their own sons. Those who have lost their (own) selves, they do not believe. ²¹ Who is more evil than the one who forges a lie against God, or calls His signs a lie? Surely the evildoers will not prosper. ²² On the Day when We shall gather them – all (of them) – We shall say to those who associated, 'Where are your associates whom you used to claim (as gods)?' ²³ Then their only excuse will be to claim, 'By God, our Lord! We have not been idolaters.' ²⁴ See how they lie against themselves, and (how) what they forged has abandoned them!

²⁵ (There are) some of them who listen to you, but We have made coverings over their hearts, so that they do not understand it, and a heaviness in their ears.

6.20 – *Those to whom We have given the Book recognize it, as they recognize their own sons*

This sūra portrays the People of the Book in a completely different way from Sūras 2–5. Here they "recognize" the recitations of the messenger in a positive way.

6.22 – *On the Day when We shall gather them*

The Quran pictures judgment scenes on the Day of Resurrection in which Allah converses with those who resisted his signs and chose to worship idols (vv. 22–23, 27, 30). Such scenes appear frequently to warn listeners or readers about judgment to come. See "Eschatology in the Quran" (p. 604).

6.25 – *This is nothing but old tales*

Some who listen to the messenger say he is simply telling old tales. This may mean that they are already familiar with the stories from elsewhere. This response repeats eight more times in the Quran. See "Apocryphal Details in Quranic Stories" (p. 299).

If they see any sign, they do not believe in it, so that when they come to dispute with you, those who disbelieve say, 'This is nothing but old tales.' [26] They keep (others) from it, and keep (themselves) from it, but they only destroy themselves, though they do not realize (it). [27] If (only) you could see when they are made to stand before the Fire: they will say, 'Would that we (could) be returned, and had not called the signs of our Lord a lie, but were among the believers.' [28] No! What they were hiding before has (now) become apparent to them. Even if they were returned, they would indeed return to what they were forbidden. Surely they are liars indeed!

[29] They say, 'There is nothing but our present life. We are not going to be raised up.' [30] If (only) you could see when they are made to stand before their Lord: He will say, 'Is this not the truth?' They will say, 'Yes indeed! By our Lord!' He will say, 'Taste the punishment for what you were disbelieving.' [31] Lost (are) those who call the meeting with God a lie – until, when the Hour comes upon them unexpectedly, they say, 'Alas for us, because of what we neglected concerning it!' They bear their burdens on their backs. Is it not a fact that evil is what they bear? [32] This present life is nothing but jest and diversion. Yet the Home of the Hereafter is indeed better for the ones who guard (themselves). Will you not understand?

[33] We know that what they say causes you sorrow. Yet surely they do not call you a liar, but the evildoers are denying the signs of God. [34] Certainly messengers have been called liars before you, yet they patiently endured being called liars, and suffered harm, until Our help came to them. No one can change the words of God. Certainly some of the story has (already) come to you about the envoys (before you). [35] But if their aversion is hard on you, (even) if you were able to seek out an opening in the earth, or a ladder into the sky, to bring them

---

6.31 – *Lost (are) those who call the meeting with God a lie*

The Day of Resurrection and what will take place afterwards is a very important topic in the Quran. References to the "Day" or the "Hour" (as in this verse) become especially frequent in Sūras 11–46. See "Eschatology in the Quran" (p. 604).

6.33 – *We know that what they say causes you sorrow*

The Quran speaks directly to the messenger to encourage him, telling him that messengers experienced resistance in the past.

6.34 – *No one can change the words of God*

This verse states that "there is no changer" of the words of Allah. The context here is the reassurance that Allah helped his messengers in the past. The statement that Allah's word is unchangeable repeats in slightly different forms later in this sūra at verse 115 and also at 10.64 and 18.27. See a summary of these verses at 18.27 (p. 303).

a sign [. . .]. If God had (so) pleased, He would indeed have gathered them to the guidance. Do not be one of the ignorant. ³⁶ Only those who hear respond, but the dead – God will raise them up. Then to Him they will be returned.

³⁷ They (also) say, 'If only a sign were sent down on him from his Lord.' Say: 'Surely God is able to send down a sign,' but most of them do not know (it). ³⁸ (There is) no creature on the earth, nor (any) bird flying with both its wings, but (they are) communities like you. We have not neglected anything in the Book. Then to their Lord they will be gathered. ³⁹ Those who call Our signs a lie are deaf and speechless in the darkness. Whomever God pleases, He leads astray, and whomever He pleases, He places him on a straight path. ⁴⁰ Say: 'Do you see yourselves? If the punishment of God comes upon you, or the Hour comes upon you, will you call on (any god) other than God, if you are truthful?' ⁴¹ No! You will call on Him, and He will remove what you call on Him for, if He pleases, and you will forget what you associate.

⁴² Certainly We have sent to communities before you, and We seized them with violence and hardship, so that they might humble themselves. ⁴³ If only they had humbled themselves when Our violence came upon them! But their hearts were hard, and Satan made what they were doing appear enticing to them. ⁴⁴ So when they forgot what they were reminded of, We opened on them the gates of everything, until they gloated over what they were given, when (once again) We seized them unexpectedly, and suddenly they were in despair. ⁴⁵ So the last remnant of the people who did evil was cut off. Praise (be) to God, Lord of the worlds!

⁴⁶ Say: 'Do you see? If God takes away your hearing and your sight, and sets a seal on your hearts, who is a god other than God to bring it (back) to you?' See how We vary the signs? Then they (still) turn away. ⁴⁷ Say: 'Do you see yourselves? If the punishment of God comes upon you, unexpectedly or openly, will any be destroyed but the people who are evildoers?' ⁴⁸ We send the envoys only as bringers of good news and warners. Whoever believes and sets (things) right – (there will be) no fear on them, nor will they sorrow. ⁴⁹ But those who call Our signs a lie – the punishment will touch them because they were acting wickedly.

⁵⁰ Say: 'I do not say to you, "The storehouses of God are with me." I do not know the unseen, nor do I say to you, "I am an angel." I only follow what I am inspired (with).' Say: 'Are the blind and the sighted equal? Will you not reflect?'

6.48 – *We send the envoys only as bringers of good news and warners*

In this sūra the role of the "messengers" is only to bring good news and warn (see also vv. 10, 34, 51). There is no trace here of making judgments and commanding obedience (see vv. 66, 107).

⁵¹ Warn by means of it those who fear that they will be gathered to their Lord – they have no ally and no intercessor other than Him – so that they may guard (themselves). ⁵² And do not drive away those who call on their Lord in the morning and the evening, desiring His face. Nothing of their account (falls) on you, and nothing of your account (falls) on them, (that) you should drive them away and so become one of the evildoers. ⁵³ In this way We have tested some of them by means of others, so that they will say, 'Are these (the ones) on whom God has bestowed favor among us?' Is it not God (who) knows the thankful? ⁵⁴ When those who believe in Our signs come to you, say: 'Peace (be) upon you! Your Lord has prescribed mercy for Himself. Whoever of you does evil in ignorance, (and) then turns (in repentance) after that and sets (things) right – surely He is forgiving, compassionate.' ⁵⁵ In this way We make the signs distinct, and (We do this) so that the way of the sinners may become clear.

⁵⁶ Say: 'Surely I am forbidden to serve those whom you call on instead of God.' Say: 'I do not follow your (vain) desires, (for) then I would indeed have gone astray, and not be one of the (rightly) guided.' ⁵⁷ Say: 'I (stand) on a clear sign from my Lord, but you have called it a lie. What you seek to hurry is not in my power. Judgment (belongs) only to God. He recounts the truth, and He is the best of judges.' ⁵⁸ Say: 'If what you seek to hurry were in my power, the matter would indeed have been decided between you and me. God knows about the evildoers.'

⁵⁹ With Him are the keys of the unseen. No one knows them but Him. He knows whatever is on the shore and the sea. Not a leaf falls but He knows of it. (There is) not a grain in the darkness of the earth, and nothing ripe or withered, but (it is recorded) in a clear Book. ⁶⁰ He (it is) who takes you in the night, and He knows what you have earned in the day. Then He raises you up in it, so that an appointed time may be completed. Then to Him is your return, (and) then He will inform you about what you have done. ⁶¹ He is the Supreme One over His servants. He sends watchers over you, until, when death comes to one of you, Our messengers take him – and they do not neglect (their duty). ⁶² Then they are returned to God, their true Protector. Is it not a fact that judgment (belongs) to Him? He is the quickest of reckoners.

⁶³ Say: 'Who rescues you from the dangers of the shore and the sea? You call on Him in humility and in secret: "If indeed He rescues us from this, we shall

---

6.59 – *With Him are the keys of the unseen*

These words begin one of this sūra's several striking descriptions of Allah (vv. 59–65), here highlighting his omniscience, omnipotence, and judgment.

6.63 – *Who rescues you from the dangers of the shore and the sea?*

The messenger draws attention to the way in which Allah saves people from

indeed be among the thankful."' ⁶⁴ Say: 'God rescues you from it, and from every distress, (but) then you associate.' ⁶⁵ Say: 'He is the One able to raise up punishment against you, from above you or from beneath your feet, or to confuse you (into different) parties, and make some of you taste violence from others.' See how We vary the signs, so that they may understand. ⁶⁶ But your people have called it a lie, when it is the truth. Say: 'I am not a guardian over you. ⁶⁷ Every prophecy will come true. Soon you will know!'

⁶⁸ When you see those who banter about Our signs, turn away from them until they banter about some other topic. If Satan makes you forget (this), do not sit, after (you give) the Reminder, with the people who are evildoers. ⁶⁹ Nothing of their account (falls) on the ones who guard (themselves), but (it is) a reminder, so that they (too) may guard (themselves). ⁷⁰ Leave those who take their religion as jest and diversion. This present life has deceived them. Remind (them) by means of it, in case a person be given up to destruction for what he has earned. He has no ally and no intercessor other than God. Even if he were to offer any equal compensation, it would not be accepted from him. Those are the ones who are given up to destruction for what they have earned. For them (there will be) a drink of boiling (water) and a painful punishment, because they were disbelieving.

⁷¹ Say: 'Shall we call on what does not benefit us or harm us, instead of God (alone), and turn back on our heels after God has guided us? – Like the one whom the satans have lured on the earth, (and he is) confused, though he has companions who call him to the guidance (saying): "Come to us"?' Say: 'Surely the guidance of God – it is the (true) guidance, and we have been commanded to submit to the Lord of the worlds, ⁷² and (to say), "Observe the prayer and guard (yourselves) against Him, (for) He is the One to whom you will be gathered."' ⁷³ He (it is) who created the heavens and the earth in truth. On the day when He says 'Be!' it is. His word is the truth, and the kingdom (will belong) to Him on the Day when there will be a blast on the trumpet. (He is) the Knower of the unseen and the seen. He is the Wise, the Aware.

⁷⁴ (Remember) when Abraham said to his father Āzar: 'Do you take idols

---

dangers on land and at sea. This is another sign of Allah's presence and power. However, the people are ungrateful and continue to serve other gods.

The language of salvation (*najjā*, also in v. 64) usually appears in stories about figures familiar from the Old Testament. See "Salvation in the Quran" (p. 180).

6.74 – *when Abraham said to his father Āzar: "Do you take idols as gods?"*

Abraham opposes the idol worship practiced by his father and his people. He learns from experience not to worship the creation but rather the Creator (vv. 75–79).

as gods? Surely I see you and your people are clearly astray.' [75] In this way We were showing Abraham the kingdom of the heavens and the earth, and (this took place) so that he might be one of those who are certain. [76] When night descended on him, he saw a star. He said, 'This is my Lord.' But when it set, he said, 'I do not love what vanishes.' [77] When he saw the moon rising, he said, 'This is my Lord.' But when it set, he said, 'Surely if my Lord does not guide me, I shall indeed be one of the people who go astray.' [78] When he saw the sun rising, he said, 'This is my Lord – this is greater!' But when it set, he said, 'My people! Surely I am free of what you associate. [79] Surely I have turned my face to Him who created the heavens and the earth – (being) a Ḥanīf. Yet I am not one of the idolaters.' [80] But his people disputed with him. He said, 'Do you dispute with me about God, when He has indeed guided me? I do not fear what you associate with Him, unless (it be) that my Lord wills something (against me). My Lord comprehends everything in knowledge. Will you not take heed? [81] How should I fear what you have associated, when you are not afraid to associate with God what He has not sent down on you any authority for?' Which of the two groups has (more) right to security, if you know? [82] Those who have believed, and have not confused their belief with evildoing, those – for them (there is) the (true) security, and they are (rightly) guided. [83] That (was) Our argument. We gave it to Abraham against his people. We raise in rank whomever We please. Surely your Lord is wise, knowing.

[84] And We granted him Isaac and Jacob – each one We guided, and Noah We guided before (them) – and of his descendants (were) David, and Solomon, and Job, and Joseph, and Moses, and Aaron – in this way We repay the doers of good – [85] and Zachariah, and John, and Jesus, and Elijah – each one was of the righteous – [86] and Ishmael, and Elisha, and Jonah, and Lot – each one We favored over the worlds [87] – and some of their fathers, and their descendants,

---

Stories of Abraham in confrontation with idolaters appear in different versions throughout the Quran. See "Abraham in the Quran" (p. 90).

The Quran here names Abraham's father as Āzar, whereas in the Bible his father is Teraḥ (Genesis 11:24–32).

6.84 – *And We granted him Isaac and Jacob – each one We guided*

Immediately after the story of Abraham, the Quran lists many other names, all of them biblical characters, and gives them a high status (vv. 86–87).

Isaac is mentioned first as the son Allah granted to Abraham, while Ishmael appears only near the end of the list. This may come as a surprise to readers who are familiar with the importance of Ishmael in Islam. The same pattern is followed in a number of other quranic passages. See a discussion of this pattern at 21.72 (p. 335).

and their brothers. We chose them and guided them to a straight path. [88] That is the guidance of God. He guides by means of it whomever He pleases of His servants. If they had associated, what they did would indeed have come to nothing for them. [89] Those are the ones to whom We gave the Book, and the judgment, and the prophetic office. If these (people) disbelieve in it, We have already entrusted it to a people who do not disbelieve in it. [90] Those are the ones whom God has guided. Follow their guidance. Say: 'I do not ask you for any reward for it. It is nothing but a reminder to the worlds.'

[91] They have not measured God (with) due measure, when they said, 'God has not sent down anything on a human being.' Say: 'Who sent down the Book which Moses brought as a light and a guidance for the people? You make it (into) sheets of papyrus – you reveal (some of) it, but you hide much (of it). And you were taught what you did not know – neither you nor your fathers.' Say: 'God,' and leave them in their banter (while) they jest.

[92] This is a Book: We have sent it down, blessed, confirming that which was before it. And (We sent it down) so that you may warn the Mother of Towns and those around it. Those who believe in the Hereafter believe in it, and they keep guard over their prayers. [93] Who is more evil than the one who forges a lie

---

6.91 – *Who sent down the Book which Moses brought as a light and a guidance for the people?*

The sending down of a book to Moses is used here as a proof that Allah reveals to humankind. As is the rule whenever a pre-Islamic scripture is actually named (or here in other words), the Quran speaks only in the most positive and respectful ways. Interestingly, the messenger seems to say that he has seen the "sheets of papyrus" (*qarāṭīs*). The messenger also accuses his listeners of hiding much of the Torah, without giving an indication of what they have hidden. This accusation of concealment appears relatively frequently in the Quran. See "Tampering with the Pre-Islamic Scriptures" (p. 142).

6.92 – *This is a Book: We have sent it down, blessed, confirming that which was before it*

After mentioning the "Book which Moses brought," the Quran claims that the present recitation is also revealed by Allah. See this "self-referential" style of verse in "Different Kinds of Literature" in the general introduction (p. 14).

The Quran frequently states that its contents confirm (*muṣaddiq*) what came before it – in this case apparently the Torah. For an analysis of the Quran's claim of confirmation, see 46.12 (p. 502).

6.93 – *Who is more evil than the one who . . . says, "I am inspired," when he is not inspired at all . . . ?*

The questions in this verse are indeed important for non-Muslim readers. Were the

against God, or says, 'I am inspired,' when he is not inspired at all, or the one who says, 'I will send down the equivalent of what God has sent down'?

If (only) you could see when the evildoers are in the throes of death, and the angels are stretching out their hands (saying): 'Out with yourselves! Today you are repaid (with) the punishment of humiliation because you spoke about God (something) other than the truth, and (because) you behaved arrogantly toward His signs.' ⁹⁴ 'Certainly you have come to Us individually, as We created you the first time, and you have left what We bestowed on you behind your backs. Nor do We see with you your intercessors, whom you claimed to be associates (with God) on your behalf. Certainly (the bond) between you has been cut, and what you used to claim (as gods) has abandoned you.'

⁹⁵ Surely God is the splitter of the grain and the date seed. He brings forth the living from the dead, and brings forth the dead from the living. That is God. How are you (so) deluded? ⁹⁶ (He is) the splitter of the dawn, and has made the night for rest, and the sun and moon for reckoning. That is the decree of the Mighty, the Knowing. ⁹⁷ He (it is) who has made the stars for you, so that you might be guided by them in the darkness of the shore and the sea. We have made the signs distinct for a people who know. ⁹⁸ And He (it is) who produced you from one person, and (gave you) a dwelling place and a place of deposit. We have made the signs distinct for a people who understand. ⁹⁹ He (it is) who has sent down water from the sky, and We have brought forth by means of it vegetation of every (kind), and brought forth green (leaves). We bring forth from it thick-clustered grain, and from the date palm, from its sheath, (We bring forth) bunches of dates near (at hand), and gardens of grapes, and olives, and pomegranates, alike and different. Look at its fruit, when it bears fruit, and its ripening. Surely in that are signs indeed for a people who believe.

¹⁰⁰ They make the jinn associates with God, when He created them, and

---

contents of the Quran truly "sent down"? Was the reciter of these verses "inspired"? These questions also bring to mind the prophetic test found in Deuteronomy 18:20: "But a prophet who presumes to speak in my name anything I have not commanded him to say ... ."

6.95 – *Surely God is the splitter of the grain and the date seed*

These words begin a lovely passage (vv. 95–99) about the "signs" (*āyāt*) of Allah's presence and power, such as the land's large variety of fruit (v. 99).

6.100 – *They make the jinn associates with God, when He created them*

This verse offers the first appearance of *jinn* – invisible created beings between angels and humankind. Further mention of jinn comes in this sūra at verses 112, 128, and 130. See the discussion of jinn in the Quran at 72.1 (p. 593).

they assign to Him sons and daughters without any knowledge. Glory to Him! He is exalted above what they allege. [101] Originator of the heavens and the earth – how can He have a son when He has no consort, (and) when He created everything and has knowledge of everything? [102] That is God, your Lord. (There is) no god but Him, Creator of everything. So serve Him! He is guardian over everything. [103] Sight does not reach Him, but He reaches sight. He is the Gentle, the Aware.

[104] Now evidence has come to you from your Lord: whoever sees – it is to his advantage, and whoever is blind – it is to his disadvantage. I am not a watcher over you. [105] In this way We vary the signs, so that they will say, 'You have studied,' and that We may make it clear to a people who know. [106] Follow what you are inspired (with) from your Lord – (there is) no god but Him – and turn away from the idolaters. [107] If God had (so) pleased, they would not have been idolaters. We have not made you a watcher over them, nor are you a guardian over them. [108] Do not revile those (gods) on whom they call instead of God, or they will revile God in enmity without any knowledge. In this way We make their deed(s) appear enticing to every community. Then to their Lord is their return, and He will inform them about what they have done.

[109] They have sworn by God the most solemn of their oaths: if indeed a sign comes to them, they will indeed believe in it. Say: 'The signs (are) only

---

6.101 – *how can He have a son when He has no consort . . . ?*

With this question, the Quran seems to claim that it is impossible for Allah to have a son (*walad*) because he has no consort (*ṣāḥiba*). Though there is no mention of Christians in the verse or its context, this line of questioning is common in many Muslim-Christian conversations. If Christians are indeed in mind here, they could ask a return question: When God the Father called Jesus his Son in the Gospel accounts, did he mean to imply a relationship between God and a woman? See "Son of God in the Quran" (p. 352).

6.108 – *Do not revile those (gods) on whom they call instead of Allah*

The Quran commands believers not to insult or abuse (*sabba*) the objects of people's worship apart from Allah. This verb appears only here in the Quran, but in later Islamic history this became one of the main verbs used to allege "blasphemy" against Muhammad.

6.109 – *The signs (are) only with God*

The listeners ask for a sign so that they may believe. The answer is that they would not believe even if a convincing sign came to them (v. 111). On verses that question whether the Quran's messenger performs miracles, see the comments at 43.40 (p. 490).

with God.' What will make you realize that, when it does come, they will not believe? [110] We shall turn their hearts and their sight away (from the sign), just as (We did when) they did not believe in it the first time, and We shall leave them in their insolent transgression, wandering blindly. [111] Even if We had sent down the angels to them, and the dead had spoken to them, and (even if) We had gathered together everything against them head on, they would (still) not believe, unless God (so) pleased. But most of them are ignorant.

[112] In this way We have assigned to every prophet an enemy – satans of the humans and jinn – some of them inspiring others (with) decorative speech as a deception. If your Lord had (so) pleased, they would not have done it. So leave them and what they forge. [113] And (it is) so that the hearts of those who do not believe in the Hereafter may incline to it, and that they may be delighted by it, and that they may acquire what they are acquiring. [114] Shall I seek (anyone) other than God as a judge? He (it is) who has sent down to you the Book, set forth distinctly. Those to whom We have (already) given the Book know that it is sent down from your Lord with the truth. Do not be one of the doubters.

[115] Perfect is the word of your Lord in truth and justice. No one can change His words. He is the Hearing, the Knowing. [116] If you obey the majority of those on the earth, they will lead you astray from the way of God. They only follow conjecture and they only guess. [117] Surely your Lord – He knows who goes astray from His way and He knows the ones who are (rightly) guided.

6.112 – *In this way We have assigned to every prophet an enemy*

Quranic statements that characterize "every prophet" raise the question of the extent to which they correspond to the accounts of prophets in the Bible. See an analysis of such statements at 25.20 (p. 365).

6.114 – *Those to whom We have (already) given the Book know that it is sent down from your Lord with the truth*

This characterization of the People of the Book is quite different from most of Sūras 2–5. Here they say that the messenger's recitations are revealed (see also v. 20). Does this mean they have converted to Islam, as 5.83–85 seems to suggest?

6.115 – *No one can change His words*

This verse states that there is no changer of the words of Allah (*lā mubaddila li-kalimātihi*). Interestingly, in the preceding verse the people to whom Allah has previously "given the Book" are said to recognize the present recitations. The statement that Allah's words are unchangeable repeats in slightly different forms at 6.34; 10.64; and 18.27.

6.118 – *Eat of that over which the name of God has been mentioned*

This verse and the following extended passage (vv. 118–46) contain a number

[118] Eat from that over which the name of God has been mentioned, if you are believers in His signs. [119] What is (the matter) with you that you do not eat from that over which the name of God has been mentioned, when He has already made distinct for you what He has forbidden you (to eat), unless you are forced to (eat) it? Surely many are indeed led astray by their (vain) desires without realizing (it). Surely your Lord – He knows about the transgressors. [120] Forsake (both) obvious and hidden sin. Surely those who earn sin will be repaid for what they have earned. [121] Do not eat that over which the name of God has not been mentioned. Surely it is wickedness indeed! Surely the satans inspire their allies, so that they may dispute with you. If you obey them, surely you will be idolaters indeed! [122] Is the one who was dead, and We gave him life (again), and made for him a light to walk by among the people, like the one who is to be compared to (a person) in the darkness from which he never emerges? In this way what they have done was made to appear enticing to the disbelievers.

[123] In this way We have placed in every town great ones among its sinners, so that they might scheme there. Yet they do not scheme against (anyone) but themselves, though they do not realize (it). [124] When a sign comes to them, they say, 'We will not believe until we are given (something) similar to what was given to the messengers of God.' God knows where He places His message. Disgrace in God's sight will smite those who have sinned, and (also) a harsh punishment, for what they were scheming. [125] Whomever God intends to guide, He expands his heart to Islam, and whomever He intends to lead astray, He makes his heart narrow (and) constricted, as if he were climbing up into the sky. In this way God places the abomination on those who do not believe. [126] This is the path of your Lord – straight. We have made the signs distinct for a people who take heed. [127] For them (there is) the Home of peace with their Lord. He is their ally for what they have done.

[128] On the Day when He will gather them all together: 'Assembly of the jinn! You have acquired many of humankind.' And their allies among humankind will say, 'Our Lord, some of us have profited by others, but (now) we have

---

of references to permitted foods, including another verse about various fruit (v. 141) and a short description of prohibitions for Jews (v. 146).

6.127 – *For them (there is) the Home of peace with their Lord*

The Arabic translated "the Home of peace" here is the lovely *dār al-salām*.

6.128 – *On the Day when He will gather them all together*

A conversation between Allah and humans who were seduced by *jinn* introduces a vision of a judgment scene on the Day of Resurrection (vv. 128–35). See "Eschatology in the Quran" (p. 604).

reached our time which You appointed for us.' He will say, 'The Fire is your dwelling place, there to remain' – except for whomever God pleases. Surely your Lord is wise, knowing. [129] In this way We make some of the evildoers allies of others for what they have earned.

[130] 'Assembly of the jinn and humans! Did messengers not come to you from among you, recounting to you My signs and warning you of the meeting of this Day of yours?' They will say, 'We bear witness against ourselves.' This present life deceived them, and they bear witness against themselves that they were disbelievers. [131] That (is because) your Lord was not one to destroy the towns in an evil manner, while their people were oblivious. [132] And for each (there are) ranks according to what they have done, and your Lord is not oblivious of what they do. [133] Your Lord is the wealthy One, the One full of mercy. If He (so) pleases, He will do away with you, and appoint as a successor after you whomever He pleases, just as He produced you from the descendants of another people. [134] Surely what you are promised will indeed come, and you cannot escape (it). [135] Say: 'My people! Do as you are able. Surely I am going to do (what I can). Soon you will know to whom the final Home (belongs). Surely he – the evildoers will not prosper.'

[136] They assign to God a portion of the crops and the livestock which He created, and they say, 'This is for God' – so they claim – 'and this is for our associates.' But what is for their associates does not reach God, and what is for God reaches their associates. Evil is what they judge! [137] In this way their associates made the killing of their children appear enticing to many of the idolaters, in order that they might bring them to ruin and confuse their religion for them. If God had (so) pleased, they would not have done it. So leave them and what they forge. [138] They say, 'These livestock and crops are forbidden. No one may eat them, except for whomever we please' – so they claim – 'and livestock whose backs have been forbidden, and livestock over which the name of God is not to be mentioned' – forging (lies) against Him. He will repay them for what they have forged. [139] They say, 'What is in the bellies of these livestock is exclusively for our males and forbidden to our wives. But if it is (born) dead, they will (all) be partakers in it.' He will repay them for their attributing (these things to Him). Surely He is wise, knowing. [140] Lost (are) those who kill their children in foolishness, without any knowledge, and forbid what God has provided them, forging (lies) against God. They have gone astray and are not (rightly) guided.

[141] He (it is) who produces gardens, trellised and untrellised, and date palms and crops of diverse produce, and olives and pomegranates, alike and different. Eat from its fruits when it bears fruit, and give its due (portion) on the day of its

harvest. But do not act wantonly. Surely He does not love the wanton. [142] And of the livestock (there are some for) burden and (some for) slaughter. Eat from what God has provided you, and do not follow the footsteps of Satan. Surely he is clear enemy to you.

[143] Eight pairs: two of the sheep, and two of the goats. Say: 'Has He forbidden the two males or the two females? Or what the wombs of the two females contain? Inform me with knowledge, if you are truthful.'

[144] And two of the camels, and two of the cows. Say: 'Has He forbidden the two males or the two females? Or what the wombs of the two females contain? Or were you witnesses when God charged you with this (command)? Who is more evil than the one who forges a lie against God, in order to lead the people astray without (their) realizing (it)? Surely God does not guide the people who are evildoers.'

[145] Say: 'I do not find in what I have been inspired (with anything) forbidden to one who eats of it, unless it is (already) dead, or blood (which is) shed, or swine's flesh – surely it is an abomination – or – something wicked – it has been dedicated to (a god) other than God.' But whoever is forced (by necessity), not desiring or (deliberately) transgressing – surely your Lord is forgiving, compassionate.

[146] To those who are Jews We have forbidden every (animal) with claws, and of the cows and the sheep and goats We have forbidden to them their fat, except what their backs carry, or their entrails, or what is mixed with the bone. We repaid them that for their envy. Surely We are truthful indeed. [147] If they call you a liar, say: 'Your Lord is full of abundant mercy, but His violence will not be turned back from the people who are sinners.'

[148] The idolaters will say, 'If God had (so) pleased, we would not have been idolaters, nor our fathers, nor would we have forbidden anything.' In this way the people before them called (it) a lie, until they tasted Our violence. Say: 'Do you have any knowledge? Bring it forth for us! You only follow conjecture and you only guess.' [149] Say: 'To God (belongs) the conclusive argument. If He had (so) pleased, He would indeed have guided you all.' [150] Say: 'Produce your witnesses who (will) bear witness that God has forbidden this.' If they do bear witness, do not bear witness with them. Do not follow the desires of those who

---

6.141 – *Surely He does not love the wanton*

The Quran contains twenty-four statements about the kinds of people whom Allah does not love. The Arabic word translated "wanton" is *musrifūn*, also commonly translated "prodigals." This statement repeats at 7.31. See "The Language of Love in the Quran" (p. 560).

call Our signs a lie, and who do not believe in the Hereafter, and (who) equate (others) with their Lord.

[151] Say: 'Come! I will recite what your Lord has forbidden to you: Do not associate anything with Him, and (do) good to parents, and do not kill your children because of poverty – We shall provide for you and them – and do not go near (any) immoral deeds, neither what is obvious of them nor what is hidden, and do not kill the person whom God has forbidden (to be killed), except by right. That is what He has charged you with, so that you may understand. [152] Do not go near the property of the orphan, except to improve it, until he reaches his maturity. Fill up the measure and the scale in justice. We do not burden anyone beyond their capacity. When you speak, be fair, even if he is a family member. Fulfill the covenant of God. That is what He has charged you with, so that you may take heed. [153] And (know) that this is My straight path. So follow it, and do not follow the ways (of others), or it will diverge with you from His way. That is what He has charged you with, so that you may guard (yourselves).'

[154] Then We gave Moses the Book, complete for the one who does good, and a distinct setting forth of everything, and a guidance and mercy, so that they might believe in the meeting with their Lord. [155] And this is a Book: We have sent it down, blessed. Follow it and guard (yourselves), so that you may receive compassion. [156] Otherwise you would say, 'The Book has only been sent down on two contingents (of people) before us, and we were indeed oblivious of their studies.' [157] Or you would say, 'If (only) the Book had been sent down to us, we would indeed have been better guided than them.' Yet a clear sign has come to you from your Lord, and a guidance and mercy. Who is more evil than

---

6.151 – *Come! I will recite what your Lord has forbidden to you*

This list of duties that the "Lord" requires is strong on justice to the disadvantaged and in the market (vv. 151–52). The practice of families killing their children, here forbidden, is mentioned earlier in the sūra at verses 137 and 140. Fulfilling these duties is called Allah's straight path (v. 153).

6.154 – *Then We gave Moses the Book, complete for the one who does good, and a distinct setting forth of everything, and a guidance and a mercy*

The sūra once more describes the Torah in the most positive and respectful way (also v. 91). Also once more, the sūra seems to launch its claims for a new book (vv. 155, 157) from an affirmation of revelation to "two contingents" of people in the past (v. 156). There is no sense here, as one felt in Sūra 5, that the new recitations serve as judge over the pre-Islamic scriptures. Nevertheless, the sūra insists that the recitations be accepted as "a clear sign (*bayyina*) . . . from your Lord" (v. 157).

the one who calls the signs of God a lie, and turns away from them? We shall repay those who turn away from Our signs (with) an evil punishment for their turning away. [158] Do they expect (anything) but the angels to come to them, or your Lord to come, or one of the signs of your Lord to come? On the Day when one of the signs of your Lord comes, belief will not benefit anyone who did not believe before, or (who did not) earn some good through his belief. Say: '(Just) wait! Surely We (too) are waiting.'

[159] Surely those who have divided up their religion and become (different) parties – you are no part of them. Their affair (belongs) only to God, and He will inform them about what they have done. [160] Whoever brings a good deed will have ten equal to it, but whoever brings an evil deed will only be paid the equal of it – and they will not be done evil. [161] Say: 'Surely my Lord has guided me to a straight path, a right religion, the creed of Abraham the Ḥanīf. He was not one of the idolaters.'

[162] Say: 'Surely my prayer and my sacrifice, and my living and my dying, are for God, Lord of the worlds. [163] He has no associate. With that I have been commanded, and I am the first of those who submit.'

[164] Say: 'Shall I seek a Lord other than God, when He is the Lord of everything? No one earns (anything) except against himself, and no one bearing a burden bears the burden of another. Then to your Lord is your return, (and) then He will inform you about your differences.' [165] He (it is) who has made you successors on the earth, and raised some of you above others in rank, so that He might test you by what He has given you. Surely your Lord is quick in retribution, yet surely He is indeed forgiving, compassionate.

6.159 – *Surely those who have divided up their religion*
See the comments on division and differences at 98.4 (p. 642).

THE HEIGHTS
AL-AʿRĀF

7

The task of the unnamed messenger in this sūra is to warn humankind of the destruction to come if they do not heed the "signs" of Allah. The sūra contains a series of stories about messengers in the past that illustrate divine destruction of those who denied the signs. These stories seem to lead up to a long story about Moses and the Children of Israel.

Many messenger stories seem to follow a pattern in which each people resists the preaching of its messenger until Allah destroys the people and saves the messenger and his followers. The Adam story in this sūra does not follow this pattern. But the long Moses story, after offering many details, ultimately ends with destruction of the unbelievers by Allah. Moses emerges here as the exemplary prophet of the Quran. See "Moses in the Quran" (p. 388) and the table of Moses stories (p. 390).

In the middle of the Moses story, the Quran instructs the messenger to declare, "People! Surely I am the messenger of Allah to you," and to command belief not only in Allah, but also in his messenger (v. 158). The passage also declares that an "ummī prophet" ("prophet of the common people") would be found written "in their Torah and Gospel" (v. 157).

In the Name of God, the Merciful, the Compassionate

[1] Alif Lām Mīm Ṣād.

[2] A Book sent down to you – so let there be no heaviness in your heart because of it – in order that you may warn by means of it, and as a reminder to the believers. [3] Follow what has been sent down to you from your Lord, and do not follow any allies other than Him. Little do you take heed!

7.2 – *A Book sent down to you – so let there be no heaviness in your heart because of it*

The sūra opens with direct address to the "messenger," to encourage him and to claim that his recitations are "sent down." Such seemingly self-conscious verses, set in the second-person singular, begin many sūras in the 10–46 range. See "Different Kinds of Literature" (p. 14).

⁴ How many a town have We destroyed! Our violence came upon it at night, or (while) they were relaxing at midday. ⁵ Their only cry, when Our violence came upon them, was that they said, 'Surely We were evildoers!' ⁶ We shall indeed question those to whom (a messenger) was sent, and We shall indeed question the envoys. ⁷ We shall indeed recount to them with knowledge, (for) We were not absent. ⁸ The weighing on that Day (will be) the true (weighing). Whoever's scales are heavy, those – they are the ones who prosper, ⁹ but whoever's scales are light, those are the ones who have lost their (own) selves, because of the evil they have done to Our signs.

¹⁰ Certainly We have established you on the earth, and provided for you a means of living on it – little thanks you show! ¹¹ Certainly We created you, (and) then fashioned you. Then We said to the angels, 'Prostrate yourselves before Adam,' and they prostrated themselves, except Iblīs. He was not one of those who prostrated themselves. ¹² He said, 'What kept you from prostrating yourself when I commanded you?' He said, 'I am better than him. You created me from fire, but You created him from clay.' ¹³ He said, 'Go down from here! It is not for you to be arrogant here. Get out! Surely you are one of the disgraced.' ¹⁴ He said, 'Spare me until the Day when they are raised up.' ¹⁵ He said, 'Surely you are one of the spared.' ¹⁶ He said, 'Because you have made me err, I shall indeed sit (in wait) for them (on) Your straight path. ¹⁷ Then I shall indeed

---

7.4 – *How many a town have We destroyed!*

Destruction of peoples who do not heed the signs of Allah is an important theme in the stories of prophets in this sūra.

7.8 – *Whoever's scales are heavy, . . . they are the ones who prosper*

The image of weigh scales is important in the judgment that the Quran envisions for the Day of Resurrection. See "The Place of the Scale(s) in the Reckoning" (p. 481).

7.11 – *Then We said to the angels, "Prostrate yourselves before Adam"*

In this second quranic version of the Adam story (vv. 11–27; cf. 2.30–39), Adam and his wife (unnamed in the Quran) are commanded not to go near a certain tree (v. 19). Tempted by Satan, they taste of the tree (v. 22). When their Lord calls them to account, they say they have "done ourselves evil" and confess their need for forgiveness (v. 23). This detail of accepting personal responsibility is different from the version of the story in Sūra 2. There Satan simply causes them to slip (2.36).

A third version of the Adam story comes at 20.115–24. See an analysis of the Quran's Adam stories at 20.121 (p. 327).

7.12 – *I am better than him. You created me from fire, but You created him from clay*

On the subplot of Iblīs's refusal to bow down (vv. 11–12), see the analysis and response at 38.73–74 (p. 458).

come upon them, from before them and from behind them, and from their right and from their left, and You will not find most of them thankful.' [18] He said, 'Get out of here, detested (and) rejected! Whoever of them follows you – I shall indeed fill Gehenna with you – all (of you)!'

[19] 'Adam! Inhabit the Garden, you and your wife, and eat freely of it wherever you please, but do not go near this tree, or you will both be among the evildoers.' [20] Then Satan whispered to them both, to reveal to them both what was hidden from them of their shameful parts. He said, 'Your Lord has only forbidden you both from this tree to keep you both from becoming two angels, or from becoming two of the immortals.' [21] And he swore to them both, 'Surely I am indeed one of your trusty advisers.' [22] So he caused them both to fall by means of deception. And when they both had tasted the tree, their shameful parts became apparent to them, and they both began fastening on themselves some leaves of the Garden. But their Lord called to them both, 'Did I not forbid you both from that tree, and say to you both, "Surely Satan is a clear enemy to you"?' [23] They both said, 'Our Lord, we have done ourselves evil. If You do not forgive us, and have compassion on us, we shall indeed be among the losers.' [24] He said, 'Go down, some of you an enemy to others! The earth is a dwelling place for you, and enjoyment (of life) for a time.' [25] He said, 'On it you will live and on it you will die, and from it you will be brought forth.'

[26] Sons of Adam! We sent down on you clothing – it covers your shameful parts – and feathers. Yet the clothing of guarding (yourselves) – that is better. That is one of the signs of God, so that they may take heed.

[27] Sons of Adam! Do not let Satan tempt you, as he drove your parents out of the Garden, stripping both of them of their clothing in order to show both of them their shameful parts. Surely he sees you – he and his ilk – from where you do not see them. Surely We have made the satans allies of those who do not believe.

[28] When they commit immorality, they say, 'We found our fathers doing it, and God has commanded us (to do) it.' Say: 'Surely God does not command immorality. Do you say about God what you do not know?' [29] Say: 'My Lord has commanded justice. Set your faces in every mosque, and call on Him, devoting (your) religion to Him. As He brought you about, (so) will you return. [30] (One) group He has guided, and (another) group – their going astray was deserved. Surely they have taken the satans as allies instead of God, and they think that they are (rightly) guided.'

7.26 – *Sons of Adam! We sent down on you clothing*

These words begin an extended section of instructions addressed to the "Sons of Adam" (vv. 26–37).

³¹ Sons of Adam! Take your adornment in every mosque, and eat and drink, but do not act wantonly. Surely He does not love the wanton. ³² Say: 'Who has forbidden the adornment of God which He has brought forth for His servants, and the good things of (His) provision?' Say: 'It is exclusively for those who have believed in this present life on the Day of Resurrection.' In this way We make the signs distinct for a people who know.

³³ Say: 'My Lord has only forbidden immoral deeds – (both) what is obvious of them and what is hidden – and all sin and envy – without any right – and that you associate with God what He has not sent down any authority for, and that you say about God what you do not know.' ³⁴ For every community (there is) a time. When their time comes, they will not delay (it) by an hour, nor will they advance (it by an hour).

³⁵ Sons of Adam! If messengers from among you should come to you, recounting to you My signs, whoever guards (himself) and sets (things) right – (there will be) no fear on them, nor will they sorrow. ³⁶ But those who call Our signs a lie, and become arrogant about it – those are the companions of the Fire. There they will remain. ³⁷ Who is more evil than the one who forges a lie against God, or calls His signs a lie? Those – their portion of the Book will reach them, until, when Our messengers come to them, to take them, they say, 'Where is what you used to call on (as gods) instead of God?' They will say, 'They have abandoned us,' and they will bear witness against themselves that they were disbelievers.

³⁸ He will say, 'Enter into the Fire, among the communities of jinn and humans who have passed away before you.' Whenever a (new) community enters, it curses its sister (community), until, when they have all followed each other into it, the last of them will say to the first of them, 'Our Lord, these led us astray, so give them a double punishment of the Fire.' He will say, 'To each

---

7.31 – *Surely He does not love the wanton*

The Quran contains twenty-four statements about the kinds of people whom Allah does not love. The object translated "wanton" also appears in 6.141. See "The Language of Love in the Quran" (p. 560).

7.38 – *Enter into the Fire, among the communities of jinn and humans*

The Quran pictures a judgment scene on the Day of Resurrection in which Allah speaks to the condemned and the condemned speak to one another (vv. 37–39). Those who enter the "Garden" praise Allah and thank the messengers who brought them the truth (v. 43). Then the "companions of the Garden" and the "companions of the Fire," separated by a veil, carry on a longer conversation (vv. 44–51).

Verse 38 calls the *jinn* a "community." See the discussion of jinn at 72.1 (p. 593).

a double, but you do not know.' [39] And the first of them will say to the last of them, 'You have no advantage over us, so taste the punishment for what you have earned.'

[40] Surely those who call Our signs a lie, and are arrogant about it – the gates of the sky will not be opened for them, nor will they enter the Garden, until the camel passes through the eye of the needle. In this way We repay the sinners. [41] They have a bed in Gehenna, and coverings above them. In this way We repay the evildoers. [42] But those who believe and do righteous deeds – We do not burden anyone beyond their capacity – those are the companions of the Garden. There they will remain. [43] We shall strip away whatever rancor is in their hearts. Beneath them rivers will flow, and they will say, 'Praise (be) to God, who has guided us to this! We would not have been guided if God had not guided us. Certainly the messengers of our Lord have brought the truth.' And they will be called out to: 'That is the Garden! You have inherited it for what you have done.' [44] The companions of the Garden will call out to the companions of the Fire: 'We have found what our Lord promised us (to be) true. So have you found what your Lord promised (to be) true?' They will say, 'Yes!' And then a caller will call out among them: 'The curse of God is on the evildoers, [45] who keep (people) from the way of God and desire (to make) it crooked, and they are disbelievers in the Hereafter.'

[46] Between both (groups) of them (there is) a partition, and on the heights (there are) men who recognize each (of them) by their marks, and they call out to the companions of the Garden: 'Peace (be) upon you! They have not entered it, as much as they were eager (to do so).' [47] And when their sight is turned toward the companions of the Fire, they say, 'Our Lord, do not place us among the people who are evildoers.' [48] The men of the heights will call out to men whom they recognize by their marks, (and) say, 'Your hoarding is of no use to you, nor what you were arrogant (about). [49] Are these the ones whom you swore God would not reach with (His) mercy? Enter the Garden! (There will be) no fear on you, nor will you sorrow.'

[50] And the companions of the Fire will call out to the companions of the Garden: 'Pour some water on us, or some of what God has provided you!' They will say, 'Surely God has forbidden both to the disbelievers, [51] who have taken their religion as diversion and jest. This present life has deceived them.'

7.40 – *until the camel passes through the eye of the needle*

Is this possibly a place where an expression of Jesus in the Gospel accounts (Matthew 19:24; Mark 10:25; Luke 18:25) has made its way into the text of the Quran? If so, the route was more likely verbal – heard in the course of conversation – than literary.

So today We forget them as they forgot the meeting of this Day of theirs, and because they have denied Our signs.

⁵² Certainly We have brought them a Book – We have made it distinct on (the basis of) knowledge – as a guidance and mercy for a people who believe. ⁵³ Do they expect anything but its interpretation? On the Day when its interpretation comes, those who forgot it before will say, 'The messengers of our Lord have brought the truth. Have we any intercessors to intercede for us? Or (may) we return so that we might do other than what we have done?' They have lost their (own) selves, and what they forged has abandoned them.

⁵⁴ Surely your Lord is God, who created the heavens and the earth in six days. Then He mounted the throne. The night covers the day, which it pursues urgently, and the sun, and the moon, and the stars are subjected, (all) by His command. Is it not (a fact) that to Him (belong) the creation and the command? Blessed (be) God, Lord of the worlds!

⁵⁵ Call on your Lord in humility and in secret. Surely He does not love the transgressors. ⁵⁶ Do not foment corruption on the earth after it has been set right, and call on Him in fear and in eagerness. Surely the mercy of God is near to the doers of good. ⁵⁷ He (it is) who sends the winds as good news before His mercy, until, when it brings a cloud heavy (with rain), We drive it to some barren land, and send down water by means of it, and bring forth by means of it every (kind of) fruit. In this way We bring forth the dead, so that you may take heed. ⁵⁸ (As for) the good land, its vegetation comes forth by the permission of its Lord, but (as for) the bad, (its vegetation) comes forth only poorly. In this way We vary the signs for a people who are thankful.

⁵⁹ Certainly We sent Noah to his people, and he said, 'My people! Serve God!

7.55 – *Surely He does not love the transgressors*

The "transgressors" make up one of the groups most often denied Allah's love in the Quran (also 2.190; 5.87). See "The Language of Love in the Quran" (p. 560).

7.59 – *Certainly We sent Noah to his people*

Noah is an important character in the Quran, and different versions of his story appear seven times. He is portrayed mainly as a messenger whom Allah sends to his people. This version (vv. 59–64) features a long speech from Noah in which he defends himself from the accusation of leading the people astray. The detail of the ark or "ship" (v. 64) seems almost incidental. The focus is on how God rescued Noah and drowned Noah's opponents.

Further versions of the Noah story come at 10.71–3; 11.25–48; 23.23–30; 26.105–20; 54.7–17; and 71.1–28.

This story of Noah is the first in a series of stories in this sūra in which messengers

You have no god other than Him. Surely I fear for you the punishment of a great Day.' [60] The assembly of his people said, 'Surely we see you are indeed clearly astray.' [61] He said, 'My people! There is nothing astray in me, but I am a messenger from the Lord of the worlds. [62] I deliver to you the messages of my Lord and I offer advice to you. I know from God what you do not know. [63] Are you amazed that a reminder has come to you from your Lord by means of a (mere) man from among you, so that he may warn you, and that you may guard (yourselves), and that you may receive compassion?' [64] But they called him a liar, so We rescued him and those with him in the ship, and We drowned those who called Our signs a lie. Surely they were a blind people.

Salvation in the Quran
Peter Riddell

Salvation is far less clearly defined as a doctrine in the Quran than in the Bible. Nevertheless, the Quran contains elements that help Muslims prepare for a positive outcome on the Day of Judgment.

Quranic Arabic makes use of the verb *najā* to express the notion of "deliver" or "save." The use of this verb is less associated with an expression of hope and more commonly coupled with delivery from punishment for those who follow the divine commands, as well as delivery denied to those who disbelieve.

The verb rarely appears in sūras usually associated with the earliest part of Muhammad's ministry in Mecca. At this early stage the architecture of quranic doctrine was somewhat in flux; the messenger is believed to have been engaging with and responding to challenges in the marketplace as he preached. The single reference from this period at 70.14 is concerned with a divine rebuke to disbelievers who will be ready to "ransom" (v. 11) family members on the Day of Judgment in order to save themselves, but to no

are sent to various peoples. Similar material appears in many of the sūras starting with Sūra 10 and continuing up to Sūra 46. Some scholars of the Quran call these stories "punishment narratives." Other examples of a series of such stories – involving the same five characters presented in this sūra – are given in Sūras 11 (which adds Abraham before Lot) and 26.

7.64 – *But they called him a liar, so We rescued him and those with him in the ship*
The language of salvation (*anjā*) appears in this series of stories of past prophets or messengers (also vv. 72, 83, 141, 165).

avail. The medieval commentator Ibn Kathīr expands on the quranic idea of salvation in this verse in the following terms: "Even the child that he had who was dearer to him than the last beat of his heart in the life of this world, he would wish to use the child as a ransom for himself against the torment of Allah on the Day of Judgment when he sees the horrors. However, even this child would not be accepted from him as a ransom."

In chapters seen by Muslims as reflecting the messenger in a later period in Mecca, the Arabic form *anjā* occurs with increasing frequency. The dichotomy between believers and unbelievers takes shape more clearly in these chapters. At this stage the Quran was issuing both promises of reward and increasingly stern warnings of divine punishment. The concept of deliverance or salvation hinges on several key elements. First, God remains in control of the distribution or denial of salvation. He saves the obedient and leaves others to stray (19.72) or destroys them (21.9). In some cases God predestines some to miss out on salvation (27.57). God's sovereignty is spelled out clearly, rewarding the obedient and punishing the sinners (7.72, 165; cf. 12.110: "Those whom We pleased were rescued. But Our violence was not turned back from the people who were sinners").

A second key element is the method of God's identification of who is to be delivered or saved. At 27.53 we encounter a clear statement that God saves "those who believed and guarded (themselves)" (cf. 21.88). Elsewhere the Quran makes it clear that God delivers certain people or groups as "a blessing" or a reward to "the one who is thankful" (54.34–35; cf. 39.61; 41.18).

The prophets are often identified in the Quran as the beneficiaries of God's salvation, because they have believed and provided a righteous model for others (10.103). For example, Abraham was saved from the fire (29.24), while Moses was saved from being apprehended after he slew the Egyptian slave master (20.40; 26.66). Lot was saved "from the town which was doing bad things" (21.71, 74; 29.32), Noah was delivered when he cried out and was heard by God (21.76; 10.73; 29.15), and Hud was saved, along with his fellow believers (11.58), as were Salih (11.66) and Shu'ayb (11.94).

The deliverance or salvation represented by the verb *anjā* not only relates to end-time salvation. Indeed, the Quran uses the verb on occasion to refer to saving a physical person who then turns away through ingratitude (6.64; 10.23; 17.67). The famous Jalalayn commentary is specific on identifying the sin after salvation in 6.64: "Say, to them: 'God delivers you from that and from every distress, [from every] other anxiety. Yet you associate others with Him.'"

In the sūras attributed by Muslims to Muhammad's Medinan period, the verb *anjā* occurs infrequently. By this stage, in terms of Muslim understanding, Muhammad's authority as the messenger of God has been firmly established, and the message of deliverance/salvation and reward has been clearly articulated. What predominates in these chapters is a resounding warning of the dire punishments awaiting disbelievers and the disobedient. Even when the verb *anjā* does occur, it is collocated with references to punishment: "You who believe! Shall I direct you to a transaction that will rescue you from a painful punishment?" (61.10).

Apart from the specific use of the verb *anjā*, how does the Quran advise Muslims to avoid eternal punishment in the hereafter? The core notion is through obedience to God's commands by following the guidance of the prophets and the divine Law. This is well summarized in 103.2–3, which Muslims consider to originate from the early part of Muhammad's ministry, where the message of following the Law and the Prophets is clearly articulated: "Surely the human is indeed in (a state of) loss – except for those who believe and do righteous deeds, and exhort (each other) in truth, and exhort (each other) in patience."

⁶⁵ And to ʿĀd (We sent) their brother Hūd. He said, 'My people! Serve God! You have no god other than Him. Will you not guard (yourselves)?' ⁶⁶ The assembly of those who disbelieved among his people said, 'Surely we see you are indeed in foolishness, and surely we think you are indeed one of the liars.' ⁶⁷ He said, 'My people! There is no foolishness in me, but I am a messenger from the Lord of the worlds. ⁶⁸ I deliver to you the messages of my Lord and I am a trustworthy adviser for you. ⁶⁹ Are you amazed that a reminder has come to you from your Lord by means of a (mere) man from among you, so that he may warn you? (Remember) when He made you successors after the people of Noah,

---

7.65 – And to ʿĀd (We sent) their brother Hūd

Hūd is the first of three characters in this sūra who are thought to be Arabian messengers but are not known from the Bible or Jewish traditions. The other two figures are Ṣāliḥ (v. 73) and Shuʿayb (v. 85). Hūd preaches to his people, called ʿĀd, and the people reject his message. Then Allah rescues Hūd and cuts off the unbelievers. The story of Hūd appears elsewhere in the Quran at 11.50–60; 26.123–40; and 46.21–26.

Early Muslim writings supply many details to the story of Hūd and ʿĀd, but these writings offer no helpful evidence for a historical identification.

and increased you in size abundantly. Remember the blessings of God, so that you may prosper.' [70] They said, 'Have you come to us (with the message) that we should serve God alone, and forsake what our fathers have served? Bring us what you promise us, if you are one of the truthful.' [71] He said, 'Abomination and anger from your Lord have fallen upon you. Will you dispute with me about names which you have named, you and your fathers? God has not sent down any authority for it. (Just) wait! Surely I shall be one of those waiting with you.' [72] So We rescued him and those with him by a mercy from Us, and We cut off the last remnant of those who called Our signs a lie and were not believers.

[73] And to Thamūd (We sent) their brother Ṣāliḥ. He said, 'My people! Serve God! You have no god other than Him. A clear sign has come to you from your Lord: this is the she-camel of God, a sign for you. Let her graze on God's earth, and do not touch her with evil, or a painful punishment will seize you. [74] Remember when He made you successors after 'Ād and settled you on the earth: you took palaces from its plains, and carved houses out of the mountains. Remember the blessings of God, and do not act wickedly on the earth, fomenting corruption.' [75] The assembly of those who were arrogant among his people said to those who were weak, to those of them who believed, 'Do you (really) know that Ṣāliḥ is an envoy from his Lord?' They said, 'Surely We are believers in what he has been sent with.' [76] Those who were arrogant said, 'Surely we are disbelievers in what you have believed.' [77] So they wounded the she-camel, and disdained the command of their Lord, and said, 'Ṣāliḥ! Bring us what you promise us, if you are one of the envoys.' [78] And then the earthquake seized them, and morning found them leveled in their home(s). [79] So he turned away from them, and said, 'My people! Certainly I have delivered to you the message of my Lord and I offered advice to you, but you do not like advisers.'

[80] And Lot, when he said to his people, 'Do you commit (such) immorality

---

7.73 – And to Thamūd (We sent) their brother Ṣāliḥ.

Ṣāliḥ preaches to his people, named Thamūd, but the leaders of the people discourage the believers. A special detail of the resistance of the leaders is that they hamstring a certain "she-camel of Allah" in opposition to the clear preaching of Ṣāliḥ (vv. 73–77). As punishment, an earthquake seizes the people (v. 78).

Different versions of the Ṣāliḥ story appear six times in the Quran. As with Hūd (v. 65 above), early Muslim writings expand the story of Ṣāliḥ, but it cannot be connected with any known past story, and pre-Islamic mention of the name Ṣāliḥ is very rare.

7.80 – And Lot, when he said to his people, "Do you commit (such) immorality . . . ?"

The story of Lot and the punishment of his people appears in eight versions in the Quran. This first version of the story identifies the abomination or "immorality"

(as) no one in all the worlds has committed before you? [81] Surely you approach
men with lust instead of women. Yes! You are a wanton people.' [82] But the only
response of his people was that they said, 'Expel them from your town, (for)
surely they are men who keep themselves clean.' [83] So We rescued him and his
family, except his wife – she was one of those who stayed behind. [84] And We
rained down on them a rain. See how the end was for the sinners!

[85] And to Midian (We sent) their brother Shuʿayb. He said, 'My people!
Serve God! You have no god other than Him. A clear sign has come to you
from your Lord. Fill up the measure and the scale, and do not shortchange the
people of their wealth, and do not foment corruption on the earth after it has
been set right. That is better for you, if you are believers. [86] And do not sit in
every path making threats, and keeping from the way of God those who believe
in Him, and desiring (to make) it crooked. Remember when you were few (in
number) and He multiplied you. And see how the end was for the fomenters of
corruption! [87] If (there is) a contingent of you who believe in that with which
I have been sent, and a contingent who do not believe, be patient until God
judges between us, (for) He is the best of judges.' [88] The assembly of those who
were arrogant among his people said, 'We shall indeed expel you, Shuʿayb, and
those who believe with you, from our town, or else you will indeed return to our
creed.' He said, 'Even if we are unwilling? [89] We would have forged a lie against
God, if we returned to your creed after God rescued us from it. It is not for us
to return to it, unless God our Lord (so) pleases. Our Lord comprehends everything in knowledge. In God we have put our trust. Our Lord, disclose the truth
between us and our people, (for) You are the best of disclosers.' [90] The assembly
of those who disbelieved among his people said, 'If indeed you follow Shuʿayb,
surely then you will be losers indeed.' [91] And then the earthquake seized them,
and morning found them leveled in their home(s). [92] Those who called Shuʿayb

---

(fāhisha) of the people as approaching "men with lust instead of women" (v. 81). Lot's
wife stays behind (v. 83).

7.85 – *And to Midian (We sent) their brother Shuʿayb.*

The preaching of Shuʿayb calls for justice in the market and safety on the roads
(vv. 85–86). A part of the people of Midian (*Madyan*) accept Shuʿayb's message, but
the leaders threaten to drive them out. An earthquake seizes the leaders.

The story of Shuʿayb repeats at 11.84–95 and 26.176–90. At 26.176 Midian is called
"the people of the Grove." Because Shuʿayb is sent to Midian, some readers have suggested that he is the biblical Jethro (Exodus 3:1; 4:18; 18:1–27). However, the Quran
does not make this identification, and otherwise Shuʿayb's story does not match that
of any known figure.

a liar – (it was) as if they had not lived in prosperity there. Those who called Shuʿayb a liar – they were the losers. [93] So he turned away from them, and said, 'My people! Certainly I have delivered to you the messages of my Lord and I offered advice to you. How shall I grieve over a disbelieving people?'

[94] We have not sent any prophet to a town, except that We seized its people with violence and hardship, so that they might humble themselves. [95] Then We exchanged good for evil, until they forgot (about it), and said, 'Hardship and prosperity have touched our fathers.' So we seized them unexpectedly, when they did not realize (it). [96] Yet if the people of the towns had believed and guarded (themselves), We would indeed have opened on them blessings from the sky and the earth. But they called (it) a lie, so We seized them for what they had earned.

[97] Do the people of the towns feel secure that Our violence will not come upon them at night, while they are sleeping? [98] Or do the people of the towns feel secure that Our violence will not come upon them in the daylight, while they jest? [99] Do they feel secure against the scheme of God? No one feels secure against the scheme of God except the people who are losers. [100] Or is it not a guide for those who inherit the earth after its (former) people that, if We (so) please, We could smite them because of their sins, and We could set a seal on their hearts so that they do not hear?

[101] Those were the towns – We recount to you some of their stories. Certainly their messengers brought them the clear signs, but they were not (able) to believe what they had called a lie before. In this way God sets a seal on the hearts of the disbelievers. [102] We did not find any covenant with most of them, but We found most of them wicked.

[103] Then, after them, We raised up Moses with Our signs to Pharaoh and his assembly, but they did evil to them. See how the end was for the fomenters

---

7.94 – *We have not sent any prophet to a town, except*

After the series of stories, starting with Noah and ending with Shuʿayb, the Quran seems to explain the lessons that the reader is to take from the stories.

Statements that characterize every prophet raise the question of the extent to which they correspond to the accounts of prophets in the Bible. See the analysis of categorical statements about prophets at 25.20 (p. 365).

7.103 – *Then, after them, We raised up Moses with Our signs to Pharaoh and his assembly*

This long story about Moses and the Children of Israel (vv. 103–71) offers more details than any of the many other Moses narratives in the Quran. This version starts out with Allah sending Moses to Pharaoh and includes many of the narrative elements

of corruption! [104] Moses said, 'Pharaoh! Surely I am a messenger from the Lord of the worlds. [105] (There is) an obligation on (me) that I do not say about God (anything) but the truth. I have brought you a clear sign from your Lord, so send forth the Sons of Israel with me.' [106] He said, 'If you have come with a sign, bring it, if you are one of the truthful.' [107] So he cast (down) his staff, and suddenly it became a real snake. [108] And he drew forth his hand, and suddenly it became white to the onlookers. [109] The assembly of the people of Pharaoh said, 'Surely this man is a skilled magician indeed. [110] He wants to expel you from your land. So what do you command?' [111] They said, 'Put him and his brother off (for a while), and send searchers into the cities [112] to bring you every skilled magician.'

[113] And the magicians came to Pharaoh, (and) said, 'Surely for us (there will be) a reward indeed, if we are the victors.' [114] He said, 'Yes, and surely you will indeed be among the ones brought near.' [115] They said, 'Moses! Are you going to cast (first), or are we to be the ones who cast?' [116] He said, 'Cast!' So when they cast, they bewitched the eyes of the people, and terrified them, and produced a great (feat of) magic. [117] And We inspired Moses: 'Cast (down) your staff!,' and suddenly it swallowed up what they were falsely contriving. [118] So the truth came to pass, and what they were doing was invalidated. [119] They were overcome there, and turned back disgraced. [120] And the magicians were cast (down) in prostration. [121] They said, 'We believe in the Lord of the worlds, [122] the Lord of Moses and Aaron.' [123] Pharaoh said, 'You have believed in Him before I gave you permission. Surely this is indeed a scheme which you have schemed in the city to expel its people from it. But soon you will know! [124] I shall indeed cut off your hands and your feet on opposite sides, (and) then I shall indeed crucify you – all (of you)!' [125] They said, 'Surely we are going to return to our Lord. [126] You are not taking vengeance on us (for any other reason) than that we believed in the signs of our Lord when they came to us. Our Lord, pour out on us patience, and take us as ones who have submitted.'

[127] The assembly of the people of Pharaoh said, 'Will you leave Moses and his people to foment corruption on the earth and to forsake you and your gods?' He said, 'We shall kill their sons and keep their women alive. Surely we shall be supreme over them!' [128] Moses said to his people, 'Seek help from God and be patient. Surely the earth (belongs) to God. He causes whomever He pleases of

---

familiar from the account of Moses in the Torah. However, three elements not known from the Old Testament are (also in Sūra 2.49–73) Allah commanding the Children of Israel to enter a town prostrate (vv. 161–62); Allah raising a mount above the people (v. 171); and the Children of Israel transgressing the Sabbath (v. 163). See the table of quranic Moses stories plotted against familiar narrative elements (p. 390).

His servants to inherit it. The outcome (belongs) to the ones who guard (themselves).' [129] They said, 'We have suffered harm before you came to us and after you came to us.' He said, 'It may be that your Lord will destroy your enemy and make you successors on the earth, and then see how you will act.'

[130] Certainly We seized the house of Pharaoh with years (of famine), and scarcity of fruits, so that they might take heed. [131] But when good came to them, they said, 'This (belongs) to us,' but if evil smote them, they attributed it to the evil omen of Moses and those with him. Is it not a fact that their evil omen was with God? But most of them did not know (it). [132] And they said, 'Whatever kind of sign you bring us, to bewitch us by means of it, we are not going to believe in you.' [133] So We sent on them the flood, and the locusts, and the lice, and the frogs, and the blood, as distinct signs. But they became arrogant and were a sinful people. [134] When the wrath fell upon them, they said, 'Moses! Call on your Lord for us by whatever covenant He has made with you. If indeed you remove this wrath from us, we shall indeed believe in you, and send forth the Sons of Israel with you.' [135] But when We removed the wrath from them, until a time they reached (later), suddenly they broke (their promise). [136] So We took vengeance on them and drowned them in the sea, because they called Our signs a lie and were oblivious of them. [137] And We caused the people who were weak to inherit the land We had blessed – the east (parts) and the west (parts) of it – and the best word of your Lord was fulfilled for the Sons of Israel, because they were patient. And We destroyed what Pharaoh and his people had been making and what they had been building.

[138] We crossed the sea with the Sons of Israel, and they came upon a people devoted to their idols. They said, 'Moses! Make for us a god like the gods they have.' He said, 'Surely you are an ignorant people. [139] Surely these – what they (are engaged) in (will be) destroyed, and what they are doing is worthless.' [140] He said, 'Shall I seek a god for you other than God, when He has favored you over the worlds?'

[141] (Remember) when We rescued you from the house of Pharaoh. They were inflicting on you the evil punishment, killing your sons and sparing your women. In that was a great test from your Lord. [142] And We appointed for Moses (a period of) thirty night(s), and We completed them with ten (more), so the meeting with his Lord was completed in forty night(s). And Moses said to his brother Aaron, 'Be my successor among my people, and set (things) right, and do not follow the way of the fomenters of corruption.' [143] And when Moses came to Our meeting, and his Lord spoke to him, he said, 'My Lord, show me (Yourself), so that I may look at You.' He said, 'You will not see Me, but look at the mountain. If it remains in its place, you will see Me.' But when his Lord

revealed His splendor to the mountain, He shattered it, and Moses fell down thunderstruck. And when he recovered, he said, 'Glory to You! I turn to You (in repentance), and I am the first of the believers.' ¹⁴⁴ He said, 'Moses! I have chosen you over the people for My messages and for My word. So take what I have given you, and be one of the thankful.'

¹⁴⁵ And We wrote for him on the Tablets an admonition of everything, and a distinct setting forth of everything: 'So hold it fast, and command your people to take the best of it. I shall show you the home of the wicked. ¹⁴⁶ I shall turn away from My signs those who are arrogant on the earth without any right. Even if they see every sign, they will not believe in it. And if they see the right way, they will not take it as a way, but if they see the way of error, they will take it as a way. That (is) because they called Our signs a lie and were oblivious of them. ¹⁴⁷ Those who have called Our signs a lie, and (also) the meeting of the Hereafter – their deeds come to nothing. Will they be repaid (for anything) except for what they have done?'

¹⁴⁸ And the people of Moses, after he (was gone), made a calf out of their ornaments – a (mere) image of it (having) a mooing sound. Did they not see that it could not speak to them or guide them to a way? (Yet) they made it and became evildoers. ¹⁴⁹ But when they stumbled and saw that they had gone astray, they said, 'If indeed our Lord does not have compassion on us, and does not forgive us, we shall indeed be among the losers.' ¹⁵⁰ When Moses returned to his people, in anger (and) grief, he said, 'Evil is what you have done as my successors, after I (left you). Have you sought to hurry the command of your Lord?' And he cast (down) the Tablets, and seized his brother's head, dragging him toward himself. He said, 'Son of my mother! Surely the people thought me weak, and nearly killed me. So do not let (my) enemies gloat over me, and do not place me among the people who are evildoers.' ¹⁵¹ He said, 'My Lord, forgive me and my brother, and cause us to enter into Your mercy, (for) You are the most compassionate of the compassionate.' ¹⁵² Surely those who made the calf – anger from their Lord will reach them, and humiliation in this present life. In this way We repay the forgers (of lies). ¹⁵³ But those who do evil deeds, (and) then turn (in repentance) after that, and believe – surely after that your Lord is indeed forgiving, compassionate.

7.144 – *Moses! I have chosen you over the people for My messages and for My word*

The Quran contains more verses related to Moses than to any other character, and one scholar has suggested that Moses is the Quran's main character. Here the Quran makes some very reverent statements about Moses, saying that Allah chose Moses above humankind.

¹⁵⁴ When the anger of Moses abated, he took (up) the Tablets, and in their inscription (there was) a guidance and mercy for those who fear their Lord. ¹⁵⁵ And Moses chose his people – seventy men – for Our meeting. So when the earthquake seized them, he said, 'My Lord, if You had pleased, You could have destroyed them before, and me (as well). Will You destroy us for what the foolish among us have done? It is only Your test by which You lead astray whomever You please and guide whomever You please. You are our ally, so forgive us and have compassion on us, (for) You are the best of forgivers. ¹⁵⁶ And prescribe for us good in this world and in the Hereafter. Surely we have turned to You.' He said, 'My punishment – I smite with it whomever I please, but My mercy comprehends everything. I shall prescribe it for the ones who guard (themselves), and give the alms, and those who – they believe in Our signs – ¹⁵⁷ those who follow the messenger, the prophet of the common people, whom they find written in their Torah and Gospel. He will command them what is right and forbid them what is wrong, and he will permit them good things and forbid them bad things, and he will deliver them of their burden and the chains that were on them. Those who believe in him, and support him and help him,

---

7.157 – *the prophet of the common people, whom they find written in their Torah and Gospel*

In the middle of the Moses story and just after a description of Moses that casts him as the ultimate example of a prophet (vv. 142–55) comes a pair of verses that shifts the focus elsewhere. The action jumps forward from the prayer of Moses (vv. 155–56) and God's answer (v. 156) to a time when people possess both Torah and Gospel (v. 157). In those scriptures, according to this verse, they find a prophet "written with them" (*maktūban ʿindahum*).

The Arabic original for the expression here translated "of the common people" is *ummī*, a term that some Muslim translators have rendered "who can neither read nor write" (e.g., Pickthall). Muslim commentators connected this verse with 29.48, which mentions reading and writing.

This prophet is a lawmaker who calls humanity to believe not only in Allah but also in "His messenger" (v. 158). The expression "the prophet," with definite article, does not occur frequently in the Quran. See the analysis of the uses of this expression at 66.9 (p. 579).

Muslim commentators identified the "*ummī* prophet" with Muhammad and said this verse means that references to Muhammad are found in the Torah and Gospel. This claim seems to have given rise to two kinds of polemic from the Muslim community: one that attempts to find passages in the Bible that Muslims then claim are references to Muhammad; and another that claims that since references to Muhammad

and follow the light which has been sent down with him, those – they are the ones who will prosper.'

¹⁵⁸ Say: 'People! Surely I am the messenger of God to you – all (of you) – (the messenger of) the One to whom (belongs) the kingdom of the heavens and the earth. (There is) no god but Him. He gives life and causes death. So believe in God and His messenger, the prophet of the common people, who believes in God and His words, (and) follow him, so that you may be (rightly) guided.'

¹⁵⁹ Among the people of Moses (there was) a community which guided by the truth, and by means of it acted fairly. ¹⁶⁰ We divided them (into) twelve tribes as communities, and We inspired Moses, when his people asked him for water: 'Strike the rock with your staff,' and (there) gushed forth from it twelve springs – each tribe knew its drinking place – and We overshadowed them (with) the cloud, and We sent down on them the manna and the quails: 'Eat from the good things which We have provided you.' They did not do Us evil, but they did themselves evil.

¹⁶¹ (Remember) when it was said to them, 'Inhabit this town and eat of it wherever you please, and say: "Ḥiṭṭa," and enter the gate in prostration. We shall forgive you your sins and increase the doers of good.' ¹⁶² But those of them who did evil exchanged a word other than that which had been spoken to them. So We sent down on them wrath from the sky, because of the evil they were doing.

¹⁶³ Ask them them about the town which was near the sea, when they transgressed in (the matter of) the sabbath, when their fish came to them on the day of their sabbath, (swimming) right to the shore. But on the day when they did not observe the sabbath, they did not come to them. In this way We were testing them because they were acting wickedly. ¹⁶⁴ (Remember) when a (certain) community of them said, 'Why do you admonish a people whom God is going to destroy or punish (with) a harsh punishment?' They said, '(As) an excuse to your Lord, and so that they might guard (themselves).' ¹⁶⁵ So when they forgot what they were reminded of, We rescued those who had been forbidding evil,

---

cannot be found in the Bible, Jews and Christians must have changed or erased the references. See the analysis of the Quran's "Gospel" verses at 57.27 (p. 548).

Some scholars believe verses 157–58 to be an insertion. The Moses story flows quite smoothly from verse 103 to verse 156, then picks up at verse 159 until verse 171. The descriptions of this *ummī* prophet in verse 157–58 seem out of place in Sūra 7, where the messenger is otherwise only a "warner" (v. 188) like messengers from Noah to Shu'ayb. Understood from a different angle, however, if the Quran's intention is to recommend its own messenger, it would make sense to place these verses directly after the very favorable portrait of Moses. See "Moses in the Quran" (p. 388).

and We seized the evildoers with a violent punishment because they were acting wickedly. ¹⁶⁶ So when they disdained what they had been forbidden from,
We said to them, 'Become apes, skulking away!'

¹⁶⁷ (Remember) when your Lord proclaimed (that) He would indeed raise
up against them – until the Day of Resurrection – those who would inflict
them (with) evil punishment. Surely your Lord is indeed quick in retribution,
yet surely He is indeed forgiving, compassionate.

¹⁶⁸ We divided them (into) communities on the earth, some of them righteous and some of them other than that, and We tested them with good things
and bad, so that they might return. ¹⁶⁹ And after them came successors (who)
inherited the Book, taking (the fleeting) goods of this lower (world) and saying, 'It will be forgiven us.' And if there comes to them goods like that (again),
they will take them. Has the covenant of the Book not been taken upon them,
(namely) that they should not say about God (anything) but the truth? And
have they (not) studied what is in it? The Home of the Hereafter is better for
the ones who guard (themselves). Will you not understand? ¹⁷⁰ Those who hold
fast the Book and observe the prayer – surely We do not let the reward of those
who set (things) right go to waste.

¹⁷¹ (Remember) when We shook the mountain above them, as if it were a
canopy, and they thought it was going to fall on them: 'Hold fast what We have
given you, and remember what is in it, so that you may guard (yourselves).'

¹⁷² (Remember) when your Lord took from the sons of Adam – from their
loins – their descendants, and made them bear witness about themselves: 'Am
I not your Lord?' They said, 'Yes indeed! We bear witness.' (We did that) so
that you would not say on the Day of Resurrection, 'Surely we were oblivious of
this,' ¹⁷³ or say, 'Our fathers were idolaters before (us), and we are descendants
after them. Will You destroy us for what the perpetrators of falsehood did?'
¹⁷⁴ In this way We make the signs distinct, so that they will return.

¹⁷⁵ Recite to them the story of the one to whom We gave Our signs, but he
passed them by, and Satan followed him, and he became one of those who are
in error. ¹⁷⁶ If We had (so) pleased, We would indeed have raised him by it, but
he clung to the earth and followed his (vain) desire. So his parable is like the
parable of the dog: If you attack it, it lolls its tongue out, or if you leave it alone,
it (still) lolls its tongue out. That is the parable of the people who called Our
signs a lie. So recount the account, that they may reflect.

¹⁷⁷ Evil is the parable of the people who called Our signs a lie, but (who
only) did themselves evil. ¹⁷⁸ Whoever God guides is the (rightly) guided one,
and whoever He leads astray, those – they are the losers. ¹⁷⁹ Certainly We have
created for Gehenna many of the jinn and humans: they have hearts, but they

do not understand with them; they have eyes, but they do not see with them; they have ears, but they do not hear with them. Those (people) are like cattle – No! They are (even) farther astray! Those – they are the oblivious.

[180] To God (belong) the best names. So call on Him with them, and leave those who pervert His names. They will be repaid for what they have done.

[181] Among those whom We have created is a community which guides by the truth and by means of it acts fairly. [182] But those who call Our signs a lie – We shall lead them on step by step without their realizing it, [183] and I shall spare them – surely My plan is strong. [184] Do they not reflect? Their companion is not possessed. He is only a clear warner. [185] Do they not look into the kingdom of the heavens and the earth, and whatever things God has created, and that it may be that their time has already drawn near? So in what (kind of) proclamation will they believe after this? [186] Whoever God leads astray has no guide. He leaves them in their insolent transgression, wandering blindly.

[187] They ask you about the Hour: 'When is its arrival?' Say: 'Knowledge of it is only with my Lord. No (one) will reveal it at its (appointed) time but He. It is heavy in the heavens and the earth, (but) it will only come upon you unexpectedly.' They ask you as if you are well informed about it. Say: 'Knowledge of it is only with God, but most of the people do not know (it).' [188] Say: 'I have no power to (cause) myself benefit or harm, except for whatever God pleases. If I had knowledge of the unseen, I would indeed have acquired much good, and evil would not have touched me. I am only a warner and bringer of good news to a people who believe.'

[189] He (it is) who created you from one person, and made from him his spouse, so that he might dwell with her. And when he covered her, she bore a light burden and passed on with it (unnoticed). But when she became heavy, they both called on God their Lord, 'If indeed You give us a righteous (son), we shall indeed be among the thankful.' [190] But when He gave them a righteous

---

7.187 – *They ask you about the Hour: "When is its arrival?"*

Verses about "the Hour" usually seem to refer to the Day of Resurrection, but in this case "they" may be asking the messenger about the arrival of judgment on "disbelievers" in this world on the pattern of the punishment narratives in this sūra. References to the "Day" or the "Hour" become especially frequent in Sūras 11–47. See "Eschatology in the Quran" (p. 604).

7.188 – *I am only a warner and bringer of good news to a people who believe*

Here the messenger says, "I am only a warner." In many sūras of the Quran, the messenger is a preacher, not a ruler, lawgiver, or warrior. Notice how the identity of the messenger changes in the next two sūras – Sūras 8 and 9.

(son), they set up associates for Him in (return for) what He had given them. Yet God is exalted above what they associate. [191] Do they associate (with Him) what does not create anything, since they are (themselves) created? [192] They cannot (give) them any help, nor can they (even) help themselves. [193] If you call them to the guidance, they will not follow you. (It is) the same for you whether you call them or you remain silent.

[194] Surely those you call on instead of God are servants like you. So call on them and let them respond to you, if you are truthful. [195] Do they have feet with which they walk, or do they have hands with which they grasp, or do they have eyes with which they see, or do they have ears with which they hear? Say: 'Call on your associates, (and) then plot against me and do not spare me! [196] Surely my ally is God, who has sent down the Book. He takes the righteous as allies. [197] Those you call on instead of Him cannot help you, nor can they (even) help themselves.' [198] If you call them to the guidance, they do not hear. You see them looking at you, but they do not see.

[199] Take the excess, and command what is right, and turn away from the ignorant. [200] If any provocation from Satan provokes you, take refuge with God. Surely He is hearing, knowing. [201] Surely the ones who guard (themselves), when a circler from Satan touches them, remember, and suddenly they see (clearly). [202] But their brothers increase them in error, (and) then they do not stop.

[203] When you do not bring them a sign, they say, 'If only you would choose (to do) it.' Say: 'I only follow what I am inspired (with) from my Lord. This is evidence from your Lord, and a guidance and mercy for a people who believe.' [204] When the Qur'ān is recited, listen to it and remain silent, so that you may receive compassion.

[205] Remember your Lord within yourself, in humility and in fear, and without loud words, in the mornings and the evenings. Do not be one of the oblivious. [206] Surely those who are with your Lord are not too proud to serve Him. They glorify Him and prostrate themselves before Him.

THE SPOILS
AL-ANFĀL

8

This sūra signals immediately that it is connected with conflict: "The spoils (belong) to Allah and the messenger." Though subsequent verses do not provide a context for the action, the sūra explicitly mentions battle (*qitāl*; v. 16), war (*harb*; v. 57), fighting (*qātala*; v. 39, 64), killing (*qatala*; v. 17, 30), holding captives (vv. 67, 70), military advance (*zahf*, v. 15), and other vocabulary of armed engagement.

The sūra provides instruction and encouragement to the "believers" for their encounter with the enemy. Both Allah and "the messenger" are to be obeyed in the heat of battle. Not only are the unbelievers to be attacked, but the believers themselves are repeatedly threatened in order to motivate them to advance to the front lines.

A number of verses in this sūra offer a strong theological interpretation of the conflict. Here Allah promises, plans, and guides the battle, sends his angels to back the believers, and himself kills the enemy (v. 17). Though the sūra names no persons or places, tradition associates it with a famous military engagement in the Muslim story of Islamic origins – the "battle of Badr" (*Sīra*, 321–27, *Raids*, 66–70).

In the Name of God, the Merciful, the Compassionate

[1] They ask you about the spoils. Say: 'The spoils (belong) to God and the messenger. So guard (yourselves) against God, and set right what is between you. Obey God and His messenger, if you are believers.'

8.1 – *The spoils (belong) to God and the messenger*

The abrupt change of content and tone from Sūra 7 to Sūra 8 is striking. Here suddenly the Quran tells about spoils of battle, or war loot (*anfāl*, the sūra's title). This kind of change is a characteristic of the Quran that has raised questions for many readers. On the face of it, these are two different kinds of writing.

From the beginning of Sūra 8, the messenger has a very different profile from the messenger described in the preceding two sūras (6 and 7). In Sūra 7, the messenger is

[2] Only those are believers who, when God is mentioned, their hearts become afraid, and when His signs are recited to them, it increases them in belief. They put their trust in their Lord. [3] Those who observe the prayer, and contribute from what We have provided them, [4] those – they are the true believers. For them (there are) ranks (of honor) with their Lord, and forgiveness and generous provision.

[5] – As your Lord brought you forth from your house with the truth, when a group of the believers were indeed unwilling, [6] disputing with you about the truth after it had become clear, as if they were being driven to death with their eyes wide open.

"only a warner" (7:188). His task there is to recite the signs of Allah and to urge people to respond appropriately to Allah.

Muslim scholars have accounted for the differences between sūras 6 and 7 on the one hand, and sūras 8 and 9 on the other, by asserting that they belong to different periods in the life of Muhammad. They claim that the messenger of Islam recited sūras 6 and 7 while in Mecca, then recited sūras 8 and 9 later in Medina, according to the traditional story. The Quran itself does not indicate the times or places of these recitations. Some scholars suggest that the chronology was rather imposed from outside of the Quran – especially from Muslim stories about Islamic origins written in the second and third centuries of Islam. See "Muslim Story of Islamic Origins" (p. 16).

Islamic Studies scholar David Marshall makes the case that Sūra 8 represents a transition in the Quran from the understanding that Allah alone punishes unbelievers to the idea that Allah uses "believers" to punish unbelievers by defeating them militarily in this world. See "Divine Punishment of Unbelievers in This World" (p. 507).

8.1 – *Obey Allah and His messenger, if you are believers*

The command to obey both Allah and "His messenger" appears more frequently in Sūra 8 than in any other sūra (also vv. 20, 46; cf. v. 24). Sūra 8 also associates the messenger with Allah for spoils of war (vv. 1, 41), in opposition (v. 13), and in betrayal (v. 27), compared with only one occurrence of such pairing in the preceding two sūras (7.158).

These commands to obey both Allah and his messenger became very important in the writings of the influential Muslim jurist al-Shāfiʿī (d. 820), who insisted that they gave divine authority to the sayings ("hadith") attributed to Muhammad. See the summary and analysis of these commands at 64.12 (p. 574).

8.5 – *As your Lord brought you forth from your house with the truth*

These words, addressed to the messenger, begin an extended passage that brings to mind a military battle (*qitāl*, v. 16). "A group of the believers" are evidently unwilling to participate (vv. 5–6).

Muslim tradition has connected the remainder of the sūra with "the battle of Badr."

⁷ (Remember) when God was promising you that one of the two contingents would be yours, and you were wanting the unarmed one to be yours, but God wished to verify the truth by His words, and to cut off the last remnant of the disbelievers, ⁸ so that He might verify the truth and falsify the false, even though the sinners disliked (it). ⁹ (Remember) when you were calling on your Lord for help, and He responded to you: 'I am going to increase you with a thousand angels following behind.' ¹⁰ God did it only as good news, and that your hearts might be satisfied by it. Help (comes) only from God. Surely God is mighty, wise.

¹¹ (Remember) when He covered you with slumber as a security from Him, and sent down on you water from the sky, so that He might purify you by means of it, and take away from you the abomination of Satan, and that he might strengthen your hearts and make firm (your) feet by means of it. ¹² When your Lord inspired the angels: 'I am with you, so make firm those who believe. I shall cast dread into the hearts of those who disbelieve. So strike above (their) necks, and strike (off) all their fingers!' ¹³ That was because they broke with God and His messenger, and whoever breaks with God and His messenger – surely God is harsh in retribution. ¹⁴ 'That is for you! So taste it! And (know) that the punishment of the Fire is for the disbelievers.'

¹⁵ You who believe! When you encounter those who disbelieve advancing (for battle), do not turn (your) backs to them. ¹⁶ Whoever turns his back to them on that day – unless turning aside to fight or to join (another) cohort – he

---

8.9 – *I am going to increase you with a thousand angels*

This passage (vv. 9–19) seems to give the battle a theological interpretation. The Quran promises Allah's presence in the battle and the help of a thousand angels (v. 9) to fight the "disbelievers." Allah commands the angels to "strike above (their) necks, and strike (off) all their fingers" (v. 12). In this way (as the Quran tells the "believers"), "You did not kill them, but Allah killed them" (v. 17). The reason for the killing, according to verse 13, is that the disbelievers "broke with Allah and His messenger."

8.12 – *I shall cast dread into the hearts of those who disbelieve*

The Quran describes Allah as terrorizing the enemy. He casts terror or "dread" (*ruʻb*) into hearts. The expression repeats at 3.151; 33.26; and 59.2. Here the reason for this terrorizing is that those who disbelieve "broke with Allah and His messenger" (v. 13). Later in this sūra the Quran commands "believers" themselves to terrify (*arhaba*) their enemies (v. 60). See the discussion of terror and terrorizing at 59.2 (p. 554).

8.13 – *whoever breaks with Allah and His messenger – surely Allah is harsh in retribution*

has incurred the anger of God. His refuge will be Gehenna – and it is an evil destination!

¹⁷ You did not kill them, but God killed them, and you did not throw when you threw, but God threw, and (He did that) in order to test the believers (with) a good test from Himself. Surely God is hearing, knowing. ¹⁸ That is for you! (Know) that God weakens the plot of the disbelievers. ¹⁹ If you ask for a victory, the victory has already come to you. And if you stop, it will be better for you. But if you return, We shall return (too), and your cohort will be of no use to you, even if it should be numerous. (Know) that God is with the believers.

²⁰ You who believe! Obey God and His messenger, and do not turn away from him when you hear (him). ²¹ Do not be like those who say, 'We hear,' when they do not hear. ²² Surely the worst of creatures in the sight of God are the deaf (and) the speechless – those which do not understand. ²³ If God had known any good in them, He would indeed have made them hear. But (even) if He had made them hear, they would indeed have turned away in aversion.

²⁴ You who believe! Respond to God and to the messenger, when he calls you to what gives you life. Know that God stands between a person and his (own) heart, and that to Him you will be gathered. ²⁵ Guard (yourselves) against trouble, which will indeed smite not just the evildoers among you, and know that God is harsh in retribution.

²⁶ Remember when you were few (and) weak on the earth, (and) you feared that the people might snatch you away, and He gave you refuge, and supported you with His help, and provided you with good things, so that you might be thankful. ²⁷ You who believe! Do not betray God and the messenger, and do not betray your pledges when you know (better). ²⁸ Know that your wealth and your children are a test, and that God – with Him (there is) a great reward. ²⁹ You who believe! If you guard (yourselves) against God, He will grant deliverance for you, and absolve you of your evil deeds, and forgive you. God is full of great favor.

In the midst of the battle scene, the Quran makes a number of theological points. This particular characterization of Allah, that he is "harsh," or terrible, "in retribution" (*shadīdu 'l-ʿiqāb*), appears four times in the sūra (vv. 13, 25, 48, 52).

8.17 – *You did not kill them, but God killed them*

This sūra seems to synchronize the actions of the messenger and the "believers" with the actions of Allah. Here the action is killing people. In the heat of battle, how clearly can warriors discern whether their actions are godly or carnal? Where does the Quran deal with the temptation to justify human actions by claiming they are God's?

[30] (Remember) when those who disbelieved were scheming against you, to confine you, or kill you, or expel you. They were scheming but God was scheming (too), and God is the best of schemers. [31] When Our signs are recited to them, they say, 'We have already heard (this). If we wished, we could indeed say (something) like this. This is nothing but old tales.' [32] And (remember) when they said, 'God! If this is the truth from You, rain down on us stones from the sky or bring us a painful punishment.' [33] But God was not one to punish them while you were among them, and God was not one to punish them while they were asking for forgiveness. [34] But what (excuse) have they (now) that God should not punish them, when they are keeping (people) from (going to) the Sacred Mosque, and they are not its (true) allies? Its only allies are the ones who guard (themselves), but most of them do not know (it). [35] Their prayer at the House is nothing but whistling and clapping of hands. So taste the punishment for what you disbelieve!

[36] Surely those who disbelieve spend their wealth to keep (people) from the way of God – and they will (continue to) spend it. Then it will be a (cause of) regret for them, (and) then they will be overcome. Those who disbelieve will be gathered into Gehenna, [37] so that God may separate the bad from the good, and place the bad one on top of the other, and so pile them all up, and place them in Gehenna. Those – they are the losers. [38] Say to those who disbelieve (that) if they stop, whatever is already past will be forgiven them, but if they return, the customary way of those of old has already passed away. [39] Fight them until (there) is no persecution and the religion – all of it – (belongs) to God. If they

---

8.30 – *They were scheming but God was scheming (too), and God is the best of schemers.*

The Arabic verb translated "scheme," *makara*, means to deceive or dupe. The same verb is used in 3.54 and applied by Muslim commentators to 3.55 and the question of 'Īsā's death.

8.31 – *If we wished, we could indeed say (something) like this*

In response to the recitations of the messenger, the "disbelievers" (v. 31) seem to say they could speak the same words because they are familiar with the stories.

8.34 – *But what (excuse) have they (now) that God should not punish them*

Those who prevent access to the sacred mosque (*al-masjid al-ḥarām*) have no way of escape from Allah's punishment.

8.39 – *Fight them until (there) is no persecution and the religion – all of it – (belongs) to God*

This verse commands the reader or listener to fight, using the Arabic verb *qātala*. It follows the same wording as 2.193 except for the additional word here translated

stop – surely God sees what they do. [40] If they turn away, know that God is your Protector. Excellent is the Protector, and excellent is the Helper!

[41] Know that whatever spoils you take, a fifth of it (belongs) to God and to the messenger, and to family, and the orphans, and the poor, and the traveler, if you believe in God and what We sent down on Our servant on the Day of Deliverance, the day the two forces met. God is powerful over everything.

[42] (Remember) when you were on the nearer side, and they on the farther side, and the caravan was below you. (Even) if you had set a time (to fight), you would indeed have failed to keep the appointment. But (the battle took place) so that God might decide the affair – it was done! – (and it took place) so that those who perished might perish on (the basis of) a clear sign, and that those who lived might live on (the basis of) a clear sign. Surely God is indeed hearing, knowing.

[43] (Remember) when God showed them to you in your dream as (only) a few, and if had He shown them as many, you would indeed have lost courage, and indeed argued about the matter. But God kept (you) safe. Surely He knows what is in the hearts. [44] (Remember) when He showed them to you – when you met – as few in your eyes, and He made you (appear as) few in their eyes. (This took place) so that God might decide the affair – it was done! To God all affairs are returned.

[45] You who believe! When you encounter a (hostile) cohort, stand firm, and remember God often, so that you may prosper. [46] Obey God and His messenger, and do not argue, so that you lose courage and your strength fails. And be patient. Surely God is with the patient. [47] Do not be like those who went forth from their homes boastfully, and to show off to the people, and to keep (them) from the way of God. God encompasses what they do.

[48] (Remember) when Satan made their deeds appear enticing to them, and said, '(There is) no one among the people to defeat you today. Surely I am your

---

"all." The enemy seems to be "those who disbelieve" mentioned in the preceding verses (36–38). Similarly, the reason for fighting seems to be that those who "disbelieve" keep people from the way of Allah (v. 36). Fighting is to continue until there is no more "persecution" (*fitna*) and until all of the religion is Allah's. See "Fighting and Killing in the Quran" (p. 220).

8.42 – *and the caravan was below you*

Muslim interpretations of this verse have picked up on the word *caravan* to match it to the traditional story of a raid on a Meccan caravan by Muslims from Medina.

8.48 – *when Satan made their deeds appear enticing to them, and said*

In addition to the involvement of Allah and angels in the battle on behalf of the "believers," Satan is portrayed as being on the side of the enemy "disbelievers."

neighbor.' But when the two cohorts saw each other, he turned on his heels, and said, 'Surely I am free of you, (for) surely I see what you do not see. Surely I fear God, (for) God is harsh in retribution.'

⁴⁹ (Remember) when the hypocrites and those in whose hearts is a sickness were saying: 'Their religion has deceived these (people).' But whoever puts his trust in God – surely God is mighty, wise. ⁵⁰ If (only) you could see when the angels take those who have disbelieved, striking their faces and their backs, and (saying): 'Taste the punishment of the burning (Fire)! ⁵¹ That is for what your (own) hands have sent forward, and (know) that God is not an evildoer to (His) servants.' ⁵² (It will be) like the case of the house of Pharaoh, and those who were before them: they disbelieved in the signs of God, so God seized them for their sins. Surely God is strong, harsh in retribution. ⁵³ That is because God is not one to change the blessing with which He has blessed a people, until they change what is within themselves. (Know) that God is hearing, knowing. ⁵⁴ Like the case of the house of Pharaoh, and those who were before them: they called the signs of their Lord a lie, so We destroyed them for their sins, and We drowned the house of Pharaoh. All were evildoers.

⁵⁵ Surely the worst of creatures in the sight of God are those who disbelieve – and they will not believe – ⁵⁶ those of them with whom you have made a treaty, (and) then they break their treaty every time, and they do not guard (themselves). ⁵⁷ If you come upon them in war, scatter with them those who are behind them, so that they may take heed. ⁵⁸ If you fear treachery from a people, toss (the treaty) back at them likewise. Surely God does not love the treacherous. ⁵⁹ Do not let those who disbelieve think they have gotten away. Surely they

---

8.50 – *If (only) you could see when the angels take those who have disbelieved*

In this case, the angels seem to be tormenting the "disbelievers" who come to them after death (cf. vv. 9, 12).

8.52 – *like the case of the house of Pharaoh, and those who were before them*

The Quran very briefly refers to the story of Pharaoh's people (vv. 52–54), apparently to suggest that the enemies in battle have the same "disbelief" and will also be destroyed "for their sins." A second suggestion seems to be that the signs (*āyāt*) of Allah through the Quran's messenger are comparable to the signs through Moses.

8.57 – *If you come upon them in war*

This verse makes explicit that the context of the recitation is "war" (*ḥarb*) and refers to scattering the enemy, perhaps by frightening them (see also v. 12, 60).

8.58 – *Surely God does not love the treacherous*

The Quran contains twenty-four expressions for the kinds of people whom Allah does not love. See "The Language of Love in the Quran" (p. 560).

will not escape. [60] Prepare for them whatever force and cavalry you can, to terrify by this means the enemy of God and your enemy, and others besides them. You do not know them, but God knows them. Whatever you contribute in the way of God will be repaid to you in full, and you will not be done evil. [61] If they incline toward peace, you incline toward it (as well). Put (your) trust in God. Surely He is the Hearing, the Knowing. [62] But if they intend to deceive you – surely God is enough for you. He (it is) who supported you with His help and with the believers, [63] and He has brought their hearts together. If you had spent what is on the earth – all (of it) – you could not have brought their hearts together. But God has brought their hearts together. Surely He is mighty, wise.

[64] Prophet! God is enough for you, and whoever follows you of the believers. [65] Prophet! Urge on the believers to the fighting. If (there) are twenty of you (who are) patient, they will overcome two hundred, and if (there) are a hundred of you, they will overcome a thousand of those who disbelieve, because they are a people without understanding. [66] Now God has lightened (the task) for you, and He knows that (there is) weakness in you. If (there) are a hundred of you (who are) patient, they will overcome two hundred, and if (there) are a

---

8.60 – *Prepare for them whatever force and cavalry you can, to terrify by this means the enemy of God and your enemy*

The concept of terrorizing the enemy is clearly indicated here through the use of the Arabic verb *arhaba*, when earlier in the sūra it was Allah who cast terror (*ruʿb*) into the hearts of the "disbelievers" (v. 12). The Quran also portrays the enemy of the "believers" as Allah's enemy. Both statements serve to further blur the line between Allah's punishments and the fighting of humans. See a discussion of terror and terrorizing at 59.2 (p. 554).

8.61 – *If they incline toward peace, you incline toward it (as well)*

In this battle, if the enemy is willing to agree to terms, the messenger must also "incline toward peace." Elsewhere, the Quran commands the "believers" that if the battle is going their way, they must not "grow weak and call for peace" (47.35).

8.65 – *Prophet! Urge on the believers to the fighting*

Direct addresses to "the prophet" are not very frequent in the Quran, and most of the occurrences come in this sūra (vv. 64, 65, 70) and in Sūras 33 and 66. Known as the "vocative," direct address here instructs the prophet in the conduct of battle (*qitāl*, v. 65) and the treatment of captives (v. 70). See the analysis of the contexts in which "Prophet!" occurs at 66.1 (p. 577).

Notice that the exhortation to "believers" – that one of them can overcome ten of "those who disbelieve" – changes to a ratio of 1:2 in the following verse. See "Fighting and Killing in the Quran" (p. 220).

thousand of you, they will overcome two thousand by the permission of God. God is with the patient.

[67] It is not for a prophet to have captives, until he has subdued (the enemy) on the earth. You desire (the fleeting) goods of this world, but God desires the Hereafter. God is mighty, wise. [68] Were it not for a preceding Book from God, a great punishment would indeed have touched you for what you took. [69] So eat from what you have taken as spoils as permitted (and) good, and guard (yourselves) against God. Surely God is forgiving, compassionate.

[70] Prophet! Say to the captives in your hands: 'If God knows of any good in your hearts, He will give you (something) better than what has been taken from you, and He will forgive you. Surely God is forgiving, compassionate.' [71] But if they intend to betray you, they have already betrayed God before (that). So He has given (you) power over them. God is knowing, wise.

[72] Surely those who have believed and emigrated, and struggled with their wealth and their lives in the way of God, and those who have given refuge and help, those – they are allies of each other. But those who have believed and not emigrated – their protection is not (an obligation) on you at all, until they emigrate. Yet if they seek your help in the (matter of) religion, (their) help is

---

8.67 – *It is not for a prophet to have captives, until he has subdued (the enemy) on the earth*

Instead of the mild "subdued," a number of translators render the difficult verb *athkhana* as "made slaughter" (Pickthall, Arberry, Mohsin Khan) or even "inflicted a massacre" (Sahih International). The verb appears again at 47.4.

Statements that assert certain behaviors of "every prophet" raise the question of the extent to which they correspond to the accounts of prophets in the Bible. See an analysis of this question at 25.20 (p. 365).

8.71 – *So He has given (you) power over them*

About the treatment of captives taken in the battle, the Quran tells the prophet (see v. 70) that Allah has given him power over them. This message seems to contradict many other parts of the Quran where the messenger has no permission or power to hurt others.

8.72 – *Surely those who have believed and emigrated, and struggled with their wealth and their lives in the way of God*

The closing verses of this sūra provide a good opportunity to enquire into the meaning of *jihad* in the Quran. See also "Jihad in the Quran" (p. 368).

The Arabic verb at the root of the term, *jāhada*, appears in verses 72, 74, and 75. The verb is here translated "struggled," but what kind of struggle is meant? The context of this sūra is about fighting (vv. 39, 65), taking captives (v. 70), and dividing

(an obligation) on you, unless (it be) against a people with whom you have a treaty. God sees what you do.

[73] Those who disbelieve are allies of each other. Unless you do this, (there) will be trouble on the earth and great corruption. [74] But those who have believed, and emigrated, and struggled in the way of God, and those who have given refuge and help, those – they are the true believers. For them (there is) forgiveness and generous provision. [75] But those who have believed after that, and emigrated, and struggled (along) with you, they (too) belong to you. Yet those related by blood are closer to one another in the Book of God. Surely God has knowledge of everything.

---

up the spoils (vv. 1, 41, 69). In such a context, it is reasonable to understand the "struggling" as physical, military, and armed.

The classical Muslim commentator al-Ṭabarī (d. 923) consistently interpreted *jihād* and *jāhada* to mean fighting, even when the context is not as suggestive as in the eighth sūra.

REPENTANCE
AL-TAWBA

9

Sūra 9 is unique in being the only sūra among the Quran's 114 that lacks the *basmala* ("In the name of God, the merciful, the compassionate"). Muslim tradition suggested that the reason for the missing *basmala* was that the contents of the sūra are also unique.

For example, Sūra 9 associates "the messenger" with Allah more frequently than any other sūra. "Allah and His messenger" are joined together for a truly remarkable variety of actions and reactions: renunciation of idolaters (vv. 1, 3), proclaiming (v. 3), making treaties (v. 7), being taken as allies (v. 16), being "dearer" (v. 24), forbidding (v. 29), being believed in or disbelieved in (vv. 54, 80, 84), giving (v. 59), being pleased (v. 62), being opposed or obeyed (vv. 63, 71), being mocked (v. 65), enriching (v. 74), being lied to (v. 90), being shown sincerity (v. 91), seeing the conduct of people (vv. 94, 105), and being fought against (v. 107).

Sūra 9 also contains more commands to fight and kill than any other sūra. The commands are peppered throughout the first part of the sūra. See "Fighting and Killing in the Quran" (p. 220).

Amid these commands comes one of the strongest denials of the deity of the Messiah in the entire Quran. This theological denial seems to take on a dangerous military edge from the surrounding emphasis on fighting and conquest.

According to the Muslim story of Islamic origins, the first part of this sūra was initially recited after the Muslim conquest of Mecca in the eighth year after the Muslims' migration to Medina. Verses 38–99, however, are associated with a military campaign to Tabūk (*Raids*, 519–27; cf. *Sīra* 602–9).

A command to fight the disbelievers near the end of the sūra further instructs the "believers" to "let them find sternness in you" (v. 123). According to one Muslim tradition, ʿAlī ibn Abī Ṭālib suggested that it was for this harshness toward non-Muslims that Sūra 9 gained no *basmala*.

¹ A renunciation from God and His messenger to those of the idolaters with whom you have made a treaty: ² 'Move about (freely) on the earth for four months, and know that you cannot escape God, and that God will disgrace the disbelievers.'

³ And a proclamation from God and His messenger to the people on the day of the great pilgrimage: 'God renounces the idolaters, and (so does) His messenger. If you turn (in repentance), it will be better for you, but if you turn away, know that you cannot escape God.'

Give those who disbelieve news of a painful punishment, ⁴ except those of the idolaters with whom you have made a treaty, (and who) since then have not failed you in anything and have not supported anyone against you. Fulfill their treaty with them until their term. Surely God loves the ones who guard (themselves).

⁵ Then, when the sacred months have passed, kill the idolaters wherever you find them, and seize them, and besiege them, and sit (in wait) for them at every place of ambush. If they turn (in repentance), and observe the prayer and give

---

9.1 – *A renunciation from God and His messenger*

Throughout this sūra, the Quran pairs Allah with "His messenger" in a variety of actions and reactions. In this first part of the sūra, for example, Allah and the messenger renounce the idolaters (vv. 1, 3), proclaim (v. 3), and make treaties together (v. 7).

9.4 – *Surely God loves the ones who guard (themselves)*

The Quran contains twenty-two statements about the kinds of people whom Allah loves. In this verse the objects of Allah's love are the godfearing or "ones who guard" (also v. 7). See "The Language of Love in the Quran" (p. 560).

9.5 – *kill the idolaters wherever you find them*

The ninth sūra contains more commands to fight and kill than any other sūra of the Quran. Because these commands have much to do with the Muslim treatment of non-Muslims, both in the Quran and in history up to the present, these commands are carefully explained.

Commands to fight and kill often come with conditions as to reason and purpose, the objects of the fighting, the scope of hostilities, and so on. The command to kill (*qatala*) in verse 5 comes with three qualifications: (1) after the "sacred months" have passed, (2) kill the *mushrikūn*, and (3) if the objects of war choose to observe the Muslim ritual practices, let them go.

The question of the "sacred months" is taken up below at verse 36. Droge's translation of "idolaters" for the Arabic *mushrikūn* misses an important possibility in the meaning. The word actually means people who "associate" anything or anyone with Allah. In the minds of many Muslims, Christians "associate" a merely human Messiah

the alms, let them go their way. Surely God is forgiving, compassionate. [6] If one of the idolaters seeks your protection, grant him protection until he hears the word of God. Then convey him to his place of safety – that is because they are a people who have no knowledge.

[7] How can the idolaters have a treaty with God and with His messenger, except those with whom you have made a treaty at the Sacred Mosque? So long as they go straight with you, go straight with them. Surely God loves the ones who guard (themselves). [8] How (can there be a treaty with them)? If they were to prevail over you, they would not respect any bond or agreement with you. They please you with their mouths, but their hearts refuse (you). Most of them are wicked. [9] They have sold the signs of God for a small price, and kept (people) from His way. Surely evil is what they have done. [10] They do not respect any bond or agreement with a believer. Those – they are the transgressors. [11] If they turn (in repentance), and observe the prayer and give the alms, (they are) your brothers in the religion. We make the signs distinct for a people who know. [12] But if they break their oaths, after their treaty, and vilify your religion, fight the leaders of disbelief – surely they have no (binding) oaths – so that they stop (fighting).

[13] Will you not fight (against) a people who have broken their oaths, and are determined to expel the messenger, and started (to attack) you the first time?

---

with Allah (see v. 31, 33). See a summary of verses that accuse the People of the Book of "associating" at 61.9 (p. 565).

This verse says that those who "turn (in repentance), and observe the prayer and give the alms" may be allowed to go their way. In this sūra, the prayers (*ṣalāh*) and the alms (*zakāh*) seem to represent the Muslim ritual practices (also v. 18, 71; cf. v. 54). If so, this verse means that the *mushrikūn* may be spared if they "submit" and become Muslims. Support for this understanding comes in verse 11: repenting, observing the prayer, and giving alms makes people "brothers in the religion" to the "believers."

Muslim scholars have traditionally called 9.5 the "sword verse." In setting out Islamic Law, this verse became important in defining the relationship of Muslims to non-Muslims. For some Muslim scholars, among them Ibn Salama (d. 1020) and Ibn al-'Atā'iqī (d. 1308), 9.5 had the distinction of abrogating more quranic verses than any other – a total of 124 verses. See the discussion of verses related to abrogation at 16.101 (p. 282) and "Fighting and Killing in the Quran" (p. 220).

9.12 – *fight the leaders of disbelief . . . so that they stop (fighting)*

This verse commands the reader or listener to fight, using the Arabic verb *qātala*. The enemies to be fought are the "leaders of disbelief," and the purpose of the fighting is to stop the enemy from defaming the religion of the Muslims.

Are you afraid of them? God – (it is more) right that you should fear Him, if you are believers. [14] Fight them! God will punish them by your hands, and disgrace them, and help you against them, and heal the hearts of a people who believe, [15] and take away (all) rage from their hearts. God turns (in forgiveness) to whomever He pleases. God is knowing, wise.

[16] Or did you think that you would be left (in peace), when God did not (yet) know those of you who have struggled, and have not taken any ally other than God and His messenger and the believers? God is aware of what you do. [17] It is not for the idolaters to inhabit the mosques of God, (while) bearing witness against themselves of disbelief. Those – their deeds have come to nothing, and in the Fire they will remain. [18] Only he will inhabit the mosques of God who believes in God and the Last Day, and observes the prayer and gives the alms, and does not fear (anyone) but God. It may be that those – they will be among the (rightly) guided ones.

[19] Do you make the giving of water to the pilgrims and the inhabiting of the Sacred Mosque like the one who believes in God and the Last Day and struggles in the way of God? They are not equal with God, and God does not guide the people who are evildoers. [20] Those who have believed, and emigrated, and struggled in the way of God with their wealth and their lives are higher in rank with God. Those – they are the triumphant. [21] Their Lord gives them good news of mercy from Himself, and approval, and (there are) Gardens for them in which (there is) lasting bliss, [22] there to remain forever. Surely God – with Him is a great reward.

[23] You who believe! Do not take your fathers and your brothers as allies, if they prefer disbelief over belief. Whoever among you takes them as allies, those – they are the evildoers. [24] Say: 'If your fathers, and your sons, and your brothers, and your wives, and your clan, and wealth you have acquired,

---

9.14 – *Fight them! God will punish them by your hands, and disgrace them*

Here the "believers" are addressed (v. 13), and the objects of the fighting are people who have broken their oaths and – according to verse 13 – intended to expel the messenger. The purpose of the fighting here is so that the hearts of the believers will be healed and their rage assuaged (v. 15).

Among the Quran's twelve commands to fight, this particular command is unique in specifying that Allah will punish the enemy by the physical hands of the "believers." Some scholars have suggested that this verse represents a shift from an understanding that Allah will himself punish sinful nations to an understanding that "believers" will deliver the punishment on behalf of Allah. See "Divine Punishment of Unbelievers in This World" (p. 507).

and (business) transaction(s) you fear (may) fall off, and dwellings you take pleasure in are dearer to you than God and His messenger, and struggling in His way, then wait until God brings His command. God does not guide the people who are wicked.'

²⁵ Certainly God has helped you on many (battle)fields, and on the day of Ḥunayn, when your multitude impressed you but was of no use to you at all, and the earth was too narrow for you, despite its breadth, and you turned back, retreating. ²⁶ Then God sent down His Sakīna on His messenger and on the believers, and He sent down forces you did not see, and punished those who disbelieved – that was the payment of the disbelievers. ²⁷ Then, after that, God turns (in forgiveness) to whomever He pleases. God is forgiving, compassionate.

²⁸ You who believe! Only the idolaters are impure, so let them not go near the Sacred Mosque after this, their (final) year. If you fear poverty, God will enrich you from His favor, if He pleases. Surely God is knowing, wise.

²⁹ Fight those who do not believe in God or the Last Day, and do not forbid what God and His messenger have forbidden, and do not practice the religion

---

9.24 – *and struggling in His way*

"Struggling" here translates the Arabic word *jihād*. This word only appears four times in the Quran, and this verse is its first appearance in the canonical progression. The sense of *jihad* that the Quran intends in each of these occurrences may be partly determined by context. If the context is a battle scene, and *jihad* appears close to commands to fight (*qātala*, e.g., vv. 12, 14, 29), *jihad* picks up the sense of fighting. See "Jihad in the Quran" (p. 368).

9.26 – *Then God sent down His Sakīna on His messenger and on the believers*

This description of battle contains the word *Sakīna* (also v. 40). Here Allah sends down the *Sakīna* on the messenger and the "believers" when they are fleeing the battle (v. 25). Allah helps them to prevail over their enemies, the "disbelievers." See the comment on *Sakīna* at 2.248 (p. 71).

9.29 – *Fight those . . . who have been given the Book*

This verse commands the "believers" (v. 28) to fight "those who have been given the Book" – the People of the Book – until they pay an extra tax (*jizya*) and have been humiliated (*ṣāghirūn*).

Describing the People of the Book as those who "do not believe in Allah or the Last Day" seems to clash with what many Jews and Christians would say about themselves. It is true, however, that they do not accept the authority of Islam's messenger to "forbid" and determine law on God's behalf, nor do they follow "the religion of truth," if this expression is exclusive to Islam (see v. 33).

In this verse the enemies are the People of the Book, and they are to be fought

of truth – from among those who have been given the Book – until they pay tribute out of hand, and they are disgraced.

[30] The Jews say, 'Ezra is the son of God,' and the Christians say, 'The Messiah is the son of God.' That is their saying with their mouths. They imitate the saying of those who disbelieved before (them). (May) God fight them. How are they (so) deluded? [31] They have taken their teachers and their monks as Lords instead of God, and (also) the Messiah, son of Mary, when they were only commanded to serve one God. (There is) no god but Him. Glory to Him

---

until they pay tribute and accept subjection. Otherwise, the reason for fighting is not obvious. There is no indication here that the People of the Book have attacked the Muslims. This and the following verses seem to suggest that the fighting is simply because the Quran accuses Jews and Christians of believing wrongly.

Along with 9.5, Muslim jurists who formulated Islamic Law considered verse 29 to be one of the most important verses for defining the relationship of Muslims to non-Muslims. Muslim scholars know this verse as the "verse of tribute (*jizya*)." The necessity to "pay tribute" was important to the concept of Jewish and Christian *dhimmi* communities living within Muslim dominions and is even called for today by some Islamist groups. See "Fighting and Killing in the Quran" (p. 220).

9.30 – *the Christians say: "The Messiah is the son of God."*

Amid this warlike sūra, with its many commands to fight, come two powerful verses against the Christian practices of confessing the Messiah as the Son of God and taking the Messiah as Lord (vv. 30–31). These verses evidently represent a strongly felt denial of the deity of Jesus and opposition to those who believe in it. In response to Christians who make this confession, the Quran declares, "May Allah fight them."

The verse's description of Christian belief and confession is accurate. From their earliest days following the death and resurrection of Jesus, Christians have declared that the Messiah is the Son of God (e.g., Acts 9:20; Romans 1:4). In fact, the Gospel often uses "Messiah" and "Son of God" interchangeably (e.g., Matthew 16:16; John 20:31). On the name "Messiah" in the Quran, see the comment at 3.45 (p. 85).

The Quran here uses the expression *ibn Allāh*, whereas all other quranic passages about "son" of Allah use the word *walad*. See "Son of God in the Quran" (p. 352). The accusation that the Jews say, "Ezra is the son of Allah," however, does not seem to be based in historical reality.

9.31 – *They have taken their teachers and their monks as Lords instead of God, and (also) the Messiah*

The accusation in this verse is that Christians have taken the Messiah as Lord (*rabb*). This is accurate. The New Testament says, "If you confess with your mouth, 'Jesus is Lord,' and believe in your heart that God raised him from the dead, you will

above what they associate! ³² They want to extinguish the light of God with their mouths, but God refuses (to do anything) except perfect His light, even though the disbelievers dislike (it). ³³ He (it is) who has sent His messenger with the guidance and the religion of truth, so that He may cause it to prevail over religion – all of it – even though the idolaters dislike (it).

³⁴ You who believe! Surely many of the teachers and the monks consume the wealth of the people by means of falsehood, and keep (people) from the way of God. Those who hoard the gold and the silver, and do not spend it in the way of God – give them news of a painful punishment. ³⁵ On the Day when it will be heated in the Fire of Gehenna, and their foreheads and their sides and their backs will be branded with it: 'This is what you hoarded for yourselves, so taste what you have hoarded!'

³⁶ Surely the number of months with God is twelve, (written) in the Book of God on the day when He created the heavens and the earth. Of them, four are sacred. That is the right religion. Do not do yourselves evil during them, but fight (against) the idolaters all together, as they fight you all together, and know

---

be saved" (Romans 10:9). The Quran's issue with the term *rabb* is that it implies the deity of Jesus and his supreme authority to command humanity how to live. See the analysis of the Quran's denials of the deity of ʿĪsā at 43.59 (p. 491).

Verse 31 continues with the words "they were only commanded to serve one God. (There is) no god but Him" – a statement very close to the first part of the Muslim confession of faith. Here again the Quran says that Christians are "associating" (*ashraka*, also v. 33; see the comment at 9.5). The Quran contains characterizations of Christians, Jews, and others that almost none of the followers of those faiths would give. See a summary of verses that accuse the People of the Book of "associating" at 61.9 (p. 565).

9.33 – *so that He may cause it to prevail over religion – all of it*

Here is a further clue to the reason for the command to fight the People of the Book (v. 29). Allah wants the "religion of truth" to prevail over all other religion. Once more, the translation "idolaters" for *mushrikūn* does not seem to pay attention to the group of people discussed in the context (vv. 29–34).

The same wording appears in 61.9 and in 48.28 with slight differences, and it was written above the north door of the Dome of the Rock when it was built in AD 691. See the discussion of verses that describe the People of the Book as "associators" at 61.9 (p. 565).

9.36 – *fight (against) the idolaters all together, as they fight you all together*

This verse commands the "believers" (vv. 34, 38) to fight the enemy, here identified as the idolaters (*mushrikūn*). The verse seems to take away any limits to the

that God is with the ones who guard (themselves). [37] The postponement is an increase of disbelief by which those who disbelieve go astray. They make it profane (one) year, and make it sacred (another) year, to adjust the number (of months) God has made sacred, and to profane what God has made sacred. The evil of their deeds is made to appear enticing to them, but God does not guide the people who are disbelievers.

[38] You who believe! What is (the matter) with you? When it is said to you, 'Go forth in the way of God,' you slump to the earth. Are you pleased with this present life, rather than the Hereafter? Yet what enjoyment (there is) of this present life is only a little (thing) in (comparison to) the Hereafter. [39] If you do not go forth, He will punish you (with) a painful punishment, and exchange a people other than you. You will not harm Him at all, (for) God is powerful over everything. [40] If you do not help him, God has already helped him, when those who disbelieved expelled him, the second of two: when the two were in the cave, (and) when he said to his companion, 'Do not sorrow, (for) surely God is with us.' Then God sent down His Sakīna on him, and supported him with forces which you did not see, and made the word of those who disbelieved the lowest, while the word of God is the highest. God is mighty, wise.

[41] Go forth, light and heavy, and struggle in the way of God with your

---

fighting in terms of "sacred" months and to envision a reciprocal response to the fighting of the enemy.

Here also is a brief explanation of the "sacred months" referred to in verse 5.

9.38 – *When it is said to you, "Go forth in the way of God," you slump to the earth*

Writers of the earliest Muslim stories of Islamic origins connected this and the following ninety verses with the story of a raid on Tabūk (*Raids*, 519–27; cf. *Sīra*, 602–9). According to Muslim tradition, Muhammad leads an army of Muslims to northwest Arabia to engage the Byzantines in battle. However, when the Muslim army arrives in Tabūk, they find no Byzantine presence there.

9.41 – *Go forth, light and heavy, and struggle in the way of God with your wealth and your lives*

"Struggle" translates the Arabic verb *jāhada*, from which the word *jihād* comes, and here it appears in the form of a command. There are seven such commands in the Quran, and three of those come in Sūra 9 (also vv. 73, 86). The sense of *struggle* that the Quran intends in each imperative may be partly determined by context. If the context is a battle scene, and *struggle* appears close to commands to fight (*qātala*, e.g., v. 36), *struggle* tends to pick up the sense of fighting.

See the analysis of these commands at 66.9 (p. 579) and "Jihad in the Quran" (p. 368).

wealth and your lives. That is better for you, if (only) you knew. ⁴² If it were (some fleeting) gain near (at hand), and an easy journey, they would indeed have followed you, but the distance is (too) far for them. (Still) they will swear by God, 'If we had been able, we would indeed have gone out with you.' (In this way) they destroy themselves. But God knows: 'Surely they are liars indeed!

⁴³ God pardon you! Why did you give them permission, before (it was) clear to you (who were) those who spoke the truth, and (before) you knew (who) the liars (were)? ⁴⁴ Those who believe in God and the Last Day do not ask your permission, so that they may struggle with their wealth and their lives. God knows the ones who guard (themselves). ⁴⁵ Only those who do not believe in God and the Last Day ask your permission, and their hearts are filled with doubt, and they waver in their doubt. ⁴⁶ If they had intended to go forth, they would indeed have made some preparation for it. But God disliked their rising up, so He held them back, and it was said (to them), 'Sit (at home) with the ones who sit.' ⁴⁷ If they had gone forth with you, they would have added to you nothing but ruin, and would indeed have run around in your midst, seeking to stir up trouble among you – and some of you would have listened to them. But God knows the evildoers. ⁴⁸ Certainly they sought to stir up trouble before (this), and upset matters for you, until the truth came and the command of God prevailed, even though they were unwilling. ⁴⁹ (There is) one of them who says, 'Give me permission, and do not tempt me.' Is it not (a fact) that they have (already) fallen into temptation? Surely Gehenna will indeed encompass the disbelievers.

⁵⁰ If some good smites you, it distresses them, but if some smiting smites you, they say, 'We took hold of our affair before (this),' and they turn away, gloating. ⁵¹ Say: 'Nothing smites us except what God has prescribed for us. He is our Protector, and in God let the believers put (their) trust.' ⁵² Say: 'Do you wait for anything in our case except for one of the two good (rewards)? But we are waiting in your case for God to smite you with punishment from Him or at our hands. (Just) wait! Surely we shall be waiting with you.'

⁵³ Say: 'Contribute willingly or unwillingly, it will not be accepted from you. Surely you are a wicked people.' ⁵⁴ Nothing prevents their contributions being accepted from them, except that they have not believed in God and in His messenger, and they do not come to the prayer, except in a lazy fashion, and they do not contribute, except unwillingly.

⁵⁵ Do not let their wealth and their children impress you. God only intends to punish them by means of it in this present life, and (that) they themselves should pass away while they are disbelievers. ⁵⁶ They swear by God that they indeed belong to you, but they do not belong to you. They are a people who

are afraid. [57] If they could find a shelter, or caves, or a place to hide, they would indeed resort to it and rush off.

[58] (There is) one of them who finds fault with you concerning freewill offerings. Yet if they are given (a share) of it, they are pleased, but if they are not given (a share) of it, they are angry. [59] If (only) they had been pleased with what God gave them, and His messenger, and had said, 'God is enough for us. God will give us (more) of His favor, and (so will) His messenger. Surely we turn in hope to God.' [60] Freewill offerings are only for the poor and the needy, and the ones who collect it, and the ones whose hearts are united, and for the (freeing of) slaves, and the (relief of) debtors, and for the way of God, and the traveler. (That is) an obligation from God. God is knowing, wise.

[61] (There are) some of them who hurt the prophet, and say, 'He is all ears!' Say: 'Good ears for you! He believes in God and believes in the believers, and (he is) a mercy for those of you who believe. But those who hurt the messenger of God – for them (there is) a painful punishment.' [62] They swear to you by God in order to please you, but God and His messenger – (it is more) right that they should please Him, if they are believers. [63] Do they not know that the one who opposes God and His messenger – surely for him (there is) the Fire of Gehenna, there to remain? That is the great humiliation!

[64] The hypocrites are afraid that a sūra will be sent down against them, informing them of what is in their hearts. Say: 'Go on mocking! Surely God will bring forth what you are afraid of.' [65] If indeed you ask them, they will indeed say, 'We were only bantering and jesting.' Say: 'Were you mocking God, and His signs, and His messenger? [66] Do not make excuses! You have disbelieved after your believing. If We pardon (one) contingent of you, We will punish (another) contingent because they have been sinners.' [67] The hypocrite men and the hypocrite women are all alike. They command wrong and forbid right, and they withdraw their hands. They have forgotten God, so He has forgotten them. Surely the hypocrites – they are the wicked. [68] God has promised the hypocrite men and the hypocrite women, and the disbelievers, the Fire of Gehenna, there to remain. It will be enough for them. God has cursed them, and for them (there is) a lasting punishment. [69] Like those before you: they were stronger than you in power and (had) more wealth and children, and they took enjoyment in their share. You have taken enjoyment in your share, as those before you took enjoyment in their share. You have bantered as they bantered.

9.61 – *(There are) some of them who hurt the prophet, and say*

This verse promises a painful punishment to those who hurt the messenger. This promise repeats in 33.57, which adds Allah's curse in this world.

Those – their deeds have come to nothing in this world and the Hereafter. And those – they are the losers. [70] Has no story come to them of those who were before them: the people of Noah, and ʿĀd, and Thamūd, and the people of Abraham, and the companions of Midian, and the overturned (cities)? Their messengers brought them the clear signs. God was not one to do them evil, but they did themselves evil.

[71] The believing men and the believing women are allies of each other. They command right and forbid wrong, they observe the prayer and give the alms, and they obey God and His messenger. Those – God will have compassion on them. God is mighty, wise. [72] God has promised the believing men and the believing women Gardens through which rivers flow, there to remain, and good dwellings in Gardens of Eden – but the approval of God is greater. That is the great triumph!

[73] Prophet! Struggle against the disbelievers and the hypocrites, and be stern with them. Their refuge is Gehenna – and it is an evil destination! [74] They swear by God that they did not say (it), but certainly they have said the word of disbelief, and have disbelieved after their submission. They determined (to do) what they did not attain, and they took vengeance for no other reason than that God and His messenger had enriched them from His favor. If they turn (in repentance) it will be better for them, but if they turn away, God will punish them (with) a painful punishment in this world and the Hereafter. They have no ally and no helper on the earth.

[75] (There is) one of them who has made a covenant with God: 'If He gives us some of His favor, we shall indeed make contributions and indeed be among the righteous.' [76] But when He gave them some of His favor, they were stingy with it and turned away in aversion. [77] So He placed hypocrisy in their hearts until the Day when they meet Him, because they broke (with) God (concerning) what they promised Him, and because they have lied. [78] Do they not know

---

9.73 – *Prophet! Struggle against the disbelievers and the hypocrites, and be stern with them*

This second occurrence of the command to "struggle" applies to "the prophet" in particular. The sense of *struggle* that the Quran intends by this imperative may be partly determined by context. See the analysis of these commands at 66.9 (p. 579) and "Jihad in the Quran" (p. 368). On "be stern with them," see 9.123, 48.29, and 66.9.

Direct addresses to "the prophet" are not frequent in the Quran, and most of the occurrences come in Sūras 8, 33, and 66. Known as the "vocative," this direct address instructs the prophet in how to deal with non-Muslims. See an analysis of the contexts of "Prophet!" at 66.1 (p. 577).

that God knows their secret and their secret talk, and that God is the Knower of the unseen? [79] Those who find fault with those of the believers who contribute voluntarily, and those who ridicule those (believers) who do not find (anything to offer) but their effort – God has ridiculed them, and for them (there is) a painful punishment. [80] Ask forgiveness for them or do not ask forgiveness for them. (Even) if you ask forgiveness for them seventy times, God will not forgive them. That is because they have disbelieved in God and His messenger. God does not guide the wicked.

[81] The ones who stayed behind gloated over their sitting (at home) behind the messenger of God, and disliked (it) that they should (have to) struggle with their wealth and their lives in the way of God. They said, 'Do not go forth in the heat.' Say: 'The Fire of Gehenna is hotter!' If (only) they understood! [82] So let them laugh a little (now) and weep a lot in payment for what they have earned. [83] If God brings you back to some contingent of them, and they ask your permission to go forth, say: 'You will never go forth with me, nor will you ever fight any enemy with me. Surely you were pleased with sitting (at home) the first time, so sit with the ones who stay behind.'

[84] Never pray over anyone of them who has died, nor stand over his grave. Surely they disbelieved in God and His messenger, and died while they were wicked. [85] Do not let their wealth and their children impress you. God only intends to punish them by means of it in this world, and (that) they themselves should pass away while they are disbelievers.

[86] When a sūra is sent down (stating): 'Believe in God, and struggle alongside His messenger,' the wealthy among them ask your permission, and say,

---

9.80 – *if you ask forgiveness for them seventy times, God will not forgive them*

In this verse the disbelievers are beyond hope of forgiveness because they did not believe in "Allah and His messenger." The belief required here is quite specific – not simply a general kind of religious faith (see the comment at 2.4). The theme of not asking for forgiveness for "disbelievers" continues in this sūra at verses 84 and 113–14.

9.83 – *You will never go forth with me, nor will you ever fight any enemy with me*

This verse pairs "going forth" with fighting (*qātala*) in a way that suggests the meaning of the otherwise vague expression "going forth" in this battle scene (e.g., vv. 38, 41).

9.86 – *When a sūra is sent down (stating): "Believe in God, and struggle alongside His messenger..."*

This third command to "stuggle" claims that it is "sent down" as part of a sūra. See the analysis of commands to struggle (*jāhada*) at 66.9 (p. 579) and "Jihad in the Quran" (p. 368).

'Let us be with the ones who sit (at home).' ⁸⁷ They are pleased to be with the ones who stay behind, and a seal is set on their hearts, and so they do not understand. ⁸⁸ But the messenger and those who believe with him have struggled with their wealth and their lives. And those – for them (there are) the good things, and those – they are the ones who prosper. ⁸⁹ God has prepared for them Gardens through which rivers flow, there to remain. That is the great triumph!

⁹⁰ The excuse-makers among the Arabs came to get permission for themselves, and those who lied to God and His messenger sat (at home). A painful punishment will smite those of them who disbelieve. ⁹¹ There is no blame on the weak or on the sick or on those who find nothing to contribute, if they are true to God and His messenger. (There is) no way against the doers of good – God is forgiving, compassionate – ⁹² nor against those (to) whom, when they came to you for you to give them mounts, you said, 'I cannot find a mount for you.' They turned away, and their eyes were full of the tears of sorrow, because they did not find anything to contribute. ⁹³ The way is only open against those who ask your permission when they are rich. They are pleased to be with the ones who stay behind. God has set a seal on their hearts, but they do not know (it).

⁹⁴ They will make excuses to you when you return to them. Say: 'Do not make excuses, (for) we do not believe you. God has already informed us of the reports about you. God will see your deed, and (so will) His messenger. Then you will be returned to the Knower of the unseen and the seen, and He will inform you about what you have done.' ⁹⁵ They will swear to you by God, when you turn back to them, that you may turn away from them. Turn away from them, (for) surely they are an abomination. Their refuge is Gehenna – a payment for what they have earned. ⁹⁶ They will swear to you in order that you may be pleased with them. Yet (even) if you are pleased with them, surely God will not be pleased with the people who are wicked.

⁹⁷ The Arabs are (even) stronger in disbelief and hypocrisy, and more likely not to know the limits of what God has sent down on His messenger. God is knowing, wise. ⁹⁸ Among the Arabs (there is) one who regards what he contributes as a fine, and waits for the wheels (of fortune to turn) against you. The wheel of evil (will turn) against them! God is hearing, knowing. ⁹⁹ Among the Arabs (there is) one who believes in God and the Last Day, and takes what he contributes as a (means of) drawing near to God, and (likewise) the prayers of the messenger. Is it not a fact that it is a (means of) drawing near for them? God will cause them to enter into His mercy. God is forgiving, compassionate.

9.90 – *The excuse-makers among the Arabs*
The "Arabs" in this passage (vv. 90–101) are often described as nomadic Bedouin.

[100] The foremost – the first of the emigrants and the helpers, and those who have followed them in doing good – God is pleased with them and they are pleased with Him. He has prepared for them Gardens through which rivers flow, there to remain forever. That is the great triumph! [101] Some of the Arabs who (dwell) around you are hypocrites, and some of the people of the city (also). They have become obstinate in (their) hypocrisy. You do not know them, (but) We know them, (and) We shall punish them twice. Then they will be returned to a great punishment. [102] Others have acknowledged their sins. They have mixed a righteous deed and another (that is) evil. It may be that God will turn (in forgiveness) to them. Surely God is forgiving, compassionate. [103] Take from their wealth a contribution, to cleanse them and purify them by means of it, and pray over them. Surely your prayers are a rest for them. God is hearing, knowing. [104] Do they not know that God – He accepts repentance from His servants and takes (their) contributions, and that God – He is the One who turns (in forgiveness), the Compassionate? [105] Say: 'Work! God will see your deed, and (so will) His messenger and the believers, and you will be returned to the Knower of the unseen and the seen, and He will inform you about what you have done.' [106] (There are) others (who will be) deferred to the command of God, (to see) whether He will punish them or turn (in forgiveness) to them. God is knowing, wise.

[107] Those who have taken a mosque (to cause) harm and disbelief and division among the believers, and (to provide) a place of ambush for those who fought against God and His messenger before – they will indeed swear, 'We wanted nothing but good!' But God bears witness: 'Surely they are liars indeed!' [108] Never stand in it! A mosque founded from the first day on the (obligation of) guarding (oneself) is indeed (more) worthy for you to stand in. In it (there are) are men who love to purify themselves, and God loves the ones who purify themselves. [109] So is someone who founded his building on (the obligation of) guarding (oneself) against God, and (on His) approval, better, or someone

---

9.100 – *The foremost – the first of the emigrants and the helpers*

The Muslim story of Islamic origins describes the "emigrants" (*muhājirūn*) as those who migrated from Mecca to Medina with Muhammad and the "helpers" (*anṣār*) as the people in Medina who received and helped the Muslims. This verse says that Allah is pleased with both groups and has prepared "Gardens" for them in the afterlife.

9.108 – *God loves the ones who purify themselves*

The objects of love here are the "purifiers" (also 2.222) in relation to ritual prayer. See "The Language of Love in the Quran" (p. 560).

who founded his building on the brink of a crumbling precipice, (which) then collapsed with him into the Fire of Gehenna? God does not guide the people who are evildoers. [110] Their building which they have built will continue (to be a cause of) doubt in their hearts, unless their hearts are cut (to pieces). God is knowing, wise.

[111] Surely God has purchased from the believers their lives and their wealth with (the price of) the Garden (in store) for them. They fight in the way of God, and they kill and are killed. (That is) a promise binding on Him in the Torah, and the Gospel, and the Qur'ān. Who fulfills his covenant better than God? So welcome the good news of the bargain you have made with Him. That is the great triumph! [112] The ones who turn (in repentance), the ones who serve, the ones who praise, the ones who wander, the ones who bow, the ones who prostrate themselves, the ones who command right, and the ones who forbid wrong, (and) the ones who keep the limits of God – give good news to the believers.

[113] It is not for the prophet and those who believe to ask forgiveness for the idolaters, even though they may be family, after it has become clear to them

9.111 – *They fight in the way of God, and they kill and are killed*

When the Quran describes believers as fighting "in the way of Allah," it makes a theological claim by associating Allah with human fighting. See the analysis of these expressions at 73.20 (p. 597).

9.111 – *a promise binding on Him in the Torah, and the Gospel, and the Qur'ān*

This is the only verse in the Quran that brings the Torah (*tawrāt*), Gospel (*injīl*), and *qur'ān* (lit. "recitation") together. The Quran claims here that the particular point on which the Torah and Gospel agree with the Muslim recitation is that believers "fight in the way of Allah, and they kill and are killed."

This verse makes the reader question whether the Quran has a clear idea of the contents of the Torah and Gospel. A similar question is raised by 61.14, which appears to say that ʿĪsā and his disciples fought against their enemies (cf. 3.52). Along with these misunderstandings, the Quran gives no information about the peaceable teaching and example of Jesus in the Gospel accounts. See the analysis of the Quran's verses on the "Gospel" at 57.27 (p. 549).

Do the Torah and Gospel in fact contain such a promise? See the comment on this characterization of the Bible at 61.14 (p. 566).

9.113 – *It is not for the prophet ... to ask forgiveness for the idolaters*

This verse seems be an example of the freedom from obligation or "renunciation" mentioned at the beginning of Sūra 9 (vv. 1, 3). The unnamed "prophet" makes a decisive break with the associators (*mushrikūn*), even close relatives, and abandons them to hell. In order to support this approach, the Quran refers to Abraham (v. 114).

that they are the companions of the Furnace. [114] Abraham's asking forgiveness for his father was only because of a solemn promise he had made to him. But when it became clear to him that he was an enemy to God, he disowned him. Surely Abraham was indeed kind (and) forbearing. [115] God is not one to lead a people astray after He has guided them, until He makes clear to them what they should guard (themselves) against. Surely God has knowledge of everything. [116] Surely God – to Him (belongs) the kingdom of the heavens and the earth. He gives life and causes death. You have no ally and no helper other than God.

[117] Certainly God has turned (in forgiveness) to the prophet, and (to) the emigrants and the helpers who followed him in the hour of hardship, after the hearts of a group of them had nearly turned aside. Then He turned to them (in forgiveness). Surely He was kind (and) compassionate with them. [118] And to the three who stayed behind, when the earth became narrow for them despite its breadth, and they themselves were constrained, and they thought that (there was) no shelter from God except (going) to Him, then He turned to them (in forgiveness), so that they might (also) turn (in repentance). Surely God – He is the One who turns (in forgiveness), the Compassionate.

[119] You who believe! Guard (yourselves) against God, and be with the truthful. [120] It is not for the people of the city, and those of the Arabs who (dwell) around them, to lag behind the messenger of God, nor should they prefer their lives to his. That is because no thirst and no weariness and no emptiness smites them in the way of God, nor do they make any attack (that) enrages the disbelievers, nor do they take any gain from an enemy, except that a righteous deed is thereby written down for them. Surely God does not let the reward of the doers of good go to waste. [121] Nor do they make any contribution, small or great, nor cross any wādī, except that it is written down for them, so that God may repay them (for the) best of what they have done.

[122] It is not for the believers to go forth all together. Why not have a contingent of every group of them go forth, so that they may gain understanding in

---

But it first needs to account for Abraham's prayers for forgiveness for his idolatrous father (e.g., 14.41, 19.47, 26.86). It argues that Abraham reached a point where he "disowned" his father. The Quran makes a similar argument at 60.4 after commanding the "believers" not to take their enemies for friends (60.1–3). There Abraham says to his people, "We repudiate you." Yet even then, Abraham appears to keep his promise to ask forgiveness for his father. See "Abraham in the Quran" (p. 90).

9.120 – *It is not for the people of the city . . . to lag behind the messenger of God*

This passage (vv. 120–21) claims that Allah rewards "believers" who fight. Another important passage of this type is 4.74.

religion, and that they may warn their people when they return to them, so that they (in turn) may beware?

[123] You who believe! Fight those of the disbelievers who are close to you, and let them find sternness in you, and know that God is with the ones who guard (themselves).

Fighting and Killing in the Quran
Ayman S. Ibrahim

Fighting is a central theme in the Quran. The verb *kill* occurs in seventy-seven verses in various forms, *fight* in thirty-nine, and the participle *fighting* in ten. In Arabic, the commands to kill and to fight, as well as the noun for *battles*, all have the same root letters *qtl*. While the Quran is not a military guide, it repeatedly directs the reader to engage in fighting and killing for Allah's cause. For the early hearers of the Quran who used to raid each other, incursions and expeditions became wars for Allah.

Fighting is now prescribed by Allah as a duty for the believers (2.216; 4.77; 47.20). Allah instructs the "prophet," the Quran's recipient, to urge and exhort the believers to fight (8.65). Only weak believers do not pursue fighting (3.167). It is for Allah's cause (2.244) and is divinely ordained (4.77; 47.20). Allah loves those fighting in his cause (61.4), and he is sufficient for them (33.25). Faithful believers pursue fighting in Allah's path (2.244–246; 3.13, 146, 195; 4.84; 9.111; 73.20), while unbelievers fight for the devil (4.75–76). In their fighting, believers sell the present life for the hereafter (4.74). They will be rewarded with gardens with flowing rivers (3.195). Fighting is thus sanctioned by Allah, but the question remains: Whom should the believers fight?

The Quran calls for fighting several groups: the polytheists (or "associators," *mushrikūn*; 9.36), the infidels (*kuffār*; 8.39; 9.12–14; 9.123), the people

---

9.123 – *You who believe! Fight those of the disbelievers who are close to you, and let them find sternness in you*

The Quran commands the "believers" to fight and identifies their enemy as the "disbelievers." The reasons for the fighting and the limits of the hostilities are not clear. However, the attitude that the Quran intends the "disbelievers" to experience from the "believers" is clear and of interest to non-Muslims: it is *ghilẓa*, here translated "sternness" but also commonly defined as "harshness" or "ruthlessness" (see also vv. 73; 48.29; 66.9). See "Fighting and Killing in the Quran" above.

who received the Scripture (9.29–30, presumably Jews and Christians), and the unjust quranic believers (49.9). The Quran despises those who remain at home instead of fighting (3.167; 5.24; 9.83; 48.16). It instructs both defensive (2.190; 4.90; 22.39) and offensive (2.193, 244–46; 4.84; 8.39; 9.5, 29, 36, 111) fighting and promises divine support and victory (3.111; 48.22). While fighting does not necessarily mean killing, the Quran often uses the command "kill" explicitly in relation to fighting.

In fighting, the believers are to kill the infidels (4.89) and strike their necks (47.4). While one is supposed to kill only for justifiable reasons (5.32; 6.151; 17.33; 18.74; 20.40; 25.68), the Quran refers to polytheism as a greater evil than killing (2.217) and thus instructs killing polytheists wherever they are caught (2.191; 4.89). It also commands the believers to kill the People of the Book (33.26), the hypocrites (33.61), and those who do not want peace (4.91). The Quran's believers are not allowed to kill their fellow believers except mistakenly or unintentionally (4.92, 93; 5.27, 28, 30). Like many prophets and messengers who are killed by unbelievers (2.61, 87, 91; 3.21, 112, 181, 183; 4.155, 157; 5.70; 8.30), the believers, when killed in battle, are martyrs for Allah's cause (2.154; 3.157, 169, 195; 4.74; 22.58).

The Quran is not primarily about warfare, but the reader cannot avoid the loud call for war throughout. The commands "kill" and "fight," as well as the noun "fighting," signify aspects, reasons, and targets of divinely prescribed warfare. Quranic fighting is distinct, as Allah sanctions it and identifies specifically whom are to be fought by the believers. While a few verses mandate fighting and killing only in self-defense, the vast majority of warfare references are read as an open call, universal and timeless.

Trying to find a context for many quranic passages – including those with imperatives to kill and fight – can be very difficult. The reader cannot know clearly whether a command is time-bound and limited or timeless and universal. This is one reason why Muslims today can be confused as to whether the commands are applicable in our day or are merely descriptive of past events. The challenge for Muslims is that the earliest commentaries on the Quran by renowned Muslim scholars take these commands as prescriptive and mandatory. It thus becomes the decision of the reader as to which commands to follow – a significant decision with huge implications.

[124] Whenever a sūra is sent down, some of them say, 'Which of you has this increased in belief?' As for those who believe, it increases them in belief, and

they welcome the good news. [125] But as for those in whose hearts is a sickness, it increases them in abomination (added) to their abomination, and they die while they are disbelievers. [126] Do they not see that they are tested every year once or twice? Yet still they do not turn (in repentance), nor do they take heed.

[127] Whenever a sūra is sent down, some of them look at others: 'Does anyone see you?' Then they turn away. God has turned away their hearts, because they are a people who do not understand.

[128] Certainly a messenger has come to you from among you. What you suffer is a mighty (weight) on him, (for he has) concern over you, (and he is) kind (and) compassionate with the believers.

[129] If they turn away, say: 'God is enough for me. (There is) no god but Him. In Him have I put my trust. He is the Lord of the great throne.'

9.128 – *Certainly a messenger has come to you from among you*

After commanding the messenger to be harsh with the "disbelievers" (vv. 73, 123), the Quran describes the messenger as compassionate (*ra'ūf*) and merciful (*raḥīm*) with the "believers." For this "self-referential" language of the Quran, see "Different Kinds of Literature" (p. 14).

Elsewhere in the Quran, the adjective pair *ra'ūf raḥīm* is only associated with Allah, including in 9.117.

JONAH
YŪNUS

10

The vocabulary used in Sūra 6 – "signs" of the Creator's presence and power – appears strongly again in this sūra and is an interesting and important component of many sūras in the long series to follow.

The first part of the sūra mixes the content of the messenger's preaching with a call for response to Allah and announcement of reward and punishment. The audience does not accept the preaching. They raise a number of objections (whether sincere or not), and the messenger answers back vigorously with speeches introduced by the word *say*.

The preaching is addressed to "people" (e.g., v. 23) rather than "People of the Book" or "Children of Israel." There is little sense here of Jews and Christians in the audience, except possibly in the discussion of "Allah has taken a son" in verse 68.

Nevertheless, the tone is polemical, and the messenger probes the trust of the unbelievers in "associates" while making his case for Allah (e.g., vv. 34–36). At one point, the voice of the Quran comforts the messenger in the midst of the rejection of his message.

The sūra is named after Jonah, described here as history's only successful preacher. Readers may be interested to read Sūras 10–15 closely in order to test a scholar's recent argument that these six sūras share a unifying theme. See the discussion in the introduction to Sūra 15.

In the Name of God, the Merciful, the Compassionate

¹ Alif Lām Rā'. Those are the signs of the wise Book.

² Is it amazing to the people that We have inspired a man from among them:

10.1 – *Those are the signs of the wise Book*

The sūra begins with seemingly self-conscious and "self-referential" claims for itself and for a man "among them" who preaches (v. 2). Notice that the following five sūras open with similar verses – as do many other sūras of the Quran. See "Different Kinds of Literature" (p. 14).

'Warn the people, and give good news to those who believe, that for them (there is) a sure footing with their Lord'? (But) the disbelievers say, 'Surely this (man) is a clear magician indeed.'

³ Surely your Lord is God, who created the heavens and the earth in six days. Then He sat down on the throne. He directs the (whole) affair. (There is) no intercessor without His permission. That is God, your Lord, so serve Him! Will you not take heed? ⁴ To Him is your return – all (of you) – the promise of God in truth! Surely He brought about the creation, (and) then He restores it, so that He may repay those who believe and do righteous deeds in justice. But those who disbelieve – for them (there is) a drink of boiling (water) and a painful punishment, because they were disbelieving.

Creation in the Quran
Jon Hoover

Creation is at the core of the Quran's theology. As in the Bible, God is the one, all-powerful Creator of everything (13.16). God created the heavens and the earth (14.19), the angels (43.19), the sun and the moon and the day and the night (41.37), the mountains and the rivers (13.3), trees, fruit, grain, and herbs (55.11–12), the animals (24.45), humankind (23.12–14), and the jinn, a world of invisible beings parallel to the human world (55.15). God did not just originate the world to let it run on its own but continuously sustains it: "Or (is He not better) who brings about the creation, (and) then restores it, and who provides for you from the sky and the earth?" (27.64). Moreover, everything that God creates is good (32.7), and he creates nothing in vain (3.191).

10.3 – *Surely your Lord is God, who created the heavens and the earth in six days*

Just as the change of content and tone at the beginning of Sūra 8 was worthy of special note, so is the change from the battle atmosphere of Sūra 9 to the comparatively placid setting of Sūra 10.

The theme of Allah as Creator (10:3–6) is strong in many sūras that Muslims call "Meccan" and is often beautifully expressed. This passage draws attention to the "signs" of Allah's presence (vv. 5–6). The theme of creation echoes an important theological emphasis of the Bible and seems to be a theme common to Judaism, Christianity, and Islam.

The Quran says that there is no intercession with God except with his permission. See the analysis of verses on intercession at 39.44 (p. 464).

Creation in the Quran serves profoundly moral and religious purposes. God created the world as an arena to test humankind (18.7), and God's original creation of the world is cited as proof establishing his ability to resurrect the dead for punishment (46.33). Every created thing is a sign pointing to God, and the Quran is full of exhortation to understand and think about these signs in order to remember God, believe in him, and worship him: "He is the Lord of the heavens and the earth and all that is between them. Worship Him and be steadfast in your worship of Him" (19.65, Muhammad Sarwar). While humans were created fretful, anxious, and grudging (70.19–21) and the angels questioned God's wisdom in creating them because they would shed blood (2.30), their ultimate purpose, along with the jinn, is to worship God: "I did not create the jinn and humankind except to worship" (51.56; Droge has "serve me" instead of "worship").

According to the Quran, God created the world in six days (11.7). The biblical notion that God rested on the seventh day is not mentioned. Instead, it is implicitly denied: "Certainly, We created the heavens and the earth, and whatever is between them, in six days. No weariness touched Us in (doing) that" (50.38). Sūra 41.9–12 appears to indicate that creation took eight days – two for the earth, four for the mountains and the earth's nourishment, and two for the seven heavens – but commentators included the first two days within the four days mentioned immediately thereafter in order to bring the total back down to six. Otherwise, the Quran does not specify what God created on each of the six days, although such accounts are found in traditions ascribed to Muhammad.

Both Christian and Muslim theologians have pondered whether the world is eternal or had a beginning. Patristic theologians argued that the world had a beginning – God created it out of nothing (*ex nihilo*) in time – and the medieval church established this as Christian orthodoxy. Many Muslim theologians argued in similar fashion that God's creation of the world had a beginning, and they found this affirmed in the Quran, "When [God] decrees something, He simply says to it, 'Be!' and it is" (2.117). This remains the most common Muslim view. However, Muslim philosophers influenced by Neoplatonism countered that the perfection of God entails his production of the world from eternity. If God had at some point begun to create, that would have subjected God to change. The theologian Fakhr al-Dīn al-Rāzī (d. 1210) argued that the Quran does not support one position or the other clearly and that rational arguments cannot decide the matter either. The only thing that can be known is that the world depends on God for its existence. The Christian theologian Thomas Aquinas (d. 1274) also took rational arguments to be inconclusive but held on the basis of faith that the world had a beginning. The Muslim philosopher Ibn Rushd, known in the west as Averroes (d. 1198), and theologian Ibn Taymiyya (d. 1328) argued that the Quran in fact supports creation out of preexisting matter. It affirms that God's throne was on water prior to the creation of this world (11.7) and that God called forth the heaven and the earth from preexisting smoke (41.11). Both Muslim scholars thus concluded that God created the world continuously from eternity, and Ibn Taymiyya even appealed to the mention of preexisting water in Genesis 1:1–2 to add weight to his argument. Some modern biblical scholars have likewise claimed that Genesis does not necessarily support creation *ex nihilo*.

[5] He (it is) who made the sun an illumination, and the moon a light, and determined it by stations, so that you might know the number of the years and the reckoning (of time). God created that only in truth. He makes the signs distinct for a people who know. [6] Surely in the alternation of the night and the day, and (in) what God has created in the heavens and the earth, (there are) signs indeed for a people who guard (themselves).

[7] Surely those who do not expect to meet Us, and are satisfied with this present life and feel secure in it, and those who are oblivious of Our signs, [8] those – their refuge is the Fire for what they have earned. [9] Surely those who believe and do righteous deeds – their Lord guides them for their belief. Beneath them rivers flow in Gardens of Bliss. [10] Their call there is: 'Glory to You, God!,' and their greeting there is: 'Peace!,' and the last (part) of their call is: 'Praise (be) to God, Lord of the worlds!'

[11] If God were to hurry the evil for the people, (as) their seeking to hurry the good, their time would indeed have been completed for them. But We leave those who do not expect the meeting with Us in their insolent transgression, wandering blindly.

[12] When hardship touches a person, he calls on Us, (whether lying) on his side or sitting or standing. But when We have removed his hardship from him, he continues on, as if he had not called on Us about the hardship (that)

10.12 – *When hardship touches a person, he calls on Us*

Many people call on Allah when they are in trouble, but according to this verse, after Allah helps them they forget all about him (see also vv. 22–23).

had touched him. In this way what the wanton do is made to appear enticing to them.

[13] Certainly We destroyed the generations before you when they did evil, when their messengers brought them the clear signs and they would not believe. In this way We repay the people who are sinners. [14] Then, after them, We made you successors on the earth, so that We might see how you would do.

[15] When Our signs are recited to them as clear signs, those who do not expect the meeting with Us say, 'Bring a different Qur'ān than this one, or change it.' Say: 'It is not for me to change it of my own accord. I only follow what I am inspired (with). Surely I fear, if I disobey my Lord, the punishment of a great Day.' [16] Say: 'If God had (so) pleased, I would not have recited it to you, nor would He have made it known to you. I had already spent a lifetime among you before it (came to me). Will you not understand?' [17] Who is more evil than the one who forges a lie against God, or calls His signs a lie? Surely the sinners will not prosper.

[18] They serve what neither harms them nor benefits them, instead of God (alone), and they say, 'These are our intercessors with God.' Say: 'Will you inform God about what He does not know either in the heavens or on the earth? Glory to Him! He is exalted above what they associate.' [19] The people were (once) one community, then they differed. Were it not for a preceding word from your Lord, it would indeed have been decided between them concerning their differences. [20] They say, 'If only a sign were sent down on him from his Lord.' Say: 'The unseen (belongs) only to God. (Just) wait! Surely I shall be one of those waiting with you.' [21] When We give the people a taste of mercy, after hardship has touched them, suddenly they (devise) some scheme against Our signs. Say: 'God is quicker (at devising) a scheme. Surely Our messengers are writing down what you are scheming.'

[22] He (it is) who enables you to travel on the shore and the sea, until, when you are on the ship, and they sail with them by means of a fair wind, and they gloat over it, a violent wind comes upon it and the waves come at them from every side, and they think they are encompassed by them. (Then) they call on

---

10.15 – *When Our signs are recited to them as clear signs*

The preaching may be peaceful, but in many parts of this sūra the audience does not accept the message (see vv. 2–3, 15–18, 20–21, 31–35, 48–53, 68–69). These passages give the sense of a controversial encounter in progress between a speaker and an audience. The audience evidently asks for a different recitation (*qur'ān*) than the speaker is giving. The speaker responds that he can only recite what Allah has inspired him to say.

God, devoting (their) religion to Him: 'If indeed you rescue us from this, we shall indeed be among the thankful.' ²³ Yet when He has rescued them, suddenly they become greedy on the earth without any right. People! Your envy is only against yourselves – (the fleeting) enjoyment of this present life. Then to Us is your return, and We shall inform you about what you have done.

²⁴ A parable of this present life: (It is) is like water which We send down from the sky, and (there) mingles with it the vegetation of the earth from which the people and livestock eat, until, when the earth takes on its decoration and is adorned, and its people think that they have power over it, Our command comes on it by night or by day, and We cut it down, as if it had not flourished the day before. In this way We make the signs distinct for a people who reflect.

²⁵ God calls to the Home of peace, and guides whomever He pleases to a straight path. ²⁶ For those who have done good, (there is) the good (reward) and more (besides). Neither dust nor humiliation will cover their faces. Those are the companions of the Garden. There they will remain. ²⁷ But those who have done evil deeds – (the) payment for an evil deed is (an evil) like it – humiliation will cover them. They will have no protector from God. (It will be) as if their faces were covered (with) pieces of the darkness of night. Those are the companions of the Fire. There they will remain.

²⁸ On the Day when We shall gather them all together, then We shall say to those who associated: '(Take) your place, you and your associates!' Then We shall separate them, and their associates will say, 'You were not serving us. ²⁹ God is sufficient as a witness between us and you that we were indeed oblivious of your service.' ³⁰ There every person will stand trial (for) what he has done, and they will be returned to God, their true Protector, and (then) what they forged will abandon them.

³¹ Say: 'Who provides for you from the sky and the earth? Or who has power over hearing and sight? Who brings forth the living from the dead, and brings forth the dead from the living, and who directs the (whole) affair?' Then they will say, 'God.' So say: 'Will you not guard (yourselves)?' ³² That is God, your true Lord. And what (is there) after the truth except straying (from it)? How (is it that) you are turned away? ³³ In this way the word of your Lord has proved true against those who acted wickedly: 'They will not believe.' ³⁴ Say: '(Is there) any of your associates who (can) bring about the creation, (and) then restore it?' Say: 'God – He brings about the creation, (and) then He restores it. How are you (so) deluded?' ³⁵ Say:

10.30 – *There every person will stand trial (for) what he has done*

The reckoning for humanity will come on "the Day" that Allah will gather all people together for judgment (v. 28).

'(Is there) any of your associates who (can) guide to the truth?' Say: 'God – He guides to the truth. Is He who guides to the truth more worthy to be followed, or he who does not guide unless he is guided? What is (the matter) with you? How do you judge?' ³⁶ Most of them only follow conjecture, (and) surely conjecture is of no use at all against the truth. Surely God is aware of what they do.

³⁷ This Qur'ān is not the kind (of Book) that it could have been forged apart from God. (It is) a confirmation of what was before it, and a distinct setting forth of the Book – (there is) no doubt about it – from the Lord of the worlds. ³⁸ Or do they say, 'He has forged it'? Say: "Then bring a sūra like it, and call on anyone you can, other than God, if you are truthful.' ³⁹ No! They have called a lie what they cannot encompass in (their) knowledge of it, and when the interpretation of it has not (yet) come to them. Those who were before them called (it) a lie (too), and see how the end was for the evildoers!

⁴⁰ (There is) one of them who believes in it, and (there is) one of them who does not believe in it, but your Lord knows the ones who foment corruption. ⁴¹ If they call you a liar, say: 'To me my deed, and to you your deed. You are free of what I do, and I am free of what you do.' ⁴² (There is) one of them who listens to you, but can you make the deaf hear, when they do not understand? ⁴³ (There is) one of them

---

10.37 – *This Qur'ān is not is not the kind (of Book) that it could have been forged apart from God*

The Quran makes many claims for itself and its messenger. The audience says that the messenger is simply inventing his recitations (v. 38). The accusation of human forgery or "inventing" appears at least seventeen times in the Quran. Verse 37 preempts that accusation with an assertion that this is impossible. See the discussion on verses that accuse the messenger of inventing at 69.44 (p. 587). On the word *qur'ān*, see the comment at 2.185 (p. 61).

Also in this verse, the Quran claims a relationship of confirmation or attestation with the pre-Islamic scriptures. See the analysis of this claim at 46.12 (p. 502).

10.38 – *Or do they say, "He has forged it"? Say: "Then bring a sūra like it ..."*

The audience does not believe that the messenger's recitation is "sent down." The Quran's response is to command the messenger to challenge the audience to compose a *sūra* like the recitation. Similar challenges appear at 2.23; 11.13; 17.88; 28.49; and 52.34. In Muslim tradition these verses became known as the *taḥaddī* ("challenge") verses. See the analysis of these verses at 52.34 (p. 529).

10.41 – *You are free of what I do, and I am free of what you do*

The work of the messenger in this sūra – as in many sūras of the Quran – is to recite the message faithfully. He gives freedom to the listeners to respond, does not compel people to believe (v. 99), and waits patiently for Allah to act (v. 109).

who looks to you, but can you guide the blind, when they do not see? [44] Surely God does not do the people any evil at all, but the people do themselves evil.

[45] On the Day when He gathers them, (it will seem) as if they had remained (in the grave) only for an hour of the day, (and) they will recognize each other. Lost (are) those who called the meeting with God a lie, and were not (rightly) guided. [46] Whether We show you some of that which We promise them, or take you, to Us is their return. Then God is a witness over what they do. [47] For every community (there is) a messenger. When their messenger comes, it will be decided between them in justice – and they will not be done evil.

[48] They say, 'When (will) this promise (come to pass), if you are truthful?' [49] Say: 'I do not have power to (cause) myself harm or benefit – except whatever God pleases. For every community (there is) a time. When their time comes, they will not delay (it) by an hour, nor will they advance (it by an hour).' [50] Say: 'Do you see? If His punishment comes to you by night or by day, what (part) of it would the sinners seek to hurry? [51] When it falls, will you believe in it? Now? When you had been seeking to hurry it?' [52] Then it will be said to those who have done evil: 'Taste the punishment of eternity! Are you being repaid (for anything) except for what you have earned?'

[53] They ask you to inform them: 'Is it true?' Say: 'Yes, by my Lord! Surely it is true indeed! You will not escape (it).' [54] If each person who has done evil had all that is on the earth, he would indeed (try to) ransom (himself) with it. They will be full of secret regret when they see the punishment. It will be decided between them in justice – and they will not be done evil. [55] Is it not a fact that to God (belongs) whatever is in the heavens and the earth? Is it not a fact that the promise of God is true? But most of them do not know (it). [56] He gives life and causes death, and to Him you will be returned.

10.46 – *Whether We show you some of that which We promise them, or take you*

The Quran addresses the messenger directly to tell him that Allah may not necessarily show him his judgment of the people.

In this verse, Droge translates the Arabic verb *tawaffā* as "take" (see also v. 104) adding "in death" in a footnote. Several Muslim translations render the verb as "cause to die" (Pickthall, Shakir, Mohsin Khan, Sahih International, Muhammad Sarwar). Yet none of these five translates *tawaffā* in the same way at 3.55, where 'Īsā is the object of the verb. See the comments at 3.55 (p. 87) and "The Death of Jesus in the Quran" (p. 314).

10.47 – *For every community (there is) a messenger*

An important concept in the Quran is that Allah would send a messenger to every human community (*umma*), including to Arabic speakers. See the discussion about categorical statements concerning messengers and prophets at 25.20 (p. 365).

⁵⁷ People! An admonition has come to you from your Lord, and a healing for what is in the hearts, and a guidance and mercy for the believers. ⁵⁸ Say: 'In the favor of God and in His mercy – let them gloat over that, (for) it is better than what they accumulate.' ⁵⁹ Say: 'Have you seen what God has sent down for you from (His) provision, yet you have made some of it forbidden and (some) permitted?' Say: 'Has God given permission to you, or do you forge (lies) against God?' ⁶⁰ What will they think who forge lies against God on the Day of Resurrection? Surely God is indeed full of favor to the people, but most of them are not thankful (for it).

⁶¹ You are not (engaged) in any matter, nor do you recite any recitation of it, nor do you do any deed, except (that) We are witnesses over you when you are busy with it. Not (even) the weight of a speck on the earth or in the sky escapes from your Lord, nor (is there anything) smaller than that or greater, except (that it is recorded) in a clear Book. ⁶² Is it not a fact that the allies of God – (there will be) no fear on them, nor will they sorrow? ⁶³ Those who believe and guard (themselves) – ⁶⁴ for them (there is) good news in this present life and in the Hereafter. No one can change the words of God. That is the great triumph! ⁶⁵ Do not let their speech cause you sorrow. Surely honor (belongs) to God altogether. He is the Hearing, the Knowing.

⁶⁶ Is it not a fact that to God (belongs) whoever is in the heavens and who-ever is on the earth? They follow – those who call on associates other than God – they only follow conjecture and they only guess. ⁶⁷ He (it is) who made the night for you to rest in and the day to see. Surely in that are signs indeed for a people who hear.

⁶⁸ They say, 'God has taken a son.' Glory to Him! He is the wealthy One.

10.57 – *People! An admonition has come to you from your Lord*

The Quran proclaims itself to be an exhortation from the Lord. This verse is addressed to humankind in general (also vv. 104, 108).

10.64 – *No one can change the words of God*

This verse states that there is no change in the words of Allah. The context seems to be an encouragement to the messenger in the midst of resistance to his message. The statement that Allah's words are unchangeable repeats in slightly different forms at 6.34; 6.116; and 18.27.

10.65 – *Do not let their speech cause you sorrow*

The Quran speaks directly to the messenger to encourage him. See "Different Kinds of Literature" (p. 14).

10.68 – *They say: "God has taken a son." Glory to Him! He is the wealthy One*

The expression, "Allah has taken a son," appears ten times in the Quran. Here it is

To Him (belongs) whatever is in the heavens and whatever is on the earth. You have no authority for this (claim). Do you say about God what you do not know? [69] Say: 'Surely those who forge lies against God will not prosper.' [70] A (little) enjoyment in this world, then to Us is their return. Then We (shall) make them taste the harsh punishment for what they have disbelieved.

[71] Recite to them the story of Noah: when he said to his people, 'My people! If my stay (here) and my reminding (you) by the signs of God are hard on you, yet in God have I put my trust. So put together your plan, (you) and your associates. Then do not let your plan (be a cause of) distress for you. Then decide about me and do not spare me. [72] If you turn away, (know that) I have not asked you for any reward. My reward (depends) only on God, and I have been commanded to be one of those who submit.' [73] But they called him a liar, so We rescued him and those who were with him in the ship, and We made them successors, and We drowned those who called Our signs a lie. See how the end was for the ones who were warned!

[74] Then, after him, We raised up messengers for their people, and they brought them the clear signs. But they would not believe in what they had called a lie before. In this way We set a seal on the hearts of the transgressors.

[75] Then, after them, We raised up Moses and Aaron for Pharaoh and his assembly with Our signs, but they became arrogant and were a sinful people.

---

not clear who "they" are, but the context does not seem to have Christians in mind. In any case, the Quran is clear in its response: this expression is a lie against Allah (v. 69) because Allah is sovereign over the universe and is the "wealthy One."

Muslim commentators on the Quran took this to mean that Allah is sufficient in himself and has no need of anything. In this sense for Allah to "take a son" would mean that he needed help or a partner (v. 66). See "Son of God in the Quran" (p. 352).

10.71 – *Recite to them the story of Noah*

Noah is an important character in the Quran, and different versions of his story appear seven times. This short version starts out with a speech of Noah in which he tells his people about his call from Allah (vv. 71–73). Like the version in 7.59–64, mention of the ark, or "ship," seems to be incidental. The focus is on how Allah rescued Noah and drowned his opponents.

Additional versions of Noah's story come at 11.25–34; 23.23–30; 26.105–20; 54.7–17; and 71.1–28.

10.75 – *Then, after them, We raised up Moses and Aaron for Pharaoh*

Among the many Moses stories in the Quran, the two most common episodes are the scene in Pharaoh's court (vv. 75–83), and God's delivery of the Children of Israel at the sea crossing (v. 90). In this version, Moses and the people pray for deliverance

⁷⁶ When the truth came to them from Us, they said, 'Surely this is clear magic indeed.' ⁷⁷ Moses said, 'Do you say (this) about the truth, when it has come to you? Is this magic? Yet magicians do not prosper.' ⁷⁸ They said, 'Have you come to us in order to turn us away from what we found our fathers doing, and (in order that) you two (might) have greatness on the earth? We do not believe in you two.' ⁷⁹ And Pharaoh said, 'Bring me every skilled magician.' ⁸⁰ When the magicians came, Moses said to them, 'Cast (down) what you are going to cast.' ⁸¹ Then, when they had cast, Moses said, 'What you have brought is magic. Surely God will invalidate it. Surely God does not set right any deed of the fomenters of corruption. ⁸² God verifies the truth by His words, even though the sinners dislike (it).' ⁸³ So no one believed in Moses, except for the descendants of his people, out of fear that Pharaoh and their assembly would persecute them. Surely Pharaoh was indeed haughty on the earth. Surely he was indeed one of the wanton.

⁸⁴ Moses said, 'My people! If you believe in God, put your trust in Him, if you have submitted.' ⁸⁵ They said, 'In God we have put our trust. Our Lord, do not make us an (object of) persecution for the people who are evildoers, ⁸⁶ but rescue us by Your mercy from the people who are disbelievers.' ⁸⁷ And We inspired Moses and his brother: 'Establish houses for your people in Egypt, and make your houses a direction (of prayer), and observe the prayer, and give good news to the believers.' ⁸⁸ Moses said, 'Our Lord, surely You have given Pharaoh and his assembly splendor and wealth in this present life, Our Lord, so that they might lead (people) astray from Your way. Our Lord, obliterate their wealth and harden their hearts, so that they do not believe until they see the painful punishment.' ⁸⁹ He said, 'The request of both of you has been answered. So both of you go straight, and do not follow the way of those who do not know.'

⁹⁰ And We crossed the sea with the Sons of Israel, and Pharaoh and his forces followed them (out of) envy and enmity, until, when the drowning overtook him, he said, 'I believe that (there is) no god but the One in whom the

---

from persecution and punishment for Pharaoh and his people (vv. 84–90). See "Moses in the Quran" and the table of the Quran's Moses narratives (p. 388).

10.90 – *when the drowning overtook him, he said, "I believe that (there is) no god but the One in whom the Sons of Israel believe*

Pharaoh repents at the last moment and God rescues him (vv. 90–92). This surprising plot twist seems to echo a detail in some Jewish rabbinic writings. Pharaoh's confession of faith is very close to the Islamic confession of faith (*lā ilāha illā 'lladhī...*).

Sons of Israel believe. I am one of those who submit.' [91] 'Now? When you had disobeyed before and were one of the fomenters of corruption? [92] Today We rescue you with your body, so that you may be a sign for those who succeed you. Yet surely many of the people are indeed oblivious of Our signs.' [93] Certainly We settled the Sons of Israel in a sure settlement and provided them with good things. They did not (begin to) differ until (after) the knowledge had come to them. Surely your Lord will decide between them on the Day of Resurrection concerning their differences.

[94] If you are in doubt about what We have sent down to you, ask those who have been reciting the Book before you. The truth has come to you from your Lord, so do not be one of the doubters. [95] And do not be one of those who call the signs of God a lie, or you will be one of the losers. [96] Surely those against whom the word of your Lord has proved true will not believe, [97] even though every sign comes to them, until they see the painful punishment. [98] Why was there no town which believed, and its belief benefited it, except the people of Jonah? When they believed, We removed from them the punishment of disgrace in this present life and gave them enjoyment (of life) for a time.

10.94 – *If you are in doubt about what We have sent down to you, ask those who have been reciting the Book before you*

The Quran commands the messenger to check with others if he is in doubt. Since this comes just after a story about Moses and the Children of Israel, and "those who have been reciting the Book before you" closely matches "the People of the Book," it is reasonable to assume that the Quran is instructing the messenger to consult the custodians of the Torah – the Jews.

If so, this would be one of several quranic expressions that seem to show an unqualified acceptance of the authority of the Torah (also 3.23, 93). This is not to say that these verses prove the authority of the pre-Islamic scriptures – or even that this is the consistent attitude of the Quran. In fact, the Quran is rather confused and confusing about the pre-Islamic scriptures: always positive and respectful when actually naming them, but often suspicious of their treatment by their custodians. See "Tampering with the Pre-Islamic Scriptures" (p. 142).

10.98 – *Why was there no town which believed . . . except the people of Jonah?*

Jonah gets special mention for the way in which God lifted the punishment from the town to which Jonah preached (the Quran does not give the name of the town). As a rule, the Quran's "punishment narratives" end with Allah destroying the people. This sūra is named after him (*Yūnus*). Jonah's name appears elsewhere in lists of prophets and he is also referred to in two different ways as "the one of the fish," but the fullest version of his story comes at 37.139–49.

[99] If your Lord had (so) pleased, whoever was on the earth would indeed have believed – all of them together. Will you compel the people until they become believers? [100] It is not for any person to believe, except by the permission of God. He places abomination on those who do not understand.

[101] Say: 'See what is in the heavens and the earth!' But signs and warnings are of no use to a people who do not believe. [102] Do they expect (anything) but the same as the days of those who passed away before them? Say: '(Just) wait! Surely I shall be one of those waiting with you.' [103] Then We rescue Our messengers and those who believe. In this way – (it is) an obligation on Us – We shall rescue the believers.

[104] Say: 'People! If you are in doubt about my religion, (know that) I do not serve those whom you serve instead of God, but I serve God, the One who takes you. I have been commanded to be one of the believers.' [105] And: 'Set your face to the religion (as) a Ḥanīf, and do not be one of the idolaters. [106] Do not call on what can neither benefit nor harm you, instead of God (alone). If you do, surely then you will be one of the evildoers. [107] If God touches you with any harm, (there is) no one to remove it but Him, and if He intends for you any good, (there is) no one to turn back His favor. He smites with it whomever He pleases of His servants. He is the Forgiving, the Compassionate.'

10.99 – *Will you compel the people until they become believers?*

The Quran asks the messenger whether he will compel the people, using the same Arabic root as the famous "no compulsion" verse (*akraha*, 2.256). The implied answer is no – that this would not be appropriate to the messenger's role. Coming so soon after Sūras 8 and 9, this expectation of no compulsion sets up a contrast to the messenger's assignment in verses like 4.84; 8.39; and 9.5.

10.103 – *Then We rescue Our messengers and those who believe*

The language of salvation usually appears in stories of past prophets, for example in this sūra at verses 73 and 92. Sūra 10.103 seems to make this pattern into a principle and adds that Allah makes it obligatory upon himself to deliver the believers from harm. See "Salvation in the Quran" (p. 180).

10.104 – *I serve God, the One who takes you*

On Droge's translation of the Arabic verb *tawaffā* as "take," see the comment at 10.46. See also comments at 3.55 (p. 87) and "The Death of Jesus in the Quran" (p. 314).

10.105 – *Set your face to the religion (as) a Ḥanīf*

The word *Ḥanīf* is often translated as "a man by nature upright" or "of pure faith" and is usually associated with Abraham elsewhere in the Quran. See the comments at 2.135 (p. 55) and "Abraham in the Quran" (p. 90).

[108] Say: 'People! The truth has come to you from your Lord. Whoever is (rightly) guided, is guided only for himself, and whoever goes astray, goes astray only against himself. I am not a guardian over you.'

[109] Follow what you are inspired (with), and be patient until God judges, (for) He is the best of judges.

HŪD
HŪD

11

A long story about Noah sets the tone for this sūra, in which a series of messengers faithfully preach yet experience resistance from their audiences. The sūra also includes a substantial version of the story of the messengers who came to Abraham and Lot. The characters named and the sequence of their stories is very similar to Sūras 7 and 26.

This sūra gets its name from the story of Hūd, thought by some to be an Arabian prophetic figure (vv. 50–60). Hūd is one of a few figures in this sūra who are not familiar from the Bible; the others are Ṣāliḥ and Shuʿayb. In each case the Quran describes the people to whom each messenger was sent. Scholars have speculated on the identity of these three figures but have not been able to discover their place in history.

The sūra begins with the general preaching of the "messenger" and the responses of his audience. Each of the stories in the sūra end with God's destruction of people who do not heed the messenger's warning. After all the stories are presented, the Quran speaks directly to the messenger to tell him that the purpose of all these narratives is to strengthen his heart.

In the Name of God, the Merciful, the Compassionate

¹ Alif Lām Rāʾ. A Book – its verses have been clearly composed (and) then made distinct – (sent down) from One (who is) wise, aware.

² 'Do not serve (anyone) but God! Surely I am a warner and bringer of good news to you from Him.' ³ And: 'Ask forgiveness from your Lord, then turn to Him (in repentance). He will give you good enjoyment (of life) for an appointed time, and give His favor to everyone (deserving) of favor. If you turn away – surely I fear for you the punishment of a great Day. ⁴ To God is your return. He is powerful over everything.'

11.2 – *Surely I am a warner and bringer of good news to you from Him*

The messenger describes himself as a warner and bringer of good news. Notice that in this opening passage there is no command from the voice of the Quran to "say."

⁵ Is it not a fact that they cover their hearts to hide from Him? Is it not (a fact) that (even) when they cover themselves with their clothing, He knows what they keep secret and what they speak aloud? Surely He knows what is in the hearts. ⁶ (There is) not a creature on the earth but its provision (depends) on God. He knows its dwelling place and its storage place. Everything is (recorded) in a clear Book. ⁷ He (it is) who created the heavens and the earth in six days – and His throne was upon the water – that He might test you (to see) which of you is best in deed.

If indeed you say, 'Surely you will be raised up after death,' those who disbelieve will indeed say, 'This is nothing but clear magic.' ⁸ If indeed We postpone the punishment from them until a set period (of time), they will indeed say, 'What is holding it back?' Is it not (a fact) that on the Day when it comes to them, it will not be diverted from them, and what they were mocking will overwhelm them? ⁹ If indeed We give a person a taste of mercy from Us, (and) then We withdraw it from him, surely he is indeed despairing (and) ungrateful. ¹⁰ But if indeed We give him a taste of blessing, after hardship has touched him, he will indeed say, 'The evils have gone from me.' Surely he is indeed gloating (and) boastful ¹¹ – except those who are patient and do righteous deeds. Those – for them (there is) forgiveness and a great reward.

¹² Perhaps you are leaving out part of what you are inspired (with), and your heart is weighed down by it, because they say, 'If only a treasure were sent down on him or an angel came with him.' You are only a warner. God is guardian over everything. ¹³ Or do they say, 'He has forged it'? Say: 'Then bring ten sūras forged like it, and call on whomever you can, other than God, if you are truthful.' ¹⁴ If they do not respond to you, know that it has been sent down with the knowledge of God, and that (there is) no god but Him. So (will) you submit? ¹⁵ Whoever desires this present life and its (passing) splendor – We shall pay them in full for their deeds in it, and they will not be shortchanged in it. ¹⁶ Those are the ones who – for them there is nothing in the Hereafter but the Fire. What they have done will come to nothing there. What they have done will be in vain.

11.13 – *Or do they say, "He has forged it"? Say: "Then bring ten sūras forged like it . . ."*
The audience does not believe that the messenger's recitation is true. They accuse the messenger of simply inventing the words. The Quran commands the messenger to challenge the audience to compose ten *sūras* like the recitation. Similar challenges appear at 2.23; 10.38; 17.88; 28.49; and 52.34. In Muslim tradition these verses became known as the *taḥaddī* ("challenge") verses. See the analysis of these verses at 52.34 (p. 529). On verses that accuse the messenger of inventing, see the discussion at 69.44 (p. 587).

[17] Is the one who (stands) on a clear sign from his Lord, and recites it as a witness from Him, and before it was the Book of Moses as a model and mercy [. . .]? Those believe in it, but whoever disbelieves in it from the factions – the Fire is his appointed place. So do not be in doubt about it. Surely it is the truth from your Lord, but most of the people do not believe.

[18] Who is more evil than the one who forges a lie against God? Those will be presented before their Lord, and the witnesses will say, 'These are those who lied against their Lord.' Is it not (a fact) that the curse of God is on the evildoers, [19] who keep (people) from the way of God and desire (to make) it crooked, and they are disbelievers in the Hereafter? [20] Those – they cannot escape (Him) on the earth, and they have no allies other than God. The punishment will be doubled for them. They could not hear and did not see. [21] Those are the ones who have lost their (own) selves, and what they forged has abandoned them. [22] (There is) no doubt that they will be the worst losers in the Hereafter. [23] Surely those who believe, and do righteous deeds, and humble themselves to their Lord – those are the companions of the Garden. There they will remain. [24] The parable of the two groups is like the blind and the deaf, and the sighted and the hearing. Are they equal in comparison? Will you not take heed?

[25] Certainly We sent Noah to his people: 'I am a clear warner for you.

11.17 – *before it was the Book of Moses as a model and mercy*

Wherever the Quran names the pre-Islamic scriptures or – as in this case – the Torah by another name, it consistently describes them only in the most positive and respectful ways. The Arabic word here translated "model" (*imām*) can also mean standard, criterion, or even "plumb line."

11.23 – *Surely those who believe, and do righteous deeds, and humble themselves to their Lord*

In Sūra 11 and in many other sūras like it, this is an important summary of the preaching of the messenger. Those who follow this will be rewarded after death in the "Gardens."

11.25 – *Certainly We sent Noah to his people*

Noah is an important character in the Quran, and different versions of his story appear seven times. This version (vv. 25–48) is the most extensive. It begins with an animated conversation between Noah and the people who oppose him (vv. 25–34). Then God commands Noah to build the "ship," gives instructions on how to fill it, and sets Noah and his family off on the waves (vv. 36–44). When the waters recede, Noah talks with his Lord about the loss of his son (vv. 45–48).

Other versions of Noah's story come at 7.59–64; 10.71–3; 23.23–30; 26.105–20; 54.7–17; and 71.1–28.

²⁶ Do not serve (anyone) but God! Surely I fear for you the punishment of a painful Day.' ²⁷ The assembly of those who disbelieved of his people said, 'We do not see you as (anything) but a human being like us, and we do not see following you (any) but the worst (and) most gullible of us. We do not see in you any superiority over us. No! We think you are liars.' ²⁸ He said, 'My people! Do you see? If I (stand) on a clear sign from my Lord, and He has given me mercy from Himself, but it has been obscured for you, shall we compel you (to accept) it when you are unwilling? ²⁹ My people! I do not ask you for any money for it. My reward (depends) only on God. I am not going to drive away those who believe. Surely they are going to meet their Lord, but I see that you are an ignorant people. ³⁰ My people! Who would help me against God if I drove them away? Will you not take heed? ³¹ I do not say to you, "I possess the storehouses of God," nor do I know the unseen. And I do not say, "I am an angel," nor do I say to those your eyes look down on, "God will not give them any good." God knows what is in them. Surely then I would indeed be one of the evildoers.' ³² They said, 'Noah! You have disputed with us, and disputed (too) much with us. Bring us what you promise us, if you are one of the truthful.' ³³ He said, 'Only God will bring it to you, if He (so) pleases, and you will not escape. ³⁴ My advice will not benefit you – (even) if I wish to advise you – if God wishes to make you err. He is your Lord, and to Him you will be returned.'

³⁵ Or do they say, 'He has forged it'? Say: 'If I have forged it, my sin is on me, but I am free of the sins you commit.'

³⁶ And Noah was inspired: 'None of your people will believe, except for the one who has (already) believed, so do not be distressed by what they have done. ³⁷ Build the ship under Our eyes and Our inspiration, and do not address Me concerning those who have done evil. Surely they are going to be drowned.' ³⁸ And he was building the ship, and whenever the assembly of his people passed

---

11.28 – *shall we compel you (to accept) it when you are unwilling?*

Noah asks the same question that the quranic messenger asks in 10.99, using a different verb for "compel," *alzama*. The implied answer is no – Noah leaves the audience freedom to respond to his preaching.

11.35 – *Or do they say, "He has forged it"?*

The people question Noah's preaching in the same way that the audience of the Quran's messenger question his preaching (v. 13). Noah, however, does not challenge his listeners to produce an equivalent recitation.

11.36 – *do not be distressed by what they have done*

The portrait of the messenger in this story of Noah is that he faithfully does what God commands him and leaves the judgment to God.

by him, they ridiculed him. He said, 'If you ridicule us, surely we shall ridicule you as you ridicule. [39] Soon you will know (on) whom punishment will come, disgracing him, and on whom a lasting punishment will descend.' [40] – Until, when Our command came and the oven boiled, We said, 'Load into it two of every kind, a pair, and your family – except for the one against whom the word has (already) gone forth – and whoever has believed.' But only a few had believed with him. [41] And he said, 'Sail in it! In the name of God (is) its running and its anchoring. Surely my Lord is indeed forgiving, compassionate.' [42] It ran with them in (the midst of) wave(s) like mountains, and Noah called out to his son, since he was in a place apart, 'My son! Sail with us and do not be with the disbelievers!' [43] He said, 'I shall take refuge on a mountain (that) will protect me from the water.' He said, '(There is) no protector today from the command of God, except for the one on whom He has compassion.' And the waves came between them, and he was among the drowned.

[44] And it was said: 'Earth! Swallow your water! And sky! Stop!' And the waters subsided, and the command was accomplished, and it came to rest on al-Jūdī. And it was said: 'Away with the people who were evildoers!' [45] And Noah called out to his Lord, and said, 'My Lord, surely my son is one of my family, and surely Your promise is the truth, and You are the most just of judges.' [46] He said, 'Noah! Surely he is not one of your family. Surely it is an unrighteous deed. So do not ask Me about what you have no knowledge of. Surely I admonish you not to be one of the ignorant.' [47] He said, 'My Lord, surely I take refuge with You for asking You about what I have no knowledge of, and unless You forgive me

---

11.42 – *Noah called out to his son*

Noah's son thinks he can survive the flood by climbing a mountain, but the water reaches him there and he drowns (v. 43). After the flood, Noah seems to argue with Allah about his son (v. 45), but Allah says the disobedience of the son separates him from Noah's family (v. 46). Interestingly, the Quran also says elsewhere that the wife of Noah disobeys and is commanded to "enter the Fire!" (66.10).

11.44 – *it came to rest on al-Jūdī*

The Torah account of Noah states that "the ark came to rest on the mountains of Ararat" (Genesis 8:4). Al-Jūdī is a name that reflects postbiblical Jewish and Christian speculations about the particular mountain on which the ark landed.

11.47 – *unless You forgive me and have compassion on me, I shall be one of the losers*

Noah asks forgiveness for appealing to his Lord about his son. In the Quran, biblical prophets generally acknowledge their faults and ask forgiveness. This clashes with the Muslim doctrine of the sinlessness of prophets known by the Arabic term 'iṣma. In fact, the Islamic interpretive tradition debated who is guilty of "an unrighteous

and have compassion on me, I shall be one of the losers.' [48] It was said, 'Noah! Go down with peace from Us, and blessings on you and on the communities of those who are with you. But (to other) communities We shall give enjoyment (of life), (and) then a painful punishment from Us will touch them.' [49] That is one of the stories of the unseen. We inspired you (with) it. You did not know it, (neither) you nor your people, before (this). So be patient. Surely the outcome (belongs) to the ones who guard (themselves).

[50] And to 'Ād (We sent) their brother Hūd. He said, 'My people! Serve God! You have no god other than Him. You are nothing but forgers (of lies). [51] My people! I do not ask you for any reward for it. My reward (depends) only on the One who created me. Will you not understand?' [52] And: 'My people! Ask forgiveness from your Lord, (and) then turn to Him (in repentance). He will send the sky (down) on you in abundance (of rain), and increase you in strength upon your strength. Do not turn away as sinners.' [53] They said, 'Hūd! You have not brought us any clear sign, and we are not going to abandon our gods on your saying, (for) we do not believe in you. [54] We (can) only say (that) one of our gods has seized you with evil.' He said, 'Surely I call God to witness, and you bear witness (too), that I am free of what you associate, [55] other than Him. So plot against me, all of you, (and) then do not spare me. [56] Surely I have put my trust in God, my Lord and your Lord. (There is) no creature He does not seize by its hair. Surely my Lord is on a straight path. [57] If you turn away, I have delivered to you what I was sent to you with, and my Lord will make another people succeed you, and you will not harm Him at all. Surely my Lord is a watcher over everything.' [58] And when Our command came, We rescued Hūd, and those who believed with

---

deed" in verse 46, and how to interpret this verse so that it leaves no stain on Noah's claimed sinlessness. See the analysis of verses on the sins of prophets at 48.2 (p. 513).

11.49 – *That is one of the stories of the unseen. We inspired you (with) it. You did not know it*

After the Noah story, the Quran addresses the messenger to state that he did not know the story prior to reciting it. Similar expressions come at 3.44 (after the story of Mary); 12.102 (story of Joseph); and 28.44 (story of Moses). See the analysis of this claim at 28.44 (p. 395).

11.50 – *And to 'Ād (We sent) their brother Hūd*

On 'Ād and Hūd (vv. 50–60), see the explanation at 7.65 (p. 182).

11.58 – *We rescued Hūd, and those who believed with him*

The language of salvation is usually found in stories about figures familiar from the Old Testament. In this sūra, however, the expression "We rescued" is associated with Hūd, Ṣāliḥ (v. 66), and Shu'ayb (v. 94). See "Salvation in the Quran" (p. 180).

him, by a mercy from Us, and We rescued them from a stern punishment. [59] That was 'Ād: they denied the signs of their Lord, and disobeyed His messengers, and followed the command of every stubborn tyrant. [60] And they were followed in this world (by) a curse, and on the Day of Resurrection: 'Is it not a fact that 'Ād disbelieved their Lord? Is it not, "Away with 'Ād, the people of Hūd"?'

[61] And to Thamūd (We sent) their brother Ṣāliḥ. He said, 'My people! Serve God! You have no god other than Him. He produced you from the earth and settled you in it. So ask forgiveness from Him, (and) then turn to Him (in repentance). Surely my Lord is near (and) responsive.' [62] They said, 'Ṣāliḥ! You were among us as someone in whom hope was placed before. Do you forbid us to serve what our fathers have served? Surely we are in grave doubt indeed about what you call us to.' [63] He said, 'My people! Do you see? If I (stand) on a clear sign from my Lord, and He has given me mercy from Himself, who would help me against God if I disobeyed Him? You would only increase my loss. [64] My people! This is the she-camel of God, a sign for you. Let her graze on God's earth, and do not touch her with evil, or a punishment near (at hand) will seize you.' [65] But they wounded her, and he said, 'Enjoy (yourselves) in your home(s) for three days – that is a promise not to be denied.' [66] And when Our command came, We rescued Ṣāliḥ, and those who believed with him, by a mercy from Us, and from the disgrace of that day. Surely your Lord – He is the Strong, the Mighty. [67] And the cry seized those who did evil, and morning found them leveled in their homes. [68] (It was) as if they had not lived in prosperity there. 'Is it not a fact that Thamūd disbelieved their Lord? Is it not, "Away with Thamūd"?'

[69] Certainly Our messengers brought Abraham the good news. They said,

---

11.61 – *And to Thamūd (We sent) their brother Ṣāliḥ*

On Thamūd and Ṣāliḥ (vv. 61–68), see the comment at 7.73 (p. 183).

11.69 – *Certainly Our messengers brought Abraham the good news*

In this narrative (vv. 69–83), messengers bring Abraham good news of the birth of Isaac (*Isḥāq*, v. 71) and say they are on their way to the people of Lot (v. 70). Abraham's wife (not named) laughs to hear about Isaac, then reflects on the strangeness of bearing a child at her age (v. 72).

The messengers visit Lot and urge him and his family to flee the city (vv. 77–83). This version refers to the evil deeds of the townspeople in a roundabout way (vv. 78–81, with frightening echoes of the Genesis 19 story), while other quranic versions specify the sin that brings judgment. The messengers say that Lot's wife will be punished along with the rest of the town (v. 81).

The story about Abraham and the messengers appears in four other versions in the Quran. See "Abraham in the Quran" (p. 90). This story of Lot is the second of eight

'Peace!' He said, 'Peace!,' and did not delay in bringing a roasted calf. [70] When he saw their hands not reaching for it, he became suspicious of them and began to feel fear of them. They said, 'Do not fear! Surely we have been sent to the people of Lot.' [71] His wife was standing (there), and she laughed. And so We gave her the good news of Isaac, and after Isaac, Jacob. [72] She said, 'Woe is me! Shall I give birth when I am an old woman and my husband here is an old man? Surely this is an amazing thing indeed!' [73] They said, 'Are you surprised by the command of God? The mercy of God and His blessings (be) upon you, People of the House! Surely He is indeed praiseworthy, glorious.' [74] When the fright had left Abraham and the good news had come to him, he was disputing with Us concerning the people of Lot. [75] Surely Abraham was indeed tolerant, kind, (and) turning (in repentance). [76] 'Abraham! Turn away from this! Surely it has come – the command of your Lord. Surely they – a punishment is coming upon them which cannot be turned back.'

[77] And when Our messengers came to Lot, he became distressed about them, and felt powerless (to protect) them, and he said, 'This is a hard day.' [78] His people came to him, rushing to him, (for) they had been in the habit of doing evil deeds before (this). He said, 'My people! These are my daughters, they are purer for you. So guard (yourselves) against God, and do not disgrace me concerning my guests. Is (there) no one among you of right mind?' [79] They said, 'Certainly you know that we have no right to your daughters, and surely you know indeed what we want.' [80] He said, 'If only I had the strength for you, or could take refuge in a strong supporter!' [81] They said, 'Lot! Surely we are messengers of your Lord. They will not reach you. So journey with your family in a part of the night, and let none of you turn around, except your wife, (for) surely what is about to smite them is going to smite her. Surely their appointment is the morning. Is the morning not near?' [82] So when Our command came, We turned it upside down, and rained on it stones of baked clay, one after another, [83] marked in the presence of your Lord. It is not far from the evildoers.

---

versions, appearing together with Abraham and the messengers two other times (15.61–74; 29.28–34).

11.71 – *We gave her the good news of Isaac*

The particular wording of the Arabic original for "we gave her the good news," *bashsharnāhā*, helps provide a background for the question of which son is referred to in 37.101. In Sūra 37 the son of sacrifice is not named, but 37.101 says that God gave Abraham the good news (*bashsharnāhu*) "of a forbearing boy." See the discussion of this question at 37.107 (p. 451).

⁸⁴ And to Midian (We sent) their brother Shu'ayb. He said, 'My people! Serve God! You have no god other than Him. Do not diminish the measure or the scale. Surely I see you in prosperity, but surely I fear for you the punishment of an overwhelming day. ⁸⁵ My people! Fill up the measure and the scale in justice, and do not shortchange the people of their wealth, and do not act wickedly on the earth, fomenting corruption. ⁸⁶ A remnant of God is better for you, if you are believers. I am not a watcher over you.' ⁸⁷ They said, 'Shu'ayb! Does your prayer command you that we should abandon what our fathers have served, or that (we should abandon) doing what we please with our wealth? Surely you – you indeed are the tolerant (and) right-minded one.' ⁸⁸ He said, 'My people! Have you considered? If I (stand) on a clear sign from my Lord, and He has provided me with good provision from Himself [. . .]. I do not wish to go behind your backs to (do) what I forbid you from. I only wish to set (things) right, as much as I am able, but my success is only with God. In Him I have put my trust, and to Him I turn (in repentance). ⁸⁹ My people! Do not let my defiance (of you) provoke you to sin, or something will smite you similar to what smote the people of Noah, or the people of Hūd, or the people of Ṣāliḥ. And the people of Lot are not far from you. ⁹⁰ Ask forgiveness from your Lord, (and) then turn to Him (in repentance). Surely my Lord is compassionate, loving.'

⁹¹ They said, 'Shu'ayb! We do not understand much of what you say. Surely we indeed see you as weak among us. But (for) your gang (of followers) we would indeed have stoned you, (for) you are not mighty against us.' ⁹² He said, 'My people! Is my gang (of followers) mightier against you than God? Have you taken Him (as something to cast) behind you? Surely my Lord encompasses what you do. ⁹³ My people! Do as you are able. Surely I am going to do (what I can). Soon you will know the one (on) whom punishment will come, disgracing him, and the one who is a liar. (Just) watch! Surely I am watching with you.' ⁹⁴ And when Our command came, We rescued Shu'ayb, and those who believed with him, by a mercy from Us. And the cry seized those who did evil, and morning found them leveled in their homes. ⁹⁵ (It was) as if they had not lived there. 'Is it not away with Midian, (just) as Thamūd was done away with?'

11.84 – *And to Midian (We sent) their brother Shu'ayb*

On Midian and Shu'ayb (vv. 84–95), see the explanation at 7.85.

11.90 – *my Lord is compassionate, loving*

Shu'ayb urges the people of Midian to respond appropriately to their Lord, describing the Lord as kind or "loving" (*wadūd*). This description comes once more in the Quran at 85.14. See "The Language of Love in the Quran" (p. 560).

[96] Certainly We sent Moses with Our signs and clear authority [97] to Pharaoh and his assembly, but they followed the command of Pharaoh, when the command of Pharaoh was not right-minded. [98] He will precede his people on the Day of Resurrection, and lead them to the Fire. Evil is the place (to which they are) led! [99] They were followed in this (world by) a curse, and on the Day of Resurrection – evil is the gift (they will be) given!

[100] That is from the stories of the towns (which) We recount to you. Some of them are (still) standing and some (are already) cut down. [101] Yet We did not do them evil, but they did themselves evil. Their gods, on whom they called instead of God, were of no use to them at all, when the command of your Lord came, and they only added to their ruin. [102] Such was the seizing of your Lord, when He seized the towns while they were doing evil. Surely His seizing was painful (and) harsh. [103] Surely in that is a sign indeed for whoever fears the punishment of the Hereafter. That is a Day to which the people will be gathered, and that is a Day (that will be) witnessed. [104] We postpone it only for a set time. [105] (When that) Day comes, no one will speak, except by His permission. Some of them will be miserable, and some happy. [106] As for those who are miserable, (they will be) in the Fire, where (there will be) a moaning and panting for them, [107] remaining there as long as the heavens and the earth endure, except as your Lord pleases. Surely your Lord accomplishes whatever He pleases. [108] But as for those who are happy, (they will be) in the Garden, there to remain as long as the heavens and earth endure, except as your Lord pleases – an unceasing gift. [109] Do not be in doubt about what these (people) serve: they only serve as their fathers served before (them). Surely We shall indeed pay them their portion in full, undiminished.

[110] Certainly We gave Moses the Book, and then differences arose about it. Were it not for a preceding word from your Lord, it would indeed have been decided between them. Surely they are in grave doubt indeed about it. [111] Surely each (of them) – when your Lord will indeed pay them in full for their deeds. Surely He is aware of what they do.

[112] So go straight, as you have been commanded, (you) and those who have turned (in repentance) with you. Do not transgress insolently, (for) surely He sees what you do. [113] Do not incline toward those who do evil, or the Fire will touch you – you have no allies other than God – (and) then you will not be helped.

11.110 – *Certainly We gave Moses the book, and then differences arose about it*

As in verse 17, there is no criticism here for the Book of Moses, but the Quran says that people disagreed concerning that book and fell into doubt about it. See the discussion of the differences attributed to the People of the Book at 98.4 (p. 642).

¹¹⁴ And observe the prayer at the two ends of the day and at the approach of the night. Surely good (deeds) take away evil (ones). That is a reminder to the mindful. ¹¹⁵ And be patient. Surely God does not let the reward of the doers of good go to waste.

¹¹⁶ If only there had been a remnant of men, among the generations before you, to forbid the (fomenting of) corruption on the earth – aside from a few of those whom We rescued among them. But those who did evil pursued what luxury they were given to delight in, and became sinners. ¹¹⁷ Yet your Lord was not one to destroy the towns in an evil manner, while its people were setting (things) right. ¹¹⁸ If your Lord had (so) pleased, He would indeed have made the people one community, but they will continue to differ, ¹¹⁹ except for the one on whom your Lord has compassion, and for that (purpose) He created them. But the word of your Lord is fulfilled: 'I shall indeed fill Gehenna with jinn and people – all (of them)!'

¹²⁰ Everything We recount to you from the stories of the messengers (is) what We make firm your heart with, and by this means the truth has come to you, and an admonition, and a reminder to the believers. ¹²¹ Say to those who do not believe: 'Do as you are able. Surely we are going to do (what we can).' ¹²² And: '(Just) wait! Surely we (too) are waiting.'

¹²³ To God (belongs) the unseen in the heavens and the earth, and to Him the affair – all of it – will be returned. So serve Him and put your trust in Him! Your Lord is not oblivious of what you do.

11.114 – *And observe the prayer at the two ends of the day and at the approach of the night*

The Quran does not specify five times of ritual prayer (*ṣalāh*), but rather three. See the comment at a similar verse, 17.78.

11.119 – *I shall indeed fill Gehenna with jinn and people – all (of them)!*

This verse seems to say that the intention of Allah is to fill hell (*jahannam*) with people. The *jinn* in the Quran are created beings that are neither angels nor demons. See the discussion of jinn at 72.1 (p. 593).

11.120 – *Everything We recount to you from the stories of the messengers (is) what We make firm you heart with*

The Quran directly addresses the messenger to tell him that one of the main purposes of the "punishment narratives" in the sūra is to encourage him.

Joseph

Yūsuf

12

Sūra 12 is the best-known – and longest – sūra that tells a single story. Those who are familiar with the Joseph story from the Bible know its power to capture the imagination. Readers will naturally compare the biblical story with the details and the narrative style of Sūra 12. They may notice that the quranic version leaves out some of the important details from Genesis 37–50 and at the same time adds some details not found in the biblical account. For example, the sūra includes descriptions of Joseph's desires and his awareness of the state of his soul.

Before and after the story, the Quran makes a series of claims about the significance of its telling of the story. The beauty of the story and its recitation in Arabic are claimed as signs of divine origin, and the sūra seems to state that its author must be inspired, because he did not know the story before reciting it.

Scholars have written extensively about the quranic story of Joseph and frequently observed the "elliptical," "allusive," and "referential" style of the story. That is, the story leaves out names and plot details that one might expect normally. The story offers many pronouns whose antecedents are not clearly identified. John Wansbrough went so far as to suggest that for readers who are not familiar with the biblical story, the quranic story would be unintelligible without commentary to fill in the gaps (see *Quranic Studies* in the bibliography).

Wansbrough further asked what this observation might mean for questions about the origins of the Quran. If the story only alludes or refers to the basic framework of the biblical story, this suggests that the listeners were already familiar with the story. If they were already familiar with the story, were the first listeners idolatrous Arabs in central Arabia?

In the Name of God, the Merciful, the Compassionate

[1] Alif Lām Rā'. Those are the signs of the clear Book. [2] Surely We have sent it down as an Arabic Qur'ān, so that you may understand.

12.2 – *Surely We have sent it down as an Arabic Qur'ān, so that you may understand*

³ We shall recount to you the best of accounts in what We have inspired you (with of) this Qur'ān, though before it you were indeed one of the oblivious.

⁴ (Remember) when Joseph said to his father, 'My father! Surely I saw eleven stars, and the sun and the moon. I saw them prostrating themselves before me.' ⁵ He said, 'My son! Do not recount your vision to your brothers or they will hatch a plot against you. Surely Satan is a clear enemy to humankind. ⁶ In this way your Lord will choose you, and teach you about the interpretation of dreams, and complete His blessing on you and on the house of Jacob, as He completed it before on your fathers, Abraham and Isaac. Surely your Lord is knowing, wise.'

⁷ Certainly in (the story of) Joseph and his brothers (there) are signs for the ones who ask.

⁸ (Remember) when they said, 'Joseph and his brother are indeed dearer to our father than we, (even) though we are a (large) group. Surely our father is indeed clearly astray. ⁹ Kill Joseph, or cast him (into some other) land, so that your father's favor will be exclusively for you, and after that you will be a righteous people.' ¹⁰ A speaker among them said, 'Do not kill Joseph, but cast him to the bottom of the well, (and) some caravan will pick him up – if you are going to do (anything).'

¹¹ They said, 'Our father! Why do you not trust us with Joseph? Surely we shall indeed look after him. ¹² Send him out with us tomorrow to enjoy (himself) and jest. Surely we shall indeed watch over him.' ¹³ He said, 'Surely I – it sorrows me indeed that you should take him away – I fear that the wolf may eat him while you are oblivious of him.' ¹⁴ They said, 'If indeed the wolf eats him, when we are (so large) a group, surely then we (would be) losers indeed.'

¹⁵ When they had taken him away, and agreed to put him in the bottom of

---

Before presenting the story of Joseph, the Quran makes a series of claims for the source of its version of the story and the inspiration of the messenger. Here *qur'ān* does not necessarily mean the Muslim scripture as it is known today. The word *qur'ān* simply means "recitation." However, the expression "Arabic Qur'ān" becomes very important in the claims that the Quran makes for itself, especially in Sūras 39–46. This verse indicates that one of the reasons for an "Arabic" recitation is "that you may understand" (also at 43.2). See the analysis of the claims for "Arabic" at 43.2–3 (p. 487).

12.4 – *when Joseph said to his father*

The lack of names for Joseph's father and brothers, including the other brother who was dearer to the father (v. 6), raises a number of interesting questions about the original audience of this sūra. For example, if the reciter or author knew these names, why did he not provide them? If the original listeners or readers already knew the names, who were they?

the well, We inspired him: 'You will indeed inform them about this affair (of theirs), though they will not realize (who you are).' [16] And they came to their father in the evening, weeping. [17] They said, 'Our father! Surely we went off racing (one another), and we left Joseph (behind) with our things, and the wolf ate him. But you will not believe us, even though we are truthful.' [18] And they brought his shirt with fake blood on it. He said, 'No! You have only contrived a story for yourselves. Patience is becoming (for me), and God is the One to be sought for help against what you allege.'

[19] A caravan came, and they sent their water-drawer, and he let down his bucket. He said, 'Good news! This is a young boy (here).' And they hid him as merchandise, but God knew what they were doing. [20] And they sold him for a small price, a number of dirhams, (for) they had no interest in him. [21] The one who bought him, (being) from Egypt, said to his wife, 'Make his dwelling place honorable. It may be that he will benefit us, or we may adopt him as a son.' In this way We established Joseph in the land, and (this took place) in order that We might teach him about the interpretation of dreams. God is in control of His affair, but most of the people do not know (it). [22] When he reached his maturity, We gave him judgment and knowledge. In this way We repay the doers of good.

[23] She, in whose house he was, tried to seduce him. She closed the doors and said, 'Come here, you!' He said, 'God's refuge! Surely he is my lord, and he has given me a good dwelling place. Surely the evildoers do not prosper.' [24] Certainly she was obsessed with him, and he would have been obsessed with her, if (it had) not (been) that he saw a proof of his Lord. (It happened) in this way in order that We might turn evil and immorality away from him. Surely he was one of Our devoted servants. [25] They both raced to the door, and she tore his shirt from behind. They both met her husband at the door. She said, 'What penalty (is there) for (someone) who intended (to do) evil to your family, except that he

---

12.21 – *The one who bought him, (being) from Egypt, said to his wife*

No names are given to the man and his wife.

12.24 – *he would have been obsessed with her*

The Quran says that Joseph would have desired the woman (*hamma bihā*) just like the woman desired him. The only thing that prevents him from immorality is that he sees "a proof of his Lord." On this point, the biblical account does not agree. There is no mention of any desire for the woman, only that Joseph refused (Genesis 39:8–12).

The earliest Muslim commentaries on the Quran were quite frank in imagining the scene according to the claim that Joseph "would have been obsessed with her." However, this expression became a point of controversy in Muslim commentaries after Islamic orthodoxy declared that prophets are sinless.

should be imprisoned or (suffer) a painful punishment?' ²⁶ He said, 'She tried to seduce me!' (Just then) a witness of her household bore witness: 'If his shirt is torn from the front, she has been truthful, and he is one of the liars. ²⁷ But if his shirt is torn from behind, she has lied, and he is one of the truthful.' ²⁸ So when he saw his shirt torn from behind, he said, 'Surely it is a plot of you women! Surely your plot is grave. ²⁹ Joseph, turn away from this. And you (woman), ask forgiveness for your sin. Surely you are one of the sinners!'

³⁰ Some women in the city said, 'The wife of that mighty one has been trying to seduce her young man. He has affected her deeply (with) love. Surely we see (that) she is indeed clearly astray.' ³¹ When she heard their cunning (gossip), she sent for them, and prepared a banquet for them, and gave each one of them a knife. Then she said (to Joseph), 'Come forth to (wait on) them.' When they saw him, they admired him, and cut their hands, and said, 'God preserve (us)! This is no (mere) mortal. This is nothing but a splendid angel!' ³² She said, 'That is the one you blamed me about. I certainly did try to seduce him, but he defended himself, and (now) if he does not do what I command him, he will indeed be imprisoned, and become one of the disgraced.' ³³ He said, 'My Lord, prison is preferable to me than what they invite me to. But unless You turn their plot away from me, I shall give in to them, and I shall become one of the ignorant.' ³⁴ Then his Lord responded to him, and turned their plot away from him. Surely He – He is the Hearing, the Knowing.

³⁵ Then it became apparent to them, after they had seen the signs, (that) they should imprison him for a time. ³⁶ And two young men entered the prison with him. One of them said, 'Surely I saw myself (in a dream) pressing wine,' and the other said, 'Surely I saw myself (in a dream) carrying bread on my head, from which the birds were eating. Inform us about its interpretation. Surely we see you are one of the doers of good.' ³⁷ He said, 'Before any food comes to either of

---

12.31 – *When she heard their cunning (gossip), she sent for them*

In the Torah account, at this point Joseph's master put him in prison (Genesis 39:20). In contrast, the Quran slips in a tale to dramatize how Joseph "was well-built and handsome" (Genesis 39:6).

When the woman hears the gossip of other women in the city, she invites them to a banquet to make a point. She gives each woman a paring knife and then calls Joseph into the room. The women are so amazed by Joseph's beauty that they cut their hands with the knives they are holding. This detail is not found in the biblical account of Joseph (Genesis 39:13–20), but a similar story is found in Jewish commentary on the Torah (*Midrāsh Yalkut, Midrāsh Haggādōl*). See "Apocryphal Details in Quranic Stories" (p. 299).

you for provision, I shall inform each of you about its interpretation before it comes to you. That is part of what my Lord has taught me. Surely I have forsaken the creed of a people (who) do not believe in God and (who) are disbelievers in the Hereafter, [38] and I have followed the creed of my fathers, Abraham, and Isaac, and Jacob. (It) was not for us to associate anything with God. That is part of the favor of God to us and to the people, but most of the people are not thankful (for it). [39] My two companions of the prison! Are various Lords better, or God, the One, the Supreme? [40] Instead of Him, you only serve names which you have named, you and your fathers. God has not sent down any authority for it. Judgment (belongs) only to God. He has commanded you not to serve (anyone) but Him. That is the right religion, but most of the people do not know (it). [41] My two companions of the prison! As for one of you, he will give his lord wine to drink, and as for the other, he will be crucified, and birds will eat from his head. The matter about which you two asked for a pronouncement has been decided.' [42] He said to the one of them he thought would be released, 'Mention me in the presence of your lord.' But Satan made him forget to mention (him) to his lord. So he remained in the prison for several years.

[43] The king said, 'Surely I saw (in a dream) seven fat cows, (and) seven lean ones are eating them, and seven green ears (of corn) and others dry. Assembly! Make a pronouncement to me about my vision, if you can interpret visions.' [44] They said, 'A jumble of dreams. We know nothing of the interpretation of dreams.' [45] But the one who had been released (from prison) said – (for) he remembered after a period (of time) – 'I shall inform you about its interpretation. So send me.'

[46] 'Joseph, you truthful man! Make a pronouncement to us about the seven fat cows (and) seven lean ones eating them, and the seven green ears (of corn) and others dry, in order that I may return to the people, so that they will know.' [47] He said, 'You will sow for seven years as usual, but what you harvest leave in its ear, except a little from which you may eat. [48] Then, after that, will come seven hard (years), (which will) eat up what you stored up for them, (all) except a little of what you preserved. [49] Then, after that, will come a year in which the people will have rain, and in which they will press.'

[50] The king said, 'Bring him to me!' But when the messenger came to him, he said, 'Return to your lord and ask him, "What (about the) case of the women who cut their hands?" Surely my Lord knew of their plot.' [51] He said, 'What is this business of yours, when you tried to seduce Joseph?' They said, 'God preserve (us)! We know no evil against him.' The wife of the mighty one said, 'Now the truth has come to light. I tried to seduce him, but surely he is indeed one of the truthful.' [52] 'That (is) so that he may know that I did not betray him

in secret, and that God does not guide the plot of the treacherous. [53] Yet I do not pronounce myself innocent, (for) surely the self is indeed an instigator of evil, except as my Lord has compassion. Surely my Lord is forgiving, compassionate.'

[54] The king said, 'Bring him to me! I want him for myself.' So when he spoke to him, he said, 'Surely this day you are secure with us (and) trustworthy.' [55] He said, 'Set me over the storehouses of the land. Surely I am a skilled overseer.' [56] In this way We established Joseph in the land. He settled in it wherever he pleased. We smite whomever We please with Our mercy, and We do not let the reward of the doers of good go to waste. [57] But the reward of the Hereafter is indeed better for those who believe and guard (themselves).

[58] The brothers of Joseph came, and they entered upon him. He recognized them, but they did not know him. [59] When he had supplied them with their supplies, he said, 'Bring me a brother of yours from your father. Do you not see that I fill up the measure, and that I am the best of hosts? [60] But if you do not bring him to me, (there will be) no measure for you with me, and you will not come near me.' [61] They said, 'We shall solicit his father for him. Surely we shall indeed do (so).' [62] He said to his young men, 'Put their merchandise (back) in their packs, so that they will recognize it when they turn back to their family, (and) so that they will return (here).'

[63] When they returned to their father, they said, 'Our father! The measure was refused us, so send our brother (back) with us, (and) we shall get the measure. Surely we shall indeed watch over him.' [64] He said, 'Shall I trust you with him as I trusted you with his brother before? God is the best Watcher, and He (is) the most compassionate of the compassionate.' [65] When they opened their belongings, they found their merchandise returned to them. They said, 'Our father, what (more) do we desire? This is our merchandise returned to us. We shall supply (food for) our family, and watch over our brother, and get an extra measure of a camel(-load). That is an easy measure.' [66] He said, 'I shall not send him with you until you give me a promise from God that you will indeed bring him (back) to me, unless you are surrounded.' When they had given him their pledge, he said, 'God is guardian over what we say.' [67] And he said, 'My sons!

12.53 – *surely the self is indeed an instigator of evil*

The Quran shows Joseph to be innocent in the matter of the "wife of the mighty one" (vv. 50–52). However, Joseph himself says that he does not consider himself innocent, then offers this striking statement about the human soul (*nafs*), which can also be translated "the soul surely commands evil." It is one of several verses in the Quran that hint at a deeper diagnosis of human nature. See the analysis of verses on human nature at 79.40 (p. 612).

Do not enter by one gate, but enter by different gates. I am of no use to you at all against God. Judgment (belongs) only to God. In Him have I put my trust, and in Him let the trusting put their trust.'

⁶⁸ When they had entered in the way their father commanded them – it was of no use to them at all against God, but (it was only) a need in Jacob himself which he satisfied. Surely he was indeed full of knowledge because of what We had taught him, but most of the people do not know (it). ⁶⁹ And when they entered upon Joseph, he took his brother to himself and said, 'Surely I am your brother, so do not be distressed at what they have done.'

⁷⁰ When he had supplied them with their supplies, he put the drinking cup in the pack of his brother. Then a crier cried out, 'Caravan! Surely you are thieves indeed!' ⁷¹ They said as they approached them, 'What is it you are missing?' ⁷² They said, 'We are missing the king's cup. To the one who brings it a camel-load (will be given). I guarantee it.' ⁷³ They said, 'By God! Certainly you know (that) we did not come to foment corruption on the earth. We are not thieves.' ⁷⁴ They said, 'What will the penalty for it be, if you are liars?' ⁷⁵ They said, 'The penalty for it (will be): the one in whose pack it is found, he (will be) liable for it. In this way we repay the evildoers.' ⁷⁶ So he began with their packs before (searching) his brother's pack, (and) then he brought it out of his brother's pack. In this way We plotted for (the sake of) Joseph. He was not one to take his brother, in (accord with) the religion of the king, unless God had (so) pleased. We raise in rank whomever We please, and above everyone who has knowledge is the One who knows.

⁷⁷ They said, 'If he steals, a brother of his has stolen before.' But Joseph kept it secret within himself and did not reveal it to them. He said, 'You are (in) a bad situation. God knows what you are alleging.' ⁷⁸ They said, 'Great one! Surely he has a father (who is) very old, so take one of us (in) his place. Surely we see (that) you are one of the doers of good.' ⁷⁹ He said, 'God's refuge! That we should take (anyone) except (the one) in whose possession we found our things! Surely then we (would be) evildoers indeed.' ⁸⁰ So when they had given up hope of (moving) him, they withdrew in private conversation. The eldest of them said, 'Do you not know that your father has already taken you under a promise from God? And (that) before that you neglected (to keep your promise) concerning Joseph? I shall not leave the land until my father gives me permission or (until) God judges for me. He is the best of judges. ⁸¹ Return to your father and say, "Our father! Surely your son has stolen. We bear witness only about what we know. We were not observers of the unseen. ⁸² Ask (the people of) the town where we were, and (those in) the caravan in which we have come. Surely we are truthful indeed."'

⁸³ He said, 'No! You have only contrived a story for yourselves. Patience is becoming (for me). It may be that God will bring them all to me. Surely He – He

is the Knowing, the Wise.' [84] He turned away from them and said, 'My sorrow for Joseph!' And his eyes became white from the grief, and he choked back his sadness. [85] They said, 'By God! You will never stop mentioning Joseph until you are frail or are on the verge of death.' [86] He said, 'I only complain (of) my anguish and my grief to God, (for) I know from God what you do not know. [87] My sons! Go and search out news of Joseph and his brother, and do not despair of the comfort of God. Surely everyone has hope of the comfort of God, except for the people who are disbelievers.'

[88] When they entered upon him, they said, 'Great one! Hardship has touched us and our house, and we have brought merchandise of little value. Fill up the measure for us and be charitable to us. Surely God rewards the charitable.' [89] He said, 'Do you know what you did with Joseph and his brother, when you were ignorant?' [90] They said, 'Are you indeed Joseph?' He said, 'I am Joseph, and this is my brother. God has bestowed favor on us. Surely the one who guards (himself) and is patient – surely God does not let the reward of the doers of good go to waste.' [91] They said, 'By God! Certainly God has preferred you over us, and we have been sinners indeed.' [92] He said, '(There is) no reproach on you today. God will forgive you, (for) He is the most compassionate of the compassionate. [93] Go with this shirt of mine and cast it on my father's face. He will regain (his) sight. And (then) bring me your family all together.'

[94] When the caravan set forth, their father said, 'Surely I do indeed perceive the scent of Joseph, though you may think me senile.' [95] They said, 'By God! Surely you are indeed in your (same) old error.' [96] So when the bringer of good news came (to him), he cast it on his face and (his) sight returned. He said, 'Did I not say to you, "Surely I know from God what you do not know"?' [97] They said, 'Our father! Ask forgiveness for us for our sins. Surely we have been sinners.' [98] He said, 'I shall ask my Lord for forgiveness for you. Surely He – He is the Forgiving, the Compassionate.'

[99] When they entered upon Joseph, he took his parents to himself and said, 'Enter Egypt, if God pleases, secure.' [100] He raised his parents on the throne, and they (all) fell down before him in prostration. And he said, 'My father! This is the interpretation of my vision from before. My Lord has made it (come) true. He has been good to me, when He brought me out of the prison, and when He brought you out of the desert, after Satan had caused strife between me and my brothers. Surely my Lord is astute to whatever He pleases. Surely He – He is the Knowing, the Wise. [101] My Lord, you have given me some of the kingdom, and taught me some of the interpretation of dreams. Creator of the heavens and the

---

12.101 – *Take me as one who has submitted, and join me with the righteous*

In this prayer of Joseph, Droge translates the Arabic verb *tawaffā* as "take," adding

earth, You are my ally in this world and the Hereafter. Take me as one who has submitted, and join me with the righteous.'

[102] That is one of the stories of the unseen. We inspired you (with) it. You were not with them when they agreed on their plan and were scheming. [103] Most of the people are not going to believe, even if you are eager (for that). [104] You do not ask them for any reward for it. It is nothing but a reminder to the worlds. [105] How many a sign in the heavens and the earth do they pass by! Yet they turn away from it. [106] Most of them do not believe in God, unless they associate. [107] Do they feel secure that a covering of God's punishment will not come upon them, or that the Hour will not come upon them unexpectedly, when they do not realize (it)? [108] Say: 'This is my way. I call (you) to God on (the basis of) evidence – I and whoever follows me. Glory to God! I am not one of the idolaters.'

[109] We have not sent (anyone) before you except men whom We inspired from the people of the towns. Have they not traveled on the earth and seen how the end was for those who were before them? The Home of the Hereafter is indeed better for those who guard (themselves). Do you not understand? [110] – Until, when the messengers had given up hope, and thought that they had been lied to, Our help came to them, and those whom We pleased were rescued. But Our violence was not turned back from the people who were sinners. [111] Certainly in their accounts (there is) a lesson for those with understanding.

It is not a forged proclamation, but a confirmation of what was before it, and a distinct setting forth of everything, and a guidance and mercy for a people who believe.

"in death" in a footnote. Several Muslim translations simply give "cause to die" or similar expressions related to death (Pickthall, Shakir, Mohsin Khan, Sahih International, Muhammad Sarwar; cf. Yusuf Ali). Yet none of these six translates *tawaffā* in the same way at 3.55, where ʿĪsā is the object of the verb. See the comments at 3.55 (p. 87) and "The Death of Jesus in the Quran" (p. 314).

12.102 – *You were not with them when they agreed on their plan*

After the story of Joseph is told, the Quran addresses the messenger directly in a self-conscious way to assure him that he was not present to observe the events of the story. The implication seems to be that if he did not witness the story, his telling of the story must be "inspired" (*awḥā*, also in v. 3). See a discussion of this and similar verses at 28.44 (p. 395).

12.111 – *It is not a forged proclamation, but a confirmation of what was before it*

In a self-affirming way similar to verse 102, the Quran claims confirmation or attestation by the pre-Islamic scriptures. See the analysis of this claim, and a response, at 46.12 (p. 502). On verses that accuse the messenger of inventing, see the discussion at 69.44 (p. 587).

THE THUNDER
AL-RAʿD

13

The Creator of the universe has displayed the signs of his presence and power in the natural world and expects an appropriate response from humankind. This is the message of a large part of this sūra. In fact, the sūra is named after one of those signs: "the thunder (al-raʿd) glorifies (Him) with His praise" (v. 13).

The sūra also contains a number of verses that indicate an encounter between the messenger and his audience and the questions or speeches of resistance from the audience. In reply, the Quran dictates the preaching of the messenger, introduced by the word *say*.

The response of the audience to the message carries consequences, and there are several descriptions of rewards and punishments.

In this sūra the messenger is "only a warner" and is apparently vulnerable to discouragement. The Quran reassures the messenger at a number of points, claiming that his recitations are from Allah and telling him that being mocked was also an experience of messengers in the past.

In the Name of God, the Merciful, the Compassionate

[1] Alif Lām Mīm Rāʾ. Those are the signs of the Book. What has been sent down to you from your Lord is the truth, but most of the people do not believe.

[2] (It is) God who raised up the heavens without pillars that you (can) see. Then He mounted the throne, and subjected the sun and the moon, each one running (its course) for an appointed time. He directs the (whole) affair. He makes the signs distinct, so that you may be certain of the meeting with your Lord. [3] He (it is) who stretched out the earth, and placed on it firm mountains and rivers. And of all the fruits He has placed on it two in pairs. He covers the day with the night. Surely in that are signs indeed for a people who reflect.

13.2 – *(It is) God who raised up the heavens without pillars that you (can) see*

These words begin an extended passage (vv. 2–18) that tells of the "signs" (āyāt) of creation and the need for an appropriate human response to the Creator.

⁴ On the earth (there are) parts neighboring (each other), and gardens of grapes, and (fields of) crops, and palm trees, (growing in) bunches and singly, (all) watered with one water. Yet We favor some of it over others in fruit. Surely in that are signs indeed for a people who understand.

⁵ If you are amazed, their saying is amazing: 'When we have turned to dust, shall we indeed (return) in a new creation?' Those are the ones who have disbelieved in their Lord, and those – the chains will be on their necks – those are the companions of the Fire. There they will remain. ⁶ They seek to hurry you with the evil before the good, though the examples (of punishment) have already happened before them. Surely your Lord is indeed full of forgiveness for the people, despite their evildoing, yet surely your Lord is (also) indeed harsh in retribution.

⁷ Those who disbelieve say, 'If only a sign were sent down on him from his Lord.' You are only a warner, and for every people (there is) a guide.

⁸ God knows what every female bears, and (in) what (way) the womb shrinks and (in) what (way) it swells. Everything with Him has (its) measure. ⁹ (He is) the Knower of the unseen and the seen, the Great, the Exalted. ¹⁰ (It is) the same (for) any of you who keeps (his) saying secret or who makes it public, and (for) anyone who hides in the night or goes about in the day. ¹¹ For him (there is) a following, before him and behind him, who watch over him by the command of God. Surely God does not change what is in a people, until they change what is in themselves. And when God wishes evil for a people, (there is) no turning (it) back for them. They have no ally other than Him.

¹² He (it is) who shows you the lightning – in fear and desire – and He produces the clouds heavy (with rain). ¹³ The thunder glorifies (Him) with His praise, and the angels (too) out of awe of Him. He sends the thunderbolts,

---

13.5 – *When we have turned to dust, shall we indeed (return) in a new creation?*

The audience raises an objection to the messenger's preaching about the resurrection.

13.7 – *Those who disbelieve say, "If only some sign were sent down on him from his Lord."*

This speech of the disbelievers seems to indicate an encounter between a messenger and his audience in which the audience is not accepting his message. The Quran then tells the messenger what to "say" in response. The speech repeats in verse 27 and draws a second response from the messenger.

In this verse the messenger is "only a warner" and guide (also vv. 30–31, 36, 40, 43). He delivers Allah's message and leaves the outcome to Allah. On whether the messenger performs miracles, see discussion at 43.40 (p. 490).

and smites with it whomever He pleases. Yet they dispute about God, when He is mighty in power. ¹⁴ The true call (is) to Him, and those whom they call on instead of Him do not respond to them at all. (They are) only like someone stretching out his hands toward water, so that it may reach his mouth, but it does not reach it. The call of the disbelievers only goes astray. ¹⁵ Whatever is in the heavens and the earth prostrates itself before God, willingly or unwillingly, and (so do) their shadows in the morning and the evenings.

¹⁶ Say: 'Who is Lord of the heavens and the earth?' Say: 'God.' Say: 'Have you taken allies other than Him? They do not have power to (cause) themselves benefit or harm.' Say: 'Are the blind and the sighted equal, or are the darkness and the light equal? Or have they set up associates for God who have created a creation like His, so that the creation is (all) alike to them?' Say: 'God is the Creator of everything. He is the One, the Supreme.'

¹⁷ He sends down water from the sky, and the wādīs flow, (each) in its measure, and the torrent carries a rising (layer of) froth (on top), like the froth that arises from what they heat in the fire, seeking some ornament or utensil. In this way God strikes (a parable of) the true and the false. As for the froth, it becomes worthless, but as for what benefits the people, it remains on the earth. In this way God strikes parables.

¹⁸ For those who respond to their Lord (there is) the good (reward), but those who do not respond to Him – (even) if they had what is on the earth – all (of it) – and as much again, they would indeed (try to) ransom (themselves) with it. Those – for them (there is) the evil reckoning. Their refuge is Gehenna – it is an evil bed!

¹⁹ Is the one who knows that what has been sent down to you from your Lord is the truth, like the one who is blind? Only those with understanding take heed: ²⁰ those who fulfill the covenant of God and do not break the compact, ²¹ and who join together what God has commanded to be joined with it, and fear their Lord, and are afraid of the evil reckoning, ²² and who are patient in seeking the face of their Lord, and observe the prayer, and contribute from what We have provided them, in secret and in open, and avert evil by means of the good. Those – for them (there is) the outcome of the Home: ²³ Gardens of Eden which they (will) enter, and (also) those who were righteous among their fathers, and their wives, and their descendants. The angels (will) come in to them from every gate:

13.20 – *those who fulfill the covenant of God and do not break the compact*
This and the following verses detail an appropriate response to the Creator, reward for those who do this, and punishment for those who break the covenant of Allah (vv. 20–26).

[24] 'Peace (be) upon you because you were patient! Excellent is the outcome of the Home!'

[25] But those who break the covenant of God, after its ratification, and sever what God has commanded to be joined, and foment corruption on the earth, those – for them (there is) the curse, and for them (there is) the evil Home. [26] God extends (His) provision to whomever He pleases, and restricts (it). They gloat over this present life, but this present life is nothing but a (fleeting) enjoyment in (comparison to) the Hereafter.

[27] Those who disbelieve say, 'If only a sign were sent down on him from his Lord?' Say: 'Surely God leads astray whomever He pleases and guides to Himself whoever turns (to Him).' [28] Those who believe and whose hearts are secure in the remembrance of God – surely hearts are secure in the remembrance of God – [29] those who believe and do righteous deeds – for them (there is) happiness and a good (place of) return.

[30] In this way We have sent you among a community – before it (other) communities have already passed away – in order that you might recite to them what We have inspired you (with). Yet they disbelieve in the Merciful. Say: 'He is my Lord – (there is) no god but Him. In Him I have put my trust, and to Him is my turning (in repentance).' [31] If (only there were) a Qur'ān by which the mountains were moved, or by which the earth were split open, or by which the dead were spoken to. No! The affair (belongs) to God altogether. Have those who believe no hope that, if God (so) pleased, He would indeed guide all the people? (As for) those who disbelieve, a striking will continue to smite them for what they have done, or it will descend near their home(s), until the promise of God comes. Surely God will not break the appointment. [32] Certainly messengers have been mocked before you, but I spared those who disbelieved. Then I seized them – and how was my retribution?

[33] Is He who stands over every person for what he has earned [. . .]? They have set up associates for God. Say: 'Name them! Or will you inform Him about what He does not know on the earth, or about what is said openly?' No!

13.27 – *Surely God leads astray whomever He pleases*

The free will of humans to choose the right path, on the one hand, and the authority of Allah to determine their steps, on the other, are important themes in the Quran that many readers – including Muslims – have found contradictory (see also v. 33; 14:4; 16:95; 17:97).

13.30 – *In this way We have sent you among a community*

The Quran speaks directly to the messenger to claim that Allah sends and inspires him. See "Different Kinds of Literature" (p. 14).

Their scheming is made to appear enticing to those who disbelieve, and they are kept from the way. Whoever God leads astray has no guide. [34] For them (there is) punishment in this present life, yet the punishment of the Hereafter is indeed harder. They have no defender against God.

[35] A parable of the Garden which is promised to the ones who guard (themselves): through it rivers flow, its fruit is unending, and (also) its shade. That is the outcome for the ones who guard (themselves), but the outcome for the disbelievers is the Fire.

[36] Those to whom We have given the Book rejoice in what has been sent down to you, though some among the factions reject part of it. Say: 'I am only commanded to serve God, and not to associate (anything) with Him. To Him do I call (you), and to Him is my return.'

[37] In this way We have sent it down as an Arabic judgment. If indeed you follow their (vain) desires, after what has come to you of the knowledge, you will have no ally and no defender against God. [38] Certainly We sent messengers before you, and gave them wives and descendants, but it was not for any messenger to bring a sign, except by the permission of God. For every (period of)

13.34 – *For them (there is) punishment in this present life, yet the punishment of the Hereafter is indeed harder*

Punishment of unbelievers in the "Hereafter" is the main message of this sūra, but this verse also anticipates punishment in the present life.

13.36 – *Those to whom We have given the Book rejoice in what has been sent down to you*

The setting for this verse seems different from many other passages in the Quran. If the People of the Book approve of the recitations of the messenger, what is their relationship to him and his message?

13.37 – *In this way We have sent it down as an Arabic judgment*

The Quran claims that this Arabic judgment is revealed. Verses that highlight the Arabic nature of the recitation become very important in the claims that the Quran makes for itself. See the analysis of claims for "Arabic" at 43.2–3 (p. 487).

13.38 – *it was not for any messenger to bring a sign, except by the permission of God*

This is another statement in the Quran's series of characterizations of "all" messengers or prophets. This verse asserts that no messenger brings a sign (*āya*) without Allah's permission, perhaps in response to what the audience is demanding in verse 7.

But this is not actually true. The Gospel accounts report many miracles of Jesus and describe them as signs of his glory (John 2:11). See the discussion of verses making categorical statements about all messengers and prophets at 25.20 (p. 365).

time (there is) a written decree. [39] God blots out whatever He pleases, and He confirms (whatever He pleases). With Him is the mother of the Book.

[40] Whether We let you see part of what We promise them, or We take you, only (dependent) on you is the delivery (of the message). (Dependent) on Us is the reckoning. [41] Do they not see that We come to the land, pushing back its borders? God judges, (and there is) no revision of His judgment. He is quick at the reckoning.

[42] Those who were before them schemed, but the scheme (belongs) to God altogether. He knows what every person earns, and soon the disbelievers will know to whom the outcome of the Home (belongs). [43] Those who disbelieve say, 'You are not an envoy.' Say: 'God is sufficient as a witness between me and you, and (so is) whoever has knowledge of the Book.'

13.39 – *God blots out whatever He pleases, and He confirms (whatever He pleases)*

This verse states literally that Allah erases (*maḥā*) what he wants. As such, it seems to fit in with a series of verses that say Allah cancels (2.106, 22.52) or exchanges (16.101) material in the Quran. For an explanation of the Islamic theory of abrogation, see the comments at 16.101 (p. 282).

13.39 – *With Him is the mother of the Book*

The expression "mother of the Book" appears here and at 3.7 and 43.4. It seems to refer to a concept of an original book in heaven from which all revelation comes. See the discussion of the "doctrine of scripture" within the Quran at 85.21–22 (p. 624).

13.40 – *Whether We let you see part of what We promise them, or We take you*

In this verse addressed to the messenger, Droge translates the Arabic verb *tawaffā* as "take," adding "in death" in a footnote. Several Muslim translations give "make die" or similar expressions related to death (Pickthall, Shakir, Mohsin Khan, Sahih International, Muhammad Sarwar). Yet none of these five translates *tawaffā* in the same way at 3.55, where ʿĪsā is the object of the verb. See the comments at 3.55 (p. 87) and "The Death of Jesus in the Quran" (p. 314).

ABRAHAM
IBRĀHĪM

14

The words of a prayer spoken by Abraham stand out in this sūra and give the sūra its name. The sūra also presents a kind of pattern of what happens when prophets preach Allah's message to their peoples and the people do not respond appropriately.

The sūra opens with a direct address to the Quran's messenger and a statement that Allah sends each of his messengers to speak in the language of his people. The message here is that God created the universe and expects a good response from the people he has created.

Human response to the message comes with consequences, and this sūra contains a number of graphic descriptions of the punishments that the disobedient will receive after death. The sūra pictures the Day of Judgment in two extended passages.

Abraham's prayer here includes a reference to settling some of his descendants in an uncultivable valley near the Lord's holy house. The biblical account makes no such reference, and it seems that this story exists only in the Quran.

In the Name of God, the Merciful, the Compassionate

[1] Alif Lām Rāʾ. A Book – We have sent it down to you, so that you may bring the people out of the darkness to the light, by the permission of their Lord, to the path of the Mighty, the Praiseworthy. [2] God who – to Him (belongs) whatever is in the heavens and whatever is on the earth. Woe to the disbelievers because of a harsh punishment! [3] Those who love this present life more than the Hereafter, and keep (people) from the way of God, and desire (to make) it crooked – those are far astray!

14.1 – *A Book – We have sent it down to you*

The Quran speaks directly to the messenger in many seemingly self-conscious passages that claim both a divine origin for the book and prophethood for the messenger. Here the Quran gives a reason for "sending down" material for the messenger's recitations.

[4] We have not sent any messenger except in the language of his people, so that he might make (things) clear to them. Then God leads astray whomever He pleases and guides whomever He pleases. He is the Mighty, the Wise.

[5] Certainly We sent Moses with Our signs: 'Bring your people out of the darkness to the light, and remind them of the days of God.' Surely in that are signs indeed for every patient (and) thankful one.

[6] (Remember) when Moses said to his people, 'Remember the blessing of God on you, when He rescued you from the house of Pharaoh. They were inflicting on you the evil punishment, and slaughtering your sons and sparing your women. In that was a great test from your Lord.' [7] And (remember) when your Lord proclaimed, 'If indeed you are thankful, I shall indeed give you more, but if indeed you are ungrateful, surely My punishment is harsh indeed.' [8] And Moses said, '(Even) if you disbelieve, you and whoever is on the earth all together – surely God is indeed wealthy, praiseworthy.'

[9] Has no story come to you of those who were before you: the people of Noah, 'Ād, Thamūd, and those who (came) after them? No one knows them but God. Their messengers brought them the clear signs, but they put their hands in their

---

14.4 – *We have not sent any messenger except in the language of his people*

Listeners cannot respond unless they can understand the message. This verse seems to go along with verses that specify that the recitations are in Arabic (e.g., 12.2; 13.37).

14.5 – *Certainly We sent Moses with Our signs*

This brief reference to the story of Moses (vv. 5–8) highlights the need for Moses' people to be thankful to Allah for the way he delivered them from Pharaoh.

14.9 – *Their messengers brought them the clear signs*

Many of the Quran's stories of messengers and prophets follow a similar pattern. This passage (vv. 9–14) sets out the pattern handily by collectively describing the response of 'Ād, Thamūd, and the people of Noah to the preaching of their messengers. Here the messengers bring their peoples a message, but the people will not receive it (v. 9). This initiates an encounter in which the messengers attempt to persuade the people but the people still resist the message (vv. 10–12). Finally the people prepare to physically harm the messengers (v. 13a). At this point, however, the Lord destroys the resisting people and saves and prospers the messengers (vv. 13b–14).

This verse seems to say that no one but Allah knows these stories. This may be the case for stories of messengers to 'Ād and Thamūd, but the Bible contains a great deal of information about prophets that is not found in the Quran. On 'Ād and Thamūd, see the explanations at 7.65 and 7.73 (p. 182–83).

mouths, and said, 'Surely We disbelieve in what you are sent with, and surely we are in grave doubt indeed about what you call us to.' [10] Their messengers said, '(Is there any) doubt about God, Creator of the heavens and the earth? He calls you so that He may forgive you of your sins and spare you for an appointed time.' They said, 'You are nothing but human beings like us. You want to keep us from what our fathers have served. Bring us some clear authority (for this).' [11] Their messengers said to them, 'We are nothing but human beings like you, but God bestows favor on whomever He pleases of His servants. It is not for us to bring you any authority, except by the permission of God. In God let the believers put their trust. [12] Why should we not put our trust in God, when He has guided us to our ways. Indeed we shall patiently endure whatever harm you do us. In God let the trusting put their trust.' [13] Those who had disbelieved said to their messengers, 'We shall indeed expel you from our land, or (else) you will return to our creed.' Then their Lord inspired them: 'We shall indeed destroy the evildoers [14] and cause you to inhabit the land after them. That is for whoever fears My position and fears My promise.'

[15] They asked for victory, and every stubborn tyrant despaired. [16] Behind him is Gehenna, and he is given a drink of filthy water. [17] He gulps it but can hardly swallow it. Death comes upon him from every side, yet he does not die, and behind him is a stern punishment.

[18] A parable of those who disbelieve in their Lord: their deeds are like ashes, on which the wind blows strongly on a stormy day. They have no power over anything of what they have earned. That is straying far.

[19] Do you not see that God created the heavens and the earth in truth? If He (so) pleases, He will do away with you and bring a new creation. [20] That is no great matter for God.

[21] They will come forth to God all together, and the weak will say to those who were arrogant, 'Surely we were your followers, so are you going relieve us (now) of any of the punishment of God?' They will say, 'If God had guided us, we would indeed have guided you. (It is) the same for us whether we become

---

14.12 – *Indeed we shall patiently endure whatever harm you do us*

This is the attitude of many of the messengers referred to in the Quran and indeed of biblical prophets in general. Interestingly, elsewhere in the Quran the same verb for harming, *ādhā*, is used to threaten punishment for "those who hurt Allah and His messenger" (33.57).

14.16 – *Behind him is Gehenna*

Verses 16 and 17 give a particularly graphic description of life in hell (*jahannam*, also vv. 49–51). See "Eschatology in the Quran" (p. 604).

distressed or are patient. (There is) no place of escape for us.' ²² And Satan will say, when the matter is decided, 'Surely God promised you a true promise, and I (too) promised you, (but) then I broke (my promise) to you. I had no authority over you, except that I called you and you responded to me. So do not blame me, but blame yourselves. I am not going to help you, nor are you going to help me. Surely I disbelieved in your associating me (with God) before.' Surely the evildoers – for them (there is) a painful punishment. ²³ But those who believe and do righteous deeds – they are made to enter Gardens through which rivers flow, there to remain by the permission of their Lord. Their greeting there is: 'Peace!'

²⁴ Do you not see how God has struck a parable? A good word is like a good tree. Its root is firm and its branch (reaches) to the sky, ²⁵ giving its fruit every season by the permission of its Lord. God strikes parables for the people so that they may take heed. ²⁶ But the parable of a bad word is like a bad tree, uprooted from the earth, without any support for it. ²⁷ God makes firm those who believe by the firm word in this present life and in the Hereafter. But God leads astray the evildoers. God does whatever He pleases.

²⁸ Do you not see those who have exchanged the blessing of God for disbelief, and caused their people to descend to the home of ruin – ²⁹ Gehenna – where they will burn? It is an evil dwelling place! ³⁰ They have set up rivals to God in order to lead (people) astray from His way. Say: 'Enjoy (yourselves)! Surely your destination is to the Fire!'

³¹ Say to My servants who believe (that) they should observe the prayer, and contribute from what We have provided them, in secret and in open, before a Day comes when (there will be) no bargaining and no friendship.

³² (It is) God who created the heavens and the earth, and sent down water from the sky, and brought forth fruits by means of it as a provision for you. And He subjected the ship to you, to run on the sea by His command, and subjected the rivers to you. ³³ And He subjected the sun and the moon to you, both being constant (in their courses), and subjected the night and the day to you. ³⁴ He has given you some of all that you have asked Him for. If you (try to) number God's blessing, you will not (be able to) count it. Surely the human is indeed an evildoer (and) ungrateful!

³⁵ (Remember) when Abraham said, 'My Lord, make this land secure, and keep

---

14.22 – *And Satan will say, when the matter is decided*

Satan says he is not responsible for the painful doom that is coming to many. The people obeyed him when he called to them, so they only have themselves to blame.

14.35 – *when Abraham said, "My Lord, make this land secure..."*

This passage (vv. 35–41) offers the precise words of a prayer of Abraham for

me and my sons away from serving the idols. [36] My Lord, surely they have led many of the people astray. Whoever follows me, surely he belongs to me, and whoever disobeys me – surely You are forgiving, compassionate. [37] Our Lord, I have settled some of my descendants in a wādī without any cultivation, near your Sacred House, Our Lord, in order that they may observe the prayer. So cause the hearts of some of the people to yearn toward them, and provide them with fruits, so that they may be thankful. [38] Our Lord, You know what we hide and what we speak aloud. Nothing is hidden from God (either) on the earth or in the sky. [39] Praise (be) to God, who has granted me Ishmael and Isaac in (my) old age. Surely my Lord is indeed the Hearer of the call. [40] My Lord, make me observant of the prayer, and (also) some of my descendants, our Lord, and accept my call. [41] Our Lord, forgive me, and my parents, and the believers, on the Day when the reckoning takes place.'

[42] Do not think (that) God is oblivious of what the evildoers do. He is only sparing them for a Day when (their) eyes will stare, [43] (as they go) rushing with their heads raised up, unable to turn back their gaze, and their hearts empty. [44] Warn the people (of) a Day when the punishment will come to them, and those who have done evil will say, 'Our Lord, spare us for a time near (at hand)! We shall respond to Your call and follow the messengers.' 'Did you not swear before that (there would be) no end for you? [45] You dwell in the (same) dwelling places as those who did themselves evil, and it became clear to you how We dealt with them, and (how) We struck parables for you. [46] They schemed their scheme, but their scheme was known to God, even though their scheme was (such as) to remove the mountains by it.'

---

himself and his descendants. He praises Allah for giving him Ishmael and Isaac in his old age (v. 39) and asks forgiveness for himself, his parents, and his people (v. 41).

This expression that Allah granted Ishmael to Abraham (v. 39) is unique in the Quran. It appears among a series of verses that say Allah granted Isaac and Jacob to Abraham (6.84; 19.49; 27.27). See the analysis of verses related to Isaac at 21.72 (p. 335) and 37.101, 107 (p. 450–51). For a discussion of prophets asking Allah for forgiveness, see 48.2 (p. 513).

14.37 – *Our Lord, I have settled some of my descendants in a wādī without any cultivation, near your Sacred House*

Muslim commentaries have interpreted "your Sacred House" to mean the *Ka'ba* in Mecca. In 5:97 the Quran calls the *Ka'ba* the "Sacred House," though Abraham does not appear in the context. On the "House," see the comment at 2.124 (p. 54); and on the quranic idea that Abraham travelled deep into the Arabian Peninsula, see analysis at 22.26 (p. 341).

See also "Abraham in the Quran" (p. 90).

⁴⁷ Do not think (that) God is going to break His promise to His messengers. Surely God is mighty, a taker of vengeance. ⁴⁸ On the Day when the earth will be changed (into something) other (than) the earth, and the heavens (as well), and they will go forth to God, the One, the Supreme, ⁴⁹ and you will see the sinners on that Day bound together in chains, ⁵⁰ their clothing (made) of pitch, and the Fire will cover their faces, ⁵¹ so that God may repay everyone for what he has earned. Surely God is quick at the reckoning.

⁵² This is a delivery for the people, and (it is delivered) so that they may be warned by means of it, and that they may know that He is one God, and that those with understanding may take heed.

AL-ḤIJR
AL-ḤIJR

15

This sūra refers to "those who have cut the Qur'ān (into) parts" (v. 91). The sūra itself – and many others like it – gives the impression of being a collection of "parts" covering numerous topics: destruction of townships, accusations against the messenger, Allah's treatment of the mockers, a creation passage, a story of Iblīs, punishment and reward, stories of Abraham and Lot, and a closing section that leaves multiple mysteries for commentators.

One English translation that has attempted to map out this apparently fragmentary nature of the sūra in a visual way is that of Arthur Arberry, *The Koran Interpreted*.

Other scholars have argued not only for the coherent nature of such sūras but also for clusters of sūras belonging together. One recent argument makes Sūra 15 the final sūra of a series of six that reveal a shift in the thinking of the messenger (Sūras 10–15). The scholar suggests that these sūras are telling the messenger to give up hope of people's conversion and to instead expect a new way that Allah will bring about his will.

In the Name of God, the Merciful, the Compassionate

¹ Alif Lām Rā'. Those are the signs of the Book and a clear Qur'ān.

² Perhaps those who disbelieve (will) wish, if they had submitted [. . .]. ³ Leave them (to) eat and enjoy (themselves), and (let their) hope divert them. Soon they will know! ⁴ We have not destroyed any town without its having a known decree. ⁵ No community precedes its time, nor do they delay (it).

⁶ They have said: 'You on whom the Reminder has been sent down! Surely you are possessed indeed! ⁷ Why do you not bring the angels to us, if you are one of the truthful?' ⁸ We only send down the angels with the truth, and then they

---

15.6 – *You on whom the Reminder has been sent down!*

The audience evidently accuses the messenger of being possessed by *jinn* and asks him why he does not bring angels to confirm his message (v. 7). This begins a kind of reflection on Allah's treatment of unbelievers and their responses (vv. 8–15).

will not be spared. [9] Surely We have sent down the Reminder, and surely We are indeed its Watchers. [10] Certainly We sent (messengers) before you among the parties of old, [11] yet not one messenger came to them whom they did not mock. [12] In this way We put it into the hearts of the sinners – [13] they do not believe in it, though the customary way of those of old has already passed away. [14] (Even) if We opened on them a gate of the sky, and they were going up through it continually, [15] they would (still) indeed say, 'Our sight is bewildered! No! We are a bewitched people!'

[16] Certainly We have made constellations in the sky, and made it appear enticing for the onlookers, [17] and protected it from every accursed satan [18] – except any who (may) steal in to overhear, then a clear flame pursues him. [19] And the earth – We stretched it out, and cast on it firm mountains, and caused everything (that is) weighed to sprout in it. [20] We have made for you a means of living on it, and (for those creatures) for which you are not providers. [21] The storehouses of everything are only with Us, and We send it down only in a known measure. [22] We send the fertilizing winds, and We send down water from the sky and give it to you to drink. You are not the storekeepers of it. [23] Surely We – We indeed give life and cause death, and We are the inheritors. [24] Certainly We know the ones who press forward among you, and certainly We know the ones who lag behind. [25] Surely your Lord – He will gather them. Surely He is wise, knowing.

[26] Certainly We created the human from dry clay, from molded mud, [27] and the (ancestor of the) jinn, We created him before (that) from scorching fire.

[28] (Remember) when your Lord said to the angels: 'Surely I am going to create a human being from dry clay, from molded mud. [29] When I have fashioned him,

---

15.11 – *yet not one messenger came to them whom they did not mock*

The Quran seems to reassure the messenger by saying that his experience of rejection is the lot of a messenger. See the analysis of the Quran's categorical statements about messengers and prophets at 25.20 (p. 365).

15.16 – *Certainly We have made constellations in the sky*

The Quran offers another passage about the activities of the Creator (vv. 16–27), including some beautiful expressions. See "Creation in the Quran" (p. 224).

15.27 – *and the (ancestor of the) jinn, We created him before (that) from scorching fire*

On the Quran's concept of *jinn*, see the summary at 72.1 (p. 593).

15.28 – *when your Lord said to the angels: "Surely I am going to create a human being from dry clay …"*

The story that Iblīs refuses to bow down to the first created human has already appeared twice in the canonical progression (2.34; 7.11). On the name *Iblīs*, see the comment at 2.34. Here is a long conversation between Allah and Iblīs (vv. 28–48) in

and breathed some of My spirit into him, fall down before him in prostration.' ³⁰ So the angels prostrated themselves – all of them together ³¹ – except Iblīs. He refused to be with the ones who prostrated themselves. ³² He said, 'Iblīs! What is (the matter) with you that you are not with the ones who prostrated themselves?' ³³ He said, 'I am not (one) to prostrate myself before a human being whom you have created from dry clay, from molded mud.' ³⁴ He said, 'Get out of here! Surely you are accursed! ³⁵ Surely the curse (is going to remain) on you until the Day of Judgment.' ³⁶ He said, 'My Lord, spare me until the Day when they are raised up.' ³⁷ He said, 'Surely you are one of the spared ³⁸ – until the Day of the known time.' ³⁹ He said, 'My Lord, because You have made me err, I shall indeed make (things) appear enticing to them on the earth, and I shall indeed make them err – all (of them) ⁴⁰ – except for Your devoted servants among them.' ⁴¹ He said, 'This is the straight path (incumbent) on Me. ⁴² Surely My servants – you will not have any authority over them, except for whoever follows you of the ones who are in error. ⁴³ Surely Gehenna is indeed their appointed place – all (of them). ⁴⁴ It has seven gates: to each gate a part of them is assigned. ⁴⁵ (But) surely the ones who guard (themselves) will be in (the midst of) gardens and springs: ⁴⁶ "Enter it in peace, secure!" ⁴⁷ We shall strip away whatever rancor is in their hearts. (As) brothers (they will recline) on couches, facing each other. ⁴⁸ No weariness will touch them there, nor will they be expelled from it.'

⁴⁹ Inform My servants that I am the Forgiving, the Compassionate, ⁵⁰ and that My punishment is the painful punishment. ⁵¹ And inform them about the guests of Abraham: ⁵² when they entered upon him, and said, 'Peace!,' he said, 'Surely we are afraid of you.' ⁵³ They said, 'Do not be afraid. Surely we give you good news of a knowing boy.' ⁵⁴ He said, 'Do you give me good news, even though old age has touched me? What good news do you give me?' ⁵⁵ They said, 'We give you good news in truth, so do not be one of the despairing.' ⁵⁶ He said, 'Who despairs of the mercy of his Lord, except for the ones who go astray?' ⁵⁷ He said, 'What is your business, you envoys?' ⁵⁸ They said, 'Surely we have been sent

---

which Iblīs gives his reason for not bowing down (v. 33), the Lord punishes Iblīs but leaves him some room to work (vv. 37–38), and Iblīs promises to pervert humankind (v. 39). Curiously, the "human being" is not named.

On Iblīs's refusal to bow down, see the analysis at 38.73–74 (p. 458).

15.51 – *And inform them about the guests of Abraham*

Abraham's guests bring him good news of a son and inform Abraham of their mission to Lot's city (vv. 51–60). In this second quranic version of the story (see also 11:69–76), the son is simply "a knowing boy" (v. 53) rather than Isaac (11:71), and Abraham's wife does not appear in the story.

to a people who are sinners, [59] except for the house(hold) of Lot. Surely we shall indeed rescue them – all (of them) [60] – except his wife. We have determined that she indeed (will be) one of those who stay behind.'

[61] When the envoys came to the house(hold) of Lot, [62] he said, 'Surely you are a people unknown (to me).' [63] They said, 'No! We have brought you what they were in doubt about. [64] We have brought you the truth. Surely we are truthful indeed. [65] So journey with your family in a part of the night, but you follow behind them. Let none of you turn around, but proceed where you are commanded.' [66] We decreed for him that command, that the last remnant of these (people) would be cut off in the morning. [67] The people of the city came welcoming the good news. [68] He said, 'Surely these are my guests, so do not shame me. [69] Guard (yourselves) against God, and do not disgrace me.' [70] They said, 'Did we not forbid you from the worlds?' [71] He said, 'These are my daughters, if you would do (it).' [72] By your life! Surely they were wandering blindly in their drunkenness. [73] So the cry seized them at sunrise. [74] We turned (the city) upside down and rained on them stones of baked clay. [75] Surely in that are signs indeed for the discerning. [76] Surely it is indeed on a (path)way (which still) exists. [77] Surely in that is a sign indeed for the believers.

[78] The people of the Grove were evildoers indeed, [79] so We took vengeance on them. Surely both of them are indeed in a clear record.

15.61 – *When the envoys came to the house(hold) of Lot*

In this version of the Lot story, the sin of the people for which the guests bring judgment is described in general terms (vv. 67–71, similar to 11.77–80). Before and after these two versions, however, the Quran is more specific (7.81; 26:165–66). Here the wife of Lot stays behind (v. 60).

To compare this version with the biblical account, readers can turn to Genesis 18–19.

15.75 – *Surely in that are signs indeed for the discerning*

The preceding stories and the activities of the Creator are signs (*āyāt*) of Allah's power, mercy, and judgment.

15.78 – *The people of the Grove were evildoers indeed*

The following passage (vv. 78–91) is a good example of quranic text that makes little sense apart from explanation. There are four expressions: the people of the Grove, the people of al-Ḥijr (v. 80), seven of the oft-repeated (v. 87), cut the Quran into parts (v. 91). If readers/listeners know that the expression "people of the Grove" also appears at 26.176, they might assume that this is another name for the people of Midian because the same messenger (Shu'ayb) preached to both (26.176; cf. 7.85). The other three expressions are even more obscure.

On the observation of such scattered fragments, see the introduction to this sūra.

⁸⁰ Certainly the people of al-Ḥijr called the envoys liars. ⁸¹ We gave them Our signs, but they turned away from it. ⁸² They carved secure houses out of the mountains, ⁸³ but the cry seized them in the morning. ⁸⁴ What they had earned was of no use to them.

⁸⁵ We did not create the heavens and the earth, and whatever is between them, except in truth. Surely the Hour is coming indeed, so excuse (them) gracefully. ⁸⁶ Surely your Lord – He is the Creator, the Knowing.

⁸⁷ Certainly We have given you seven of the oft-repeated (stories), and the great Qur'ān.

⁸⁸ Do not yearn after what We have given classes of them to enjoy, and do not sorrow over them, but lower your wing to the believers, ⁸⁹ and say: 'Surely I am the clear warner.'

⁹⁰ – As We have sent (it) down on the dividers, ⁹¹ those who have cut the Qur'ān (into) parts. ⁹² By your Lord! We shall indeed question them all ⁹³ about what they have done.

⁹⁴ Break forth with what you are commanded, and turn away from the idolaters. ⁹⁵ Surely We are sufficient for you (against) the mockers, ⁹⁶ who set up another god with God. Soon they will know! ⁹⁷ Certainly We know that you – your heart is distressed by what they say. ⁹⁸ Glorify your Lord with praise, and be one of those who prostrate themselves, ⁹⁹ and serve your Lord, until the certainty comes to you.

THE BEE
AL-NAHL

16

The signs of the Creator's power and presence is the main theme in several substantial passages in this sūra. In one of these passages, the Creator speaks to the bee – after which the sūra is named. A couple of these passages also include refrains, suggesting a liturgical use of some of the verses.

The Creator then looks for an appropriate response from his creation. Animals, birds, and insects respond naturally, but humans have difficulty showing thankfulness for the provisions of their Creator. This sūra urges idolaters to consider whether their idols have the power to create.

Human response, whether appropriate or not, brings consequences. The sūra promises rewards and punishments on the Day of Resurrection, beyond the judgments that Allah may execute on peoples in the present life.

There are no messenger stories in this sūra, but Abraham is called a *Hanīf* and his character is spotlighted as an example for the messenger. The sūra addresses several other passages directly to the messenger, encouraging him to be patient in the face of resistance.

In the Name of God, the Merciful, the Compassionate

¹ The command of God has come! Do not seek to hurry it. Glory to Him! He is exalted above what they associate.

² He sends down the angels with the spirit of His command on whomever He pleases of His servants: 'Give warning that (there is) no god but Me, so guard (yourselves) against Me!'

16.2 – *He sends down the angels with the spirit of His command*

Allah reveals his word to whomever he chooses. The expression "the spirit of His command" also appears at 40.15 and 42.52, and "the spirit of my Lord's command" at 17.85. Here this spirit seems to descend with the angels, leaving a question as to what kind of being is envisioned. Further on in the sūra it is the "holy spirit" who "sends down" the recitations of the messenger (v. 102). On "the spirit of [Allah's] command," see the comment at 42.52 (p. 486).

[3] He created the heavens and the earth in truth. He is exalted above what they associate. [4] He created the human from a drop, and suddenly he (becomes) a clear adversary. [5] And the cattle – He created them for you. (There is) warmth in them and (other) benefits, and from them you eat. [6] And (there is) beauty in them for you, when you bring them in and when you lead them out. [7] They carry your loads to a land you would (otherwise) not reach without exhausting yourselves. Surely your Lord is indeed kind, compassionate. [8] (He also created) horses and mules and donkeys for you to ride, and for display. And He creates what you do not know. [9] (It is incumbent) on God (to set the) direction of the way, yet (there is) deviation from it. If He had (so) pleased, He would indeed have guided you all.

[10] He (it is) who sends down water from the sky. From it you have (something to) drink, and from it vegetation (grows) on which you pasture (livestock). [11] By means of it He causes the crops to grow for you, and (also) olives, and date palms, and grapes, and all (kinds of) fruit. Surely in that is a sign indeed for a people who reflect. [12] He subjected the night and the day for you, and the sun and the moon, and the stars (are) subjected by His command. Surely in that are signs indeed for a people who understand. [13] And whatever He has scattered for you on the earth (with) its various colors – surely in that is a sign indeed for a people who take heed. [14] He (it is) who subjected the sea, so that you may eat fresh fish from it, and bring out of it an ornament which you wear, and you see the ship cutting through it, and (it is) so that you may seek some of His favor, and that you may be thankful. [15] And He cast on the earth firm mountains, so that it does not sway with you (on it), and rivers and (path)ways, that you may guide

---

16.3 – *He created the heavens and the earth in truth*

This verse begins a creation passage in which there are a number of beautiful expressions (vv. 3–21). The passage leads up to a verdict on the false objects that many people worship: these objects cannot create but are themselves created.

16.4 – *suddenly he (becomes) a clear adversary*

The Quran says that the human is an opponent or "adversary." See the discussion of the Quran's view of human nature at 79.40 (p. 612).

16.11 – *Surely in that is a sign indeed for a people who reflect*

This is one of the refrains that repeat throughout two creation passages in this sūra (see also vv. 12, 13, 65, 67).

16.14 – *so that you may seek some of His favor, and that you may be thankful*

The proper human response to the Creator and his provisions is to be thankful. This is an important theme in the Quran as well as in the Hebrew Bible and the New Testament. See "Creation in the Quran" (p. 224).

yourselves, [16] and landmarks (too). And by the stars they guide (themselves). [17] Is the One who creates like the one who does not create? Will you not take heed? [18] If you (try to) number God's blessing, you will not (be able to) count it. Surely God is indeed forgiving, compassionate.

[19] God knows what you keep secret and what you speak aloud. [20] Those they call on instead of God do not create anything, since they are (themselves) created. [21] (They are) dead, not alive, and they do not realize when they will be raised up. [22] Your God is one God. Those who do not believe in the Hereafter – their hearts are defiant, and they are arrogant. [23] (There is) no doubt that God knows what they keep secret and what they speak aloud. Surely He does not love the arrogant.

[24] When it is said to them, 'What has your Lord sent down?,' they say, 'Old tales!' [25] – that they may bear their own burdens fully on the Day of Resurrection, and (also) some of the burdens of those whom they led astray without (their) realizing (it). Evil is what they will bear! [26] Those who were before them schemed, but God came (against) their building from the foundations, and the roof fell down on them from above them, and the punishment came upon them from where they did not realize (it would). [27] Then on the Day of Resurrection He will disgrace them, and say, 'Where are My associates for whose sake you broke away?' Those who were given the knowledge will say, 'Surely today disgrace and evil are on the disbelievers, [28] those who – the angels take them (while they are

---

16.23 – *Surely He does not love the arrogant*

The Quran contains twenty-four statements about the kinds of people whom Allah does not love. See "The Language of Love in the Quran" (p. 560).

16.24 – *When it is said to them, "What has your Lord sent down?," they say, "Old tales!"*

With this answer, does the audience mean to say that they have heard the messenger's stories before? This expression appears nine times in the Quran. See "Apocryphal Details in Quranic Stories" (p. 299).

16.27 – *Where are My associates for whose sake you broke away?*

The Quran pictures a judgment scene on the Day of Resurrection, in which first the disbelievers (vv. 27–29) and then the believers (vv. 30–32) are questioned. See "Eschatology in the Quran" (p. 604).

16.28 – *those who – the angels take them (while they are doing) themselves evil*

In this verse Droge translates the Arabic verb *tawaffā* as "take" (also in v. 32), adding "in death" in a footnote. Several Muslim translations give "cause to die" or similar expressions related to death at both verses (e.g., Pickthall, Shakir, Sahih International). Yet none of these three translates *tawaffā* in the same way at 3.55,

doing) themselves evil.' They will offer peace: 'We were not doing anything evil.' 'Yes indeed (you were)! Surely God is aware of what you have done. ²⁹ So enter the gates of Gehenna, there to remain. Evil indeed is the dwelling place of the arrogant!'

³⁰ And it is said to those who guard (themselves), 'What has your Lord sent down?' They say, 'Good!' For those who do good in this world (there is) good, but the Home of the Hereafter is indeed better. Excellent indeed is the Home of the ones who guard (themselves) ³¹ – Gardens of Eden, which they will enter, through which rivers flow, where they will have whatever they please. In this way God repays the ones who guard (themselves), ³² those who – the angels take them (while they are doing) good. They will say, 'Peace (be) upon you! Enter the Garden for what you have done.'

³³ Do they expect (anything) but the angels to come to them, or the command of your Lord to come? So did those who were before them. God did not do them evil, but they did themselves evil. ³⁴ So the evils of what they had done smote them, and what they were mocking overwhelmed them.

³⁵ The idolaters say, 'If God had (so) pleased, we would not have served anything other than Him, neither we nor our fathers, and we would not have forbidden anything other than Him.' So did those who were before them. (Does anything depend) on the messengers except the clear delivery (of the message)? ³⁶ Certainly We have raised up in every community a messenger (saying): 'Serve God and avoid al-Ṭāghūt!' (There were) some of them whom God guided, and some whose going astray was deserved. Travel the earth and see how the end was for the ones who called (it) a lie. ³⁷ If you are eager for their guidance – surely God does not guide those whom He leads astray. They will have no helpers.

³⁸ They have sworn by God the most solemn of their oaths: 'God will not raise up anyone who dies!' Yes indeed! (It is) a promise (binding) on Him in truth, but most of the people do not know (it). ³⁹ (They will be raised) so that He may make clear their differences to them, and so that those who disbelieved may know that they were liars. ⁴⁰ Our only word to a thing, when We intend it, is that We say to it, 'Be!' and it is.

⁴¹ Those who emigrate in (the way of) God, after they have been done evil – We shall indeed give them a good settlement in this world, but the reward of the Hereafter is indeed greater, if (only) they knew. ⁴² (They are) those who are patient and put their trust in their Lord.

---

where 'Īsā is the object of the verb. See the comments at 3.55 (p. 87) and "The Death of Jesus in the Quran" (p. 314).

[43] We have not sent (anyone) before you except men whom We inspired – just ask the People of the Reminder, if you do not know (it) – [44] with the clear signs and the scriptures, and We have sent down to you the Reminder, so that you may make clear to the people what has been sent down to them, and that they will reflect.

[45] Do those who have schemed evils feel secure that God will not cause the earth to swallow them, or that the punishment will not come upon them from where they do not realize? [46] Or that He will not seize them in their comings and goings, and they will not be able to escape? [47] Or that He will not seize them with a (sudden) fright? Surely your Lord is indeed kind, compassionate.

[48] Do they not see anything of what God has created? (How) its shadows revolve from the right and the left, prostrating themselves before God, and they are humble? [49] Whatever is in the heavens and whatever is on the earth prostrates itself before God – every living creature and the angels (too) – and they are not arrogant. [50] They fear their Lord above them, and they do what they are commanded.

[51] God has said: 'Do not take two gods. He is only one God. So Me – fear Me (alone)!' [52] To Him (belongs) whatever is in the heavens and the earth, and to Him (belongs) the religion forever. Will you guard (yourselves) against (anyone) other than God? [53] Whatever blessing you have is from God. Then when hardship touches you, (it is) to Him you cry out. [54] Then when He removes the hardship from you, suddenly a group of you associates with their Lord, [55] to show ingratitude for what We have given them. Enjoy (yourselves)! Soon you will know!

[56] They assign to what they do not know a portion of what We have provided them. By God! Surely you will indeed be questioned about what you have forged. [57] And they assign daughters to God – glory to Him! – and to themselves (they assign) what they desire. [58] When one of them is given news of a female (child), his face turns dark and he chokes back his disappointment. [59] He hides himself from the people because of the evil of what he has been given news about. Should he keep it in humiliation or bury it in the dust? Is it not evil what they judge? [60] An evil parable (is fitting) for those who do not believe in the Hereafter, but (only) the highest parable (is fitting) for God. He is the Mighty, the Wise.

[61] If God were to take the people to task for their evildoing, He would not

---

16.43 – *just ask the People of the Reminder, if you do not know*

In this verse the Quran seems to reach out to pre-Islamic revelations for support. The "People of the Reminder" seems to function like the "People of the Book," similar to 10.94 ("ask those who have been reciting the Book before you"). The next verse goes on to claim that the "reminder" has also been sent down to the Quran's messenger.

16.61 – *If God were to take the people to task for their evildoing, He would not leave on it any living creature*

leave on it any living creature. But He is sparing them until an appointed time. When their time comes, they will not delay (it) by an hour, nor will they advance (it by an hour). ⁶² They assign to God what they (themselves) dislike, and their tongues allege the lie that the best is for them. (There is) no doubt that the Fire (is fitting) for them, and that they (will) be rushed (into it).

⁶³ By God! Certainly We sent messengers to communities before you, but Satan made their deeds appear enticing to them. So he is their ally today, and for them (there is) a painful punishment. ⁶⁴ We have not sent down on you the Book, except for you to make clear their differences to them, and (We have sent it down) as a guidance and mercy for a people who believe.

⁶⁵ (It is) God (who) sends down water from the sky, and by means of it gives the earth life after its death. Surely in that is a sign indeed for a people who hear. ⁶⁶ And surely in the cattle is a lesson indeed for you: We give you to drink from what is in their bellies – between excretions and blood – pure milk, pleasant tasting to the drinkers. ⁶⁷ And from the fruits of the date palms and the grapes, from which you take an intoxicating drink and a good provision – surely in that is a sign indeed for a people who understand.

⁶⁸ And your Lord inspired the bee: 'Make hives among the mountains, and among the trees, and among what they construct. ⁶⁹ Then eat from all the fruits, and follow the ways of your Lord subserviently.' (There) comes forth from their bellies a drink of various colors, in which (there is) healing for the people. Surely in that is a sign indeed for a people who reflect.

⁷⁰ (It is) God (who) creates you. Then He will take you. But among you (there is) one who is reduced to the worst (stage) of life, so that he knows nothing after (having had) knowledge. Surely God is knowing, powerful.

This verse seems to indicate a view of the seriousness of human sin (*ẓulm*) and the judgment it deserves from the divine perspective. There are not many verses in the Quran that express this view, though this particular wording also appears at 35.45. See the discussion of the Quran's view of human nature at 79.40 (p. 612).

16.64 – *We have not sent down on you the Book, except for you*

The Quran addresses the messenger directly to claim that his recitations are "sent down" (also v. 89). This verse suggests that the recitations would solve some of the differences among his listeners. On differences among the People of the Book, see the comments at 98.4 (p. 642).

16.68 – *And your Lord inspired the bee: "Make hives among the mountains..."*

This striking thought – that the Lord inspires the bee – is part of another creation and provision passage (vv. 65–73) with a number of lovely expressions. This theme continues in verses 78–81.

[71] God has favored some of you over others in the (matter of) provision, but those who have been favored do not give over their provision to what their right (hands) own, so (that) they are (all) equal in that respect. Is it the blessing of God they deny? [72] God has given you wives from yourselves, and from your wives He has given you sons and grandsons, and He has provided you with good things. Do they believe in falsehood, and do they disbelieve in the blessing of God? [73] Do they serve, instead of God, what has no power to provide anything for them from the heavens or the earth, nor are they able (to do anything)? [74] Do not strike any parables for God. Surely God knows and you do not know.

[75] God strikes a parable: a slave (who is) owned – he has no power over anything – and (another) whom We have provided with a good provision from Us, and he contributes from it in secret and in public. Are they equal? Praise (be) to God! No! But most of them do not know (it).

[76] God strikes a parable: two men, one of them cannot speak – he has no power over anything, and he is a burden on his master – wherever he directs him, he does not bring (back anything) good. Is he equal to the one who commands justice and is himself on a straight path?

[77] To God (belongs) the unseen of the heavens and the earth, and the affair of the Hour is only like a blink of the eye, or it is nearer. Surely God is powerful over everything.

[78] (It is) God (who) brought you forth from the bellies of your mothers – you did not know a thing – and made for you hearing and sight and hearts, so that you may be thankful. [79] Do they not see the birds, subjected in the midst of the sky? No one holds them (up) but God. Surely in that are signs indeed for a people who believe.

[80] God has made (a place of) rest for you from your houses, and made houses for you from the skins of the livestock, which you find light (to carry) on the day of your departure and on the day of your encampment. And from their wool and their fur and their hair (He has made for you) furnishings and enjoyment for a time.

[81] God has made (places of) shade for you from what He has created, and made (places of) cover for you from the mountains, and made clothing for you to guard you from the heat, and clothing to guard you from your (own) violence. In this way He completes His blessing on you, so that you will submit. [82] If they turn away – only (dependent) on you is the clear delivery (of the message).

16.82 – *If they turn away – only (dependent) on you is the clear delivery*

The responsibility of the messenger addressed in this passage (vv. 78–83) is only to preach. His message is the pleasant "signs" of the Creator.

⁸³ They recognize the blessing of God, (and) then they reject it. Most of them are ungrateful.

⁸⁴ On the Day when We raise up a witness from every community, then no permission (to speak) will be given to those who have disbelieved, nor will they be allowed to make amends. ⁸⁵ When those who have done evil see the punishment, it will not be lightened for them, nor will they be spared.

⁸⁶ When those who were idolaters see their associates, they will say, 'Our Lord, these are our associates, on whom we used to call instead of You.' But they will cast (back) at them the word: 'Surely you are liars indeed!' ⁸⁷ And they will offer peace to God on that Day, and (then) what they have forged will abandon them.

⁸⁸ Those who disbelieve and keep (people) from the way of God – We shall increase them in punishment upon punishment because they were fomenting corruption.

⁸⁹ On the Day when We raise up in every community a witness against them from among them, and bring you as a witness against these (people) [. . .]. We have sent down on you the Book as an explanation for everything, and as a guidance and mercy, and as good news for those who submit.

⁹⁰ Surely God commands justice and good, and giving to family, and He forbids immorality, and wrong, and envy. He admonishes you so that you may take heed.

⁹¹ Fulfill the covenant of God, when you have made a covenant, and do not break (your) oaths after their confirmation, when you have made God a guarantor over you. Surely God is aware of what you do.

⁹² Do not be like the one who unraveled her yarn, after (it was) firmly spun, (into) broken strands, (by) taking your oaths as a (means of) deception between you, because (one) community is more numerous than (another) community. God is only testing you by means of it. He will indeed make clear to you your differences on the Day of Resurrection. ⁹³ If God had (so) pleased, He would indeed have made you one community, but He leads astray whomever He pleases and guides whomever He pleases. You will indeed be questioned about what you have done.

⁹⁴ Do not take your oaths as a (means of) deception between you, so that

---

16.89 – *We have sent down on you the Book as an explanation for everything*
The Quran addresses the messenger directly to make high claims for his recitations (also v. 64).

16.93 – *He leads astray whomever He pleases and guides whomever He pleases*
In this sūra people are held responsible for their choices, while at the same time other verses seem to say that Allah determines all things (also v. 37).

a foot should slip after its standing firm, and you taste evil for having kept (people) from the way of God, and (there be) for you a great punishment. ⁹⁵ Do not sell the covenant of God for a small price. Surely what is with God is better for you, if (only) you knew. ⁹⁶ What is with you fails, but what is with God lasts, and We shall indeed pay those who are patient their reward for the best of what they have done. ⁹⁷ Whoever does righteousness – whether male or female – and he is a believer – We shall indeed give him a good life, and We shall indeed pay them their reward for the best of what they have done.

⁹⁸ When you recite the Qur'ān, take refuge with God from the accursed Satan. ⁹⁹ Surely he has no authority over those who believe and put their trust in their Lord. ¹⁰⁰ His authority is only over those who take him as an ally, and those who associate (other gods) with Him.

¹⁰¹ When We exchange a verse in place of (another) verse – and God knows what He sends down – they say, 'You are only a forger!' No! But most of them do not know (anything).

16.98 – *When you recite the Qur'ān, take refuge with God from the accursed Satan*

Verse 98 begins a passage (vv. 98–105) that brings together a series of challenges to Muslim claims for the source of the Quran.

First comes a suggestion that Satan may attempt to attack at the time of recitation, and therefore the reciter needs to deliberately seek refuge in Allah. The following verses state that Satan has no power over those who trust their Lord but does exert his power over others. In Muslim tradition, the influence of Satan becomes a live issue in the story known as the "satanic verses" (see the comments at 22.52 and 53.19). Sūras 113 and 114 also contain the expression "I take refuge."

"Qur'ān" in verse 98 does not necessarily mean the book now known as Muslim scripture but can simply mean a unit of the messenger's recitation. On the word *qur'ān*, see the comment at 2.185 (p. 61).

16.101 – *When We exchange a verse in place of (another) verse*

The second challenge comes from opponents who say that the messenger is merely inventing his recitations. See the discussion on verses that accuse the messenger of inventing at 69.44 (p. 587).

Verse 101 suggests that Allah may substitute (*baddala*) one verse for another. To the audience, however, the exchange of verses seems to be an arbitrary action of the messenger.

This verse (along with 2.106; 13.39; and 22.52) became one of the most important props for the Islamic theory of "abrogation" – that in certain cases, verses believed to have been recited by Muhammad later in his career abrogate or cancel the rulings of verses believed to have been recited earlier.

[102] Say: 'The holy spirit has brought it down from your Lord in truth, to make firm those who believe, and as a guidance and good news for those who submit.'

For many Muslim scholars, this theory of abrogation has provided a way to deal with the contradictions within the Quran on a number of important themes, including response to conflict and the treatment of non-Muslims. Scholars placed the contents of the Quran on a timeline according to the Muslim story of Islamic origins and then declared that in case of contradiction, the verse recited later in the story would overrule the earlier verse.

As an example, some Muslim scholars asserted that since – according to their chronology – Sūra 9 was the last or second to last sūra to be recited, 9.5 should have abrogating power over all verses that suggest a gentler treatment of non-Muslims. David Powers found in his study of the subject that for some scholars, 9.5 abrogates "every other verse in the Quran which commands or implies anything less than a total offensive against the non-believers" (see Powers's article, "The Exegetical Genre," in the bibliography). In this case, Muslim agreement with the theory of abrogation would prove very dangerous for non-Muslims!

A related action in both 2.106 and 87.6–7 is that Allah would cause or allow a verse (*āya*) to be forgotten. This possibility gave rise to speculation among some early Muslim scholars that the messenger of Islam recited certain verses that did not find their way into the final edition of the Quran.

16.102 – *The holy spirit has brought it down from your Lord in truth*

In response to the accusation of inventing in verse 101, the messenger is commanded to say that the "holy spirit" brought him the substituted verse. A second response comes in verse 105: the "disbelievers" are lying (using the same verb as v. 101).

This is the last of only four occurrences of the expression "holy spirit" (*rūḥ al-qudus*, lit. "the spirit of the holy") in the Quran (also 2.87; 2.253; 5.110). In the three other occurrences, "holy spirit" is used only in connection with 'Īsā.

What does the Quran mean by this expression? Muslim commentators came to identify "holy spirit" in the Quran with Gabriel. In 2.97, Gabriel (*jibrīl*) "brought it down on your heart." If readers understand 2.97 to be in parallel with 16.102, they would tend to identify the holy spirit with Gabriel.

One consequence of these few and confusing references to the holy spirit is that there is no development in the Quran of the presence of God's own spirit with people to, for example, "guide you into all truth" (John 16:8). A biblical understanding of God's Holy Spirit could also have prevented the needless controversy of 61.6. When Jesus described to his disciples the "Counselor" who was to come after him, he clearly indicated that the Counselor was the Holy Spirit (John 14:26), not a human leader. See the comment at 61.6 on the "Holy Spirit" described by Jesus in the Gospel (p. 564).

¹⁰³ Certainly We know that they say, 'Only a human being teaches him.' The language of the one to whom they perversely allude is foreign, but this language is clear Arabic. ¹⁰⁴ Surely those who do not believe in the signs of God – God will not guide them, and for them (there is) a painful punishment. ¹⁰⁵ Only they forge lies who do not believe in the signs of God. Those – they are the liars!

¹⁰⁶ Whoever disbelieves in God after having believed – except for someone who is compelled, yet his heart is (still) secure in belief – and whoever expands his heart in disbelief – on them is anger from God, and for them (there is) a great punishment. ¹⁰⁷ That is because they loved this present life over the Hereafter, and because God does not guide the disbelievers. ¹⁰⁸ Those – God has set a seal on their hearts and their hearing and their sight. And those – they are the oblivious. ¹⁰⁹ (There is) no doubt that in the Hereafter they (will be) the losers.

¹¹⁰ Then surely your Lord – to those who emigrated after having been persecuted, (and) then struggled and were patient – surely your Lord after that is indeed forgiving, compassionate, ¹¹¹ on the Day when each person will come disputing on his own behalf, and each person will be paid in full for what he has done – and they will not be done evil.

¹¹² God strikes a parable: a town was secure (and) at rest, its provision coming to it in abundance from every place, but it was ungrateful for the blessings of

---

16.103 – *Only a human being teaches him*

The third challenge is an accusation from the audience that the messenger has simply learned his preaching from someone else (see also 25:4–5). No name is given for the alleged teacher, so Muslim commentaries on the Quran supplied a number of names to identify the teacher, including a Christian slave. The Quran's response, however, is that the teacher the audience is thinking of speaks a foreign language.

Readers who would like a taste of traditional Muslim interpretation in translation can see the commentary of Zamakhsharī (d. 1144) on this verse in Helmut Gätje's *The Qur'án and its Exegesis* (see bibliography).

16.103 – *this language is clear Arabic*

The Quran seems to put forward, as a kind of proof, that the messenger could not be preaching what another has taught him because his recitation is in Arabic. The assertion is that the recitations must be "sent down." See the analysis of claims for "Arabic" at 43.2–3 (p. 487).

16.106 – *Whoever disbelieves in God after having believed*

This verse is one of a series of verses that are discussed in relation to apostasy (also 2.217; 3.86–91; 4.89, 137; 88.23, 24). Here disbelief after belief brings Allah's wrath and punishment, apparently in the "Hereafter" (v. 109). However, some Muslim scholars have justified the penalty of death for apostates from this verse.

God. So God caused it to wear the clothing of hunger and fear for what they had been doing. [113] Certainly a messenger had come to them from among them, but they called him a liar. So the punishment seized them while they were doing evil.

[114] Eat from what God has provided you as permitted (and) good, and be thankful for the blessing of God, if it is Him you serve. [115] He has only forbidden you: the dead (animal), and the blood, and swine's flesh, and what has been dedicated to (a god) other than God.' But whoever is forced (by necessity), not desiring or (deliberately) transgressing – surely God is forgiving, compassionate. [116] (As for what your tongues (may) allege, do not speak the (following) lie: 'This is permitted but that is forbidden,' so that you forge lies against God. Surely those who forge lies against God – they will not prosper. [117] A little enjoyment (of life), and (then) for them (there is) a painful punishment.

[118] To those who are Jews, We have forbidden what We recounted to you before. We did not do them evil, but they did themselves evil. [119] Then surely your Lord – to those who have done evil in ignorance, (and) then repented and set (things) right – surely your Lord after that is indeed forgiving, compassionate.

[120] Surely Abraham was a community obedient before God – a Ḥanīf – yet he was not one of the idolaters. [121] (He was) thankful for His blessings. He chose him and guided him to a straight path. [122] We gave him good in this world, and surely in the Hereafter he will indeed be among the righteous. [123] Then We inspired you: 'Follow the creed of Abraham the Ḥanīf. He was not one of the idolaters.'

[124] The sabbath was only made for those who differed concerning it. Surely on the Day of Resurrection your Lord will judge between them concerning their differences.

[125] Call to the way of your Lord with wisdom and good admonition, and dispute with them by means of what is better. Surely your Lord – He knows who goes astray from His way, and He knows the ones who are (rightly) guided.

16.120–23 – *Surely Abraham was a community obedient before God – a Ḥanīf*

Here "community" translates the Arabic term *umma*, which Muslims understand to mean the community of Islam. *Ḥanīf* is often taken to mean "upright" or "of pure faith." On *Ḥanīf*, see the comment at 2.135 (p. 55) and "Abraham in the Quran" (p. 90). The Quran recommends the character of Abraham as an example for the messenger to follow.

16.125 – *Call to the way of your Lord with wisdom and good admonition, and dispute with them by means of what is better*

The messenger encounters much resistance to his preaching, but the Quran counsels him to argue (*jādala*) with his audience in the best way. This is great advice for anyone who makes a case for the truth.

[126] If you take retribution, take it in the same way as retribution was taken against you. But if indeed you are patient – it is indeed better for the ones who are patient. [127] And you be patient (too). Yet your patience (comes) only with (the help of) God. Do not sorrow over them, and do not be in distress because of what they are scheming. [128] Surely God is with those who guard (themselves), and those who do good.

Calling to Islam (*da'wa*)
Matthew Kuiper

The Arabic term *da'wa* can be translated as "calling," "inviting," or "summoning." Like *jihād*, Muslims historically have used *da'wa* for a diverse set of ideas and practices. In modern times, the term is overwhelmingly used for Islamic missionary activity ("inviting" to Islam). In the Quran, *da'wa* and variants occur over two hundred times. Along with the noun *da'wa*, there are many occurrences of the verb *da'ā* (to invite) and the participle *dā'ī* (one who invites). Sometimes *da'wa* has a "secular" meaning (e.g., calling witnesses in 2.282; inviting to a meal in 33.53), but most often, *da'wa* and variants are used in the Quran for prayer: calling upon God or upon false gods (e.g., 2.186; 6.17; 13.14; 17.56; 18.14; 34.22).

Before one can offer *da'wa* to God in prayer, however, one must hear and respond to God's own *da'wa*. Not unlike the theological concept of *missio Dei* (mission of God) – wherein God takes the initiative in redemption – God is pictured in the Quran as the first practitioner of missionary *da'wa*. In the Quran, one hears the voice of a preacher, and very often that preacher is God delivering to humanity his summons (*da'wa*) to repentance and submission (*islām*) (10.25). According to the Quran, this divine *da'wa* demands several human responses.

First, responding to God's *da'wa* entails resisting the false *da'wa*s of Satan and others (2.221; 14.22; 28.41). Underlying its warnings on this theme is the Quran's assumption that *da'wa* takes place in a competitive space in which multiple *da'wa*s vie for human attention. Second, responding to God's *da'wa* entails heeding the *da'wa* of God's prophets and messengers. Prophets who communicate God's *da'wa* in the Quran include Noah, Moses, Elijah, Joseph, and Jesus. The Quran also narrates the *da'wa*s of several ordinary believers (40.28–43). Muslim preachers today cite the latter to argue that *da'wa* is the responsibility of every Muslim.

For Muslims, of course, the most important quranic prophet is Muhammad. Setting aside scholarly questions concerning the identity of the Quran's prophet (the name "Muhammad" appears only four times in the Quran), how do Muslims understand the Quran's teaching on Muhammad and his *da'wa*? For Muslims, God's *da'wa* is now made decisively through Muhammad (8.20–24, 33.45–46, 46.31–32). Muhammad's *da'wa*, moreover, supersedes the *da'wa*s of earlier prophets and is universal. In part for this reason, Muhammad's quranic *da'wa* is pervaded by interreligious debates with unbelievers (*kāfirūn*), "polytheists" (*mushrikūn*), Jews (*yahūd*), and Christians (*naṣāra*). Muhammad's *da'wa* aims not only to persuade skeptics and unbelievers but also to admonish "believers" (*mu'minūn*) (e.g., 9.38–9). Today, too, *da'wa* is as often directed toward Muslims as toward non-Muslims. In either case, Muhammad's quranic *da'wa* is always made with urgency, in light of the terrible coming Day of Judgment (14.44; 40.10–14; 40.49–50).

Third, responding to God's *da'wa* entails engaging in *da'wa* as a community. Though the early quranic community (*umma*) should not be too quickly equated with the Muslim *umma* of later centuries, it is still clear that the Quran speaks to a community of believers and endows it with certain responsibilities, *da'wa* among them. One of the most important texts on this theme is 16.125: "Call to the way of your Lord with wisdom and good admonition, and dispute with them by means of what is better." Similar to the way many Christians understand the New Testament's "Great Commission" (Matthew 28:19–20), contemporary *da'wa*-minded Muslims believe this quranic verse gives them a mandate to spread Islam to the whole world. Another frequently quoted verse is 3.104: "Let there be (one) community of you, calling (people) to good, and commanding right and forbidding wrong" (cf. 3.110). In this verse, *da'wa* is related to the duty to command the right and forbid the wrong. Some modern Muslims understand this to mean that *da'wa* is part of a larger project of promoting *shari'a* (Islamic Law) around the world. Sūra 9.71, which also mentions commanding right and forbidding wrong, is used by modern activists to substantiate the idea that Muslim women should be engaged in *da'wa*.

Among the Quran's primary purposes is to persuade its audience to heed God's *da'wa* by heeding his prophets and messengers, especially Muhammad. In this sense, we might say that Quran not only *contains* but *is* the original *da'wa* of Islam. In the Quran, this *da'wa* results in a community – a community which offers *da'wa* to God in prayer, resists false *da'wa*s, and which carries out missionary *da'wa* after the pattern of the prophets.

THE JOURNEY
AL-ISRĀ'

17

At this point in the Quran, if read in the canonical arrangement, the reader may begin to feel that many sūras are collections of prophetic-sounding material from predictable types of literature. In Sūra 17, for example, we find polemic, law, brief references to peoples of the past, descriptions of how Allah deals with humans, and the human response. We also find several passages of the characteristic, seemingly self-conscious verses in which the Quran makes claims for itself.

Worthy of note in this sūra is a passage of law that in some ways resembles the Ten Commandments of Exodus 20. There are also a couple of passages addressed to the messenger in which the Quran says that messengers are going to have a difficult time and that the present "warner" should not expect any better.

Some of the verses in this sūra seem to defy comprehension and have challenged Muslim commentators and modern scholars alike.

In the Name of God, the Merciful, the Compassionate

¹ Glory to the One who sent His servant on a journey by night from the Sacred Mosque to the Distant Mosque, whose surroundings We have blessed, so that We might show him some of Our signs. Surely He – He is the Hearing, the Seeing.

17.1 – *Glory to the One who sent His servant on a journey by night*

This verse is a good example of how a single verse in the Quran can be associated with a quite extensive tradition about its meaning. The verse itself gives few clues. No names or places are given, only the unidentified "his servant," "sacred (*ḥarām*) mosque," and "distant (*aqṣā*) mosque." The immediate context gives no further information, nor are there other passages in the Quran that fill in the picture. However, Muslim tradition connects this verse with an elaborate story about a "night journey" of Muhammad from Mecca to Jerusalem and from there up into heaven. One version of the story is given in Ibn Isḥāq's *Sīra* (pp. 181–87).

² We gave Moses the Book, and made it a guidance for the Sons of Israel: 'Do not take any guardian other than Me!' ³ (They were) descendants of those whom We carried with Noah. Surely he was a thankful servant. ⁴ And We decreed for the Sons of Israel in the Book: 'You will indeed foment corruption on the earth twice, and you will indeed rise to a great height.' ⁵ When the first promise came (to pass), We raised up against you servants of Ours, men of harsh violence, and they invaded (your) homes, and it was a promise fulfilled. ⁶ Then We returned to you (another) chance against them, and increased you with wealth and sons, and made you more numerous. ⁷ 'If you do good, you do good for yourselves, but if you do evil, (it is likewise) for yourselves.' When the second promise came (to pass), (We raised up against you servants of Ours) to cause you distress, and to enter the Temple as they entered it the first time, and to destroy completely what they had conquered. ⁸ It may be that your Lord will have compassion on you. But if you return, We shall return, and We have made Gehenna a prison for the disbelievers.

⁹ Surely this Qur'ān guides to that which is more upright, and gives good news to the believers who do righteous deeds, that for them (there is) a great reward, ¹⁰ and that those who do not believe in the Hereafter – We have prepared for them a painful punishment. ¹¹ But the human calls for evil (as if) calling for good, (for) the human is (always) hasty.

¹² We have made the night and the day as two signs: We have blotted out the sign of the night and made the sign of the day to (let you) see, so that you may seek some favor from your Lord, and that you may know the number of the years and the reckoning (of time). Everything – We have made it distinct.

¹³ And every human – We have fastened his fate to him on his neck, and We shall bring forth a book for him on the Day of Resurrection, which he will find unrolled. ¹⁴ 'Read your book! You are sufficient today as a reckoner against yourself.'

17.2 – *We gave Moses the Book, and made it a guidance for the Sons of Israel*

This positive description of the Torah is typical of all quranic passages where the pre-Islamic scriptures are named or clearly referred to.

17.4 – *You will indeed foment corruption on the earth twice*

Because the following passage (vv. 4–8) contains so many unidentified pronouns, it is difficult to know what the Quran has in mind with these two corruptions.

17.9 – *Surely this Qur'ān guides to that which is more upright*

This is the first of several passages in the sūra in which the Quran makes claims for itself in this self-affirming way (also vv. 41, 45, 82, 86, 88, 105–6). See "Different Kinds of Literature" (p. 14). On the word *qur'ān*, see the comment at 2.185 (p. 61).

¹⁵ Whoever is (rightly) guided, is guided only for himself, and whoever goes astray, goes astray only against himself. No one bearing a burden bears the burden of another. We never punish until We have raised up a messenger.

¹⁶ When We wish to destroy a town, We (first) command its affluent ones, and they act wickedly in it, so that the word against it is proved true, and We destroy it completely. ¹⁷ How many generations have We destroyed after Noah! Your Lord is sufficient (as One who) is aware of (and) sees the sins of His servants.

¹⁸ Whoever desires this hasty (world) – We hasten to (give) him in it whatever We please to whomever We wish. Then We have made Gehenna for him, (where) he will burn, condemned (and) rejected. ¹⁹ But whoever desires the Hereafter and strives with effort for it, and he is a believer, those – their striving will be thanked. ²⁰ Each one We increase – these and those – with some gift of your Lord. The gift of your Lord is not limited. ²¹ See how We have favored some of them over others. Yet the Hereafter is indeed greater in ranks (of honor) and greater in favor.

²² Do not set up another god with God, or you will sit down condemned (and) forsaken.

²³ Your Lord has decreed that you do not serve any but Him, and (that you do) good to your parents, whether one or both of them reaches old age with you. Do not say to them, 'Uff,' and do not repulse them, ²⁴ but speak to them an honorable word. And conduct yourself humbly toward them out of mercy, and say: 'My Lord, have compassion on both of them, as they brought me up (when I was) small.' ²⁵ Your Lord knows what is in you. If you are righteous, surely He is forgiving to those who regularly turn (to Him in repentance).

²⁶ Give the family member his due, and the poor and the traveler, but do not squander (your wealth) wastefully. ²⁷ Surely the squanderers are brothers of the satans, and Satan is ungrateful to his Lord. ²⁸ But if you turn away from them, seeking a mercy from your Lord that you expect, speak to them a gentle word. ²⁹ Do not keep your hand chained to your neck, nor extend it all the way, or you will sit down blamed (and) impoverished. ³⁰ Surely your Lord extends (His) provision to whomever He pleases, and restricts (it). Surely He is aware of His servants (and) sees (them).

17.22 – *Do not set up another god with God*

These words begin an extended passage of commandments (vv. 22–39) that show some similarities to the Ten Commandments of Exodus 20. The passage ends with a recap of the command not to set up another god with Allah (v. 39).

This law passage also treats behavior toward parents (v. 23); justice to kinsmen, the poor, and the traveler (v. 26); killing and adultery (vv. 31–33); and honesty in the marketplace (v. 35).

[31] Do not kill your children for fear of poverty. We will provide for them and for you. Surely their killing is a great sin.

[32] Do not go near adultery. Surely it is an immoral act and evil as a way.

[33] Do not kill the person whom God has forbidden (to be killed), except by right. Whoever is killed in an evil manner – We have given authority to his ally, but he should not be excessive in the killing, (for) surely he has been helped.

[34] Do not go near the property of the orphan, except to improve it, until he reaches his maturity.

Fulfill the covenant. Surely you are responsible for a covenant.

[35] Fill up the measure when you measure, and weigh with the straight balance. That is better and fairer in interpretation.

[36] Do not pursue what you have no knowledge of. Surely the hearing and the sight and the heart – all those you are responsible for.

[37] Do not walk on the earth in jubilation. Surely you will not plumb the depths of the earth, nor reach the mountains in height.

[38] All that – the evil of it – is hateful in the sight of your Lord. [39] That is some of the wisdom your Lord has inspired you (with).

Do not set up another god with God, or you will be cast into Gehenna, blamed (and) rejected. [40] Has your Lord distinguished you with sons and taken (for Himself) females from the angels? Surely you speak a dreadful word indeed! [41] Certainly We have varied (the signs) in this Qur'ān, so that they may take heed, but it only increases them in aversion (to it). [42] Say: 'If there were (other) gods with Him, as they say, they would indeed have sought a way to the Holder of the throne.' [43] Glory to Him! He is exalted a great height above what they say. [44] The seven heavens and the earth, and whatever is in them, glorify Him, and (there is) nothing that does not glorify (Him) with His praise, but you do not understand their glorifying. Surely He is forbearing, forgiving.

[45] When you recite the Qur'ān, We place between you and those who do not believe in the Hereafter an obscuring veil. [46] And We make coverings over their hearts, so that they do not understand it, and a heaviness in their ears. When you mention your Lord alone in the Qur'ān, they turn their backs in aversion (to it). [47] We know what they listen to when they listen to you, and when they (are in) secret talk, when the evildoers say, 'You are only following a man (who is) bewitched.' [48] See how they strike parables for you! But they have gone astray and cannot (find) a way.

17.45 – *When you recite the Qur'ān*

These words begin a passage of controversy or polemic (vv. 45–57) in which the objections of the listeners are apparently recorded, along with the responses of the messenger ("Say!").

⁴⁹ They say, 'When we have become bones and fragments, shall we indeed be raised up as a new creation?' ⁵⁰ Say: 'Become stones or iron, ⁵¹ or something greater still in your estimation!' And then they will say, 'Who will restore us?' Say: '(He) who created you the first time.' And then they will shake their heads at you, and say, 'When will it be?' Say: 'It may be that it is near ⁵² – the Day when He will call you, and you will respond with His praise, and you will think that you remained (in the grave) only for a little (while).'

⁵³ Say to My servants (that) they should say that which is best. Surely Satan provokes discord among them. Surely Satan is a clear enemy to humankind. ⁵⁴ Your Lord knows about you. If He pleases, He will have compassion on you, or if He pleases, He will punish you. We have not sent you as a guardian over them. ⁵⁵ Your Lord knows whatever is in the heavens and the earth. Certainly We have favored some of the prophets over others, and We gave David (the) Psalms.

⁵⁶ Say: 'Call on those whom you have claimed (as gods) instead of Him. They have no power (to) remove hardship from you, nor (to) change (it).' ⁵⁷ Those whom they call on seek access to their Lord, whichever of them (may be) nearest, and they hope for His mercy and fear His punishment. Surely the punishment of your Lord is something to beware of.

⁵⁸ (There is) no town that We are not going to destroy before the Day of Resurrection, or are not going to punish (with a) harsh punishment. That is written in the Book.

⁵⁹ Nothing prevented Us from sending the signs, except that those of old

---

17.49 – *When we have become bones and fragments, shall we indeed be raised up as a new creation?*

The audience tries to pose clever questions in order to deny the resurrection, but the messenger answers that the One who created humans is able to raise them up as well (v. 51).

17.55 – *Certainly We have favored some of the prophets over others, and We gave David (the) Psalms*

This is the second mention of the Psalms (*zabūr*) being given to David (also 4.163; cf. 21.105).

17.58 – *(There is) no town that We are not going to destroy*

The Quran says that every town is destined for either destruction or harsh punishment.

17.59 – *Nothing prevented Us from sending the signs*

This verse raises the question of whether Allah's messengers come accompanied by "signs" (*āyāt*), understood as miracles.

In the conversations and debates that sprang up between the conquering Arabs

called them a lie. We gave Thamūd the she-camel as a visible (sign), but they did her evil. We send the signs only to frighten.

⁶⁰ (Remember) when We said to you, 'Surely your Lord encompasses the people,' and We made the vision which We showed you only a test for the people, and (also) the cursed tree in the Qur'ān. We frighten them, but it only increases them in great(er) insolent transgression.

⁶¹ (Remember) when We said to the angels, 'Prostrate yourselves before Adam,' and they prostrated themselves, except Iblīs. He said, 'Shall I prostrate myself before one whom You have created (from) clay?' ⁶² He said, 'Do You see this (creature) whom You have honored above me? If indeed You spare me until the Day of Resurrection, I shall indeed root out his descendants, except for a few.' ⁶³ He said, 'Go, and any of them who follows you! Surely Gehenna will be your payment – an ample payment! ⁶⁴ Scare any of them you can with your voice, and assemble against them with your cavalry and your infantry, and associate with them in (their) wealth and children, and make promises to them.' Yet Satan does not promise them (anything) but deception. ⁶⁵ 'Surely My servants – you will have no authority over them.' Your Lord is sufficient as a guardian.

⁶⁶ Your Lord (it is) who drives the ship on the sea for you, so that you may seek some of His favor. Surely He is compassionate with you. ⁶⁷ When hardship touches you on the sea, (all those) whom you call on abandon (you), except Him, but when He has delivered you (safely) to the shore, you turn away. The human is ungrateful. ⁶⁸ Do you feel secure that He will not cause the shore to swallow you, or send a sandstorm against you? Then you will find no guardian for yourselves. ⁶⁹ Or do you feel secure that He will not send you back into it a second time, and send a hurricane against you, and drown you because you were ungrateful? Then you will find no attendant (to help) you with it against Us.

⁷⁰ Certainly We have honored the sons of Adam, and carried them on the

---

and the Christians and Jews in the Islamic Empire, it was not unusual for non-Muslims to ask whether the messenger of Islam had any miracles to show in support of the Muslim claim for the divine origin of the Quran. In available documents from that early period, some Christians and Jews cited Q 17.59 and 17.90–96. Non-Muslims asserted that miracles by Moses and Jesus supported the truth of the Torah and Gospel. See the discussion of miracles and the messenger of the Quran at 43.40 (p. 490), and see also "Early Christian Exegesis of the Quran" (p. 129).

17.61 – *when We said to the angels, "Prostrate yourselves before Adam..."*
Once more the Quran tells the story of the refusal of *Iblīs* to bow before Adam, and once more it focuses this particular detail apart from the Adam story. See an analysis of the story of Iblīs at 38.73–74 (p. 458).

shore and the sea, and provided them with good things, and favored them greatly over many of those whom We have created. [71] On the Day when We shall call all people with their record, whoever is given his book in his right (hand) – those will read their book, and they will not be done evil in the slightest. [72] Whoever is blind in this (world will be) blind in the Hereafter, and farther astray (from the) way.

[73] Surely they almost tempted you away from what We inspired you (with), so that you might forge against Us (something) other than it, and then they would indeed have taken you as a friend. [74] And had We not made you (stand) firm, you would almost have been disposed toward them a little. [75] Then We would have made you taste the double of life and the double of death, (and) then you would have found no helper for yourself against Us. [76] They almost scared you from the land, so that they might expel you from it, but then they would not have remained (there) after you, except for a little (while). [77] (That was Our) customary way (concerning) those of Our messengers whom We sent before you, and you will find no change in Our customary way.

[78] Observe the prayer at the setting of the sun until the darkness of the night, and (deliver) a recitation at the dawn – surely a recitation at the dawn is witnessed. [79] And a part of the night – keep watch in it as a gift for you. It may be that your Lord will raise you up to a praised position. [80] And say: 'My Lord, cause me to enter a truthful entrance, and cause me to exit a truthful exit, and grant me authority from Yourself (to) help (me).' [81] And say: 'The truth has come and falsehood has passed away. Surely falsehood is (bound) to pass away.'

[82] What We send down of the Qur'ān is a healing and mercy for the believers, but it only increases the evildoers in loss. [83] When We bless a person, he turns away and distances himself, but when evil touches him, he is in despair. [84] Say: 'Each does according to his own disposition, but your Lord knows who is best guided (as to the) way.'

[85] They ask you about the spirit. Say: 'The spirit (comes) from the command of my Lord. You have only been given a little knowledge (of it).'

17.78 – *Observe the prayer at the setting of the sun until the darkness of the night*

Sunni Muslim practice prescribes five daily times of ritual prayer (*ṣalāh*). In the Quran, the times of prayer seem to be no more than three (also 11.114). This passage mentions prayer when the sun goes down, again later in the evening, and in the morning at dawn. Instructions about five times of ritual prayer come rather from the hadith, the sayings attributed to Muhammad, first recorded in the third century of Islam (ninth century AD).

17.85 – *They ask you about the spirit*

The identity of "the spirit" (*al-rūḥ*) seems to be a matter of mystery. In this verse

[86] If We (so) pleased, We could indeed take away what We have inspired you (with). Then you would find no guardian for yourself against Us concerning it, [87] except as a mercy from your Lord. Surely His favor toward you is great.

[88] Say: 'If indeed humankind and the jinn joined together to produce something like this Qur'ān, they would not produce anything like it, even if they were supporters of each other.' [89] Certainly We have varied (the signs) for the people in this Qur'ān by means of every (kind of) parable, yet most of the people refuse (everything) but disbelief.

[90] They say, 'We shall not believe you until you cause a spring to gush forth for us from the earth, [91] or (until) you have a garden of date palms and grapes, and cause rivers to gush forth abundantly in the midst of it, [92] or (until) you make the sky fall on us in fragments, as you have claimed, or (until) you bring

---

the listeners seem to know very little about the spirit, and they ask the messenger about it. But little information is provided, either here or in other verses that mention the spirit. "The spirit (comes) from the command of my Lord" is similar to "the spirit of his command" at 16:2; 40:15; and 42:52. Those verses relate the spirit to warning and guidance.

The Muslim story of Islamic origins provided a narrative context or "occasion of recitation" for this verse. A group of Jewish rabbis in Medina come to ask four things of Muhammad, the third of which is "Tell us about the spirit." Islam's messenger answers, "Do you not know it is Gabriel . . . ?" (*Sīra*, 255).

For an analysis of "the spirit" in the Quran, see the comments at 97.4 (p. 639).

17.86 – *If We (so) pleased, We could indeed take away what We have inspired you*

The Quran seems to take a rather harsh tone toward the messenger in this passage. Does this relate to uncertainty about the spirit?

17.88 – *If indeed humankind and the jinn joined together to produce something like this Qur'ān*

Amid passages that show the audience resisting the recitations of the messenger, the Quran declares that no one could produce anything like the recitations. Similar claims appear at 2.23; 10.38; 11.13; 28.49; and 52.34. In Muslim tradition these verses became known as the *taḥaddī* ("challenge") verses. See the analysis of these verses at 52.34 (p. 529), and on the Quran's concept of jinn, see the summary at 72.1 (p. 593).

17.90 – *We shall not believe you until you cause a spring to gush forth*

The audience presses the messenger for signs and wonders (vv. 90–93) before they will believe in him. The messenger answers modestly that he is a mere mortal (vv. 93–94) and that "Allah is sufficient as a witness between me and you" (v. 96). See the comments at verse 59 and a discussion of verses about miracles and the Quran's messenger at 43.40 (p. 490).

God and the angels before (us), [93] or (until) you have a decorative house, or (until) you ascend into the sky. And we shall not believe in your ascent until you bring down on us a book, so that we may read it.' Say: 'Glory to my Lord! Am I anything but a human being, a messenger?'

[94] What prevented the people from believing when the guidance came to them, except that they said, 'Has God raised up a human being as a messenger?' [95] Say: 'If there were angels walking contentedly on the earth, We would indeed have sent down on them an angel from the sky as a messenger.' [96] Say: 'God is sufficient as a witness between me and you. Surely He is aware of His servants (and) sees (them).' [97] Whoever God guides is the (rightly) guided one, and whoever He leads astray – you will not find for them any allies other than Him. We shall gather them on the Day of Resurrection on their faces – without sight, or speech, or hearing. Their refuge is Gehenna – whenever it dies down We increase (for) them a blazing (Fire). [98] That is their payment because they disbelieved in Our signs, and said, 'When we have become bones and fragments, shall we indeed be raised up as a new creation?' [99] Do they not see that God, who created the heavens and the earth, is able to create their equivalent? He has appointed a time for them – (there is) no doubt about it – yet the evildoers refuse (everything) but disbelief.

[100] Say: '(Even) if you possessed the storehouses of my Lord's mercy, you would (still) hold back (out of) a fear (of) spending (it). Humankind is stingy.'

[101] Certainly We gave Moses nine clear signs – (just) ask the Sons of Israel. (Remember) when he came to them, and Pharaoh said to him, 'Moses! Surely I think you are bewitched indeed.' [102] He said, 'Certainly you know that no one has sent down these (signs) as clear proofs except the Lord of the heavens and the earth. Pharaoh! Surely I think you are doomed indeed.' [103] He wanted to scare them from the land, but We drowned him and those who were with him – all (of them). [104] After that We said to the Sons of Israel, 'Inhabit the land, and when the promise of the Hereafter comes, We shall bring you (all together) as a mob.'

[105] With the truth We have sent it down, and with the truth it has come down, and We have sent you only as a bringer of good news and a warner. [106] (It is) a Qur'ān – We have divided it, so that you may recite it to the people at intervals, and We have sent it down once and for all. [107] Say: 'Believe in it, or do

---

17.106 – *a Qur'ān – We have divided it, so that you may recite it to the people at intervals*

This verse is important for the Muslim belief that the messenger's recitations were "sent down" to him in parts over a period of twenty-two years (AD 610–32). On the Quran's doctrine of scripture, see the discussion at 85.21–22 (p. 624).

not believe. Surely those who were given the knowledge before it – when it is recited to them, they fall down on their chins in prostration, [108] and say, "Glory to our Lord! Surely our Lord's promise has been fulfilled indeed." [109] They fall down on their chins weeping, and it increases them in humility.'

[110] Say: 'Call on God or call on the Merciful – whichever you call on, to Him (belong) the best names.' And do not be loud in your prayer, nor silent in it, but seek a way between that.

[111] Say: 'Praise (be) to God, who has not taken a son, nor has He any associate in the kingdom, nor has He any (need of) an ally (to protect Him) from disgrace.' Magnify Him (with all) magnificence.

17.110 – *whichever you call on, to Him (belong) the best names*

Here *Allāh* and *Raḥmān* seem to be equally appropriate names for God. The verse adds that God has many beautiful names.

17.111 – *Praise (be) to God, who has not taken a son, nor has He any associate in the kingdom*

The Quran denies that Allah has taken a son. This verse does not clarify the identity of the audience, and the rest of the sūra does not seem to be concerned with Christians. However, the same words appear in the inscriptions within the Dome of the Rock, built in AD 691, where they were likely intended to target the Christian majority in Jerusalem at that time.

In any case, the verse offers a strong suggestion of the reason for the denial. The concern is theological. Allah has no partner (*sharīk*) in his rule and no need for an ally (*walīy*). To say that he has taken a son seems to be considered a statement that impinges on Allah's sovereignty. See "Son of God in the Quran" (p. 352) and a summary of verses that accuse the People of the Book of "associating" at 61.9 (p. 565).

THE CAVE
AL-KAHF

> Three unusual stories dominate this sūra: stories about young men in a cave, Moses and a mysterious riddler, and a character named Dhū 'l-Qarnayn, who builds a barrier. Unlike many other stories in the Quran, these three stories do not seem to serve an obvious purpose. The Moses story, for example, seems to be a kind of folk tale that could be attached to any character. It makes no imaginable connection to the account of Moses in the Torah, and it is also categorically different from all of the Quran's other Moses stories.
>
> Muslim tradition connects the tales about Moses and the companions of the cave with a story about a "test of prophethood."
>
> Some recent scholars have sensed an anti-Christian tone in the first verses of the sūra and have suggested that perhaps the story of men in the cave is presented in a competitive or polemical way. The theme of worshiping gods other than Allah certainly appears in the story of the cave, and "associating" (*shirk*) with Allah dots the sūra until the final verse.

In the Name of God, the Merciful, the Compassionate

¹ Praise (be) to God, who has sent down on His servant the Book! He has not made in it any crookedness. ² (He has made it) right: to warn of harsh violence from Himself, and to give good news to the believers who do righteous deeds, that for them (there is) a good reward ³ in which they will remain forever, ⁴ and to warn those who have said, 'God has taken a son.' ⁵ They have no knowledge

---

18.4 – *and to warn those who say, "God has chosen a son."*

The opening passage of this sūra (vv. 1–8) contains a good deal of feeling ("Monstrous is the word," v. 5) and perhaps even hints of force ("harsh violence," v. 2). The reason seems to be the statement, "Allah has chosen a son (*walad*)." The Quran calls this a lie (v. 5) but offers no further explanation, except perhaps at verse 26.

The close proximity in the canonical progression of these verses to other verses about a son of Allah (17.111, and ahead to 19:35, 88) is intriguing. See "Son of God in the Quran" (p. 352).

about it, nor (did) their fathers. Monstrous is the word (that) comes out of their mouths! They say nothing but a lie. [6] Perhaps you are going to destroy yourself by following after them, if they do not believe in this proclamation. [7] Surely We have made what is on the earth a splendor for it, so that We may test them (to see) which of them is best in deed. [8] And surely We shall make what is on it barren soil.

Apocryphal Details in Quranic Stories
Mateen Elass

The accusation that the Quran contains stories "borrowed" from foreign sources did not originate in the West but can actually be traced to those who first heard the recitations. Nine times the Quran records that the messenger was faced with the scoffing of disbelievers who labeled his accounts "tales of the ancient ones" (6.25; 8.31; 16.24; 23.83; 25.5; 27.68; 46.17; 68.15; 83.13). It is hard to deny that the Quran was heavily influenced by oral folklore of its day rooted in Jewish, Christian, Persian, and other traditions. For example:

- In 18.83–99, we meet the mysterious character of Dhu'l-Qarnayn (or "Possessor of the Two Horns," likely a reference to a great kingdom stretching from east to west). Traditional Muslim commentators identify him as Alexander the Great (which raises problems, since the Quran portrays him as obedient to Allah), who locates the place on earth where the sun sets daily (according to 18.86, it slides into a pool of warm/murky water). Of course, nothing in the Old or New Testament speaks of Dhu'l-Qarnayn or his exploits, but we find extremely close parallels in the Syriac *Christian Legend Concerning Alexander* and other "Alexander Romance" stories circulating among Arab Christian communities prior to the rise of Islam.
- Also in Sūra 18, we find a curious account known as "the companions of the cave" (vv. 9–18). Several young men sleep in a cave for some three hundred years before waking and discovering that the cause of their persecution has long since disappeared. From at least the sixth century AD, this same story had been told among Christians with more specificity than the quranic account and was known as "the seven sleepers of Ephesus."
- In 19.22–26, a distressed and very pregnant Mary is pictured alone under a palm tree in the wilderness, about to deliver. She cries out in anguish and a voice answers her that Allah has provided a stream beneath her to quench

her thirst and that if she will shake the palm tree, ripened dates will fall upon her to satiate her hunger. Where might this alternate birth narrative have come from? In chapter 20 of the *Gospel of Pseudo-Matthew* (also known as the *History of the Nativity of Mary and the Savior's Infancy*), written in the early seventh century AD, we find a fanciful account of Joseph, Mary, and the toddler Jesus in the midst of their flight to Egypt. A weary Mary finds shelter under a date-bearing palm and looks wistfully at Joseph, who claims the tree is too high to climb. For his part, he bemoans the fact that they have no water. The young Jesus, in his mother's arms, commands the tree to bend down and offer its dates (which it does, of course) and then further orders that it open from its roots a stream of clear, cool, sparkling water. As a result, the Holy Family is refreshed and sustained in their time of trial.

- Also in 19.29–30, the magical story of Jesus preaching from his crib as a newborn finds its antecedent in the opening chapter of the *Arabic Infancy Gospel*, dating to a Syriac origin somewhere in the fifth and sixth century AD.
- Both in 3.49 and 5.110 we find lists of Jesus' miraculous accomplishments, including something not found in the New Testament – that Jesus could fashion a bird out of clay and, breathing on it, bring it to life (by the permission of Allah). In the *Infancy Gospel of Thomas*, dating back to the second century AD, a five-year-old Jesus fashions twelve clay sparrows on the Sabbath. When he is admonished for breaking the Sabbath, he claps his hands and commands the sparrows to fly off, which they do. The Jewish witnesses to this miracle are suitably amazed.
- In Sūra 5, after Cain has slain Abel, he has no idea what to do with the body until Allah sends a raven that scratches the ground to bury its dead mate (vv. 27–31). In the third-to-sixth-century Jewish work *Pirke de Rabbi Eliezer*, we find the same story with the sole exception being that Adam witnesses the work of the raven and buries Abel.
- In 27.17–44 we read a delightfully fantastic story of Solomon (who can speak the languages of animals) and a hoopoe that is missing from the court when Solomon summons all his subjects. The king is angry until the hoopoe returns and tells him of its discovery of the Queen of Sheba, which leads ultimately to the Queen's visit to Solomon's court. A parallel to this quranic account is found in the *Second Targum of Esther*, the dating of which makes it roughly contemporary with traditional dating of the Quran.
- Lastly, seven times the Quran tells the story of the fall of Iblis (Satan) and his interactions with Adam. When Allah commands the angels to prostrate

themselves before Adam, Iblis refuses, reasoning that he was created prior to Adam and of more noble material. As a result, Iblis is cast from the court of heaven. This same understanding is detailed in Jewish/Christian literature of the third and fifth centuries AD, especially in *Vita Adae et Evae* 13:1–16:4 and *Gospel of Bartholomew* 4:51–55.

When all is said and done, the Quran seems to have drawn freely from apocryphal material circulating in oral forms throughout the Middle East and repurposed it to enhance its own message of submission.

[9] Or did you think that the companions of the cave and al-Raqīm were an amazing thing among Our signs? [10] (Remember) when the young men took refuge in the cave, and said, 'Our Lord, grant us mercy from Yourself, and furnish the right (course) for us in our situation.' [11] So We sealed up their ears in the cave for a number of years, [12] and then We raised them up (again), so that We might know which of the two factions would better count (the length of) time (they had) remained (there).

[13] We shall recount to you their story in truth: Surely they were young men who believed in their Lord, and We increased them in guidance. [14] We strengthened their hearts, when they stood up and said, 'Our Lord is the Lord of the heavens and the earth. We do not call on any god other than Him. Certainly we would then have spoken an outrageous thing. [15] These people of ours have taken

---

18.9 – *Or do you think that the companions of the cave*

In the following story (vv. 9–27), a number of young men take a stand for "the Lord of the heavens and the earth" (v. 14). In order to avoid harm from their idolatrous people, they seek refuge in a cave. There they sleep for 309 years, while their dog guards the entrance to the cave (v. 18). When the men wake up, they send one among them to the city to bring back food. The number of men is not certain (v. 23), and only God knows how long they slept in the cave (v. 27).

This story of the "companions of the cave" provides a clue about some of the sources for a variety of materials that found their way into the Quran. Most modern scholars draw attention to the Christian legend of the "seven sleepers of Ephesus," which circulated in the Middle East in the sixth century and can be found today in two Syriac homilies attributed to Jacob of Serūgh. The Christian legend is about idolatry during the reign of the Roman emperor Decius, who ruled from AD 249–51. The young men are Christians who escaped prison in Ephesus and then sought refuge in a cave.

gods other than Him. If only they would bring some clear authority concerning them! Who is more evil than the one who forges a lie against God? [16] When you have withdrawn from them and what they serve instead of God, take refuge in the cave. Your Lord will display some of His mercy to you, and will furnish some relief for you in your situation.'

[17] And you (would) see the sun when it rose, inclining from their cave toward the right, and when it set, passing them by on the left, while they were in the open part of it. That was one of the signs of God. Whoever God guides is the (rightly) guided one, and whoever He leads astray – you will not find for him an ally guiding (him). [18] And you (would) think them awake, even though they were asleep, and We were turning them (now) to the right and (now) to the left, while their dog (lay) stretched out (with) its front paws at the door (of the cave). If you (had) observed them, you would indeed have turned away from them in flight, and indeed been filled (with) dread because of them.

[19] So We raised them up (again) that they might ask questions among themselves. A speaker among them said, 'How long have you remained (here)?' Some said, 'We have (only) remained (here) a day, or part of a day.' Others said, 'Your Lord knows how long you have remained (here). So send one of you with this paper (money) of yours to the city, and let him see which (part) of it (has the) purest food, and let him bring you a supply of it. But let him be astute, and let no one realize (who) you (are). [20] Surely they – if they become aware of you – they will stone you, or make you return to their creed, and then you will never prosper.' [21] So We caused (the people of the city) to stumble upon them, in order that they might know that the promise of God is true, and that the Hour – (there is) no doubt about it.

When they argued among themselves about their situation, they said, 'Build over them a building. Their Lord knows about them.' Those who prevailed over their situation said, 'We shall indeed take (to building) a place of worship over them.'

[22] Some say, '(There were) three, the fourth of them was their dog.' But others say, '(There were) five, the sixth of them was their dog' – guessing about what is unknown. Still others say, '(There were) seven, the eighth of them was their dog.' Say: 'My Lord knows about their number. No one knows (about) them except a few.' So do not dispute about them, except (on) an obvious point, and do not ask for a pronouncement about them from any of them. [23] And do not say of

---

18.23–24 – *And do not say of anything: "Surely I am going to do that tomorrow," except (with the proviso): "If God pleases."*

This expression is similar to the thought in James 4:13–15: "Instead, you ought to

anything, 'Surely I am going to do that tomorrow,' ²⁴ except (with the proviso): 'If God pleases.' And remember your Lord, when you forget, and say, 'It may be that my Lord will guide me to something nearer the right (way) than this.'

²⁵ They remained in their cave for three hundred years and (some) add nine (more). ²⁶ Say: 'God knows about how long they remained (there). To Him (belongs) the unseen of the heavens and the earth. How well He sees and hears! They have no ally other than Him, and He does not associate anyone in His judgment.'

²⁷ Recite what you have been inspired (with) of the Book of your Lord. No one can change His words, and you will find no refuge other than Him. ²⁸ Be patient within yourself with those who call on their Lord in the morning and the evening, desiring His face, and do not let your eyes turn away from them, desiring the (passing) splendor of this present life. Do not obey (anyone) whose heart We have made oblivious of Our remembrance, and (who only) follows his desire and whose concern is (only) excess.

²⁹ Say: 'The truth is from your Lord. Whoever pleases, let him believe, and whoever pleases, let him disbelieve.' Surely We have prepared a Fire for the evil-doers – its walls will encompass them. If they call for help, they will be helped with water like molten metal (which) will scald their faces. Evil is the drink

---

say, 'If it is the Lord's will, we will live and do this or that.'" Interestingly, the Quran puts this expression into a conversation within the story of the companions of the cave – which seems to be a version of a legend about Christian characters.

18.26 – *They have no ally other than Him, and He does not associate anyone in His judgment*

Because this statement ends the story of the men in the cave, some scholars have suggested that this verse and verse 4 form a kind of parentheses around the story – to use the story as a warning against belief in a son of Allah. If so, the reason for the warning seems to be that belief in a son of Allah implies that Allah needs help.

18.27 – *No one can change His words*

The Quran states that no one can change the words of Allah (*lā mubaddila li-kalimātihi*) as part of an encouragement to the messenger to recite from the Lord's book. By this point in the Quran, readers have seen this statement in three other verses (6.34, 115; and similarly *lā tabdīla li-kalimāti 'llāh* in 10.64). This statement must be taken into account when evaluating the Muslim claim that the Quran accuses the Bible of being corrupt or falsified. See "Tampering with the Pre-Islamic Scriptures" (p. 142).

18.29 – *If they call for help, they will be helped with water like molten metal*

The Quran gives graphic descriptions of its concept of hell, as well as its concept of heaven ("Gardens of Eden," v. 31).

and evil the resting place! [30] Surely those who believe and do righteous deeds – surely We do not allow the reward of anyone who does a good deed to go to waste. [31] Those – for them (there are) Gardens of Eden through which rivers flow. There they will be adorned with bracelets of gold, and they will wear green clothes of silk and brocade, reclining there on couches. Excellent is the reward, and good the resting place!

[32] Strike for them a parable of two men: We made for one of them two gardens of grapes, and surrounded both with date palms, and placed between them (a field of) crops. [33] Each of the two gardens produced its fruit and did not fail in any way. And We caused a river to gush forth between them. [34] And he had fruit. So he said to his companion, while he was talking with him, 'I am greater than you in wealth, and mightier in family.' [35] And he entered his garden, doing himself evil, (for) he said, 'I do not think that this will ever perish, [36] nor do I think the Hour is coming. If indeed I am returned to my Lord, I shall indeed find a better (place of) return than this.' [37] His companion said to him, while he was talking with him, 'Do you disbelieve in Him who created you from dust, then from a drop, (and) then fashioned you as a man? [38] But as for us, He is God, my Lord, and I do not associate anyone with my Lord. [39] Why did you not say, when you entered your garden, "What God pleases," (for there is) no power except in God? If you see me as inferior to you in wealth and children, [40] it may be that my Lord will give me (something) better than your garden, and send on it a reckoning from the sky, so that it becomes slippery soil, [41] or its water sinks (into the earth), so that you will not be able to find it.' [42] And (all) his fruit was overwhelmed, and in the morning he began wringing his hands over what he had spent on it, (for) it had collapsed on its trellises, and he said, 'I wish I had not associated anyone with my Lord!' [43] But there was no cohort to help him, other than God, and he was helpless. [44] In such a case protection (belongs only) to God, the True One. He is best in reward, and best in final outcome.

[45] Strike for them a parable of this present life: (It is) like water which We send down from the sky, and the vegetation of the earth mingles with it, and it becomes stubble which the winds scatter. God is powerful over everything. [46] Wealth and sons are the (passing) splendor of this present life, but the things that endure – righteous deeds – are better in reward with your Lord, and better in hope.

18.32 – *Strike for them a parable of two men*

This parable tells about two men who have gardens side by side (vv. 32–44). One man raises himself above the other while the second man urges the first to live by "what Allah pleases" (v. 39). Another difference between the men is that the second man does not associate anyone with Allah (vv. 38, 42).

⁴⁷ On the Day when We shall cause the mountains to move, and you see the earth coming forth, and We gather them so that We do not leave any of them behind, ⁴⁸ and they are presented before your Lord in lines: 'Certainly you have come to Us as We created you the first time. Yet you claimed that We had not set an appointment for you!' ⁴⁹ And the Book will be laid down, and you will see the sinners apprehensive because of what is in it, and they will say, 'Woe to us! What (kind of) Book is this? It omits nothing small or great, but it has counted it?' And they will find what they have done presented (to them), and your Lord will not do anyone evil.

⁵⁰ (Remember) when We said to the angels: 'Prostrate yourselves before Adam,' and they prostrated themselves, except Iblīs. He was one of the jinn, and acted wickedly (against) the command of his Lord. Do you take him and his descendants as allies instead of Me, when they are your enemy? Evil is the exchange for the evildoers! ⁵¹ I did not make them witnesses of the creation of the heavens and the earth, nor of the creation of themselves. I am not one to take those who lead (others) astray (for) support.

⁵² On the Day when He will say, 'Call those who you claimed were My associates,' they will call them, but they will not respond to them – (for) We have set between them a place of destruction. ⁵³ The sinners will see the Fire and think that they are about to fall into it, but they will find no escape from it.

⁵⁴ Certainly We have varied (the signs) for the people in this Qur'ān by means of every (kind of) parable, yet the people remain contentious for the most part. ⁵⁵ Nothing prevented the people from believing, when the guidance came to

---

18.49 – *And the Book will be laid down, and you will see the sinners apprehensive because of what is in it*

The "Book" in this case is one in which all of a person's deeds are recorded.

18.50 – *when We said to the angels: "Prostrate yourselves before Adam"*

Once more the Quran mentions Iblīs's refusal to bow down to the first human. In this verse Iblīs is one of the *jinn*, and he is cited in order to pose a question about taking "allies" apart from Allah. See an analysis of the story of Iblīs at 38.73–74 (p. 458) and a summary of verses about jinn at 72.1 (p. 593).

18.54 – *Certainly We have varied (the signs) for the people in this Qur'ān by means of every (kind of) parable*

This verse begins a passage (vv. 54–59) about how Allah deals with people. On the word *qur'ān*, see the comment at 2.185 (p. 61).

18.54 – *yet the people remain contentious for the most part*

The Quran sometimes makes general statements about people – in this verse that they are quarrelsome or "contentious" (*jadalan*). See the discussion of the Quran's concept of human nature at 79.40 (p. 612).

them, and from asking forgiveness from their Lord, except that the customary way of those of old should come upon them, or the punishment come upon them head on. ⁵⁶ We send the envoys only as bringers of good news and warners, but those who disbelieve dispute by means of falsehood in order to refute the truth with it. They have taken My signs and what they were warned about in mockery. ⁵⁷ Who is more evil than the one who, having been reminded by the signs of his Lord, turns away from them, and forgets what his hands have sent forward? Surely We have made coverings over their hearts, so that they do not understand it, and a heaviness in their ears. Even if you call them to the guidance, they will never be guided. ⁵⁸ Yet your Lord is the Forgiving, the One full of mercy. If He were to take them to task for what they have earned, He would indeed hurry the punishment for them. Yet for them (there is) an appointment from which they will find no escape. ⁵⁹ Those towns – We destroyed them when they did evil, and We set an appointment for their destruction.

⁶⁰ (Remember) when Moses said to his young man, 'I shall not give up until I reach the junction of the two seas, or (else) I shall go on for a long time.' ⁶¹ When they reached the junction of them, they forgot their fish, (for) it had taken its way into the sea, swimming off. ⁶² So when they had passed beyond (that place), he said to his young man, 'Bring us our morning meal. We have indeed become weary from this journey of ours.' ⁶³ He said, 'Did you see when we took refuge at the rock? Surely I forgot the fish – none other than Satan made me forget to remember it – and it took its way into the sea – an amazing thing!' ⁶⁴ He said, 'That is what we were seeking!' So they returned, retracing their footsteps. ⁶⁵ And they found a servant, one of Our servants to whom We had given mercy from Us, and whom We had taught knowledge from Us. ⁶⁶ Moses said to him, 'Shall I follow you on (the condition) that you teach me some of what you have been taught (of) right (knowledge)?' ⁶⁷ He said, 'Surely you will not be able (to have) patience with me. ⁶⁸ How could you have patience for what you cannot encompass in (your) awareness of it?' ⁶⁹ He said, 'You will find me, if God pleases, patient, and I shall not disobey you in any command.' ⁷⁰ He said, 'If you follow (me), do not ask me about anything, until I mention it to you.'

18.56 – *We send the envoys only as bringers of good news and warners*

Statements that assert certain behaviors of "every messenger" raise the question of the extent to which they correspond to the accounts of messengers in the Bible. See an analysis of this question at 25.20 (p. 365).

18.60 – *when Moses said to his young man*

These words begin a curious story about Moses and a kind of riddler (vv. 60–82). What is the purpose of this story?

⁷¹ So they both set out (and continued on) until, when they sailed in the ship, he made a hole in it. He said, 'Have you made a hole in it in order to drown its passengers? You have indeed done a dreadful thing!' ⁷² He said, 'Did I not say, "Surely you will not be able (to have) patience with me?"' ⁷³ He said, 'Do not take me to task for what I forgot, and do not burden me (with) hardship in my affair.' ⁷⁴ So they both set out (and continued on) until, when they met a young boy, he killed him. He said, 'Have you killed an innocent person, other than (in retaliation) for a person? Certainly you have done a terrible thing!' ⁷⁵ He said, 'Did I not say to you, "Surely you will not be able (to have) patience with me?"' ⁷⁶ He said, 'If I ask you about anything after this, do not keep me as a companion. You have had enough excuses from me.' ⁷⁷ So they both set out (and continued on) until, when they came to the people of a town, they asked its people for food, but they refused to offer them hospitality. They both found in it a wall on the verge of collapse, and he set it up. He said, 'If you had wished, you could indeed have taken a reward for that.' ⁷⁸ He said, 'This is the parting between me and you. (Now) I shall inform you about the interpretation of what you were not able (to have) patience with. ⁷⁹ As for the ship, it belonged to poor people working on the sea, and I wanted to damage it, (because) behind them (there) was a king seizing every ship by force. ⁸⁰ As for the young boy, his parents were believers, and we feared that he would burden them both (with) insolent transgression and disbelief. ⁸¹ We wanted their Lord to give to them both in exchange (one) better than him in purity, and closer (to them) in affection. ⁸² As for the wall, it belonged to two orphan boys in the city, and underneath it was a treasure belonging to them both, (for) their father had been a righteous man. Your Lord wanted them both to reach their maturity, and bring forth their treasure as a mercy from your Lord. I did not do it on my (own) command. That is the interpretation (of) what you were not able (to have) patience with.'

⁸³ They ask you about Dhū-l-Qarnayn. Say: 'I shall recite to you a remembrance of him. ⁸⁴ Surely We established him on the earth and gave him a way of access to everything. ⁸⁵ He followed (one such) way of access ⁸⁶ until, when he reached the setting of the sun, he found it setting in a muddy spring, and he found next to it a people. We said, "Dhū-l-Qarnayn! Either punish (them) or do them (some) good." ⁸⁷ He said, "As for the one who does evil, we shall punish him. Then he will be returned to his Lord, and He will punish him (with) a

---

18.83 – *They ask you about Dhū-l-Qarnayn*

Dhū 'l-Qarnayn, literally "he of the two horns," is thought to refer to Alexander the Great. Here he builds a barrier between the people and *Yajūj* and *Majūj*. See "Apocryphal Details in Quranic Stories" (p. 299).

terrible punishment. ⁸⁸ But as for the one who believes, and does righteousness, for him (there is) the good payment, and we shall speak to him something easy from our command."

⁸⁹ Then he followed (another) way of access ⁹⁰ until, when he reached the rising (place) of the sun, he found it rising on a people for whom We had not provided any shelter from it. ⁹¹ So (it was), but We had already encompassed what his situation was in (our) awareness. ⁹² Then he followed (another) way of access ⁹³ until, when he arrived (at the place) between the two barriers, he found on this side of them a people hardly able to understand (his) speech. ⁹⁴ They said, "Dhū-l-Qarnayn! Surely Yajūj and Majūj are fomenting corruption on the earth. Shall we pay tribute to you on (the condition) that you construct a barrier between us and them?" ⁹⁵ He said, "What my Lord has established me with is better. Help me with a force, (and) I shall construct a rampart between you and them. ⁹⁶ Bring me blocks of iron!" – Until, when he had made level (the gap) between the two cliffs, he said, "Blow!" – Until, when he had made it a fire, he said, "Bring me (blocks of brass)! I will pour molten brass over it." ⁹⁷ So they were not able to surmount it, nor were they able (to make) a hole in it. ⁹⁸ He said, "This is a mercy from my Lord. But when the promise of my Lord comes, He will shatter it. The promise of my Lord is true."'

⁹⁹ We shall leave some of them on that Day crashing into each other, and there will be a blast on the trumpet, and We shall gather them all together. ¹⁰⁰ We shall present Gehenna on that Day to the disbelievers, ¹⁰¹ whose eyes were covered from My remembrance and (who) were not capable (of) hearing. ¹⁰² Do those who disbelieve think that they can take My servants as allies instead of Me? Surely We have prepared Gehenna as a reception for the disbelievers.

¹⁰³ Say: 'Shall We inform you about the worst losers in (regard to their) deeds? ¹⁰⁴ (They are) those whose striving goes astray in this present life, even though they think that they are doing good in (regard to their) work. ¹⁰⁵ Those – (they are) those who disbelieve in the signs of their Lord and in the meeting with Him. So their deeds have come to nothing. We shall not assign any weight to them on the Day of Resurrection. ¹⁰⁶ That is their payment – Gehenna – because they

---

18.94 – *Surely Yajūj and Majūj are fomenting corruption on the earth*

Yajūj and *Majūj* seem to echo the ruler "Gog" and the people of "Magog" in Ezekiel 38–39 (also Q 21.96). Here they are associated with Alexander, as they are also in postbiblical Christian writings such as the Syriac "Legend of Alexander." In Muslim tradition *Yajūj* and *Majūj* have become part of the end time events.

disbelieved and took My signs and My messengers in mockery. [107] (But) surely those who believe and do righteous deeds – for them (there will be) Gardens of Paradise as a reception, [108] there to remain. They will not desire any removal from there.'

[109] Say: 'If the sea were ink for the words of my Lord, the sea would indeed give out before the words of my Lord would give out, even if We brought (another sea) like it as an extension.'

[110] Say: 'I am only a human being like you. I am inspired that your God is one God. So whoever expects the meeting with his Lord, let him do righteous deeds and not associate anyone in the service of his Lord.'

18.107 – *surely those who believe and do righteous deeds – for them (there will be) Gardens of Paradise*

The Quran frequently describes heaven as "Gardens," but the word "Paradise" (*firdaws*), appears only here and in 23.11.

18.109 – *If the sea were ink for the words of my Lord*

The sūra ends with a beautiful expression of the vastness of the words of the Lord, and a modest self-estimate from the messenger.

MARY
MARYAM

19

The stories of Zechariah and Mary open this sūra with a whimsical, storybook quality. This sūra contains the third of three longer passages about 'Īsā, the quranic Jesus. In this case the information about 'Īsā comes from a heavenly messenger sent to Mary and from the infant 'Īsā, who speaks from the cradle.

This sūra tells readers to "remember in the Book" Abraham, Moses, Ishmael, and Idrīs. This introductory formula is found only in this sūra. The sūra also refers to a line of prophets beginning with Adam whom God guided and chose.

However, according to the sūra, the generations following those prophets – including the generations of Christians – went astray and therefore need to be warned about a Judgment Day to come. The sūra refers to rewards and punishments and, in a famous verse, seems to suggest that believers and unbelievers alike will first go to hell.

Along with information about 'Īsā, this sūra contains two pointed denials of the belief that God has a Son. The second of these denials seems to contain a good deal of emotion, which could make the reader curious to understand the reason for such vehemence over this belief.

In the Name of God, the Merciful, the Compassionate
¹ Kāf Hā' Yā' 'Ayn Ṣād.
  ² A remembrance of the mercy of your Lord (to) His servant Zachariah:

19.2 – *A remembrance of the mercy of your Lord (to) His servant Zachariah*

With the name of Zachariah (*Zakariyya*; spelled "Zechariah" in the English New Testament), this sūra begins an extended and important passage on Zachariah, John, Mary, and 'Īsā, the quranic Jesus. This is the third of the Quran's three longer passages on 'Īsā (see also 3.33–60; 5.109–20).

First, verses 2–15 tell a story about Zachariah, his unnamed wife, and the birth of John (the Baptist, *Yaḥyā*).

³ When he called on his Lord in secret, ⁴ he said, 'My Lord, surely I – (my) bones have become weak within me, and (my) head is aflame (with) white (hair), but I have not been disappointed in calling on You (before), my Lord. ⁵ Surely I fear (who) the heirs (will be) after me, (for) my wife cannot conceive. So grant me from Yourself an heir, ⁶ (who) will inherit from me and inherit from the house of Jacob, and make him, my Lord, pleasing.'

⁷ 'Zachariah! Surely We give you good news of a boy. His name (will be) John. We have not given (this) name to anyone before.' ⁸ He said, 'My Lord, how shall I have a boy, when my wife cannot conceive and I have already reached extreme old age?' ⁹ He said, 'So (it will be)! Your Lord has said, "It is easy for Me, seeing that I created you before, when you were nothing."' ¹⁰ He said, 'My Lord, give me a sign.' He said, 'Your sign is that you will not speak to the people for three days exactly.' ¹¹ So he came out to his people from the place of prayer and inspired them: 'Glorify (Him) morning and evening.'

¹² 'John! Hold fast the Book!' And We gave him the judgment as a child, ¹³ and grace from Us, and purity. He was one who guarded (himself) ¹⁴ and was dutiful to his parents. He was not a tyrant (or) disobedient. ¹⁵ Peace (be) upon him the day he was born, and the day he dies, and the day he is raised up alive.

¹⁶ And remember in the Book Mary: When she withdrew from her family to an eastern place, ¹⁷ and took a veil apart from them, We sent to her Our spirit, and it took for her the form of a human being exactly. ¹⁸ She said, 'Surely I take refuge with the Merciful from you, if you are one who guards (yourself).'

19.15 – *Peace (be) upon him the day he was born, and the day he dies, and the day he is raised up alive*

The wording of this verse is significant in view of the fact that the same three verbs used here are also used about 'Īsā in verse 33 (see below). The Quran describes John in a strikingly positive way (vv. 12–14).

19.17 – *We sent to her Our spirit, and it took for her the form of a human being exactly*

The way that Allah made Mary pregnant with 'Īsā is described in a couple of different ways in the Quran. Here Allah's spirit appears in a human form and simply says he will grant Mary a son (v. 19). At 21.91 and 66.12, the Quran says, "We breathed into her some of Our spirit." For an analysis of "the spirit" (*rūḥ*) in the Quran, see the comments at 97.4 (p. 639).

19.18 – *Surely I take refuge with the Merciful from you*

Here Mary speaks of God as "the Merciful" (*al-raḥmān*), and this name for God is used throughout the sūra.

[19] He said, 'I am only a messenger of your Lord (sent) to grant you a boy (who is) pure.' [20] She said, 'How can I have a boy, when no human being has touched me, nor am I a prostitute?' [21] He said, 'So (it will be)! Your Lord has said: "It is easy for Me. And (it is) to make him a sign to the people and a mercy from Us. It is a thing decreed."'

[22] So she conceived him, and withdrew with him to a place far away. [23] The pains of childbirth drove her to the trunk of the date palm. She said, 'I wish I had died before (this) and was completely forgotten!' [24] And then he called out

---

19.19 – *(sent) to grant you a boy (who is) pure*

The Arabic word describing ʿĪsā (*zakīy*), translated here as "pure," is also commonly rendered "faultless," "blameless," or "sinless." This particular adjective is only used with ʿĪsā in the Quran.

19.21 – *Your Lord has said, "It is easy for Me. . . ."*

The answer of the "messenger" sent by Allah to Mary's question, "How can I have a boy . . . ?" is different from the parallel speech of the angels at 3.47. Here there is no mention of Allah creating ʿĪsā in Mary's womb. However, the same statement that Allah "simply says to it, 'Be!' and it is" appears later at verse 35. Muslim commentators have interpreted this to mean that Allah created ʿĪsā.

The Quran offers two stories of the encounter between Mary and heavenly beings, here called "Our spirit" (v. 17) and in Sūra 3 called "angels" (3.42–46). When we compare these stories to the Gospel accounts in Matthew 1 and Luke 1–2, we find two striking omissions and an influential addition. Gabriel in Luke 1 announced the birth of the "Son of God" (see discussion at Q 9.35 below); and Gabriel, as well as the angel in Matthew 1, specified that Mary name her child "Jesus" (Luke 1:31; Matthew 1:20–21). This omission may not seem significant, but in the Gospel accounts, the angel also gave a reason: "because he will save his people from their sins." The Hebrew meaning of *Yēshūaʿ* or *Yehōshūaʿ* is "the Lord [Yahweh] saves" – a rich meaning utterly lost in the quranic name ʿĪsā.

One influential addition in the quranic stories of the encounter is the claim that Allah creates ʿĪsā (3.47, see the comment above). Strikingly opposite, the Gospel according to John states that "through him [Jesus, the Word] all things were made; without him nothing was made that has been made" (John 1:3; cf. 1 Corinthians 8:6; Colossians 1:16; Hebrews 1:2).

19.22 – *So she conceived him, and withdrew with him to a place far away*

Mary's journey to the trunk of a date palm (vv. 22–26) does not appear in the New Testament accounts but resembles a story in a Christian apocryphal writing known as the *Gospel of Pseudo-Matthew* (thought to have been written in the early 600s AD). See "Apocryphal Details in Quranic Stories" (p. 299).

to her from beneath her, 'Do not sorrow! Your Lord has made a stream beneath you. ²⁵ Shake the trunk of the date palm toward you, and it will drop on you fresh ripe (dates). ²⁶ Eat and drink and be comforted. If you see any human being, say: "Surely I have vowed a fast to the Merciful, and so I shall not speak to any human today."'

²⁷ Then she brought him to her people, carrying him. They said, 'Mary! Certainly you have brought something strange. ²⁸ Sister of Aaron! Your father was not a bad man, nor was your mother a prostitute.' ²⁹ But she referred (them) to him. They said, 'How shall we speak to one who is in the cradle, a (mere) child?' ³⁰ He said, 'Surely I am a servant of God. He has given me the Book and made me a prophet. ³¹ He has made me blessed wherever I am, and He has charged me with the prayer and the alms as long as I live, ³² and (to be) respectful to my mother. He has not made me a tyrant (or) miserable. ³³ Peace (be) upon me the day I was born, and the day I die, and the day I am raised up alive.'

19.28 – *Sister of Aaron! Your father was not a bad man*

Mary's kinfolk address her as the sister of Aaron – the brother of Moses and Miriam (Exodus 15:20). This verse, together with 3.35–36 and 66.12, seems to indicate a conflation of Miriam with Maryam the mother of 'Īsā in the Quran.

19.30 – *He has given me the Book and made me a prophet*

'Īsā speaks from the cradle to say that Allah has already given him "the Book." Verses like this (also 5.46; 57.27) seem to be behind the Muslim misconception that the Gospel (*injīl*) is a book given to 'Īsā rather than an account of Jesus' birth, life, death, and resurrection. Other verses say that Allah teaches 'Īsā the Gospel (3.48; 5.110) or "sends down" the Gospel (3.3, 65). See the analysis of the Quran's "Gospel" verses at 57.27 (p. 549).

19.33 – *Peace (be) upon me the day I was born, and the day I die, and the day I am raised up alive*

Here the infant 'Īsā speaks about his own birth, death, and resurrection in a way that seems to match the Gospel affirmations of the same events in the life of Jesus. There is nothing in the context of the verse, or even in the entire sūra, that would contradict this impression. In fact, the Arabic verbs 'Īsā uses for his birth, death, and resurrection are the very same verbs and tenses that the Quran uses about John the Baptist in verse 15.

Muslim commentators, however, have tended to assert that in this verse 'Īsā is referring to a death that will happen only after his return as part of the end times scenario in Muslim tradition. His resurrection would then simply be part of the general resurrection on the Day of Resurrection.

This verse is the third of only three verses in the Quran that touch on the death of Jesus (also 3.55; 4.157; cf. 5.75).

The Death of Jesus in the Quran

Gordon Nickel

Given the amount of material devoted to the description and application of the death of Jesus in the New Testament, Christian readers may be surprised to learn that a later scripture from the same region – the Quran – touches on the death of 'Īsā in only three verses.

Even more striking is the fact that of those three verses, only one addresses the question of whether or not 'Īsā was crucified (4.157). In that verse the question is limited to the alleged actions of the Jews, and a key Arabic phrase in the verse has challenged both translators and exegetes.

The other two verses are 3.55 and 19.33. The Quran deals with the death of Jesus in only these three passages, and their meaning is far from clear.

The Quran claims that the Jews did not kill or crucify 'Īsā (4.157). What happened then? The verse indicates only disagreement, doubt, and conjecture and provides the difficult expression *shubbiha lahum*, which Marmaduke Pickthall translates "it appeared so to them." Translators have struggled with this Arabic expression and rendered it in a dozen different ways (Droge translates it as "it (only) seemed like (that) to them").

The second verse on the death of Jesus adds to the confusion. At issue is another difficult expression, *mutawaffīka* (3.55). Pickthall translates it as "I am gathering you," while several other translations render the expression as "I am causing you to die" (e.g., Sale). See the discussion of the verb *tawaffā* below.

The third verse offers a speech from the infant 'Īsā: "Peace be upon me the day I was born, and the day I die, and the day I am raised up alive!" (19.33). This seems to follow the Gospel sequence, and the same three verbs are used about John the Baptist in 19.15. Also adding to the confusion is 5.75, which, while claiming that 'Īsā is nothing by a messenger, says that "messengers had passed away before him."

It is surely a matter of great curiosity that many translators relate every occurrence of the verb *tawaffā* to "death" except in verses about 'Īsā (3.55; 5.117). This seems to show a desire on the part of translators to be consistent with their understanding of 4.157. Verses in which *tawaffā* is commonly related to death include 10.46, 104; 12.101; 13.40; 16.28; and 40.77. Several of these verses are addressed to the messenger of the Quran.

The difficult expression *shubbiha lahum* in 4.157 has challenged translators and Muslim commentators alike. In order to explain the claim that the Jews did not crucify 'Īsā, "but it (only) seemed like (that) to them," many commentators composed a tale about the appearance of 'Īsā attaching onto another person. They suggested a variety of names for this substitute. They then wrote that the substitute was crucified while 'Īsā escaped. Sūra 4.158 claims that "Allah took him up." Commentators thus proposed an ascension without a death and resurrection.

What then could the infant 'Īsā mean at 19.33, where he speaks about his death and resurrection? Muslim commentators put his death far in the future among the events of the end times and his subsequent resurrection alongside the resurrection of all humankind.

This uncertainty about the death of 'Īsā in the Quran can be seen in Muslim commentaries over a thousand-year period. Some of these interpretations are fascinating. For example, al-Rāzī (d. 1209) wrote that saying the witnesses of the crucifixion were mistaken challenges the whole idea of sense perception and the possibility of history. He also wrote that saying God deceived the witnesses is saying something unworthy of the almighty God. Even so, al-Rāzī denied the death of 'Īsā because he perceived the denial to come from the messenger of Islam.

This unaccountable ambiguity about the death of 'Īsā in the Quran raises one of the largest questions about the reliability of the Arabic scripture and its messenger. The Gospel accounts and the apostolic writings of the New Testament are unanimous that Jesus died on the cross, and secular sources of the time corroborate Jesus' death. It is a matter of history and a matter of truth. But beyond this factual concern, the denial of Jesus' death cuts the deniers off from the cross's tangible demonstration of the love of God in human history and society, as well as from the salvation that the gospel says comes to humanity through his sacrificial death.

According to the New Testament, Jesus' death was a sacrifice of atonement, and God makes righteous all those who accept his redemptive death by faith (Romans 3:21–28).

[34] That was Jesus, son of Mary – a statement of the truth about which they are in doubt. [35] It is not for God to take any son. Glory to Him! When He decrees something, He simply says to it, 'Be!' and it is. [36] 'Surely God is my Lord and your Lord, so serve Him! This is a straight path.'

19.34 – *That was Jesus, son of Mary – a statement of the truth about which they are in doubt*

For the quranic name 'Īsā, see the explanation at 2.87 (p. 48). This verse can be

[37] But the factions differed among themselves. So woe to those who disbelieve on account of (their) witnessing a great Day! [38] How well they will hear on it! How well they will see on the Day when they come to Us! But the evildoers today are clearly astray. [39] Warn them of the Day of Regret, when the matter will be decided while they are (still) oblivious and disbelieving. [40] Surely We shall inherit the earth, and whoever is on it, and to Us they will be returned.

[41] And remember in the Book Abraham: Surely he was a man of truth,

---

understood to call 'Īsā himself a "statement of the truth" (*qawla 'l-ḥaqq*), thereby matching what the Quran says about 'Īsā in 3.45 and 4.171.

In a more straightforward sense, the verse represents well the quranic presentation of 'Īsā: a tone of finality, a claim to truth about the matter (see also 3.60–62; 4.174), and a suggestion that the People of the Book are in dispute (see also v. 37).

As for the "factions" (v. 37) doubting or differing about 'Īsā, during the seventh century Byzantine, Nestorian, and Monophysite Christians all believed in the death and deity of Jesus. They differed about how to express Jesus' humanity. See the comments on the theme of disagreements at 98.4 (p. 624).

19.35 – *It is not for God to take any son. Glory to Him!*

The Quran denies that Allah has taken a son (*walad*). Coming as it does at the end of a long passage on 'Īsā, Mary, and other Gospel characters, this verse may be taken as a denial of Christian belief in the divine Sonship of Jesus. The reason for the denial in this case seems to be that the Christian belief is understood to impinge on the exclusive authority of Allah.

This denial of divine Sonship shortly after a story about the birth of 'Īsā is curious because the words of the "spirit" in verses 19–21 make a glaring omission of a Gospel detail about Jesus that contradicts verse 35 (also the speech of the "angels" in Q 3.42–46). In the Gospel according to Luke, Gabriel said to Mary that the child "will be great and will be called the Son of the Most High." Gabriel added – as if to emphasize this point – that because "the power of the Most High" would overshadow Mary, "the holy one to be born will be called the Son of God" (Luke 1:32, 35).

The expression "Allah has taken a son" appears six other times in the Quran, including at verses 88–92 of this sūra. See "Son of God in the Quran" (p. 352).

19.36 – *God is my Lord and your Lord, so serve Him!*

If this verse is taken to be a statement spoken by 'Īsā, it matches several other verses in which 'Īsā himself is "quoted" as denying his own deity (3.51; 5.72, 116–17; 43.64; cf. 4.172). See an analysis of these statements at 43.64 (p. 492).

19.41 – *And remember in the Book Abraham*

Abraham challenges his father persistently about his idol worship (vv. 42–44),

a prophet. [42] When he said to his father, 'My father! Why do you serve what does not hear and does not see, and is of no use to you at all? [43] My father! Surely some knowledge has come to me that has not come to you. So follow me, and I shall guide you to an even path. [44] My father! Do not serve Satan! Surely Satan is disobedient to the Merciful. [45] My father! I fear that punishment from the Merciful will touch you, and you become an ally of Satan.' [46] He said, 'Do you forsake my gods, Abraham? If indeed you do not stop, I shall indeed stone you. So leave me for a long time!' [47] He said, 'Peace (be) upon you! I shall ask forgiveness for you from my Lord. Surely He has been gracious to me. [48] I shall withdraw from you and what you call on instead of God, and I shall call on my Lord. It may be that I shall not be disappointed in calling on my Lord.' [49] So when he had withdrawn from them and what they were serving instead of God, We granted him Isaac and Jacob, and each one We made a prophet. [50] We granted them some of Our mercy, and We assigned to them a true (and) high reputation.

[51] And remember in the Book Moses: Surely he was devoted, and he was a messenger, a prophet. [52] We called him from the right side of the mountain, and We brought him near in conversation. [53] And We granted him some of Our mercy: his brother Aaron, a prophet.

[54] And remember in the Book Ishmael: Surely he was true to the promise, and he was a messenger, a prophet. [55] He commanded his people with the prayer and the alms, and he was pleasing before his Lord.

---

but his father does not appreciate the challenge (v. 46). Abraham promises his father to ask forgiveness on his behalf (v. 47) but also departs from his father and his idolatry (vv. 48–49).

Stories of Abraham's opposition to idolatry appear frequently in the Quran, each adding details that are not included in other quranic versions. In most of the stories, Abraham preaches to his people as well; only in this version is Abraham's father the main focus.

19.49 – *We granted him Isaac and Jacob, and each one We made a prophet*

That Isaac, not Ishmael, is mentioned as the son God granted to Abraham may come as a surprise to readers who are familiar with the importance of Ishmael in Islam. In this sūra Ishmael's name only appears at verse 54, with no connection made to Abraham. The same pattern is followed in a number of quranic passages. See the analysis of this pattern at 21.72 (p. 335).

Elsewhere, the Quran offers a brief story about Abraham that features only Ishmael (2.125–127). See "Abraham in the Quran" (p. 90).

⁵⁶ And remember in the Book Idrīs: Surely he was a man of truth, a prophet. ⁵⁷ We raised him up to a high place.

⁵⁸ Those were the ones whom God has blessed among the prophets from the descendants of Adam, and from those We carried with Noah, and from the descendants of Abraham and Israel, and from those whom We have guided and chosen. When the signs of the Merciful were recited to them, they fell down in prostration and weeping. ⁵⁹ But after them came successors (who) neglected the prayer and followed (their own) desires. Soon they will meet error ⁶⁰ – except for the one who turns (in repentance), and believes, and does righteousness. Those will enter the Garden, and they will not be done evil at all ⁶¹ – Gardens of Eden, which the Merciful has promised to His servants in the unseen. Surely He – His promise will come to pass. ⁶² There they will not hear any frivolous talk, only 'Peace!' And there they will have their provision morning and evening. ⁶³ That is the Garden which We give as an inheritance to those of Our servants who guard (themselves).

⁶⁴ 'We only come down by the command of your Lord. To Him (belongs) whatever is before us and whatever is behind us, and whatever is between that. Your Lord is not forgetful ⁶⁵ – Lord of the heavens and the earth, and whatever is between them. So serve Him and be patient in His service! Do you know (another) name for Him?'

⁶⁶ The human says, 'When I am dead, shall I indeed be brought forth alive?' ⁶⁷ Does the human not remember that We created him before, when he was nothing? ⁶⁸ By your Lord! We shall indeed gather them together, and (also) the satans. Then We shall indeed bring them around Gehenna (on) bended knees. ⁶⁹ Then We shall indeed draw out from each party those of them (who are) most (in) rebellion against the Merciful. ⁷⁰ Then indeed We shall know those who most deserve burning with it. ⁷¹ (There is) not one of you (who is) not coming to it – (that) is for your Lord an inevitability decreed. ⁷² Then We

---

19.56 – *And remember in the Book Idrīs*

The identity of the name Idrīs is uncertain (mentioned only here and 21.85). Some scholars suggest this may refer to Enoch; others say Ezra.

19.60 – *Those will enter the Garden, and they will not be done evil at all*

This passage (vv. 60–63) describes heaven as the "Gardens of Eden."

19.71 – *(There is) not one of you (who is) not coming to it*

This passage appears to say that all people will first go down to hell, if the "it" of verse 72 is taken to be the "Gehenna" mentioned in verse 68. The evildoers would remain there, while the Lord would save from hell those who guarded themselves (v. 72).

shall rescue the ones who guarded (themselves), and leave the evildoers in it (on) bended knees.

[73] When Our signs are recited to them as clear signs, those who disbelieve say to those who believe, 'Which of the two groups is better in status and better as a cohort?' [74] But how many a generation We have destroyed before them! They were better in wealth and outward appearance. [75] Say: 'Whoever is astray, let the Merciful prolong his life until, when they see what they are promised – either the punishment or the Hour – they will know who is worse in position and weaker in forces.' [76] But God will increase in guidance those who are guided. And the things that endure – righteous deeds – are better with your Lord, and better in return.

[77] Have you seen the one who disbelieves in Our signs, and says, 'I shall indeed be given wealth and children'? [78] Has he looked into the unseen, or has he taken a covenant with the Merciful? [79] By no means! We shall write down what he says, and We shall increase the punishment for him. [80] We shall inherit from him what he says, and he will come to Us alone.

[81] They have taken gods other than God, so that they might be a (source of) honor for them. [82] By no means! They will deny their service, and they will be opposed to them. [83] Do you not see that We have sent the satans against the disbelievers to incite them. [84] So do not be in a hurry with them. We are only counting for them a (certain) number (of years). [85] On the Day when We shall gather to the Merciful the ones who guarded (themselves) like a delegation, [86] and drive the sinners into Gehenna like a herd, [87] they will have no power of intercession, except for the one who has made a covenant with the Merciful.

[88] They say, 'The Merciful has taken a son.' [89] Certainly you have put forth

---

19.73 – *When Our signs are recited to them as clear signs*

In this final section (vv. 73–92), the sūra discusses the unbelievers, their behavior, and how Allah will deal with them. This seems to be the context for the verses about Son of God (vv. 88–92).

19.87 – *they will have no power of intercession*

This verse makes an exception for "the one who has made a covenant with the Merciful." See the analysis of verses on intercession at 39.44 (p. 464).

19.88 – *They say, "The Merciful has taken a son"*

Up to this point the Quran has made many references to the "son of God," and earlier in this sūra we saw the expression, "It is not for God to take any son" (v. 35). Looking further back, these verses seem to be part of a series of verses against sonship alongside 17.111 and 18.4.

However, there seems to be an extra depth of feeling in this passage (vv. 88–92).

something abhorrent! [90] The heavens are nearly torn apart because of it, and the earth split open, and the mountains collapse in pieces [91] – that they should attribute to the Merciful a son, [92] when it is not fitting for the Merciful to take a son.

[93] (There is) no one in the heavens and the earth who comes to the Merciful except as a servant. [94] Certainly He has counted them and numbered them exactly. [95] Each one of them will come to Him on the Day of Resurrection alone. [96] Surely those who believe and do righteous deeds – to them the Merciful will show (His) love.

[97] Surely We have made it easy in your language, so that you may give good news by means of it to the ones who guard (themselves), and warn by means of it a contentious people. [98] But how many a generation We have destroyed before them! Do you see a single one of them, or hear (even) a whisper of them?

Here, it is a terrible thing to say that the Merciful (*raḥmān*) has taken to himself a son (v. 89), and the universe starts to disintegrate at the mere mention of it (v. 90). The claim is that it is not appropriate for the Merciful to take a son (v. 92).

The expression "Allah has taken a son" appears six other times in the Quran; these verses give a variety of reasons for why the Quran does not consider the statement theologically appropriate. See "Son of God in the Quran" (p. 352).

19.96 – *Surely those who believe and do righteous deeds – to them the Merciful will show this love*

In this verse the Merciful will appoint affection or "love" (*wudd*) for those who believe and do good works. Coming directly after verses 88–95, this "belief" cannot be just any kind of "religious faith." Rather, it is specific to claims for the Quran's Allah, his messenger, and the recitations "sent down" to him.

The noun *wudd* only appears here in the Quran. See "The Language of Love in the Quran" (p. 560).

ṬĀ' HĀ'

ṬĀ' HĀ'

20

The story of Moses' encounter with God at the burning bush is retold in this sūra in the first of three quranic versions. This account is interesting because of the names that Allah uses to introduce himself to Moses and because of the long ensuing conversation in which Allah commissions Moses.

The sūra begins with the seemingly self-conscious first-person-plural ("We") assertion to the messenger that the contents of his recitation are sent down from the Creator. This language of reassurance appears twice more in the sūra.

The largest part of the sūra is taken up by a series of episodes in the life of Moses. This is one of the longest narratives about Moses in the Quran. In terms of the first part of the familiar Moses story, it is the most complete. This version includes Moses' infancy, his killing of a man, his sojourn in Midian, his commission and appearance before Pharaoh, and the deliverance of the Children of Israel from Egypt. The episode of the golden calf is unique in specifying that a Samaritan leads the people astray.

Another important passage in this sūra is the third of three quranic versions of the story of Adam. This version is striking in offering a strong verb to characterize Adam's behaviour.

In the Name of God, the Merciful, the Compassionate

[1] Ṭā' Hā'. [2] We have not sent down the Qur'ān on you for you to be miserable, [3] but as a reminder to the one who fears [4] – as a sending down from the One

---

20.2 – *We have not sent down the Qur'ān on you for you to be miserable*

The seemingly self-conscious, first-person language of this verse, addressed to the messenger and making claims for his recitation, is typical of the voice of the Quran at many points – often at the beginnings or endings of sūras. The same kind of language also appears in this sūra at verses 99 and 113–14. Here the Quran claims that its material is a sending down (*tanzīl*) "from the One who created the earth and the high heavens" (v. 4). See "Different Kinds of Literature" (p. 14).

On the word *qur'ān*, see the comment at 2.185 (p. 61).

who created the earth and the high heavens. ⁵ The Merciful is mounted upon the throne. ⁶ To Him (belongs) whatever is in the heavens and whatever is on the earth, and whatever is between them, and whatever is beneath the ground. ⁷ If you speak the word publicly, surely He knows the secret and (what is even) more hidden. ⁸ God – (there is) no god but Him. To Him (belong) the best names.

⁹ Has the story of Moses come to you? ¹⁰ When he saw a fire, he said to his family, 'Stay (here). Surely I perceive a fire. Perhaps I shall bring you a flaming torch from it, or I shall find at the fire guidance.' ¹¹ But when he came to it, he was called: 'Moses! ¹² Surely I am your Lord, so take off your shoes. Surely you are in the holy wādī of Ṭuwā. ¹³ I have chosen you, so listen to what is inspired. ¹⁴ Surely I am God – (there is) no god but Me. So serve Me, and observe the prayer for My remembrance! ¹⁵ Surely the Hour is coming – I almost hide it, so that every person may be repaid for what he strives after. ¹⁶ So do not let anyone who does not believe in it, and who (only) follows his (own) desire, keep you from it, or you will be brought to ruin.'

¹⁷ 'What is that in your right (hand), Moses?' ¹⁸ He said, 'It is my staff. I lean on it, and I bring down leaves with it to (feed) my sheep, and I have other uses for it.' ¹⁹ He said, 'Cast it (down), Moses!' ²⁰ So he cast it, and suddenly it became a slithering snake. ²¹ He said, 'Take hold of it, and do not fear. We shall restore it to its former state. ²² Now draw your hand to your side. It will come out white, unharmed – another sign. ²³ (We have done this) to show you one of Our greatest signs.'

²⁴ 'Go to Pharaoh! Surely he has transgressed insolently.' ²⁵ He said, 'My Lord,

---

20.9 – *Has the story of Moses come to you?*

This question starts one of the longest and most detailed versions of the Moses story in the Quran (vv. 9–98). The question itself seems to imply that the story is generally known or readily available. This version starts out with the burning bush episode and then goes back to recount Moses' childhood.

The story includes many of the narrative elements familiar from the Torah. However, one plot detail here is not found in the Bible. The Quran says that a character called *al-Sāmirī* led the people astray (vv. 85–98). See the table of Moses narratives plotted against familiar narrative elements (p. 390).

20.10 – *When he saw a fire*

The episode known to many as the "burning bush" is recounted in the Quran in three different versions. Among the many interesting details in these stories are the names that God gives for himself to Moses. Here God introduces himself as "your Lord" (*rabb*, v. 12) and "Allah" (v. 14). The other versions of the story are found at 27:7–12 and 28:29–35.

expand my heart for me, ²⁶ and make my task easy for me. ²⁷ Untie the knot from my tongue, ²⁸ so that they may understand my words. ²⁹ And appoint an assistant for me from my family: ³⁰ Aaron, my brother. ³¹ Strengthen me through him, ³² and associate him in my task, ³³ so that we may glorify You often, ³⁴ and remember You often. ³⁵ Surely you see us.' ³⁶ He said, 'You are granted your request, Moses.'

³⁷ 'Certainly We bestowed favor on you another time, ³⁸ when We inspired your mother (with) what was inspired: ³⁹ "Cast him into the ark, and cast it into the sea, and let the sea throw it up on the shore, and an enemy to Me and an enemy to him will take him." But I cast love on you from Me, and (I did this) so that you might be brought up under My eye. ⁴⁰ When your sister went out, she said, "Shall I direct you to (someone) who will take charge of him?" And We returned you to your mother, so that she might be comforted and not sorrow. And (then) you killed a man, and We rescued you from that distress, and We tested you thoroughly. So you remained for (some) years with the people of Midian, (and) then you came (here), according to a decree, Moses.'

⁴¹ 'I have brought you up for Myself. ⁴² Go, you and your brother, with My signs, and do not be lax in My remembrance. ⁴³ Go, both of you, to Pharaoh. Surely he has transgressed insolently. ⁴⁴ But speak to him a soft word. Perhaps he may take heed or fear.' ⁴⁵ They said, 'Our Lord, surely we are afraid that he may act rashly against us, or that he may transgress insolently.' ⁴⁶ He said, 'Do not be afraid! Surely I am with both of you. I hear and I see. ⁴⁷ So go to him, both of you, and say: "We are two messengers of your Lord, so send forth the Sons of Israel with us, and do not punish them. We have brought you a sign from your Lord. Peace (be) upon anyone who follows the guidance! ⁴⁸ Surely we have been inspired that the punishment (will fall) on anyone who calls (it) a lie and turns away."'

⁴⁹ He said, 'And who is your Lord, Moses?' ⁵⁰ He said, 'Our Lord is the One who gave everything its creation, (and) then guided (it).' ⁵¹ He said, 'What

---

20.39 – *I cast love on you from Me*

This tender statement of Allah to Moses contains the only occurrence of one of the main Arabic nouns for love – *maḥabba* – in the Quran. See "The Language of Love in the Quran" (p. 560).

20.49 – *He said, "And who is your Lord, Moses?"*

This story of the interactions between Moses, Pharaoh, and the sorcerers (vv. 49–73) is remarkable for its length and detail. The sorcerers are so impressed with the signs of Moses that they immediately convert (vv. 70, 72–73), in spite of the fearsome punishments threatened by Pharaoh (v. 71).

(about the) case of the former generations?' ⁵² He said, 'The knowledge of it is with my Lord in a Book. My Lord does not go astray, nor does He forget. ⁵³ (It is He) who made the earth as a cradle for you, and put (path)ways in it for you, and sent down water from the sky. And by means of it We brought forth pairs of various (kinds of) vegetation. ⁵⁴ Eat (of it) and pasture your livestock (on it). Surely in that are signs indeed for those with reason. ⁵⁵ We created you from it, and into it We shall return you, and from it We shall bring you forth another time.'

⁵⁶ Certainly We showed him Our signs, all of them, but he called (them) a lie and refused. ⁵⁷ He said, 'Have you come to bring us forth from our land by your magic, Moses? ⁵⁸ We shall indeed bring you magic like it. So set an appointment between us and you – We shall not break it, nor will you – at a fair place.' ⁵⁹ He said, 'Your appointment is on the Day of Splendor. Let the people be gathered at morning light.'

⁶⁰ So Pharaoh turned away, and put together his plot. Then he came (again). ⁶¹ Moses said to them, 'Woe to you! Do not forge a lie against God, or He will destroy you with a punishment. Whoever forges (a lie) has failed.' ⁶² So they disputed their situation among themselves, but they kept their talk secret. ⁶³ They said, 'Surely these two magicians want to expel you from your land by their magic, and to do away with your exemplary way (of life). ⁶⁴ So put together your plot, (and) then line up. He who has the upper hand today will indeed prosper.' ⁶⁵ They said, 'Moses! Are you going to cast or shall we be first to cast?' ⁶⁶ He said, 'No! You cast (first)!' And suddenly their ropes and their staffs seemed to him to be moving as a result of their magic. ⁶⁷ So Moses felt fear within himself. ⁶⁸ We said to him, 'Do not be afraid! Surely you will be the superior one. ⁶⁹ Cast (down) what is in your right (hand), and it will swallow up what they have made. What they have done is only a magician's trick, and the magician does not prosper, (no matter) where he comes.'

⁷⁰ And the magicians were cast (down) in prostration. They said, 'We believe in the Lord of Aaron and Moses.' ⁷¹ He said, 'Have you believed in him before I gave you permission? Surely he indeed is your master, the (very) one who taught you magic? I shall indeed cut off your hands and your feet on opposite sides, and I shall indeed crucify you on the trunks of date palms, and you will indeed know which of us is harsher in punishment, and more lasting.' ⁷² They said, 'We shall not prefer you over the clear signs which have come to us, nor (over) Him who created us. So decree whatever you are going to decree. You can only decree for this present life. ⁷³ Surely we have believed in our Lord, so that He may forgive us our sins and the magic you forced us to (practice). God is better and more lasting.'

⁷⁴ Surely the one who comes to his Lord as a sinner, surely for him (there is)

Gehenna, where he will neither die nor live. [75] But whoever comes to Him as a believer, (and) he has done righteous deeds, those – for them (there are) the highest ranks: [76] Gardens of Eden, through which rivers flow, there to remain. That is the payment for the one who purifies himself.

[77] Certainly We inspired Moses: 'Journey with My servants, and strike for them a dry passage in the sea, without fear of being overtaken or being afraid.' [78] So Pharaoh followed them with his forces, but (there) covered them of the sea what covered them. [79] Pharaoh led his people astray and did not guide (them).

[80] Sons of Israel! We have rescued you from your enemy, and made a covenant with you at the right side of the mountain, and sent down on you the manna and the quails: [81] 'Eat from the good things which We have provided you, but do not transgress insolently in that, or My anger will descend on you. Whoever My anger falls on has perished. [82] Yet surely I am indeed forgiving to whoever turns (in repentance) and believes, and does righteousness, (and) then is (rightly) guided.'

[83] 'What has made you hurry (ahead) of your people, Moses?' [84] He said, 'They are close on my footsteps, but I have hurried (ahead) to you, my Lord, in order that You might be pleased.' [85] He said, 'Surely We have tempted your people after you (left them), and al-Sāmirī has led them astray.' [86] So Moses returned to his people, angry (and) sorrowful. He said, 'My people! Did your Lord not promise you a good promise? Did (the time of) the covenant last too long for you, or did you wish that the anger of your Lord would descend on you, and so you broke (your) appointment with me?' [87] They said, 'We did not break (our) appointment with you by our (own) will, but we were loaded with burdens of the ornaments of the people, and we cast them (down), and so did al-Sāmirī.' [88] Then he brought forth for them a calf, a (mere) image of it (having) a mooing sound, and they said, 'This is your god, and the god of Moses, though he has forgotten.' [89] Did they not see that it did not return a word to them, and had no power to (cause) them harm or benefit? [90] Certainly Aaron had said to them before, 'My people! You are only being tempted by it. Surely your Lord is the Merciful, so follow me and obey my command!' [91] They said, 'We shall continue (to be) devoted to it until Moses returns to us.'

20.85 – *Surely We have tempted your people after you (left them), and al-Sāmirī has led them astray*

Here the Lord says to Moses that *al-Sāmirī* is responsible for leading the people astray. Perhaps meaning "the Samaritan," this reference (also vv. 87, 95) is otherwise incomprehensible. Meanwhile Aaron, whom Moses had left in charge, offers a lame excuse (v. 94).

⁹² He said, 'Aaron! What prevented you, when you saw them going astray, ⁹³ from following me? Did you disobey my command?' ⁹⁴ He said, 'Son of my mother! Do not seize (me) by my beard or by my head! Surely I was afraid that you would say, "You have caused a division among the Sons of Israel, and you have not respected my word."' ⁹⁵ He said, 'What was this business of yours, al-Sāmirī?' ⁹⁶ He said, 'I saw what they did not see, and I took a handful (of dust) from the footprint of the messenger, and I tossed it. In this way my mind contrived (it) for me.' ⁹⁷ He said, 'Go! Surely it is yours in this life to say, "Do not touch (me)!" And surely for you (there is) an appointment – you will not break it. Look at your god which you remained devoted to! We shall indeed burn it (and) then scatter it as dust in the sea. ⁹⁸ Your only god is God – (there is) no god but Him – who comprehends everything in knowledge.'

⁹⁹ In this way We recount to you some of the stories of what has already gone before, and We have given you a reminder from Us. ¹⁰⁰ Whoever turns away from it, surely he will bear a burden on the Day of Resurrection. ¹⁰¹ [. . .] there to remain, and evil (will be the) load for them on the Day of Resurrection.

¹⁰² On the Day when there is a blast on the trumpet – and We shall gather the sinners on that Day blue – ¹⁰³ they will murmur among themselves: 'You have remained (in the grave) only for ten (days).' ¹⁰⁴ We know what they will say, when the best of them in way (of life) will say, 'You have remained only for a day.'

¹⁰⁵ They ask you about the mountains. Say: 'My Lord will scatter them as dust, ¹⁰⁶ and He will leave it a barren plain ¹⁰⁷ in which you will not see any crookedness or curve.'

¹⁰⁸ On that Day they will follow the Caller, in whom (there is) no crookedness, and voices will be hushed before the Merciful, so that you will hear nothing but a faint murmur. ¹⁰⁹ On that Day intercession will not be of any benefit, except for the

---

20.99 – *In this way We recount to you some of the stories of what has already gone before*

In such statements, the Quran seems to claim that its stories are a sign of its divine origin (see vv. 2–4). As we have noted, however, this quranic version of the well-known Moses story adds a strange detail not found in the Torah.

20.102 – *On the Day when there is a blast on the trumpet*

These words begin a judgment scene on the Day of Resurrection (*yawm al-qiyāma*), which gives the terrified speech of the guilty (vv. 102–12). Another short judgment scene comes in verses 124–27. See "Eschatology in the Quran" (p. 604).

20.109 – *On that Day intercession will not be of any benefit, except*

This verse starts out like a prohibition but then – as in a number of other quranic passages – makes an exception. The Merciful will give permission for intercession

one to whom the Merciful gives permission, and whose word He approves. [110] He knows what is before them and what is behind them, but they do not encompass Him in knowledge. [111] Faces will be humbled before the Living, the Everlasting. Whoever carries (a load of) evildoing will have failed, [112] but whoever does any righteous deeds – and he is a believer – he will not fear (any) evil or dispossession.

[113] In this way We have sent it down as an Arabic Qur'ān, and We have varied some of the promise(s) in it, so that they may guard (themselves), or so that it may arouse in them a reminder. [114] Exalted is God, the true King! Do not be in a hurry with the Qur'ān, before its inspiration is completed to you, but say: 'My Lord, increase me in knowledge.'

[115] Certainly We made a covenant with Adam before, but he forgot, and We found in him no determination. [116] (Remember) when We said to the angels, 'Prostrate yourselves before Adam,' and they prostrated themselves, except Iblīs. He refused. [117] And We said, 'Adam! Surely this is an enemy to you and to your wife. Do not let him expel you both from the Garden, and you become miserable. [118] Surely it is yours not to hunger there or go naked, [119] nor to thirst there or be exposed to the sun.' [120] But Satan whispered to him. He said, 'Adam! Shall I direct you to the Tree of Immortality, and (to) a kingdom that does not decay?' [121] So they both ate from it, and their shameful parts became apparent to them, and they both began fastening on themselves some leaves of the Garden, and Adam disobeyed his Lord and erred. [122] Then his Lord chose him, and turned

---

to someone whose word he approves. See the analysis of verses on intercession at 39.44 (p. 464).

20.113 – *In this way We have sent it down as an Arabic Qur'ān*

The Quran claims that it is revealed. The word *qur'ān* does not necessarily mean the Muslim scripture as it is known today. See the comment on "Qur'ān" at 2.185 (p. 61) and an analysis of claims for "Arabic" at 43.2–3 (p. 487).

20.115 – *Certainly We made a covenant with Adam before, but he forgot*

This verse begins the Quran's third version of the Adam story. Adam is immediately introduced as forgetful and lacking determination (*'azm*).

20.116 – *they prostrated themselves, except Iblīs*

On Iblīs's refusal to bow down, see the analysis and response at 38.73–74 (p. 458).

20.121 – *Adam disobeyed his Lord and erred*

This third version introduces a strong verb into its description of Adam's action. Satan tells Adam about "the tree of immortality" (v. 120), and "they both ate from it" (v. 121). The stark judgment on the action here is that "Adam disobeyed (*'aṣā*) his Lord and erred."

This is significantly different from the characterization of Adam's culpability in

to him (in forgiveness), and guided (him). [123] He said, 'Go down from it, both of you together, some of you an enemy to others. If any guidance comes to you from Me, whoever follows My guidance will not go astray, nor become miserable. [124] But whoever turns away from My reminder, surely for him (there will be) a life of deprivation, and We shall gather him blind on the Day of Resurrection.' [175] He will say, 'My Lord, why have you gathered me blind, when I had sight before?' [126] He will say, 'So (it is). Our signs came to you, but you forgot them, so today you are forgotten.' [127] In this way We repay anyone who acts wantonly and does not believe in the signs of his Lord. Yet the punishment of the Hereafter is indeed harsher and more lasting.

[128] Is it not a guide for them how many generations We destroyed before them, (seeing that) they walk in (the midst of) their dwelling places? Surely in that are signs indeed for those with reason. [129] Were it not for a preceding word from your Lord, it would indeed be close at hand – but (there is) a time appointed (for punishment). [130] So be patient with what they say, and glorify your Lord with praise before the rising of the sun, and before its setting, and during the hours of the night, and glorify (Him) at the ends of the day, so that you may find satisfaction. [131] Do not yearn after what We have given classes of them to enjoy – the flower of this present life – that We may test them by means

---

the two other versions of the Adam story at 2.30–39 and 7.10–27. The first of these simply says that Satan caused Adam and his spouse to "slip," with no responsibility on Adam's part (2.36). In the second version the role of Satan also seems to be dominant, but Adam and his spouse acknowledge "We have wronged ourselves" and ask for forgiveness (7.23). Only in the third version does the Quran put the responsibility where it belongs: "Adam disobeyed his Lord." The verb *'aṣā* has the sense of revolt, rebellion, and breaking relationship.

The discrepancy among the three versions produces a kind of ambivalence about human sinfulness and its seriousness before God. In the first version, Allah forgives or "relents toward" Adam with no acknowledgment of sin from Adam (2.37; cf. 20.122). In the second version, Allah holds Adam to account but says that half of Adam's sin was failing to heed God's warning about Satan (7.22; cf. 20.117). All three versions seem distracted by the tale of Iblīs's refusal to bow. The biblical account, by contrast, portrays a detailed encounter between God and each guilty human, as well as serious, individualized punishments proportionate to their sin (Genesis 2:15–3:19).

The Quran's Adam stories include a promise of guidance to come (2.38; 20.123), but notably absent is the Bible's promise of a deeper treatment of the evil in Eden: the offspring of the woman will crush the head of the tempter, the serpent (Genesis 3:15). See also the analysis of verses on human nature at 79.40 (p. 612).

of it. The provision of your Lord is better and more lasting. [132] Command your family (to observe) the prayer, and be patient in it. We do not ask you for provision. We provide for you, and the outcome (is) for the guarding (of yourself).

[133] They say, 'If only he would bring us a sign from his Lord.' Has there not come to them a clear sign (of) what was in the former pages? [134] If We had destroyed them with a punishment before him, they would indeed have said, 'Our Lord, if only you had sent us a messenger, so that we might have followed your signs before we were humiliated and disgraced?' [135] Say: 'Each one is waiting, so you wait (too), and then you will know who are the followers of the even path, and who is (rightly) guided.'

20.133 – *Has there not come to them a clear sign (of) what was in the former pages?*
The expression "former pages" (*al-ṣuḥuf al-ūlā*) may refer to earlier scriptures and, if so, indicates a favorable attitude toward pre-Islamic scriptures.

THE PROPHETS
AL-ANBIYĀ'

21

> This sūra lives up to its name by touching on the stories of several prophets, most of whom are recognizable from the Bible. The majority of these references are short, but there is a longer story about Abraham in conflict with his father and his people over the worship of idols. There is also some interesting information about David and Solomon, and Mary is referred to as the one into whom Allah breathed some of his spirit.
>
> The sūra begins with a long passage about an encounter between the messenger and his audience. We seem to hear the audience's objections and personal criticisms of the messenger and the messenger's speeches in response. There is a warning about peoples of the past who did not listen and who were destroyed as a result. The Quran promises strict accounting on the Day of Resurrection and punishments that will come to some. This sūra also reassures the messenger and encourages him to continue to preach in spite of opposition.

In the Name of God, the Merciful, the Compassionate

[1] Their reckoning has drawn near to the people, while they are turning away oblivious. [2] No new reminder comes to them from their Lord, without their listening to it while they jest, [3] their hearts diverted. Those who do evil keep their talk secret: 'Is this (anything) but a human being like you? Will you surrender to magic when you see (it)?' [4] Say: 'My Lord knows the words (spoken) in the sky

---

21.3 – *Those who do evil keep their talk secret: "Is this (anything) but a human being like you?..."*

This question seems to suggest the kinds of responses that the audience gives to the messenger's preaching. Their main point is to say that he has invented his message (v. 5). When they ask for a "sign" (*āya*) like earlier messengers brought (v. 5), the audience may be thinking of the miracles that Moses and Jesus were known to have done. On miracles and the messenger of the Quran, see the discussion at 43.40 (p. 490).

21.4 – *My Lord knows the words*

This translation by Droge conceals an interesting challenge related to the Arabic

and the earth. He is the Hearing, the Knowing.' [5] 'No!' they say, '(It is) a jumble of dreams! No! He has forged it! No! He is a poet! Let him bring us a sign, as the ones of old were sent (with signs).' [6] Not one town which We destroyed before them believed. Will they believe?

[7] We have not sent (anyone) before you except men whom We inspired – just ask the People of the Reminder, if you do not know (it) – [8] nor did We give them a body not eating food, nor were they immortal. [9] But We were true to them in the promise, so We rescued them and whomever We pleased, and We destroyed

---

text of the Quran. The first word in the verse is *qāla*, which means, "he said." The same word begins the last verse in this sūra. Most translations render *qāla* as "he said," but Droge has chosen an alternate reading. The source of the confusion is the ambiguity in the earliest Quran manuscripts: in the earliest manuscripts, the writing of "he said" and "Say!" (*qul*) was exactly the same, because Arabic at that point had neither an *alif* for the long "a" in *qāla*, nor a mark for the short "a" at the end of *qāla*. The issue for interpretation is whether the Quran means to say that a human speaker composes and speaks the following words, or that Allah commands the messenger to say words that the messenger then recites. Andrew Rippin explains this point further in his book, *Muslims* (see bibliography). See also "Manuscripts of the Quran" (p. 407).

21.5 – *No! He is a poet!*

The negative sense of "poet" and "poetry" (*shi'r*) in a number of passages seems to come from a concept in the Quran that poetry is associated with the inspiration of devils or *jinn*. Some scholars also suggest that in the seventh century Arabic poetry was increasingly used for obscenity or curses.

In fact, many parts of the Quran are made up of lines that rhyme. Scholars refer to this as "rhymed prose" rather than poetry. The rhyme is constructed through a vowel plus the final consonant at the end of each verse. In the longer narrative sūras the rhyme is created by the use of stock phrases such as "Allah is all-knowing, all-wise."

On the accusation in this verse that the messenger is inventing, see the discussion at 69.44 (p. 587).

21.7 – *just ask the People of the Reminder, if you do not know (it)*

This verse is one of a number of verses in the Quran that seem to come out of a positive assumption about Jews and Christians and their scriptures (16.43 has the same wording; see also 10.94). "People of the Reminder" is an expression similar to "People of the Book."

21.9 – *so We rescued them and whomever We pleased, and We destroyed the wanton*

The language of salvation (*anjā*) appears a number of times in this sūra's stories of past prophets (also vv. 71, 74, 76, 88). See "Salvation in the Quran" (p. 180).

the wanton. [10] Certainly We have sent down to you a Book in which (there is) your reminder. Will you not understand?

[11] How many a town (which) was doing evil have We smashed, and produced another people after it! [12] And when they sensed Our violence, suddenly they began fleeing from it. [13] 'Do not flee, but return to what luxury you were given to delight in, and (to) your dwellings, so that you may be questioned.' [14] They said, 'Woe to us! Surely we have been evildoers.' [15] This cry of theirs did not stop until We cut them down (and) snuffed (them) out.

[16] We did not create the sky and the earth, and whatever is between them, in jest. [17] If We wanted to choose a diversion, We would indeed have chosen it from Ourselves, if We were going to do (anything). [18] No! We hurl the truth against falsehood, and it breaks its head, and suddenly it passes away. Woe to you for what you allege!

[19] To Him (belongs) whoever is in the heavens and the earth, and those who are in His presence are not (too) proud for His service, nor do they grow weary (of it). [20] They glorify (Him) night and day – they do not cease.

[21] Or have they taken gods from the earth? Do they raise (the dead)? [22] If there were any gods in the two of them other than God, the two would indeed go to ruin. So glory to God, Lord of the throne, above what they allege! [23] He will not be questioned about what He does, but they will be questioned. [24] Or have they taken gods other than Him? Say: 'Bring your proof! This is a Reminder (for) those who are with me, and a Reminder (for) those who were before me.' But most of them do not know the truth, so they turn away. [25] We have not sent any messenger before you except that We inspired him: '(There is) no god but Me, so serve Me!'

[26] They say, 'The Merciful has taken a son.' Glory to Him! No! (They are) honored servants. [27] They do not precede Him in speech, but they act on His command. [28] He knows what is before them and what is behind them, and they do not intercede, except for the one whom He approves, and they are

---

21.26 – They say: "The Merciful has taken a son"

Once more the Quran disputes with those who speak about a son of Allah. The expression here is that Allah has *taken* a son. The Quran argues that any human figure whom people may claim is Allah's son is rather merely a servant of Allah who acts on Allah's command (v. 27). Anyone who would say, "I am a god" (*ilāh*), will be punished in hell (v. 29). See "Son of God in the Quran" (p. 352).

21.28 – *they do not intercede, except for the one whom He approves*

Intercession between humans and Allah is generally denied in the Quran, but this verse leaves open the possibility that Allah may approve someone for this role. See the analysis of verses on intercession at 39.44 (p. 464).

apprehensive because of fear of Him. [29] Whoever of them says, 'Surely I am a god instead of Him,' We repay that one with Gehenna. In this way We repay the evildoers.

[30] Do those who disbelieve not see that the heavens and the earth were (once) a solid mass, and We split the two of them apart, and We made every living thing from water? Will they not believe? [31] We have placed on the earth firm mountains, so that it does not sway with them (on it), and placed in it passes (to serve) as (path)ways, so that they might be guided. [32] And We have made the sky as a guarded roof. Yet they (still) turn away from its signs. [33] He (it is) who created the night and the day, and the sun and the moon, each floating in (its own) orbit.

[34] We have not granted immortality to any human being before you. If you die, will they live forever? [35] Every person will taste death. We try you with evil and good as a test, and to Us you will be returned. [36] When those who disbelieve see you, they take you only in mockery: 'Is this the one who makes mention of your gods?' Yet they (become) disbelievers at any mention of the Merciful. [37] The human was created out of haste. I shall show you My signs, so do not ask Me to hasten (them). [38] But they say, 'When (will) this promise (come to pass), if you are truthful?' [39] If (only) those who disbelieved knew the time when they will not be able to hold off the Fire from their faces and from their backs, nor will they be helped! [40] No! It will come upon them unexpectedly and confound them, and they will not be able to turn it back, nor will they be spared. [41] Certainly messengers have been mocked before you, but those of them who ridiculed (were) overwhelmed (by) what they were mocking.

[42] Say: 'Who will guard you in the night and the day from the Merciful?' No! They (still) turn away from (any) reminder of their Lord. [43] Or do they have gods other than Us to protect them? They are not able to help themselves, nor will they have any companions (to shield them) from Us. [44] No! We gave these (people) and their fathers enjoyment (of life), until life had lasted a long time for them. Do they not see that We come to the land, pushing back its borders? Are they the victors? [45] Say: 'I warn you only by means of inspiration.' But the deaf do

---

21.37 – *The human was created out of haste*

The Quran contains several statements about the condition in which humans were created, in this verse "created out of haste" ('*ajalin*, also 4.28; 7.11; 70.19). See the analysis of verses about human nature at 79.40 (p. 612).

21.41 – *Certainly messengers have been mocked before you*

The Quran speaks directly to the messenger to reassure him that if he is mocked in the course of his preaching, he is in good company.

not hear the call when they are warned. [46] If indeed a whiff of the punishment of your Lord should touch them, they would indeed say, 'Woe to us! Surely we – we have been evildoers.' [47] We shall lay down the scales of justice for the Day of Resurrection, and no one will be done any evil. (Even) if there is (only) the weight of a mustard seed, We shall produce it, and We are sufficient as reckoners.

[48] Certainly We gave Moses and Aaron the Deliverance, and a light, and a reminder to the ones who guard (themselves), [49] who fear their Lord in the unseen, and they are apprehensive of the Hour. [50] And this is a blessed Reminder. We have sent it down. Will you reject it?

[51] Certainly We gave Abraham his right (path) before (them), (for) We knew him. [52] (Remember) when he said to his father and his people: 'What are these images which you are devoted to?' [53] They said, 'We found our fathers serving them.' [54] He said, 'Certainly you and your fathers were clearly astray.' [55] They said, 'Have you brought us the truth, or are you one of those who jest?' [56] He said, 'No! Your Lord – Lord of the heavens and the earth – is the One who created them, and I am one of the witnesses to this. [57] By God! I shall indeed plot (to destroy) your idols after you have turned away, withdrawing.' [58] So he broke them into pieces, (all) except a big one they had, so that they would return to it. [59] They said, 'Who has done this with our gods? Surely he is indeed one of the evildoers.' [60] They said, 'We heard a young man mentioning them – he is called Abraham.' [61] They said, 'Bring him before the eyes of the people, so that they may bear witness.' [62] They said, 'Have you done this with our gods, Abraham?'

21.47 – *We shall lay down the scales of justice for the Day of Resurrection*

The weigh scales of Allah make for precise judgements on the Day of Resurrection, down to the weight of a mustard seed. Here Allah is the reckoner watching which way the scales will tip. See "The Place of the Scale(s) in the Reckoning" (p. 481).

21.48 – *Certainly we gave Moses and Aaron the Deliverance*

"Deliverance" translates the Arabic term *furqān*, often also translated as "criterion." See the comment at 25.1 on *furqān*, its seven occurrences in the Quran, and what they refer to (p. 363).

21.51 – *Certainly We gave Abraham his right (path) before (them), (for) We knew him*

Abraham preaches against the idolatry of his father and his people and breaks all their idols except one (v. 58). When the people ask who broke the idols, however, Abraham says that the remaining idol broke the others (v. 63).

Abraham's lie in this story posed a problem to later Muslim commentators who claimed that prophets cannot sin. Readers who would like a taste of this discussion can find it in a helpful article by Norman Calder, "Tafsīr from Ṭabarī to Ibn Kathīr" (see bibliography). See also "Abraham in the Quran" (p. 90).

[63] He said, 'No! This big one of them did it. Just ask them, if they are able to speak.' [64] And they turned to each other, and said, 'Surely you – you are the evildoers.' [65] Then they became utterly confused: 'Certainly you know (that) these do not speak.' [66] He said, 'Do you serve what does not benefit you at all, or harm you, instead of God (alone)? [67] Uff to you and to what you serve instead of God! Will you not understand?' [68] They said, 'Burn him, and help your gods, if you are going to do (anything).' [69] We said, 'Fire! Be coolness and peace for Abraham!' [70] They intended a plot against him, but We made them the worst losers, [71] and We rescued him, and Lot, (and brought them) to the land which We have blessed for the worlds.

[72] And We granted him Isaac, and Jacob as a gift, and each (of them) We made righteous. [73] And We made them leaders (who) guide (others) by Our command, and We inspired them (with) the doing of good deeds, and the observance of the prayer and the giving of the alms, and they served Us.

[74] And Lot – We gave him judgment and knowledge, and we rescued him from the town which was doing bad things. Surely they were an evil people (and) wicked. [75] And We caused him to enter Our mercy. Surely He was one of the righteous.

[76] And Noah – when he called out before (that), and We responded to him, and rescued him and his family from great distress. [77] We helped him against

---

21.68 – *Burn him, and help your gods*

In response to Abraham's polemic, and his destruction of their idols, the people throw Abraham into a fire, but God rescues him (v. 71) by making the fire cool (v. 69). This episode is not part of the biblical account, and Bible readers will no doubt think of the story of Shadrach, Meshach, and Abednego in Daniel 3. However, a similar story about Abraham appears in *Midrāsh Rabbah Genesis*, an early Jewish commentary dated to the sixth century.

21.72 – *And We granted him Isaac, and Jacob as a gift, and each of them We made righteous*

That Isaac, not Ishmael, is mentioned here as the son Allah gave to Abraham, may surprise readers who are familiar with the importance of Ishmael in Islam. The name of Ishmael only appears at verse 85, with no clear connection to Abraham. The same pattern is followed in a number of other quranic passages (6.84; 19.49; cf. 38.45). Worth noting in these passages is not only the spotlighting of Isaac but also the high praise that the Quran gives to Isaac and Jacob at 6.84; 19.49–50; 21.72–73; and 38.45–47.

This kind of material in the Quran seems to represent a historical situation in which there was no particular controversy with the "Children of Israel."

the people who called Our signs a lie. Surely they were an evil people, and so We drowned them – all (of them)!

⁷⁸ And David and Solomon – when they rendered judgment concerning the field, when the people's sheep had grazed in it – We were witnesses to their judgment. ⁷⁹ We caused Solomon to understand it, and to each We gave judgment and knowledge. (Along) with David We subjected the mountains and the birds to glorify (Us) – We were the doers (of it). ⁸⁰ We taught him the making of clothing to protect you from your (own) violence. Are you thankful? ⁸¹ And to Solomon (We subjected) the wind, blowing strongly at his command to the land which We have blessed – We have knowledge of everything. ⁸² And among the satans, (there were) those who dived for him and did other work besides – We were watching over them.

⁸³ And Job – when he called on his Lord, 'Surely hardship has touched me, and You are the most compassionate of the compassionate.' ⁸⁴ We responded to him, and removed what hardship was upon him, and We gave him his family, and as much again, as a mercy from Us, and a reminder to the ones who serve.

⁸⁵ And Ishmael, and Idrīs, and Dhū-l-Kifl – each one was among the patient. ⁸⁶ And We caused them to enter Our mercy. Surely they were among the righteous.

⁸⁷ And Dhū-l-Nūn – when he went away angry, and thought that We had no power over him, but he called out in the darkness: '(There is) no god but You. Glory to You! Surely I – I have been one of the evildoers.' ⁸⁸ We responded to him and rescued him from (his) distress. In this way We rescue the believers.

⁸⁹ And Zachariah – when he called out to his Lord: 'My Lord, do not leave

---

21.78 – *And David and Solomon – when they rendered judgment concerning the field*

These verses about David and Solomon (78–82) refer to Solomon's wisdom as well as to extrabiblical traditions about the two figures. That mountains and birds are subjected to David (v. 80) seems to refer to expressions in the Psalms that exhort nature to praise God. The Quran says that Solomon has authority over "satans" (v. 82) and *jinn* (34.12–13).

21.83 – *And Job – when he called on his Lord, "Surely hardship has touched me . . ."*

This passage (vv. 83–84) is one of two passages in the Quran that present identifiable characteristics of Job (*Ayyūb*, also 38.41–44).

21.87 – *And Dhū-l-Nūn – when he went away angry*

Dhū 'l-Nūn means "he of the fish" and is another name for Jonah in the Quran (vv. 87–88). A longer passage on Jonah is 37.139–48.

me alone, when You are the best of inheritors.' ⁹⁰ We responded to him, and granted him John, and set his wife right for him. Surely they were quick in the (doing of) good deeds, and they used to call on Us in hope and fear, and humble (themselves) before Us.

⁹¹ And she who guarded her private part – We breathed into her some of Our spirit, and made her and her son a sign to the worlds: ⁹² 'Surely this community of yours is one community, and I am your Lord. So serve Me!' ⁹³ But they cut up their affair among them. (Yet) all (of them) will return to Us. ⁹⁴ Whoever does any righteous deeds – and he is a believer – (there will be) no ingratitude for his striving. Surely We are writing (them) down for him.

⁹⁵ (There is) a ban on any town which We have destroyed: they shall not return ⁹⁶ until, when Yajūj and Majūj are opened, and they come swooping down from every height, ⁹⁷ and the true promise draws near, and suddenly (there) it (is)! The eyes of those who disbelieved (will be) staring (and they will say): 'Woe to us! We were oblivious of this. No! We were evildoers.' ⁹⁸ 'Surely you, and what you were serving instead of God, are stones for Gehenna – you will go down to it.' ⁹⁹ If these had been gods, they would not have gone down to it, but everyone (of them) will remain in it. ¹⁰⁰ In it (there is) a moaning for them, and in it they do not hear (anything else).

¹⁰¹ Surely those for whom the best (reward) has gone forth from Us – those will be (kept) far from it. ¹⁰² They will not hear (even) a slight sound of it, and they will remain in what they themselves desired. ¹⁰³ The great terror will not cause them sorrow, and the angels will meet them: 'This is your Day which you were promised.'

¹⁰⁴ On the Day when We shall roll up the sky like the rolling up of a scroll for the writings: as We brought about the first creation, (so) We shall restore it

---

21.91 – *We breathed into her some of Our spirit*

The way that Allah made Mary (not named here) pregnant with ʿĪsā is described in a couple of different ways in the Quran. The expression in this verse is also found at 66.12, while at 19.17 "the spirit" comes to Mary in human form to simply "give" her a son. On "spirit" in the Quran, see the analysis at 97.4 (p. 639).

21.96 – *until, when Yajūj and Majūj are opened*

Yajūj and *Majūj* seem to be an echo of the ruler "Gog" and the people "Magog" in Ezekiel 38–39. At 18.94 they are associated with *Dhū ʾl-Qarnayn* ("he of the two horns," referring to Alexander the Great). The association with Alexander was also made in postbiblical Christian writings such as the Syriac "Legend of Alexander." See the focus article "Apocryphal Details in Quranic Stories" (p. 299).

– (it is) a promise (binding) on Us. Surely We shall do (it)! [105] Certainly We have written in the Psalms, after the Reminder: 'The earth – My righteous servants will inherit it.' [106] Surely in this (there is) a delivery indeed for a people who serve.

[107] We have sent you only as a mercy to the worlds. [108] Say: 'I am only inspired that your God is one God. Are you going to submit?' [109] If they turn away, say: 'I have proclaimed to all of you equally, but I do not know whether what you are promised is near or far. [110] Surely He knows what is spoken publicly and He knows what you conceal. [111] I do not know. Perhaps it is a test for you, and enjoyment (of life) for a time.' [112] Say: 'My Lord, judge in truth! Our Lord is the Merciful – the One to be sought for help against what you allege.'

21.105 – *Certainly We have written in the Psalms, after the Reminder*

This is the Quran's third and final mention of *Zabūr* (Psalms, see also 4.163; 17.55), here without mentioning David. Does the Quran offer the following wording as a quotation from the Psalms?

THE PILGRIMAGE
AL-ḤAJJ

22

The story of Abraham setting up the pilgrimage (*al-ḥajj*) in this sūra is one of the key passages that form the basis of the Muslim belief that Abraham entered Arabia. This sūra also provides extensive commentary on the use of animals as part of the pilgrimage rituals.

Warnings about Judgment Day and details about rewards and punishments form a large part of this sūra. The sūra responds to people who dispute about God with arguments about the Creator's presence and power. The two criteria of admittance into heaven (the "Gardens") are stated repeatedly in this sūra: belief and righteous deeds.

This sūra also contains one of the two quranic passages that many Muslim commentators have associated with the story known as the "satanic verses" (see explanations at 22.52 and 53.19). In 22.52, Satan is able to cast recitations into the minds of messengers and prophets.

Seemingly out of line with much of the content in this sūra, three additional passages refer to conflict. One passage tells of people who keep others from the way of Allah and the sacred mosque, while another promises "victory in the world" to the messenger. The third passage is famous for permitting "believers" to fight.

In the Name of God, the Merciful, the Compassionate

[1] People! Guard (yourselves) against your Lord! Surely the earthquake of the Hour is a great thing. [2] On the Day when you see it, every nursing woman will forget what she has nursed, and every pregnant female will deliver her burden, and you will see the people drunk when they are not drunk – but the punishment of God is harsh! [3] Yet among the people (there is) one who disputes about God without any knowledge, and follows every rebellious satan. [4] It is written

---

22.1 – *Surely the earthquake of the Hour is a great thing*

The sūra begins with a warning about judgment to come and offers graphic details. Much of the sūra develops this theme.

about him: 'He who takes him as an ally – he will lead him astray and guide him to the punishment of the blazing (Fire).'

⁵ People! If you are in doubt about the raising up – surely We created you from dust, then from a drop, then from a clot, (and) then from a lump, formed and unformed, so that We may make (it) clear to you. We establish in the wombs what We please for an appointed time, then We bring you forth as a child, (and) then (We provide for you) so that you may reach your maturity. Among you (there is) one who is taken, and among you (there is) one who is reduced to the worst (stage) of life, so that he knows nothing after (having had) knowledge. And you see the earth withered, but when We send down water on it, it stirs and swells, and grows (plants) of every beautiful kind. ⁶ That is because God – He is the Truth, and because He gives the dead life, and because He is powerful over everything, ⁷ and because the Hour is coming – (there is) no doubt about it – and because God will raise up those who are in the graves.

⁸ Yet among the people (there is) one who disputes about God without any knowledge or guidance or illuminating Book, ⁹ (who) turns away in scorn to lead (people) astray from the way of God. For him (there is) disgrace in this world, and on the Day of Resurrection We shall make him taste the punishment of the burning (Fire): ¹⁰ 'That is for what your (own) hands have sent forward, and (know) that God is not an evildoer to (His) servants.' ¹¹ Among the people (there is also) one who serves God sitting on the fence. If some good smites him, he is satisfied with it, but if some trouble smites him, he is overturned (by it). He loses this world and the Hereafter. That – it is the clearest loss! ¹² Instead of God, he calls on what does not harm him, and what does not benefit him. That – it is straying the farthest! ¹³ He calls indeed on one whose harm is nearer than his benefit. Evil indeed is the protector, and evil indeed the friend!

¹⁴ Surely God will cause those who believe and do righteous deeds to enter Gardens through which rivers flow. Surely God does whatever He wills.

22.5 – *surely We created you from dust, then from a drop, then from a clot*

In answer to those who deny the Day of Resurrection, the Quran affirms that Allah creates humans and gives life to the natural world. The picture of Allah creating human life in the womb is noteworthy.

22.15 – *Whoever thinks that God will not help him in this world and the Hereafter*

The first words of this verse strike a note that sounds dissonant from most of the sūras since Sūra 10. Muslim commentators understood these words to mean that Allah would help the messenger to triumph (*naṣara*) in the world. Though later in the sūra the messenger claims to be "only a clear warner" (v. 49), verse 15 seems to signal additional tasks: fighting, commanding right, and forbidding wrong (vv. 39–41).

¹⁵ Whoever thinks that God will not help him in this world and the Hereafter, let him stretch a rope to the sky. Then let him cut (it), and see whether his scheme will take away what enrages (him). ¹⁶ In this way We have sent it down as signs – clear signs – and because God guides whomever He wills.

¹⁷ Surely those who believe, and those who are Jews, and the Sabians, and the Christians, and the Magians, and the idolaters – surely God will distinguish between them on the Day of Resurrection. Surely God is a witness over everything. ¹⁸ Do you not see that God – whoever is in the heavens and whoever is on the earth prostrates before Him, and (so do) the sun, and the moon, and the stars, and the mountains, and the trees, and the animals, and many of the people? But (there are) many for whom the punishment is justified, and whomever God humiliates, (there is) no one to honor him. Surely God does whatever He pleases.

¹⁹ These two disputants dispute about their Lord. But those who disbelieve – clothes of fire have been cut for them, and boiling (water) will be poured (on them) from above their heads, ²⁰ by which what is in their bellies and (their) skins will be melted. ²¹ And for them (there are) hooked rods of iron. ²² Whenever they want to come out of it, because of (their) agony, they will be sent back into it, and: 'Taste the punishment of the burning (Fire)!' ²³ Surely God will cause those who believe and do righteous deeds to enter Gardens through which rivers flow. There they will be adorned with bracelets of gold and (with) pearls, and there their clothes (will be of) silk. ²⁴ They have been guided to good speech, and they have been guided to the path of the Praiseworthy.

²⁵ Surely those who disbelieve and keep (people) from the way of God and the Sacred Mosque, which We have made for the people equally – the resident there and the visitor – and whoever intends to pervert it in an evil manner – We shall make him taste a painful punishment.

²⁶ (Remember) when We settled the place of the House for Abraham: 'Do not associate anything with Me, but purify My House for the ones who go

---

22.17 – *those who believe, and those who are Jews, and the Sabians and the Christians*

This verse starts out like 2.62, which suggests that Jews and Christians alongside the believers may be rewarded. In this case, however, the Quran simply says that God will distinguish between these different groups on the Day of Resurrection.

22.19 – *But those who disbelieve – clothes of fire have been cut for them*

This passage (vv. 19–24) offers rather graphic details of the punishments and rewards in store for unbelievers and believers.

22.26 – *when We settled the place of the House for Abraham*

"The House" (*bayt*) associated here with Abraham, also called the "ancient house"

around (it), and the ones who stand, and the ones who bow, (and) the ones who prostrate themselves. ²⁷ And proclaim the pilgrimage among the people. Let them come to you on foot and on every lean animal. They will come from every remote mountain pass, ²⁸ so that they may witness things of benefit to them, and mention the name of God, on (certain) specified days, over whatever animal of the livestock He has provided them: "Eat from them, and feed the wretched poor." ²⁹ Then let them bring an end to their ritual state, and fulfill their vows, and go around the ancient House.'

³⁰ That (is the rule). Whoever respects the sacred things of God – it will be better for him with his Lord. Permitted to you (to eat) are the livestock, except for what is recited to you. Avoid the abomination of the idols, and avoid the speaking of falsehood, ³¹ (being) Ḥanīfs before God, not associating (anything) with Him. Whoever associates (anything) with God – (it is) as if he has fallen from the sky, and the birds snatched him away, or (as if) the wind has swept him away to some far off place.

³² That (is the rule). Whoever respects the symbols of God – surely that (comes) from the guarding of (your) hearts. ³³ (There are) benefits for you in this up to an appointed time. Then their lawful place is to the ancient House.

³⁴ For every community We have appointed a ritual: that they should mention the name of God over whatever animal of the livestock He has provided them. Your God is one God, so submit to Him. And give good news to the humble, ³⁵ those who, when God is mentioned, their hearts become afraid, and the ones who are patient with whatever smites them, and the ones who observe the prayer, and contribute from what We have provided them. ³⁶ The (sacrificial) animals – We have appointed them for you among the symbols of God: there is good for you in them. So mention the name of God over them, (as they stand) in lines. Then when their sides fall (to the ground), eat from them, and feed the

---

(vv. 29, 33), is not further identified in this passage (vv. 26–38). The passage tells of ritual acts of pilgrimage and sacrifice.

Muslims have traditionally interpreted "the House" to be the *Ka'ba* in Mecca. At 14.37 the Quran associates Abraham with "the Sacred House," and at 5.97 "the Sacred House" is called the *Ka'ba*. See the comment on "the House" at 2.124 (p. 54).

This is the final passage from which Muslims take their belief that Abraham traveled deep into the Arabian Peninsula (also 2.125–27; 3.96–97; 14.37). The Quran is the only source for the story of Abraham's journey to Mecca. The Bible gives no hint of this. However, Jewish *Midrāsh* – interpretation of the Hebrew Bible – contains a story of Abraham visiting Ishmael in the "Desert of Paran" (*Pirqē Rabbi Eli'ezer*, ch. 30).

See also "Abraham in the Quran" (p. 90).

needy and the beggar. In this way We have subjected them to you, so that you may be thankful. [37] Its flesh will not reach God, nor its blood, but the guarding (of yourselves) will reach Him from you. In this way He has subjected them to you, so that you may magnify God because He has guided you. Give good news to the doers of good. [38] Surely God will repel (evil) from those who believe. Surely God does not love any traitor (or) ungrateful one.

[39] Permission is given to those who fight because they have been done evil – and surely God is indeed able to help them – [40] those who have been expelled from their homes without any right, only because they said, 'Our Lord is God.' But if God had not repelled some of the people by the means of others, many monasteries, and churches, and synagogues, and mosques, in which the name of God is mentioned often, would indeed have been destroyed. God will indeed help the one who helps Him – surely God is indeed strong, mighty – [41] those who, if We establish them on the earth, observe the prayer and give the alms, and command right and forbid wrong. To God (belongs) the outcome of all affairs.

22.37 – *Its flesh will not reach God, nor its blood*

After the description of the importance of sacrifice (vv. 28–36), this verse seems to comment on a concept of sacrifice in which God "needs" sacrifice. If so, the response here is that devotion or "guarding" oneself (*taqwā*) is what matters to Allah.

22.38 – *Surely God does not love any traitor (or) ungrateful one*

The Quran contains twenty-four statements about the kinds of people whom Allah does not love. In this verse, Allah does not love the ungrateful (*kafūr*). See "The Language of Love in the Quran" (p. 560).

22.39 – *Permission is given to those who fight because they have been done evil*

The Quran declares here that Allah gives "believers" permission to fight (*qātala*). The following verse offers a justification for this permission: if people did not fight, their places of worship would be destroyed (v. 40). In this case, Allah helps people, but first he needs them to help him. Allah repels "some of the people by the means of others."

The Muslim story of Islamic origins gave prominence to this verse by specifying that it was first recited just before Muhammad commanded his followers in Mecca to emigrate to Medina. According to Ibn Isḥāq (d. 767), this was the first verse "sent down" on the subject of fighting (*Sīra*, 212–13).

Several scholars suggest that verses 39–41 represent an important "transitional moment" from an understanding that Allah will punish unbelievers himself to a concept that "believers" will take the punishment of unbelievers into their own hands. Whether this means a transition with time or simply two different concepts, these verses certainly spotlight a pivot point. See "Fighting and Killing in the Quran" (p. 220).

[42] If they call you a liar, the people of Noah called (him) a liar before you, and (so did) 'Ād, and Thamūd, [43] and the people of Abraham, and the people of Lot, [44] and the companions of Midian, and Moses was called a liar (too). I spared the disbelievers, then I seized them, and how was My loathing (of them)! [45] How many a town have We destroyed while it was doing evil, so it is (now) collapsed on its supports! (How many) an abandoned well and well-built palace! [46] Have they not traveled on the earth? Do they have hearts to understand with or ears to hear with? Surely it is not the sight (which) is blind, but the hearts which are within the chests are blind. [47] They seek to hurry you with the punishment. God will not break His promise. Surely a day with your Lord is like a thousand years of what you count. [48] How many a town have I have spared while it was doing evil! Then I seized it. To Me is the (final) destination. [49] Say: 'People! I am only a clear warner for you.' [50] Those who believe and do righteous deeds – for them (there is) forgiveness and generous provision. [51] But those who strive against Our signs to obstruct (them) – those are the companions of the Furnace.

[52] We have not sent any messenger or any prophet before you, except that, when he began to wish, Satan cast (something) into his wishful thinking. But God cancels what Satan casts, (and) then God clearly composes His verses – surely God is knowing, wise – [53] so that He may make what Satan casts a test for those in whose hearts is a sickness, and whose hearts are hardened – and surely

---

22.52 – *Satan cast (something) into his wishful thinking. But God cancels what Satan casts, (and) then God clearly composes His verses*

This is the second of only two occurrences of the Arabic verb *nasakha*, meaning "to abrogate." The other is at 2.106, where it became an important prop for the Islamic theory of abrogation. See the discussion of verses related to abrogation at 16.101 (p. 282).

Early Muslim commentaries and histories explained verse 52 and the two following verses by telling the Muslim story of the "satanic verses." The Muslim story is that Muhammad wishes to gain the favor of the people of Mecca, so Satan takes the opportunity to cast into his mind words that are not from Allah. Muhammad then recites that the intercession of the Meccan idols may be hoped for (see al-Ṭabarī's *History*, vol. 6, pp. 107–12). Commentaries also connected this story with 53.19–20.

Verse 52 claims that this is an experience common to all messengers. Like other categorical statements about messengers in the Quran, however, it deserves some careful consideration. According to the Gospel accounts, Jesus was indeed tempted by the devil, but Jesus, "full of the Holy Spirit," successfully resisted all Satanic suggestions and sent the devil packing (Matthew 4; Luke 4; cf. Hebrews 2:18; 4:15). See the analysis of categorical statements about messengers at 25.20 (p. 365).

the evildoers are indeed in extreme defiance – [54] and so that those who have been given the knowledge may know that it is the truth from your Lord, and may believe in it, and so that their hearts may be humble before Him. Surely God is indeed guiding those who believe to a straight path.

[55] Those who disbelieve will continue (to be) in doubt about it, until the Hour comes upon them unexpectedly, or the punishment of a barren Day comes upon them. [56] The kingdom on that Day (will belong) to God. He will judge between them. Those who believe and do righteous deeds (will be) in Gardens of Bliss, [57] but those who disbelieve and call Our signs a lie – for them (there will be) a humiliating punishment.

[58] Those who have emigrated in the way of God, (and) then were killed or died, God will indeed provide them (with) a good provision. Surely God – He indeed is the best of providers. [59] He will indeed cause them to enter by an entrance with which they will be pleased. Surely God is indeed knowing, forbearing. [60] That (will be so). And whoever takes retribution with the same retribution he suffered, (and) then is sought out – God will indeed help him. Surely God is indeed pardoning, forgiving.

[61] That is because God causes the night to pass into the day, and causes the day to pass into the night, and because God is hearing, seeing. [62] That is because God – He is the Truth, and because what they call on instead of Him, that is the falsehood, and because God is the Most High, the Great. [63] Do you not see that God sends down water from the sky, (and) then the earth becomes green? God is astute, aware. [64] To Him (belongs) whatever is in the heavens and whatever is on the earth. Surely God – He indeed is the wealthy One, the Praiseworthy. [65] Do you not see that God has subjected to you whatever is on the earth, and the ship that runs on the sea by His command, and He (that) holds up the sky so that it does not fall upon the earth, except by His permission? Surely God is indeed kind (and) compassionate with the people. [66] He (it is) who gave you life, then He causes you to die, (and) then He will give you life (again). Surely the human is ungrateful indeed.

[67] For every community we have appointed a ritual which they practice. So let them not argue with you about the matter, but call (them) to your Lord. Surely you are indeed on a straight guidance. [68] If they dispute with you, say: 'God

---

22.58 – *Those who have emigrated in the way of God, (and) then were killed or died*

The idea that believers who die fighting are martyrs who go straight to heaven has its quranic basis in verses like this. Here fighters are promised provision from Allah and entry into "Gardens of Bliss" (vv. 59, 56). Other verses like this are 2.154; 3.157–58, 169–72, 195; and 47.4–6. See an analysis of these verses at 47.4 (p. 509).

knows what you do. [69] God will judge between you on the Day of Resurrection concerning your differences.' [70] Do you not know that God knows whatever is in the sky and the earth? Surely that is in a Book. Surely that is easy for God.

[71] Instead of God, they serve what He has not sent down any authority for, and what they have no knowledge of. The evildoers will have no helper. [72] When Our signs are recited to them as clear signs, you recognize defiance in the faces of those who disbelieve – they all but attack those who recite Our signs to them. Say: 'Shall I inform you about (something) worse than that? The Fire! God has promised it to those who disbelieve – and it is an evil destination!'

[73] People! A parable is struck, so listen to it. Surely those you call on instead of God will not create a fly, even if they joined together for it. And if a fly were to snatch anything away from them, they would not (be able to) rescue it from it. Weak is the seeker and the sought (alike)! [74] They have not measured God (with) the measure due Him. Surely God is indeed strong, mighty.

[75] God chooses messengers from the angels and from the people. Surely God is hearing, seeing. [76] He knows what is before them and what is behind them. To God all affairs are returned.

[77] You who believe! Bow and prostrate yourselves, and serve your Lord, and do good, so that you may prosper. [78] And struggle for God with the struggling due Him. He has chosen you, and has not placed any difficulty on you in the (matter of) religion: the creed of your father Abraham. He named you Muslims, (both) before and in this, so that the messenger might be a witness against you, and that you might be witnesses against the people. So observe the prayer and give the alms, and hold fast to God. He is your Protector. Excellent is the Protector, and excellent is the Helper!

22.78 – *And struggle for God with the struggling due Him*

"Struggle" translates the Arabic verb *jāhada*, and "struggling" translates the word *jihād*. Here *struggle* appears in the form of a command. The sense of *struggle* that the Quran intends in this imperative may be partly determined by context. In this case, there seems to be nothing in the verse or its immediate context to bring fighting to mind, though elsewhere in this sūra the Quran gives permission to fight (v. 39). See the analysis of these commands at 66.9 (p. 579)

Muslim commentaries disagreed about the meaning of *struggle* in this verse. At an early stage, al-Ṭabarī (d. 923) seems to have understood a physical struggle against associators. Two centuries later, however, Zamakhsharī (d. 1144) offered a traditional saying about struggling against inner human desire. See "Jihad in the Quran" (p. 368).

THE BELIEVERS
AL-MU'MINŪN

23

The ways in which Allah deals with people and the responses of people to the signs of Allah are explained in several substantial passages in this sūra. Allah sends messengers to deliver his message, and in this sūra the representative messenger is Noah.

Most of the listeners resist the message that the messengers do their best to deliver. Whether in Noah's day or at the time of the Quran's first recitation, this sūra anticipates the questions and objections of the listeners and provides the answers that the messenger is commanded to say. In the case of Noah, Allah delivered Noah and his family and drowned the opposition.

Sūra 23 is also notable for an opening psalm-like passage and a judgment scene conversation between Allah and certain inhabitants of Gehenna near the sūra's end.

In the Name of God, the Merciful, the Compassionate

[1] The believers have prospered [2] who are humble in their prayers, [3] and who turn away from frivolous talk, [4] and who give the alms, [5] and who guard their private parts, [6] except from their wives or what their right (hands) own – surely then they are not (to be) blamed, [7] but whoever seeks beyond that, those – they are the transgressors – [8] and those who keep their pledges and their promise(s), [9] and who guard their prayers. [10] Those – they are the inheritors [11] who will inherit Paradise. There they will remain.

[12] Certainly We created the human from an extract of clay. [13] Then We made

---

23.1–2 – *The believers have prospered who are humble in their prayers*

The opening passage of this sūra (vv. 1–11) is made up of short verses that have a Psalm-like quality.

23.12 – *Certainly We created the human from an extract of clay*

The details of the creation of a human in this verse are intriguing. In the larger passage (vv. 12–22), Allah's creation is full of lessons (v. 21), including that Allah has the power to raise up humanity on the Day of Resurrection.

him a drop in a secure dwelling place, [14] then We made a clot (from) the drop, then We made a lump (from) the clot, then We made bones (from) the lump, then We clothed the bones (with) flesh, (and) then We (re)produced him as another creature. So blessed (be) God, the best of creators! [15] Then, after that, you will indeed die, [16] (and) then surely on the Day of Resurrection you will be raised up.

[17] Certainly We created above you seven orbits, and We were not oblivious of the creation. [18] We send down water from the sky in (due) measure, and cause it to settle in the earth – and surely We are able indeed to take it away. [19] By means of it We produce gardens of date palms and grapes for you, in which (there are) many fruits for you, and from which you eat, [20] and a tree (which) comes forth from Mount Sinai (which) bears oil and seasoning for eaters. [21] Surely in the cattle is a lesson indeed for you: We give you to drink from what is in their bellies, and in them (there are) many benefits for you, and from them you eat. [22] On them, and on the ship (as well), you are carried.

[23] Certainly We sent Noah to his people, and he said, 'My people! Serve God! You have no god other than Him. Will you not guard (yourselves)?' [24] But the assembly of those who disbelieved among his people said, 'This is nothing but a human being like you. He wants to gain superiority over you. If God had (so) pleased, He would indeed have sent down angels. We have not heard of this among our fathers of old. [25] He is nothing but a man possessed. Wait on him for a time.' [26] He said, 'My Lord, help me, because they are calling me a liar.' [27] So We inspired him: 'Build the ship under Our eyes and Our inspiration, and when Our command comes and the oven boils, put into it two of every kind, a pair, and your family – except for him against whom the word has (already) gone forth. Do not address Me concerning those who have done evil. Surely they are going to be drowned! [28] When you have boarded the ship – you and (those) who are with you – say: "Praise (be) to God, who has rescued us from the people who were evildoers!" [29] And say: "My Lord, bring me to land (at) a blessed landing

---

23.23 – *Certainly We sent Noah to his people*

Noah is an important character in the Quran, and his story appears seven times in different versions. The Quran portrays Noah as a messenger whom God only later instructs to build the ark. Here (vv. 23–30) the disbelievers among Noah's people say why they will not listen to Noah, and Noah asks for help against them. Allah commands Noah to build the ark and promises that he will punish the people who opposed Noah.

Other versions of the Noah story come at 7.59–64; 10.71–3; 11.25–48; 26.105–20; 54.7–17; and 71.1–28. See 51.24 for a discussion of the repetition of stories in the Quran (p. 526).

place, (for) You are the best of those who bring to land."' ³⁰ Surely in that are signs indeed. Surely We have been testing (people) indeed.

³¹ Then, after them, We produced another generation, ³² and We sent among them a messenger from among them: 'Serve God! You have no god other than Him. Will you not guard (yourselves)?' ³³ But the assembly of his people, those who disbelieved and called the meeting of the Hereafter a lie, even though We had given them luxury in this present life, said, 'This is nothing but a human being like you. He eats from what you eat from, and drinks from what you drink. ³⁴ If indeed you obey a human being like you, surely then you will be the losers indeed. ³⁵ Does he promise you that when you are dead, and become dust and bones, that you will be brought forth? ³⁶ Away! Away with what you are promised! ³⁷ There is nothing but our present life. We die, and we live, and we are not going to be raised up. ³⁸ He is nothing but a man who has forged a lie against God. We are not believers in him.' ³⁹ He said, 'My Lord, help me, because they are calling me a liar.' ⁴⁰ He said, 'In a little (while) they will indeed be full of regret.' ⁴¹ Then the cry seized them in truth, and We turned them into ruins. Away with the people who are evildoers!

⁴² Then, after them, We produced other generations. ⁴³ No community precedes its time, nor do they delay (it). ⁴⁴ Then We sent Our messengers in succession: whenever its messenger came to a community, they called him a liar. So We caused some of them to follow others, and We turned them (into) stories. Away with a people who do not believe!

⁴⁵ Then We sent Moses and his brother Aaron, with Our signs and clear authority, ⁴⁶ to Pharaoh and his assembly, but they became arrogant and were a haughty people. ⁴⁷ They said, 'Shall we believe in two human beings like us, when their people are serving us?' ⁴⁸ So they called them both liars, and were among the destroyed.

⁴⁹ Certainly We gave Moses the Book, so that they might be (rightly) guided. ⁵⁰ And We made the son of Mary and his mother a sign, and We gave them both

---

23.32 – *We sent among them a messenger from among them*
The Quran here offers a story similar to the preceding Noah story, but this time it does not name the messenger or the people to whom he preached (vv. 31–41). As such, this passage serves as a good example of the typical plot lines in many of the Quran's messenger stories. As if to affirm this template, verses 42–44 summarize the story in even simpler terms. Notice the repeating response from the audience to the messenger: "This is nothing but a human being like you" (vv. 24, 33; cf. 47, 69).

23.49 – *Certainly We gave Moses the Book, so that they might be (rightly) guided*
The Quran speaks of the pre-Islamic scriptures only in the most positive and

refuge on high ground, (where there was) a hollow (as) a dwelling place and a flowing spring: ⁵¹ 'Messengers! Eat from the good things, and do righteousness! Surely I am aware of what you do. ⁵² Surely this community of yours is one community, and I am your Lord. So guard (yourselves) against Me!' ⁵³ But they cut their affair (in two) between them (over the) scriptures, each faction gloating over what was with them. ⁵⁴ Leave them in their flood (of confusion) for a time. ⁵⁵ Do they think that in increasing them with wealth and children ⁵⁶ We are quick to do them good? No! But they do not realize (it).

⁵⁷ Surely those who – they are apprehensive on account of fear of their Lord, ⁵⁸ and those who – they believe in the signs of their Lord, ⁵⁹ and those who – they do not associate (anything) with their Lord, ⁶⁰ and those who give what they give, while their hearts are afraid because they are going to return to their Lord – ⁶¹ (it is) those who are quick in the (doing of) good deeds, and they are foremost in them.

⁶² We do not burden anyone beyond his capacity, and with Us is a Book (which) speaks in truth – and they will not be done evil. ⁶³ No! But their hearts are in a flood (of confusion) about this, and they have deeds other than that, which they (will continue to) do ⁶⁴ – until, when We seize their affluent ones with the punishment, suddenly they cry out. ⁶⁵ 'Do not cry out today! Surely you will receive no help from Us. ⁶⁶ My signs were recited to you, but you turned on your heels, ⁶⁷ being arrogant toward it, (and) forsaking (one who was) conversing by night.'

⁶⁸ Have they not contemplated the word? Or did (there) come to them what did not come to their fathers of old? ⁶⁹ Or did they not recognize their messenger, and so rejected him? ⁷⁰ Or do they say, 'He is possessed'? No! He brought them the truth, but most of them were averse to the truth. ⁷¹ If the truth had followed their desires, the heavens and the earth and whatever is in them would indeed have been corrupted. No! We brought them their Reminder, but they turned away from their Reminder. ⁷² Or do you ask them for payment? Yet the

---

respectful way. This verse refers to the Torah as the book given to Moses, and describes it as guidance. The following verses seem to say that problems came when Jews and Christians divided over the scriptures (v. 53). On disagreement and division among the People of the Book, see the discussion at 98.4 (p. 642).

23.50 – *And We made the son of Mary and his mother a sign*

This very brief mention of ʿĪsā refers to him simply as the "son of Mary." The details in this verse, like the details of 19.22–26, are similar to those in a Christian apocryphal work, the *Gospel of Pseudo-Matthew*. See "Apocryphal Details in Quranic Stories" (p. 299).

23.62 – *with Us is a Book (which) speaks in truth*

The "Book" (*kitāb*) in this verse does not refer to a scripture, but rather to a just accounting of people's deeds with Allah.

payment of your Lord is better, and He is the best of providers. ⁷³ Surely you indeed call them to a straight path, ⁷⁴ and surely those who do not believe in the Here-after are indeed deviating from the path. ⁷⁵ Even if We had compassion on them, and removed whatever hardship they had, they would indeed persist in their insolent transgression, wandering blindly. ⁷⁶ Certainly We have seized them with the punishment (already), but they did not submit themselves to their Lord, nor were they humble. ⁷⁷ – Until, when We open a gate of harsh punishment on them, suddenly they are in despair about it.

⁷⁸ He (it is) who has produced for you hearing and sight and hearts – little thanks you show! ⁷⁹ He (it is) who has scattered you on the earth, and to Him you will be gathered. ⁸⁰ He (it is) who gives life and causes death, and to Him (belongs) the alternation of the night and the day. Will you not understand? ⁸¹ No! They said just what those of old said. ⁸² They said, 'When we are dead, and turned to dust and bones, shall we indeed be raised up? ⁸³ We have been promised this before – we and our fathers. This is nothing but old tales.'

⁸⁴ Say: 'To whom (does) the earth and whatever is on it (belong), if you know?' ⁸⁵ They will say, 'To God.' Say: 'Will you not take heed?' ⁸⁶ Say: 'Who is Lord of the seven heavens, and Lord of the great throne?' ⁸⁷ They will say, 'To God.' Say: 'Will you not guard (yourselves)?' ⁸⁸ Say: 'Who is (it) in whose hand is the kingdom of everything, (who) protects and needs no protection, if you know?' ⁸⁹ They will say, 'To God.' Say: 'How are you (so) bewitched?' ⁹⁰ No! We have brought them the truth. Surely they are liars indeed! ⁹¹ God has not taken a son, nor is there any (other) god with Him. Then each god would indeed have

---

23.81 – *No! They said just what those of old said*

This verse begins another passage that seems to describe a conversation between the messenger and his audience (vv. 81–100). "They said / will say" introduces the speeches of the audience, and "Say" introduces the preaching or replies of the messenger.

23.91 – *God has not taken a son, nor is there any (other) god with Him*

This verse seems to connect the concept that Allah has taken a son with the idea of a separate second god. Verse 92 links it further with associating (*shirk*) someone with Allah. See a summary of verses that accuse the People of the Book of "associating" at 61.9 (p. 565).

The context of this denial of Son of God does not suggest that the Quran is addressing Christians. However, the logic of verse 91 is worth noting. If Allah had a son, according to this verse, the result would be two gods; the two gods would then compete and exalt themselves over each other.

Among the three persons of the one God of the New Testament, however, there is no rivalry but rather mutual submission and a fellowship of love.

gone off with what he had created, and some of them would indeed have exalted (themselves) over others. Glory to God above what they allege! [92] (He is the) Knower of the unseen and the seen. He is exalted above what they associate.

Son of God in the Quran

Gordon Nickel

The Quran takes issue with a number of important Gospel affirmations about Jesus. Among these, the affirmation that the Quran seems to make the strongest efforts to deny is the confession that Jesus is the Son of God.

The denial of the Son of God is also noteworthy because it comes with a historical context. The Dome of the Rock, built on the Temple Mount in Jerusalem in 691 AD, contains an Arabic inscription that some scholars call the earliest written expression of the faith of Islam. This inscription warned the city's Christian inhabitants against believing that God has a Son. These four warnings also appear in the Quran.

The Quran states, similar to the Dome inscriptions, that Allah "has not begotten and was not begotten" (112.3). It further explains, also like the Dome, that Allah "has not taken a son" and "has no associate in the kingdom, nor has He any (need of) an ally (to protect Him) from disgrace" (17.111). The longest theological passage in the Dome inscriptions shares the wording of 4.171–2, including the statement, "Allah is only one god. Glory to him! (Far be it) that he should have a son!" The fourth passage appears in the Quran at the end of the third of three longer passages on 'Īsā: "It is not for God to take any son. Glory to Him!" (19.35).

These quranic "Dome" passages introduce the main lines of the denial of Son of God and suggest some reasons for the denial. At its most basic, the Quran denies the perceived confession, "Allah has taken a son (*walad*)" (2.116; 10.68; 17.111; 18.4; 19.88, 92; 21.26, *Raḥmān*; cf. 19.35; 23.91; 25.2). The Quran curiously never specifies that it is Christians who are saying this, but the "People of the Book" are sometimes addressed or mentioned in the context of the verses.

The main reasons for the denials are theological: Allah has no need of anything, including a partner (*sharīk*) or helper (2.116; 4.171; 10.68; 17.111; cf. 112.2). In several verses, belief in a "son" is perceived to threaten Allah's exclusive sovereignty (2.116; 17.111; 18.4; 21.26). Two verses say it is "not appropriate" for Allah to take a son (19.92, 35). One verse asks, "How can [Allah] have a child, if he has no consort?" (6.101). Another verse seems to claim that a son would be like another god and then suggests that this would result in competition and conflict between them (23.91).

The tone of the denials can be as harsh as any of the Quran's polemical passages. At 9.30, in response to the perceived confessions of Jews and Christians, the Quran seems to boil over with anger, "Allah fights them! How they are perverted!" But nothing exceeds the apparent depth of feeling in 19.89–91, where "they say: '*al-Raḥmān* has taken a son.'" This confession is called a disastrous (*idd*) utterance that almost causes the universe to fall apart.

One Muslim scholar has suggested that the main Islamic objection to the Christian confession is not the phrase "son of God" – that could be understood figuratively, he writes. The actual objection is to the perception that Son of God ascribes deity to Jesus.

Some scholars have written that when the Quran denies a *walad* ("son" or "child") of Allah, it has in mind Arab idolaters and not Christians. But the choice of three *walad* texts for the Dome inscriptions does not suggest that they target idolaters. At 9.30 the Quran also denies that the Messiah is the son of Allah using another term for son – *ibn Allāh*.

One response to the quranic denials might be to say that Christians do not actually believe that God "took" a son, nor do Christians "associate" a mere human with God. Such an approach, however, would miss the depth of revulsion that Muslims have felt against calling Jesus the Son of God throughout history up to the present day.

It is noteworthy that as the Dome inscriptions place 'Īsā's status far below the Gospel's Son of God, the inscriptions raise up another. The wording of 33.56 appears twice, with its high claim that Allah and his angels "pray upon" (or "for," *ṣalla 'alā*) the prophet of Islam. The inscriptions claim that Allah has sent "his messenger" with the "religion of truth," so that he may cause it to "prevail over all religion" (9.33; 48.28; 61.9).

Meanwhile, the New Testament writings are unanimous in reporting that it was God the Father who called Jesus his Son. Peter testifies, "We ourselves heard this voice" (2 Peter 1:18).

[93] Say: 'My Lord, if You show me what they are promised, [94] my Lord, do not place me among the people who are evildoers.' [95] Surely We are able indeed to show you what We promise them. [96] Repel the evil with that which is better. We know what they allege. [97] And say: 'My Lord, I take refuge with You from

the incitements of the satans, [98] and I take refuge with You, my Lord, from their being present with me.'

[99] – Until, when death comes to one of them, he says, 'My Lord, send me back, [100] so that I may do righteousness concerning what I left (undone).' By no means! Surely it is (only) a word which he says. Behind them is a barrier, until the Day when they will be raised up.

[101] When there is a blast on the trumpet, (there will be) no (claims of) kinship among them on that Day, nor will they ask each other questions. [102] Whoever's scales are heavy, those – they are the ones who prosper, [103] but whoever's scales are light, those are the ones who have lost their (own) selves – remaining in Gehenna. [104] The Fire will scorch their faces, while they grimace in it. [105] 'Were My signs not recited to you, and did you not call them a lie?' [106] They will say, 'Our Lord, our miserableness overcame us, and we were a people in error. [107] Our Lord, bring us out of it! Then if we return (to evil), surely we shall be evildoers.' [108] He will say, 'Skulk away into it, and do not speak to Me! [109] Surely there was a group of My servants (who) said, "Our Lord, we believe, so forgive us, and have compassion on us, (for) You are the best of the compassionate." [110] But you took them (in) ridicule, until they made you forget My remembrance, and you were laughing at them. [111] Surely I have repaid them today for their patience. Surely they – they are the triumphant!' [112] He will say, 'How long did you remain in the earth, (by) number of years?' [113] They will say, 'We remained a day, or part of a day. Ask those who keep count.' [114] He will say, 'You remained only a little (while) – if only you knew! [115] Did you think that We created you in vain, and that you would not be returned to Us?'

[116] Exalted is God, the true King! (There is) no god but Him, Lord of the honorable throne. [117] Whoever calls on another god with God – for which he has no proof – his reckoning is with his Lord. Surely he will not prosper, (nor will) the disbelievers. [118] Say: 'My Lord, forgive and have compassion, (for) You are the best of the compassionate.'

23.101 – *When there is a blast on the trumpet*

The trumpet blast introduces a striking judgment scene that includes a conversation between the Lord and the inhabitants of Gehenna (vv. 105–15).

Bible readers may be reminded of the hell scene in the parable of poor Lazarus and the rich man in the Gospel according to Luke (16:19–31). See "Eschatology in the Quran" (p. 604).

23.102 – *Whoever's scales are heavy, those – they are the ones who prosper*

The image of weigh scales (*mawāzīn*, sing. *mīzān*) is very important in the Quran's concept of the Day of Judgment and the reckoning of good deeds against evil deeds. See "The Place of the Scale(s) in the Reckoning" (p. 481).

THE LIGHT
AL-NŪR

24

Sūra 24 immediately engages the reader by stipulating a punishment for adultery or fornication. The following passage then deals with the inevitable problem of false accusations. The language of law continues throughout the sūra and is applied to such detailed areas as treatment of slaves, modesty, and entering houses.

Perhaps because of the mention of adultery and fornication in the first verses, a substantial anonymous passage in this sūra has been associated with a story in Muslim tradition about an accusation of adultery (vv. 11–20).

The last third of the sūra associates "the messenger" with Allah for belief, obedience, and judgment a total of seven times. In fact, the last major unit of the sūra instructs believers about their behavior with the messenger.

Other noteworthy features of this sūra are the beautiful "light" or "niche" verse, a pair of similes about unbelievers, and a lovely creation passage.

In the Name of God, the Merciful, the Compassionate

[1] A sūra – We have sent it down and made it obligatory, and We have sent down in it clear signs, so that you may take heed.

[2] The adulterous woman and the adulterous man – flog each one of them a hundred lashes, and let no pity for the two of them affect you concerning the

---

24.1 – *A sūra – We have sent it down and made it obligatory*

This sūra brings a change in tone and audience. The preceding fourteen sūras contain a style of preaching that tells many stories and warns listeners but leaves them free to respond. The opening verse of Sūra 24 announces that Allah imposes or makes "obligatory" (*faraḍa*) its laws. Indeed, the next verse prescribes a law and commands a punishment.

24.2 – *The adulterous woman and the adulterous man – flog each one of them a hundred lashes*

The Quran prescribes the punishment for adultery as one hundred lashes. The Arabic verb *zanā* can also mean to fornicate, and translators are divided on how to

religion of God, if you believe in God and the Last Day. And let a group of the believers witness their punishment. ³ The adulterous man shall marry no one but an adulterous woman or an idolatrous woman, and the adulterous woman – no one shall marry her but an adulterous man or an idolatrous man. That is forbidden to the believers.

⁴ Those who hurl (accusations) against women of reputation, (and) then do not bring four witnesses, flog them eighty lashes, and do not accept their testimony ever (again). Those – they are the wicked, ⁵ except for those who turn (in repentance) after that and set (things) right. Surely God is forgiving, compassionate. ⁶ Those who hurl (accusations) against their wives, and have no witnesses except themselves, the testimony of such a person shall be to bear witness four times 'by God,' that he is indeed one of the truthful, ⁷ and the fifth time, that the curse of God (be) upon him if he is one of the liars. ⁸ And it shall avert the punishment from her that she bear witness four times 'by God,' that he is indeed one of the liars, ⁹ and the fifth time, that the anger of God (be) upon her if he is one of the truthful. ¹⁰ And if (it were) not (for the) favor of God on you, and His mercy, and that God turns (in forgiveness), wise [. . .].

¹¹ Surely those who brought the lie are a group of you. Do not think it a bad (thing) for you – No! It is good for you! Each one of them will bear what sin he

---

render the verb in this case. This is the only verse in the Quran that specifies a punishment for adultery (*zinā'*). A different verse deals with sexual immorality (*fāḥisha*, 4.15).

In contrast, the punishment for adultery in Islamic Law is death by stoning. The clash between the Quran's punishment and early Muslim understandings sparked a crisis among the jurists who formulated Islamic Law. Most jurists chose the punishment of stoning rather than flogging, based on what they understood to be the practice (*sunna*) of Muhammad. Some early Muslim figures claimed that a verse commanding stoning for adultery had once been part of the Quran.

In any case, the Quran warns against letting compassion or "pity" divert from "the religion of Allah" when punishing the guilty pair. For more on how the Muslim tradition has connected the stoning punishment to Muhammad's example, see the comments at 5.41.

24.4 – *Those who hurl (accusations) against women of reputation*

Along with the punishment for adultery, the Quran prescribes a punishment for those who falsely accuse women of adultery. The following verses (6–9) deal with accusations that men make against their wives.

24.11 – *Surely those who brought the lie are a group of you*

The passage starting with this verse (vv. 11–20) is a good example of a unit of text that means very little on its own but that Muslim tradition has connected to a story.

has earned, and the one who took upon himself the greater part of it – for him (there will be) a great punishment. [12] Why, when you heard it, did the believing men and the believing women not think better of themselves, and say, 'This is a clear lie'? [13] Why did they not bring four witnesses concerning it? Since they did not bring the witnesses, they are liars in the sight of God. [14] If (it were) not (for the) favor of God on you, and His mercy, in this world and the Hereafter, a great punishment would have touched you for what you spread about. [15] When you were receiving it with your tongues, and speaking with your mouths what you had no knowledge of, and thought it was a trivial (thing), when with God it was a mighty (thing) – [16] why, when you heard it, did you not say, 'It is not for us to speak about this. Glory to You! This is a great slander'? [17] God admonishes you from ever returning to such a thing (again), if you are believers. [18] God makes clear to you the signs. God is knowing, wise. [19] Surely those who love (allegations of) immorality to circulate among those who believe – for them (there is) a painful punishment in this world and the Hereafter. God knows, and you do not know. [20] If (it were) not (for the) favor of God on you, and His mercy, and that God is kind, compassionate [. . .].

[21] You who believe! Do not follow the footsteps of Satan. Whoever follows the footsteps of Satan – surely he commands (what is) immoral and wrong. If (it were) not (for the) favor of God on you, and His mercy, not one of you would ever have been pure. God purifies whomever He pleases. God is hearing, knowing.

[22] Let not those of you who possess favor and abundance swear against giving (support) to family, and the poor, and the ones who emigrate in the way of God, but let them pardon and excuse (them). Would you not like God to forgive you? God is forgiving, compassionate.

[23] Surely those who hurl (accusations) against chaste women – the oblivious (but) believing women – are accursed in this world and the Hereafter. For them (there is) a great punishment. [24] On the Day when their tongues, and their hands, and their feet will bear witness against them about what they have done, [25] on that Day God will pay them their just due in full, and they will know that God – He is the clear Truth.

The passage is full of pronouns that have no antecedent; therefore, it is impossible to know who "you" and "those" are.

The Muslim story of Islamic origins linked this passage to an episode in which 'Ā'isha, the young wife of Muhammad, gets separated from the main group of Muslims on the way back from a military campaign. The "slander" is the accusation that while she is away from the main group, 'Ā'isha is unfaithful with a young soldier who brings her back (*Sīra*, 494–97).

²⁶ The bad women for the bad men, and the bad men for the bad women. And the good women for the good men, and the good men for the good women – those are (to be declared) innocent of what they say. For them (there is) forgiveness and generous provision.

²⁷ You who believe! Do not enter houses other than your (own) houses, until you ask permission and greet its inhabitants. That is better for you, so that you may take heed. ²⁸ But if you do not find anyone inside, do not enter it until permission is given to you. If it is said to you, 'Go away,' go away. It is purer for you. God is aware of what you do. ²⁹ There is no blame on you that you enter uninhabited houses, where (there is) enjoyment for you. God knows what you reveal and what you conceal.

³⁰ Say to the believing men (that) they (should) lower their sight and guard their private parts. That is purer for them. Surely God is aware of what they do. ³¹ And say to the believing women (that) they (should) lower their sight and guard their private parts, and not show their charms, except for what (normally) appears of them. And let them draw their head coverings over their breasts, and not show their charms, except to their husbands, or their fathers, or their husbands' fathers, or their sons, or their husbands' sons, or their brothers, or their brothers' sons, or their sisters' sons, or their women, or what their right (hands) own, or such men as attend (them who) have no (sexual) desire, or children (who are) not (yet) aware of women's nakedness. And let them not stamp their feet to make known what they hide of their charms. Turn to God (in repentance) – all (of you) – believers, so that you may prosper.

³² Marry off the unmarried among you, and (also) the righteous among your male slaves and your female slaves. If they are poor, God will enrich them from His favor. God is embracing, knowing. ³³ Let those who do not find (the means for) marriage abstain, until God enriches them from His favor. Those who seek the writ, among what your right (hands) own, write (it) for them, if you know any good in them, and give them some of the wealth of God which He has given you. And do not force your young women into prostitution, if they wish

---

24.31 – *And let them draw their head coverings over their breasts, and not show their charms*

The Quran gives instructions about human modesty in a number of verses. These instructions to believing women follow similar instructions to believing men (v. 30). This verse adds that women draw their "head coverings" (*khumur*, sing. *khimār*) over their breasts, except in the presence of close male family members.

On women's coverings, See "Women in the Quran" (p. 429).

(to live in) chastity, so that you may seek (the fleeting) goods of this present life. Whoever forces them – surely God is forgiving (and) compassionate (to them) after their being forced.

³⁴ Certainly We have sent down to you clear signs, and an example of those who passed away before you, and an admonition for those who guard (themselves).

³⁵ God (is the) light of the heavens and the earth. A parable of His light (is) like a niche in which (there is) a lamp, the lamp in a glass, the glass as it were a brilliant star, lit from a blessed tree, an olive (tree) neither (of the) East nor (of the) West, whose oil would almost shine, even if no fire touched it – light upon light – God guides to His light whomever He pleases, and God strikes parables for the people, and God has knowledge of everything – ³⁶ in houses (which) God permitted to be raised up and in which His name was remembered. Glorifying Him there, in the mornings and the evenings, ³⁷ were men (whom) neither (any business) transaction nor (any) bargaining would divert from the remembrance of God, or (from) observing the prayer and giving the alms. They feared a Day on which the hearts and the sight would be overturned, ³⁸ so that God might repay them (for the) best of what they had done, and increase them from His favor. God provides for whomever He pleases without reckoning.

³⁹ But those who disbelieve – their deeds are like a mirage in a desert which the thirsty man thinks (to be) water, until, when he comes to it, he finds it (to be) nothing, but he finds God beside him, and then He pays him his account in full. God is quick at the reckoning. ⁴⁰ Or (he is) like the darkness in a deep sea – a wave covers him, above which is (another) wave, above which is a cloud – darkness upon darkness. When he puts out his hand, he can hardly see it. The one to whom God does not give light has no light (at all).

24.34 – *Certainly We have sent down to you clear signs*

The Quran addresses the messenger directly to claim that the verses or "signs" (*āyāt*) he recites are from a divine source (also v. 46). See "Different Kinds of Literature" (p. 14).

24.35 – *God (is the) light of the heavens and the earth*

The picture of a lamp in a niche is used in this verse to make a remarkable and justly famous statement about Allah. It is one of the most striking theological statements in the Quran and a favorite verse for posting on walls in beautiful Arabic calligraphy.

24.39 – *But those who disbelieve – their deeds are like a mirage in a desert*

Here the Quran offers two similes (vv. 39–40) to illustrate unbelief.

⁴¹ Do you not see that God – whatever is in the heavens and the earth glorifies Him, and (so do) the birds spreading (their wings in flight)? Each one knows its prayer and its glorifying, and God is aware of what they do. ⁴² To God (belongs) the kingdom of the heavens and the earth. To God is the (final) destination. ⁴³ Do you not see that God drives the clouds, then gathers them, then makes them (into) a mass, and then you see the rain come forth from the midst of it? He sends down mountains (of them) from the sky, in which (there is) hail, and He smites whomever He pleases with it, and turns it away from whomever He pleases. The flash of His lightning almost takes away the sight. ⁴⁴ God alternates the night and the day. Surely in that is a lesson indeed for those who have sight. ⁴⁵ God has created every living creature from water. (There are) some of them who walk on their bellies, and some of them who walk on two feet, and some of them who walk on four. God creates whatever He pleases. Surely God is powerful over everything. ⁴⁶ Certainly We have sent down clear signs. God guides whomever He pleases to a straight path.

⁴⁷ They say, 'We believe in God and the messenger, and we obey.' Then, after that, a group of them turns away. Those are not with the believers. ⁴⁸ When they are called to God and His messenger, so that he may judge between them, suddenly a group of them turns away. ⁴⁹ But if (they think) the truth is on their side, they come to him readily. ⁵⁰ (Is there) a sickness in their hearts, or do they doubt, or do they fear that God will be unjust to them, and His messenger (too)? No! Those – they are the evildoers. ⁵¹ The only saying of the believers, when they are called to God and His messenger so that he may judge between them, is that they say, 'We hear and obey.' Those – they are the ones who prosper. ⁵² Whoever obeys God and His messenger, and fears God, and guards (himself) against Him, those – they are the triumphant. ⁵³ They have sworn by God the most solemn of their oaths: if indeed you command them, they will indeed go forth. Say: 'Do not swear! Honorable obedience (is sufficient). Surely God is aware of what you do.' ⁵⁴ Say: 'Obey God and obey the messenger! If you turn away, (there is) only on him what is laid on him, and (only) on you what is laid

---

24.41 – *whatever is in the heavens and the earth glorifies Him*

Among the beautiful expressions in this creation passage (vv. 41–45) are the birds praising the Creator in their flight and the Creator gathering and layering the clouds (v. 43).

24.54 – *Obey God and obey the messenger!*

Commands to obey the messenger appear mainly in Sūras 4; 8; and 33. But Sūra 24 contains two notable commands (also v. 56) and a couple of other mentions (vv. 51–52, cf. 47). Such verses associate "the messenger" with Allah for obedience,

on you. But if you obey him, you will be (rightly) guided. Nothing (depends) on the messenger except the clear delivery (of the message).'

⁵⁵ God has promised those of you who believe and do righteous deeds that He will indeed make them successors on the earth, (even) as He made those who were before them successors, and (that) He will indeed establish their religion for them – that which He has approved for them – and (that) He will indeed give them security in exchange for their former fear: 'They will serve Me, not associating anything with Me. Whoever disbelieves after that, those – they are the wicked.' ⁵⁶ Observe the prayer and give the alms, and obey the messenger, so that you may receive compassion. ⁵⁷ Do not think (that) those who disbelieve are able to escape (God) on the earth. Their refuge is the Fire – and it is indeed an evil destination!

⁵⁸ You who believe! Let those whom your right (hands) own, and those of you who have not reached the (age of) puberty, ask permission of you at three times (of the day) – before the dawn prayer, and when you lay down your clothes at the noon hour, and after the evening prayer – the three (times) of nakedness for you. But beyond those (times) there is no blame on you or on them in going about among each other. In this way God makes clear to you the signs. God is knowing, wise. ⁵⁹ When your children reach the (age of) puberty, let them ask permission (before entering), as those before them asked permission. In this way God makes clear to you His signs. God is knowing, wise. ⁶⁰ And your women who are past childbearing and have no hope of marriage, there is no blame on them that they lay down their clothes, (as long as there is) no flaunting of (their) charms. But that they abstain is better for them. God is hearing, knowing.

⁶¹ There is no blame on the blind, and no blame on the disabled, and no blame on the sick, nor on yourselves, that you eat at your houses, or your fathers'

---

judgment (vv. 48, 51), and belief (v. 62, cf. 47). However, verse 56 commands obedience to the messenger alone.

The Quran's commands to obey the messenger became very important in the writings of the influential Muslim jurist al-Shāfiʿī (d. 820), who insisted they gave divine authority to the sayings (hadith) attributed to Muhammad outside the Quran. See the summary and analysis of these commands at 64.12 (p. 574).

24.56 – *Observe the prayer and give the alms, and obey the messenger*

In other parts of the Quran, performing ritual prayer and giving alms seem to represent *islām* ("submission"). And this verse adds obedience to the messenger. All three are required in order to receive mercy.

This command to obey "the messenger" also appears without the accompanying "obey Allah" (see the comment at v. 54).

houses, or your mothers' houses, or your brothers' houses, or your sisters' houses, or your paternal uncles' houses, or your paternal aunts' houses, or your maternal uncles' houses, or your maternal aunts' houses, or (at houses) of which you possess the keys, or (at the house) of your friend. There is no blame on you that you eat together or in separate groups. When you enter (these) houses, greet one another (with) a greeting from God, blessed (and) good. In this way God makes clear to you the signs, so that you may understand.

⁶² Only those are believers who believe in God and His messenger, and who, when they are with him on some common matter, do not go away until they ask his permission. Surely those who ask your permission – those are the ones who believe in God and His messenger. When they ask your permission for some affair of theirs, give permission to whomever you please of them, and ask forgiveness for them from God. Surely God is forgiving, compassionate.

⁶³ Do not make the messenger's calling of you like the calling of some of you to others. God already knows those of you who slip away secretly. Let those who go against his command beware, or trouble will smite them, or a painful punishment will smite them.

⁶⁴ Is it not a fact that to God (belongs) whatever is in the heavens and the earth? He already knows what you are up to, and on the Day when they will be returned to Him, He will inform them about what they have done. God has knowledge of everything.

24.62 – *Only those are believers who believe in God and His messenger*

This verse makes explicit what is implicit – and often seemingly invisible – in many other quranic passages. In the Quran, true belief is not just any kind of religious faith (see 2.4) but is specific to "Allah and His messenger." In Muslim daily life today, this is reflected emphatically in the Islamic *shahāda* (confession of faith) and in the public call to ritual prayer.

The instructions in verses 62 and 63 for how to behave in the presence of "the messenger" provide a good example of "personal situation" passages. Such passages are most extensive in Sūra 33. See "Different Kinds of Literature" (p. 14).

THE DELIVERANCE
AL-FURQĀN

25

Sūra 25 jumps quickly into the middle of an encounter between the messenger and an audience that resists him. The audience finds fault with both the message and the messenger. They accuse the recitation of being a lie or a fable. The listeners resist bowing down to the Merciful. They ask why the entire recitation (qur'ān) is not sent down all at once. Why should they accept a message from one who simply eats and walks in the markets rather than from one who is recommended by the help of an angel or – better! – receives a treasure? The listeners fear that the messenger will lead them astray from their gods.

In response, the messenger on the one hand warns of future punishments for disbelievers and on the other appeals to the signs of the presence and power of the Creator. At one point, the messenger complains to his Lord about the rejection of his message. The Quran reassures the messenger and promises punishment to the unresponsive audience.

The last part of the sūra offers a striking description of the "servants of the Merciful."

In the Name of God, the Merciful, the Compassionate

[1] Blessed (be) the One who sent down the Deliverance on His servant, so that he may be a warner to the worlds [2] – the One who – to Him (belongs) the kingdom

---

25.1 – *Blessed (be) the One who sent down the Deliverance on His servant*

"Deliverance" translates the Arabic term *furqān*, which gives this sūra its name. In most of its seven occurrences in the Quran, *furqān* appears to indicate a scripture sent from Allah, for example to Moses at 2.53 and 21.48 (cf. 3.4). In 25.1, the Quran claims that Allah also sends down the *furqān* to the messenger ("His servant").

The term itself is difficult to translate. Arthur Jeffery traced *furqān* through Syriac to the Aramaic word for "salvation" or "deliverance" – which seems to match its use in 8.29, 41. Muslim commentators, however, often related the term to the Arabic verb *faraqa*, which means "to discriminate." This meaning may suit its use at 2.185. See Jeffery's *Foreign Vocabulary of the Qur'ān* in the bibliography.

of the heavens and the earth. He has not taken a son, nor has He any associate in the kingdom. He created everything and decreed it exactly. [3] Yet they have taken gods other than Him. They do not create anything, since they are (themselves) created, and do not have power to (cause) themselves harm or benefit, and do not have power over death or life or raising up.

[4] Those who disbelieve say, 'This is nothing but a lie! He has forged it, and other people have helped him with it.' So they have come to evil and falsehood. [5] And they say, 'Old tales! He has written it down, and it is dictated to him morning and evening.' [6] Say: 'He has sent it down – He who knows the secret in the heavens and earth. Surely He is forgiving, compassionate.'

[7] They say, 'What is wrong with this messenger? He eats food and walks about in the markets. If only an angel were sent down to him to be a warner with him, [8] or a treasure were cast (down) to him, or he had a garden from which to eat.' The evildoers say, 'You are only following a man (who is) bewitched.' [9] See how they strike parables for you! But they have gone astray and cannot (find) a way. [10] Blessed is He who, if He pleases, will give you (what is) better than that – Gardens through which rivers flow – and He will give you palaces.

25.2 – *He has not taken a son, nor has He any associate in the kingdom*

The warning against saying that "Allah has taken a son" appears many times in the Quran. Here this perceived confession is grouped with believing that Allah shares his sovereignty with a partner and with taking gods other than Allah (v. 3). See "Son of God in the Quran" (p. 352) and a summary of verses that accuse the People of the Book of "associating" at 61.9 (p. 565).

25.4 – *Those who disbelieve say, "This is nothing but a lie! He has forged it . . ."*

This passage seems to indicate a verbal encounter between a messenger and his audience (vv. 4–10). The speeches of the listeners show that they doubt the message and, especially, its source. They say the messenger puts his message together with help from others who dictate to him what to recite (vv. 4–5). The listeners instead demand an angel or a treasure from above (vv. 7–8).

Their expression, "Old tales!" (v. 5), repeats eight additional times in the Quran and seems to accuse the messenger of telling stories with which the audience is already familiar. See "Apocryphal Details in Quranic Stories" (p. 299). On verses that accuse the messenger of inventing, see the discussion at 69.44 (p. 587).

25.6 – *He has sent it down – He who knows the secret of the heavens and the earth*

In response to the accusation of "forging" (v. 4), the Quran commands the messenger to make this bold assertion.

¹¹ No! They have called the Hour a lie – and We have prepared a blazing (Fire) for whoever calls the Hour a lie. ¹² When it sees them from a place far off, they will hear its raging and moaning. ¹³ When they are cast into a narrow part of it, bound in chains, they will call out there (for) destruction. ¹⁴ 'Do not call out today (for) one destruction, but call out (for) many destruction(s)!' ¹⁵ Say: 'Is that better, or the Garden of Eternity which is promised to the ones who guard (themselves)? It is their payment and (final) destination.' ¹⁶ Remaining there, they will have whatever they please. It is a promise (binding) on your Lord, (something) to be asked for.

¹⁷ On the Day when He will gather them and what they serve instead of God, He will say, 'Did you lead astray these servants of Mine, or did they (themselves) go astray from the way?' ¹⁸ They will say, 'Glory to You! It was not fitting for us to take any allies other than You, but You gave them and their fathers enjoyment (of life), until they forgot the Reminder and became a ruined people.' ¹⁹ 'So they have called you a liar in what you say, and you are incapable of turning (it) aside or (finding any) help. Whoever among you does evil – We shall make him taste a great punishment.'

²⁰ We have not sent any of the envoys before you, except that they indeed ate food and walked about in the markets. We have made some of you a test for

---

25.11 – *No! They have called the Hour a lie – and We have prepared a blazing*

Those who resist the preaching of the messenger will face a great punishment when Allah gathers humanity for judgment (vv. 11–21). Verses 17–18 picture a conversation on the "Day" of resurrection. Similar verses in this sūra are verses 22–29 and 69. See "Eschatology in the Quran" (p. 604).

25.20 – *We have not sent any of the envoys before you, except that they indeed ate food*

The Quran makes many categorical statements about prophets and messengers (here *mursalūn*) in the style of this verse. The statement that all messengers eat food seems to be a response to the question of the audience in verse 7.

That pre-Islamic messengers and prophets ate food and walked in the markets is not in dispute. However, many other quranic statements warrant comparison to messengers and prophets as the Bible portrays them. Among the more straightforward statements are that Allah sent all envoys as good news bringers and warners (6.48; 18.56), that Allah sent all messengers in the language of the people (14.4), and that all messengers and prophets were mocked (15.11; 43.6–7). The Bible, on the other hand, does not confirm the Quran's claims that God sent messengers to every community (Q 10.47; 16.36), that God assigned an enemy to every prophet ("satans of

others: 'Will you be patient?' Your Lord is seeing. [21] Those who do not expect to meet Us say, 'If only the angels were sent down on us, or we saw our Lord.' Certainly they have become arrogant within themselves and behaved with great disdain.

[22] On the Day when they see the angels, (there will be) no good news that Day for the sinners, and they will say, 'An absolute ban!' [23] We shall press forward to whatever deeds they have done, and make them scattered dust. [24] The companions of the Garden on that Day (will be in) a better dwelling place and a finer resting place. [25] On the Day when the sky is split open, (along) with the clouds, and the angels are sent down all at once, [26] the true kingdom that Day (will belong) to the Merciful, and it will be a hard Day for the disbelievers. [27] On the Day when the evildoer bites down on both his hands, he will say, 'Would that I had taken a way with the messenger! [28] Woe to me! Would that I had not taken So-and-so as a friend! [29] Certainly he led me astray from the Reminder, after it came to me. Satan is the betrayer of humankind.'

[30] The messenger said, 'My Lord! Surely my people have taken this Qur'ān (as a thing to be) shunned.' [31] In this way We have assigned to every prophet

---

the humans and jinn," 6.112), or that Satan "casts" into the wishful thinking of every messenger and prophet (22.52).

More consequential are the categorical statements about political power and force. "How many a prophet has fought (*qātala*)?" asks the Quran (3.146), apparently commenting on a battle scene in which the survival of Muhammad (3.144) was in doubt. To what extent were messengers sent to be obeyed (4.64)? Is it true that no prophet may take captives "until he makes wide slaughter in the land" (8.67, trans. Arberry; cf. Pickthall)? These statements do not match the Quran's portrayal of most prophets and messengers, much less the biblical accounts.

As for envoys who ate food in 25.20, the Quran seems to use this statement to deny deity to 'Īsā at 5.75. The reference to walking about in the markets (*aswāq*) is also intriguing because of polemical controversy over Isaiah's first "Song of the Suffering Servant" (Isaiah 42:1–7). The song says that the servant "will not raise his voice in the streets" (v. 2), and the Gospel accounts find this prophecy fulfilled in the behavior of Jesus (e.g., Matthew 12:15–21). However, several early Muslim writers cited a tradition resembling Isaiah 42:2 about a person who "will not be clamorous in the markets," which they claimed to be a mention of the messenger of Islam in the Torah. (Further details in my book *The Gentle Answer*, ch. 19. See bibliography.)

25.30 – *The messenger said, "My Lord! Surely my people have taken this Qur'ān..."*
This is the sūra's second passage that appears to give the objections of the listeners (vv. 32a, 41–42), the complaint of the messenger (v. 30), and the reassurance of

an enemy from the sinners. Yet your Lord is sufficient as a guide and helper. [32] Those who disbelieve say, 'If only the Qur'ān were sent down on him all of one piece.' (It has been sent down) in this way, so that We may make firm your heart by means of it. We have arranged it very carefully. [33] They do not bring you any parable, except (that) We have (already) brought you the truth, and (something) better in exposition. [34] Those who are going to be gathered to Gehenna on their faces – those will be worse in position and farther astray (from the) way.

[35] Certainly We gave Moses the Book, and appointed his brother Aaron as an assistant with him. [36] We said, 'Both of you go to the people who have called Our signs a lie.' We destroyed them completely. [37] And the people of Noah – when they called the messengers liars – We drowned them, and made them a sign for the people. We have prepared for the evildoers a painful punishment. [38] And 'Ād, and Thamūd, and the companions of al-Rass, and many generations between that. [39] Each – We struck parables for it, and each We destroyed completely. [40] Certainly they have come upon the town which was rained on by an evil rain. Have they not seen it? No! They do not expect any raising up.

[41] When they see you, they take you only in mockery: 'Is this the one whom God has raised up as a messenger? [42] He would indeed have led us astray from our gods, had we not been patient toward them.' Soon they will know, when they see the punishment, who is farther astray (from the) way. [43] Do you see the one who takes his own desire as his god? Will you be a guardian over him? [44] Or do you think that most of them hear or understand? They are just like cattle – No! They are (even) farther astray (from the) way!

[45] Have you not regarded your Lord, how He has stretched out the shadow? If He had (so) pleased, He would indeed have made it stand still. Then We made the sun a guide for it, [46] (and) then We drew it to Us gradually. [47] He (it is) who has made the night as a covering for you, and made sleep as a rest, and He has made the day as a raising up. [48] He (it is) who has sent the winds as good news before His mercy, and We have sent down pure water from the sky, [49] so that We might give some barren land life by means of it, and give it as a drink to some of what We have created – livestock and many people. [50] Certainly We have

---

the Quran (vv. 32b–34). The brief references to the people of Noah, Moses, 'Ād, and Thamūd (vv. 35–38) also seem to be part of the encouragement to the messenger.

On the word *qur'ān*, see the comment at 2.185 (p. 61).

25.45 – *Have you not regarded your Lord, how He has stretched out the shadow?*

This question introduces a remarkable passage in which the blessings of creation are beautifully described (vv. 45–62). The appropriate response of humankind is to glorify the Merciful (v. 58, cf. 50).

varied it among them so that they might take heed, yet most of the people refuse (everything) but disbelief. [51] If We had (so) pleased, We would indeed have raised up a warner in every town. [52] So do not obey the disbelievers, but struggle mightily against them by means of it.

Jihad in the Quran
David Cook

The Arabic root verb from which the important concept of *jihād* is derived literally means "to struggle, to exert." But since the rise of Islam, specifically since the period of the great Islamic conquests (635–732), the verb has taken on the sense of "divinely sanctioned warfare."

The root *jhd* occurs in the Quran about forty-one times. In the Quran the root is not the primary locus for fighting or warfare but conveys a range of different meanings. These include struggling against opponents in terms of argumentation or remonstration, as well as the struggle with one's (evil) self or soul – a doctrine that would later be developed in Islamic mystical beliefs.

Although *jihād* is not considered to be fundamental to Islam, it does often appear together with believing in Allah and the Last Day (end of the world), which are central to Islamic theology. As 9.44 states, "Those who believe in God and the Last Day do not ask your permission, so that they may struggle with their lives and their wealth." Here, *jihād* has both a physical as well as a financial aspect to it (see 49.15). Those who want to enter the Garden (Paradise) must be tested on earth by *jihād* (3.142), which is most likely fighting, that will separate the true believers from the false.

Those who have passed this test are considered to be at a level higher than other believers (9.16). "Those of the believers who sit (at home) – other

---

25.52 – *So do not obey the disbelievers, but struggle mightily against them by means of it*

The second clause of this verse is literally "struggle against them with a great struggling." "Struggle" translates the Arabic verb *jāhada*, and here it appears in the form of a command to the messenger in particular. "Struggling" translates the word *jihād*. The sense of *jihad* that the Quran intends in this verse may be partly determined by context. Since this sūra gives no sense of a battle scene and features no commands to fight, *struggle* likely refers to the preaching of the messenger.

See the analysis of commands to "strive" at 66.9 (p. 579).

than the injured – are not equal with the ones who struggle in the way of God with their wealth and their lives" (4.95). Several other verses affirm this idea as well, such as 9.20: "Those who have believed, and emigrated, and struggled in the way of God with their wealth and their lives are higher in rank with God. Those – they are the triumphant."

When *jihād* does have the sense of "divinely sanctioned warfare," it is often followed by the phrase "in the way [or path] of God" (5.54; 61.11). The fighting process is made explicit occasionally: "Go forth, light and heavy, and struggle in the way of God with your wealth and lives" (9.41). There are, however, verses in which the nature of the *jihād* is not clear: "And struggle for God with the struggling due to Him" (22.78).

In the Quran *jihād* often appears as part of the process of joining the Muslim community, who are described as believing, emigrating, and then participating in *jihād* (8.72, 74, 75; 2.218). This theme of personal commitment enjoined upon the believers is a community-building factor inside the Quran.

In general, the messenger and the believers are encouraged to use *jihād* against unbelievers: "Prophet! Struggle against the disbelievers and the hypocrites, and be stern with them" (66.9; cf. 9.73). Occasionally *jihād* is described as a practice that is the opposite of what the unbelievers want and thus desirable to the believers: "So do not obey the disbelievers, but struggle mightily against them by means of it" (25.52).

It is possible for *jihād* to be associated with the self or soul (*nafs*), "Whoever struggles, struggles for himself" (or "his soul"; 29.6). One should remember that the soul is said to be the locus of evil (12.53), and therefore this type of *jihād* is said to be practiced against the lower nature and is closely associated with Sufi mystical practices. In general, *jihād* is a choice between the things of this world, such as close relatives, one's beloved, and possessions on the one hand and violence on the other hand – which might cause one to die and lose everything (9.24).

The quranic material from the root *jhd* is not very large, and as a religious, political, and military concept, *jihād* does not seem to be singled out as important within the text. The primary quranic root word for fighting is *qtl* (closely related to the Hebrew and Aramaic root words), meaning "fighting, killing," and it is with these verses that one finds a more fully fleshed out doctrine of warfare. See "Fighting and Killing in the Quran" (p. 220).

What is distinctive about *jihād* is the religious nature of it, which is most likely the reason the term ultimately came to be the best-known Muslim term concerning fighting. This religious aspect to fighting was fairly unique during the seventh century, as neither the Byzantine (Christian Roman) nor Sasanian (Persian) empire emphasized it as part of its political theology.

⁵³ He (it is) who has let loose the two seas, this one sweet and fresh, and this (other) one salty (and) bitter, and placed between them a barrier, and an absolute ban. ⁵⁴ He (it is) who created a human being from water, and made him related by blood and by marriage, (for) Your Lord is powerful. ⁵⁵ Yet they serve what neither benefits them nor harms them, instead of God (alone). The disbeliever (always) allies himself against his Lord. ⁵⁶ We have sent you only as a bringer of good news and a warner. ⁵⁷ Say: 'I do not ask you for any reward for it, except for whoever pleases to take a way to his Lord.' ⁵⁸ Put your trust in the Living One who does not die, and glorify (Him) with His praise. He is sufficient (as One who) is aware of the sins of His servants, ⁵⁹ who created the heavens and the earth, and whatever is between them, in six days. Then He mounted the throne (as) the Merciful. Ask anyone (who is) aware about Him! ⁶⁰ But when it is said to them, 'Prostrate yourselves before the Merciful,' they say, 'What is the Merciful? Shall we prostrate ourselves before what you command us?' And it (only) increases them in aversion (to Him). ⁶¹ Blessed is He who has made constellations in the sky, and has made a lamp in it, and an illuminating moon. ⁶² He (it is) who has made the night and the day a succession – for anyone who wishes to take heed or wishes to be thankful.

⁶³ The servants of the Merciful are those who walk humbly on the earth, and when the ignorant address them, say: 'Peace!' ⁶⁴ (They are) those who spend the night prostrating themselves and standing before their Lord, ⁶⁵ and those who say, 'Our Lord, turn away from us the punishment of Gehenna. Surely its punishment is torment! ⁶⁶ Surely it is an evil dwelling and resting place!' ⁶⁷ And (they are) those who, when they contribute, are neither wanton nor stingy,

25.56 – *We have sent you only as a bringer of good news and a warner*
When the messenger's role has no forceful or military dimension, the audience is free to accept or reject his message. Is it this limitation of the messenger's task that could account for the peaceful tone of this sūra?

25.63 – *The servants of the Merciful are those who walk humbly on the earth*
This is a remarkable and positive vision (vv. 63–76) of a community that answers even the ignorant with a greeting of "Peace!" These believers keep to their prayers (vv. 64–65, 74) and stay away from sin (v. 68).

but right between that, [68] and those who do not call on another god with God, and do not kill the person whom God has forbidden (to be killed), except by right, and do not commit adultery – whoever does that will meet (his) penalty. [69] The punishment will be doubled for him on the Day of Resurrection, and he will remain in it humiliated, [70] except for the one who turns (in repentance), and believes, and does a righteous deed – and those, God will change their evil deeds (into) good ones, (for) God is forgiving, compassionate. [71] Whoever turns (in repentance) and does righteousness, surely he turns to God in complete repentance. [72] (They are) those who do not bear false witness, and, when they pass by any frivolous talk, they pass by with dignity, [73] and those who, when they are reminded by the signs of their Lord, do not fall down over it, deaf and blind, [74] and those who say, 'Our Lord, grant us comfort (to our) eyes from our wives and descendants, and make us a model for the ones who guard (themselves).' [75] Those will be repaid with the exalted room because they were patient, and there they will meet a greeting and 'Peace!' [76] There they will dwell – it is good as a dwelling and resting place.

[77] Say: 'My Lord would not care about you, if it were not for your prayer. But you have called (it) a lie, so it will be close at hand.'

THE POETS
AL-SHU'ARĀ'

26

This sūra begins with a first-person-plural address to the messenger about the people who deny his message. Very quickly, however, the reader enters a series of stories about Moses, Abraham, Noah, Hud, Salih, Lot, and Shu'ayb.

The sūra shows a definite structure that is not often clear in other sūras. A refrain repeats between the stories, starting with the words, "Surely in that is a sign indeed" (e.g., vv. 8–9). Several of the stories about the prophets also repeat a substantial passage of preaching beginning with "Will you not guard (yourselves)?" (e.g., vv. 105–9). This suggests a concept that prophetic characters of the past not only shared the same mission but also preached the same words.

The long narrative about Moses at the beginning of the series is interesting especially for its extensive scene in Pharaoh's court. The names Moses uses for God are noteworthy. This sūra seems to use the name Allah quite sparingly.

In the Name of God, the Merciful, the Compassionate

¹ Ṭā' Sīn Mīm. ² Those are the signs of the clear Book.

³ Perhaps you are going to destroy yourself because they do not believe. ⁴ If We (so) please, We shall send down on them a sign from the sky, and their necks will stay bowed before it. ⁵ But no new reminder comes to them from the Merciful without their turning away from it. ⁶ They have called (it) a lie, so the story of what they were mocking will come to them. ⁷ Do they not look at the earth – how many (things) of every excellent kind We have caused to grow

---

26.1–2 – *Ṭā' Sīn Mīm. Those are the signs of the clear Book*

On the disconnected Arabic letters that begin this sūra, see the comment at 2.1 (p. 35). The sūra opens with a claim that it is made up of verses or "signs" (*āyāt*) of a clarifying book.

Most of the sūras from 26 through 46 begin with various disconnected Arabic letters, and of these sūras, most also start with self-referential claims to be revealed.

in it? [8] Surely in that is a sign indeed, but most of them are not believers. [9] Surely your Lord – He indeed is the Mighty, the Compassionate.

[10] (Remember) when your Lord called to Moses: 'Go to a people who are evildoers, [11] the people of Pharaoh. Will they not guard (themselves)?' [12] He said, 'My Lord, surely I fear that they will call me a liar, [13] and my heart will be distressed, and my tongue will not work. So send for Aaron. [14] And they (also) have a crime against me, and I fear they will kill me.' [15] He said, 'By no means! Go, both of you, with Our signs. Surely We shall be with you, hearing (everything). [16] So come, both of you, to Pharaoh, and say: "Surely we are the messenger of the Lord of the worlds. [17] Send forth the Sons of Israel with us."'

[18] He said, 'Did we not bring you up among us as a child, and did you not remain among us for some years of your life? [19] Yet you did the deed you did, and were one of the ungrateful.' [20] He said, 'I did it when I was one of those who had gone astray, [21] and I fled from you when I became afraid of you. But my Lord granted me judgment, and made me one of the envoys. [22] And that is a blessing you bestow on me, that you have enslaved the Sons of Israel.'

[23] Pharaoh said, 'What is the Lord of the worlds?' [24] He said, 'The Lord of the heavens and the earth, and whatever is between them, if you (would) be

---

26.8 – *Surely in that is a sign indeed, but most of them are not believers*
Verses 8 and 9 make up a refrain that repeats at verses 67–68, 103–4, 121–22, 139–40, 158–59, 174–75, and 190–91.

26.10 – *when your Lord called Moses: "Go to a people who are evildoers …"*
This verse begins another important version of the story of Moses, focusing (similarly to 20.49–73) mainly on the scene in Pharaoh's court (vv. 18–51). Here the Lord delivers the Children of Israel at the sea (vv. 63–66). See the table of the Quran's Moses narratives (p. 390).

26.14 – *And they (also) have a crime against me, and I fear they will kill me*
Moses notes to God that the Egyptians have a sin (*dhanb*) against him. Then when Moses tries to establish his presence before Pharaoh, Pharaoh reminds Moses about the "crime," and Moses replies that he did it "when I was one of those who had gone astray" (*al-ḍāllīn*, v. 20).
See the analysis of the sins of prophets and messengers at Q 48.2 (p. 513).

26.23 – *Pharaoh said, "What is the Lord of the worlds?"*
The names that Moses uses for God in Pharaoh's presence are worth noting: "Lord" (v. 21), "Lord of the worlds" (*rabb al-'ālamīn*, v. 16), "Lord of the heavens and the earth" (v. 24), "your Lord and the Lord of your fathers" (v. 26), and "Lord of the East and the West" (v. 28).

certain.' He said to those who were around him, ²⁵ 'Do you not hear?' ²⁶ He said, 'Your Lord and the Lord of your fathers of old.' ²⁷ He said, 'Surely your messenger who has been sent to you is possessed indeed.' ²⁸ He said, 'The Lord of the East and the West, and whatever is between them, if you (would) understand.' ²⁹ He said, 'If indeed you take a god other than me, I shall indeed make you one of the imprisoned.' ³⁰ He said, 'Even if I brought you something clear?' ³¹ He said, 'Bring it, if you are one of the truthful.' ³² So he cast (down) his staff, and suddenly it became a real snake, ³³ and he drew forth his hand, and suddenly it became white to the onlookers. ³⁴ He said to the assembly around him, 'Surely this is a skilled magician indeed. ³⁵ He wants to expel you from your land by his magic. So what do you command?' ³⁶ They said, 'Put him and his brother off (for a while), and raise up searchers in the cities ³⁷ to bring you every skilled magician.' ³⁸ So the magicians were gathered together for the meeting on a day made known. ³⁹ And it was said to the people, 'Will you (too) gather together?' ⁴⁰ 'Perhaps we will follow the magicians, if they are the victors.'

⁴¹ When the magicians came, they said to Pharaoh, '(Will there) surely (be) for us a reward indeed, if we are the victors?' ⁴² He said, 'Yes, and surely then you will indeed be among the ones brought near.' ⁴³ Moses said to them, 'Cast (down) what you are going to cast.' ⁴⁴ So they cast their ropes and their staffs, and said, 'By the honor of Pharaoh! Surely we shall be the victors indeed.' ⁴⁵ And then Moses cast his staff, and suddenly it swallowed up what they were falsely contriving. ⁴⁶ And the magicians were cast (down) in prostration. ⁴⁷ They said, 'We believe in the Lord of the worlds, ⁴⁸ the Lord of Moses and Aaron.' ⁴⁹ He said, 'You have believed in him before I gave you permission. Surely he is indeed your master, the (very) one who taught you magic. But soon indeed you will know! I shall indeed cut off your hands and your feet on opposite sides, and I shall indeed crucify you – all (of you)!' ⁵⁰ They said, 'No harm! Surely we are going to return to our Lord. ⁵¹ Surely we are eager that our Lord should forgive us our sins, because we are the first of the believers.'

⁵² And We inspired Moses: 'Journey with My servants. Surely you will be followed.' ⁵³ So Pharaoh sent searchers into the cities: ⁵⁴ 'Surely these (people) are indeed a small band, ⁵⁵ and surely they are indeed enraging us, ⁵⁶ but surely we are indeed all vigilant.' ⁵⁷ So We brought them forth from gardens and springs, ⁵⁸ and treasures and an honorable place. ⁵⁹ So (it was), and We caused the Sons of Israel to inherit them. ⁶⁰ So they followed them at sunrise, ⁶¹ and when the two forces saw each other, the companions of Moses said, 'Surely we are indeed overtaken!' ⁶² He said, 'By no means! Surely my Lord is with me. He will guide me.' ⁶³ And so We inspired Moses: 'Strike the sea with your staff!' And it parted, and each part was like a great mountain. ⁶⁴ We brought the others near to that place,

⁶⁵ and We rescued Moses and those who were with him – all (of them). ⁶⁶ Then We drowned the others. ⁶⁷ Surely in that is a sign indeed, but most of them do not believe. ⁶⁸ Surely your Lord – He indeed is the Mighty, the Compassionate.

⁶⁹ Recite to them the story of Abraham: ⁷⁰ When he said to his father and his people, 'What do you serve?' ⁷¹ They said, 'We serve idols, and continue (to be) devoted to them.' ⁷² He said, 'Do they hear you when you call, ⁷³ or do they benefit you or harm (you)?' ⁷⁴ They said, 'No! But we found our fathers doing so.' ⁷⁵ He said, 'Do you see what you have been serving, ⁷⁶ you and your fathers who preceded (you)? ⁷⁷ Surely they are an enemy to me – except the Lord of the worlds, ⁷⁸ who created me, and He guides me, ⁷⁹ and who – He gives me food and gives me drink, ⁸⁰ and when I am sick, He heals me. ⁸¹ He (it is) who causes me to die, (and) then gives me life, ⁸² and who – I am eager that He should forgive me my sin on the Day of Judgment. ⁸³ My Lord, grant me judgment, and join me with the righteous, ⁸⁴ and assign to me a good reputation among later (generations). ⁸⁵ Make me one of the inheritors of the Garden of Bliss. ⁸⁶ And forgive my father, (for) surely he is one of those who have gone astray. ⁸⁷ Do not disgrace me on the Day when they are raised up, ⁸⁸ the Day when neither wealth nor children will benefit (them), ⁸⁹ except for the one who comes to God with a sound heart. ⁹⁰ The Garden will be brought near for the ones who guard themselves, ⁹¹ and the Furnace will come forth for the ones who are in error. ⁹² And it will be said to them, "Where is what you were serving ⁹³ instead of God? (Can) they defend you or defend themselves?" ⁹⁴ And then they will be tossed into it – they and the ones who are in error – ⁹⁵ and the forces of Iblīs – all (of them). ⁹⁶ They will say, as they are disputing there, ⁹⁷ "By God! We were indeed far astray, ⁹⁸ when we

---

26.65 – *We rescued Moses and those who were with him*

The language of salvation (*anjā*) appears in several passages in this sūra, here in a story of Moses and later in stories of Noah and Lot. Frequently the deliverance of the messenger and "those with him" is accompanied by the destruction of those who resisted the message (e.g., v. 66). See "Salvation in the Quran" (p. 180).

26.69 – *Recite to them the story of Abraham*

Abraham challenges his father and his people about their worship of idols (vv. 70–77) and bears witness to the Creator – the "Lord of the worlds" (vv. 77–82). Abraham then prays for wisdom (v. 83) and asks forgiveness for his father (v. 86).

Here Abraham acknowledges his sin (*khaṭiʾa*) and his need for forgiveness (v. 82). See the analysis of the sins of prophets and messengers at 48.2 (p. 513).

Stories of Abraham's opposition to idolatry appear eight times in the Quran, each adding unique details. One striking difference between this version and the final version is Abraham's "hatred" for his people at 60.4. See "Abraham in the Quran" (p. 90).

made you equal with the Lord of the worlds. ⁹⁹ (It was) only the sinners who led us astray. ¹⁰⁰ (Now) we have no intercessors, ¹⁰¹ and no true friend. ¹⁰² If only we had (another) turn, and (could) be among the believers!'" ¹⁰³ Surely in that is a sign indeed, but most of them do not believe. ¹⁰⁴ Surely your Lord – He indeed is the Mighty, the Compassionate.

¹⁰⁵ The people of Noah called the envoys liars: ¹⁰⁶ When their brother Noah said to them, 'Will you not guard (yourselves)? ¹⁰⁷ Surely I am a trustworthy messenger for you, ¹⁰⁸ so guard (yourselves) against God and obey me. ¹⁰⁹ I do not ask you for any reward for it. My reward (depends) only on the Lord of the worlds. ¹¹⁰ Guard (yourselves) against God and obey me.' ¹¹¹ They said, 'Shall we believe you, when (only) the worst (people) follow you?' ¹¹² He said, 'What do I know about what they have done? ¹¹³ Their reckoning is only with my Lord, if (only) you realized (it). ¹¹⁴ I am not going to drive away the believers. ¹¹⁵ I am only a clear warner.' ¹¹⁶ They said, 'If indeed you do not stop, Noah, you will indeed be one of the stoned.' ¹¹⁷ He said, 'My Lord, surely my people have called me a liar, ¹¹⁸ so disclose (the truth) decisively between me and them, and rescue me and those of the believers who are with me.' ¹¹⁹ So We rescued him, and those who were with him, in the loaded ship. ¹²⁰ Then, after that, We drowned the rest. ¹²¹ Surely in that is a sign indeed, but most of them do not believe. ¹²² Surely your Lord – He indeed is the Mighty, the Compassionate.

¹²³ 'Ād called the envoys liars: ¹²⁴ When their brother Hūd said to them, 'Will you not guard (yourselves)? ¹²⁵ Surely I am a trustworthy messenger for you, ¹²⁶ so guard (yourselves) against God and obey me. ¹²⁷ I do not ask you for any reward for it. My reward (depends) only on the Lord of the worlds. ¹²⁸ Do you build a sign on every high place in vain, ¹²⁹ and take strongholds in the hope that you may remain there? ¹³⁰ And when you attack (someone), do you attack like tyrants? ¹³¹ Guard (yourselves) against God and obey me. ¹³² Guard (yourselves) against the One who has increased you with what you know. ¹³³ He has increased you with livestock

---

26.105 – *The people of Noah called the envoys liars*

In this version of the Noah story (vv. 105–20), the audience asks why they should believe Noah when only – in their opinion – the worst kind of people follow him. Noah replies that reckoning with the believers is God's concern, but Noah is hardly going to drive the believers away!

Other versions of the Noah story appear at 7.59–64; 10.71–73; 11.25–49; 23.23–30; 54.7–17; and 71.1–28. See the discussion of the Quran's repetition of stories at 51.24 (p. 526).

26.123–24 – *'Ād called the envoys liars: When their brother Hūd said to them*

On 'Ād and Hūd (vv. 123–39), see the explanation at 7.65 (p. 182).

and sons, ¹³⁴ and gardens and fountains. ¹³⁵ Surely I fear for you the punishment of a great day.' ¹³⁶ They said, '(It is) the same for us whether you admonish (us) or are not one of the admonishers. ¹³⁷ This is nothing but the creation of those of old. ¹³⁸ We are not going to be punished.' ¹³⁹ So they called him a liar, and We destroyed them. Surely in that is a sign indeed, but most of them do not believe. ¹⁴⁰ Surely your Lord – He indeed is the Mighty, the Compassionate.

¹⁴¹ Thamūd called the envoys liars: ¹⁴² When their brother Ṣāliḥ said to them, 'Will you not guard (yourselves)? ¹⁴³ Surely I am a trustworthy messenger for you, ¹⁴⁴ so guard (yourselves) against God and obey me. ¹⁴⁵ I do not ask you for any reward for it. My reward (depends) only on the Lord of the worlds. ¹⁴⁶ Will you be left secure in what is here, ¹⁴⁷ in gardens and springs, ¹⁴⁸ and (fields of) crops and date palms (with) its slender sheath? ¹⁴⁹ Will you (continue to) carve houses out of the mountains with skill? ¹⁵⁰ Guard (yourselves) against God and obey me. ¹⁵¹ Do not obey the command of the wanton, ¹⁵² those who foment corruption on the earth and do not set (things) right.' ¹⁵³ They said, 'You are only one of the bewitched. ¹⁵⁴ You are nothing but a human being like us. Bring (us) a sign, if you are one of the truthful.' ¹⁵⁵ He said, 'This is a she-camel: to her a drink and to you a drink, on a day made known. ¹⁵⁶ Do not touch her with evil, or the punishment of a great day will seize you.' ¹⁵⁷ But they wounded her, and morning found them full of regret, ¹⁵⁸ and the punishment seized them. Surely in that is a sign indeed, but most of them do not believe. ¹⁵⁹ Surely your Lord – He indeed is the Mighty, the Compassionate.

¹⁶⁰ The people of Lot called the envoys liars: ¹⁶¹ When their brother Lot said to them, 'Will you not guard (yourselves)? ¹⁶² Surely I am a trustworthy messenger for you, ¹⁶³ so guard (yourselves) against God and obey me. ¹⁶⁴ I do not ask you for any reward for it. My reward (depends) only on the Lord of the worlds. ¹⁶⁵ Do you approach the males of all peoples, ¹⁶⁶ and leave your wives whom your Lord created for you? Yes! You are a people who transgress!' ¹⁶⁷ They said, 'If indeed you do not stop, Lot, you will indeed be one of the expelled.' ¹⁶⁸ He said, 'Surely I am

---

26.141–42 – *Thamūd call the envoys liars: When their brother Ṣāliḥ said to them*
On Thamūd and Ṣāliḥ (vv. 141–158), see the comment at 7.73 (p. 183).

26.160 – *The people of Lot called the envoys liars*
Lot preaches to his people and asks them, "Do you approach the males of all peoples, and leave your wives whom your Lord created for you?" (vv. 165–66).

This passage (vv. 160–73) is the fourth of eight versions of the Lot story in the Quran and unique in indicating a concept of a created order that echoes Genesis 2. Another difference is that while the woman who is left behind is Lot's wife in the earlier three versions, here she is "an old woman" who stays behind (v. 171).

one of those who despise what you do. [169] My Lord, rescue me and my family from what they do.' [170] So We rescued him and his family – all (of them) – [171] except for an old woman among those who stayed behind. [172] Then We destroyed the others. [173] We rained down on them a rain, and evil was the rain on those who had been warned! [174] Surely in that is a sign indeed, but most of them do not believe. [175] Surely your Lord – He indeed is the Mighty, the Compassionate.

[176] The people of the Grove called the envoys liars: [177] When Shu'ayb said to them, 'Will you not guard (yourselves)? [178] I am a trustworthy messenger for you, [179] so guard (yourselves) against God and obey me. [180] I do not ask you for any reward for it. My reward (depends) only on the Lord of the worlds. [181] Fill up the measure, and do not be cheaters, [182] and weigh with the even scale, [183] and do not shortchange the people of their wealth, and do not act wickedly on the earth, fomenting corruption. [184] Guard (yourselves) against the One who created you and the multitudes of old.' [185] They said, 'You are only one of the bewitched. [186] You are nothing but a human being like us. Surely we think (that) you are indeed one of the liars. [187] Make fragments of the sky fall on us, if you are one of the truthful.' [188] He said, 'My Lord knows what you are doing.' [189] But they called him a liar, and the punishment of the Day of Shadow seized them. Surely it was the punishment of a great day. [190] Surely in that is a sign indeed, but most of them do not believe. [191] Surely your Lord – He indeed is the Mighty, the Compassionate.

[192] Surely it is indeed a sending down from the Lord of the worlds. [193] The trustworthy spirit has brought it down [194] on your heart, so that you may be one of the warners, [195] in a clear Arabic language. [196] Surely it is indeed in the scriptures of

---

26.176 – *The people of the Grove called the envoys liars: When Shu'ayb said to them*

On the people of the Grove and Shu'ayb (vv. 176–89), see the explanation at 7.85, also the discussion on repetition of stories in the Quran at 51.24 (p. 526).

26.192 – *Surely it is indeed a sending down from the Lord of the worlds*

The Quran returns to direct address to the messenger (as at v. 3), not only reassuring the messenger but also making the claim that his message is a "sending down" (*tanzīl*). This verse and the following verses are important for the Muslim doctrine of scripture. See a discussion of this theme at 85.21–22 (p. 624).

26.193–94 – *The trustworthy spirit has brought it down on your heart*

The Quran claims that the recitation comes to the messenger by way of "the trustworthy [or faithful] spirit." Elsewhere Gabriel (2.97) or the holy spirit (16.102) brings the recitation down. This may be one reason why many Muslim commentators equate the spirit with Gabriel. On "spirit" (*rūḥ*) in the Quran, see the analysis at 97.4 (p. 639).

26.195 – *in a clear Arabic language*

Verses that highlight the Arabic nature of the recitation often become very

those of old. [197] Was it not a sign for them that it was known to the learned of the Sons of Israel? [198] If We had sent it down on one of the foreigners, [199] and he had recited it to them, they would not have believed in it. [200] In this way We put it into the hearts of the sinners. [201] They will not believe in it until they see the painful punishment, [202] and it will come upon them unexpectedly, when they do not realize (it), [203] and they will say, 'Are we going to be spared?' [204] Do they seek to hurry Our punishment? [205] Have you considered? If We give them enjoyment (of life) for (some) years, [206] (and) then what they were promised comes upon them, [207] what use will the enjoyment they were given be to them? [208] We have not destroyed any town without its having warners [209] as a reminder. We have not been evildoers.

[210] The satans have not brought it down. [211] It is not fitting for them (to do), nor are they able (to). [212] Surely they are removed indeed from the hearing (of it). [213] Do not call on another god (along) with God, or you will be one of the punished. [214] Warn your clan, [215] and lower your wing to whoever follows you of the believers. [216] If they disobey you, say: 'I am free of what you do.' [217] Put your trust in the Mighty, the Compassionate, [218] who sees you when you stand, [219] and when you turn about among the ones who prostrate themselves. [220] Surely He – He is the Hearing, the Knowing.

[221] Shall I inform you on whom the satans come down? [222] They come down on every liar (and) sinner. [223] They listen attentively, but most of them are liars. [224] And the poets – the ones who are in error follow them. [225] Do you not see that they wander in every wādī, [226] and that they say what they do not do? [227] – except for those who believe, and do righteous deeds, and remember God often, and defend themselves after they have suffered evil. Those who have done evil will come to know what a complete overturning they will suffer.

---

important in the claims the Quran makes for itself. In the context of the following two verses, the description "clear Arabic language" seems to suggest a claim to be an Arabic version of the message of earlier scriptures. See the analysis of claims for "Arabic" at 43.2–3 (p. 487).

26.196 – *Surely it is indeed in the scriptures of those of old*

This verse seems to represent a positive view of the pre-Islamic scriptures (*zubur*), as well as an appeal to the earlier scriptures for authority. The following verse, which indicates that the learned men (*'ulamā'*) among the Children of Israel "knew" (perhaps the stories presented in this sūra?), also suggests a positive attitude toward the Jews.

26.224 – *And the poets – the ones who are in error follow them*

On the negative sense of the word *poets* in the Quran, see the comment at 21.5 (p. 331). This passage characterizes poets as leading people astray and not practicing what they preach (v. 226). The word *poets* gives this sūra its name.

THE ANT
AL-NAML

27

The name of this sūra, "the Ant," comes from a curious story about Solomon. Solomon musters his forces for review, including *jinn*, men, and birds. As the forces advance, Solomon overhears an ant telling his fellow ants to run for cover.

Apart from this story, the sūra contains a second version of the burning bush story and stories about Ṣāliḥ and Lot. Preceding and following this set of stories, the Quran claims to provide guidance for the believers and portrays a scene of controversy between the messenger and an audience that does not accept his preaching.

Like several other sūras of this type, this sūra contains a striking appeal to the presence and power of the Creator. The last part of the sūra presents a scenario of the "Day" on which all human communities will be gathered for judgment.

In the Name of God, the Merciful, the Compassionate

[1] Ṭā' Sīn. Those are the signs of the Qur'ān and a clear Book, [2] a guidance and good news for the believers, [3] who observe the prayer and give the alms, and they are certain of the Hereafter. [4] Those who do not believe in the Hereafter – We have made their deeds appear enticing to them, and they wander blindly. [5] Those are the ones for whom (there is) an evil punishment, and in the Hereafter they will be the worst losers. [6] Surely you have indeed received the Qur'ān from One (who is) wise, knowing.

[7] (Remember) when Moses said to his family: 'Surely I perceive a fire. I shall bring you some news of it, or I shall bring you a flame – a torch – so that you may

---

27.1 – *Ṭā' Sīn. Those are the signs of the Qur'ān and a clear Book*

On the disconnected Arabic letters that begin this sūra, see the comment at 2.1. The Quran claims to be "a guidance" (v. 2) that the messenger receives (v. 6). See "Different Kinds of Literature" (p. 14). On the word *qur'ān*, see the comment at 2.185 (p. 61).

27.7 – *when Moses said to his family: "Surely I perceive a fire . . ."*

This second version of the burning bush episode (vv. 7–13) is unique in the

warm yourselves.' [8] But when he came to it, he was called: 'Blessed is He who is in the fire, and whoever is around it. Glory to God, Lord of the worlds! [9] Moses! Surely I am God, the Mighty, the Wise.' [10] And: 'Cast (down) your staff!' When he saw it wiggling as if it were a snake, he turned around, retreating, and did not look back. 'Moses! Do not fear! Surely in My presence the envoys do not fear [11] – except for the one who has done evil, (and) then has exchanged good after evil – surely I am forgiving, compassionate. [12] Put your hand inside your cloak. It will come out white, unharmed – (these are two) among nine signs for Pharaoh and his people. Surely they are a wicked people.' [13] But when Our signs came to them visibly, they said, 'This is clear magic.' [14] They denied them, even though they were convinced of them in themselves, out of evil and haughtiness. See how the end was for the fomenters of corruption!

[15] Certainly We gave David and Solomon knowledge, and they said, 'Praise (be) to God, who has favored us over many of His believing servants!' [16] Solomon inherited (it) from David, and said, 'People! We have been taught the speech of birds, and we have been given (some) of everything. Surely this – it indeed is clear favor.' [17] Gathered before Solomon were his forces – jinn, and men, and birds – and they were arranged (in rows) [18] – until, when they came upon the Wādī of the Ants, an ant said, 'Ants! Enter your dwellings, or Solomon and his forces will crush you without realizing (it).' [19] But he smiled, laughing at its words, and said, 'My Lord, (so) dispose me that I may be thankful for your blessing with which You have blessed me and my parents, and that I may do righteousness (that) pleases You, and cause me to enter, by Your mercy, among your righteous servants.'

[20] He reviewed the birds, and said, 'Why do I not see the hudhud? Or is it one of the absent? [21] I shall indeed punish it severely, or slaughter it, or it will

number of names it gives for God. Moses addresses God as *Allah* and "Lord of the worlds" (*rabb al-ʿālamīn*) in verse 8, while Allah describes himself as "the Mighty" (*ʿazīz*) and "the Wise" (*ḥakīm*) in verse 9 and as "forgiving" (*ghafūr*) and "compassionate" (*raḥīm*) in verse 11.

The two other versions of the burning bush story are at 20:10–48 and 28:29–35.

27.15 – *Certainly We gave David and Solomon knowledge*

The Quran introduces David and Solomon once more (see 21.78–82), but the following substantial passage (27.16–44) is really all about Solomon. Their "knowledge" includes the language of birds (v. 16).

27.17 – *Gathered before Solomon were his forces – jinn, and men, and birds*

Solomon not only knows the language of birds (v. 16), but the language of ants as well (vv. 18–19). A hoopoe bird arrives late to Solomon's review of the birds. For the Quran's concept of *jinn*, see the summary at 72.1 (p. 593).

bring me a clear authority.' ²² But it did not stay (away) for long, and said, 'I have encompassed what you have not encompassed, and I have brought you reliable news from (the people of) Sheba. ²³ Surely I found a woman ruling over them, and she has been given (some) of everything, and she has a great throne. ²⁴ I found her and her people prostrating themselves before the sun instead of God. Satan has made their deeds appear enticing to them, and he has kept them from the way, and they are not (rightly) guided. ²⁵ (He did this) so that they would not prostrate themselves before God, who brings forth what is hidden in the heavens and the earth. He knows what you hide and what you speak aloud. ²⁶ God – (there is) no god but Him, Lord of the great throne.' ²⁷ He said, 'We shall see whether you have spoken the truth or are one of the liars. ²⁸ Go with this letter of mine, and cast it (down) to them. Then turn away from them and see what they return.'

²⁹ She said, 'Assembly! Surely an honorable letter has been cast (down) to me. ³⁰ Surely it is from Solomon, and surely it (reads): "In the Name of God, the Merciful, the Compassionate. ³¹ Do not exalt yourselves over me, but come to me in surrender."' ³² She said, 'Assembly! Make a pronouncement to me about my affair. I do not decide any affair until you bear me witness.' ³³ They said, 'We are full of strength and full of harsh violence, but the affair (belongs) to you. See what you will command.' ³⁴ She said, 'Surely kings, when they enter a town, corrupt it, and make the upper class of its people the lowest, and that is what they will do. ³⁵ Surely I am going to send a gift to them, and see what the envoys bring back.'

³⁶ When he came to Solomon, he said, 'Would you increase me with wealth, when what God has given me is better than what He has given you? No! (It is) you (who) gloat over your own gift. ³⁷ Return to them! We shall indeed come upon them with forces which they have no power to face, and we shall indeed expel them from there in humiliation, and they will be disgraced.' ³⁸ He said, 'Assembly! Which of you will bring me her throne before they come to me in surrender?' ³⁹ A crafty one of the jinn said, 'I shall bring it to you before you (can)

27.22 – *I have brought you reliable news from (the people of) Sheba*

A hoopoe bird tells Solomon about a woman who rules over the people of Sheba (*Sabā'*, vv. 23–26). In the passage that follows, Solomon sends a letter to the people of Sheba via the hoopoe (vv. 28–32), the queen sends a gift to Solomon (vv. 35–36), and the people of Sheba end up surrendering to Solomon and his Lord (vv. 39–44). The only other mention of the people of Sheba in the Quran is at 34.15–19, but there the queen does not appear.

27.30 – *In the name of God, the Merciful, the Compassionate*

Solomon's letter to the queen of Sheba starts with the Islamic *basmala*.

rise from your place. Surely I have strength for it (and am) trustworthy.' [40] One who had knowledge of the Book said, 'I will bring it to you in the wink of an eye.' So when he saw it set before him, he said, 'This is from the favor of my Lord to test me (to see) whether I am thankful or ungrateful. Whoever is thankful is thankful only for his own good, and whoever is ungrateful – surely my Lord is wealthy, generous.' [41] He said, 'Disguise her throne for her. We shall see whether she is (rightly) guided or is one of those who are not (rightly) guided.' [42] So when she came, it was said, 'Is your throne like this?' She said, 'It seems like it.' 'And we had been given the knowledge before her, and were in surrender, [43] but what she served, instead of God, kept her back. Surely she was from a disbelieving people.' [44] It was said to her, 'Enter the palace.' When she saw it, she thought it was a pool (of water), and she uncovered her legs. He said, 'Surely it is a polished palace of crystal.' She said, 'My Lord, surely I have done myself evil. I surrender with Solomon to God, Lord of the worlds.'

[45] Certainly We sent to Thamūd their brother Ṣāliḥ: 'Serve God!' And suddenly they were two groups disputing each other. [46] He said, 'My people! Why do you seek to hurry the evil before the good? Why do you not ask forgiveness from God, so that you may receive compassion?' [47] They said, 'We have an evil omen about you and those who are with you.' He said, 'Your evil omen is with God. But you are a people being tested!' [48] In the city (there) was a group of nine persons who were fomenting corruption on the earth, and not setting (things) right. [49] They said, 'Swear to each other by God, "We shall indeed attack him and his family by night." Then we shall indeed say to his ally, "We were not witnesses of the destruction of his family" and "Surely we are truthful indeed."' [50] They schemed a scheme, but We (too) schemed a scheme, though they did not realize (it). [51] See how the end of their scheme was: We destroyed them and their people – all (of them)! [52] Those are their houses, collapsed because of the evil they did. Surely in that is a sign indeed for a people who know. [53] And We rescued those who believed and guarded (themselves).

[54] And Lot, when he said to his people: 'Do you commit immorality with

---

27.45 – *Certainly We sent to Thamūd their brother Ṣāliḥ*

This version of the story of Ṣāliḥ and Thamūd (vv. 45–53) is almost completely different from the other five versions of the story in the Quran, lacking the distinctive "camel of Allah" and reference to the particular punishment that came to the people. On the basic story of Ṣāliḥ and Thamūd, see the comment at 7.73 (p. 183).

27.54 – *And Lot, when he said to his people: "Do you commit immorality...?"*

Lot asks his people, "Do you indeed approach men with lust instead of women?" (v. 55) and describes their intention as "immorality." Allah decrees that the wife of Lot

your eyes open? ⁵⁵ Do you indeed approach men with lust instead of women? But you are an ignorant people!' ⁵⁶ The only response of his people was that they said, 'Expel the house(hold) of Lot from your town, (for) surely they are men who keep themselves clean.' ⁵⁷ So We rescued him and his family, except for his wife. We decreed that she (would be) one of those who stayed behind. ⁵⁸ And We rained down on them a rain. Evil was the rain on those who had been warned!

⁵⁹ Say: 'Praise (be) to God, and peace (be) upon His servants whom He has chosen!' Is God better, or what they associate? ⁶⁰ Or (is He not better) who created the heavens and earth, and sent down water from the sky for you, and then by means of it We cause orchards to grow, full of beauty, whose trees you could never grow? (Is there any other) god with God? No! But they are a people who equate (others to Him). ⁶¹ Or (is He not better) who made the earth a dwelling place, and placed rivers in the midst of it, and made firm mountains for it, and placed a partition between the two seas? (Is there any other) god with God? No! But most of them do not know (it). ⁶² Or (is He not better) who responds to the distressed (person) when he calls on Him and removes the evil, and establishes you as successors on the earth? (Is there any other) god with God? Little do you take heed! ⁶³ Or (is He not better) who guides you in the darkness of the shore and the sea, and who sends the winds as good news before His mercy? (Is there any other) god with God? God is exalted above what they associate! ⁶⁴ Or (is He not better) who brings about the creation, (and) then restores it, and who provides for you from the sky and the earth? (Is there any other) god with God? Say: 'Bring your proof, if you are truthful.'

⁶⁵ Say: 'No one in the heavens or the earth knows the unseen except God. They do not realize when they will be raised up. ⁶⁶ No! Their knowledge is confused concerning the Hereafter. No! They are in doubt about it. No! They are blind to it.'

⁶⁷ Those who disbelieve say, 'When we have become dust, and our fathers (too), shall we indeed be brought forth? ⁶⁸ Certainly we have been promised this before, we and our fathers. This is nothing but old tales.' ⁶⁹ Say: 'Travel the earth and see how the end was for the sinners.' ⁷⁰ Do not sorrow over them, nor be in distress because of what they are scheming.

---

will stay behind (v. 57) when the "rain" begins to fall. This is the fifth of eight versions of the Lot story in the Quran.

27.59 – *Is God better, or what they associate?*

This verse begins a striking passage of preaching (vv. 59–66), appealing to the audience with probing theological questions and repeating the refrain, "(Is there any other) god with Allah?" (e.g., v. 60).

⁷¹ They say, 'When (will) this promise (come to pass), if you are truthful?' ⁷² Say: 'It may be that part of what you seek to hurry is bearing down on you (now).' ⁷³ Surely your Lord is indeed full of favor to the people, but most of them are not thankful (for it). ⁷⁴ Surely your Lord indeed knows what their hearts conceal and what they speak aloud. ⁷⁵ (There is) nothing hidden in the sky or the earth, except (that it is recorded) in a clear Book.

⁷⁶ Surely this Qur'ān recounts to the Sons of Israel most of their differences, ⁷⁷ and surely it is indeed a guidance and mercy to the believers. ⁷⁸ Surely your Lord will decide between them by His judgment. He is the Mighty, the Knowing. ⁷⁹ Put your trust in God, (for) surely you (stand) on the clear truth. ⁸⁰ Surely you cannot make the dead to hear, nor can you make the deaf to hear the call, when they turn away, withdrawing. ⁸¹ Nor can you guide the blind out of their straying. You cannot make (anyone) hear, except the one who believes in Our signs, and so they submit.

⁸² When the word falls upon them, We shall bring forth for them a creature from the earth, (which) will speak to them: 'The people were not certain of Our signs.' ⁸³ On the Day when We shall gather from every community a crowd of those who have called Our signs a lie, and they are arranged (in rows) ⁸⁴ – until, when they come, He will say, 'Did you call My signs a lie, when you did not encompass them in knowledge, or what (it was) you were doing?' ⁸⁵ And the word will fall upon them because of the evil they have done, and they will not speak.

⁸⁶ Do they not see that We made the night for them to rest in, and the day to see? Surely in that are signs indeed for a people who believe. ⁸⁷ On the Day when there is a blast on the trumpet, and whoever is in the heavens and whoever is on the earth will be terrified, except for whomever God pleases, and all will come to Him humbled, ⁸⁸ and you see the mountains, supposedly solid, yet passing by (as) the clouds pass by – (such is) the work of God who has perfected everything.

27.76 – *Surely this Qur'ān recounts to the Sons of Israel most of their differences*

In this self-referential statement the Quran seems to claim that it not only tells stories known from the Hebrew Bible but also corrects the Jews. On the differences among the People of the Book, see the discussion at 98.4 (p. 642), and on the word *qur'ān* see the comment at 2.185 (p. 61).

27.79 – *Put your trust in God, (for) surely you (stand) on the clear truth*

Much of the remainder of the sūra is directly addressed to the messenger, claiming truth for him, describing the limitations of his preaching (vv. 80–81, 91–92), and encouraging him with the assurance of judgment to come for those who resist his preaching (vv. 83–90).

Surely He is aware of what you do. [89] (On that Day) whoever brings a good (deed) will have a better one than it, and they will be secure from the terror of that Day. [90] But whoever brings an evil (deed), they will be cast down face first into the Fire: 'Are you repaid (for anything) except for what you have done?'

[91] 'I have only been commanded to serve the Lord of this land, who has made it sacred. To Him everything (belongs). And I have been commanded to be one of those who submit, [92] and to recite the Qur'ān. Whoever is (rightly) guided is guided only for himself, and whoever goes astray [...].' Say: 'I am only one of the warners.' [93] And say: 'Praise (be) to God! He will show you His signs and you will recognize them. Your Lord is not oblivious of what you do.'

THE STORY
AL-QAṢAṢ

28

This sūra is known as "The Story" (*al-qaṣaṣ*), and at this point in reading through the Quran, the reader certainly will have noticed the high number of narrative passages (and perhaps also wonder at the frequent repetition of stories). More than half of this sūra contains one of the most extensive and detailed versions of the Moses story in the Quran. The sūra later returns to the time of Moses to tell a story about Korah.

After stating that Allah gave the "Book" to Moses, the sūra claims that the Quran's messenger now receives a similar revelation for a people who had no previous warning. The response of the listeners, however, is mixed. Some say they disbelieve in both books, which they call "two magics." In this case it is the People of the Book who say they believe in the recitations.

In the Name of God, the Merciful, the Compassionate

¹ Ṭā' Sīn Mīm. ² Those are the signs of the clear Book.

³ We recite to you some of the story of Moses and Pharaoh in truth, for a people who believe: ⁴ Surely Pharaoh had exalted himself on the earth, and divided its people (into) parties, weakening one contingent of them (by) slaughtering their sons and sparing their women. Surely he was one of the fomenters

---

28.1 – *Ṭā' Sīn Mīm. Those are the signs of the clear Book*

On the disconnected Arabic letters that begin this sūra, see the comment at 2.1. The sūra opens with a claim that it is made up of verses or "signs" (*āyāt*) of a clarifying book.

28.3 – *We recite to you some of the story of Moses and Pharaoh in truth*

Set right at the beginning of this sūra is one of the four longest passages about Moses and the Children of Israel (vv. 3–46). This version follows the chronology of the biblical account more closely than any other. Note the new narrative elements: Pharaoh's wife asks that baby Moses be spared (v. 9), and Pharaoh tells Haman to build a tower (v. 38).

of corruption. [5] But We wanted to bestow favor on those who were weak on the earth, and make them leaders, and make them the inheritors, [6] and to establish them on the earth, and show Pharaoh and Haman, and their forces, what they had to beware of from them.

Moses in the Quran
Gordon Nickel

The material on Moses in the Quran is abundant, varied, and interesting. His name appears some 136 times. Verses related to Moses number more than 500 in a book of just over 6,000 verses, and 36 of the Quran's 114 *sūras* mention Moses in 50 separate passages. This is more material than exists about any other figure: more than twice as much as the material on Abraham, the next most-mentioned figure; and more than five times the material on 'Īsā.

Even more striking than this abundance is the special profile that the Quran gives to Moses. In the canonical progression of the Quran this is first signaled in the fourth *sūra*, when after a list of names of prophets that appear repeatedly, we read, "[Allah] spoke to Moses directly" (4.164). Further on, in a scene of divine revelation to Moses, Allah says, "Moses, I have chosen you over the people for My messages and for My word" (7.144). Later, the quranic voice declares about Moses, "We called him from the right side of the mountain, and We brought him near in conversation" (19.52). Still later, in the midst of another extensive Moses narrative, Allah says to Moses, "I cast love (*maḥabba*) on you from Me" (20.39). This is the only appearance of this particular noun for love, *maḥabba*, in the Quran. Finally, a couple of verses after this, Allah says to Moses, "I have brought you up for Myself" (20.41).

These are remarkable expressions in the context of the Quran. In fact, none of these expressions occur in association with any other figure. John Wansbrough concluded from these passages, "The [quranic] scriptural

---

28.6 – *and to establish them on the earth, and show Pharaoh and Haman*

The Quran pairs Haman with Pharaoh in this sūra at verses 6, 8, and 38 and elsewhere at 29.39; 40.24; and 40.36. In the Bible, Hāmān (with the very same pronunciation) is a character in the story of Esther at a very different period in Israel's history (e.g., Est. 3:1).

material may be enlisted to support the particular position of Moses in the prophetical hierarchy, but hardly that of Muhammad." Wansbrough means that the name Muhammad only appears four times in the Quran, in striking contrast to the name Moses (see Wansbrough's *Quranic Studies* in the bibliography).

However, Moses and the messenger, traditionally understood to be Muhammad, come together in the middle of one of the Quran's longest Moses narratives at 7.156. The verses leading up to 156 are among the highest accolades of any prophet: Moses spoke with Allah, saw Allah's splendor, and was chosen over all people. Immediately before verse 156, Moses receives the tablets a second time, "and in their inscription (there was) a guidance and mercy for those who fear their Lord" (v. 154). At verse 157, however, the subject changes to the "*ummi* prophet," whom the Quran claims would be found "written with them in the Torah and the Gospel." Verses 157–58 include the following: a call to follow this messenger, who will make law; a first-person declaration of being Allah's messenger; and a command to believe in Allah's messenger before returning to Moses and his people.

Does the Quran use its picture of the ultimate prophetic figure to launch a new figure, here called the *ummi* prophet, and to assert his authority? Another tantalizing suggestion of this possibility is the way that shortly after promising punishment to those "those who hurt (*ādhā*) God and his messenger" (33.57), the Quran uses the very same verb in 33.69: "Do not be like those who hurt Moses, but Allah cleared him of what they said, and he was eminent in the sight of Allah" (see also 61.5).

The accompanying table gives an idea of the contents of thirteen of the Quran's most important Moses passages. Down the left-hand side are listed twenty of the narrative elements in the Torah account of Moses. Thirteen Quran passages about Moses are listed across the top. The numbers in each vertical column show which narrative elements from the Torah list are included in each Quran passage. The order of the numbers in each column indicates the sequence of the elements in each Quran passage. The asterisks beside the numbers in the vertical column under 44.17-33 indicate narrative elements in a Moses passage that does not include his name.

Across the bottom of the table is a list of narrative elements that are not part of the Torah account. This table raises many intriguing questions about the Quran's Moses passages and their differences, as well as about the ways in which the many narrative elements found their way into the Quran.

NARRATIVE ELEMENTS	Sura 2.49-93	5.20-26	7.103-71	10.75-93
I. Baby Moses saved				
II. Moses kills a man				
III. Moses' sojourn in Midian				
IV. Moses sees a fire				
V. God encounters Moses				
VI. God sends Moses to Pharaoh			1	1
VII. Moses asks for help from Aaron				
VIII. Scene in Pharaoh's court			2	2
IX. God sends the plagues			3	
X. God tells Moses to lead Israel out of Egypt				
XI. God delivers the Children of Israel	1		4, 5	3
XII. God sends manna and quails	5		12	
XIII. Moses draws water from rock	7		11	
XIV. Moses goes away for 40 nights	2		6	
XV. Moses appoints 70 leaders			10	
XVI. God gives Moses the Tablets			8	
XVII. God gives Moses 'the Book'	4, 10			
XVIII. Children of Israel worship a calf	3, 11		9	
XIX. Moses asks to see God			7	
XX. Moses commands to enter the land		1		

	Sura 2.49-93	5.20-26	7.103-71	10.75-93
A. Allah says enter a township prostrate	6		13	
B. Allah raises a "mount" above the people	8, 12		15	
C. Children of Israel transgress the Sabbath	9		14	
D. Pharaoh believes before he dies				4
E. Moses follows a strange riddling "servant"				
F. A Samaritan leads the people astray				
G. Pharaoh's wife asks that Moses be spared				
H. Pharaoh tells Haman to build a tower				
I. Haman and Qarun present with Pharaoh				
J. A "believer" defends Moses in court				

18.60-82	20.9-98	26.10-66	27.7-14	28.3-46	37.114-21	40.23-54	44.17-33	79.15-25
	5			1				
	6			3				
	7			4				
	1		1	5				
	2		2	6				1
	3, 8	1				1	1*	2
	4	2		7				
	9	3	3	8		3	2*	3
	10	4					3*	
	11	5		10	1		4*	
	12							
				11	2	6		
	14							
1								
	13							
				2				
				9		5		
						2		
						4		

* These narrative elements occur in a Moses story that does not mention Moses' name.

 [7] We inspired Moses' mother: 'Nurse him, and when you fear for him, cast him into the sea, but do not fear and do not sorrow. Surely We are going to return him to you, and make him one of the envoys.' [8] And the house of Pharaoh picked him up, so that he might be an enemy to them and a (cause of) sorrow. Surely Pharaoh and Haman, and their forces, were sinners. [9] The wife of Pharaoh said, '(He is) a comfort to me and to you. Do not kill him! It may be that he will benefit us, or we may adopt him as a son.' But they did not realize (what they were doing). [10] The next day the heart of Moses' mother was empty. She would almost have betrayed him, if We had not strengthened her heart, so that she might be one of the believers. [11] She said to his sister, 'Follow him.' So she watched him on the sly, though they did not realize (it). [12] Before (this) We had forbidden any wet nurses for him, so she said, 'Shall I direct you to the people of a household who will take charge of him for you, and look after him?' [13] And We returned him to his mother, so that she might be comforted and not sorrow, and that she might know that the promise of God is true. But most of them do not know (it). [14] When he reached his maturity and established (himself), We gave him judgment and knowledge. In this way We reward the doers of good.

 [15] He entered the city at a time when its people were oblivious, and in it he found two men fighting: the one of his (own) party, and the other of his enemies. The one who was of his (own) party called him for help against the one who was of his enemies. So Moses struck him, and finished him off. He said, 'This is the work of Satan. Surely he is a clear enemy (who) leads (people) astray.' [16] He said, 'My Lord, surely I have done myself evil. Forgive me!' So God forgave him. Surely He – He is the Forgiving, the Compassionate. [17] He said, 'My Lord, because of the blessing with which You have blessed me, I shall not be a supporter of the sinners.'

 [18] The next day he was in the city, afraid (and) watchful, when suddenly the one who had sought his help the day before cried out to him for help (again). Moses said to him, 'Surely you are in error indeed!' [19] But when he was about to attack the one who was an enemy to them both, he said, 'Moses! Do you intend to kill me as you killed (that) person yesterday? You only want to be a tyrant

---

28.9 – *(He is) a comfort to me and to you*

Pharaoh's wife steps in to urge the Pharaoh not to kill the baby Moses.

28.16 – *He said, "My Lord, surely I have done myself evil. Forgive me!"*

Moses strikes and kills a man (v. 15). He then acknowledges his guilt (*ẓalamtu nafsī*) and asks his Lord for forgiveness. When Allah forgives him, Moses promises not to support sinners (v. 17). See the analysis of the sin of prophets and messengers at 48.2 (p. 513).

on the earth, and you do not want to be one of those who set (things) right.'
²⁰ And (just then) a man came running from the farthest part of the city. He said, 'Moses! Surely the assembly is taking counsel about you, to kill you. So get out! Surely I am one of your trusty advisers.' ²¹ So he went forth from it, afraid (and) watchful. He said, 'My Lord, rescue me from the people who are evildoers.'

²² When he turned his face toward Midian, he said, 'It may be that my Lord will guide me to the right way.' ²³ And when he came to the water of Midian, he found by it a community of the people watering (their flocks), and besides them he found two women driving off their flocks. He said, 'What is the matter with you two?' They said, 'We may not water (our flocks) until the shepherds drive off (their flocks), and our father is very old.' ²⁴ So he watered (their flocks) for them. Then he turned aside to the shade, and said, 'My Lord, surely I am in need of whatever good You may send down to me.' ²⁵ Then one of the two women came to him, walking shyly. She said, 'My father calls you, so that he may pay you a reward for your watering (our flocks) for us.' When he had come to him and recounted the story to him, he said, 'Do not fear! You have escaped from the people who are evildoers.' ²⁶ One of the two women said, 'My father! Hire him, (for) surely the best man whom you can hire is the strong (and) the trustworthy one.' ²⁷ He said, 'Surely I wish to marry you to one of these two daughters of mine, on (the condition) that you hire yourself to me for eight years. But if you complete ten, that will be of your own accord, (for) I am not about to make it a hardship for you. You will find me, if God pleases, one of the righteous.' ²⁸ He said, 'That is between me and you. No matter which of the two terms I fulfill, (let there be) no enmity against me. God is guardian over what we say.'

²⁹ When Moses had fulfilled the term and traveled with his family, he perceived a fire on the side of the mountain. He said to his family, 'Stay (here). Surely I perceive a fire. Perhaps I shall bring you some news of it, or some wood from the fire, so that you may warm yourselves.' ³⁰ But when he came to it, he was called out to from the right side of the wādī, in the blessed hollow, from the tree:

28.27 – *on (the condition) that you hire yourself to me for eight years*

The man from Midian in the biblical account is named Jethro (Exodus 2:15–3:1). Some scholars make a connection between Jethro and the quranic Shuʿayb, because Midian was the people to whom Shuʿayb was sent. On Shuʿayb, see the comment at 7.85.

28.29 – *he perceived a fire on the side of the mountain*

This third of three versions of the burning bush episode (vv. 29–35) is the only one that specifies that Moses was called from the tree on "the right side of the wādī, in the blessed hollow" (v. 30). Here God introduces himself as Allah, "Lord of the

'Moses! Surely I am God, Lord of the worlds.' ³¹ And: 'Cast (down) your staff!' And when he saw it wiggling as if it were a snake, he turned around, retreating, and did not look back. 'Moses! Come forward and do not fear! Surely you are one of the secure. ³² Put your hand into your cloak. It will come out white, unharmed. Now draw your hand to your side from fear. Those are two proofs from your Lord for Pharaoh and his assembly. Surely they are a wicked people.' ³³ He said, 'My Lord, surely I have killed one of them, and I fear that they will kill me. ³⁴ My brother Aaron – he is more eloquent than me in speech. Send him with me as a support (who) will confirm me. Surely I fear that they will call me a liar.' ³⁵ He said, 'We shall strengthen your arm by means of your brother, and give authority to both of you, so that they will be no match for you because of Our signs. You two, and whoever follows you, will be the victors.'

³⁶ When Moses brought them Our clear signs, they said, 'This is nothing but a magic trick. We have not heard of this among our fathers of old.' ³⁷ But Moses said, 'My Lord knows who brings the guidance from Him, and to whom the final Home (belongs). Surely the evildoers will not prosper.' ³⁸ Pharaoh said, 'Assembly! I know of no other god for you than me. So light a fire for me, Haman, on the clay, and make a tower for me, so that I may look at the god of Moses. Surely I think he is indeed one of the liars.' ³⁹ He and his forces became arrogant on the earth without any right, and thought that they would not be returned to Us. ⁴⁰ So We seized him and his forces, and tossed them into the sea. See how the end was for the evildoers! ⁴¹ We made them leaders (who) call (others) to the Fire, and on the Day of Resurrection they will not be helped. ⁴² We pursued them in this world with a curse, and on the Day of Resurrection they will be among the scorned.

⁴³ Certainly We gave Moses the Book, after We had destroyed the former

---

worlds." Compare this with the other two versions of this story found at 20:10–48 and 27:7–12.

Because the biblical account of Moses and the burning bush (Exodus 3) is so important for God's call of Moses and the Children of Israel, some readers may be interested to compare the names God gives for himself in the two scriptures. The Quran does not come close to the name God gives in the Torah account: "I AM WHO I AM," or "Yahweh" (Exodus 3:14). However, the Quran gives God several meaningful names in its versions, especially at 27.8–11, and the three passages indicate a great deal of divine affection toward Moses.

28.38 – *So light a fire for me, Haman, on the clay, and make a tower for me*
Pharaoh commands Haman to build a tower in a way that seems to echo some parts of the Tower of Babel story in Genesis 11.

generations, as evidence for the people, and a guidance and mercy, so that they might take heed. [44] You were not on the western side when We decreed the command to Moses, nor were you among the witnesses. [45] But We produced (other) generations, and life was prolonged for them. You were not dwelling among the people of Midian, reciting to them Our signs, when We were sending (messengers). [46] You were not on the side of the mountain when We called out (to Moses), but (you were sent) as a mercy from your Lord, so that you might warn a people to whom no warner had come before you, so that they might take heed. [47] If (it were) not that a smiting might smite them for what their hands have sent forward, and (that) they might say, 'Our Lord, why did You not send a messenger to us, so that we might have followed Your signs, and (so) been among the believers [. . .]?' [48] Yet when the truth did come to them from Us, they said, 'If only he were given the same as what Moses was given.' Did they not disbelieve in what was given to Moses before? They said, 'Two magic (tricks) supporting each other,' and they said, 'Surely we are disbelievers in all (of it).' [49] Say: 'Bring a Book from God that is a better guide than these two – I shall follow it, if you are truthful.' [50] If they do not respond to you, know that they are only following their (vain) desires. And who is farther astray than the one who follows his

---

28.44 – *You were not on the western side when We decreed the command to Moses*

The Quran says to the messenger that he was not present in Egypt during the time of Moses to witness the events of verses 3–42. The implication seems to be that this story must have been revealed by Allah to the messenger. This matches the claim in verse 3 that it is Allah who "recites" this story to the messenger (also 12.3).

This is the most extensive of such passages in the Quran, with "You were not . . ." in verses 45 and 46 as well. Similar statements appear at 3.44 (story of Mary); 11.49 (Noah); and 12.102 (Joseph). Several of the statements add that Allah "reveals" or "inspires" the story in the messenger, and 11.49 specifies that neither the messenger nor his people knew the story prior to its recitation by the messenger.

In response: How effective is this claim for a divine source? The Quran's versions of biblical stories provide enough familiar parts to show that these are the same basic stories. But does this prove that the quranic versions are inspired? Moses stories circulated widely in the Middle East during the seventh century. And what about the evidence of details in the Quran's versions that are not in the Bible but are also found in Jewish rabbinic or Christian apocryphal writings from before the seventh century?

28.49 – *Bring a Book from God that is a better guide than these two*

The audience does not believe that the messenger's recitation is true. The Quran commands the messenger to challenge the audience to compose a book, or "writing" (*kitāb*), like the recitation. Similar challenges appear at 2.23; 10.38; 11.13; 17.88;

desire without guidance from God? Surely God does not guide the people who are evildoers. ⁵¹ Certainly We have caused the word to reach them, so that they may take heed.

⁵² Those to whom We gave the Book before it – they believe in it. ⁵³ When it is recited to them, they say, 'We believe in it. Surely it is the truth from our Lord. Surely we were Muslims before it.' ⁵⁴ Those – they will be given their reward twice over for what they have endured. They avert evil by means of the good, and contribute from what We have provided them. ⁵⁵ When they hear any frivolous talk, they turn away from it, and say, 'To us our deeds and to you your deeds. Peace (be) upon you! We do not seek out the ignorant.'

⁵⁶ Surely you will not guide whomever you like, but God guides whomever He pleases, and knows the ones who are (rightly) guided. ⁵⁷ They say, 'If we follow the guidance with you, we shall be snatched from our land.' Have We not established a secure sanctuary for them, where fruits of every kind are brought as a provision from Us? But most of them do not know (it). ⁵⁸ How many a town have We destroyed (which) boasted of its means of livelihood! Those are their dwelling places (which remain) uninhabited after them, except for a few. We became the inheritors! ⁵⁹ Yet your Lord was not one to destroy the towns until He had raised up a messenger in their mother (city), reciting Our signs to them. We would not have destroyed the towns unless their people had been evildoers.

⁶⁰ Whatever thing you have been given is (only) an enjoyment of this present life, and its (passing) splendor, but what is with God is better and more lasting. Will you not understand? ⁶¹ Is the one whom We have promised a good promise, and (who) receives it, like the one whom We have given the enjoyment of this present life, (and) then on the Day of Resurrection will be one of those brought forward (to the punishment)?

⁶² On the Day when He will call them, and say, 'Where are My associates

---

and 52.34. In Muslim tradition these verses became known as the *taḥaddī* (challenge) verses. See the analysis of these challenge verses at 52.34 (p. 529).

Interestingly, in this version of the challenge, the Quran holds together the book given to Moses (Torah) with the messenger's recitations. There does not seem to be any hint of an accusation of corruption against the Torah or even suspicion about the Jewish handling of the Torah in these verses (41–51). See also the tone of the following verses (52–55).

28.52 – *Those to whom We gave the Book before it – they believe in it*

This and the following verse indicate a scenario in which the People of the Book – presumably Jews and/or Christians – believe in the recitations of the messenger. They describe themselves as Muslims (v. 53). Are these "believers" converts to Islam?

whom you used to claim (as gods)?,' ⁶³ those against whom the word has proved true will say, 'Our Lord, these are those whom we made err. We made them err as we had erred. We disown (them) before You. They were not serving us.' ⁶⁴ And it will be said, 'Call your associates!' And they will call them, but they will not respond to them, and they will see the punishment. If only they had been guided!

⁶⁵ On the Day when He will call them, and say, 'What response did you give the envoys?' ⁶⁶ The news will be dark for them on that Day, nor will they ask each other questions. ⁶⁷ But as for the one who turns (in repentance), and believes, and does righteousness, it may be that he will be one of those who prosper.

⁶⁸ Your Lord creates whatever He pleases, and chooses (whomever He pleases) – the choice is not theirs. Glory to God! He is exalted above what they associate. ⁶⁹ Your Lord knows what their hearts conceal and what they speak aloud. ⁷⁰ He is God – (there is) no god but Him. To Him (be) praise, at the first and at the last! To Him (belongs) the judgment, and to Him you will be returned.

⁷¹ Say: 'Have you considered? If God makes the night continuous for you until the Day of Resurrection, what god other than God will bring you light? Will you not hear?' ⁷² Say: 'Have you considered? If God makes the day continuous for you until the Day of Resurrection, what god other than God will bring you night to rest in? Will you not see? ⁷³ But out of His mercy He has made the night and the day for you, so that you may rest in it, and that you may seek some of His favor, and that you may be thankful.'

⁷⁴ On the Day when He will call them, and say, 'Where are My associates whom you used to claim (as gods)?' ⁷⁵ We shall draw out a witness from every community, and say, 'Bring your proof!' And then they will know that the truth (belongs) to God, and what they have forged will abandon them.

28.76 – *Surely Qārūn was one of the people of Moses, and acted oppressively toward them*

This story of Korah, or *Qārūn* (vv. 76–82), portrays him as possessing great wealth but neglecting "the Home of the Hereafter" (v. 77). Allah caused the earth to swallow him (v. 81). Korah is also named at 29.39 and 40.24.

The Torah account of Korah (Heb. *Qōraḥ*) is found in Numbers 16; there, as in Jude 11, he is the quintessential example of rebellion.

28.76 – *Surely God does not love those who gloat*

The Quran contains twenty-four statements about the kinds of people whom Allah does not love. In addition to the statement in this verse, the following verse says that Allah withholds his love from "the fomenters of corruption" (*mufsidūn*, v. 77; also 5.64). See "The Language of Love in the Quran" (p. 560).

⁷⁶ Surely Qārūn was one of the people of Moses, and acted oppressively toward them. We had given him treasures, the keys of which would indeed have been a burden for a group (of men) endowed with strength. (Remember) when his people said to him, 'Do not gloat! Surely God does not love those who gloat. ⁷⁷ But seek the Home of the Hereafter by means of what God has given you, and do not forget your portion of this world. Do good, as God has done good to you, and do not seek to foment corruption on the earth. Surely God does not love the fomenters of corruption.' ⁷⁸ He said, 'I have been given it only because of the knowledge (that is) in me.' Did he not know that God had destroyed those of the generations before him who were stronger than him and had accumulated more? The sinners will not be questioned about their sins. ⁷⁹ So he went forth to his people in his splendor. Those who desired this present life said, 'Would that we had the same as what has been given to Qārūn! Surely he is indeed the possessor of great good luck.' ⁸⁰ But those to whom knowledge had been given said, 'Woe to you! The reward of God is better for the one who believes and does righteousness. But no one will obtain it except the patient.' ⁸¹ So We caused the earth to swallow him and his home, and he had no cohort to help him, other than God, and he was not one of those who could help themselves. ⁸² In the morning those who had longed (to be in) his place the day before were saying, 'Woe (to Qārūn)! Surely God extends (His) provision to whomever He pleases of His servants, and restricts (it). If God had not bestowed favor on us, He would indeed have caused (the earth) to swallow us (too). Woe to him! The disbelievers will not prosper.'

⁸³ That is the Home of the Hereafter: We assign it to those who do not desire haughtiness on the earth, nor corruption. The outcome (belongs) to the ones who guard (themselves). ⁸⁴ Whoever brings a good (deed) will have a better one than it, and whoever brings an evil (deed) – those who have done evil deeds will only be repaid for what they have done.

⁸⁵ Surely He who made the Qur'ān obligatory for you will indeed return you to (your) home. Say: 'My Lord knows who brings the guidance, and who is clearly astray.' ⁸⁶ You did not expect that the Book would be cast (down) to you, except as a mercy from your Lord. So do not be a supporter of the disbelievers. ⁸⁷ Let them not keep you from the signs of God, after they have been sent down to you, but call (people) to your Lord, and do not be one of the idolaters. ⁸⁸ Do not call on another god (along) with God. (There is) no god but Him. Everything perishes except His face. To Him (belongs) the judgment, and to Him you will be returned.

THE SPIDER
AL-'ANKABŪT

29

This sūra begins and ends with controversy between the messenger and his audience. The listeners look for help and protection from every source except Allah. The Quran illustrates their situation with a simile about a spider. Taking protection apart from Allah is like a spider's web, "the most feeble of houses" (v. 41).

In the middle of the sūra are brief references to Noah, Shu'ayb, Korah, Pharaoh and Haman, and to the peoples of 'Ād and Thamūd, plus longer stories about Abraham and Lot.

Much of the last part of the sūra instructs and encourages the messenger directly and states that Allah inspires and "sends down" his recitations.

In the Name of God, the Merciful, the Compassionate

¹ Alif Lām Mīm.

² Do the people think that they will be left (in such a position) that they (can) say, 'We believe,' but (that) they will not be tested? ³ Certainly We tested those who were before them, and God will indeed know those who are truthful, and He will indeed know the liars. ⁴ Or do those who do evil deeds think that they will escape Us? Evil is what they judge! ⁵ Whoever expects the meeting with God – surely the time of God is coming indeed! He is the Hearing, the Knowing. ⁶ Whoever struggles, struggles only for himself. Surely God is indeed wealthy beyond the worlds. ⁷ Those who believe and do righteous deeds – We shall indeed absolve them of their evil deeds, and indeed repay them (for the) best of what they have done.

⁸ We have charged each person (to do) good to his parents, but if they both

---

29.6 – *Whoever struggles, struggles only for himself*

The uses of the Arabic verb *jāhada* ("to struggle") in this sūra offer a chance to study its meaning when the context is not a battle scene (see also v. 8 and the comments at v. 69).

29.8 – *We have charged each person (to do) good to his parents*

Obey your parents – except when they force you to associate (*ashrak*) something or someone with Allah.

struggle with you – to make you associate with Me what you have no knowledge of – do not obey them. To Me is your return, and I shall inform you about what you have done. ⁹ Those who believe and do righteous deeds – We shall indeed cause them to enter among the righteous.

¹⁰ Among the people (there is) one who says, 'We believe in God,' but when he is hurt in (the way of) God, he takes the persecution of the people as the punishment of God. But if indeed help comes to you from your Lord, they indeed say, 'Surely we were with you.' Does God not know what is in the hearts of all? ¹¹ God indeed knows those who believe, and He indeed knows the hypocrites.

¹² Those who disbelieve say to those who believe, 'Follow our way, and let us bear your sins.' Yet they cannot bear a single one of their own sins. Surely they are liars indeed! ¹³ But they will indeed bear their burdens, and (other) burdens with their burdens, and on the Day of Resurrection they will indeed be questioned about what they have forged.

¹⁴ Certainly We sent Noah to his people, and he stayed among them a thousand years, minus fifty years, and then the flood seized them while they were doing evil. ¹⁵ But We rescued him and (his) companions on the ship, and made it a miracle for all peoples.

¹⁶ And Abraham, when he said to his people: 'Serve God, and guard (yourselves) against Him. That is better for you, if (only) you knew. ¹⁷ Instead of God, you only serve idols, and you create a lie. Surely those whom you serve, instead

---

29.15 – *But We rescued him and (his) companions on the ship*

The language of salvation (*anjā*) usually appears in stories of figures familiar from the Old Testament, as it does in this sūra alongside Noah, Abraham (v. 24), and Lot (v. 32). See "Salvation in the Quran" (p. 180).

29.16 – *And Abraham, when he said to his people: "Serve God, and guard (yourselves)…"*

Abraham challenges his people about their idol worship in this substantial passage (vv. 16–27) and implores them to acknowledge their Creator. But the people respond with a call to kill Abraham (v. 24).

Stories of Abraham opposing idolatry appear frequently in the Quran, each adding details that are not included in the other versions. The call to burn Abraham and Allah's subsequent rescue of him from the fire is more fully narrated in 21.68–71. It is not found in the Bible, but a similar story about Abraham appears in *Midrāsh Rabbah Genesis* – early Jewish commentary dated to the sixth century.

29.19 – *Do they not see how God brings about the creation, (and) then restores it?*

This passage (vv. 19–23) returns to the situation of the messenger and seems to interrupt the flow of the Abraham story.

of God, do not possess any provision for you. Seek (your) provision from God, and serve Him, and be thankful to Him – to Him you will be returned. [18] But if you call (it) a lie, (know that) communities called (it) a lie before you. Nothing (depends) on the messenger except the clear delivery (of the message).'

[19] Do they not see how God brings about the creation, (and) then restores it? Surely that is easy for God. [20] Say: 'Travel the earth and see how He brought about the creation. Then God produces the latter growth. Surely God is powerful over everything. [21] He punishes whomever He pleases and has compassion on whomever He pleases – and to Him you will be turned. [22] You cannot escape (Him) either on the earth or in the sky, and you have no ally and no helper other than God.' [23] Those who disbelieve in the signs of God and the meeting with Him – those have no hope of My mercy, and those – for them (there is) a painful punishment.

[24] But the only response of his people was that they said, 'Kill him, or burn him!' And then God rescued him from the fire. Surely in that are signs indeed for a people who believe. [25] And he said, 'Instead of God, you have only taken idols (in a bond of) friendship among you in this present life. Then on the Day of Resurrection some of you will deny others, and some will curse others, and your refuge will be the Fire, and you will have no helpers.' [26] Lot believed in him, and said, 'I am going to flee to my Lord. Surely He – He is the Mighty, the Wise.' [27] And We granted him Isaac and Jacob, and We placed among his descendants the prophetic office and the Book. We gave him his reward in this world, and in the Hereafter he will indeed be among the righteous.

[28] And Lot, when he said to his people: 'Surely you commit (such) immorality

---

29.27 – And We granted him Isaac and Jacob

Not only is Ishmael not mentioned in this sūra, but here the descendants of Isaac and Jacob are associated with "the prophetic office and the Book" (v. 27; cf. 19.49–50). Such verses seem to reflect a more sanguine view of the Children of Israel.

If Allah established "the prophetic office and the Book" among Abraham's descendants, then the identity of Abraham's seed can become a point of controversy, as indeed seems to be the case in 2.124–40 and 3.65–68 (cf. Galatians 3:16).

29.28 – And Lot, when he said to his people

Lot confronts his people and asks, "Do you indeed approach men . . . ?" (v. 29). He describes their actions as "immorality" (*fāḥisha*) and "wrong" (or abomination, *munkar*, v. 29). In this sixth of eight versions of Lot's story in the Quran, the people challenge him to bring Allah's doom upon them. Lot's wife stays behind when the rest of the family flees (v. 33).

In the middle of this Lot story, Allah's messengers bring Abraham the "good news," but give no details of either a son or Isaac (v. 31).

(as) no one in all the worlds has committed before you. ²⁹ Do you indeed approach men, and cut off the way, and commit wrong in your meeting?' But the only response of his people was that they said, 'Bring us the punishment of God, if you are one of the truthful.' ³⁰ He said, 'My Lord, help me against the people who foment corruption.' ³¹ When Our messengers brought Abraham the good news, they said, 'Surely we are going to destroy the people of this town, (for) its people are evildoers.' ³² He said, 'Surely Lot is in it.' They said, 'We know who is in it. We shall indeed rescue him and his family, except his wife. She will be one of those who stay behind.' ³³ When Our messengers came to Lot, he became distressed about them, and felt powerless (to protect) them, but they said, 'Do not fear and do not sorrow. Surely we are going to rescue you and your family, except your wife. She will be one of those who stay behind. ³⁴ Surely We are going to send down wrath from the sky on the people of this town, because they have acted wickedly.' ³⁵ Certainly We have left some of it as a clear sign for a people who understand.

³⁶ And to Midian (We sent) their brother Shuʿayb. He said, 'My people! Serve God and expect the Last Day. Do not act wickedly on the earth, fomenting corruption.' ³⁷ But they called him a liar, so the earthquake seized them, and morning found them leveled in their home(s).

³⁸ And ʿĀd and Thamūd – it is clear to you from their dwellings. Satan made their deeds appear enticing to them, and kept them from the way, though they saw (it) clearly.

³⁹ And Qārūn, and Pharaoh, and Haman – certainly Moses brought them the clear signs, but they became arrogant on the earth. Yet they did not outrun (Us). ⁴⁰ We seized each one for his sin. We sent a sandstorm against one of them, and another of them was seized by the cry, and We caused the earth to swallow (yet) another of them, and We drowned (still) another of them. Yet God was not one to do them evil, but they did themselves evil.

⁴¹ The parable of those who take allies other than God is like the parable of the spider: it takes a house, but surely the house of the spider is indeed the most feeble of houses – if (only) they knew. ⁴² Surely God knows whatever they call on instead of Him. He is the Mighty, the Wise. ⁴³ Those parables – We strike them for the people, but no one understands them except the ones who know.

29.39 – *And Qārūn, and Pharaoh, and Haman – certainly Moses brought them the clear signs*

The Quran places Korah and Haman in Pharaoh's court. In the biblical account, Korah is well clear of Pharaoh at Numbers 16 (see the comment at 28.76). For the dislocation of Haman, see the comment at 28.6.

⁴⁴ God created the heavens and the earth in truth. Surely in that is a sign indeed for the believers.

⁴⁵ Recite what you have been inspired (with) of the Book, and observe the prayer. Surely the prayer forbids immorality and wrong, yet the remembrance of God is indeed greater. God is aware of what you do. ⁴⁶ Do not dispute with the People of the Book except with what is better – except for those of them who do evil. And say: 'We believe in what has been sent down to us, and what has been sent down to you. Our God and your God is one, and to Him we submit.' ⁴⁷ In this way We have sent down the Book to you. Those to whom We have given the Book believe in it, and among these (people) (there are) some who believe in it. No one denies Our signs but the disbelievers.

⁴⁸ You were not accustomed to read from any book before it, or to write it with your right (hand), (for) then the perpetrators of falsehood would indeed have had (reason to) doubt (you). ⁴⁹ No! It is clear signs in the hearts of those who have been given knowledge. No one denies Our signs but the evildoers.

⁵⁰ They say, 'If only signs were sent down on him from his Lord.' Say: 'The signs are only with God. I am only a clear warner.' ⁵¹ Is it not sufficient for them that We have sent down on you the Book to be recited to them? Surely in that is a mercy indeed, and a reminder to a people who believe. ⁵² Say: 'God is sufficient as a witness between me and you.' He knows whatever is in the heavens and the earth. Those who believe in falsehood and disbelieve in God, those – they are the losers.

⁵³ They seek to hurry you with the punishment. If it were not for an appointed

---

29.46 – *Do not dispute with the People of the Book except with what is better*

This and the following verse seem to reflect a situation in which relations with the People of the Book were good and the messenger understood his recitations to agree with the pre-Islamic scriptures. See a discussion of the Quran's approach to the People of the Book at 98.1 (p. 641).

29.47 – *In this way We have sent down the Book to you*

The Quran claims that Allah "sends down" the book to the messenger, and here the People of the Book believe in his recitations.

29.48 – *You were not accustomed to read from any book before it, or to write it with your right (hand)*

The Quran continues to address the messenger directly (vv. 45–54), here apparently claiming that his recitations could only come from Allah. If the messenger could neither read nor write, according to this claim, then he could have neither copied from another book nor written out of his own thoughts (see also comments at 7.157).

time, the punishment would indeed have come upon them (already). Yet it will indeed come upon them unexpectedly, when they do not realize (it). [54] They seek to hurry you with the punishment. Surely Gehenna will indeed encompass the disbelievers. [55] On the Day when the punishment will cover them – from above them and from beneath their feet – (then) He will say, 'Taste what you have done!'

[56] My servants who believe! Surely My earth is wide, so serve Me! [57] Every person will taste death, then to Us you will be returned. [58] Those who have believed and done righteous deeds – We shall indeed settle them in exalted rooms of the Garden, through which rivers flow, there to remain. Excellent is the reward of the doers, [59] who are patient and trust in their Lord.

[60] How many a creature (there is which) does not carry its own provision, yet God provides for it and for you. He is the Hearing, the Knowing. [61] If indeed you ask them, 'Who created the heavens and the earth, and subjected the sun and the moon?,' they will indeed say, 'God.' How then are they (so) deluded? [62] God extends (His) provision to whomever He pleases of His servants, and restricts (it) from him (whom He pleases). God has knowledge of everything. [63] If indeed you ask them, 'Who sends down water from the sky, and by means of it gives the earth life after its death?,' they will indeed say, 'God.' Say: 'Praise (be) to God!' But most of them do not understand.

[64] This present life is nothing but jest and diversion. Surely the Home of the Hereafter – it is life indeed, if (only) they knew. [65] When they sail in the ship, they call on God, devoting (their) religion to Him. But when He brings them safely to the shore, suddenly they associate (other gods with Him). [66] Let them be ungrateful for what We have given them, and enjoy (themselves). Soon they will know! [67] Do they not see that We established a secure sanctuary (for them), while all around them the people are plundered? Do they believe in falsehood, but disbelieve in the blessing of God?

29.61 – *If indeed you ask them, "Who created the heavens and the earth . . . ?" they will indeed say, "God."*

The point of the questions in this and the following verses seems to be that if people acknowledge Allah as creator and sustainer of the universe, they should also believe in him and serve him. Another suggestion of these verses is that *Allāh* is not a name that originated with Islam but was well known to those who heard the recitations.

29.64 – *This present life is nothing but jest and diversion*

This concept that the hereafter is more important than the "present life" is a key component of many sūras and is familiar to Bible readers.

⁶⁸ Who is more evil than the one who forges a lie against God, or calls the truth a lie when it comes to him? Is there not in Gehenna a dwelling place for the disbelievers? ⁶⁹ But those who struggle for Us, We shall indeed guide them in Our ways. Surely God is indeed with the doers of good.

29.69 – *But those who struggle for Us, We shall indeed guide them in Our ways*

This is another good example of the use of the verb *jāhada* (translated here as "struggle") that does not give any sense of physical fighting (also vv. 6, 8; cf. 22.78). See "Jihad in the Quran" (p. 368).

THE ROMANS
AL-RŪM

30

Sūra 30 is an example of a sūra made up of a collection of short text units that one scholar has called "prophetical *logia*" – that is, sayings that listeners or readers tend to associate with divine utterances.

In such sūras the subject, voice, audience, and style of literature change every few verses, and units may repeat later. In this case, the Quran tells how Allah deals with humans, describes two scenes of the Day of Resurrection, shows the Creator's presence and power, includes at least four separate passages addressed directly to the messenger (and others to the messenger's audience), has an example of what the Quran calls "parables," and, of course, in the opening verses may refer to a historical event.

In the Name of God, the Merciful, the Compassionate
[1] Alif Lām Mīm.

[2] The Romans have been conquered [3] in the nearest (part) of the land, but after their conquering, they will conquer [4] in a few years. The affair (belongs) to God before and after, and on that day the believers will gloat [5] over the help of God. He helps whomever He pleases. He is the Mighty, the Compassionate.

30.2–3 – *The Romans have been conquered in the nearest (part) of the land*

Some scholars identify verses 2–5 as the only passage in the Quran that refers to a historical event that could be confirmed by other sources. The "Romans" (*al-rūm*), meaning the Eastern Roman Empire, or Byzantines, were a major world power in the seventh century but are mentioned only here in the Quran. The Byzantines were in conflict with the Sasanian Empire during the years AD 602–28.

As it happens, the two verbs in verses 2–3 can be read as either active or passive – that is, either "have conquered" or "have been conquered." The reason for this is that the earliest manuscripts of the Quran have no vowel markings that would allow a reader to distinguish between active and passive. Therefore, though this verse seems to refer to a historical event, it is not certain which event it reports.

Manuscripts of the Quran
Daniel A. Brubaker

The existence and study of Bible manuscripts is by now widely known. In recent years, interest in Quran manuscripts has begun to grow.

The Hebrew Bible and the New Testament proliferated in manuscript over many centuries with various scribal issues that have by now been well-studied, but neither set of writings was ever apparently systematically and comprehensively revised, with variants destroyed. In contrast, the physical Quran weathered at least two major campaigns of suppression in its first century. These campaigns, if the earliest narrative accounts of them are substantially correct, destroyed evidence that would have been valuable to scholars today. They proceeded under the pretext of standardization, in the first case at the direction of the third caliph, ʿUthmān, within twenty years of the reported death of Muhammad. For reasons that require more elaboration than possible in this short article, it is evident to scholars that the central stated motivations for the suppression – namely variations in the manuscripts relating to dialect – could hardly have been the actual motivating factors since quranic materials written from this early stage did not supply the short vowels that would have indicated dialect variations. If these campaigns did happen, the removal of dialect variants is most likely a façade for a larger and more problematic motivating cause or causes.

These circumstances notwithstanding, there is today no shortage of extant manuscripts of the Quran, including some appearing to predate even ʿUthmān's suppression.

In particular, many surviving Quran manuscripts date back to the early centuries of its history, and some of them have been very well preserved. Their endurance in large numbers owes partly to the fact that by the seventh century AD, parchment, which is quite durable, had generally supplanted papyrus as the most commonly used writing material. Radiocarbon dating of one Quran fragment has recently returned a date range that includes or even precedes the reported lifetime of Muhammad. This does not necessarily mean that this manuscript predates Muhammad, but it does open the possibility. Nevertheless, most believe that several of these manuscripts, including the palimpsests studied by quranic scholars Elisabeth Puin, Alba Fedeli, and Asma Hilali, for example, are reasonably attributed to the latter part of the seventh century, in the decades following Muhammad's reported death.

Quran manuscripts are important to historians and theologians since they stand as witnesses from the time of their production and have the potential to answer questions that the earliest narrative accounts, which were written more than a century after the events they describe, cannot.

Today early Quran fragments exist in both public and private collections as well as in some notable institutions around the world. Important, early, near-complete Qurans are held in Cairo, Istanbul, Tashkent, and Sanaʿā. Further important collections of early manuscript fragments exist in the National Library of France in Paris, the British Library in London, the National Library of Russia in St. Petersburg, the Oriental Institute in St. Petersburg, the Dar al-Makhtutāt in Sanaʿā, the private Nasser D. Khalili Collection, the Museum of Islamic Art in Doha, the Chester Beatty Library in Dublin, the Dar Museum and Sabah Collection in Kuwait, the Beit al-Quran in Manama, the Tareq Rajab Museum in Kuwait, the Cambridge University Library, the Oxford Bodleian Library, the Topkapi Palace Library, the Biruni Institute in Tashkent, and the Cadbury Research Library at the University of Birmingham. This is a partial list but highlights many of the important collections.

Access to Quran manuscripts in facsimile is increasing as many institutions, sometimes aided by government funding, are digitizing their collections. Online technology has recently made possible the digital reunion of fragments that belonged originally to the same codex despite being now physically separated between different institutions or collections.

There remains much work to be done in the study of early Quran manuscripts, but the increasing availability of, accessibility of, interest in, and openness to their study will permit this field of study to grow and flourish in the coming years. Key questions surround the nature of the transmission and development of the physical representation of the Quran text, the relationship of the written word to its oral transmission, the development of the pluralities of readings (both canonical and noncanonical), and the ordinary study of variants and corrections for what they may tell us about the Quran as a tangible object situated in history.

The Quran Gateway website, qurangateway.org, developed by myself and Andy Bannister, features research on physical corrections that exist in early Quran manuscripts, including detailed descriptions and many photographs.

[6] The promise of God! God will not break His promise, but most of the people do not know (it). [7] They perceive (only) what is obvious in this present

life, but they are oblivious of the Hereafter. ⁸ Do they not reflect within themselves? God did not create the heavens and the earth, and whatever is between them, except in truth and (for) an appointed time. Yet surely many of the people are indeed disbelievers in the meeting with their Lord. ⁹ Have they not traveled on the earth and seen how the end was for those who were before them? They were stronger than them in power, and they ploughed the earth and populated it more than they have populated it. Their messengers brought them the clear signs. God was not one to do them evil, but they did themselves evil. ¹⁰ Then the end of those who had done evil was evil, because they had called the signs of God a lie and mocked them.

¹¹ God brings about the creation, then restores it, (and) then to Him you will be returned. ¹² On the Day when the Hour strikes, the sinners will despair. ¹³ They will not have any intercessors among their associates, but they (will come to) disbelieve in their associates. ¹⁴ On the Day when the Hour strikes, on that Day they will be separated. ¹⁵ As for those who have believed and done righteous deeds, they will be made happy in a meadow. ¹⁶ But as for those who have disbelieved, and called Our signs a lie, and the meeting of the Hereafter, those will be brought forward to the punishment. ¹⁷ So glory to God, when you come to evening and when you come to morning. ¹⁸ Praise (be) to Him in the heavens and the earth – and at night and when you appear (in the day)! ¹⁹ He brings forth the living from the dead, and brings forth the dead from the living. He gives the earth life after its death, and in this way you (too) will be brought forth.

²⁰ (One) of His signs is that He created you from dust, and now you are human beings spreading (far and wide). ²¹ (Another) of His signs is that He created spouses for you from yourselves, so that you may live with them, and He

30.8 – *God did not create the heavens and the earth . . . except in truth and (for) an appointed time*

The Creator's presence and power is an important theme in this sūra (vv. 11, 17–27, 40, 46, 48–50, 54). See the focus article about "Creation in the Quran" (p. 224).

30.15 – *As for those who have believed and done righteous deeds, they will be made happy in a meadow*

Verses 14–16 set out the criteria for reward and punishment on "that day" in a concise and handy way. "Signs" in verse 16 translates the Arabic *āyāt*.

30.21 – *He has established love and mercy between you*

This verse offers one of the most beautiful expressions in the Quran about the relationship between husbands and wives. "Love" translates the Arabic noun *mawadda*. See "The Language of Love in the Quran" (p. 560).

has established love and mercy between you. Surely in that are signs indeed for a people who reflect. ²² (Another) of His signs is the creation of the heavens and the earth, and the variety of your languages and colors. Surely in that are signs indeed for those who know. ²³ (Another) of His signs is your sleeping by night and day, and your seeking some of His favor. Surely in that are signs indeed for a people who hear. ²⁴ (Another) of His signs (is that) He shows you lightning – in fear and desire – and He sends down water from the sky, and by means of it gives the earth life after its death. Surely in that are signs indeed for a people who understand. ²⁵ (Another) of His signs is that the sky and the earth stand (fast) by His command. Then, when He calls you out of the earth once and for all, suddenly you will come forth. ²⁶ To Him (belongs) whoever is in the heavens and the earth: all are obedient before Him. ²⁷ He (it is) who brings about the creation, then restores it – it is easy for Him. (Only) the highest parable in the heavens and the earth (is fitting) for Him. He is the Mighty, the Wise.

²⁸ He has struck a parable for you from yourselves: Among what your right (hands) own, do you have associates in what We have provided you with, so that you are (all) equal in that respect – (you) fearing them as you fear each other? In this way We make the signs distinct for a people who understand.

²⁹ No! Those who do evil follow their own (vain) desires without any knowledge. So who will guide those whom God has led astray? They have no helpers. ³⁰ Set your face to the religion (as) a Ḥanīf – the creation of God for which He created humankind. (There is) no change in the creation of God. That is the

30.21 – *Surely in that are signs indeed for a people who reflect*

This refrain, with changing descriptions of the "people," appears four times (vv. 21–24) in the midst of the larger passage about creation.

30.26 – *To Him (belongs) whoever is in the heavens and the earth: all are obedient before Him*

All of creation responds to its Creator in obedience – except most of humankind!

30.28 – *He has struck a parable for you from yourselves*

Here is an example of the kind of parable (*mathal*) that this sūra claims to offer (v. 58). As a master does not consider one of his slaves to be his associate (*sharīk*) – equal to him – so the Creator does not consider one of his creatures to be his partner.

30.30 – *Set your face to the religion (as) a Ḥanīf*

This striking instruction addressed to the messenger (or perhaps to the listener or reader) tells him to act like a *Ḥanīf*, a difficult word often translated as "an upright person" and usually associated with Abraham in the Quran. A similar instruction appears at verse 43. For further discussion of *Ḥanīf*, see the comment at 2.135 (p. 55) and "Abraham in the Quran" (p. 90).

right religion, but most of the people do not know (it) – [31] turning to Him (in repentance). Guard (yourself) against Him, and observe the prayer, and do not be one of the idolaters, [32] one of those who have divided up their religion and become parties, each faction gloating over what was with them. [33] When hardship touches the people, they call on their Lord, turning to Him (in repentance). Then, when He gives them a taste of mercy from Himself, suddenly a group of them associates (other gods) with their Lord. [34] Let them be ungrateful for what We have given them: 'Enjoy (yourselves)! Soon you will know!' [35] Or have We sent down any authority on them (for this), and does it speak about what they associate with Him?

[36] When We give the people a taste of mercy, they gloat over it, but if some evil smites them because of what their (own) hands have sent forward, suddenly they despair. [37] Do they not see that God extends (His) provision to whomever He pleases, and restricts (it)? Surely in that are signs indeed for a people who believe.

[38] Give the family its due, and the poor, and the traveler – that is better for those who desire the face of God, and those – they are the ones who prosper. [39] Whatever you give in usury, in order that it may increase on the wealth of the people, does not increase with God, but what you give in alms, desiring the face of God – those are the ones who gain double.

[40] (It is) God who created you, then provided for you, then causes you to die, (and) then gives you life. (Are there) any of your associates who (can) do any of that? Glory to Him! He is exalted above what they associate. [41] Corruption has appeared on the shore and the sea because of what the hands of the people have earned, so that He may give them a taste of what they have done, that they may return. [42] Say: 'Travel the earth and see how the end was for those who were before (you). Most of them were idolaters.'

[43] Set your face to the right religion, before a Day comes from God which cannot be turned back. On that Day they will be divided: [44] whoever disbelieves – his disbelief (will be) on him, but whoever does righteousness – they are smoothing (the way) for themselves, [45] so that He may repay from His favor those who believe and do righteous deeds. Surely He does not love the disbelievers.

[46] (One) of His signs is that He sends the winds as bringers of good news, so that He may give you a taste of His mercy, and that the ship may run by His command, and that you may seek some of His favor, and that you may be thankful.

30.45 – *Surely He does not love the disbelievers*

The Quran contains twenty-four statements about the kinds of people whom Allah does not love. This object, "the disbelievers," also appears at 3.32. See "The Language of Love in the Quran" (p. 560).

[47] Certainly We sent messengers to their people before you, and they brought them the clear signs. Then We took vengeance on those who sinned, but it was an obligation on Us (to) help the believers. [48] (It is) God who sends the winds, and it stirs up a cloud, and He spreads it in the sky as He pleases, and breaks it into fragments, and you see the rain coming forth from the midst of it. When He smites with it whomever He pleases of His servants, suddenly they welcome the good news, [49] though before (this), before it was sent down on them, they were in despair. [50] Observe the traces of the mercy of God, how He gives the earth life after its death. Surely that One will indeed give the dead life. He is powerful over everything. [51] If indeed We send a wind, and they see it growing yellow, they indeed remain disbelievers after that. [52] You cannot make the dead to hear, nor can you make the deaf to hear the call when they turn away, withdrawing. [53] You cannot guide the blind out of their straying, nor can you make (anyone) hear, except for those who believe in Our signs, and so they submit. [54] (It is) God who created you from weakness, then after weakness He made strength, (and) then after strength He made weakness and grey hair. He creates whatever He pleases. He is the Knowing, the Powerful.

[55] On the Day when the Hour strikes, the sinners will swear they remained (in the grave) only for an hour – that is how deluded they were – [56] but those who have been given knowledge and belief will say (to them), 'You have remained in the Book of God until the Day of Raising Up, and this is the Day of Raising Up, but you did not know (it).' [57] On that Day their excuses will not benefit those who have done evil, nor will they be allowed to make amends.

[58] Certainly We have struck for the people every (kind of) parable in this Qur'ān. But if indeed you bring them a sign, those who disbelieve will indeed say, 'You are nothing but perpetrators of falsehood.' [59] In this way God sets a seal on the hearts of those who do not know. [60] So be patient! Surely the promise of God is true. And (let) not those who are uncertain unsettle you.

30.47 – *Certainly We sent messengers to their people before you*

This verse states the pattern of messenger stories in a nutshell: Allah sends messengers to their own peoples; the messengers preach; Allah takes vengeance on those who resist the preaching and saves the believers.

30.52 – *You cannot make the dead to hear*

In this sūra the abilities and the duties of the messenger are limited (vv. 52–53); therefore, the Quran counsels patience (v. 60).

LUQMĀN
LUQMĀN

31

A character named Luqmān appears at the center of this sūra, warning of the dangers of ascribing partners to Allah. The name Luqmān appears only here in the Quran and is not known from the Bible or from other writings prior to the Quran.

Apart from the warning against ascribing partners (*ashraka*), the sūra tells of the signs of creation and the human responses to them, and offers a lovely expression about the abundance of the words of Allah.

It is interesting that the sūra claims to contain signs of the "wise" (*ḥakīm*) book (v. 2), because Luqmān's exhortations to his "son" (vv. 12–19) bring to mind the Bible's "wisdom literature," especially the book of Proverbs.

In the Name of God, the Merciful, the Compassionate

[1] Alif Lām Mīm. [2] Those are the signs of the wise Book, [3] a guidance and mercy for the doers of good, [4] who observe the prayer and give the alms, and they are certain of the Hereafter. [5] Those (depend) on guidance from their Lord, and those – they are the ones who prosper. [6] But among the people (there is) one who buys a diverting tale to lead (others) astray from the way of God without any knowledge, and to take it in mockery. Those – for them (there is) a humiliating punishment. [7] When Our signs are recited to him, he turns away arrogantly, as if he had not heard them, as if (there were) a heaviness in his ears. So give him news of a painful punishment! [8] Surely those who believe and do righteous deeds

---

31.1–2 – *Alif Lām Mīm. Those are the signs of the wise Book*

On the disconnected Arabic letters that begin this sūra, see the comment at 2.1. The sūra opens by claiming that its contents are the verses or "signs" (*āyāt*) of the "wise" book.

31.6 – *But among the people (there is) one who buys a diverting tale to lead (others) astray*

Instead of accepting the recitations as "sent down" by Allah, some listeners mock the message and lead others astray.

– for them (there are) Gardens of Bliss, [9] there to remain. The promise of God in truth! He is the Mighty, the Wise.

[10] He created the heavens without any pillars you (can) see, and He cast on the earth firm mountains, so that it does not sway with you (on it), and He scattered on it all (kinds of) creatures. And We sent down water from the sky, and caused (things) of every excellent kind to grow in it. [11] This is the creation of God. Show me what those (whom you worship) instead of Him have created. No! The evildoers are clearly astray.

[12] Certainly We gave Luqmān wisdom: 'Be thankful to God. Whoever is thankful is thankful only for himself, and whoever is ungrateful – surely God is wealthy, praiseworthy.'

[13] (Remember) when Luqmān said to his son, when he was admonishing him, 'My son! Do not associate (anything) with God. Surely the association (of anything) with God is a great evil indeed.'

[14] We have charged the human concerning his parents – his mother bore him in weakness upon weakness, and his weaning took two years – 'Be thankful to Me and to your parents. To Me is the (final) destination.' [15] But if they both struggle with you – to make you associate with Me what you have no knowledge of – do not obey them. Keep rightful company with them in this world, but follow the way of the one who turns to Me (in repentance). Then to Me is your return, and I shall inform you about what you have done.'

[16] 'My son! Surely it – if it should be (only) the weight of a mustard seed, and it should be in a rock, or in the heavens, or on the earth, God will bring it forth. Surely God is astute, aware. [17] My son! Observe the prayer, and command right and forbid wrong. Bear patiently whatever smites you – surely that is one of the determining factors in (all) affairs. [18] Do not turn your cheek to the people, and do not walk on the earth in jubilation. Surely God does not love anyone who

---

31.10 – *He created the heavens without any pillars you (can) see*

The sūra draws attention to the Creator's presence and power in this passage (vv. 10–11) and again later (vv. 20–29).

31.12 – *Certainly We gave Luqmān wisdom: "Be thankful to God…"*

The story of Luqmān features the advice of a father to his son (vv. 12–19). His warning against ascribing partners to Allah seems to invite the insertion of verses 14–15, which encourage thankfulness and obedience to parents except when parents make their children ascribe partners to Allah. The name Luqmān appears only here in the Quran and is not known from the Bible or from other writings prior to the Quran.

31.18 – *Surely God does not love anyone who is arrogant (and) boastful*

The Quran contains twenty-four statements about the kinds of people whom

is arrogant (and) boastful. [19] Be modest in your walking, and lower your voice. Surely the most hateful of voices is the voice of donkeys.'

[20] Do you not see that God has subjected to you whatever is in the heavens and whatever is on the earth, and has lavished on you His blessings, both outwardly and inwardly? But among the people (there is) one who disputes about God without any knowledge or guidance or illuminating Book. [21] When it is said to them, 'Follow what God has sent down,' they say, 'No! We will follow what we found our fathers doing.' Even if Satan were calling them to the punishment of the blazing (Fire)? [22] Whoever submits his face to God, being a doer of good, has grasped the firmest handle. To God (belongs) the outcome of all affairs. [23] Whoever disbelieves – do not let his disbelief cause you sorrow. To Us is their return, and We shall inform them about what they have done. Surely God knows what is in the hearts. [24] We give them enjoyment (of life) for a little (while), then We force them to a stern punishment. [25] If indeed you ask them, 'Who created the heavens and the earth?,' they will indeed say, 'God.' Say: 'Praise (be) to God!' But most of them do not know (it). [26] To God (belongs) whatever is in the heavens and the earth. Surely God – He is the wealthy One, the Praiseworthy.

[27] Even if all the trees on the earth were pens, and the sea (were ink) – (and) extending it (were) seven seas after it – the words of God would (still) not give out. God is mighty, wise.

[28] Your creation and your raising up are only as (that of) a single person. God is hearing, seeing.

[29] Do you not see that God causes the night to pass into the day, and causes the day to pass into the night, and has subjected the sun and the moon, each one running (its course) for an appointed time, and that God is aware of what you do? [30] That is because God – He is the Truth, and what they call on instead of Him – that is the falsehood, and because God is the Most High, the Great. [31] Do you not see that the ship runs on the sea by the blessing of God, so that He may show you some of His signs? Surely in that are signs indeed for every patient (and) thankful one. [32] And when wave(s) cover them like shadows, they call on

---

Allah does not love. The object in this verse, the "arrogant (and) boastful" (*mukhtār fakhūr*), also appears at 4.36 and 57.23. See "The Language of Love in the Quran" (p. 560).

31.27 – *Even if all the trees on the earth were pens*
This lovely statement about the words of Allah may remind Bible readers of the verse at the end of the Gospel according to John (21:25) and – for some – the hymn "The Love of God Is Greater Far."

God, devoting (their) religion to Him. But when He has brought them safely to the shore, some of them become lax. No one denies Our signs except every traitor (and) ungrateful one.

³³ People! Guard (yourselves) against your Lord, and fear a Day when no father will offer any compensation for his son, and no son will offer any compensation for his father. Surely the promise of God is true, so do not let this present life deceive you, and do not let the Deceiver deceive you about God. ³⁴ Surely God – with Him is the knowledge of the Hour. He sends down the rain, and He knows what is in the wombs, but no person knows what he will earn tomorrow, and no person knows in what (place on) earth he will die. Surely God is knowing, aware.

THE PROSTRATION
AL-SAJDA

32

Questions continue from an audience that does not accept that the words of the messenger are anything but his own. This sūra replies from several familiar angles.

The presence and power of the Creator requires an appropriate response from his creation. A reckoning will come when all of humankind are resurrected and gathered to their Lord. Allah destroyed many generations in the past who resisted the message.

The sūra also includes brief and positive references to the book God gave to Moses and to the leaders of the Children of Israel.

In the Name of God, the Merciful, the Compassionate

[1] Alif Lām Mīm. [2] The sending down of the Book – (there is) no doubt about it – (is) from the Lord of the worlds. [3] Or do they say, 'He has forged it'? No! It is the truth from your Lord, so that you may warn a people to whom no warner has come before you, so that they may be (rightly) guided.

[4] (It is) God who created the heavens and the earth, and whatever is between them, in six days. Then He mounted the throne. You have no ally and no

---

32.1–2 – *Alif Lām Mīm. The sending down of the Book – (there is) no doubt about it*

On the disconnected Arabic letters that begin this sūra, see the comment at 2.1. The sūra opens with a claim that it is the revelation or "sending down" (*tanzīl*) of a book that contains no doubt (cf. 2.2).

32.3 – *Or do they say, "He has forged it"?*

In spite of verse 2, many listeners doubt both the message and the messenger. The objection, "He has forged it," appears at least seventeen times in the Quran. This verse asserts the truth of the message and claims the necessity of the messenger. See the discussion on verses that accuse the messenger of inventing at 69.44 (p. 587).

32.4 – *(It is) God who created the heavens and the earth*

The first topic of preaching is the signs of Allah's creative activity, including the creation of humans (vv. 7–9).

intercessor other than Him. Will you not take heed? [5] He directs the (whole) affair from the sky to the earth; then it will go up to Him in a day, the measure of which is a thousand years of what you count. [6] That One is the Knower of the unseen and the seen, the Mighty, the Compassionate, [7] who made well everything He created. He brought about the creation of the human from clay, [8] then He made his progeny from an extract of despicable water, [9] then He fashioned him and breathed into him some of His spirit, and made for you hearing and sight and hearts. Little thanks you show!

[10] They say, 'When we have gotten lost in the earth, shall we indeed (return) in a new creation?' Yes! But they are disbelievers in the meeting with their Lord. [11] Say: 'The angel of death, who is put in charge of you, will take you, (and) then you will be returned to your Lord.' [12] If (only) you (could) see when the sinners are hanging their heads before their Lord: 'Our Lord, (now) we have seen and heard, so let us return (and) we shall do righteousness. Surely (now) we are certain.' [13] 'If We had (so) pleased, We would indeed have given every person his guidance. But My word has proved true: "I shall indeed fill Gehenna with jinn and people – all (of them)!" [14] So taste (the punishment) because you have forgotten the meeting of this Day of yours. Surely We have forgotten you! Taste the punishment of eternity for what you have done!'

[15] Only those believe in Our signs who, when they are reminded of them, fall down in prostration and glorify their Lord with praise. They are not arrogant. [16] They forsake their beds (during the night) to call on their Lord in fear and eagerness, and they contribute from what We have provided them. [17] No one knows what comfort is hidden (away) for them in payment for what they have done. [18] So is the one who believes like the one who is wicked? They are not equal! [19] As for those who believe and do righteous deeds, for them (there are) Gardens of the Refuge, as a reception for what they have done. [20] But as for those who act wickedly, their refuge is the Fire. Whenever they want to come out of it, they will be sent back into it, and it will be said to them: 'Taste the punishment of the Fire which you called a lie!' [21] And We shall indeed make them taste the nearer punishment, before the greater punishment, so that they

---

32.10 – *They say, "When we have gotten lost in the earth, shall we indeed (return) in a new creation?"*

A second question from the audience introduces a passage about resurrection, and reward and punishment, on the Day of Resurrection (vv. 11–22).

32.13 – *"I shall indeed fill Gehenna with jinn and people – all (of them)!"*

This striking statement of Allah's intention to fill hell (*jahannam*, also in 11.119) is an important part of the longer passage on the reckoning to come.

may return. ²² Who is more evil than the one who is reminded of the signs of his Lord, (and) then turns away from them? Surely We are going to take vengeance on the sinners.

²³ Certainly We gave Moses the Book – so do not be in doubt of meeting Him – and We made it a guidance for the Sons of Israel. ²⁴ And We appointed from among them leaders (who) guide (others) by Our command, when they were patient and were certain of Our signs. ²⁵ Surely your Lord – He will distinguish between them on the Day of Resurrection concerning their differences.

²⁶ Is it not a guide for them how many generations We have destroyed before them, (seeing that) they walk in (the midst of) their dwelling places? Surely in that are signs indeed. Will they not hear? ²⁷ Do they not see that We drive water to the barren earth, and bring forth crops by means of it, from which their livestock and they themselves eat? Will they not see? ²⁸ They say, 'When will the victory take place, if you are truthful?' ²⁹ Say: 'On the Day of Victory, their belief will not benefit those who disbelieve, nor will they be spared.' ³⁰ So turn away from them, and wait. Surely they (too) are waiting.

32.23 – *Certainly We gave Moses the book*

Wherever the Quran names the pre-Islamic scriptures or – as in this verse – the Torah by another name, it always describes them in the most positive and respectful terms. Here the Torah is "a guidance for the Sons of Israel." This passage is also positive about the Sons themselves (v. 24), but mentions that they differ and says that Allah will judge between them on the Day of Resurrection (v. 25). On the theme of disagreement, see the comments at 98.4 (p. 642).

32.28 – *They say, "When will the victory take place, if you are truthful?"*

The audience seems to taunt the messenger and his followers about a "victory" (or "opening," *fatḥ*) that the messenger has evidently promised. See "Divine Punishment of Unbelievers in This World" (p. 507).

THE FACTIONS
AL-AḤZĀB

33

> Sūra 33 is unique in the Quran for its extensive and concentrated material on "the prophet" and for the personal nature of that material. It is strikingly different in both tone and content from almost all of the sūras between Sūras 9 and 47.
>
> References to "the messenger" and "the prophet" pepper the text. "The prophet" is repeatedly addressed in the second person and described in the third person. Two statements well known among Muslims are that "the prophet is closer to the believers than they are to themselves" (v. 6) and that "certainly the messenger of God has been a good example for you" (v. 21). "The messenger" is repeatedly associated with Allah for submission and obedience (vv. 31, 33, 66, 71, cf. 36).
>
> Tradition has linked many verses from this sūra with famous events in the Muslim story of Islamic origins. The name "Muḥammad" appears in verse 40, where he is portrayed as both "the messenger of Allah" and "the seal of the prophets."

In the Name of God, the Merciful, the Compassionate

[1] Prophet! Guard (yourself) against God, and do not obey the disbelievers and the hypocrites. Surely God is knowing, wise. [2] Follow what you are inspired

---

33.1 – *Prophet! Guard (yourself) against God, and do not obey the disbelievers*

The first word of the sūra addresses "the prophet," and this expression will now appear more frequently in Sūra 33 than in any other sūra. In fact, the number of occurrences of "the prophet" here (fifteen times) is nearly as many as all other quranic occurrences combined (eighteen). Direct address from the Quran ("Prophet!") also occurs here more often than in any other sūra.

Known as the "vocative," direct address in this sūra instructs the prophet in how to deal with non-Muslims (vv. 1, 48) and how to relate to his wives (vv. 28, 50, 59), and supports his role as a witness, warner, and bringer of good news to the believers. See the analysis of the contexts in which "Prophet!" occurs at 66.1 (p. 577).

(with) from your Lord. Surely God is aware of what you do. ³ Put your trust in God, (for) God is sufficient as a guardian.

⁴ God has not placed two hearts inside anyone. He has not made your wives whom you declare to be as your mothers' backs your (real) mothers, nor has He made your adopted sons your (real) sons. That is what you say with your mouths, but God speaks the truth and guides (you) to the (right) way. ⁵ Call them by (the names of) their (real) fathers: that is more just in the sight of God. If you do not know their (real) fathers, (regard them) as your brothers in religion, and your clients. There is no blame on you in any mistakes you have made, but only in what your hearts have intended. God is forgiving, compassionate.

⁶ The prophet is closer to the believers than they are to themselves, and his wives are their mothers, but those related by blood are closer to one another in the Book of God than the believers and the emigrants – but you should do right by your allies. That is written in the Book.

⁷ (Remember) when We took a covenant with the prophets – and from you, and from Noah, and Abraham, and Moses, and Jesus, son of Mary – We took a firm covenant with them, ⁸ so that He might question the truthful about their truthfulness. He has prepared a painful punishment for the disbelievers.

⁹ You who believe! Remember the blessing of God on you, when the forces came upon you, and We sent against them a wind, and (also) forces which you did not see. God sees what you do. ¹⁰ When they came upon you from above you and from below you, and when (your) sight turned aside and (your) hearts reached (your) throats, and you were thinking about God (all kinds of) thoughts, ¹¹ there and then the believers were tested and severely shaken. ¹² And when the hypocrites, and those in whose hearts is a sickness, said, 'God and His messenger have promised us nothing but deception.' ¹³ And when a group of them said, 'People

---

33.6 – *The prophet is closer to the believers than they are to themselves*

This famous verse about the nearness of "the prophet" to the believers has encouraged great affection and veneration for the messenger of Islam among Muslims.

33.9 – *Remember the blessing of God on you, when the forces came upon you*

Verses 9–27 bring to mind a battle (v. 18) in which there are opposing factions (v. 22), death, and killing (v. 16), as well as flight from the fighting (vv. 13, 16). The Quran, however, portrays the battle as being fought by Allah (vv. 9, 25).

The Muslim story of Islamic origins connects these verses with a particular battle in the career of Islam's messenger, the "Battle of the Trench" (*khandaq*). (See *Raids*, 242–43, and *Sīra*, 466–68.)

33.13 – *And when a group of them said, "People of Yathrib!"*

"Yathrib" is one of the few places named in the Quran. Muslim tradition identifies

of Yathrib! (There is) no dwelling place for you (here), so return!' And (another) contingent of them was asking permission of the prophet, saying, 'Surely our houses are vulnerable' – yet they were not vulnerable, they only wished to flee. ¹⁴ If an entrance had been made against them from that side, (and) then they had been asked (to join in) the troublemaking, they would indeed have done it, and scarcely have hesitated with it. ¹⁵ Certainly they had made a covenant with God before (this), that they would not turn their backs, and a covenant with God is (something) to be responsible for. ¹⁶ Say: 'Flight will not benefit you. If you flee from death or killing, you will only enjoy (life) a little (while).' ¹⁷ Say: 'Who is the one who will protect you against God, if He intends evil for you, or intends mercy for you?' They will not find for themselves any ally or helper other than God.

¹⁸ God knows those of you who are a hindrance, and those who say to their brothers, 'Come to us,' but who seldom come out to the battle, ¹⁹ (in their) greed toward you. When fear comes (upon them), you see them looking at you, their eyes rolling around like one who faints at the point of death. But when fear departs, they sting you with (their) sharp tongues (in their) greed for the good (that has come to you). Those – they have not believed. God has made their deeds worthless. That is easy for God. ²⁰ They think (that) the factions have not gone away. If the factions come (again), they will wish that they were living in the desert among the Arabs, asking for news of you. Yet (even) if they were among you, they would seldom fight. ²¹ Certainly the messenger of God has been a good example for you – for the one who hopes in God and the Last Day, and remembers God often.

Yathrib with Medina, which in turn comes from the Arabic *madīnat al-nabī* ("city of the prophet").

33.16 – Say: *"Flight will not benefit you. If you flee from death or killing . . ."*

The Quran commands the messenger to urge into battle those who are hesitant to fight (vv. 16–20, cf. 11–14).

33.21 – *Certainly the messenger of God has been a good example for you*

This famous verse comes in the midst of the sūra's portrayal of a battle and at the end of a section about the willingness of various groups to fight. The Quran holds up the messenger's behavior as a "good example" (*uswa ḥasana*).

The title "the messenger of Allah," like "the prophet," has an interesting pattern of occurrence in the Quran. In most sūras it does not appear, but in Sūra 33 it appears three times as "the messenger of Allah" (vv. 21, 40, 53) and nine times in the expression "Allah and His messenger" (vv. 12, 22 (x2), 31, 33, 36 (x2), 57, 71). In this sūra the expression seems to be used interchangeably with "the prophet."

²² When the believers saw the factions, they said, 'This is what God and His messenger promised us, and God and His messenger were truthful.' It only increased them in belief and submission. ²³ Among the believers are men who have been truthful to the covenant which they made with God: some of them have fulfilled their vow, and some of them are (still) waiting (to do so). They have not changed in the least, ²⁴ so that God may repay the truthful for their truthfulness, and punish the hypocrites, if He (so) pleases, or turn to them (in forgiveness). Surely God is forgiving, compassionate. ²⁵ God turned back those who disbelieved in their rage, and they did not attain any advantage. God was sufficient for the believers in the fighting. Surely God is strong, mighty. ²⁶ He brought down from their fortifications those of the People of the Book who supported them, and cast dread into their hearts. You killed a group (of them), and took captive (another) group. ²⁷ And He caused you to inherit their land, their homes, and their wealth, and a land you had not set foot on. God is powerful over everything.

33.22 – *This is what God and His messenger promised us*

The participation of the believers in the battle (vv. 22–23) contrasts with the behavior of the hypocrites (v. 24).

Sūra 33 is one of the sūras that extensively pair Allah with "His messenger." Here the messenger is associated with Allah as deserving of obedience (vv. 31, 33, 66, 71; cf. 36) and as offering a united promise (vv. 12, 22).

33.26 – *He brought down from their fortifications those of the People of the Book*

The Quran says that Allah brings down a group from the People of the Book and gives their belongings to the "believers" (v. 27). However, it was actually the "believers" who kill the group or take them captive. Further identification of the group attacked is not given here or elsewhere in this sūra.

The Muslim stories of Islamic origins have connected these verses with a Jewish tribe in Medina called the Banū Qurayẓa (*Sīra*, 461–69; *Raids*, 244–57; *History*, 8:27–41). According to Muslim narratives, during the "Battle of the Trench" the Banū Qurayẓa tribe worked against the Muslims in Medina. When the battle ended, the Muslims dealt with the tribe by killing the men, who numbered between 600 and 900 (*Sīra*, 464, *History*, 8:35), taking the women and children captive, and seizing the tribe's land, homes, and wealth.

This verse also describes Allah as casting terror or "dread" (*ruʿb*) into the hearts of the People of the Book. This expression repeats at 3.151; 8.12; and 59.2. In this case, the reason for the terrorizing seems to be that these People of the Book supported the enemy. See a discussion of terror and terrorizing at 59.2 (p. 554) and a summary of the Quran's approach to the People of the Book at 98.1 (p. 641).

²⁸ Prophet! Say to your wives: 'If you desire this present life and its (passing) splendor, come! I shall make provision for you, and release you gracefully. ²⁹ But if you desire God and His messenger, and the Home of the Hereafter – surely God has prepared a great reward for the doers of good among you.' ³⁰ Wives of the prophet! Whoever among you commits clear immorality, for her the punishment will be doubled. That is easy for God. ³¹ But whoever among you is obedient to God and His messenger, and does righteousness – We shall give her her reward twice over. We have prepared a generous provision for her. ³² Wives of the prophet! You are not like any of the (other) women. If you guard (yourselves), do not be beguiling in (your) speech, or he in whose heart is a sickness will become lustful, but speak in a rightful fashion. ³³ Stay in your houses, and do not flaunt (yourselves) with the flaunting of the former ignorance, but observe the prayer and give the alms, and obey God and His messenger. God only wishes to take away the abomination from you, People of the House, and to purify you completely. ³⁴ Remember what is recited in your houses of the signs of God and the wisdom. Surely God is astute, aware.

³⁵ Surely the submitting men and the submitting women, the believing men and the believing women, the obedient men and the obedient women, the truthful men and the truthful women, the patient men and the patient women, the humble men and the humble women, the charitable men and the charitable women, the fasting men and the fasting women, the men who guard their private parts and the women who guard (them), the men who remember God often and the women who remember (Him) – for them God has prepared forgiveness and a great reward.

33.28–34 – *Prophet! Say to your wives: "If you desire this present life and its (passing) splendor..."*

The Quran gives the prophet a speech for his wives, but then addresses the wives directly (vv. 30–34).

33.33 – *observe the prayer and give the alms, and obey God and His messenger*

This command appears with three other verses in Sūra 33 to emphasize the importance of obedience to "the messenger." This verse seems to address the command to the "wives of the prophet." Verses 31 and 71 proclaim the rewards of obedience, and verse 36 characterizes disobedience to Allah and the messenger.

In many parts of the Quran, the "believers" are commanded to perform the ritual prayer (Ṣalāh) and almsgiving (zakāh). Here the Quran adds a command to obey the messenger.

[36] It is not for a believing man or a believing woman, when God and His messenger have decided a matter, to have the choice in their matter. Whoever disobeys God and His messenger has very clearly gone astray.

[37] (Remember) when you said to the one whom God had blessed, and whom you had blessed: 'Keep your wife to yourself, and guard (yourself) against God,' and you hid within yourself what God was going to reveal, and feared the people, when God had a better right that you feared Him. So when Zayd had gotten what he needed from her, We married her to you, so that there should not be any blame on the believers concerning the wives of their adopted sons, when they have gotten what they needed from them. The command of God was (to be) fulfilled. [38] There is no blame on the prophet concerning what God has made obligatory for him. (That was) the customary way of God concerning those who passed away before – and the command of God is a determined decree – [39] who were delivering the messages of God, and fearing Him, and not fearing anyone but Him. God is sufficient as a reckoner.

33.36 – *when God and His messenger have decided a matter*

The Quran associates the messenger with Allah for authority in decision making. This verse, as well as commands to obey the messenger, became very important in the writings of the influential Muslim jurist al-Shāfiʿī (d. 820), who insisted that they gave divine authority to the sayings attributed to Muhammad in the hadith. Al-Shāfiʿī's opinion heavily influenced the development of Islamic Law. See an analysis of commands to obey the messenger at 64.12 (p. 574).

33.37 – *when you said to the one whom God had blessed, . . . "Keep your wife to yourself . . ."*

This verse, addressed directly to the messenger, communicates very little because of the extensive use of pronouns without antecedent. However, the verse does mention Zayd – one of the few contemporary names given in the Quran. It refers to a wife who would be married to the messenger, and it says that the messenger is hiding something within himself.

The Muslim story of Islamic origins associates verses 36–40 with a story that Muhammad's adopted son, Zayd, had a beautiful wife named Zaynab. According to the story (e.g., al-Ṭabarī, *History*, 8:1–4), Islam's messenger admired Zaynab, and when Zayd learned this, he divorced Zaynab so that Islam's messenger could marry her. A variety of early Muslim commentators (e.g., Muqātil ibn Sulaymān, al-Ṭabarī, al-Qurṭubī) also told the Zaynab story in their interpretations of this verse.

[40] Muḥammad is not the father of any of your men, but the messenger of God and the seal of the prophets. God has knowledge of everything.

[41] You who believe! Remember God often, [42] and glorify Him morning and evening. [43] He (it is) who prays over you, and His angels (do too), to bring you out of the darkness to the light. He is compassionate with the believers. [44] On the Day when they meet Him, their greeting will be: 'Peace!' He has prepared a generous reward for them.

[45] Prophet! Surely We have sent you as a witness, and as a bringer of good news and a warner, [46] and as one calling to God, by His permission, and as an illuminating lamp. [47] Give good news to the believers that they have great favor from God. [48] Do not obey the disbelievers and the hypocrites. Ignore their hurt but put your trust in God. God is sufficient as a guardian.

[49] You who believe! When you marry believing women (and) then divorce them before you touch them, you have no waiting period to count for them. So make provision for them, and release them gracefully.

33.40 – *Muhammad is not the father of any of your men, but the messenger of God and the seal of the prophets*

This is the second appearance of the name "Muḥammad" in the Quran. In the preceding thirty-two sūras – more than two thirds of the content of the Quran – the name has only appeared once (at 3.144). Here the context for the name seems to be a question about paternity and a claim for special status among the prophets. This is also one of the two verses that connect the name "Muhammad" with "the messenger of Allah" (also 48.29).

The fact that the name Muhammad only appears four times in the Quran is surely striking, given that Muslims believe the Quran was revealed to Muhammad. All four occurrences are in the third person, declaring something about Muhammad, and never in the second person or vocative ("O Muhammad"). See the analysis of the four appearances of the name at 48.29 (p. 516).

The claim that Muhammad would be the "seal of the prophets" appears only here in the Quran. Muslims have understood "seal" to mean that Muhammad is the final prophet in a long sequence of prophets that begins with Adam. Many Muslim commentators take "is not the father of any of your men" to mean that there is no blame on the messenger of Islam for marrying Zayd's wife, because Zayd was adopted and not a biological son.

For a taste of classical Muslim commentary on this verse, as well as verses 37 and 50–52 of this sūra, readers can access translations of Zamakhsharī's (d. 1144) interpretations in Gätje's *The Qur'ān and its Exegesis* (see bibliography).

⁵⁰ Prophet! Surely We have made lawful for you your wives to whom you have granted their marriage gifts, and what your right (hand) owns from what God has given you, and the daughters of your paternal uncles and paternal aunts, your maternal uncles and maternal aunts, who have emigrated with you, and any believing woman, if she gives herself to the prophet, and if the prophet wishes to take her in marriage. (That is) exclusively for you, apart from the believers – We know what We have made obligatory for them concerning their wives and what their right (hands) own – so that there may be no blame on you. God is forgiving, compassionate. ⁵¹ You may put off whomever you please of them, and you may take to yourself whomever you please. And whomever you desire of those you have set aside, (there is) no blame on you (if you take her again). That is more appropriate, so that they may be comforted and not sorrow, and (that) they may be pleased with what you give them – all of them. God knows what is in your hearts. God is knowing, forbearing. ⁵² Beyond (that) women are not permitted to you, nor (is it permitted to you) to take (other) wives in exchange for them, even though their beauty pleases you, except for what your right (hand) owns. God is watching over everything.

⁵³ You who believe! Do not enter the houses of the prophet to (attend) a meal without waiting (until it) is ready, unless permission is given to you. But when you are invited, enter, and when you have eaten, disperse, and do not linger for conversation. Surely that is hurtful to the prophet, and he is ashamed of you, but God is not ashamed of the truth. When you ask them for anything, ask them from behind a veil. That is purer for your hearts and their hearts. It is not for you to hurt the messenger of God, nor to marry his wives after him – ever. Surely that is a great (offense) in the sight of God. ⁵⁴ Whether you reveal a thing or hide it, surely God has knowledge of everything.

33.50 – *Prophet! Surely We have made lawful for you your wives*

The Quran addresses the prophet directly to tell him the range of woman he is permitted to marry. The prophet may marry any believing woman who gives herself to him. This is lawful exclusively for the prophet. He may also put off any of the wives he pleases, as well as take any of them back again (v. 51).

Verses 50–53, as well as verses 35 and 37, are noticeably longer than most of the other verses in the sūra.

33.53 – *When you ask them for anything, ask them from behind a veil*

The Quran gives instructions to the believers for how they should behave in the homes of the prophet and his wives. If believers want to ask the wives for anything, they should do so from behind a veil (ḥijāb). However, the wives may receive visits from their fathers and other close relatives in their families (v. 55).

See "Women in the Quran" for an explanation of ḥijāb (p. 429).

⁵⁵ (There is) no blame on them concerning their fathers, or their sons, or their brothers, or their brothers' sons, or their sisters' sons, or their women, or what their right (hands) own. But guard (yourselves) against God. Surely God is a witness over everything.

⁵⁶ Surely God and His angels pray for the prophet. You who believe! You pray for him (too), and greet him (with a worthy) greeting. ⁵⁷ Surely those who hurt God and His messenger – God has cursed them in this world and the Hereafter, and has prepared a humiliating punishment for them. ⁵⁸ Those who hurt believing men and believing women – other than what they have earned – they will indeed bear (the burden of) slander and clear sin.

⁵⁹ Prophet! Say to your wives, and your daughters, and the believing women, to draw some of their outer clothes over themselves. That is more appropriate for their being recognized and not hurt. God is forgiving, compassionate.

33.56 – *Surely God and His angels pray for the prophet*

This is an important example of how the present translation by A. J. Droge is correct where virtually all other translations decline to translate the verse literally. This verse states that Allah and his angels pray for (or "pray upon," *Ṣalla ʿalā*) the prophet. Believers are to do the same and to wish peace upon the prophet. Many translators express this as "may peace and blessing be upon him."

In the book *Muslim Devotions*, Constance Padwick found in a survey of prayer manuals across the Muslim world that this *taṣliya* – or calling down the prayers of Allah upon the prophet – is "the commonest of phrases on Muslim lips" and in its various forms made up at least one third of the manuals she studied (see bibliography).

Discerning readers will note that 33.56 raises a profound theological question. If Allah indeed prays for or prays upon "the prophet," as this verse claims, to whom does Allah pray?

33.57 – *Surely those who hurt God and His messenger – God has cursed them in this world and the Hereafter*

The Quran associates the messenger with Allah in being "hurt" (*ādhā*). This association – and the punishments promised both in this world and the hereafter – may partly account for the extreme sensitivity surrounding perceived insults to the messenger of Islam in the modern world.

33.59 – *Prophet! Say to your wives, and your daughters, and the believing women, to draw some of their outer clothes over themselves*

In this verse, the Arabic word for "outer clothes" is *jalābīb* (sing. *jilbāb*), one of several terms that are commonly used in discussions about coverings of Muslim women today (also *ḥijāb*, see verse 53 above).

Women in the Quran
Linda Darwish

The view of women in Islam has been a contentious topic in recent public discourse, but few have a firm grasp on the quranic material about women.

The Quran presents women and men as equal in creation, created of the same *nafs*, or soul (4.1), and as having spiritual equality. Women and men make their own confessions of faith (60.12) and are accountable for themselves on the Day of Judgment (33.35, 73; 45.21–22). The Quran warns unbelievers that God will hold people accountable for female infanticide (81.8–9), allegedly practiced as a shield against excessive poverty. The Quran provides women protections against abandonment in marriage and ensures support for their them and their children (2.226–32; 4.4, 19), admonishing men to practice fairness, equity, and kindness, and reminding them to fear God in their dealings with women.

For many contemporary readers, however, the Quran's view of women is sharply at odds with principles of social equality and justice. Woman's disadvantageous position in marriage (2.223; 4.34), divorce (2.226–32; 65.1–6; though it should be noted that the most egregious disadvantages are mainly via jurisprudence), inheritance (4.11, 177), and bearing witness (2.282), among other things, are cited as evidence of the Quran's regressive attitude towards women as compared to today's standards. However, it is the exegetes, who have typically been men, who translate the Quran's references to women into normative ideas, laws, or standards of practice, while voices of women have habitually been muted, absent, or subjugated to a patriarchal hermeneutical framework. Thus in the interpretation of problematic passages of the Quran for today, presuppositions and hermeneutics are important to consider.

Amina Wadud Muhsin, an African-American feminist Muslim academic, suggests three types of interpretation regarding women in the Quran: traditional, reactive, and holistic. Traditional readings reflect a patriarchal construction; reactive readings vindicate an externally imposed feminist construction; a holistic reading, Muhsin's preference, places the female experience at the center of interpretation, while ignoring the exegetical tradition. The premise of Muhsin's approach is that the commonly perceived "problem" of women in Islam is not due to the Quran itself but to the application of a faulty, male-centered hermeneutic imposed upon the text. The aim of the holistic approach is to "unread" these patriarchal narratives.

In her interpretation of Sūra 4.34, frequently taken as proof of the inferiority of women in general and specifically in the context of marriage, Muhsin argues that the Quran's intent is not to establish male authority or to sanction punishment for female disobedience but to restore marital harmony. Her argument turns on a study of the verse's four key terms: *qānitāt* ("good"), *nushūz* ("disobedient"), *ta'a* ("obey"), and *ḍaraba* ("hit" or "beat"). Among these, her reinterpretation of *nushūz* has the most to offer, but even this is of limited value to an egalitarian exegesis. Commonly translated as "disobedient," Muhsin notes that the term is also used of men in 4.128. If a woman fears *nushūz*, translated "contempt" or "evasion" in some translations, from her husband, they should try to settle their differences amicably. Giving it the same sense in 4.34, Muhsin suggests the verse means that when either party contributes to the breakdown of the marriage, steps may be taken to restore harmony. Muhsin fails to note, however, that the husband's uncooperative behavior is criticized in 4.128 in the context of unfairness to his multiple wives. On the term *ḍaraba*, Muhsin argues that the word has broader meaning than "strike," and that it is not the much stronger Arabic second form of the verb, *ḍarraba*, meaning "to strike repeatedly," both of which do little to convince that the term is thereby rendered innocuous.

Another contentious topic in the Quran has to do with women's covering and seclusion. While eight verses use the word *ḥijāb* (7.46; 17.45; 19.17; 38.32; 41.5; 42.51; 33.53; 83.15), none refers to an article of clothing, and only two (19.17 and 33.53) have anything to do with women. Sūra 33.53, the context of which is said to be the aftermath of one of the prophet's marriages, instructs Muslim men to be respectful of Muhammad's and his wives' privacy within their domestic space. Accordingly, if men are to ask Muhammad's wives for anything, they must do so from behind a partition (*ḥijāb*). This is explained as a matter of "purity." It is added that none should marry Muhammad's wives after his death. Despite the passage's restricted reference to the prophet's domestic space, exegetes have relied on the tendency of the community to make the "mothers of the believers" role models for Muslim women a justification for extending its application to all women.

The notion of female covering is left largely to Sūras 24.31 and 33.59, neither of which uses the word *ḥijāb*, but which more effectively capture its popular meaning, evincing as they do, the notion of the outward display of modesty and the symbolism of protection from sexual harassment respectively.

In summary, the quranic view of women is neither monolithic nor static, but rather within certain boundaries remains subject to the perspectives and methods of its varied interpreters.

⁶⁰ If indeed the hypocrites do not stop – and those in whose hearts is a sickness, and those who cause commotion in the city – We shall indeed incite you against them, (and) then they will not be your neighbors there, except for a little (while). ⁶¹ (They will be) accursed! Wherever they are found, they will be seized and completely killed. ⁶² (That was) the customary way of God concerning those who have passed away before, and you will find no change in the customary way of God.

⁶³ The people ask you about the Hour. Say: 'Knowledge of it is only with God. What will make you know? Perhaps the Hour is near.' ⁶⁴ Surely God has cursed the disbelievers, and prepared for them a blazing (Fire), ⁶⁵ there to remain forever. They will not find any ally or helper. ⁶⁶ On the Day when their faces will be turned about in the Fire, they will say, 'Oh, would that we had obeyed God, and obeyed the messenger!' ⁶⁷ And they will say, 'Our Lord, surely we obeyed our men of honor and our great men, and so they led us astray from the way. ⁶⁸ Our Lord, give them a double (share) of the punishment, and curse them with a great curse!'

⁶⁹ You who believe! Do not be like those who hurt Moses, but God cleared him of what they said, and he was eminent in the sight of God. ⁷⁰ You who believe! Guard (yourselves) against God, and speak a direct word. ⁷¹ He will set right your deeds for you, and forgive you your sins. Whoever obeys God and His messenger has attained a great triumph.

⁷² Surely We offered the trust to the heavens and the earth, and the mountains, but they refused to bear it, and were afraid of it, and (instead) the human bore it. Surely he has become an evildoer (and) ignorant. ⁷³ (It is) so that God might punish the hypocrite men and the hypocrite women (alike), and the idolatrous men and the idolatrous women alike, and so that God might turn (in forgiveness) to the believing men and the believing women (alike). God is forgiving, compassionate.

33.61 – *(They will be) accursed! Wherever they are found, they will be seized and completely killed*

This and the following verse seem to say that the killing of the hypocrites is Allah's "customary way" (*sunna*).

33.66 – *Oh, would that we had obeyed God, and obeyed the messenger!*

A number of sūras contain "judgment scenes" in which people sent to hell wish they had paid attention to the warnings that came to them when they lived in the world. This passage (vv. 69–71) adds disobedience to "the messenger" to the list of regrets.

33.69 – *Do not be like those who hurt Moses*

This intriguing verse uses the same Arabic verb as the verb in verse 57 also translated "hurt," *ādhā*. Is this referring to the story in Numbers 12 about how Miriam and Aaron "spoke against" Moses?

SHEBA
SABĀ'

34

> After the intense text and claustrophobic mood of Sūra 33, the language and feel of Sūra 34 seem like a return to placid waters. Here there is no mention of "the prophet" with his wives, battles, and need for privacy. Neither is the messenger repeatedly associated with Allah. Instead, here the Quran knows only a bringer of good news and a warner (v. 28), who expects rejection from the "affluent ones" of the town (v. 34).
>
> The comments and questions from the audience in resistance to the message come thick and fast. A reckoning will indeed come to those who reject the messenger's preaching. However, the reckoning will be on the day when God gathers them all together (v. 40). The sūra features a number of "judgment scenes," including one in which the disbelievers blame each other for their bad decisions.

In the Name of God, the Merciful, the Compassionate

¹ Praise (be) to God – to Him (belongs) whatever is in the heavens and whatever is on the earth – and to Him (be) praise in the Hereafter! He is the Wise, the Aware. ² He knows what penetrates into the earth and what comes forth from it, and what comes down from the sky and what goes up into it. He is the Compassionate, the Forgiving.

³ Those who disbelieve say, 'The Hour will not come upon us.' Say: 'Yes indeed! By my Lord! It will indeed come to you! (He is the) Knower of

---

34.1 – *Praise (be) to God – to Him (belongs) whatever is in the heavens*

The Quran returns to the signs of the Creator's power and presence and the appropriate response of humankind. The abrupt change of language and content from Sūra 33 seems to indicate two completely different kinds of literature – and indeed two different writers.

34.3 – *Those who disbelieve say: "The Hour will not come upon us."*

Those who hear the preaching generally deny its truth, and the messenger answers back with speeches introduced by "Say." Here the messenger assures his listeners that a day of reckoning will come (vv. 3–9; also most of vv. 26–54).

the unseen. Not (even) the weight of a speck in the heavens and the earth escapes from Him, nor (is there anything) smaller than that or greater, except (that it is recorded) in a clear Book ⁴ – so that He may repay those who believe and do righteous deeds.' Those – for them (there is) forgiveness and generous provision. ⁵ But those who strive against Our signs to obstruct (them), those – for them (there is) a punishment of painful wrath. ⁶ But those who have been given the knowledge see (that) what has been sent down to you from your Lord is the truth, and (that) it guides to the path of the Mighty, the Praiseworthy.

⁷ Those who disbelieve say, 'Shall we direct you to a man who will inform you (that) when you have been completely torn to pieces, you will indeed (return) in a new creation? ⁸ Has he forged a lie against God, or is he possessed?' No! Those who do not believe in the Hereafter are in punishment and far astray. ⁹ Do they not look to what is before them and what is behind them of the sky and the earth? If We (so) please, We could cause the earth to swallow them, or make fragments of the sky fall on them. Surely in that is a sign indeed for every servant who turns (in repentance).

¹⁰ Certainly We gave David favor from Us: 'You mountains! Return (praises) with him, and you birds (too)!' And We made iron malleable for him: ¹¹ 'Make full (coats of armor), and measure (well) in the sewing (of them).' And: 'Do righteousness, (for) surely I see what you do.' ¹² And to Solomon (We subjected) the wind, its morning was a month's (journey), and its evening was a month's (journey), and We made a spring of molten brass to flow for him. And among the jinn, (there were) those who worked for him by the permission of his Lord. Whoever of them turns aside from Our command – We shall make him taste the punishment of the blazing (Fire). ¹³ They made for him whatever he pleased: places of prayer, and statues, and basins like cisterns, and fixed cooking pots. 'House of David! Work in

---

34.8 – *Has he forged a lie against God, or is he possessed?*

In addition to resisting the message, the audience criticizes the messenger himself (also v. 43), asking whether he is possessed by *jinn*. On verses that accuse the messenger of inventing, see the discussion at 69.44 (p. 587).

34.10 – *Certainly We gave David favor from Us*

David urges the mountains and birds to praise Allah (and in more detail in 38.17–20). Verses 10 and 11 suggest that David also had skill in making armor. A similar passage on David comes at 21.79–80, where it is Allah who subdues the mountains and birds to praise along with David (also 38.18–19).

34.12 – *And to Solomon (We subjected) the wind*

This passage again associates Solomon with occult beings, here called *jinn* (vv. 12–14; cf. "satans" at 2.102; 21.82; and 38.37–38). See the summary of verses about *jinn* at 72.1 (p. 593).

thankfulness, (for) few of My servants are thankful!' [14] And when We decreed death for him, nothing indicated his death to them except a creature of the earth devouring his staff. When he fell down, it became clear to the jinn that, if they had known the unseen, they would not have remained in the humiliating punishment.

[15] Certainly for Sheba there was a sign in their dwelling place – two gardens, on the right and left: 'Eat from the provision of your Lord, and be thankful to Him. A good land and a forgiving Lord.' [16] But they turned away, so We sent on them the flood of 'Arim, and We replaced for them their two gardens (with) two gardens producing bitter fruit, and tamarisks, and a few lote trees. [17] We repaid them that because they disbelieved. We do not repay (anyone) but the ungrateful? [18] We set between them and the towns which We have blessed (other) towns (which are still) visible, and We measured out the traveling (distance) between them: 'Travel among them by night and day in security!' [19] But they said, 'Our Lord, lengthen (the distance) between our journeys.' They did themselves evil, so We made them legendary, and We tore them completely to pieces. Surely in that are signs indeed for every patient (and) thankful one. [20] Certainly Iblīs confirmed his conjecture about them, and they followed him, except for a group of the believers. [21] But he had no authority over them, except that We might know the one who believed in the Hereafter from the one who was in doubt about it. Your Lord is a watcher over everything.

[22] Say: 'Call on those whom you claim (as gods) instead of God! They do not possess (even) the weight of a speck in the heavens or on the earth. They have no partnership in (the creation of) either of them, nor has He any support from them.' [23] Intercession will be of no benefit with Him, except for the one to whom He gives permission – until, when terror is removed from their hearts, they say, 'What did your Lord say?,' and they say, 'The truth. He is the Most High, the Great.' [24] Say: 'Who provides for you from the heavens and the earth?' Say: 'God.

34.15 – *Certainly for Sheba there was a sign in their dwelling place*

The people of Sheba are also mentioned at 27.22–44, where a woman who rules the people has a central role. Here the queen is absent, and the description focuses an ungrateful people whom Allah judges and punishes.

34.22 – *Call on those whom you claim (as gods) instead of God!*

This verse begins a series of statements from the messenger and the speeches of the audience with which he must contend.

34.23 – *Intercession will be of no benefit with Him, except for the one to whom He gives permission*

What begins as a denial of intercession is modified by an exception. See the analysis of verses on intercession at 39.44 (p. 464).

Surely (either) we or you (stand) indeed on guidance, or (are) clearly astray.'

²⁵ Say: 'You will not be questioned about what sins we have committed, nor shall we be questioned about what you do.'

²⁶ Say: 'Our Lord will gather us together, (and) then disclose the truth between us, (for) He is the Discloser, the Knowing.'

²⁷ Say: 'Show me those whom you have joined with Him as associates. By no means (can you do so)! No! He (alone) is God, the Mighty, the Wise.'

²⁸ We have sent you only as a bringer of good news and a warner to the people all together. But most of the people do not know (it).

²⁹ They say, 'When (will) this promise (come to pass), if you are truthful?' ³⁰ Say: 'For you (there is) the appointment of a Day. You will not delay it by an hour, nor will you advance (it by an hour).'

³¹ Those who disbelieve say, 'We will not believe in this Qur'ān, nor in that which was before it.' If (only) you could see when the evildoers are made to stand before their Lord, (how) some of them hurl the blame at others. Those who were weak will say to those who were arrogant, 'If not for you, we would have been believers.' ³² Those who were arrogant will say to those who were weak, 'Did we keep you from the guidance after it had come to you? No! You (yourselves) were sinners.' ³³ Those who were weak will say to those who were arrogant, 'No! (It was your) scheming by night and day, when you commanded us to disbelieve in God and to set up rivals to Him.' They will be full of secret regret when they see the punishment. We shall put chains on the necks of those who disbelieved. Will they be repaid (for anything) except for what they have done?

³⁴ We have not sent any warner to a town, except that its affluent ones said, 'Surely we are disbelievers in what you are sent with.' ³⁵ And they (also) said, 'We (have) more wealth and children, and we shall not be punished.' ³⁶ Say: 'Surely my Lord extends (His) provision to whomever He pleases, and restricts (it), but most of the people do not know (it).' ³⁷ Neither your wealth nor your children are the things which bring you near to Us in intimacy, except for whoever believes and does righteousness. And those – for them (there is) a double payment for what they have done, and they will be secure in exalted rooms. ³⁸ But those who strive against Our signs to obstruct (them) – those will be brought forward to

---

34.31 – *We will not believe in this Qur'ān*

For the word *qur'ān*, see the explanation at 2.185 (p. 61).

34.31 – *If (only) you could see when the evildoers are made to stand before their Lord*

This passage pictures how the sinners might talk to one another on the Day of Resurrection (vv. 31–33). There are two more such "judgment scenes" in this sūra (vv. 40–42, 51–54).

the punishment. ³⁹ Say: 'Surely my Lord extends (His) provision to whomever He pleases of His servants, and restricts (it) from him (whom He pleases). Whatever thing you contribute, He will replace it, (for) He is the best of providers.'

⁴⁰ On the Day when He gathers them all together, He will say to the angels, '(Was it) you these were serving?' ⁴¹ They will say, 'Glory to You! You are our ally, not they. No! They used to serve the jinn – most of them believed in them.' ⁴² 'So today none of you has power to (cause) another benefit or harm.' And We shall say to those who did evil, 'Taste the punishment of the Fire which you called a lie.'

⁴³ When Our clear signs are recited to them, they say, 'This is only a man who wants to keep you from what your fathers have served.' And they say, 'This is nothing but a forged lie.' Those who disbelieve say to the truth, when it comes to them, 'This is nothing but clear magic' ⁴⁴ – though We have not given them any Books to study, nor have We sent to them any warner before you. ⁴⁵ Those who were before them (also) called (it) a lie, though they have not reached (even) a tenth of what We gave them. They (too) called My messengers liars, and how was My loathing (of them)!

⁴⁶ Say: 'I give you only one admonition, (namely) that you stand before God, in pairs or singly, (and) then reflect: (there are) not any jinn in your companion. He is only a warner for you in the face of a harsh punishment.' ⁴⁷ Say: 'I have not asked you for any reward, but it was (only) for your own sake. My reward (depends) only on God. He is a witness over everything.' ⁴⁸ Say: 'My Lord hurls the truth – Knower of the unseen.' ⁴⁹ Say: 'The truth has come! Falsehood (can) neither bring (anything) about, nor restore (it).' ⁵⁰ Say: 'If I go astray, I go astray only against myself, but if I am guided, it is by what my Lord inspires me (with). Surely He is hearing (and) near.'

⁵¹ If (only) you could see when they are terrified and (there is) no escape, and they are seized from a place nearby, ⁵² and say, 'We believe in it (now).' Yet how will they reach (it) from a place far away, ⁵³ when they disbelieved in it before? They conjecture about the unseen from a place far away. ⁵⁴ But (a barrier) has been set between them and what they desire, as was done with their parties before. Surely they (too) were in grave doubt indeed (about it).

34.43 – *This is nothing but a forged lie*

Again, the audience accuses the messenger of inventing his recitations. This response comes more than seventeen times in the Quran. See the discussion on verses that accuse the messenger of inventing at 69.44 (p. 587). Here the listeners also go further to accuse the messenger of "magic" (*siḥr*).

34.46 – *(there are) not any jinn in your companion. He is only a warner*

The messenger defends himself against the accusation of magic in verse 43.

34.47 – *I have not asked you for any reward, but it was (only) for your own sake*

The messenger of this sūra appears humble and self-effacing, deferring to Allah.

CREATOR
FĀṬIR

35

This sūra appeals to humankind (v. 3) to respond appropriately to the signs of the Creator's power and provision. It warns of the consequences of denying the message in this world and the next. It reassures the messenger with claims that Allah sends him and inspires his recitation, and states that most people resist both the messengers and their message.

This and many other sūras give the impression that various repeated prophetic-sounding materials have been brought together without further organization.

In the Name of God, the Merciful, the Compassionate

[1] Praise (be) to God, Creator of the heavens and the earth, (who) makes the angels messengers having two, and three, and four wings. He adds to the creation whatever He pleases. Surely God is powerful over everything. [2] Whatever mercy God opens to the people, (there is) no withholder of it, and whatever (mercy) He withholds, (there is) no sender of it after that. He is the Mighty, the Wise.

[3] People! Remember the blessing of God on you. (Is there) any creator other than God, (who) provides for you from the sky and the earth? (There is) no god but Him. How are you (so) deluded? [4] If they call you a liar, (know that) messengers have been called liars before you. To God all affairs are returned.

[5] People! Surely the promise of God is true, so (do) not let this present life deceive you, and (do) not let the Deceiver deceive you about God. [6] Surely Satan is an enemy to you, so take him as an enemy. He only calls his faction so that they may be among the companions of the blazing (Fire). [7] Those who disbelieve

---

35.1 – *(who) makes the angels messengers having two, and three, and four wings*
In the Quran, angels too are messengers (*rusul*, sing. *rasūl*).

35.4 – *If they call you a liar, (know that) messengers have been called liars before you*
Several statements are directly addressed to the messenger in this sūra, apparently to encourage him (also vv. 25, 31).

– for them (there is) a harsh punishment, but those who believe and do righteous deeds – for them (there is) forgiveness and a great reward.

⁸ Is the one whose evil deed is made to appear enticing to him, and he perceives it as good, (like the one who is rightly guided)? Surely God leads astray whomever He pleases and guides whomever He pleases. So do not exhaust yourself in regrets over them. Surely God is aware of what they do.

⁹ (It is) God who sends the winds, and it stirs up a cloud, and We drive it to some barren land, and by means of it give the earth life after its death. So (too) is the raising up. ¹⁰ Whoever desires honor – honor (belongs) to God altogether. To Him good words ascend, and the righteous deed – He raises it. But those who scheme evil deeds – for them (there is) a harsh punishment, and their scheming – it will be in vain.

¹¹ God created you from dust, then from a drop, (and) then He made you pairs. No female conceives or delivers, except with His knowledge, and no one grows old who grows old, or is diminished in his life, except (it) is in a Book. Surely that is easy for God.

¹² The two seas are not alike: this one is sweet, fresh, good to drink, and this (other) one is salty (and) bitter. Yet from each you eat fresh fish, and bring out of it an ornament which you wear, and you see the ship cutting through it, so that you may seek some of His favor, and that you may be thankful. ¹³ He causes the night to pass into the day, and causes the day to pass into the night, and He has subjected the sun and the moon, each one running (its course) for an appointed time. That is God, your Lord – to Him (belongs) the kingdom, and those you call on, instead of Him, do not possess even the skin of a date seed. ¹⁴ If you call on them, they do not hear your calling, and (even) if they heard, they would not respond to you. On the Day of Resurrection they will deny your association. No one (can) inform you like One who is aware.

¹⁵ People! You are the ones in need of God, and God – He is the wealthy One, the Praiseworthy. ¹⁶ If He (so) pleases, He will do away with you and bring a new creation. ¹⁷ That is no great matter for God.

¹⁸ No one bearing a burden bears the burden of another. If one heavy-burdened calls for his load (to be carried), nothing of it will be carried, even though he be a family member. You warn only those who fear their Lord in the unseen, and (who) observe the prayer. Whoever purifies himself, only purifies (himself) for

---

35.11 – *No female conceives or delivers, except with His knowledge*

This is one of the most lovely expressions among the creation verses in this sūra.

35.18 – *No one bearing a burden bears the burden of another*

This verse says that each person will be responsible for his or her own "burden"

(the sake of) his own self. To God is the (final) destination. [19] The blind and the sighted are not equal, [20] nor are the darkness and the light, [21] nor the shade and the heat. [22] The living and the dead are not equal. Surely God causes whomever He pleases to hear. You will not cause those who are in the graves to hear [23] – you are only a warner. [24] Surely We have sent you with the truth, as a bringer of good news and a warner. (There has) not (been) any community except that a warner has passed away in it. [25] If they call you a liar, (know that) those who were before them called (their messengers) liars. Their messengers brought them the clear signs, and the scriptures, and the illuminating Book. [26] Then I seized those who disbelieved, and how was My loathing (of them)!

[27] Do you not see that God sends down water from the sky, and by means of it We bring forth fruits of various colors? And in the mountains (there are) streaks (of) white and red – their colors are diverse – and (of) deep black. [28] And among people and (wild) animals and livestock – their colors are diverse as well. Only those of His servants who have knowledge fear God. Surely God is mighty, forgiving.

[29] Surely those who recite the Book of God, and observe the prayer, and contribute from what We have provided them, in secret and in open, hope for a transaction – it will not be in vain – [30] so that He may pay them their rewards in full, and increase them from His favor. Surely He is forgiving, thankful.

[31] What We have inspired you (with) of the Book – it is the truth, confirming what was before it. Surely God is indeed aware of His servants (and) sees (them). [32] Then We caused those of Our servants whom We chose to inherit the Book. Some of them do themselves evil, and some of them are moderate, and some of them are foremost in good deeds, by the permission of God. That is the great favor!

(wizr). This statement appears elsewhere in the Quran, but here it seems especially poignant because of the way the sūra ends (v. 45).

Is this a deliberate rejection of the biblical concept of vicarious atonement? The context in Sūra 35 does not seem to have in mind the "People of the Book." However, in modern times some Muslims have used this and similar verses to deny the possibility of Jesus bearing the sins of humanity. See an analysis of these verses at 53.38 (p. 533).

35.31 – What We have inspired you (with) of the Book – it is the truth, confirming what was before it

The Quran repeatedly asserts that the recitation is "sent down" to or "inspired" in the messenger. The Quran also claims that its contents confirm (muṣaddiq) what came before it. For an analysis of the Quran's claim of confirmation, see 46.12 (p. 502).

³³ Gardens of Eden – they will enter them. There they will be adorned with bracelets of gold and (with) pearls, and there their clothes (will be of) silk. ³⁴ And they will say, 'Praise (be) to God, who has taken away all sorrow from us! Surely our Lord is indeed forgiving, thankful, ³⁵ who out of His favor has settled us in a lasting Home. No fatigue will touch us here, and no weariness will touch us here.'

³⁶ But those who disbelieve – for them (there is) the fire of Gehenna. (Death) is not decreed for them, and so they do not die, nor will any of its punishment be lightened for them. In this way We repay every ungrateful one. ³⁷ There they will cry out, 'Our Lord, bring us out! We will do righteousness instead of what we used to do.' 'Did We not give you a long life, enough of it for the one who would take heed to take heed? The warner came to you, so taste (the punishment)! The evildoers will have no helper.'

³⁸ Surely God knows the unseen (things) of the heavens and the earth. Surely He knows what is in the hearts. ³⁹ He (it is) who made you successors on the earth. Whoever disbelieves, his disbelief (will be) on him. Their disbelief only increases the disbelievers in hatred in the sight of their Lord. Their disbelief only increases the disbelievers in loss. ⁴⁰ Say: 'Have you seen your associates whom you call on instead of God? Show me what part of the earth they have created. Or do they have any partnership in (the creation of) the heavens?' Or have We given them a Book, so that they (stand) on a clear sign from it? No! The evildoers promise each other nothing but deception.

⁴¹ Surely God holds the heavens and the earth, or they would move. If indeed they moved, no one would hold them after Him. Surely He is forbearing, forgiving. ⁴² They have sworn by God the most solemn of their oaths: if a warner comes to them, they will be more (rightly) guided than one of the (other) communities. But when a warner came to them, it only increased them in aversion (to it), ⁴³ (and) in arrogance on the earth, and in scheming evil. Yet evil scheming only overwhelms its own people. Do they expect anything but the customary way of those of old? You will find no change in the customary way of God. You will find no change in the customary way of God. ⁴⁴ Have they not traveled on the earth and seen how the end was for those who were before them, though they were stronger than them in power? But God is not one that anything should

35.42 – *when a warner came to them, it only increased them in aversion*

Allah sends his messengers to deliver his message to every people (v. 24). But the response of the people is usually negative. This raises the question of whether God has limited himself to messengers and preaching in his desire to love and redeem people.

escape Him in the heavens or on the earth. Surely He is knowing, powerful. [45] If God were to take the people to task for what they have earned, He would not leave on it any living creature. But He is sparing them until an appointed time. When their time comes – surely God sees His servants.

35.45 – *If God were to take the people to task for what they have earned, He would not leave on it any living creature*

This verse seems to refer to a concept of a holy God according to whom the deeds of humankind deserve punishment (also at 16.61). Here Allah defers judgment until "an appointed time" but does not offer a way to deal with that "burden" (v. 18) before the Day of Resurrection. See the discussion of the Quran's view of human nature at 79.40 (p. 612) and "Salvation in the Quran" (p. 180).

YĀ' SĪN
YĀ' SĪN

36

Many Muslims regard Sūra 36 with special reverence because, according to tradition, Islam's messenger esteemed it highly and called it the "heart" of the Quran.

The sūra contains striking descriptions of the signs of the Creator's power and providence that invite human gratitude. On the other hand, the sūra portrays a scene of reward and punishment that awaits humans ("sons of Adam") on the Day of Resurrection.

This sūra's parable about the harsh threats that come to two of God's messengers, and a third character who rushes in to defend the messengers, has intrigued both Muslim commentators and Christian readers.

In the Name of God, the Merciful, the Compassionate

¹ Yā' Sīn.

² By the wise Qur'ān! ³ Surely you are indeed one of the envoys, ⁴ on a straight path, ⁵ a sending down of the Mighty, the Compassionate, ⁶ so that you may warn a people. Their fathers have not been warned, and so they are oblivious.

⁷ Certainly the word has proved true against most of them: 'They will not believe.' ⁸ Surely We have placed chains on their necks, and it (reaches up) to the chin, and so they (are forced to) hold their heads up. ⁹ We have made a barrier before them and a barrier behind them, and We have covered them, and so they

---

36.1–3 – *Yā' Sīn. By the wise Qur'ān! Surely you are indeed one of the envoys*

On the disconnected Arabic letters that begin this sūra, see the comment at 2.1.

The sūra starts with an oath, followed by the now characteristic claims for the messenger and his recitation (vv. 2–6). Similar claims appear at verses 69–70. On the word *qur'ān*, see the comment at 2.185 (p. 61).

36.8 – *Surely We have placed chains on their necks*

The Quran explains how Allah deals with humans – those who refuse to believe, on the one hand, and those who follow "the Reminder" (v. 11), on the other.

do not see. [10] (It is) the same for them whether you warn them or you do not warn them. They will not believe. [11] You warn only the one who follows the Reminder and fears the Merciful in the unseen. So give him the good news of forgiveness and a generous reward. [12] Surely We – We give the dead life and We write down what they have sent forward and their traces. And everything – We have counted it up in a clear record.

[13] Strike a parable for them: the companions of the town, when the envoys came to it. [14] When We sent two men to them, and they called them liars, We reinforced (them) with a third. They said, 'Surely we are envoys to you.' [15] They said, 'You are nothing but human beings like us. The Merciful has not sent down anything. You are only lying.' [16] They said, 'Our Lord knows that we are indeed envoys to you. [17] Nothing (depends) on us except the clear delivery (of the message).' [18] They said, 'Surely we have an evil omen about you. If indeed you do not stop, we shall indeed stone you, and a painful punishment from us will indeed touch you.' [19] They said, 'Your evil omen refers to yourselves. If you had taken heed – No! You are a wanton people!' [20] (Just then) a man came running from the farthest part of the city. He said, 'My people! Follow the envoys! [21] Follow those who do not ask you for any reward, and (who) are (rightly) guided. [22] Why should I not serve Him who created me? You will (all) be returned to Him. [23] Shall I take (other) gods instead of Him? If the Merciful intends any harm for me, their intercession will be of no use to me at all, nor will they save me. [24] Surely then I would indeed be far astray. [25] Surely I believe in your Lord, so listen to me!' [26] It was said, 'Enter the Garden!' He said, 'Would that my people knew [27] that my Lord has forgiven me, and made me one of the honored.' [28] We did not send down on his people after him any force from the

---

36.10 – *(It is) the same for them whether you warn them or you do not warn them*

This verse indicates the limitations of preaching and perhaps also signals that the preacher is losing hope.

36.13 – *Strike a parable for them: the companions of the town, when the envoys came to it*

Three men bring Allah's message to a city, but the people resist the messengers and threaten to stone them. Just then, however, a man comes running from the other side of the city and urges the people to listen to the messengers (vv. 13–25).

No place, time, or names are given in this parable, but classical Muslim commentaries asserted that the city is Antioch and the messengers are apostles sent by Jesus. In the book *Jesus and the Muslim*, Kenneth Cragg wonders whether the parable could possibly be an echo of the reception of Paul and Barnabas at Iconium in Acts 14:1–5 (see bibliography).

sky, nor are We (in the habit of) sending down (such a force). ²⁹ It was only a single cry, and suddenly they were snuffed out. ³⁰ Alas for the servants! Not one messenger comes to them whom they do not mock. ³¹ Do they not see how many generations We destroyed before them, (and) that they do not return to them? ³² But every one of them will be brought forward before Us.

³³ A sign for them is the dead earth: We give it life, and bring forth grain from it, and from it they eat. ³⁴ And We have placed in it gardens of date palms and grapes, and We have caused springs to gush forth in it, ³⁵ so that they may eat from its fruit and what their hands have made. Will they not be thankful? ³⁶ Glory to the One who created pairs of all that the earth grows, and of themselves, and of what they do not know.

³⁷ A sign for them is the night: We strip the day from it, and suddenly they are in darkness. ³⁸ And the sun: it runs to a dwelling place (appointed) for it. That is the decree of the Mighty, the Knowing. ³⁹ And the moon: We have determined it by stations, until it returns like an old palm branch. ⁴⁰ It is not fitting for the sun to overtake the moon, nor does the night outrun the day, but each floats in (its own) orbit.

⁴¹ A sign for them is that We carried their descendants in the loaded ship, ⁴² and We have created for them (ships) like it (in) which they sail. ⁴³ If We (so) please, We drown them, and then (there is) no cry (for help) for them, nor are they saved, ⁴⁴ except as a mercy from Us, and enjoyment (of life) for a time.

⁴⁵ When it is said to them, 'Guard (yourselves) against what is before you and what is behind you, so that you may receive compassion' – ⁴⁶ yet not a sign comes to them from the signs of their Lord without their turning away from it. ⁴⁷ When it is said to them, 'Contribute from what God has provided you,' those who disbelieve say to those who believe, 'Shall we feed one whom, if God (so) pleased, He would have fed? You are only far astray!'

36.33 – *A sign for them is the dead earth: We give it life*

This verse begins a series of three signs of the Creator's power (vv. 33–44). The passage focuses grain and fruit, and it asks for the appropriate human response of thankfulness.

36.46 – *yet not a sign comes to them from the signs of their Lord without their turning away from it*

This verse is one of several in this sūra that portray – in an extremely negative way – the people who see the Creator's signs or hear the messenger's preaching. And yet this portrayal is by now familiar. Such verses need to be taken into account when summarizing the Quran's view of human nature. See the analysis of this theme at 79.40 (p. 612).

⁴⁸ They say, 'When (will) this promise (come to pass), if you are truthful?' ⁴⁹ They are only waiting for a single cry – it will seize them while they are (still) disputing, ⁵⁰ and then they will not be able to make a bequest, nor will they return to their (own) families.

⁵¹ There will be a blast on the trumpet, and suddenly they will come swooping down from the graves to their Lord. ⁵² They will say, 'Alas for us! Who has raised us up from our sleeping place? This is what the Merciful promised, and the envoys were truthful.' ⁵³ It was only a single cry, and suddenly they are all brought forward before Us. ⁵⁴ 'Today no one will be done evil at all, nor will you be repaid (for anything) except what you have done.' ⁵⁵ Surely the companions of the Garden today are busy rejoicing ⁵⁶ – they and their spouses – reclining on couches in (places of) shade. ⁵⁷ There they have fruit, and they have whatever they call for. ⁵⁸ 'Peace!' – a word (of greeting) from a compassionate Lord. ⁵⁹ 'But separate (yourselves) today, you sinners! ⁶⁰ Did I not make a covenant with you, sons of Adam, that you should not serve Satan – surely he is a clear enemy to you – ⁶¹ and that you should serve Me? This is a straight path. ⁶² Certainly he has led astray many multitudes of you. Did you not understand? ⁶³ This is Gehenna, which you were promised. ⁶⁴ Burn in it today for what you disbelieved!'

⁶⁵ Today We will set a seal on their mouths, but their hands will speak to Us, and their feet will bear witness about what they have earned. ⁶⁶ If We (so) pleased, We would indeed have obliterated their eyes, and they would race to the path, but how could they see? ⁶⁷ And if We (so) pleased, We would indeed have transformed them where they were, and they could not go on, nor could they return. ⁶⁸ (To) whomever We grant a long life, We reverse him in (his) constitution. Do they not understand?

⁶⁹ We have not taught him the (art of) poetry, nor is it fitting for him. It is

---

36.51 – *There will be a blast on the trumpet*

A trumpet blast begins this description of end-time events from the day when Allah gathers people for judgment (vv. 51–65). Notice that those who are rewarded with the "Garden" come with their wives (v. 56).

36.60 – *Did I not make a covenant with you, sons of Adam . . . ?*

The "covenant" was not to serve Satan, who has led many astray (v. 62), but rather to serve the Merciful (vv. 61, 52).

36.69 – *We have not taught him the (art of) poetry, nor is it fitting for him*

On the negative sense of "poet" in the Quran, see the comment at 21.5 (p. 331). This verse says that instead of poetry, the recitation is a reminder. On the word *qur'ān*, see the comment at 2.185 (p. 61).

nothing but a Reminder and a clear Qur'ān, [70] so that he may warn whoever is living, and that the word may be proved true against the disbelievers. ·

[71] Do they not see that We created for them – from what Our hands have made – livestock, and (that) they are their masters? [72] We have made them subservient to them, and some of them they ride, and some they eat. [73] And they have (other) benefits in them, and drinks. Will they not be thankful? [74] But they have taken (other) gods, instead of God, so that they might be helped. [75] (But) they cannot help them, (for) they will be brought forward before them as a group. [76] So do not let their saying cause you sorrow. Surely We know what they keep secret and what they speak aloud.

[77] Does the human not see that We created him from a drop? Yet suddenly he is a clear adversary. [78] He has struck a parable for Us and forgotten (the fact of) his creation. He says, 'Who will give the bones life when they are decayed?' [79] Say: 'He will give them life who produced them the first time. He has knowledge of all creation, [80] who has made fire for you from the green tree – and so you (too) light a fire from it.' [81] Is not the One who created the heavens and the earth able to create their equivalent? Yes indeed! He is the Creator, the Knowing. [82] His only command, when He intends something, is to say to it, 'Be!' and it is. [83] Glory to the One in whose His hand is the kingdom of everything! To Him you will be returned.

36.71 – *Do they not see that We created for them … livestock … ?*

The final part of the sūra is about how Allah deals with humans and the human response. The desired response is thankfulness, but instead humans take other gods that cannot help them.

36.76 – *So do not let their saying cause you sorrow*

In the midst of describing the human response to Allah, the Quran speaks directly to the messenger to encourage him.

THE ONES WHO LINE UP

AL-ṢĀFFĀT

37

Most Muslims today believe that Ishmael was the son that Abraham was willing to sacrifice in obedience to Allah. The Quran tells its version of the story of the sacrifice in this sūra, and many readers have been bewildered to see how the story leaves out a crucial detail. The sūra also includes several other stories about biblical characters, most significant among them Elijah and Jonah.

Before and after the stories, controversy continues between the messenger and his listeners over the question of the resurrection and their rejection of his authority. The sūra presents a long and elaborate judgment scene that imagines both disconsolate conversations and "the Gardens of Bliss."

In the Name of God, the Merciful, the Compassionate

[1] By the ones who line up in lines, [2] and the shouters of a shout, [3] and the reciters of a reminder! [4] Surely your God is one, [5] Lord of the heavens and the earth, and of whatever is between them, and Lord of the Easts.

[6] Surely We have made the sky of this world appear enticing by means of the splendor of the stars, [7] and (We have made them) a (means of) protection from every rebelling satan. [8] They do not listen to the exalted Assembly, [9] but they are pelted from every side, driven off – for them (there is) punishment forever – [10] except for the one who snatches a word, and then a piercing flame pursues him. [11] So ask them for a pronouncement: 'Are they a stronger creation, or those (others) whom We have created?' Surely We created them from sticky clay.

[12] But you are amazed when they ridicule, [13] and, when they are reminded,

---

37.1–4 – *By the ones who line up in lines*

The sūra begins with a series of oaths (the second to do so after Sūra 36). This pattern of beginning with oaths will become much more prominent in Sūras 75–95.

do not take heed, ¹⁴ and, when they see a sign, ridicule, ¹⁵ and say, 'This is nothing but clear magic. ¹⁶ When we are dead, and turned to dust and bones, shall we indeed be raised up? ¹⁷ And our fathers of old (too)?' ¹⁸ Say: 'Yes, and you will be humbled.' ¹⁹ (For) it will only be a single shout, and suddenly they will see, ²⁰ and say, 'Woe to us! This is the Day of Judgment.' ²¹ 'This is the Day of Decision, which you called a lie. ²² Gather those who have done evil, and their wives, and what they used to serve, ²³ instead of God, and guide them to the path of the Furnace. ²⁴ And stop them (there), (for) they are to be questioned: ²⁵ "What is (the matter) with you (that) you do you not help each other?" ²⁶ No! Today they are resigned.' ²⁷ Some of them will approach others asking each other questions. ²⁸ They will say, 'Surely you used to come to us from the right (side).' ²⁹ They will say, 'No! You were not believers. ³⁰ We had no authority over you. No! You were a people who transgressed insolently. ³¹ So the word of our Lord has proved true against us. Surely we are indeed tasting (it). ³² We made you err (because) we were in error.' ³³ Surely on that Day they will be partners in the punishment. ³⁴ Surely in this way We deal with the sinners.

³⁵ Surely they – when it was said to them, '(There is) no god but God,' they became arrogant, ³⁶ and said, 'Are we to abandon our gods for a possessed poet?' ³⁷ 'No! He has brought the truth and confirmed the envoys. ³⁸ Surely you will indeed taste the painful punishment, ³⁹ and you will not be repaid (for anything) except what you have done.'

⁴⁰ – Except for the devoted servants of God. ⁴¹ Those – for them (there will be) a known provision ⁴² (of) fruits, and they will be honored ⁴³ in Gardens of Bliss, ⁴⁴ on couches, facing each other, ⁴⁵ (and) a cup from a flowing spring will be passed around among them – ⁴⁶ white, delicious to the drinkers, ⁴⁷ (there is) no ill effect in it, nor do they become drunk from it. ⁴⁸ With them (there will be maidens) restraining (their) glances, wide-eyed, ⁴⁹ as if they were hidden eggs.

⁵⁰ Some of them will approach others asking each other questions. ⁵¹ One of them will say, 'Surely I had a comrade, ⁵² who used to say, "Are you indeed one of the confirmers? ⁵³ When we are dead, and turned to dust and bones, shall

---

37.20 – *Woe to us! This is the Day of Judgment*

A long passage on punishments and rewards on the Day of Resurrection (vv. 20–57) begins with a "judgment scene," which imagines the conversations of evildoers with the gods they used to worship.

37.36 – *Are we to abandon our gods for a possessed poet?*

On the negative sense of "poet" in the Quran, see the comment at 21.5 (p. 331). This verse seems to make explicit what is implicit in other verses: "possessed poet" (*shāʿir majnūn*) connects poetry with possession by *jinn*.

we indeed be judged?"' ⁵⁴ (Another) will say, 'Are you looking (down)?' ⁵⁵ So he looks (down) and sees him in the midst of the Furnace. ⁵⁶ He will say, 'By God! You nearly brought me to ruin. ⁵⁷ Were it not for the blessing of my Lord, I (too) would have been one of those brought forward (to the punishment). ⁵⁸ So do we not die, ⁵⁹ except for our first death, and are we not punished? ⁶⁰ Surely this – it indeed is the great triumph! ⁶¹ Let the workers work for something like this!'

⁶² Is that better as a reception, or the tree of al-Zaqqūm? ⁶³ Surely We have made it a test for the evildoers. ⁶⁴ It is a tree which comes forth from the root of the Furnace. ⁶⁵ Its fruits are like the heads of the satans, ⁶⁶ and they eat from it, and fill their bellies from it. ⁶⁷ Then on (top of) it they have a drink of boiling (water). ⁶⁸ Then their return is to the Furnace.

⁶⁹ Surely they found their fathers astray, ⁷⁰ and they run in their footsteps. ⁷¹ Certainly most of those of old went astray before them, ⁷² even though We sent warners among them. ⁷³ See how the end was for those who were warned ⁷⁴ – except for the devoted servants of God.

⁷⁵ Certainly Noah called on Us, and excellent indeed were the responders! ⁷⁶ We rescued him and his family from great distress, ⁷⁷ and We made his descendants – they were the survivors. ⁷⁸ We left (this blessing) upon him among the later (generations): ⁷⁹ 'Peace (be) upon Noah among all peoples!' ⁸⁰ In this way We repay the doers of good. ⁸¹ Surely he was one of Our believing servants. ⁸² Then We drowned the others.

⁸³ Surely Abraham was indeed of his party: ⁸⁴ When he came to his Lord with a sound heart, ⁸⁵ when he said to his father and his people, 'What do you serve? ⁸⁶ (Is it) a lie – gods other than God – you desire? ⁸⁷ What do you think about the Lord of the worlds?' ⁸⁸ And he took a look at the stars, ⁸⁹ and said, 'Surely

37.75 – *Certainly Noah called on Us*

This brief reference to the story of Noah (vv. 75–82) highlights Allah's deliverance of Noah's household and his drowning of the others.

37.79 – *Peace (be) upon Noah among all peoples!*

This salutation becomes a refrain applied to other characters in this sūra at verses 109 (Abraham), 120 (Moses and Aaron), and 130 (Ilyās).

37.83 – *Surely Abraham was indeed of his party*

Abraham challenges his father and his people about their worship of idols, but the people only plot against him.

Stories about Abraham's opposition to idolatry appear frequently in the Quran, each adding details that are not included in the other versions. A longer narration about the "stars" (v. 88) comes at 6.75–78, about striking the idols (v. 93) at 21.57–63, and about the "blazing" (v. 97) at 21.68–71.

I am sick.' [90] So they turned away from him, withdrawing. [91] But he turned to their gods, and said, 'Do you not eat? [92] What is (the matter) with you (that) you do not speak?' [93] So he turned on them, striking (them) with the right (hand). [94] Then they came running to him. [95] He said, 'Do you serve what you carve, [96] when God created you and what you make?' [97] They said, 'Build a building for him, and cast him into the blazing (Fire)!' [98] They intended a plot against him, but We brought them down.

[99] He said, 'Surely I am going to my Lord. He will guide me. [100] My Lord, grant me one of the righteous.' [101] So We gave him the good news of a forbearing boy. [102] When he had reached the (age of) running with him, he said, 'My son! Surely I saw in a dream that I am going to sacrifice you. So look, what do you think?' He said, 'My father! Do what you are commanded. You will find me, if God pleases, one of the patient.' [103] When they both had submitted, and he had laid him face down, [104] We called out to him, 'Abraham! [105] Now you have confirmed the vision. Surely in this way We repay the doers of good. [106] Surely this

---

37.101 – *So We gave him the good news of a forbearing boy*

The Quran refers to Abraham's willingness to sacrifice his son in obedience to Allah only here (vv. 101–12). In view of this, a striking feature of this passage is that it does not name the son intended for sacrifice.

Muslim commentators on the Quran disagreed about the identity of the son. The earliest commentators up to al-Ṭabarī (d. 923) tended to identify the unnamed son as Isaac. But later in Islamic history, especially following Ibn Kathīr (d. 1373), Muslim commentators developed a near consensus that the son was Ishmael.

Verse 101 says that God gave Abraham good news (*bashshara*) of a forbearing boy. Al-Ṭabarī (AD 839–923) took this as a clue. He considered the verses where the Quran says that good news of a son came to Abraham, especially 11.71: "His wife was standing (there), and she laughed. And so we gave her the good news of Isaac" (also 37.112). Other verses that use the same verb as this announcement but that don't provide the name Isaac are 11.69; 15.53–55; 29.31; and 51.28. The verb *bashshara* is never connected to the birth of Ishmael.

Ibn Kathīr, on the other hand, argued more than 400 years after al-Ṭabarī that the son of sacrifice was Ishmael – and then went on the offensive. Ibn Kathīr alleged that the Jews had removed Ishmael's name from Genesis 22:2 and inserted Isaac's name in its place.

For more details on this shift in Muslim interpretation as well as scholarly references, see my book *The Gentle Answer*, chapter 17 (see bibliography). See also "Abraham in the Quran" (p. 90).

– it indeed was the clear test.' [107] And We ransomed him with a great sacrifice, [108] and left (this blessing) on him among the later (generations): [109] 'Peace (be) upon Abraham!' [110] In this way We repay the doers of good. [111] Surely he was one of Our believing servants.

[112] And We gave him the good news of Isaac, a prophet, one of the righteous. [113] We blessed him and Isaac, and some of their descendants are doers of good, and some clearly do themselves evil.

[114] Certainly We bestowed favor on Moses and Aaron, [115] and We rescued them and their people from the great distress. [116] We helped them, and they were the victors. [117] We gave them both the clarifying Book, [118] and guided them to the straight path, [119] and left (this blessing) on both of them among the later (generations): [120] 'Peace (be) upon Moses and Aaron!' [121] In this way We repay the doers of good. [122] Surely they were two of Our believing servants.

[123] Surely Elijah was indeed one of the envoys: [124] When he said to his people, 'Will you not guard (yourselves)? [125] Do you call on Baal, and abandon the best of creators [126] – God – your Lord and the Lord of your fathers of old?' [127] Yet they called him a liar. Surely they will indeed be brought forward (to the punishment) [128] – except for the devoted servants of God. [129] And We left (this blessing) on him among the later (generations): [130] 'Peace (be) upon Elijah!' [131] In this way We repay the doers of good. [132] Surely he was one of Our believing servants.

37.107 – *And We ransomed him with a great sacrifice*

The language of ransom (*fadā*) or sacrifice (*dhibḥ*) does not appear frequently in the Quran, so this verse has understandably attracted much attention.

The failure of the Quran to name the son of sacrifice must be seen as a significant flaw in this Muslim scripture. On the one hand, the lack of a name in verse 102 has led to serious confusion about the truth of a crucial event in salvation history, as well as to regrettable polemic like the writing of Ibn Kathīr described in the note for 37.101. The confusion continues to the present day, for example in the recently published *Study Quran*. On the other hand, the needless controversy surrounding the son's identity has distracted from the promise suggested by verse 107 for worthwhile conversation. Both the Old Testament and the Gospel accounts are deeply interested in redemption, sacrifice, and atonement, and the New Testament finds the fulfillment of the son's sacrifice in the death of Jesus for the sins of the world. The Quran does not further develop these crucial themes here or elsewhere.

37.123–32 – *Surely Elijah was indeed one of the envoys*

The prophet Elijah (*Ilyās*) appears only here and in a list at 6.85. The mention of Baal (*ba'l*) in verse 125 connects this story (vv. 123–30) with the account of Elijah and the prophets of Baal in 1 Kings 18:18–40.

¹³³ Surely Lot was indeed one of the envoys: ¹³⁴ When We rescued him and his family – all (of them) – ¹³⁵ except for an old woman among those who stayed behind. ¹³⁶ Then We destroyed the others. ¹³⁷ Surely you indeed pass near them in the morning ¹³⁸ and in the night. Will you not understand?

¹³⁹ Surely Jonah was indeed one of the envoys: ¹⁴⁰ When he ran away to the loaded ship, ¹⁴¹ and cast lots, but was one of the losers. ¹⁴² So the fish swallowed him, seeing that he was to blame. ¹⁴³ Were it not that he was one of those who glorified (God), ¹⁴⁴ he would indeed have remained in its belly until the Day when they are raised up. ¹⁴⁵ But We tossed him on the desert (shore) while he was (still) sick, ¹⁴⁶ and We caused a gourd tree to grow over him. ¹⁴⁷ We sent him to a hundred thousand, or more, ¹⁴⁸ and they believed. So We gave them enjoyment (of life) for a time.

¹⁴⁹ Ask them for a pronouncement: 'Does your Lord have daughters while they have sons? ¹⁵⁰ Or did We create the angels female while they were witnesses?' ¹⁵¹ Is it not a fact that out of their own lie they indeed say, ¹⁵² 'God has begotten'? Surely they are liars indeed! ¹⁵³ Has He chosen daughters over sons? ¹⁵⁴ What is (the matter) with you? How do you judge? ¹⁵⁵ Will you not take heed? ¹⁵⁶ Or do you have any clear authority? ¹⁵⁷ Bring your Book, if you are truthful.

37.133 – *Surely Lot was indeed one of the envoys*

This very brief story of Lot (vv. 133–38), the seventh of eight versions in the Quran, does not mention the sin for which Lot's people were destroyed, and here it is "an old woman" who remains behind when Lot and his family flee (v. 135). However, the apparent reference to passing by the ruins of Lot's city morning and evening (vv. 137–38) has intrigued scholars with its suggestion of a recitation closer to the Dead Sea.

37.139 – *Surely Jonah was indeed one of the envoys*

This story of Jonah (vv. 139–48) is the most complete of the Quran's four references. Elsewhere we only learn that "the people of Jonah" believed and were spared (10.98), that "he of the fish" fled in anger and ended up crying out in the darkness (21.87), and similarly that "he of the fish" cried out in despair (68.48).

This version touches the main points of the biblical account (Jonah 1–4) but switches the sequence of Jonah's preaching to Nineveh (the Quran does not mention the city) and his anger under the "gourd tree" (v. 146).

37.151–52 – *Is it not a fact that out of their own lie they indeed say, "God has begotten"?*

The Arabic verb, *walada*, that people use with Allah is the same as that used in 112.3 ("He has not begotten and was not begotten"). The surrounding context does not seem to suggest that it is Christians who are saying this. Some scholars suggest that the subject may be pagan Arabs. See "Son of God in the Quran" (p. 352).

¹⁵⁸ They have fabricated an affiliation between Him and the jinn. Yet certainly the jinn know that they will indeed be brought forward (to the punishment) ¹⁵⁹ – glory to God above what they allege! – ¹⁶⁰ except for the devoted servants of God.

¹⁶¹ Surely you and what you serve – ¹⁶² you will not tempt (anyone to rebellion) against Him, ¹⁶³ except for the one who is (destined) to burn in the Furnace. ¹⁶⁴ (There is) not one of us who does not have an assigned position. ¹⁶⁵ Surely we – we indeed are the ones who line up, ¹⁶⁶ and surely we – we indeed are the ones who glorify (God).

¹⁶⁷ If they were to say, ¹⁶⁸ 'If (only) we had a reminder from those of old, ¹⁶⁹ we would indeed have been the devoted servants of God.' ¹⁷⁰ Yet they have disbelieved in it. Soon they will know! ¹⁷¹ Certainly Our word has (already) gone forth to Our servants, the envoys. ¹⁷² Surely they – they indeed are the ones who will be helped. ¹⁷³ Surely Our army – they indeed are the victors. ¹⁷⁴ So turn away from them for a time, ¹⁷⁵ and observe them. Soon they will observe! ¹⁷⁶ Do they seek to hurry Our punishment? ¹⁷⁷ When it comes down in their (own) courtyard, (how) evil the morning will be for those who were warned! ¹⁷⁸ So turn from away them for a time, ¹⁷⁹ and observe (them). Soon they will observe!

¹⁸⁰ Glory to your Lord, Lord of honor, above what they allege! ¹⁸¹ Peace (be) upon the envoys, ¹⁸² and praise (be) to God, Lord of the worlds!

ṢĀD

ṢĀD

38

This sūra features several stories about biblical characters, chief among them a story about David in which two disputants ask him for a decision concerning "ninety-nine ewes." The story does not follow the usual prophet story template. Instead, David asks God for forgiveness and repents. Solomon seems to follow suit.

The stories are set amid passages about resistance to the Quran's "warner" (vv. 4, 65, 70) and graphic descriptions of heaven and hell.

The sūra closes with the final version of the refusal of Iblīs to bow down before the newly created "human being."

In the Name of God, the Merciful, the Compassionate

[1] Ṣād. By the Qur'ān, containing the Reminder! [2] – No! Those who disbelieve are in false pride and defiance. [3] How many a generation We have destroyed before them! They (all) called out, but there was no time for escape. [4] Yet they are amazed that a warner has come to them from among them. The disbelievers say, 'This (man) is a magician, a liar! [5] Has he made the gods (into) one god? Surely this is an amazing thing indeed.' [6] The assembly of them set out (saying): 'Walk (away), and remain steadfast to your gods. Surely this is a thing to be desired indeed. [7] We have not heard of this in the last creed. This is only a fabrication. [8] Has the Reminder been sent down on him (alone) among us?' No! They are in doubt about My Reminder! No! They have not yet tasted My punishment! [9] Or do they have the storehouses of the mercy of your Lord, the Mighty, the Giver? [10] Or do they have the kingdom of the heavens and the earth, and whatever is between them? Let them ascend on the ropes. [11] An army of the factions will

---

38.2 – *No! Those who disbelieve are in false pride and defiance*

The opening passage of the sūra (vv. 2–11) portrays the disbelievers, their speeches and their fate. Notice here that envy seems to be one reason for their resistance (v. 8).

454

be routed there. ¹² Before them the people of Noah called (it) a lie, and ʿĀd, and Pharaoh, he of the stakes, ¹³ and Thamūd, and the people of Lot, and the people of the Grove – those were the factions. ¹⁴ Each of them called the messengers liars, and My retribution was justified. ¹⁵ What do these (people) expect but a single cry, for which (there will be) no delay.

¹⁶ They say, 'Our Lord, hurry our share to us before the Day of Reckoning!' ¹⁷ Bear with what they say, and remember Our servant David, (who was) endowed with strength. Surely he turned regularly (in repentance). ¹⁸ Surely We subjected the mountains (along) with him to glorify (Us) in the evening and at sunrise, ¹⁹ and the birds (too), gathered together, all regularly turning to Him (in praise). ²⁰ We strengthened his kingdom, and gave him wisdom and a decisive word.

²¹ Has the story of the dispute come to you? When they climbed over the wall of the place of prayer, ²² when they entered upon David, and he was terrified of them, but they said, 'Do not fear! (We are) two disputants: one of us has acted oppressively toward the other. So judge between us in truth, and do not be unjust, and guide us to the right path. ²³ Surely this (man) is my brother. He has ninety-nine ewes, and I have (only) one ewe. He said, "Give her into my charge," and he overcame me in the argument.' ²⁴ He said, 'Certainly he has done you evil in asking for your ewe (in addition) to his ewes. Surely many (business) partners indeed act oppressively toward one another, except those who believe and do

---

38.12 – *Before them the people of Noah called (it) a lie*

The Quran provides perspective on resistance to the messenger by referring to how Allah dealt with unbelieving people in the past (vv. 12–14).

38.16 – *Our Lord, hurry our share to us before the Day of Reckoning!*

In this sūra the judgment day is called the Day of Reckoning (*ḥisāb*; also vv. 26, 53). In common usage, *ḥisāb* means "arithmetic."

38.17 – *Bear with what they say, and remember Our servant David*

A significant passage about David (*Daʾud*, vv. 17–26) starts out with the curious details that also appear at 21.79 and 34.10. Not only does David urge the mountains and birds to praise Allah, but Allah also compels them to praise him.

38.21 – *Has the story of the dispute come to you?*

This question seems to assume that at least some of the listeners or readers could answer yes or that the story was fairly well known. This raises the further questions of the makeup of the audience, the storyteller's attitude to the story, and the reasons for these particular details in a story that appears only once in the Quran.

righteous deeds – but few they are.' And David guessed that We had (somehow) tested him, so he asked his Lord for forgiveness, and fell down, bowing, and turned (in repentance). [25] So We forgave him that. Surely he has intimacy indeed with Us and a good (place of) return.

[26] 'David! Surely We have made you a ruler on the earth, so judge among the people in truth, and do not follow (vain) desire, or it will lead you astray from the way of God. Surely those who go astray from the way of God – for them (there is) a harsh punishment, because they have forgotten the Day of Reckoning.' [27] We did not create the sky and the earth, and whatever is between them, without purpose. That is the conjecture of those who disbelieve. So woe to those who disbelieve on account of the Fire! [28] Or shall We treat those who believe and do righteous deeds the same as the ones who foment corruption on the earth? Or shall We treat the ones who guard (themselves) the same as the depraved?

[29] A blessed Book – We have sent it down to you, so that those with understanding may contemplate its verses and take heed.

[30] To David We granted Solomon – an excellent servant he was! Surely he turned regularly (in repentance). [31] When the standing horses were presented before him in the evening, [32] he said, 'Surely I have loved the love of good (things)

38.24 – *And David guessed that We had (somehow) tested him, so he asked his Lord for forgiveness*

In this story, two litigants confront David in his palace with a dispute about ninety-nine ewe lambs (v. 23). This detail of the many ewes and the one ewe could reasonably be considered an echo of the parable of Nathan in 2 Samuel 12:1–4.

After giving his judgment David asks forgiveness and repents (v. 24; see also v. 17, where David is introduced as a penitent), and his Lord forgives him. Unfortunately, however, the Quran nowhere makes clear David's reason for asking forgiveness. Whatever the reason, this verse puts a question to the Islamic dogma that all prophets are sinless. Especially in terms of the biblical record, David committed the major sins of adultery and murder (commandments 6 and 7; see 2 Samuel 11–12), and the book of Psalms associates his sins with the confession of Psalm 51. See the analysis of the prayers of prophets for forgiveness at 48.2 (p. 513).

38.30 – *To David We granted Solomon – an excellent servant he was!*

The interest in this passage seems to be Solomon's horses (vv. 31–33) and his authority over the wind and "satans" (vv. 36–37). Solomon's trial in verse 34 is not clear from this passage, nor does the Quran refer to it elsewhere. Like David, Solomon repents and asks forgiveness from his Lord (vv. 34–35). The Quran asserts Solomon's power over the wind and the "satans" at 21.81–82 and over the wind and the *jinn* at 34.12–13.

more than the remembrance of my Lord, until the sun has (now) been hidden by the veil. ³³ Return them to me!' Then he began to stroke their legs and necks. ³⁴ Certainly We tested Solomon, and placed on his throne a (mere) image. Then he turned (in repentance). ³⁵ He said, 'My Lord, forgive me, and grant me a kingdom (such as) will not be fitting for anyone after me (to have). Surely You – You are the Giver.' ³⁶ So We subjected the wind to him, to blow gently at his command wherever he decided, ³⁷ and (also) the satans, every builder and diver, ³⁸ and others (as well) bound in chains: ³⁹ 'This is Our gift, so bestow or withhold without reckoning.' ⁴⁰ Surely he had intimacy indeed with Us, and a good (place of) return.

⁴¹ And remember Our servant Job: When he called out to his Lord, 'Surely I – Satan has touched me with weariness and punishment.' ⁴² 'Stamp with your foot! This (will become) a cool (place for) washing and a drink.' ⁴³ And We granted him his household, and their equivalent with them, as a mercy from Us, and a reminder to those with understanding. ⁴⁴ 'And take in your hand a bunch, and strike with it, and do not break your oath.' Surely We found him patient – an excellent servant he was! Surely he turned regularly (in repentance).

⁴⁵ And remember Our servants Abraham, and Isaac, and Jacob: endowed with strength and vision. ⁴⁶ Surely We purified them with a pure (thought): remembrance of the Home. ⁴⁷ Surely with Us they are indeed among the chosen, the good.

⁴⁸ And remember Our servants Ishmael, Elisha, and Dhū-l-Kifl: each (of them) was one of the good.

⁴⁹ This is a Reminder. Surely for the ones who guard (themselves) (there is) indeed a good (place of) return: ⁵⁰ Gardens of Eden, (where) the gates are open for them, ⁵¹ where they recline, (and) where they call for abundant fruit and drink. ⁵² With them (are maidens) restraining (their) glances, (all) of the same

---

38.41 – *And remember Our servant Job: When he called out to his Lord*

This is the final reference to Job in the canonical progression, and the longest of the two short stories about him (also 21.83–84). Recognizable from the book of Job in the Bible are his bodily distress and the restoration of his household. The other two mentions of Job come in lists of prophetic characters (4.163; 6.85).

38.45 – *And remember Our servants Abraham, and Isaac, and Jacob*

The close association of Abraham with Isaac and Jacob, as well as the high praise for them (vv. 45–47), follow a pattern seen several times in the Quran (6.84; 19.49–50; 21.72–73). Here again the name Ishmael comes only in verse 48, with no stated connection to Abraham. In other passages, however, Ishmael comes together with Abraham and Isaac (2.133, 136, 140; 3.84; 4.163; 14.39).

age. [53] 'This is what you were promised for the Day of Reckoning. [54] Surely this is indeed Our provision – (there is) no end to it. [55] (All) this!'

But surely for the insolent transgressors (there is) indeed an evil (place of) return: [56] Gehenna, (where) they will burn – it is an evil bed! [57] (All) this! So make them taste it – boiling (water) and rotten (food), [58] and other (torments) of (this) kind in pairs. [59] 'This is a crowd rushing in with you – for them (there is) no welcoming. Surely they will burn in the Fire.' [60] They say, 'No! It is you for whom (there is) no welcoming. You sent it forward for us, and it is an evil resting place!' [61] They say, 'Our Lord, whoever sent this forward for us, give him a double punishment in the Fire!' [62] And they say, 'What is (the matter) with us (that) we do not see men (here) whom we used to count among the evil? [63] Did we take them in ridicule? Or has (our) sight turned aside from them?' [64] Surely that is true indeed – the disputing of the companions of the Fire.

[65] Say: 'I am only a warner. (There is) no god but God, the One, the Supreme, [66] Lord of the heavens and the earth, and whatever is between them, the Mighty, the Forgiver.'

[67] Say: 'It is a great story [68] from which you turn away. [69] I had no knowledge of the exalted Assembly when they disputed. [70] I am only inspired that I am a clear warner.' [71] (Remember) when your Lord said to the angels: 'Surely I am going to create a human being from clay. [72] When I have fashioned him, and breathed some of My spirit into him, fall down before him in prostration.' [73] So the angels prostrated themselves – all of them together [74] – except Iblīs.

38.65 – I am only a warner. (There is) no god but God, the One, the Supreme

The wording of the messenger's confession, *mā min ilāhin illā 'llāh al-wāḥid*, seems a variation on the shahada's *lā ilāha illā 'llāh* ("no god except Allah"), except that this verse makes explicit that Allah is "One" (*wāḥid*). "The Supreme" translates *qahhār*, which has the sense of "conquering" or "vanquishing" in the direction of "forcing" or "coercing." This name for Allah appears six times in the Quran.

38.73–74 – So the angels prostrated themselves – all of them together – except Iblīs

The sūra ends with the Quran's sixth repetition of the story of Iblīs (vv. 71–85), and its second version without naming the human before whom the angels were commanded to bow. What would account for the evident interest in this particular story (also at 2.34; 7.11–12; 15.29–33; 17.61; 18.50; 20.116)? It appears more frequently than the story of Adam.

This story portrays Iblīs as giving a rational reason for his refusal to prostrate before the human. Instead of replying to Iblīs, which seems to credit Iblīs's reason as sound, the Lord punishes him. Iblīs asks for and receives a reprieve (vv. 79–80). Iblīs then announces that he make humans "err" (v. 82) – as if he has tricked the Lord into

He became arrogant, and was one of the disbelievers. ⁷⁵ He said, 'Iblīs! What prevented you from prostrating yourself before what I created with My two hands? Have you become arrogant, or are you one of the exalted?' ⁷⁶ He said, 'I am better than him. You created me from fire, but You created him from clay.' ⁷⁷ He said, 'Get out of here! Surely you are accursed! ⁷⁸ Surely My curse (is going to remain) on you until the Day of Judgment.' ⁷⁹ He said, 'My Lord, spare me until the Day when they are raised up.' ⁸⁰ He said, 'Surely you are one of the spared ⁸¹ – until the Day of the known time.' ⁸² He said, 'Then, by Your honor, I shall indeed make them err – all (of them) ⁸³ – except for Your devoted servants among them.' ⁸⁴ He said, '(This is) the truth, and the truth I say: ⁸⁵ I shall indeed fill Gehenna with you and those of them who follow you – all (of you)!'

⁸⁶ Say: 'I do not ask you for any reward for it, nor am I one of the pretenders. ⁸⁷ It is nothing but a reminder to the worlds. ⁸⁸ You will indeed know its story after a time.'

---

allowing him to do what he planned to do anyway. Indeed, the Lord promises to fill hell with Iblīs and all whom he is able to beguile (v. 85). Elsewhere, Iblīs seems to say that he will get his revenge on the Lord for "sending him astray" (15.39).

The Old Testament's account of the serpent's deception of Eve (Genesis 3) sets up a striking contrast to the Quran's repeating story of Iblīs. The serpent is "crafty" but otherwise undistinguished. Yahweh punishes the serpent not for refusing to bow down to Adam, but rather for deceiving Eve. His punishment includes enmity between the serpent and the "seed" of Eve. But then Yahweh does something very different from the Iblīs story: Yahweh promises that though the serpent may "strike his heel," the seed of the woman will "crush your head" (Genesis 3:15). This is quite different from the Quran's promise to fill hell with humans who follow Satan. The verse in the Bible sets up a story of salvation, not condemnation.

THE COMPANIES
AL-ZUMAR

39

Similar to many of the sūras since Sūra 9, Sūra 39 describes the Creator's power and provision. The Creator looks for a response of thankfulness from his creatures. Sadly, most people are thankless, and the messenger continues his appeals with a mixture of invitation and warning.

Unlike most of the sūras preceding it, however, this sūra offers no stories or even mentions of past prophets or messengers. Instead, it offers a parable (*mathal*) "so that they may take heed" (39.27).

The impression continues of repeating units of text without an evident principle of organization.

In the Name of God, the Merciful, the Compassionate

[1] The sending down of the Book is from God, the Mighty, the Wise. [2] Surely We have sent down to you the Book with the truth. So serve God, devoting (your) religion to Him.

[3] Is it not (a fact) that pure religion is for God (alone)? But those who take allies instead of Him – 'We only serve them so that they may bring us near to God in intimacy' – surely God will judge between them concerning their differences. Surely God does not guide anyone who is a liar (or) ungrateful. [4] If God wanted to take a son, He would indeed have chosen whatever He pleased from what He created. Glory to Him! He is God, the One, the Supreme.

39.1–2 – *The sending down of the Book is from God*

The sūra opens with the self-referential claim that the book is a "sending down" (*tanzīl*) to the messenger from Allah. See "Different Kinds of Literature" (p. 14).

39.3 – *But those who take allies instead of Him*

The tendency of people to give loyalty to other gods, or idols (v. 17), is an important theme in this sūra.

39.4 – *If God wanted to take a son, He would indeed have chosen whatever He pleased*

This sūra gives no indications that the audience includes Christians. In any case,

⁵ He created the heavens and the earth in truth. He wraps the night around the day, and wraps the day around the night, and He has subjected the sun and the moon, each running (its course) for an appointed time. Is He not the Mighty, the Forgiver? ⁶ He created you from one person, (and) then made from him his wife, and He sent down to you four kinds of livestock. He creates you in the bellies of your mothers, creation after creation, in three darknesses. That is God, your Lord. To Him (belongs) the kingdom. (There is) no god but Him. How (is it that) you are turned away? ⁷ If you are ungrateful – surely God is wealthy (enough) without you. Yet He does not approve ingratitude in His servants. If you are thankful, He approves it in you. No one bearing a burden bears the burden of another. Then to your Lord is your return, and He will inform you about what you have done. Surely he knows what is in the hearts.

⁸ When hardship touches a person, he calls on his Lord, turning to Him (in repentance). Then, when He bestows blessing on him from Himself, he forgets what he was calling to Him for before, and sets up rivals to God to lead (people) astray from His way. Say: 'Enjoy (life) in your disbelief for a little. Surely you will be one of the companions of the Fire.' ⁹ Or is he who is obedient in the hours of the night, prostrating himself and standing, bewaring the Hereafter and hoping for the mercy of his Lord [. . .]? Say: 'Are those who know and those who do not know equal?' Only those with understanding take heed.

---

the conditional "if" (*law*) comes as a surprise given the many quranic statements against the son of Allah. The verse seems to be a response to the statement of those who say, "We only serve them so that they may bring us near to God in intimacy" (v. 3). See "Son of God in the Quran" (p. 352).

39.5 – *He created the heavens and the earth in truth*

This verse begins the first of several passages about creation in the sūra (vv. 5–7, 21, 38, 62–63). The appropriate human response is to be thankful. A noteworthy statement in this passage is that Allah "creates you in the bellies of your mothers" (v. 6).

39.7 – *No one bearing a burden bears the burden of another*

When humans return to God, each will bear the responsibility for what he or she has done. For an analysis of this theme of bearing only one's own burden (*wizr*), see the comments at 53.38 (p. 533).

39.8 – *When hardship touches a person, he calls on his Lord*

This extended passage (vv. 8–22) compares Allah's faithful servants with those who set up rivals to Allah. The passage includes a series of "say" statements in which the messenger testifies about himself and challenges his audience (vv. 11–16). The losers are punished and the believers rewarded on the Day of Resurrection.

¹⁰ Say: 'My servants who believe! Guard (yourselves) against your Lord. For those who do good in this present world, (there is) good, and God's earth is wide. Surely the patient will be paid their reward in full without reckoning.' ¹¹ Say: 'I have been commanded to serve God, devoting (my) religion to Him, ¹² and I have been commanded to be the first of those who submit.' ¹³ Say: 'Surely I fear, if I disobey my Lord, the punishment of a great Day.' ¹⁴ Say: 'I serve God, devoting my religion to Him. ¹⁵ So serve whatever you please instead of Him.' Say: 'Surely the losers are those who lose themselves and their families on the Day of Resurrection. Is that not – it is the clearest loss! ¹⁶ For them (there are) shadows of fire above them, and shadows (of fire) below them. That is what God frightens His servants with: "My servants! Guard (yourselves) against Me!"'

¹⁷ Those who avoid al-Ṭāghūt – for fear that they serve it – and turn to God (in repentance) – for them (there is) good news. So give good news to My servants, ¹⁸ those who listen to the word and follow the best of it. Those are the ones whom God has guided, and those – they are those with understanding. ¹⁹ So is the one against whom the word of punishment is proved true – will you save the one who is (already) in the Fire? ²⁰ But those who guard (themselves) against their Lord – for them (there will be) exalted rooms, above which exalted rooms are built, (and) below which rivers flow – the promise of God! God will not break the appointment.

²¹ Do you not see that God has sent down water from the sky, and put it into the earth as springs, (and) then by means of it He brings forth crops of various colors, (and) then they wither, and you see them turning yellow, (and) then He makes them broken debris? Surely in that is a reminder indeed to those with understanding.

²² Is the one whose heart God has expanded to Islam, and so he (depends) on a light from his Lord [. . .]? Woe to those whose hearts are hardened against the remembrance of God! Those are clearly astray.

²³ God has sent down the best proclamation – a Book, resembling (itself), oft-repeating. The skins of those who fear their Lord shiver from it. Then their skins and their hearts soften to the remembrance of God. That is the guidance of God. He guides by means of it whomever He pleases, but whoever God leads astray has no guide.

²⁴ Is he who guards (himself) with his face against the evil of the punishment on the Day of Resurrection [. . .]? But it will be said to the evildoers, 'Taste what you have earned!' ²⁵ Those who were before them called (it) a lie, and the punishment came upon them from where they did not realize (it would). ²⁶ So God made them taste disgrace in this present life, but the punishment of the Hereafter is indeed greater, if (only) they knew.

²⁷ Certainly We have struck in this Qur'ān every (kind of) parable for the people, so that they may take heed ²⁸ – an Arabic Qur'ān, without any crookedness, so that they may guard (themselves). ²⁹ God has struck a parable: a man concerning whom partners are quarreling, and a man belonging to one man. Are they both equal in comparison? Praise (be) to God! No! But most of them do not know (it).

³⁰ Surely you are mortal, and surely they are mortal, ³¹ and surely on the Day of Resurrection you will dispute in the presence of your Lord. ³² Who is more evil than the one who lies against God, and calls the truth a lie when it comes to him? Is there not a dwelling place in Gehenna for the disbelievers? ³³ But the one who brings the truth and confirms it, those – they are the ones who guard (themselves). ³⁴ They will have whatever they please with their Lord. That is the payment of the doers of good ³⁵ – so that God may absolve them of the worst of what they have done, and pay them their reward for the best of what they have done. ³⁶ Is God not sufficient for His servant, when they frighten you with (gods) other than Him? Whoever God leads astray has no guide, ³⁷ but whoever God guides – no one (will) lead him astray. Is God not mighty, a taker of vengeance?

³⁸ If indeed you ask them, 'Who created the heavens and the earth?,' they will indeed say, 'God.' Say: 'Do you see what you call on instead of God? If God intends any harm for me, will they be removers of His harm? Or if He intends any mercy for me, will they be withholders of His mercy?' Say: 'God is enough for me. In Him the trusting put their trust.' ³⁹ Say: 'My people! Do as you are able. Surely I am going to do (what I can). Soon you will know ⁴⁰ on whom punishment will come, disgracing him. On him a lasting punishment will descend.'

⁴¹ Surely We have sent down on you the Book for the people with the truth. Whoever is (rightly) guided, is guided only for himself, and whoever goes astray, goes astray only against himself. You are not a guardian over them.

⁴² God takes the self at the time of its death, and that which has not died in

---

39.28 – *an Arabic Qur'ān, without any crookedness*

The word *qur'ān* need not mean the Muslim scripture as it is known today (the meaning of *qur'ān* is simply "recitation"; see the comment at 2.185, p. 61). This is the first in a remarkable series of claims for an "Arabic Qur'ān" in Sūras 39–46. See the analysis of claims for "Arabic" at 43.2–3 (p. 487).

39.38 – *If indeed you should ask them: "Who created the heavens and the earth?"*

If people know the name of the Creator is Allah, why would they worship and trust others beside Allah?

its sleep, and He retains the one for whom He has decreed death, but sends back the other until an appointed time. Surely in that are signs indeed for a people who reflect.

⁴³ Or have they taken intercessors instead of God? Say: 'Even if they possess nothing and do not understand?' ⁴⁴ Say: 'Intercession (belongs) to God altogether. To Him (belongs) the kingdom of the heavens and the earth. Then to Him you will be returned.'

⁴⁵ When God is mentioned alone, the hearts of those who do not believe in the Hereafter shrink, but when those (gods) are mentioned instead of Him, suddenly they welcome the good news. ⁴⁶ Say: 'God! Creator of the heavens and the earth, Knower of the unseen and the seen, You will judge between your servants concerning their differences.' ⁴⁷ (Even) if those who have done evil had what is on the earth – all (of it) – and as much again, they would indeed (try to) ransom (themselves) with it from the evil of the punishment on the Day of Resurrection. But what they were not counting on will become apparent to them from God, ⁴⁸ and the evils of what they have earned will become apparent to them, and what they were mocking will overwhelm them.

39.44 – *Intercession (belongs) to God altogether*

After denying the power of intercession (*shafāʿa*) to anything besides Allah (v. 43), the Quran draws attention to the one who is sovereign over the heavens and the earth.

The Quran frequently speaks of intercession, and as in this passage, the Quran denies any power of intercession to the "gods" that people choose – either in this life or on the Day of Resurrection. In several other passages, the Quran allows the possibility of intercession by one to whom Allah gives his permission (2.255; 10.3; 34.23). Going further, the Quran allows intercession from the one whom Allah accepts (21.28), from the one whose word Allah accepts (20.109), from the one who has made a covenant with his Lord (19.87), or from "the one who has borne witness to the truth" (43.86). On a popular level, these anonymous exceptions to the absolute prohibition have contributed to a widespread Muslim hope in the intercession of the messenger of Islam.

The biblical book of Isaiah promises "intercession for the transgressors" (Isaiah 53:12), and the New Testament is decisive in saying that Jesus the Messiah (Romans 8:34; Hebrews 7:25; cf. Hebrews 9:24; 1 John 2:1) and the Holy Spirit (Romans 8:26–27) intercede for humans. Jesus is intercessor because he died and rose again and is at the right hand of God the Father (Romans 8:34). Because he lives forever, Jesus is able to save completely those who come to God through him (Hebrews 7:25).

⁴⁹ When hardship touches a person, he calls on Us. Then, when We bestow blessing on him from Us, he says, 'I have only been given it because of knowledge.' No! It is a test, but most of them do not know (it). ⁵⁰ Those who were before them said it (too), but what they earned was of no use to them, ⁵¹ and the evils of what they earned smote them. And those of these (people) who have done evil – the evils of what they have earned will smite them (too), and they will not be able to escape. ⁵² Do they not know that God extends (His) provision to whomever He pleases, and restricts (it)? Surely in that are signs indeed for a people who believe.

⁵³ Say: 'My servants who have acted wantonly against themselves! Do not despair of the mercy of God. Surely God forgives sins – all (of them). Surely He – He is the Forgiving, the Compassionate. ⁵⁴ Turn to your Lord (in repentance), and submit to Him, before the punishment comes upon you, (for) then you will not be helped. ⁵⁵ Follow the best of what has been sent down to you from your Lord, before the punishment comes upon you unexpectedly, when you do not realize (it)' ⁵⁶ – in case anyone (should) say, 'Alas for me, in regard to what I neglected concerning God, for I was indeed one of the scoffers!' ⁵⁷ Or say, 'If only God had guided me, I would indeed have been one of those who guard (themselves)!' ⁵⁸ Or say, when he sees the punishment, 'If only I had (another) turn, and (could) be one of the doers of good!' ⁵⁹ 'Yes indeed! My signs did come to you, but you called them a lie, and were arrogant, and were one of the disbelievers.'

⁶⁰ On the Day of Resurrection you will see those who lied against God, their faces blackened. Is there not a dwelling place in Gehenna for the arrogant? ⁶¹ But God will rescue those who guarded (themselves) in their (place of) safety. Evil will not touch them, nor will they sorrow. ⁶² God is the Creator of everything. He is guardian over everything. ⁶³ To Him (belong) the keys of the heavens and the earth. Those who disbelieve in the signs of God, those – they are the losers.

⁶⁴ Say: 'Do you command me to serve (anyone) other than God, you ignorant ones?' ⁶⁵ You have been inspired, and those who were before you: 'If indeed you associate, your deed(s) will indeed come to nothing, and you will indeed be one of the losers.' ⁶⁶ No! Serve God, and be one of the thankful.

⁶⁷ They have not measured God (with) due measure, when the entire earth will be His handful on the Day of Resurrection, and the heavens will be rolled up in His right (hand). Glory to Him! He is exalted above what they associate.

39.49 – *When hardship touches a person, he calls on Us*

As in verse 8, Allah shows mercy to those who call on him, but humans tend to take the credit for themselves (v. 49) – or to forget altogether (v. 8).

⁶⁸ There will be a blast on the trumpet, and whoever is in the heavens and whoever is on the earth will be thunderstruck, except for those whom God pleases. Then there will be another blast on it, and suddenly they will stand up, looking around. ⁶⁹ And the earth will shine with the light of its Lord, and the Book will be laid down, and the prophets and witnesses will be brought, and it will be decided between them in truth – and they will not be done evil. ⁷⁰ Each one will be paid in full for what he has done, (for) He knows what they do.

⁷¹ Those who disbelieved will be driven in companies into Gehenna, until, when they have come to it, its gates will be opened, and its keepers will say to them: 'Did messengers not come to you from among you, reciting to you the signs of your Lord and warning you about the meeting of this Day of yours?' They will say, 'Yes indeed! But the word of punishment has proved true against the disbelievers.' ⁷² It will be said, 'Enter the gates of Gehenna, there to remain.' Evil is the dwelling place of the arrogant!

⁷³ But those who guarded (themselves) against their Lord will be driven in companies into the Garden, until, when they have come to it, and its gates will be opened, and its keepers will say to them: 'Peace (be) upon you! You have been good, so enter it, to remain (there).' ⁷⁴ They will say, 'Praise (be) to God, who has fulfilled His promise to us, and has caused us to inherit the earth! We (may) settle in the Garden wherever we please.' Excellent is the reward of the doers!

⁷⁵ And you will see the angels completely surrounding the throne, glorifying their Lord with praise. It will be decided between them in truth, and it will be said, 'Praise (be) to God, Lord of the worlds!'

39.68 – *There will be a blast on the trumpet*

The sūra ends with an extended judgment scene in which people are judged strictly on what they have done, and the unbelievers in Gehenna will be interrogated by the keepers of hell. See "Eschatology in the Quran" (p. 604).

39.75 – *And you will see the angels completely surrounding the throne, glorifying their Lord with praise*

This verse portrays an unusual vision for the Quran, but for Bible readers the scenes in Revelation 4 and 5 may come to mind.

FORGIVER
GHĀFIR

40

Amid a charged encounter between Moses and Pharaoh, with Haman and Korah looking on, a believer from Pharaoh's family urges his people to pay attention to the signs of Allah. Like the believer in this story, the entire sūra warns people about the harsh retribution that comes to those who ignore the signs.

Christians may well wonder how to think of such additions to well-known biblical narratives. Are these additions "sent down" from Allah, as the Quran repeatedly claims, or are they embellishments from a human imagination?

In the Name of God, the Merciful, the Compassionate
¹ Ḥā' Mīm.

² The sending down of the Book is from God, the Mighty, the Knowing, ³ Forgiver of sin and Accepter of repentance, harsh in retribution, full of forbearance. (There is) no god but Him. To Him is the (final) destination.

⁴ No one disputes about the signs of God, except those who disbelieve. Do not let their comings and goings in the lands deceive you. ⁵ The people of Noah before them (also) called (it) a lie, and the factions after them, and each community was determined to seize its messenger, and disputed by means of falsehood to refute the truth. So I seized them – and how was My retribution? ⁶ In this way the word of your Lord has proved true against those who disbelieve: 'They are the companions of the Fire.'

⁷ Those who bear the throne, and those around it, glorify their Lord with

---

40.1–2 – *Ḥā' Mīm. The sending down of the Book is from God*

This is the first in a series of seven sūras that start with the Arabic letters *Ḥā' mīm*. On these disconnected letters, see the comment at 2.1 (p. 35).

The sūra begins with the assertion that the "Book" is "sent down" (*tanzīl*) from Allah.

40.7 – *Those who bear the throne . . . glorify their Lord with praise*

Those who bear the throne (angels perhaps – see 39.75) ask forgiveness for the believers and intercede for them before their Lord (vv. 7–9).

praise, and believe in Him, and they ask forgiveness for those who believe: 'Our Lord, You comprehend everything in mercy and knowledge, so forgive those who turn (in repentance) and follow Your way. Guard them against the punishment of the Furnace, [8] Our Lord, and cause them to enter the Gardens of Eden, which You have promised them – and anyone who was righteous among their fathers, and their wives, and their descendants. Surely You – You are the Mighty, the Wise. [9] And guard them against evil deeds. Whoever You guard against evil deeds on that Day, You have had compassion on him. That is the great triumph!'

[10] Surely those who disbelieved will be called to: 'God's hatred is indeed greater than your hatred of one another, when you were called to belief and you disbelieved.' [11] They will say, 'Our Lord, You have caused us to die twice, and You have given us life twice. (Now) we confess our sins. (Is there) any way to get out?' [12] That is because, when God was called on alone, you disbelieved, but if (another) was associated with Him, you believed. Judgment (belongs) to God, the Most High, the Great.

[13] He (it is) who shows you His signs, and sends down provision for you from the sky, but no one takes heed except the one who turns (in repentance). [14] So call on God, devoting (your) religion to Him, (even) though the disbelievers dislike (it).

[15] Exalter of ranks, Holder of the throne, He casts the spirit of His command on whomever He pleases of His servants, to warn of the Day of Meeting. [16] On the Day when they go forth, nothing of theirs will be hidden from God. 'To whom (belongs) the kingdom today?' 'To God, the One, the Supreme! [17] Today each person will be repaid for what he has earned. (There will be) no evil (done) today. Surely God is quick at the reckoning.'

[18] Warn them of the Day of the Impending, when (their) hearts will be in (their) throats, choking (them). The evildoers will not have any loyal friend or intercessor (who) will be obeyed. [19] He knows the treachery of the eyes and what the hearts hide. [20] God will decide in truth, while those they call on instead of Him will not decide at all. Surely God – He is the Hearing, the Seeing.

40.10 – *God's hatred is indeed greater than your hatred of one another*

To claim that Allah's hatred (*maqt*) is greater than human hatred seems a strange way to motivate people to prepare to meet their Lord.

40.15 – *He casts the spirit of His command on whomever He pleases of His servants*

The expression "spirit of His command" also appears at 16.2 and 42.52 (cf. 17.85), where it seems to relate to warning and guidance. See a discussion of the Quran's verses about the "spirit" at 97.4 (p. 639).

²¹ Have they not traveled on the earth and seen how the end was for those who were before them? They were stronger than them in power, and in the traces (they left behind) on the earth. Yet God seized them in their sins, and they had no defender against God. ²² That was because they – (when) their messengers came to them with the clear signs – they disbelieved. So God seized them. Surely He is strong, harsh in retribution.

²³ Certainly We sent Moses with Our signs and clear authority ²⁴ to Pharaoh, and Haman, and Qārūn, but they said, 'A magician, a liar!' ²⁵ When he brought them the truth from Us, they said, 'Kill the sons of those who believe with him, and keep their women alive.' Yet the plot of the disbelievers always goes astray. ²⁶ Pharaoh said, 'Let me kill Moses, and let him call on his Lord. Surely I fear that he will change your religion, or that he will cause corruption to appear on the earth.' ²⁷ Moses said, 'I take refuge with my Lord and your Lord from every arrogant one (who) does not believe in the Day of Reckoning.'

²⁸ A (certain) man, a believer from the house of Pharaoh, (who) concealed his belief, said, 'Will you kill a man because he says, "My Lord is God," when he has brought you the clear signs from your Lord? If he is a liar, his lie is on him, but if he is truthful, some of what he promises you will smite you. Surely God does not guide anyone who is wanton (and) a liar. ²⁹ My people! Today the kingdom (belongs) to you (who) prevail on the earth, but who will help us against the violence of God, if it comes upon us?'

Pharaoh said, 'I only show you what I see, and I only guide you to the right way.' ³⁰ But the one who believed said, 'My people! Surely I fear for you something like the Day of the Factions, ³¹ like the case of the people of Noah, and 'Ād, and Thamūd, and those who (came) after them. Yet God does not intend any evil to (His) servants. ³² My people! Surely I fear for you the Day of Calling,

---

40.21 – *Have they not traveled on the earth and seen how the end was for those who were before them?*

The Quran often asks this question to warn the listener or reader about Allah's power to judge.

40.23–24 – *Certainly We sent Moses with Our signs and clear authority to Pharaoh, and Haman, and Qārūn*

A unique feature of this story of Moses (vv. 23–54) is the unexpected involvement of a "believer" from Pharaoh's family. The unnamed character steps forward to defend Moses and to speak God's message to his own people (vv. 28–45).

This version also repeats Pharaoh's command to Haman to build a tower (vv. 37–38; also 28.38) and once more places Korah (*Qārūn*) at Pharaoh's court. On the dislocation of these biblical characters, see the comments at 28.6 and 29.39.

33 the Day when you will turn back, retreating, having no protector from God. Whoever God leads astray has no guide. 34 Certainly Joseph brought you the clear signs before, but you did not stop doubting about what he brought you, until, when he perished, you said, "God will never raise up a messenger after him." In this way God leads astray anyone who is wanton (and) a doubter.'

35 Those who dispute about the signs of God, without any authority having come to them – (that) is a very hateful thing in the sight of God and those who believe. In this way God sets a seal on the heart of every arrogant tyrant.

36 Pharaoh said, 'Haman! Build a tower for me, so that I may reach the ropes, 37 the ropes of the heavens, and look upon the god of Moses. Surely I think he is a liar indeed.' In this way the evil of his deed was made to appear enticing to Pharaoh, and he was kept from the way. But the plot of Pharaoh only (came) to ruin.

38 Certainly the one who believed said, 'My people! Follow me, and I shall guide you to the right way. 39 My people! Surely this present life is enjoyment, but surely the Hereafter – it is the permanent Home. 40 Whoever does an evil deed will only be repaid the equal of it, but whoever does a righteous deed, whether male or female – and is a believer – those will enter the Garden, where they will be provided for without reckoning. 41 My people! Why is it that I call you to salvation, but you call me to the Fire. 42 You call me to disbelieve in God, and to associate with Him what I have no knowledge of, but I call you to the Mighty, the Forgiving. 43 (There is) no doubt that what you call me to has no calling to in this world or in the Hereafter, and that our return is to God, and that the wanton – they will be the companions of the Fire. 44 You will remember what I say to you, and (now) I commit my affair to God. Surely God sees His servants.' 45 So God guarded him against the evils of what they devised, and the evil punishment overwhelmed the house of Pharaoh. 46 The Fire – they will be presented to it morning and evening. On the Day when the Hour strikes: 'Cause the house of Pharaoh to enter the harshest punishment!'

47 When they argue with each other in the Fire, and the weak say to those who were arrogant: 'Surely we were your followers, so are you going relieve us (now) of any portion of the Fire?' 48 Those who were arrogant will say, 'Surely we are all in it. Surely God has already rendered judgment among (His) servants.'

40.41 – *My people! Why is it that I call you to salvation, but you call me to the Fire?*

It is the "believer" from Pharaoh's family who speaks the only occurrence in the Quran of the Arabic noun for salvation – *najāh*. The verb "to save," however, occurs many times in the Quran, most often in stories of the rescue of past prophets. See "Salvation in the Quran" (p. 180).

⁴⁹ Those who are in the Fire will say to the keepers of Gehenna, 'Call on your Lord to lighten for us one day of the punishment!' ⁵⁰ They will say, 'Did your messengers not bring you the clear signs?' They will say, 'Yes indeed!' They will say, 'Then call!' But the call of the disbelievers only goes astray.

⁵¹ Surely We do indeed help Our messengers and those who believe, (both) in this present life and on the Day when the witnesses arise ⁵² – the Day when their excuse will not benefit the evildoers. For them (there will be) the curse, and for them (there will be) the evil home. ⁵³ Certainly We gave Moses the guidance, and caused the Sons of Israel to inherit the Book, ⁵⁴ as a guidance and reminder to those with understanding. ⁵⁵ So be patient! Surely the promise of God is true. Ask forgiveness for your sin, and glorify your Lord with praise in the evening and the morning.

⁵⁶ Surely those who dispute about the signs of God, without any authority having come to them – they have their minds set only on greatness, but they will not reach it. So take refuge in God! Surely He – He is the Hearing, the Seeing. ⁵⁷ Indeed the creation of the heavens and earth is greater than the creation of the people, but most of the people do not know (it).

⁵⁸ The blind and the sighted are not equal, nor are those who believe and do deeds of righteousness and the evildoer. Little do you take heed! ⁵⁹ Surely the Hour is coming indeed – (there is) no doubt about it – but most of the people do not believe. ⁶⁰ Your Lord has said, 'Call on Me! I shall respond to you. Surely those who are too proud to serve Me will enter Gehenna humbled.'

⁶¹ (It is) God who made the night for you to rest in, and the day to see. Surely God is indeed full of favor to the people, but most of the people are not thankful (for it). ⁶² That is God, your Lord, Creator of everything. (There is) no god but Him. How are you (so) deluded? ⁶³ In this way those who denied the signs of God were (also) deluded. ⁶⁴ (It is) God who made the earth a dwelling place for you, and the sky a dome. He fashioned you, and made your forms well, and provided you with good things. That is God, your Lord. Blessed (be) God, Lord of

40.53 – *Certainly We gave Moses the guidance, and caused the Sons of Israel to inherit the Book*

Whenever the Quran refers to the "Book" of Moses, it always does so in the most positive and respectful way.

40.55 – *Ask forgiveness for your sin*

The Quran instructs the messenger to ask forgiveness for his sin (*dhanb*). This is one of several verses (also 47.19; 48.2) that question the Islamic doctrine that all prophets are sinless or immune (*maʿṣūm*). See a discussion of these verses at 48.2 (p. 513).

the worlds! [65] He is the Living One. (There is) no god but Him. Call on Him, devoting (your) religion to Him. Praise (be) to God, Lord of the worlds!

[66] Say: 'I am forbidden to serve those whom you call on, instead of God, when the clear signs have come to me from my Lord, and I am commanded to submit to the Lord of the worlds.' [67] He (it is) who created you from dust, then from a drop, then from a clot, then He brings you forth as children, then (He provides for you) so that you may reach your maturity, then that you may become old men – though among you (there is) one who is taken before (this) – and that you may reach an appointed time, and that you may understand. [68] He (it is) who gives life and causes death, and when He decrees something, He simply says to it, 'Be!' and it is.

[69] Do you not see those who dispute about the signs of God? How they are turned away? [70] – Those who call the Book a lie and what We sent Our messengers with? Soon they will know! [71] – When (there are) chains on their necks, and they are dragged (by) chains [72] into the boiling (water), (and) then they are poured into the Fire. [73] Then it will be said to them, 'Where is what you used to associate, [74] instead of God?' They will say, 'They have abandoned us. No! We were not calling on anything before!' In this way God leads the disbelievers astray. [75] 'That is because you gloated on the earth without any right, and because you were jubilant. [76] Enter the gates of Gehenna, there to remain.' Evil is the dwelling place of the arrogant!

[77] So be patient! Surely the promise of God is true. Whether We show you some of that which We promise them, or take you, to Us they will be returned. [78] Certainly We sent messengers before you: some of whom We have recounted to you, and some of whom We have not recounted to you. But it was not for any messenger to bring a sign, except by the permission of God. When the command of God comes, it will be decided in truth, and the perpetrators of falsehood will lose.

[79] (It is) God who made the livestock for you, for you to ride some of them

---

40.77 – *Whether We show you some of that which We promise them, or take you*

In this verse addressed to the messenger, Droge translates the Arabic verb *tawaffā* as "take," adding "in death" in a footnote. A series of Muslim translations render the verb as "cause to die" or similar expressions related to death (Pickthall, Shakir, Mohsin Khan, Sahih International, Muhammad Sarwar). The same verb appears at 10.46 and 13.40 and is similarly translated by these Muslim scholars. Yet none of these five translates *tawaffā* in the same way at 3.55, where 'Īsā is the object of the verb. See the comments on this question at 3.55 (p. 87) and "The Death of Jesus in the Quran" (p. 314).

and some of them to eat [80] – and (there are other) benefits for you in them – and for you to reach any place you set your mind on, and on them, and on the ship (as well), you are carried. [81] He shows you His signs – so which of the signs of God do you reject?

[82] Have they not traveled on the earth and seen how the end was for those who were before them? They were more numerous than them, and stronger in power, and in the traces (they left behind) on the earth. Yet what they earned was of no use to them. [83] When their messengers brought them the clear signs, they gloated over what knowledge they (already) had, and what they were mocking overwhelmed them. [84] Then, when they saw Our violence, they said, 'We believe in God alone, and we disbelieve in what we were associating (with Him).' [85] But their belief did not benefit them when they saw Our violence – the customary way of God, which has already occurred in the past concerning His servants – and then the disbelievers were lost.

MADE DISTINCT
FUṢṢILAT

41

The Quran pictures many judgment scenes to motivate the audience to respond appropriately to the Judge while there is still time. In this sūra, when the "enemies of Allah" are gathered for judgment, their ears, eyes, and skin testify against them. The bewildered enemies ask their skins, "Why?" Their skins reply, "You thought Allah did not know what you did. But we saw everything, and now we are telling about it!" (paraphrase of vv. 21-23).

Much of this sūra is about resistance to the preaching of the messenger and the punishments waiting for disbelievers in the hereafter.

In the Name of God, the Merciful, the Compassionate

[1] Ḥā Mīm.

[2] A sending down from the Merciful, the Compassionate. [3] A Book – its verses made distinct – an Arabic Qurʾān for a people who know.

[4] (He is) a bringer of good news and a warner. But most of them have turned away, and they do not hear. [5] They say, 'Our hearts are covered from what you call us to, and (there is) a heaviness in our ears, and between us and you (there is) a veil. So do (as you are able). Surely we are going to do (what we can).' [6] Say: 'I am only a human being like you. I am inspired that your God is one God. So go straight with Him, and ask forgiveness from Him. But woe to the idolaters, [7] who do not give the alms, and (who) are disbelievers in the Hereafter! [8] Surely those who believe and do righteous deeds – for them (there is) a reward without end.'

41.2 – *A sending down from the Merciful, the Compassionate*

The sūra opens with claims for the "sending down" of a book described as an Arabic *qurʾān* (v. 3). For the meaning of *qurʾān*, see the comment at 2.185 (p. 61). See also the analysis of claims for "Arabic" at 43.2–3 (p. 487).

41.5 – *Our hearts are covered from what you call us to*

Most of the listeners resist the messenger's preaching, so the messenger warns them of judgment in the world to come (vv. 6–8) and tries to persuade them by pointing out signs of the Creator's presence and power (vv. 9–12).

⁹ Say: 'Do you indeed disbelieve in the One who created the earth in two days, and do you set up rivals to Him? That is the Lord of the worlds. ¹⁰ He placed on it firm mountains (towering) above it, and blessed it, and decreed for it its (various) foods in four days, equal to the ones who ask. ¹¹ Then He mounted (upward) to the sky, while it was (still) smoke, and said to it and to the earth, "Come, both of you, willingly or unwillingly!" They both said, "We come willingly." ¹² He finished them (as) seven heavens in two days, and inspired each heaven (with) its affair. And We adorned the sky of this world with lamps, and (made them) a protection. That is the decree of the Mighty, the Knowing.'

¹³ If they turn away, say: 'I warn you of a thunderbolt like the thunderbolt of 'Ād and Thamūd.' ¹⁴ When the messengers came to them from before them and from behind them (saying): 'Do not serve (anyone) but God,' they said, 'If our Lord had (so) pleased, He would indeed have sent down angels. Surely we are disbelievers in what you are sent with.' ¹⁵ As for 'Ād, they became arrogant on the earth without any right, and said, 'Who is stronger than us in power?' Did they not see that God, who created them, was stronger than them in power? They denied Our signs. ¹⁶ So We sent a furious wind against them in the days of calamity, so that We might make them taste the punishment of disgrace in this present life. But the punishment of the Hereafter is indeed more disgraceful, and they will not be helped. ¹⁷ As for Thamūd, We guided them, but they preferred blindness over the guidance. So the thunderbolt of the punishment of humiliation took them for what they had earned. ¹⁸ But We rescued those who believed and guarded (themselves).

¹⁹ On the Day when the enemies of God are gathered to the Fire, and they are arranged (in rows) ²⁰ – until, when they have come to it, their hearing and their sight and their skins will bear witness against them about what they have done, ²¹ and they will say to their skins, 'Why did you bear witness against us?'

41.13 – *I warn you of a thunderbolt like the thunderbolt of 'Ād and Thamūd*

The messenger continues to warn the listeners by telling them of the destruction of disbelieving people in the past (vv. 13–17). On 'Ād and Thamūd, see the comments at 7.65 and 7.73 (p. 182–83).

41.19 – *On the Day when the enemies of God are gathered to the Fire*

The Quran warns listeners or readers by portraying judgment scenes on the Day of Resurrection. In this case, people in hell question their own skins – which bear witness against them (vv. 20–22). Two further such scenes come at verses 29–31 and 47–48.

Though this sūra refers to the "enemies of Allah" at verses 19 and 28, verse 34 recommends turning enemies into friends. Can Allah be less friendly than humans?

They will say, 'God, who gave speech to everything, has given us speech. He created you the first time, and to Him you are (now) returned. ²² You did not protect yourselves against your hearing and your sight and your skins bearing witness against you. You thought that God would not know much of what you had done. ²³ And that – the thought you thought about your Lord – has brought you to ruin. (Now) you are among the losers.'

²⁴ If they persist, the Fire will be a dwelling place for them, and if they ask to make amends, they will not be among the ones allowed to make amends. ²⁵ We have allotted to them comrades, and they have made what is before them and behind them appear enticing to them. The word about the communities of jinn and humankind (which) have passed away before them has proved true against them (as well). Surely they were losers.

²⁶ Those who disbelieve say, 'Do not listen to this Qur'ān, but talk frivolously about it, so that you may overcome (them).' ²⁷ We shall indeed make those who disbelieve taste a harsh punishment, and We shall indeed repay them for the worst of what they have done. ²⁸ That is the payment of the enemies of God – the Fire – where they will have the Home of Eternity as payment for their having denied Our signs.

²⁹ Those who disbelieve (will) say, 'Our Lord, show us those of the jinn and humankind who led us astray. We shall place them beneath our feet, so that they may be among the lowest.' ³⁰ Surely those who have said, 'Our Lord is God,' (and) then have gone straight – the angels will come down on them (saying): 'Do not fear, and do not sorrow, but welcome the good news of the Garden which you were promised. ³¹ We are your allies in this present life and in the Hereafter, where you will have whatever you desire, whatever you call for ³² – a reception from One forgiving, compassionate.'

³³ Who is better in speech than the one who calls (people) to God, and does righteousness, and says, 'Surely I am one of those who submit'? ³⁴ The good deed and the evil deed are not equal. Repel (evil) with that which is better, and suddenly the one with whom (there was) enmity between you and him (will behave) as if he were an ally. ³⁵ Yet no one will receive it except those who are patient, and no one will receive it except one who possesses great good luck. ³⁶ If any provocation from Satan provokes you, take refuge with God. Surely He – He is the Hearing, the Knowing.

³⁷ Among His signs are the night and the day, and the sun and the moon.

41.31 – *in the Hereafter . . . you will have whatever you desire*
The angels encourage those who say "our Lord is Allah" by telling them about future joys in paradise and providing protection (vv. 30–32).

Do not prostrate yourselves before the sun or before the moon, but prostrate yourselves before God, who created them, if you serve Him. [38] If they are (too) proud, those who are in the presence of your Lord glorify Him by night and day, and do not become tired. [39] (Another) of His signs is that you see the earth barren, (and) then, when We send down water on it, it stirs and swells. Surely the One who gives it life is indeed the giver of life to the dead. Surely He is powerful over everything. [40] Surely those who pervert Our signs are not hidden from Us. Is the one who is cast into the Fire better, or the one who comes (out) secure on the Day of Resurrection? Do whatever you please. Surely He sees what you do.

[41] Surely those who disbelieve in the Reminder when it comes to them – surely it is a mighty Book indeed! [42] Falsehood does not come to it, (either) from before it or from behind it. (It is) a sending down from One wise, praiseworthy. [43] Nothing is said to you except what has already been said to the messengers before you. Surely your Lord is indeed full of forgiveness, but (also) full of painful retribution. [44] If We had made it a foreign Qur'ān, they would indeed have said, 'Why are its signs not made distinct? Foreign and Arabic?' Say: 'It is a guidance and healing for those who believe, but those who do not believe – (there is) a heaviness in their ears, and for them it is a blindness. Those – (it is as if) they are being called from a place far away.'

[45] Certainly We gave Moses the Book, and then differences arose about it. Were it not for a preceding word from your Lord, it would indeed have been decided between them. Surely they are in grave doubt indeed about it.

[46] Whoever does righteousness, it is for himself, and whoever does evil, it is (likewise) against himself. Your Lord is not an evildoer to (His) servants.

[47] Knowledge of the Hour is reserved for Him. No fruit comes forth from

---

41.41 – *surely it is a mighty Book indeed!*

Here "mighty" translates *'azīz* – another high "self-referential" claim for the recitation.

41.43–44 – *Nothing is said to you except what has already been said to the messengers before you*

The Quran addresses the messenger directly to assert that the recitations of the messenger will match those of "the messengers before you." This seems to be one more claim that asks the reader to compare the contents of the Quran to what was said to the messengers and prophets in the Bible.

41.45 – *Certainly We gave Moses the Book, and then differences arose about it*

The Quran always speaks positively about the "Book" of Moses, but often mentions differences and doubts that arose among its custodians. See the discussion of "differences" among the People of the Book at 98.4 (p. 642).

its sheath, and no female conceives or delivers, except with His knowledge. On the Day when He will call to them, 'Where are My associates?,' they will say, 'We proclaim to You: (there is) no witness among us.' ⁴⁸ What they called on before will abandon them, and they will know (that there is) no place of escape for them.

⁴⁹ The human does not tire of calling for good, but if evil touches him, he is in despair (and) downcast. ⁵⁰ If indeed We give him a taste of mercy from Us, after hardship has touched him, he will indeed say, 'This is mine! I do not think the Hour is coming. If indeed I am returned to my Lord, surely I shall have the best (reward) indeed with Him.' We shall indeed inform those who disbelieve about what they have done, and indeed make them taste a stern punishment. ⁵¹ When We bless a person, he turns away and distances himself, but when evil touches them, he is full of long prayers.

⁵² Say: 'Do you see? If it is from God, and you disbelieve in it – who is farther astray than the one who is in extreme defiance?'

⁵³ We shall show them Our signs in the skies and in themselves, until it becomes clear to them that it is the truth. Is it not sufficient in (regard to) your Lord that He is a witness over everything? ⁵⁴ Is it not a fact that they are in doubt about the meeting with their Lord? Is it not a fact that He encompasses everything?

41.49–50 – *The human does not tire of calling for good, but if evil touches him*
Allah shows his mercy to people who are hurt, but instead of giving credit to him and thanking him, they speak as if it is their own accomplishment.

CONSULTATION
AL-SHŪRĀ

42

Sūra 42 provides a good example of how quranic text can very quickly change voice and object. The sūra begins (v. 3) with a voice speaking directly to the messenger in second person ("you") about Allah in third person ("he"). Verse 7, however, has Allah speaking in first person plural ("we") to the messenger. Verse 8 returns to third person about Allah. Verse 10 speaks to the audience in second person plural ("you") and then shifts to first person singular ("I"). Verse 13 starts with a voice speaking about Allah in third person to the audience in second person plural, then shifts to Allah speaking in first person plural to the messenger in second person singular, and then returns to discussing Allah in third person.

In the Name of God, the Merciful, the Compassionate

¹ Ḥā Mīm. ² 'Ayn Sīn Qāf.

³ In this way He inspires you, and those who were before you – God, the Mighty, the Wise. ⁴ To Him (belongs) whatever is in the heavens and whatever is on the earth. He is the Most High, the Almighty. ⁵ The heavens are nearly torn apart from above, when the angels glorify their Lord with praise, and ask forgiveness for those on the earth. Is it not a fact that God – He is the Forgiving, the Compassionate? ⁶ Those who have taken allies other than Him – God is watcher over them. You are not a guardian over them.

⁷ In this way We have inspired you (with) an Arabic Qur'ān, so that you may warn the Mother of Towns and those around it, and so that you may warn of the Day of Gathering – (there is) no doubt about it – (one) group in the Garden, and (another) group in the blazing (Fire). ⁸ If God had (so) pleased, He would indeed

---

42.3 – *In this way He inspires you, and those who were before you*

The sūra opens with the claim that Allah inspires (awḥā) the messenger with his recitation (also v. 7).

42.7 – *In this way We have inspired you (with) an Arabic Qur'ān*

The expression "Arabic qur'ān" became very important in the claims that the

will have made them one community. But He causes whomever He pleases to enter into His mercy. The evildoers will have no ally and no helper.

⁹ Or have they taken allies other than Him? God – He is the (true) Ally. He gives the dead life. He is powerful over everything. ¹⁰ Whatever you differ about, judgment of it (belongs) to God. That is God, my Lord. In Him I have put my trust, and to Him I turn (in repentance). ¹¹ (He is) the Creator of the heavens and the earth. He has made pairs for you from yourselves, and pairs (also) from the livestock. He scatters you by this means. There is nothing like Him. He is the Hearing, the Seeing. ¹² To Him (belong) the keys of the heavens and the earth. He extends (His) provision to whomever He pleases, and restricts (it). Surely He has knowledge of everything.

¹³ He has instituted for you from the religion what He charged Noah with, and that which We have inspired you (with), and what We charged Abraham, and Moses, and Jesus with: 'Observe the religion, and do not become divided in it.' What you call them to is hard on the idolaters. God chooses for Himself whomever He pleases, and He guides to Himself whoever turns (to Him in repentance). ¹⁴ They did not become divided until after the knowledge had come to them, (because of) envy among themselves. Were it not for a preceding word from your Lord, until an appointed time, it would indeed have been decided between them. Surely those who inherited the Book after them are in grave doubt indeed about it. ¹⁵ So call (them) to that, and go straight as you have been commanded, and do not follow their (vain) desires, but say: 'I believe in

---

Quran made for itself. For the meaning of *qurʾān* see the comment at 2.185 (p. 61); see also the analysis of claims for "Arabic" at 43.2–3 (p. 487).

According to Muslim tradition, the "mother of towns" is Mecca, though the name Mecca only appears once in the Quran (48.24), and there it is called a "belly" (*baṭn*), not a city.

42.10 – *In Him I have put my trust, and to Him I turn (in repentance)*

The preaching of the messenger includes his testimony of commitment to Allah.

42.13 – *He has instituted for you from the religion what He charged Noah with*

The tone and content of this verse seem to represent a peaceful and conciliatory approach toward other religious communities. Here there is only one religion (*dīn*). At the same time, the reader may enquire whether the claim is true. Is the religion of the Quran the same as that of Noah, Abraham, Moses, and Jesus?

On the theme of division over the "knowledge" (v. 14), see the comments at 98.4 (p. 642).

42.15 – *I believe in whatever Book God has sent down*

Quranic statements about pre-Islamic scriptures are generally positive, always

whatever Book God has sent down, and I have been commanded to act fairly among you. God is our Lord and your Lord. To us our deeds and to you your deeds. (There is) no argument between us and you. God will gather us together. To Him is the (final) destination.'

[16] Those who (still) argue about God, after whatever response has been made to Him – their argument is refuted in the sight of their Lord. Anger (will fall) on them, and for them (there will be) a harsh punishment. [17] (It is) God who has sent down the Book with the truth, and (also) the scale. What will make you know? Perhaps the Hour is near. [18] Those who do not believe in it seek to hurry it, but those who believe in it are apprehensive about it, and know that it is the truth. Is it not a fact that those who are in doubt about the Hour are far astray?

The Place of the Scale(s) in the Reckoning
Daniel A. Brubaker

The Quran mentions "the Scale" (*mizān*) and "the Scales" (*mawāzīn*) in the context of the Reckoning, or the Hour (i.e., the Day of Judgment), and these images are emblematic of the Quran's teaching on salvation – that a sinful person with a simple net positive of good deeds will make it into the Garden (i.e., Paradise), marking the most consequential point of difference between what the Bible and the Quran say about how people are justified before God. "(It is) Allah Who sent down the Book in truth, and (also) the scale. What will make you know? Perhaps the Hour is near" (42.17).

The core theological difference between biblical Christianity and quranic theology (and, I believe, the central mission of the latter) is that the Quran dethrones Jesus, insists he is only a man, and denies his finished work of atonement at the cross, thus rejecting salvation by grace through faith in him. The Quran explicitly and emphatically refuses the possibility of substitutionary atonement. For example, "Every human – We have fastened his fate to him on his neck. . . . No one bearing a burden bears the burden of another" (17.13, 15).

when the name of a scripture is given. In this verse the messenger says, "I believe in whatever Book Allah has sent down," indicating a positive approach to the existing scriptures. On this point there is "no argument between us and you."

42.17 – *(It is) God who has sent down the Book with the truth, and (also) the scale*
The Quran claims that Allah has sent down (*anzala*) its contents. On "the scale," see "The Place of the Scale(s) in the Reckoning" above.

The Quran's view of the universe is one in which all people will be judged by Allah based upon the weight of their deeds. If good deeds outweigh the bad, people may be admitted to the Garden, "beneath which rivers flow." If bad deeds outweigh the good, they may find themselves in the fire and a painful punishment. In both cases, the variable is the will of Allah, whose preference is the deciding factor. That Allah is "merciful, compassionate," is one of the Quran's most familiar refrains. However, various permutations of the promise of a "painful punishment," as well as the assurance that Allah is swift and strong in retribution, also abound.

The definite form *al-mīzān*, "the scale," occurs nine times in the Quran (6.152; 7.85; 11.84; 11.85; 42.17; 55.7; 55.8; 55.9; 57.25), plus once in the plural *al-mawāzīn*, "the scales" (21.47), and six times in the possessive plural *mawāzīnuhu*, "his scales" (7.8; 7.9; 23.102; 23.103; 101.6; 101.8). The past participle form *mawzūn*, "weighed," likewise occurs once (15.19), the related word for "weighing" (*waznu*) of deeds (e.g. on a scale) twice (7:8; 55:9), the word *waznan*, "an account," once (18:105), and the word *wazanūhum*, "they weigh," once as well (83:3).

> "As for the one whose scales are heavy, he will be in a pleasing life, but as for the one whose scales are light, his mother will be Hāwiya [hell or abyss]" (101.6–8).

> "But whoever's scales are light, those are the ones who have lost their (own) selves – remaining in Gehenna" (23.103, *scales* is plural in this verse).

> "We shall lay down the scales of justice for the Day of Resurrection, and no one will be done any evil. (Even) if there is (only) the weight of a mustard seed, We shall produce it, and We are sufficient as reckoners" (21.47).

Beyond reference to the Day of Judgment, scales appear in the Quran in relation to giving a minor orphan the fullness of what he is owed until he comes of age (6.152) or relating a past exhortation to the people of Midian to fulfill their obligations to each other (7.85; 11.84).

Consistent with the picture painted by the Quran, those who believe its message cannot know their final fate. Many are thus fearful of or resigned to the prospect of eternity in the fire. Although hoping to fall upon Allah's mercy, they can have no personal assurance of such.

What Does the New Testament Say about Justification?

The judgment, including an accounting for the deeds done while in the flesh, is referred to in the Hebrew Bible (e.g., Psalm 1:5) and variously in the New Testament (Matthew 10:15; Hebrews 9:27; 2 Peter 3:7; Jude 6). Beginning in Matthew 25:31, Jesus, referring to himself as the Son of Man and mirroring Ezekiel 34:17–31, promises that he will return in glory. Seated on his throne with all nations gathered before him, he will sort individuals as a shepherd separates the sheep from the goats, decreeing punishment and reward based upon what they had done.

The Bible says God is holy; no sinful person may enter his presence and live. This is the reason for the biblical sacrifices: laying the burden of sin on a lamb that is then slaughtered in place of guilty people is central in both Hebrew Bible and the New Testament. The latter reveals that the Passover and indeed the entire ongoing ritual always pointed toward a real sacrifice – that of the Messiah, as John the Baptist once exclaimed when he saw Jesus coming toward him: "Look, the Lamb of God who takes away the sin of the world!" (John 1:29).

The New Testament is emphatic and clear about the impossibility of gaining salvation by good works. Paul writes, "By the works of the Law no flesh will be justified" (Galatians 2:16; cf. Romans 3:20).

The "good news" to which the word *gospel* refers is that God did not abandon sinful humans to the hopelessness of eternal punishment, "but now apart from the Law, the righteousness of God has been manifested, being witnessed by the Law and the Prophets, even the righteousness of God through faith in Jesus Christ for all those who believe" (Romans 3:21–24; cf. Ephesians 2:8–9).

[19] God is astute with His servants, providing for whomever He pleases. He is the Strong, the Mighty.

[20] Whoever desires the harvest of the Hereafter – We shall give him increase in his harvest, and whoever desires the harvest of this world – We shall give him some of it, but he will not have any portion in the Hereafter. [21] Or do they have associates who have instituted for them from the religion what God has not given permission for? Were it not for a decisive word, it would indeed have been decided between them. Surely the evildoers – for them (there is) a painful punishment. [22] You will see the evildoers apprehensive about what they have earned, when it falls on them, while those who believe and do righteous deeds are in meadows of the Gardens. They will have whatever they please in the presence of their Lord. That is the great favor!

²³ That is the good news which God gives to His servants who believe and do righteous deeds. Say: 'I do not ask you for any reward for it, except love for family.' Whoever acquires a good (deed) – We shall increase the good for him in it. Surely God is forgiving, thankful.

²⁴ Or do they say, 'He has forged a lie against God?' If God pleases, He will set a seal on your heart, and God will blot out falsehood and verify the truth by His words. Surely He knows what is in the hearts.

²⁵ He (it is) who accepts repentance from His servants and pardons evil deeds. He knows what you do.

²⁶ He responds to those who believe and do righteous deeds, and gives them increase from His favor. But the disbelievers – for them (there is) a harsh punishment.

²⁷ If God were to extend (His) provision to His servants, they would indeed act oppressively on the earth, but He sends down in measure whatever He pleases. Surely He is aware of His servants (and) sees (them).

²⁸ He (it is) who sends down the rain after they have despaired, and displays His mercy. He is the Ally, the Praiseworthy.

²⁹ Among His signs are the creation of the heavens and the earth, and the creatures He has scattered in both of them. He has power over gathering them whenever He pleases. ³⁰ Whatever smiting may smite you is because of what your (own) hands have earned – yet He pardons much. ³¹ You cannot escape (Him) on the earth, and you have no ally and no helper other than God.

³² Among His signs are the (ships) running on the sea, like landmarks. ³³ If He pleases, He stills the wind and they remain motionless on its surface. Surely in that are signs indeed for every patient (and) thankful one. ³⁴ Or He wrecks them for what they have earned – yet He pardons much – ³⁵ and (it is so that) He may know those who dispute about Our signs. For them (there is) no place of escape.

³⁶ Whatever things you have been given are (only) the enjoyment of this present life, but what is with God is better and more lasting for those who believe

---

42.23 – *I do not ask you for any reward for it, except love for family*

In this sūra the messenger is unassuming, and his role is limited. He warns (v. 7) and delivers the message, but he is not a "watcher" over the people (v. 48).

42.36 – *Whatever things you have been given are (only) the enjoyment of this present life*

This verse and the following passage (vv. 36–43) make up an interesting expression of what Allah wants from people. Beyond trusting Allah, avoiding sins, and observing ritual prayer, the passage recommends forgiving those who do evil (vv. 40, 43).

and put their trust in their Lord [37] – and (also for) those who avoid great sins and immoral deeds, and when they are angry, they forgive, [38] and those who respond to their Lord and observe the prayer, and their affair (is a matter of) consultation among themselves, and they contribute from what We have provided them, [39] and those who, when envy smites them, defend themselves (against it). [40] (The) payment for an evil deed is an evil like it, but whoever pardons and sets (things) right – his reward (depends) on God. Surely He does not love the evildoers. [41] Whoever indeed defends himself after he has suffered evil, those – against them (there is) no way. [42] The way is only open against those who do the people evil, and act oppressively on the earth without any right. Those – for them (there is) a painful punishment. [43] But whoever indeed is patient and forgives – surely that indeed is one of the determining factors in (all) affairs.

[44] Whoever God leads astray has no ally after Him, and you will see the evildoers, when they see the punishment, saying, '(Is there) any way to return?' [45] You will see them presented to it, humbled by the disgrace, looking with furtive glance(s). And those who believe will say, 'Surely the losers are those who have lost their (own) selves and their families on the Day of Resurrection.' Is it not a fact that the evildoers (will remain) in lasting punishment? [46] They will have no allies to help them, other than God, and whoever God leads astray has no way.

[47] Respond to your Lord, before a Day comes from God which cannot be turned back. You will not have any shelter on that Day, nor any denial (of what you have done). [48] If they turn away – We have not sent you as a watcher over them. Nothing (depends) on you except the delivery (of the message). Surely We – when We give a person a taste of mercy from Us, he gloats about it, but if some evil smites them because of what their (own) hands have sent forward – surely the human is ungrateful.

[49] To God (belongs) the kingdom of the heavens and the earth. He creates whatever He pleases. He grants females to whomever He pleases, and He grants males to whomever He pleases, [50] or He pairs them males and females. He makes barren whomever He pleases. Surely He is knowing, powerful.

42.40 – *Surely He does not love the evildoers*

The Quran contains twenty-four statements about the kinds of people whom Allah does not love. The "evildoers" (*ẓālimun*) also appear as object at 3.57 and 140. See "The Language of Love in the Quran" (p. 560).

42.44 – *Whoever God leads astray has no ally after Him*

In the Quran, Allah both guides and leads astray on the one hand, and holds humans accountable for their deeds in strict justice on the other. See the comment on this theme at 13.27 (p. 260).

⁵¹ It is not (fitting) for any human being that God should speak to him, except (by) inspiration, or from behind a veil, or (that) He should send a messenger and he inspire by His permission whatever He pleases. Surely He is most high, wise. ⁵² In this way We have inspired you (with) a spirit of Our command. You did not know what the Book was, nor (what) belief (was), but We have made it a light by means of which We guide whomever We please of Our servants. Surely you will guide (people) to a straight path, ⁵³ the path of God, the One to whom (belongs) whatever is in the heavens and whatever is on the earth. Is it not a fact that all affairs are returned to God?

42.51 – *It is not (fitting) for any human being that God should speak to him*

This interesting statement tells how Allah speaks to humans through inspiration (*waḥy*), from behind a veil (*ḥijāb*), or by sending a messenger. See a discussion of the Quran's "doctrine of scripture" at 85.21–22 (p. 624).

42.52 – *In this way We have inspired you (with) a spirit of Our command*

Immediately after verse 51, the Quran asserts that Allah inspires the messenger (as at vv. 3, 7). The expression "spirit of Our command" also appears at 16.2 and 40.15 (cf. 17.85), where it seems to relate to the messenger's task of warning.

DECORATION
AL-ZUKHRUF

43

In Muslim scenarios of end time events, 'Īsā (the quranic Jesus) has a distinct role. Many Muslim commentators interpret a verse in Sūra 43 to be a reference to the second coming of 'Īsā. Readers may decide whether verse 61 has strong enough content to bear that interpretation.

In any case, this sūra contains a number of statements about 'Īsā that are the last of their kinds in the canonical progression of the Quran. Comments on this sūra include several analyses and responses to this content.

In the Name of God, the Merciful, the Compassionate
[1] Hā Mīm.

[2] By the clear Book! [3] Surely We have made it an Arabic Qur'ān, so that you

---

43.2–3 – *By the clear book! Surely we have made it an Arabic Qur'ān*

The sūra opens with the statement that the recitation is in Arabic so that the audience may understand (also 12.2). The word *qur'ān* does not necessarily mean the Muslim scripture as it is known today. See the comment on this term at 2.185 (p. 61).

Verse 3 is the final verse in a series of verses that focus an "Arabic *qur'ān*" (12.2; 20.113; 39.28; 41.3; 43.7). Other verses that highlight the Arabic language of the Quran are 13.37; 16.103; 26.195; and 46.12 (cf. 41.44). At the most basic level, these verses say that the recitation is in Arabic so that people can understand the message and be warned (20.113; 26.194; 39.28; 41.4; 42.7; 46.12). From there the verses move into claims of revelation (*anzala*, 12.2; 13.36; 20.113; *nazzala*, 16.101–2; *tanzīl*, 26.192; 41.3, 42; *āyāt*, 16.101–5) and inspiration (*awḥā*, 12.3; 42.7; *waḥy*, 20.114). In these claims Allah narrates (12.3) and coins parables (39.27, 29), and the "true spirit" brings the "revelation" down upon the heart of the messenger (26.193–4; cf. 16.102).

That people may hear or read and understand a recitation in their own language is certainly "good tidings" (46.12). However, why should the Arabic language of the recitation be a proof of revelation or inspiration? Why should retelling a well-known story (12.2–3) or claiming to "confirm" the book of Moses (46.12) or preaching what is "in the scriptures of those of old" (26.196) require a divine source? The Quran answers

may understand. ⁴ And surely it is in the mother of the Book, with Us, most high indeed, wise.

⁵ Shall We strike the Reminder away from you, on the excuse that you have been a wanton people? ⁶ How many prophets have We sent among those of old! ⁷ Yet not one prophet came to them whom they did not ridicule. ⁸ So We destroyed (those peoples who were) stronger than them in power, and the example of those of old has passed away.

⁹ If indeed you ask them, 'Who created the heavens and the earth?,' they will indeed say, 'The Mighty, the Knowing created them.' ¹⁰ (It is He) who made the earth as a cradle for you, and made (path)ways in it for you, so that you might be guided, ¹¹ and (it is He) who sends down water from the sky in measure – and by means of it We give some barren land life, and in this way you (too) will be brought forth – ¹² and (it is He) who created the pairs, all of them, and made for you what you ride on from the ship(s) and the livestock, ¹³ so that you may mount their backs, (and) then remember the blessing of your Lord when you are mounted upon them, and say, 'Glory to the One who has subjected this to us, when we (ourselves) were not fit for it. ¹⁴ Surely we are indeed going to return to our Lord.' ¹⁵ Yet they assign to Him a part of His (own) servants. Surely the human is clearly ungrateful indeed.

¹⁶ Or has He taken (for Himself) daughters from what He creates, and singled you out with sons? ¹⁷ When one of them is given news of what he has struck as a parable for the Merciful, his face turns dark and he chokes back his disappointment. ¹⁸ 'One who is brought up in luxury, and he is not clear in the (time of) dispute?' ¹⁹ Yet they have made the angels – those who are themselves servants of the Merciful – females. Did they witness their creation?

---

neither of these questions directly. Additionally, it does not address the issue that during the centuries prior to Islam, the Bible was translated into languages such as Syriac, Armenian, Coptic, and Latin. Does the Quran's teaching on inspiration imply that those translations could claim a divine origin too?

43.4 – *And surely it is in the mother of the Book, with Us*

The "mother of the Book" (*umm al-kitāb*) is a mysterious expression that may refer to a concept of a source of all the heavenly books (also 3.7; 13.39). See the discussion of the Quran's "doctrine of scripture" at 85.21–22 (p. 624).

43.6 – *How many prophets have We sent among those of old!*

According to verse 7, all prophets in the past were ridiculed by their people. The sūra provides examples to support this claim from Abraham, Moses, and 'Īsā. See the discussion of statements about all messengers or prophets at 25.20 (p. 365).

Their testimony will be written down, and they will be questioned. [20] They say, 'If the Merciful had (so) pleased, we would not have served them.' They have no knowledge about that; they are only guessing. [21] Or have We given them a Book before it, and do they hold fast to it? [22] No! They say, 'Surely we found our fathers (set) on a community, and surely we are guided in their footsteps.' [23] In this way We have not sent any warner before you to a town, except that its affluent ones said, 'Surely we found our fathers (set) on a community, and surely we are following in their footsteps.' [24] He said, 'Even if I bring you better guidance than what you found your fathers (set) on?' They said, 'Surely we are disbelievers in what you are sent with.' [25] So We took vengeance on them. See how the end was for the ones who called (it) a lie!

[26] (Remember) when Abraham said to his father and his people, 'Surely I am free of what you serve, [27] except for the One who created me. Surely He will guide me.' [28] And he made it a lasting word among his descendants, so that they might return.

[29] No! I gave these (people) and their fathers enjoyment (of life), until the truth came to them, and (also) a clear messenger. [30] But when the truth came to them, they said, 'This is magic. Surely we are disbelievers in it.'

[31] They said, 'If only this Qur'ān had been sent down on some great man of the two towns.' [32] Do they distribute the mercy of your Lord? We have distributed their livelihood among them in this present life, and raised some of them above others in rank, so that some of them may take others in slavery. But the mercy of your Lord is better than what they accumulate. [33] If it were not that humankind would be one community, We would indeed have made for those who disbelieve in the Merciful roofs of silver for their houses, and stairways on which to ascend, [34] and doors for their houses, and couches on which to recline, [35] and (all manner of) decoration. Yet all that is but the enjoyment of this present life – the Hereafter with your Lord is for the ones who guard (themselves).

[36] Whoever turns away from the Reminder of the Merciful – We allot to him a satan, and he becomes his comrade. [37] Surely they indeed keep them from the way, even though they think that they are (rightly) guided, [38] until, when he comes to Us, he says, 'Would that (there were) between me and you the distance of the two Easts!' And: 'Evil is the comrade! [39] It will not benefit you today – since you have done evil – that you are partners in the punishment.'

43.26 – *(Remember) when Abraham said to his father and his people*

A brief reference to Abraham and his people introduces a longer passage discussing the responses of people to the preaching of the messenger (vv. 31–39).

⁴⁰ Can you make the deaf to hear, or can you guide the blind and the one who is clearly astray? ⁴¹ Whether We take you away – surely We are going to take vengeance on them – ⁴² or show you what We have promised them – surely We are powerful over them. ⁴³ So hold fast to what you are inspired (with). Surely you are on a straight path. ⁴⁴ Surely it is a reminder indeed to you and to your people. Soon you will (all) be questioned. ⁴⁵ Ask those of Our messengers whom We sent before you: Did We appoint any other gods than the Merciful to be served?

⁴⁶ Certainly We sent Moses with Our signs to Pharaoh and his assembly. He said, 'Surely I am a messenger of the Lord of the worlds.' ⁴⁷ But when he brought them Our signs, suddenly they began to laugh at them, ⁴⁸ even though every sign We showed them was greater than the one before it. We seized them with the punishment, so that they might return. ⁴⁹ They said, 'Magician! Call on your Lord for us by whatever covenant He has made with you, (and) surely we shall indeed be (rightly) guided.' ⁵⁰ But when We removed the punishment from them, immediately they broke (their promise). ⁵¹ Pharaoh called out among his people: 'My people! Is the kingdom of Egypt not mine, and these rivers (which) flow beneath me? Do you not see? ⁵² Am I not better than this (man), who is despicable and scarcely makes (things) clear? ⁵³ If only bracelets of gold were cast (down) on him or the accompanying angels came with him.' ⁵⁴ So he unsettled his people, and they obeyed him. Surely they were a wicked people. ⁵⁵ When they had angered Us, We took vengeance on them and drowned them – all (of them)! ⁵⁶ We made them a thing of the past, and an example for the later (generations).

43.40 – *Can you make the deaf to hear, or can you guide the blind . . . ?*

The Quran addresses the messenger directly to note the limitations of his work and to encourage him to continue preaching faithfully. The messenger's audience asks him for a miracle or "sign" (*āya*) at a number of points (e.g., 6.109; 13.7, 27; 20.133; 29.50). The Quran's response is generally to say that the messenger is only a warner and that "signs are only with Allah" (6.109; 29.50).

The power to "make the deaf to hear" is of course what the Gospel accounts report about Jesus (Mark 7:31–37), and what Jesus freely claimed (Matthew 11.4–5; Luke 7.22; cf. Isaiah 35:5). Further on, Sūra 43 declares that "'Īsā brought the clear signs" (v. 63). See the comments at verse 63, as well as a discussion about the miracles of 'Īsā in the Quran at 5.110 (p. 153).

43.46 – *Certainly We sent Moses with Our signs to Pharaoh and his assembly*

This episode from the Moses story shows Pharaoh mocking Moses and resisting his message. Allah took vengeance on the Egyptians and drowned them (v. 55).

⁵⁷ When the son of Mary is cited as an example, suddenly your people keep (others) from it, ⁵⁸ and they say, 'Are our gods better, or is he?' They only cite him to you as a (matter of) dispute. Yes! They are a contentious people. ⁵⁹ He was only a servant whom We blessed, and We made him an example for the Sons of Israel. ⁶⁰ If We (so) pleased, We could indeed make angels out of you to be successors on the earth.

43.57 – *When the son of Mary is cited as an example*

These words begin a passage (vv. 57–64) about ʿĪsā, introduced as "the son of Mary." In verse 58 the audience seems to mention the belief in the deity of ʿĪsā in order to argue with the messenger.

43.59 – *He was only a servant whom We blessed*

In response to the "contentious people" in verse 58, the Quran asserts that ʿĪsā is nothing but a servant (or slave, ʿabd).

This verse and verse 64 are the final denials of the deity of ʿĪsā in the Quran (in its canonical progression). On this point the Quran makes a number of statements about what ʿĪsā is "only." He is "only" a servant or slave (43.59; cf. 4.172) and a messenger (4.171; 5.75; cf. 4.157; 61.6). The Quran contends that Allah created ʿĪsā in Mary's womb (3.47), created him just like Adam (3.59; also 2.117; 19.35). The quranic ʿĪsā is a mere human who eats food like his mother (5.75). ʿĪsā does miracles but only – the Quran is concerned to emphasize – by the permission of Allah (3.49; 5.110). In the Quran, ʿĪsā himself foreswears all thoughts of his deity and directs human worship toward Allah (e.g., 5.116–17, see the comments below at v. 64).

Then there is a group of verses about ʿĪsā that make even more straightforward negations, often brimming with strong feeling: Allah is not the Messiah (5.17, 72); the Messiah is not Lord (9.31; cf. 3.64); Allah is not "three" (4.171; 5.73; cf. 5.116); the Messiah is not the son of Allah (e.g., 9.30; see "Son of God in the Quran," p. 352).

In response to these verses, Christian readers may note how far this polemic places Jesus below his identity in the Gospel accounts, and may wonder at the frequency and force of the quranic denials. These verses are a reminder to the Christian community to review what the New Testament says about Jesus carefully and to recall the significance of its witness.

The early Quran commentary of Muqātil ibn Sulaymān (d. 767) tells a story of a meeting of a group of Christians from Najrān with the messenger of Islam in Medina. When the Christians arrived to make terms, the very first question they asked the messenger was, "Why do you abuse (shatama) and dishonor (ʿāba) our master (ṣāḥib)?" According to this story, the Christians perceived the messenger's preaching about ʿĪsā to be blasphemous.

⁶¹ Surely it is indeed knowledge for the Hour, so do not be in doubt about it, but follow me. This is a straight path. ⁶² Do not let Satan keep you from (it). Surely he is a clear enemy to you.

⁶³ When Jesus brought the clear signs, he said, 'I have brought you the wisdom, and (I have done so) to make clear to you some of your differences. Guard (yourselves) against God and obey me. ⁶⁴ Surely God – He is my Lord and your

---

43.61 – *Surely it is indeed knowledge for the Hour*

Many Muslims interpret this verse to refer to the second coming of ʿĪsā. Yet there seems to be little reason to do so in the verse itself (even if *it* is read as *he*). Muslim beliefs about the role of ʿĪsā in end time events were developed not in the Quran but in other early Muslim literature, such as the hadith.

43.63 – *When Jesus brought the clear signs*

For the name ʿĪsā, see the explanation at 2.97 (p. 49). The statement that ʿĪsā brought "clear signs" (*bayyināt*) also appears at 2.87; 5.110; and 61.6. The occurrence of *bayyināt* at 5.110 and 61.6 suggests that this expression may refer to the miracles of ʿĪsā. See a discussion about the miracles of ʿĪsā in the Quran at 5.110 (p. 153).

The Gospel accounts, especially the Gospel of John, call the miracles of Jesus "signs" (Gk. *sēmeia*). Earlier in this sūra the Quran asks the messenger, "Can you make the deaf to hear?" (43.40), and then there is a series of verses in which the audience asks the messenger for a miracle or sign (*āya*). The Gospel according to John says that the miraculous signs of Jesus revealed his divine glory (John 2:11; 4:54; 6:2, 14; 9:16).

43.64 – *Surely God – He is my Lord and your Lord, so serve Him!*

ʿĪsā's statement and command are similar to several other verses in which the Quran "quotes" ʿĪsā as denying his own deity (3.51; 5.72, 116–17; 19.36; cf. 4.172). This is the last such verse in the canonical progression.

Putting these words in the mouth of ʿĪsā in such passages gives the verses an apparent authority. However, the Quran is not accessing a record of the words of Jesus from eyewitnesses, nor does it point to fresh revelation of the words of Jesus six centuries after the Gospel accounts were written. It is, instead, a simple denial of the witness of the Gospel accounts – and of the New Testament generally.

Some Muslim polemicists contend that quranic "quotations" of ʿĪsā connect to the words of Jesus in John 20:17. However, they do not match. The context of the words of Jesus in the Gospel according to John is an account written to show the deity of Jesus (John 1:1–18; cf. 20:31). Immediately after John 20:17, for example, the apostle Thomas addresses Jesus as, "My Lord and my God" (John 20:28). Rather than rebuking Thomas's confession like the quranic ʿĪsā might, Jesus commends Thomas and all who believe in him without seeing him.

Lord, so serve Him! This is a straight path.' [65] But the factions differed among themselves. Woe to those who have done evil because of the punishment of a painful Day!

[66] Are they looking for anything but the Hour – that it should come upon them unexpectedly, when they do not realize (it)? [67] Friends on that Day – some of them will be enemies to others, except for the ones who guard (themselves). [68] 'My servants! (There is) no fear on you today, nor will you sorrow [69] – those (of you) who believed in Our signs and submitted. [70] Enter the Garden, you and your wives, you will be made happy!' [71] Plates and cups of gold will be passed around among them, and there (they will have) whatever they desire and their eyes delight in. And: 'There you will remain.' [72] And: 'That is the Garden which you have been given as an inheritance for what you have done. [73] There you have many fruits from which you will eat.'

[74] Surely the evildoers will remain in the punishment of Gehenna. [75] It will not subside for them, and there they will be in despair. [76] We did not do them evil, but they themselves were the evildoers. [77] They will call out, 'Master! Let your Lord finish us off!' He will say, 'Surely you will remain. [78] Certainly we brought you the truth, but most of you were averse to the truth.'

[79] Or have they woven some plot? We (too) are weaving (a plot). [80] Or do they think that We do not hear their secret and their secret talk? Yes indeed! Our messengers are present with them writing (it) down.

[81] Say: 'If the Merciful had a son, I (would be) the first of the ones who served

---

43.65 – *But the factions differed among themselves*

On the theme of differing and disagreement among Christians, see the comments at 98.4 (p. 642). It is true that the three large Christian groups in the Middle East during the seventh century (Byzantine, Nestorian, Monophysite) had differences among them. However, the Quran seems to imply that differences among Christians somehow negate the truth of the Gospel as well as Christian beliefs and practices. In fact, the three Christian groups were in agreement about the death of Jesus and the deity of Jesus – the main issues as far as the Quran is concerned. It was in describing the humanity of Jesus that differences emerged among the three Christian groups.

43.67 – *Friends on that Day – some of them will be enemies to others*

This passage (vv. 67–80) pictures a judgment scene "on that Day" when some are rewarded with the Garden and others face an eternity of torment. See "Eschatology in the Quran" (p. 604).

43.81 – *If the Merciful had a son, I (would be) the first of the ones who served (him)*

After reading many verses that declare emphatically that Allah does not and

(him). [82] Glory to the Lord of the heavens and the earth, Lord of the throne, above what they allege!' [83] So leave them! Let them banter and jest, until they meet their Day which they are promised. [84] He (it is) who is God in the sky and God on the earth. He is the Wise, the Knowing. [85] Blessed (be) the One who – to Him (belongs) the kingdom of the heavens and the earth, and whatever is between them. With Him is the knowledge of the Hour, and to Him you will be returned. [86] Those whom they call on instead of Him have no power of intercession, except for the one who has borne witness to the truth – and they know (this). [87] If indeed you ask them, 'Who created them?,' they will indeed say, 'God.' How are they (so) deluded? [88] And his saying: 'My Lord! Surely these are a people who do not believe.' [89] So excuse them, and say: 'Peace!' Soon they will know!

---

would not have a son, the reader may be surprised to encounter a verse that seems to still consider the possibility. Another verse that shares the subjunctive mood is 39.4: "If Allah wanted to take a son . . ." The verses following 43.81, however, seem to carry the sense of denial found in other passages about a "son of Allah." See "Son of God in the Quran" (p. 352).

A Christian response might be to affirm in a simple and friendly way, "According to the Gospel, God the Father called Jesus his Son (Matthew 3:17; 17.5; Mark 1:11; 9.7; Luke 3:22; 9:35). For this reason we worship and serve him."

43.86 – *no power of intercession, except for the one who has born witness to the truth*

This prohibition on intercession makes an exception. See the analysis of verses on intercession at 39.44 (p. 464).

THE SMOKE
AL-DUKHĀN

44

The Quran tells many stories involving Moses and many versions of the details in the various episodes of his life. Sūra 44 offers a story about the people of Pharaoh clearly recognizable as an episode in the life of Moses, but the sūra does not give Moses' name. Missing details like this again raise the question of the makeup of an audience so familiar with the story that the name of its chief protagonist is not necessary to state.

The remainder of this short sūra largely warns of punishment to come, beginning with the "visible smoke" (after which the sūra is named) descending from the sky to cover the people.

In the Name of God, the Merciful, the Compassionate
¹ Ḥā Mīm.

² By the clear Book! ³ Surely We sent it down on a blessed night – surely We were warning – ⁴ during which every wise command was divided out, ⁵ as a command from Us – surely We were sending – ⁶ as a mercy from your Lord. Surely He – He is the Hearing, the Knowing, ⁷ Lord of the heavens and the earth, and whatever is between them, if you (would) be certain. ⁸ (There is) no god but Him. He gives life and causes death – your Lord and the Lord of your fathers of old.

⁹ No! They are in doubt (while) they jest. ¹⁰ So watch for the Day when the sky will bring a visible smoke ¹¹ covering the people: 'This is a painful punishment!

44.1–3 – *Ḥā Mīm. By the clear Book! Surely We sent it down on a blessed night*

On these disconnected letters, see the comment at 2.1. The sūra opens with a strong self-referential claim that Allah "sent it down."

Muslim beliefs that the recitation was "sent down" disagree about whether the sending occurred all at once or "piecemeal" and at intervals. This verse and 97.1 seem to suggest all at once – and at night. See the discussion of the Quran's "doctrine of scripture" at 85.21–22 (p. 624).

44.10 – *So watch for the Day when the sky will bring a visible smoke*

The sūra is named after this painful punishment (v. 11).

[12] Our Lord, remove the punishment from us! Surely We are believers.' [13] How will the reminder be for them, when a clear messenger has already come to them? [14] Then they turned away from him, and said, '(He is) tutored, (he is) possessed!' [15] 'Surely We are going to remove the punishment a little, (but) surely you are going to revert!' [16] On the Day when We attack with the great attack, surely We are going to take vengeance.

[17] Certainly before them We tested the people of Pharaoh, when an honorable messenger came to them: [18] 'Deliver to me the servants of God! Surely I am a trustworthy messenger for you.' [19] And: 'Do not exalt yourselves against God! Surely I bring you clear authority. [20] Surely I take refuge with my Lord and your Lord, for fear that you stone me. [21] If you do not believe me, withdraw from me!' [22] So he called on his Lord: 'These are a sinful people.' [23] And: 'Journey with My servants by night. Surely you will be followed. [24] And leave the sea parted, (for) surely they are a force (to be) drowned.' [25] How many gardens and springs they left (behind), [26] and (fields of) crops, and an honorable place, [27] and prosperity in which they used to rejoice. [28] So (it was), and We caused another people to inherit them. [29] Neither the sky nor the earth wept for them, nor were they spared. [30] Certainly We rescued the Sons of Israel from the humiliating punishment, [31] (and) from Pharaoh. Surely he was haughty, one of the wanton. [32] Certainly We chose them, on (the basis of) knowledge, over the worlds, [33] and gave them signs in which (there was) a clear test.

[34] Surely these (people) indeed say, [35] 'There is nothing but our first death. We are not going to be raised. [36] Bring (back) our fathers, if you are truthful!' [37] Are they better, or the people of Tubba', and those who were before them?

44.14 – *(He is) tutored, (he is) possessed*

Two of the most common accusations against the messenger are that he is taught by others (e.g., 16.103; cf. 25.45) and that he is possessed by *jinn* (*majnūn*, e.g., 37.36; 68.2).

44.17 – *We tested the people of Pharaoh, when an honorable messenger came to them*

In this passage (vv. 17–33) the Quran clearly refers to the story of Moses without giving his name (also in 73:15). See the table of Moses stories and "Moses in the Quran" (p. 388).

44.34–35 – *Surely these (people) indeed say, "There is nothing but our first death..."*

A common objection to the warnings of judgment to come is the statement that there will be no resurrection.

44.37 – *Are they better, or the people of Tubba'...?*

This place or people is only mentioned here and at 50.14. Some scholars explain *Tubba'* as the title of the kings of the Ḥimyarites of South Arabia.

We destroyed them. Surely they were sinners. [38] We did not create the heavens and earth, and whatever is between them, in jest. [39] We created them only in truth, but most of them do not know (it). [40] Surely the Day of Decision is their meeting – all (of them) – [41] a Day when a protector will be of no use at all as a protector, and they will not be helped [42] – except for the one on whom God has compassion. Surely He – He is the Mighty, the Compassionate.

[43] Surely the tree of al-Zaqqūm [44] is the food of the sinner, [45] like molten metal boiling in the belly, [46] as hot (water) boils. [47] 'Seize him and drag him into the midst of the Furnace. [48] Then pour over his head from the punishment of hot (water)!' [49] 'Taste (it)! Surely you are the mighty, the honorable! [50] Surely this is what you doubted about.'

[51] Surely the ones who guard (themselves) are in a secure place, [52] in (the midst of) gardens and springs, [53] wearing clothes of silk and brocade, facing each other. [54] So (it is), and We shall marry them to (maidens) with dark, wide eyes. [55] There they will call for every (kind of) fruit, secure. [56] There they will not taste death, except the first death, and He will guard them against the punishment of the Furnace. [57] Favor from your Lord! That is the great triumph!

[58] Surely We have made it easy in your language, so that they may take heed. [59] So watch! Surely they (too) are watching.

44.40 – *Surely the Day of Decision is their meeting*

The Day of Decision is another of the Quran's names for the Day of Judgment. The following verses offer graphic descriptions of the punishments of hell (vv. 43–50) and delights of heaven (vv. 51–57).

44.43 – *the tree of al-Zaqqūm*

This tree, described as a plant in hell, is only named here, 37.62, and 56.52.

44.54 – *We shall marry them to (maidens) with dark, wide eyes*

What do such descriptions mean to portray about the characteristics of the heavenly "Gardens"? Droge translates the Arabic *ḥūr ʿīn* as "(maidens) with dark, wide eyes." This expression also appears at 52.20 and 56.22, and *ḥūr* alone appears at 55.72. Other verses mention "(maidens) restraining (their) glances" (38.52; 55.56), "full-breasted (maidens)" (78.33), and "virgins" (56.36).

THE KNEELING
AL-JĀTHIYA

Allah displays his signs before people in the hope that they will be thankful. However, most people do not respond appropriately to the signs; therefore, punishments of various kinds loom ahead of them. This sūra assures readers that the Creator will judge people justly on "the day" and then devotes most of its text to describing disbelievers and their fate.

In the Name of God, the Merciful, the Compassionate

¹ Ḥā Mīm.

² The sending down of the Book is from God, the Mighty, the Wise.
³ Surely in the heavens and the earth (there are) signs indeed for the believers.
⁴ And in your creation, and what He scatters of the creatures, (there are) signs for a people who are certain. ⁵ And (in the) alternation of the night and the day, and what God sends down from the sky of (His) provision, and by means of it gives the earth life after its death, and (in the) changing of the winds, (there are) signs for a people who understand. ⁶ Those are the signs of God. We recite them to you in truth. In what (kind of) proclamation – after God and His signs – will they believe?

⁷ Woe to every liar (and) sinner! ⁸ He hears the signs of God recited to him, (but) then persists in being arrogant, as if he had not heard them. Give him the news of a painful punishment. ⁹ When he comes to know any of Our signs, he

---

45.1–2 – Ḥā Mīm. The sending down of the book is from God

On these disconnected letters see the comment at Q 2.1. The sūra opens with a brief claim that its origin is divine.

45.3 – Surely in the heavens and the earth (there are) signs indeed for the believers

The Quran appeals to the signs of Allah in creation, in the natural world, and – later in this sūra – in what Allah has subjected to humans (vv. 12–13). The appropriate human response to these signs is thankfulness (v. 12)

45.7 – Woe to every liar (and) sinner!

More often than not, humans mock Allah's signs and become arrogant. For such people the future is Gehenna and painful punishment.

takes them in mockery. Those – for them (there is) a humiliating punishment. [10] Behind them is Gehenna, and what they have earned will be of no use to them at all, nor those whom they have taken as allies instead of God. For them (there is) a great punishment. [11] This is guidance, but those who disbelieve in the signs of their Lord – for them (there is) a punishment of painful wrath.

[12] (It is) God who has subjected the sea to you, so that the ship may run on it by His command, and so that you may seek some of His favor, and that you may be thankful. [13] And He has subjected to you whatever is in the heavens and whatever is on the earth – all (of it is) from Him. Surely in that are signs indeed for a people who reflect.

[14] Say to those who believe to forgive those who do not expect the days of God, so that He may repay a people for what they have earned. [15] Whoever does righteousness, it is for himself, and whoever does evil, it is (likewise) against himself – then to your Lord you will be returned.

[16] Certainly We gave the Sons of Israel the Book, and the judgment, and the prophetic office. We provided them with good things and favored them over the worlds. [17] And We gave them clear signs of the matter. They did not differ until after the knowledge had come to them, (because of) envy among themselves. Surely your Lord will decide between them on the Day of Resurrection concerning their differences. [18] Then We placed you on a pathway of the matter. So follow it, and do not follow the (vain) desires of those who do not know. [19] Surely they will be of no use to you at all against God. Surely the evildoers are allies of each other, but God is the Ally of the ones who guard (themselves).

[20] This is evidence for the people, and a guidance and mercy for a people who are certain. [21] Or do those who commit evil deeds think that We shall treat them

---

45.14 – *Say to those who believe to forgive those*

Believers should forgive "those who do not expect the days of Allah." Allah will judge people according to what they have earned.

45.16 – *Certainly We gave the Sons of Israel the Book, and the judgment, and the prophetic office*

This verse seems to represent a very positive view of the Children of Israel, including that they were favored "over the worlds" (see similar expressions at 2.47, 122; 3.33; 6.86; 7.140; 44.32). Along with this, however, the Quran states that the Children of Israel began to differ (v. 17) and that the Lord will sort them out on the Day of Resurrection. The Quran then instructs the messenger to follow the way he has been shown (v. 18).

On the differences among the Children of Israel (v. 17), see the comments at 98.4 (p. 642).

as those who believe and do righteous deeds – alike in their life and their death?
Evil is what they judge! [22] God created the heavens and the earth in truth, and so
that each person may be paid for what he has earned – and they will not be done
evil. [23] Have you seen the one who has taken his (vain) desire as his god? God has
led him astray on (the basis of) knowledge, and set a seal on his hearing and his
heart, and made a covering on his sight. Who will guide him after God? Will you
not take heed? [24] But they say, 'There is nothing but our present life. We die, and
we live, and nothing destroys us but time.' They have no knowledge about that.
They only conjecture. [25] When Our signs are recited to them as clear signs, their
only argument is that they say, 'Bring (back) our fathers, if you are truthful!' [26] Say:
'God gives you life, then causes you to die, (and) then He gathers you to the Day of
Resurrection – (there is) no doubt about it. But most of the people do not know (it).'

[27] To God (belongs) the kingdom of the heavens and the earth. On the Day
when the Hour strikes, on that Day the perpetrators of falsehood will lose.
[28] You will see each community kneeling, each community called to its Book:
'Today you will be repaid for what you have done. [29] This is Our Book – it speaks
about you in truth. Surely We have been copying down what you were doing.'
[30] As for those who have believed and done righteous deeds, their Lord will cause
them to enter into His mercy. That is the clear triumph! [31] But as for those who
have disbelieved: 'Were My signs not recited to you? Yet you became arrogant
and were a sinful people. [32] And when it was said, "Surely the promise of God is
true, and the Hour – (there is) no doubt about it," you said, "We do not know
what the Hour is. We think (it is) only conjecture, and we are not certain."'
[33] The evils of what they have done will become apparent to them, and what they
were mocking will overwhelm them. [34] And it will be said, 'Today We forget you,
as you forgot the meeting of this Day of yours. Your refuge is the Fire, and you
have no helpers. [35] That is because you took the signs of God in mockery, and
this present life deluded you.' So today they will not be brought forth from it,
nor will they be allowed to make amends.

[36] Praise (be) to God, Lord of the heavens and Lord of the earth, Lord of the
worlds! [37] To Him (belongs) the greatness in the heavens and the earth. He is
the Mighty, the Wise.

45.22 – *so that each person may be paid for what he has earned*

The remainder of this sūra is made up of a variety of text types promising the
judgment of unbelievers.

45.27 – *On the Day when the Hour strikes*

This verse introduces a series of judgment scenes concerning the nations (v. 28), the
believers (v. 30), and the unbelievers (vv. 31–35). See "Eschatology in the Quran" (p. 604).

THE SAND DUNES
AL-AḤQĀF

46

Doing good to one's parents is the theme featured in the middle of this sūra (v. 15–18). Those who do so are promised a special reward according to verse 16.

Otherwise, this sūra repeats many of the themes that have been featured in many sūras since Sūra 10: the power of the Creator, a challenge to those who call on others besides Allah, audience resistance to the recitations of the messenger, the Quran's reassurance to the messenger, and reward and punishment for human deeds on the Day of Resurrection.

In the Name of God, the Merciful, the Compassionate

[1] Ḥā Mīm.

[2] The sending down of the Book is from God, the Mighty, the Wise.

[3] We did not create the heavens and the earth, and whatever is between them, except in truth and (for) an appointed time, but those who disbelieve are turning away from what they are warned of. [4] Say: 'Do you see what you call on instead of God? Show me what (part) of the earth they have created. Or do they have any partnership in (the creation of) the heavens? Bring me any Book before this (one) or any trace of knowledge, if you are truthful.' [5] Who is farther astray than the one who, instead of God, calls on those who will not respond to him until the Day of Resurrection, while they are (otherwise) oblivious of their calling? [6] When the people are gathered, they will be enemies to them, and will deny their service.

[7] When Our signs are recited to them as clear signs, those who disbelieve say to the truth, when it has come to them, 'This is clear magic.' [8] Or do they say, 'He has forged it'? Say: 'If I have forged it, you (would) have no power at all to (help)

46.8 – Or do they say, 'He has forged it"?

A repeating statement from the audience about the messenger is that he has invented, or "forged" (*iftarā*), his recitations. See the discussion on verses that accuse the messenger of inventing at 69.44 (p. 587).

me against God. He knows what you are busy with. He is sufficient as a witness between me and you. He is the Forgiving, the Compassionate.'

⁹ Say: 'I am not the first of the messengers, and I do not know what will be done with me or with you. I only follow what I am inspired (with). I am only a clear warner.'

¹⁰ Say: 'Do you see? If it is from God, and you disbelieve in it, and a witness from the Sons of Israel has borne witness to (a Book) like it, and believed, and you become arrogant – surely God does not guide the people who are evildoers.'
¹¹ Those who disbelieve say to those who believe, 'If it had been something good, they would not have gotten to it before us' – even when they are not guided by it. And they say, 'This is an old lie!' ¹² Yet before it was the Book of Moses as a model and mercy; and this is a Book confirming (it) in the Arabic language,

---

46.9 – *I am not the first of the messengers*

The profile of the messenger in this verse is "only a clear warner." The verse seems to picture a messenger who is humble and unassuming, and who takes his message – but not himself – seriously. This portrait sets up a contrast to the role of the messenger in the following three sūras. For example, see 47.33.

46.12 – *Yet before it was the Book of Moses as a model and mercy*

Wherever the Quran names the pre-Islamic scriptures or – as in this case – refers to the "Book of Moses," it consistently describes them only in the most positive and respectful ways. The Arabic word here translated "model" (*imām*) can also mean standard, criterion, or even "plumb line" (see also 5.44; 6.154; 11.17).

46.12 – *and this is a Book confirming (it) in the Arabic language*

This verse suggests that the recitation of the messenger confirms the Torah in Arabic, as if it were an Arabic translation or paraphrase. For an analysis of claims that the Quran makes for its Arabic language (cf. 26.195), see the comments at 43.2–3 (p. 487).

Sūra 46.12 is one of sixteen verses that claim a relationship of "confirmation" between the Quran and the pre-Islamic scriptures, using the Arabic terms *muṣaddiq* and *taṣdīq*. These verses certainly show a favorable attitude toward the Torah and the Gospel. They vouch for the truth (*ṣaddaqa*) of those revelations. At the same time, these quranic verses use the authority of the Torah and the Gospel to support claims for the provenance of the recitations and the prophethood of the messenger.

The objects of the confirmation verses have the almost tactile sense of "what is with them" (six verses) and "what was before it" (*bayna yadayhi*, lit. "between his two hands"; ten verses).

However, the claim of confirmation should be examined for the extent of its realization in the Quran. Certainly many parts of the Quran offer similar content and

to warn those who do evil, and as good news for the doers of good. ¹³ Surely those who say, 'Our Lord is God,' (and) then go straight – (there will be) no fear on them, nor will they sorrow. ¹⁴ Those are the companions of the Garden, there to remain – a payment for what they have done.

¹⁵ We have charged each person (to do) good to his parents – his mother bore him with difficulty, and she delivered him with difficulty – his bearing and his weaning are thirty months – until, when he reaches his maturity, and reaches forty years, he says, 'My Lord, (so) dispose me that I may be thankful for your blessing with which You have blessed me and my parents, and that I may do righteousness pleasing to You, and do right by me concerning my descendants. Surely I turn to You (in repentance), and surely I am one of those who submit.' ¹⁶ Those are the ones from whom We shall accept the best of what they have done, and We shall pass over their evil deeds. (They will be) among the companions of the Garden – the promise of truth which they were promised. ¹⁷ But the one who says to his parents, 'Uff to both of you! Do you promise me that I shall be brought forth, when generations have already passed away before me?,' while both of them call on God for help: 'Woe to you! Believe! Surely the promise of God is true!,' and he says, 'This is nothing but old tales' – ¹⁸ those are the ones against whom the word has proved true about the communities of jinn and humankind (which) have already passed away before them. Surely they were losers.

¹⁹ For each (there are) ranks, according to what they have done, and so that He may pay them in full for their deeds – and they will not be done evil. ²⁰ On the Day when those who disbelieve are presented to the Fire: 'You squandered your good things in your present life, and enjoyed them. So today you will be

---

language as parts of the Bible. One significant similarity is the description of God as the Creator who has the right to expect a good response from his creation.

On the death and deity of Jesus, the Quran seems to be not a confirmation (*taṣdīq*) but a denial (*takdhīb*), or in the case of Jesus' death at least a confusion, of the biblical account. Similarly, in many passages the Quran's response to conflict misses the teaching of the New Testament. In the one quranic verse that claims the Torah, Gospel, and Quran agree on the same "promise," the Quran declares that the common ground is that believers "fight in the way of Allah, and they kill and are killed" (9.111). This raises the question of whether there is any genuine knowledge of the text of the New Testament behind the Quran.

46.15 – *We have charged each person (to do) good to his parents*

Doing good to parents is a sign of thankfulness to the Lord and gains a reward on the Day of Resurrection.

paid the punishment of humiliation because you became arrogant on the earth
without any right, and because you have acted wickedly.'

²¹ Remember the brother of 'Ād: When he warned his people at the sand
dunes – and warners had already passed away before him and after him – (saying): 'Do not serve (anyone) but God! Surely I fear for you the punishment of
a great Day.' ²² They said, 'Have you come to defraud us of our gods? Bring us
what you promise us, if you are one of the truthful.' ²³ He said, 'The knowledge
(of it) is only with God. I deliver to you what I was sent with, but I see you are an
ignorant people.' ²⁴ When they saw it as a cloud approaching their wādīs, they
said, 'This is a cloud (which) is going to give us rain.' 'No! It is what you were
seeking to hurry – a wind in which (there is) a painful punishment, ²⁵ destroying
everything by the command of its Lord.' And morning found them not to be
seen, except for their dwelling places. In this way We repay the people who are
sinners. ²⁶ Certainly We had established them with what We have not established
you, and We gave them hearing and sight and hearts. Yet their hearing and
their sight and their hearts were of no use to them at all, since they denied the
signs of God, and what they were mocking overwhelmed them. ²⁷ Certainly We
destroyed the towns around you, and varied the signs so that they might return.
²⁸ Why did they not help them – those gods whom they had taken, instead
of God, as a (means of) drawing near (to Him)? No! They abandoned them.
That was their lie and what they had forged.

²⁹ (Remember) when We turned a band of jinn to you to listen to the Qur'ān:
When they were in its presence, they said, 'Be silent!' And when it was finished,
they turned back to their people as warners. ³⁰ They said, 'Our people! Surely We
have heard a Book (which) has been sent down after Moses, confirming what
was before it, guiding to the truth and to a straight road. ³¹ Our people! Respond

---

46.21 – *Remember the brother of 'Ād: When he warned his people at the sand dunes*
The story of Hūd preaching to the people named 'Ād has appeared three other
times in the Quran, and this is its final version in the canonical progression. See the
comment on this messenger and people at 7.65. The story follows the pattern of the
people's resistance to the messenger's preaching followed by Allah's destruction
of the people (vv. 21–25). In this case, the Quran says that the people of 'Ād were
well established, yet Allah's blessings "were of no use to them" (v. 26) because they
denied the signs of Allah (v. 29).

46.30 – *Surely We have heard a Book (which) has been sent down after Moses*
A group of *jinn* listen to the recitation of the messenger then exhort the rest of
the *jinn* to heed the "caller of Allah" (v. 31). About the language of "confirmation," see
note at verse 12 above. See also the analysis of verses about *jinn* at 72.1 (p. 593).

to the caller of God, and believe in Him. He will forgive you some of your sins, and protect you from a painful punishment. ³² Whoever does not respond to the caller of God – there is no escaping (Him) on the earth, and he has no allies other than Him. Those are clearly astray.'

³³ Do they not see that God, who created the heavens and earth, and was not tired out by their creation, is able to give the dead life? Yes indeed! Surely He is powerful over everything. ³⁴ On the Day when those who disbelieve are presented to the Fire: 'Is this not the truth?' They will say, 'Yes indeed! By our Lord!' He will say, 'Taste the punishment for what you have disbelieved.'

³⁵ Be patient, as the messengers of firm resolve were (also) patient. Do not seek to hurry it for them. On the Day when they see what they are promised, (it will seem) as if they had remained (in the grave) for only an hour of the day. A delivery! Will any be destroyed but the people who are wicked?

Muḥammad
Muḥammad

47

After a series of sūras in which the messenger is merely a warner (e.g., 46.9), the tone and content of Sūra 47 strike a stunning contrast. Here the messenger must be obeyed, and his commands have to do with fighting. In addition to the judgment of Allah on the Day of Resurrection, "believers" are to punish "unbelievers" in the present life.

Among the "believers," however, are some who do not respond to the messenger's words in acceptable ways. To these the sūra promises various punishments and the curse of Allah.

In the Name of God, the Merciful, the Compassionate

[1] Those who disbelieve and keep (people) from the way of God – He will lead their deeds astray. [2] But those who believe and do righteous deeds, and believe in what has been sent down on Muḥammad – and it is the truth from their Lord – He will absolve them of their evil deeds, and set their case right. [3] That is because those who disbelieve follow falsehood, and because those who believe follow the truth from their Lord. In this way God strikes parables for the people.

47.2 – *and believe in what has been sent down on Muḥammad*

The name Muḥammad appears only four times in the Quran. The final two occurrences come here at the beginning of Sūra 47 (v. 2) and at the end of Sūra 48 (v. 29). These verses form a kind of parenthesis around the contents of the two sūras.

This is the only verse in the Quran that explicitly connects the language of revelation (*tanzīl*) to Muḥammad. The verse claims that the recitation "has been sent down on Muḥammad" and that it is the truth. See a summary on the four occurrences of "Muhammad" at 48.29 (p. 516).

Divine Punishment of Unbelievers in This World
David Marshall

Islam emphasizes the reward of believers and the punishment of unbelievers in the hereafter. The vivid accounts of these realities in the final book of
al-Ghazali's *The Revival of the Religious Sciences* is a classic example of the elaboration in the Islamic tradition of the already plentiful eschatological material
in the Quran. This article, however, focuses on passages in the Quran that refer
to God punishing communities of unbelievers, not after death but *in this world*.

The great majority of such passages narrate how God punished past generations of unbelievers for rejecting messengers sent by him. These stories
(almost entirely in sūras traditionally designated "Meccan") typically describe
spectacular acts of divine punishment, frequently familiar from the Bible (e.g.,
the flood or the destruction of Sodom and Gomorrah). Often several such
stories, each introducing a new messenger but linked by repeated themes
and phrases, are woven into sequences that reinforce one basic story line: God
sends a messenger; the messenger is rejected; the unbelievers are punished
(e.g., Sūras 7, 11, and 26). The Quran links these stories to the situation of the one
it addresses as called to proclaim God's message (traditionally, Muhammad):
the stories have been revealed not only to encourage him (11.120) but also to
warn unbelievers that a similar act of divine punishment in this world as has
befallen unbelievers in the past (35.43–44; 41.13). Both in stories about divine
punishments in the past and in references to the present, the overwhelming
response to the prophetic warnings is unbelief, sometimes including a derisive
challenge to the prophet to "bring on" the threatened punishment if what he
says is true (26.185–87, 204; 8.31–32).

The paradigm of divine punishment described above portrays God as acting directly. Whether narrating past punishments or warning of punishments
that could strike unbelievers in the future, the Quran speaks of *unmediated*
acts of divine intervention. Crucially, the believers are not involved. In contrast, some passages (in sūras traditionally designated "Medinan") suggest a
different paradigm of *mediated* divine punishment: God does not intervene
directly but uses believers to punish unbelievers by defeating them militarily.

Though references to this mediated punishment are comparatively rare,
they are highly significant. The clearest example occurs at 9.14, where believers
are exhorted to fight unbelievers who have broken their oaths, tried to drive
out the messenger, and attacked them first: "Fight them! God will punish them

by your hands." While there is little if any apparent acknowledgment here of the contrast between the different paradigms, the Quran does comment at other points, albeit indirectly, on the relationship between them. Traditionally Sūra 8 has been understood to address the situation after the believers defeated the unbelievers at Badr. Even if one ignores that assumption, much in this sūra is clearly commenting on a recent military victory, suggesting that it was a divine intervention against the unbelievers such as was threatened in the punishment stories discussed above. For example, 8.6–7 include verbal echoes of the punishment stories, which are also clearly in mind at 8.31–32. Also relevant here is the comment at 47.4 that God could have defeated the unbelievers himself (implying intervention without intermediaries) but has commanded the believers to fight in order to test them. Here the Quran appears to address why God is favoring one approach to punishing unbelievers over another.

If we assume, as a framework for interpreting the Quran, even just the outlines of the traditional narrative provided by the *Sīra* literature, we can develop a plausible explanation of the coexistence in the Quran of the two punishment paradigms. After the Muslims migrated to Medina according to the traditional narrative, and especially after the battle of Badr, assumptions about the role of Muhammad and his community in the Meccan "unmediated punishment paradigm" were superseded by the Medinan "mediated punishment paradigm," which involved a military dimension that previously was neither mandated by God nor expected by the believers. This transition is reflected by the almost complete absence of punishment stories in Medinan sūras, in which there emerges an increasingly explicit recognition of the believers as the instrument used by God to punish the unbelievers. Without this traditional framework, it is unclear what alternative account can be offered of the range of quranic material on God's punishment of unbelievers in this world. (For further details, see Dr. Marshall's book and article listed in the bibliography.)

[4] When you meet those who disbelieve, (let there be) a striking of the necks, until, when you have subdued them, bind (them) securely, and then either (set them free) as a favor or by ransom, until the war lays down its burdens.

47.4 – *When you meet those who disbelieve, (let there be) a striking of the necks*
The idea of "believers" striking "disbelievers" in the neck is understandably a lively concern for those whom the Quran considers disbelievers. The context of this

That (is the rule). If God had (so) pleased, He would indeed have defended Himself against them, but (He allows fighting) so that He may test some of you by means of others. Those who are killed in the way of God – He will not lead their deeds astray. [5] He will guide them and set their case right, [6] and He will cause them to enter the Garden – He has made it known to them.

[7] You who believe! If you help God, He will help you, and make firm your feet. [8] But those who disbelieve – (there will be) downfall for them, and He will lead their deeds astray. [9] That is because they disliked what God sent down, and so He has made their deeds worthless. [10] Have they not traveled on the earth and

---

activity is war (*ḥarb*), and the Quran commands believers to tighten the bonds of the unbelievers when the unbelievers are overwhelmed.

"Subdued" in this verse translates the difficult Arabic verb *athkhana*, which also appears in 8.67. Arthur Arberry translated the verb as "made wide slaughter," and the Muslim commentator Ibn Kathīr (d. 1373) also took the verse in this direction. See "Fighting and Killing in the Quran" (p. 220).

47.4 – *He would indeed have defended Himself against them, but (He allows fighting) so that He may test some of you by means of others*

This verse seems to claim that although Allah could have resolved the conflict without the need for human fighting, he chose to have the believers fight in order to "test some of you by means of others." The following passage seems to say that in times of fighting, Allah needs the help of the believers (v. 7). This is one of a number of verses that say that Allah punishes the enemy by the hands of the believers (e.g., 9.14) and thereby sorts out who are the true believers (e.g., 3.152–54; 33.11; 57.25).

47.4 – *Those who are killed in the way of God – He will not lead their deeds astray*

To be killed in the way of Allah means to die while fighting. The concept that those who die fighting will be rewarded comes from passages such as this (vv. 4–6; also 2.154; 3.157–58, 169–72; 3.195; 22:58–59).

The rewards to fighters in this passage include guidance from Allah and entry into the "Garden" – the quranic concept of heaven or paradise. Other passages promise these same rewards as well as remaining alive (2.154; 3.169), forgiveness from Allah and mercy (3.157), being gathered to Allah (3.158), freedom from fear and sorrow (3.170), absolution of evil deeds (3.195), and good provision from Allah (22.58).

These verses highlight a fundamental difference in the concept of "dying in the way of God" between the Quran and the New Testament. The New Testament has no command to fight and no promise of a reward to those who die fighting. Rather, the concept of martyrdom in the New Testament is the death of believers who die bearing faithful witness (Gk. *marturia*, e.g., Revelation 12:11) to Jesus while *not* resisting the "evil person" who is fighting them (Matthew 5:39).

seen how the end was for those who were before them? God destroyed them. The disbelievers have examples of it. [11] That is because God is the Protector of those who believe, and because the disbelievers have no protector.

[12] Surely God will cause those who believe and do righteous deeds to enter Gardens through which rivers flow. But those who disbelieve – they take their enjoyment and eat as the cattle eat. The Fire will be their dwelling place.

[13] How many a town We have destroyed that was stronger in power than your town which expelled you! And there was no helper for them. [14] Is the one who (stands) on a clear sign from his Lord like the one who – the evil of his deeds is made to appear enticing to him, and they follow their (vain) desires?

[15] A parable of the Garden which is promised to the ones who guard (themselves): In it (there are) rivers of water without pollution, and rivers of milk – its taste does not change – and rivers of wine – delicious to the drinkers – and rivers of purified honey. In it (there is) every (kind of) fruit for them, and forgiveness from their Lord. (Are they) like those who remain in the Fire? They are given boiling water to drink, and it cuts their insides (to pieces).

[16] (There are) some of them who listen to you, until, when they go forth from your presence, they say to those who have been given knowledge, 'What did he say just now?' Those are the ones on whose hearts God has set a seal, and they follow their (vain) desires. [17] But those who are (rightly) guided – He increases them in guidance, and gives them their (sense of) guarding (themselves). [18] So are they looking for anything but the Hour – that it will come upon them unexpectedly? The conditions for it have already come, and when it comes upon them, how will they have their reminder? [19] Know that He – (there is) no god but God. Ask forgiveness for your sin, and for the believing men and the believing women. God knows your comings and goings, and your dwelling place.

47.15 – *and rivers of wine – delicious to the drinkers*

The Quran shows an inconsistent attitude toward wine (*khamr*). Here rivers of wine are promised as a reward to believers. This contrasts with verses like 2.219, which says that while wine may have some benefits, its sin is greater than its benefits.

47.19 – *Ask forgiveness for your sin, and for the believing men and the believing women*

Here the messenger is told to ask forgiveness for his sin (*dhanb*). This is one of a number of verses (also 40.55; 48.2) that seem to question the Islamic doctrine that all prophets are sinless or immune (*maʿṣūm*) from sin. See the analysis and response at 48.2 (p. 513).

²⁰ Those who believe say, 'If only a sūra were sent down.' But when a clearly composed sūra is sent down, and fighting is mentioned in it, you see those in whose hearts is a sickness looking at you with the look of one who faints at the point of death. Woe to them! ²¹ Obedience and rightful words (are called for)! When the matter is determined, and if they are true to God, it will indeed be better for them. ²² Is it possible, if you turned away, that you would foment corruption on the earth, and sever your family ties? ²³ Those are the ones whom God has cursed, and made them deaf, and blinded their sight. ²⁴ Do they not contemplate the Qur'ān, or (are there) locks on their hearts? ²⁵ Surely those who have turned their backs, after the guidance has become clear to them – (it was) Satan (who) contrived (it) for them, but He has spared them. ²⁶ That is because they said to those who disliked what God had sent down, 'We will obey you in part of the matter' – but God knows their secrets. ²⁷ How (will it be) when the angels take them, striking their faces and their backs? ²⁸ That is because they have followed what angers God, and have disliked His approval, so He has made their deeds worthless.

²⁹ Or do those in whose hearts is a sickness think that God will not bring to light their malice? ³⁰ If We had (so) pleased, We would indeed have shown them to you, and you would indeed know them by their marks – indeed you do know them by their devious speech. God knows your deeds, ³¹ and We shall indeed test you, until We know those of you who struggle and those who are patient, and We shall test the reports about you. ³² Surely those who disbelieve, and keep (people) from the way of God, and break with the messenger, after the guidance has become clear to them – they will not harm God at all, and He will make their deeds worthless.

³³ You who believe! Obey God, and obey the messenger, and do not invalidate your (own) deeds. ³⁴ Surely those who disbelieve and keep (people) from the way of God, (and) then die while they are disbelievers – God will not forgive them.

47.20 – *But when a clearly composed sūra is sent down, and fighting is mentioned in it*

This verse claims that a unit of recitation (*sūra*) mentioning fighting (*qitāl*) is "sent down" by Allah. Some of the believers seem to object, and they are portrayed here as having a sickness in their hearts. See "Fighting and Killing in the Quran" (p. 220).

47.33 – *You who believe! Obey God, and obey the messenger*

This verse is the first since Sūra 33 to associate the messenger with Allah. This and the following two sūras, however, make the association a total of seven times. On commands to obey both Allah and the messenger, see the analysis and response at 64.12 (p. 574).

³⁵ Do not grow weak and call for peace, when you are the prevailing (force), and God is with you, and will not deprive you of your deeds. ³⁶ This present life is nothing but jest and diversion, but if you believe and guard (yourselves), He will give you your rewards and not ask you for your wealth. ³⁷ If He asks you for it, and presses you, you are stingy, and He brings to light your malice. ³⁸ There you are! These (people)! You are called on to contribute in the way of God, and (there are) some of you who are stingy. Whoever is stingy is stingy only to himself. God is the wealthy One, and you are the poor (ones). If you turn away, He will exchange a people other than you. Then they will not be like you.

47.35 – *Do not grow weak and call for peace, when you are the prevailing (force)*

Thus far in the sūra, the Quran has presented a scene of war (v. 4) and fighting (v. 20). Verse 35 seems to make the reasonable point that as long as the battle is going in favor of the "believers" (and Allah is with them), they must not seek to make peace with the enemy. Elsewhere, the Quran says that if the enemy "incline to peace," the messenger must also incline to it (8.61).

THE VICTORY
AL-FATḤ

48

> This sūra follows the tone and mood of Sūra 47. Like the previous sūra, this one includes a battle and associates the messenger with Allah for allegiance and obedience. In addition, Allah promises an abundance of the spoils of war and dictates speeches to the Bedouin, who do not seem to be dealing honestly with the messenger.
>
> Muslim tradition connects this sūra with two events in the story of Islamic origins. One is the peaceful entry into – and conquest of – Mecca by a large number of Muslims together with their messenger. The other is the treaty of al-Ḥudaybiyya, through which the Muslims were permitted to attack settlements previously protected by the Quraysh (the dominant tribe in Mecca), particularly the Jewish settlement of Khaybar. (See *Raids*, 304–7.)

In the Name of God, the Merciful, the Compassionate
¹ Surely We have given you a clear victory, ² so that God may forgive you what is past of your sin and what is (still) to come, and complete His blessing on you,

---

48.2 – *so that God may forgive you what is past of your sin and what is (still) to come*

This verse mentions the sin (*dhanb*) of the messenger that needs forgiveness. This is one of a number of verses (also 40.55; 47.19; cf. 3.147; 4.106; 110.3) that seem to question the Islamic doctrine that all prophets are sinless or even protected by Allah (*maʿṣūm*) from committing sins.

Prophets are sinless neither in the Bible nor in the Quran. Adam (Q 7.23), Noah (11.47), Abraham (26.82), Moses (28.16), David (38.24), and Solomon (38.35) all ask forgiveness for their sin and often repent. In 3.147, many prophets pray in unison, "Our Lord! Forgive us for our sins (*dhunūb*, sing. *dhanb*) and wasted efforts." The Arabic term *dhanb* is also defined as "offense," "crime," or "misdeed."

Notably, the quranic ʿĪsā does not ask for forgiveness in this way, but instead is described as faultless, sinless, or "pure" (*zakīy*, 19.19). This matches the teaching of the New Testament, where Jesus is the only one who "had no sin" (2 Corinthians 5:21). In the Gospel according to John, Jesus himself asked his opponents, "Can any

and guide you to a straight path, ³ and that God may help you with a mighty help. ⁴ He (it is) who sent down the Sakīna into the hearts of the believers, so that they might add belief to their belief – to God (belong) the forces of the heavens and the earth, and God is knowing, wise – ⁵ and that He may cause the believing men and the believing women to enter Gardens through which rivers flow, there to remain, and absolve them of their evil deeds – that is the great triumph in the sight of God! – ⁶ and that He may punish the hypocrite men and the hypocrite women alike, and the idolatrous men and the idolatrous women alike, and the ones who think evil thoughts about God. The wheel of evil (will turn) against them. God is angry with them, and has cursed them, and has prepared Gehenna for them – and it is an evil destination! ⁷ To God (belong) the forces of the heavens and the earth. God is mighty, wise.

⁸ Surely We have sent you as a witness, and as a bringer of good news and a warner, ⁹ so that you may believe in God and His messenger, and support him, and respect him, and that you may glorify Him morning and evening. ¹⁰ Surely those who swear allegiance to you swear allegiance to God – the hand of God is over their hands. So whoever breaks (his oath), only breaks it against himself, but whoever fulfils what he has covenanted with God – He will give him a great reward.

¹¹ Those of the Arabs who stayed behind will say to you, 'Our wealth and our families kept us busy, so ask forgiveness for us.' They say with their tongues what is not in their hearts. Say: 'Who has any power for you against God, whether He intends harm for you or intends benefit for you? No! God is aware of what

of you prove me guilty of sin?" (John 8:46). In answer, the opponents insulted Jesus, but according to the Gospel, no one took up Jesus' challenge to try to prove him guilty of sin.

48.4 – *He (it is) who sent down the Sakīna into the hearts of the believers*

The Arabic word *Sakīna* appears three times in this sūra: Allah sends down *Sakīna* on his messenger (v. 26) and on the "believers" (vv. 4, 18, 26). See the comment on *Sakīna* at 2.248 (p. 71).

48.9 – *so that you may believe in God and His messenger*

As in a number of other sūras, here the Quran associates the messenger with Allah as deserving of belief (also v. 13) and allegiance (vv. 10, 18),

48.11 – *Those of the Arabs who stayed behind will say to you*

These words introduce an extended passage about the reluctance of the Bedouin to advance with the messenger and the believers, apparently to a military engagement (vv. 11–17). The passage mentions spoils of battle (*maghānim*, v. 15; also vv. 19–20) and fighting (*qātala*, v. 16; also v. 33).

you do. [12] No! You thought that the messenger and the believers would never return to their families, and that was made to appear enticing in your hearts, and you thought evil thoughts, and became a ruined people.' [13] Whoever does not believe in God and His messenger – surely We have prepared for the disbelievers a blazing (Fire). [14] To God (belongs) the kingdom of the heavens and the earth. He forgives whomever he pleases and punishes whomever He pleases. God is forgiving, compassionate.

[15] The ones who stayed behind will say, when you set out to take spoils, 'Let us follow you.' They want to change the word of God. Say: 'You will not follow us. So God has said before.' They will say, 'No! You are jealous of us.' No! They have not understood, except for a little. [16] Say to those of the Arabs who stayed behind: 'You will be called to (fight) a people of harsh violence. You will fight them or they will surrender. If you obey, God will give you a good reward, but if you turn away, as you turned away before, He will punish you with a painful punishment.' [17] There is no blame on the blind, and no blame on the disabled, and no blame on the sick. Whoever obeys God and His messenger – He will cause him to enter Gardens through which rivers flow; but whoever turns away – He will punish him with a painful punishment.

[18] Certainly God was pleased with the believers when they were swearing allegiance to you under the tree, and He knew what was in their hearts. So He sent down the Sakīna on them, and rewarded them with a near victory, [19] and many spoils to take. God is mighty, wise. [20] And God has promised you many (more) spoils to take, and He has hurried this for you, and has restrained the hands of the people from you. (This happened) so that it might be a sign to the believers, and guide you to a straight path. [21] The other (spoils) which you were not able (to take), God has already encompassed them. God is powerful over everything.

[22] If those who disbelieve fight you, they will indeed turn their backs, (and) then they will not find any ally or any helper. [23] (That was) the customary way

---

48.23 – *the customary way of God (concerning) those who have passed away before*
The Arabic expression *sunnat Allāh*, "the customary way of Allah," appears here and at 17.77; 33.38, 62; and 40.85. What do these verses mean to communicate about the Quran's concept of God? This verse seems to mean that those who fight the "believers" will turn their backs (v. 22). At 17.77 and 40.85, the *sunnat Allāh* is Allah's treatment of peoples before Islam, while 33.62 says that the capture and killing of hypocrites at the time of that recitation is the customary way of Allah. Different from all of these is 33.38. There the *sunnat Allāh* seems to relate to the prophet's marriage to the former wife of Zayd.

of God (concerning) those who have passed away before, and you will find no change in the customary way of God. [24] He (it is) who restrained their hands from you, and your hands from them, in the heart of Mecca, after He gave you victory over them – God sees what you do. [25] They are those who disbelieved, and kept you from the Sacred Mosque, and (also) the offering, (which was) prevented from reaching its lawful place. If not for (certain) believing men and believing women, whom you did not know, or you would have trampled them, and guilt smitten you without (your) realizing (it) because of them – so that God may cause to enter into His mercy whomever He pleases – if they had been separated out (clearly), We would indeed have punished those among them who disbelieved with a painful punishment. [26] When those who disbelieved fostered a fury in their hearts – the fury of the (time of) ignorance – God sent down His Sakīna on His messenger and on the believers, and fastened to them the word of guarding (themselves). They have more right to it and are worthy of it. God has knowledge of everything.

[27] Certainly God has spoken the truth in the vision to His messenger: 'You will indeed enter the Sacred Mosque, if God pleases, in security, your heads shaved, your hair cut short, not fearing.' He knew what you did not know, and besides that produced a near victory. [28] He (it is) who has sent His messenger with the guidance and the religion of truth, so that He may cause it to prevail over religion – all of it. God is sufficient as a witness.

[29] Muḥammad is the messenger of God. Those who are with him are harsh against the disbelievers, (but) compassionate among themselves. You see them bowing and prostrating themselves, seeking favor from God and approval.

48.24 – *in the heart of Mecca*

This is the only mention in the Quran of Mecca, the town in which Muslim tradition says Muhammad spent most of his life. At 3.96 the word *bakka* appears, but it is not clear that *bakka* refers to a town or that it is connected with Mecca.

48.28 – *so that He may cause it to prevail over religion – all of it*

This striking verse appears three times in the Quran (also at 9.33, 61.9), as well as above the north door of the Dome of the Rock in Jerusalem.

48.29 – *Muḥammad is the messenger of God. Those who are with him are harsh against the disbelievers*

The name Muḥammad appears only four times in the Quran, and this is the fourth and final appearance in the canonical progression. Here the people who are with Muhammad are harsh (*ashiddāʾ*, sing. *shadīd*) against the "disbelievers" and merciful among themselves.

The fact that the name Muhammad only occurs four times in the Quran is striking,

Their marks on their faces are the trace of prostration. That is their image in the Torah, and their image in the Gospel is like a seed (that) puts forth its shoot, and strengthens it, and it becomes stout and stands straight on its stalk, pleasing the sowers – so that He may enrage the disbelievers by means of them. God has promised those of them who believe and do righteous deeds forgiveness and a great reward.

---

given that Muslims believe the Quran contains the recitations of Muhammad. All four occurrences are in the third person, declaring something about Muhammad, and never in the second person or vocative ("O Muhammad").

The Quran first mentions the name of Muhammad in a battle scene, where he is only a messenger who may die in the course of the fighting (3.144). The second mention asserts that he is not the father of Zayd but rather the messenger of Allah and the seal of the prophets (33.40). The third and fourth occurrences bracket Sūras 47 and 48. The third mention comes just before a command to strike the necks of "disbelievers" (47.2), and the final mention describes him similarly as harsh against the "disbelievers."

48.29 – *That is their image in the Torah, and their image in the Gospel*

What exactly is the "image" claimed for the "believers" in this long verse? Is it harshness against unbelievers and mercy among themselves? If their image in the Torah is "the trace of prostration" on their faces, this may relate to binding the commandments on foreheads in Deuteronomy 6:8. The Gospel image here may be one of Jesus' parables about the growth of seeds, but his parable was hardly given in order to "enrage the disbelievers."

See the analysis of the Quran's "Gospel" verses at 57.27 (p. 549).

THE PRIVATE
ROOMS
AL-ḤUJURĀT

49

> Sūra 49 seems appropriately grouped with Sūras 47 and 48. The messenger is
> again associated with Allah by belief, obedience, and decorum. High claims are
> made for "the prophet" and "the messenger of Allah." The Bedouins reappear.
>
> Yet there are differences. The first verses of this sūra are occupied with a
> seemingly private matter for the messenger. There is fighting, but this time it
> is among the believers themselves.

In the Name of God, the Merciful, the Compassionate

¹ You who believe! Do not be forward before God and His messenger, but guard
(yourselves) against God. Surely God is hearing, knowing. ² You who believe!
Do not raise your voices above the voice of the prophet, and do not be loud in
(your) speech to him, like the loudness of some of you to others, or your deeds
will come to nothing without your realizing (it). ³ Surely those who lower their
voices in the presence of the messenger of God, those are the ones whose hearts
God has tested for the guarding (of themselves). For them (there is) forgiveness
and a great reward. ⁴ Surely those who call out to you from behind the private
rooms – most of them do not understand. ⁵ If they were patient, until you

---

49.1 – *You who believe! Do not be forward before God and His messenger*

This sūra immediately addresses the "believers" with instructions for their behavior (also vv. 6, 11, 13). It also associates the messenger with Allah as deserving of
decorum (v. 1), obedience (v. 14), and belief (v. 15).

The first passage in this sūra (vv. 1–5) is another example of a text type that
concerns the personal situation of the messenger (also in Sūras 24; 33; 65; 66; see
"Different Kinds of Literature," p. 14). Here the Quran instructs believers in how to
address the messenger and behave in his presence.

The Quran here describes the messenger as "the prophet" (v. 2). This expression
occurs quite rarely in the Quran. See the analysis of "the prophet" at 66.9 (p. 579).

come out to them, it would indeed be better for them. Yet God is forgiving, compassionate.

⁶ You who believe! If a wicked person brings you some (piece of) news, be discerning, or you will smite a people in ignorance, and then become regretful over what you have done. ⁷ Know that the messenger of God is among you. If he obeyed you in much of the affair, you would indeed be in distress. But God has made belief dear to you, and made it appear enticing in your hearts, and made disbelief and wickedness and disobedience hateful to you. Those – they are the right-minded. ⁸ Favor from God and a blessing! God is knowing, wise.

⁹ If two contingents of the believers fight, set (things) right between them, and if one of them oppresses the other, fight the one which oppresses until it returns to the command of God. If it returns, set (things) right between them

---

49.7 – *Know that the messenger of God is among you*

This important self-conscious or "self-referential" claim draws attention to the messenger in a way quite different from most sūras in the Quran. The expression "the messenger of Allah" is also quite rare, appearing twice in this sūra (also in v. 3) and at 7.158; 9.61; and 48.29.

Is this a message "sent down," or is it simply a claim that the messenger makes for himself in third person (or first person, 7.158)? This sūra does not present itself as a message from Allah until verse 14 ("say"). Allah remains in third person until verse 17.

49.9 – *fight the one which oppresses until it returns to the command of God*

This verse commands the reader or listener to fight, using the Arabic verb *qātala*. Here the "believers" are commanded to fight against a contingent of other "believers" who do wrong. The reason for the fighting is to set things right between the "believers" (v. 10) in the interests of justice and fairness.

This is the final command to fight in a series of twelve commands that use the Arabic verb *qātala*. Of these, 49.9 is the only verse commanding "believers" to fight other "believers." The remaining eleven verses command fighting against people outside of the Muslim community. The targets of the fighting command are "disbelievers" (*kuffār*, 9.123), the "heads of disbelief" (9.12), "associators" (*mushrikūn*, 9.36), "those who have been given the book" (9.29), and "the allies of the devil" (4.76). Some verses seem to refer to defensive fighting (2.190; 9.36), while other verses describe objectives beyond defense (2.193; 8.39; 9.12, 14, 29, 123). Three of the verses command fighting "in the way of Allah" (2.190, 244; 4.84; cf. 4.76). Such commands raise a question about the character of Allah (see a discussion of this theological question at 73.20, p. 597).

Commands to fight pose a challenge for those who revere the Quran and its messenger and read the text as timeless divine revelation. Non-Muslims who could

with justice, and act fairly. Surely God loves the ones who act fairly. [10] Only the believers are brothers, so set (things) right between your two brothers, and guard (yourselves) against God, so that you may receive mercy.

[11] You who believe! Do not let one people ridicule (another) people who may be better than them, or women (ridicule other) women who may be better than them. Do not find fault with each other, or insult each other with nicknames. A bad name is wickedness after belief. Whoever does not turn (in repentance), those – they are the evildoers.

[12] You who believe! Avoid too much conjecture, (for) surely some conjecture is a sin. Do not pry or go behind each other's back. Would any of you like to eat the flesh of his dead brother? You would hate it! Guard (yourselves) against God. Surely God turns (in forgiveness), compassionate.

[13] People! Surely We have created you from a male and a female, and made you different peoples and tribes, so that you may recognize one another. Surely the most honorable among you in the sight of God is the one among you who guards (himself) most. Surely God is knowing, aware.

[14] The Arabs say, 'We believe.' Say: 'You do not believe. Rather say, "We submit," (for) belief has not yet entered your hearts. But if you obey God and His messenger, He will not deprive you of your deeds at all. Surely God is forgiving, compassionate. [15] The believers are only those who believe in God and

---

potentially be affected by these commands are understandably concerned about what they mean for peaceful coexistence. See also "Fighting and Killing in the Quran" (p. 220).

49.9 – *Surely God loves the ones who act fairly*

The Quran contains twenty-two statements about the kinds of people whom Allah loves. The just, or "the ones who act fairly" (*muqsiṭūn*), are among the more frequent objects of Allah's love (also 5.42; 60.8) See "The Language of Love in the Quran" (p. 560).

49.11 – *Do not let one people ridicule (another) people who may be better than them*

This passage (vv. 11–13) offers further instructions for believers.

49.14 – *The Arabs say, "We believe." Say: "You do not believe. Rather say, 'We submit'…"*

The sūra's final passage is about and addressed to the Bedouins, who seem reluctant to fight (v. 15). Several other passages refer to groups of believers who declined to fight (e.g., 3.167, 9.83, 48.16; cf. 5.24). In the book *Jihad: The Origin of Holy War in Islam*, Reuven Firestone suggests that such expressions indicate contrasting views of the legitimacy of fighting in the early Muslim community (see bibliography).

49.15 – *The believers are only those who believe in God and His messenger*

This verse makes explicit what seems implicit in many parts of the Quran: that

His messenger, (and) then have not doubted but struggled with their wealth and their lives in the way of God. Those – they are the truthful.'

[16] Say: 'Will you teach God about your religion, when God knows whatever is in the heavens and whatever is on the earth? God has knowledge of everything.'

[17] (They think) they bestow a favor on you in that they have submitted! Say: 'Do not bestow your submission on me as a favor! No! God bestows a favor on you, in that He has guided you to belief, if you are truthful. [18] Surely God knows the unseen (things) of the heavens and the earth. God sees what you do.'

"belief" is not a generic kind of "religious faith" but "only" (*innamā*) specific to Allah and the messenger. See "Allah in the Quran" (p. 572).

    Such "believers" also struggle (*jāhada*) with their wealth and their lives in the way of Allah. See "Jihad in the Quran" (p. 368).

QĀF
QĀF

50

A famous verse in this sūra states that Allah is closer to the human "than (his) jugular vein" (v. 16). The verse is treasured by Muslims who make a case for the nearness of Allah. In the context of this sūra, the verse lies between others about a book that records the deeds of unbelievers (v. 4) and about two angels who sit on the right and the left to record every word spoken (vv. 17–18). Therefore, should this famous verse be interpreted as an assurance or as a threat?

In the Name of God, the Merciful, the Compassionate

¹ Qāf. By the glorious Qur'ān! ² – No! They are amazed that a warner has come to them from among them, and the disbelievers say, 'This is an amazing thing! ³ When we are dead, and turned to dust [. . .]? That is a far return!' ⁴ We know what the earth takes away from them, and with Us is a Book (that is) keeping watch. ⁵ No! They called the truth a lie when it came to them, and they are in a confused state. ⁶ Do they not look at the sky above them, how We have built it, and adorned it, and it has no cracks? ⁷ And the earth – We stretched it out, and cast on it firm mountains, and caused every beautiful kind (of plant) to grow

---

50.2 – *They are amazed that a warner has come to them from among them*

The messenger is merely a warner in this sūra. Further on, the Quran says he is not a tyrant over the people (v. 45) and instructs him to be patient with what they say (v. 39). The idea that a messenger comes from among his people and can speak to them in their own language is an important theme in the Quran.

50.4 – *with Us is a Book (that is) keeping watch*

The "Book" that the Quran refers to is often the record of the words and deeds of each human, as in this verse.

50.6 – *Do they not look at the sky above them . . . ?*

The Quran makes an appeal to the creation in many lovely passages like this (vv. 6–11). Such passages are among the most attractive parts of the messenger's preaching.

522

on it, ⁸ as evidence and a reminder to every servant who turns (in repentance). ⁹ And We sent down blessed water from the sky, and caused gardens to grow by means of it, and grain for harvest, ¹⁰ and tall date palms with bunches (of fruit), ¹¹ as a provision for the servants, and We give a barren land life by means of it. In this way the coming forth (will take place).

¹² Before them the people of Noah called (it) a lie, and the people of al-Rass, and Thamūd, ¹³ and ʿĀd, and Pharaoh, and the brothers of Lot, ¹⁴ and the people of the Grove, and the people of Tubbaʿ – each (of them) called the messengers liars, and My promise was proved true.

¹⁵ Were We tired out by the first creation? No! They are in doubt about a new creation. ¹⁶ Certainly We created the human, and We know what his own self whispers within him, (for) We are closer to him than (his) jugular vein. ¹⁷ When the two meeters meet together, (one) seated on the right, and (one) on the left, ¹⁸ he does not utter a word without (there being) a watcher ready beside him. ¹⁹ The daze of death comes in truth: 'That is what you were trying to avoid!'

²⁰ There will be a blast on the trumpet: 'That is the Day of Promise.' ²¹ Each person will come, (and) with him a driver and a witness. ²² 'Certainly you were oblivious of this, so We have removed your covering, and today your sight is sharp.' ²³ His comrade will say, 'This is what I have ready.' ²⁴ '(You two), cast

---

50.12 – *Before them the people of Noah called (it) a lie*

Several of the peoples in this list (vv. 12–14) are not well known: the people of al-Rass (only mentioned here and 25.38), the Grove, and Tubbaʿ (only here and 44.37).

50.16 – *We are closer to him than (his) jugular vein*

This striking verse is especially treasured by Sufi Muslims because it suggests a closer relationship to Allah than orthodox Islam often projects.

Another part of this verse, "We know what his own self (*nafs*) whispers within him," is one of just a handful of verses that seems to refer to evil human desires coming from within (cf. 12.53; 75.2; 79.40). See the analysis of the Quran's teaching on "human nature" at 79.40 (p. 612).

50.17 – *When the two meeters meet together, (one) seated on the right and (one) on the left*

The picture here is of angels on either side of each person recording that person's words and deeds.

50.20 – *There will be a blast on the trumpet: "That is the Day of Promise"*

The trumpet blast begins an extended judgment scene (vv. 20–34) in which the two angels of verse 17 throw their human into Gehenna (v. 24), and the god-fearing enter the Garden in peace (v. 34). The Judgment Day is called here both the Day of Promise (*yawm al-waʿīd*, v. 20) and the Day of Eternity (*yawm al-khulūd*, v. 34).

into Gehenna every stubborn disbeliever, [25] preventer of the good, transgressor, doubter, [26] who set up another god with God. Cast him into the harsh punishment.' [27] His (other) comrade will say, 'Our Lord, I did not make him transgress insolently, but he was far astray.' [28] He will say, 'Do not dispute in My presence, when I have already sent forth the promise to you. [29] The word is not going to change with Me. I am not an evildoer to (My) servants.' [30] On the Day when We say to Gehenna, 'Are you filled?,' and it says, 'Are there any more (to come)?,' [31] and the Garden is brought near for the ones who guard (themselves) – (it is) not far: [32] 'This is what you were promised. (It is) for everyone who turns (in repentance and) keeps watch [33] – whoever fears the Merciful in the unseen, and brings a heart turning (in repentance). [34] Enter it in peace!' That is the Day of Eternity. [35] There they will have whatever they please, and with Us (there is still) more.

[36] How many a generation We have destroyed before them! They were stronger than them in power, and they searched about in the lands – was there any place of escape? [37] Surely in that is a reminder indeed to whoever has a heart or listens attentively, and he is a witness.

[38] Certainly We created the heavens and the earth, and whatever is between them, in six days. No weariness touched Us in (doing) that. [39] Be patient with what they say, and glorify your Lord with praise before the rising of the sun, and before its setting. [40] And glorify Him during part of the night, and at the ends of the prostration. [41] And listen for the Day when the caller will call from a place nearby. [42] The Day when they hear the cry in truth – that is the Day of Coming Forth. [43] Surely We – We give life and cause death, and to Us is the (final) destination.

[44] On the Day when the earth is split open from them, (and they come forth from the graves) rushing – that is an easy gathering for Us. [45] We know what they say. You are not a tyrant over them. So remind, by means of the Qur'ān, anyone who fears My promise.

50.30 – *On the Day when We say to Gehenna, "Are you filled?"*

See the discussion of the Quran's concept of human nature at 79.40 (p. 612).

50.39 – *Be patient with what they say, and glorify your Lord with praise*

The Quran directly addresses the messenger and instructs him how to behave as long as the audience resists his preaching (vv. 39–41, 45).

THE SCATTERERS
AL-DHĀRIYĀT

51

In the face of resistance from his audience, the messenger warns of a coming Judgment Day. The stories in the center of the sūra, however, focus on Allah's destruction of various peoples in this present world. In either case, says this sūra, the audience will call the warning messenger "a magician or a man possessed!" (v. 38).

In the Name of God, the Merciful, the Compassionate

¹ By the scatterers (with their) scattering, ² and the bearers (with their) burden, ³ and the runners (with their) effortlessness, ⁴ and the distributors (with their) affair! ⁵ Surely what you are promised is true indeed! ⁶ Surely the Judgment is indeed going to fall!

⁷ By the sky with all its tracks! ⁸ Surely you differ indeed in what you say! ⁹ Whoever is deluded about it is (really) deluded. ¹⁰ May the guessers perish, ¹¹ those who are in a flood (of confusion), heedless. ¹² They ask, 'When is the Day of Judgment?' ¹³ The Day when they will be tried over the Fire: ¹⁴ 'Taste your trial! This is what you were seeking to hurry.'

¹⁵ Surely the ones who guard (themselves) will be in (the midst of) gardens and springs, ¹⁶ taking whatever their Lord has given them. Surely before (this) they were doers of good. ¹⁷ Little of the night would they sleep, ¹⁸ and in the mornings they would ask for forgiveness, ¹⁹ and in their wealth (there was) a due (portion) for the beggar and the outcast.

²⁰ In the earth (there are) signs for the ones who are certain, ²¹ and (also) in yourselves. Do you not see? ²² And in the sky is your provision and what you are promised. ²³ By the Lord of the sky and the earth! Surely it is true indeed – (even) as what you (are able to) speak.

51.1 – *By the scatterers (with their) scattering*
The sūra opens with an oath that the judgment will surely come (v. 6).

51.19 – *and in their wealth (there was) a due (portion) for the beggar and the outcast*
Those who do good (v. 16) have a heart for the poor and marginalized.

[24] Has the story come to you of the honored guests of Abraham? [25] When they entered upon him, and said, 'Peace!,' he said, 'Peace! (You are) a people unknown (to me).' [26] So he turned to his family and brought a fattened calf, [27] and he placed it near them. He said, 'Will you not eat?' [28] And he began to feel a fear of them. They said, 'Do not fear!' And they gave him good news of a knowing boy. [29] And then his wife came forward in a loud voice, and struck her face, and said, 'An old woman, barren!' [30] They said, 'So (it will be)! Your Lord has said. Surely He – He is the Wise, the Knowing.' [31] He said, 'What is your business, you envoys?' [32] They said, 'Surely we have been sent to a sinful people, [33] to send (down) on them stones of clay, [34] marked by your Lord for the wanton.'

51.24 – *Has the story come to you of the honored guests of Abraham?*

This is the third version of this story (vv. 24–37) in the canonical progression of the Quran, and it is interesting to note and consider the similarities and differences among versions. Here the name Isaac is not given (as in 11.71) but only "a knowing boy" (v. 28, as also in 15.51). The wife of Abraham does not laugh and ponder the news of her pregnancy (as in 11.71–72) but seems to cry out and strike herself, calling herself "an old woman, barren" (v. 29). In Sūra 15, the wife is not mentioned.

Why the repetition of stories in the Quran, why the differences in details, and what can readers learn from both, if anything? Muslim commentators have dealt with repetition and differences by claiming that the different versions were revealed to Muhammad at different points in his career. This assumes both that the material has a divine origin and that the Muslim story about Muhammad provides the historical context and chronology of the material.

Non-Muslim scholars have treated repetition of stories and differences between the stories in various ways. Some choose to accept the general framework of the Muslim story of Muhammad, as well as the traditional chronology of the recitations, and then suggest how a prophet story may have developed over the career of Muhammad or in the emergence of the Muslim community.

Other scholars reason that since there is no evidence for the traditional chronology of the material – or for the story of Muhammad – outside of Muslim tradition, the contents of the Quran should be studied closely and reasonable suggestions made about where the material might have come from. For example, John Wansbrough has compared the different versions of the Shu'ayb story (which he terms "variant traditions") and suggests that while the differences show literary elaboration of the story, they tell us little about historical development. He speculates that in the process of the Quran's collection, different versions of such stories, perhaps coming from different regions of the expanding Arab Empire, "were incorporated more or less intact into the canonical compilation" (see *Quranic Studies* in bibliography).

 35 We (would have) brought out any of the believers who were in it, 36 but We found in it only one house of those who had submitted. 37 And We left in it a sign for those who fear the painful punishment.

 38 And (there is also a sign) in Moses: when We sent him to Pharaoh with clear authority. 39 But he turned away with his supporter(s), and said, 'A magician or a man possessed!' 40 So We seized him and his forces, and tossed them into the sea, (for) he was to blame.

 41 And (there is also a sign) in 'Ād: when We sent upon them the desolating wind. 42 It left nothing it came upon, but made it like decayed (ruins). 43 And (there is also a sign) in Thamūd: when it was said to them, 'Enjoy (yourselves) for a time!' 44 But they disdained the command of their Lord, and the thunderbolt took them while they were looking on, 45 and they were not able to stand, nor were they helped. 46 And the people of Noah before (them) – surely they were a wicked people.

 47 The sky – We built it with (Our own) hands, and surely We were (its) extenders indeed. 48 And the earth – We spread it out. Excellent were the smoothers! 49 And We created pairs of everything, so that you might take heed. 50 So flee to God! Surely I am a clear warner for you from Him. 51 And do not set up another god with God. Surely I am a clear warner for you from Him.

 52 (Even) so, not a messenger came to those who were before them, except they said, 'A magician or a man possessed!' 53 Have they bequeathed it to each other? No! They are a people who transgress insolently. 54 So turn away from them, (for) you are not to be blamed, 55 but remind (them). Surely the Reminder will benefit the believers.

 56 I did not create the jinn and humankind except to serve Me. 57 I do not desire any provision from them, nor do I desire that they should feed Me. 58 Surely God – He is the Provider, One full of power, the Firm.

 59 Surely for the ones who do evil (there will be) a portion like the portion of their companions. Let them not seek to hurry Me! 60 Woe to those who disbelieve on account of their Day which they are promised!

51.56 – *I did not create the jinn and humankind except to serve Me*

Here the Quran states the reason for which Allah created humankind. On the Quran's concept of *jinn*, see the discussion at 72.1 (p. 593).

THE MOUNTAIN
AL-ṬŪR

52

This sūra starts out very much like the previous sūra, with an opening oath leading to a promise of judgment to come. One difference is that the verses in this sūra provide much more detail about future delights to be enjoyed by "the ones who guard (themselves)" (v. 17). As for those who call the preaching of the messenger a lie, the sūra asks a long series of questions to challenge and warn them.

In the Name of God, the Merciful, the Compassionate

[1] By the mountain [2] and a Book written [3] on parchment unrolled! [4] By the inhabited House! [5] By the roof raised up [6] and the sea surging! [7] Surely the punishment of your Lord is indeed going to fall! [8] (There is) no one to repel it.

[9] On the Day when the sky will shake, [10] and the mountains fly away, [11] woe that Day to the ones who called (it) a lie, [12] who – they were playing around in (their) banter. [13] On the Day when they will be shoved forcefully into the fire of Gehenna: [14] 'This is the Fire which you called a lie! [15] Is this magic or do you not see? [16] Burn in it! Bear it patiently or do not bear it patiently – (it is) the same for you. You are only being repaid for what you have done.'

[17] Surely the ones who guard (themselves) will be in Gardens and bliss, [18] rejoicing in what their Lord has given them, and (because) their Lord has guarded them against the punishment of the Furnace. [19] 'Eat and drink with satisfaction, (in return) for what you have done.' [20] (There they will be) reclining on couches lined up, and We shall marry them to (maidens) with dark, wide eyes. [21] (For) those who believe, and whose descendants followed them in belief, We shall join their descendants with them, and We shall not deprive them of any of their deeds. Each person (is held) in pledge for what he has earned. [22] We shall

---

52.20 – We shall marry them to (maidens) with dark, wide eyes

Such descriptions have attracted the attention of non-Muslims. What do they mean to say about the characteristics of the heavenly "Gardens"? See the comment at 44.54 on "(maidens) with dark, wide eyes" (p. 497).

increase them with fruits and meat of whatever (kind) they desire. ²³ There
they will pass (around) a cup to each other in which there is no frivolous or
sinful talk, ²⁴ and among them will circulate boys of their own, as if they were
hidden pearls. ²⁵ Some of them will approach others asking each other questions.
²⁶ They will say, 'Surely we were fearful among our family before, ²⁷ but God has
bestowed favor on us, and guarded us against the punishment of the scorching
(Fire). ²⁸ Surely we used to call on Him before. Surely He – He is the Beneficent,
the Compassionate.'

²⁹ So remind (them)! By the blessing of your Lord, you are neither an
oracle-giver nor possessed. ³⁰ Or do they say, 'A poet, for whom we await the
uncertainty of Fate'? ³¹ Say: '(Just) wait! Surely I shall be one of those waiting
with you.' ³² Or do their minds command them (to do) this, or are they a people
who transgress insolently? ³³ Or do they say, 'He has invented it?' No! They
do not believe. ³⁴ Let them bring a proclamation like it, if they are truthful.

52.29 – *By the blessing of your Lord, you are neither an oracle-giver nor possessed*
The Quran reassures the messenger in the face of accusations from his audience.
The audience also seems to characterize the messenger as a poet (v. 30). On the
negative sense of "poet," see the comment at 21.5 (p. 331).

52.34 – *Let them bring a proclamation like it, if they are truthful*
The listeners do not believe that the messenger's recitation is true. They say that
he has simply invented the words (v. 33). See the discussion on verses that accuse
the messenger of inventing at 69.44 (p. 587). In response, the Quran challenges the
audience to compose a proclamation (ḥadīth) like the recitation.

This is the final verse in a series of six verses known as the *tahaddī* (challenge)
verses (also 2.23; 10.38; 11.13; 17.88; 28.49). The six verses do not report whether the
audience accepts the challenge, but the Quran says that they will not (2.24) and
cannot (17.88), or perhaps may not even respond (11.14; 28.49). Later Muslim writers
concluded that the audience was unable to compose comparable recitations. In the
third and fourth centuries of Islam, Muslim scholars developed an elaborate doctrine
of the inimitability of the Quran. They claimed that the language of the Quran is so
marvelous that it could not have been composed by a human; they then asserted
that their claim proves the divine origin of the Quran and the prophethood of Islam's
messenger.

The doctrine of the inimitability of the Quran (*i'jāz*) became an article of faith for
most Muslims. Andrew Rippin notes in his book *Muslims* that this claim is difficult
for non-Muslims to evaluate because it is in the eye (or ear) of the beholder. Rippin
cites an early work attributed to an Arabic-speaking Christian living within the Arab
Empire, 'Abd al-Masīḥ al-Kindī. To the contrary, al-Kindī suggested that the literary

³⁵ Or were they created out of nothing? Or were they the creators? ³⁶ Or did they create the heavens and the earth? No! They are not certain. ³⁷ Or are the storehouses of your Lord with them, or are they the record-keepers? ³⁸ Or do they have a ladder on which they (can) listen? Then let their listener bring clear authority. ³⁹ Or does He have daughters while you have sons? ⁴⁰ Or do you ask them for a reward, so that they are burdened with debt? ⁴¹ Or is the unseen in their keeping, so that they are writing it down? ⁴² Or do they intend a plot? Then those who disbelieve will be the ones plotted against. ⁴³ Or do they have a god other than God? Glory to God above what they associate! ⁴⁴ Even if they see fragments of the sky falling, they will say, 'A heap of clouds!' ⁴⁵ So leave them, until they meet their Day on which they will be thunderstruck ⁴⁶ – the Day when their plot will be of no use to them at all, and they will not be helped. ⁴⁷ Surely for those who do evil (there is) a punishment before that, but most of them do not know (it).

⁴⁸ Be patient for the judgment of your Lord. Surely you are in Our sight. Glorify your Lord with praise when you arise, ⁴⁹ and glorify Him during part of the night, and (at) the setting of the stars.

---

state of the Quran was so poor that he questioned any possibility of its being "sent down" from above (see also Muir, *The Apology of Al Kindy*, and Tien, "The Apology of al-Kindi," in the bibliography.)

Christians tend to evaluate the provenance of the Quran from the truth or falsehood of its contents. It is interesting to note that the Bible does not contain self-conscious claims to be the Word of God based on the excellence of its language, whether Hebrew, Aramaic, or Greek. More typical of the Bible is the claim that it presents a true account (e.g., Luke 1:1–4) based on eyewitness testimony (e.g., John 19:37, 21:24).

52.35 – *Or were they created out of nothing?*

The Quran asks a long series of questions (vv. 35–43) about the ones who call the preaching of the messenger a lie (v. 11), designed to expose their desperate need.

THE STAR
AL-NAJM

53

An Islamic story of "satanic verses" was widely recounted by Muslim commentators in the early centuries of Islam to explain several verses in this sūra and in Sūra 22. Since 1988, discussion of the story has become extraordinarily controversial because of global Muslim reaction to a novel called *The Satanic Verses* written by Salman Rushdie. The story is important, however, because it raises the question of the sources of the recitations gathered into the Quran.

In the Name of God, the Merciful, the Compassionate

[1] By the star when it falls! [2] Your companion has not gone astray, nor has he erred, [3] nor does he speak on a whim. [4] It is nothing but an inspiration inspired. [5] One harsh in power has taught him [6] – One full of strength! He stood poised, [7] while He was at the highest horizon, [8] then He drew near and came down. [9] He was two bow-lengths tall, or nearly. [10] And so He inspired His servant (with) what He inspired. [11] His heart did not lie about what it saw. [12] Will you dispute with him about what he sees?

[13] Certainly he saw Him at a second descent, [14] by the Lote Tree of the Boundary, [15] near which is the Garden of the Refuge, [16] when (there) covered the Lote Tree what covered (it). [17] His sight did not turn aside, nor did it transgress. [18] Certainly he saw one of the greatest signs of his Lord.

[19] Have you seen al-Lāt, and al-'Uzzā, [20] and Manāt, the third, the other?

53.2 – *Your companion has not gone astray, nor has he erred*

The Quran claims in this self-referential statement that the messenger speaks by inspiration (*waḥy*). The following verses (6–18) seem to refer to a vision; but again, the meaning is uncertain because of many pronouns without antecedents.

53.19 – *Have you seen al-Lāt, and al-'Uzzā, and Manāt . . . ?*

According to Muslim tradition, al-Lāt, al-'Uzzā, and Manāt were three gods worshiped by idolaters in Mecca. Early Muslim commentators and historians explained verses 19–25 by telling the story of the "satanic verses" (see al-Ṭabarī, *History*, 6:107–12). The story is that Muhammad wished to gain the favor of the Meccans, so he

[21] Do you have male (offspring) while He has female? [22] Then that (would be) an unfair division! [23] They are only names which you have named, you and your fathers. God has not sent down any authority for it. They only follow conjecture and whatever they themselves desire – when certainly the guidance has come to them from their Lord. [24] Or will a person have whatever he longs for? [25] To God (belongs) the last and the first.

[26] How many an angel there is in the heavens whose intercession is of no use at all, until God gives permission to whomever He pleases and approves. [27] Surely those who do not believe in the Hereafter indeed name the angels with the names of females. [28] But they have no knowledge about it. They only follow conjecture, and surely conjecture is of no use at all against the truth. [29] So turn away from the one who turns away from Our reminder and desires nothing but this present life. [30] That is the extent of their knowledge. Surely your Lord – He knows who goes astray from His way, and He knows who is (rightly) guided. [31] To God (belongs) whatever is in the heavens and whatever is on the earth, so that He may repay those who do evil for what they have done, and repay those who do good with the best (reward).

[32] Those who avoid great sins and immoral deeds, except for inadvertent ones – surely your Lord is embracing in forgiveness. He knows about you, when He produced you from the earth, and when you were (still) embryos in the bellies of your mothers. So do not claim purity for yourselves. He knows the one who guards (himself).

[33] Do you see the one who turns away, [34] and gives little, and (then) grudgingly?

---

proclaimed that the Meccans may hope for the intercession of these gods. Gabriel then informed Muhammad that these words were not revealed by Allah but were cast into him by Satan. Mention of Satan casting words into the minds of messengers and prophets is found in 22.52–54, which is the other passage associated with the "satanic verses" story in Muslim commentaries.

In the book *Before Orthodoxy*, Shahab Ahmed presented translations of fifty different versions of the "satanic verses" story from early Muslim commentaries. Ahmed wondered why – since virtually all Muslims during Islam's first two centuries believed the story to be historical – it has since 1800 become practically impossible for Muslims to consider it true. A handy translation of Zamakhsharī's discussion of 22.52 and 53.19 in the fifth Islamic century (twelfth century AD) is included in Helmut Gätje's *The Qur'ān and its Exegesis* (see bibliography).

53.26 – *until God gives permission to whomever He pleases and approves*

This verse denies the power of intercession to angels but allows the possibility to others (or another?) whom Allah approves. See the analysis of verses on intercession at 39.44 (p. 464).

³⁵ Is knowledge of the unseen in his keeping, and so he sees (it)? ³⁶ Or has he not been informed about what is in the pages of Moses ³⁷ and Abraham, who paid (his debt) in full? ³⁸ – That no one bearing a burden bears the burden of another; ³⁹ and that a person will receive only what he (himself) strives for; ⁴⁰ and that his striving will be seen, ⁴¹ (and) then he will be paid for it with the fullest payment; ⁴² and that to your Lord is the (ultimate) goal; ⁴³ and that He causes laughter and causes weeping; ⁴⁴ and that He causes death and gives life; ⁴⁵ and that He created pairs, the male and the female, ⁴⁶ from a drop, when it is emitted; ⁴⁷ and that the second growth (depends) on Him; ⁴⁸ and that He enriches (people) and gives wealth; ⁴⁹ and that He is the Lord of Sirius; ⁵⁰ and that He destroyed ʿĀd of old, ⁵¹ and Thamūd – He did not spare (them) ⁵² – or the people of Noah before (them) – surely they were – they (were) evil and insolent transgressor(s) – ⁵³ and the overturned (cities) He overthrew, ⁵⁴ when (there) covered them what covered (them). ⁵⁵ So which of the blessings of your Lord will you dispute?

⁵⁶ This (man) is a warner, of the warners of old. ⁵⁷ The impending (Hour) is impending! ⁵⁸ There is no one to remove it, other than God. ⁵⁹ Are you amazed at this proclamation? ⁶⁰ And do you laugh and not weep, ⁶¹ while you amuse yourselves? ⁶² Prostrate yourselves before God and serve (Him)!

53.36–37 – *in the pages of Moses and Abraham*

This expression seems to indicate a concept that a scripture was given to Abraham as well as to Moses. "Pages" translates the Arabic *ṣuḥuf*, which literally means "leaves" or "sheets." A similar expression appears at 87.19.

53.38 – *no one bearing a burden bears the burden of another*

This verse is the last in a series of similar verses that declare that no human can bear the "burden" (*wizr*) of another human. Other examples come at 6.164; 17.15; 35.18; and 39.7. The verses that follow this final occurrence explain that people will only receive what they strive for (vv. 38–41).

Do such verses intend a deliberate denial of the biblical teaching that Jesus "bore the sin of many" (Isaiah 53:4, 11, 12; Hebrews 9:28; 1 Peter 2:24)? Christians sometimes call this teaching "vicarious" or "substitutionary" atonement.

Sūra 53 does not seem to address the People of the Book to deny their faith. In any case, the word "burden" in 53.38 brings to mind a number of interesting biblical materials. Jesus says, "Come to me, all you who are weary and burdened, and I will give you rest" (Matthew 11:28). Paul encourages the believers to "carry each other's burdens, and in this way you will fulfill the law of Christ" (Galatians 6:2). As for substitutionary atonement, Isaiah 53 seems to answer Sūra 53 when it says, "We all, like sheep, have gone astray, each of us has turned to his own way; and the LORD has laid on him the iniquity of us all" (Isaiah 53:6).

THE MOON
AL-QAMAR

The theme of this sūra is the sure approach of the hour of judgment, whether people pay attention to the warning signs or not. The sūra refers to stories of various peoples who turned away from the signs and denied the messengers sent to them. "Certainly We have destroyed your parties (before), yet (is there) anyone who takes heed?" (v. 51) seems to capture the sūra's dark mood.

In the Name of God, the Merciful, the Compassionate

[1] The Hour has drawn near, and the moon has been split open! [2] Yet if they see a sign, they turn away, and say, 'Non-stop magic!' [3] They call (it) a lie, and follow their (own vain) desires, yet everything is set. [4] Certainly enough of the story has come to them to act as a deterrent – [5] far-reaching wisdom (it is) – but warnings are of no use. [6] So turn away from them. On the Day when the Caller will call to a terrible thing: [7] with sight downcast, they will come forth from the graves as if they were locusts spreading, [8] rushing to the Caller. The disbelievers will say, 'This is a hard day!'

[9] The people of Noah called (it) a lie before them, and they called Our servant a liar, and said, 'A man possessed!' He was deterred [10] and called on his Lord:

54.1 – *The Hour has drawn near, and the moon has been split open!*

Even such a dramatic warning sign (āya) has no effect on some people. With them, the messenger can only wait until the day when all are summoned.

54.9 – *The people of Noah called (it) a lie before them*

This short version of the Noah story first highlights the resistance of the people of Noah to Noah's preaching. Noah calls on the Lord for help (v. 10). Here the Quran presents the flood as the Lord's response to Noah's prayer (vv. 11–12). Noah survived because the Lord "carried him on a vessel of planks and nails" (v. 13). Other versions of the Noah story come at 7.59–64; 10.71–73; 11.25–49; 23.23–30; 26.105–20; and 71.1–28.

'I am overcome. Help (me)!' [11] So We opened the gates of the sky with water pouring (down), [12] and made the earth gush forth with springs, and the water met for a purpose already decreed. [13] We carried him on a vessel of planks and nails, [14] running before Our eyes – a payment for the one who was disbelieved. [15] Certainly We left it as a sign, yet (is there) anyone who takes heed? [16] How were My punishment and My warnings?

[17] Certainly We have made the Qur'ān easy for remembrance, yet (is there) anyone who takes heed?

[18] 'Ād called (it) a lie. How were My punishment and My warnings? [19] Surely We sent a furious wind against them on a day of the non-stop calamity. [20] It snatched the people away as if they were trunks of uprooted date palms. [21] How were My punishment and My warnings?

[22] Certainly We have made the Qur'ān easy for remembrance, yet (is there) anyone who takes heed?

[23] Thamūd called the warnings a lie, [24] and said, 'Shall we follow a single human being from among us? Surely then we would indeed be astray and raving mad. [25] Has the Reminder been cast (down) on him (alone) among us? No! He is an impudent liar.' [26] 'Tomorrow they will know who the impudent liar is! [27] We are sending the she-camel as a test for them, so watch them and be patient. [28] And inform them that the water is to be divided between them, each drink is to be brought (in turn).' [29] But they called their companion, and he took (a sword) and wounded (her). [30] How were My punishment and My warnings? [31] Surely We sent against them a single cry, and they were like the rubble (used by) the fence maker.

[32] Certainly We have made the Qur'ān easy for remembrance, yet (is there) anyone who takes heed?

54.11–12 – *So We opened the gates of the sky with water pouring (down), and made the earth gush forth with springs*

Unique among the Quran's seven versions of the Noah story, this description of the flood is very similar to the biblical account at Genesis 7:11. Other quranic versions, however, use the expression "the oven boiled" (11.40; 23.27).

54.17 – *Certainly We have made the Qur'ān easy for remembrance*

This verse repeats as a refrain at verses 22, 32, and 40. On the word *qur'ān*, see the comment at 2.185 (p. 61).

54.18 – *'Ād called (it) a lie*

On 'Ād and Hūd (vv. 18–21), see the explanation at 7.65 (p. 182).

54.23 – *Thamūd called the warnings a lie*

On Thamūd and Ṣāliḥ (vv. 23–31), see the explanation at 7.73 (p. 183).

³³ The people of Lot called the warnings a lie. ³⁴ Surely We sent a sandstorm against them, except for the house(hold) of Lot. We rescued them at dawn ³⁵ – a blessing from Us. In this way We repay the one who is thankful. ³⁶ Certainly he had warned them of Our attack, and they disputed the warnings. ³⁷ Certainly they solicited him for his guest(s), but We obliterated their eyes: 'Taste My punishment and My warnings!' ³⁸ Certainly in the morning a set punishment came upon them: ³⁹ 'Taste My punishment and My warnings!'

⁴⁰ Certainly We have made the Qur'ān easy for remembrance, yet (is there) anyone who takes heed?

⁴¹ Certainly the warnings came to the house of Pharaoh. ⁴² They called Our signs a lie – all of it – so We seized them with the seizing of a mighty, powerful (One).

⁴³ Are your disbelievers better than those? Or do you have an exemption in the scriptures?

⁴⁴ Or do they say, 'We shall all be victorious'? ⁴⁵ They will be routed and turn their back! ⁴⁶ Yes! The Hour is their appointed time, and the Hour is grievous and bitter.

⁴⁷ Surely the sinners are astray and raving mad! ⁴⁸ On the Day when they are dragged on their faces into the Fire: 'Taste the effect of Saqar!' ⁴⁹ Surely We have created everything in measure, ⁵⁰ and Our command is but a single (act), like a blink of the eye. ⁵¹ Certainly We have destroyed your parties (before), yet (is there) anyone who takes heed?

⁵² Everything they have done is in the scriptures, ⁵³ and every small and great (deed) is inscribed. ⁵⁴ Surely the ones who guard (themselves) will be in (the midst of) gardens and a river, ⁵⁵ in a sure seat in the presence of a powerful King.

54.33 – *The people of Lot called the warnings a lie*

This brief story of Lot (vv. 33–39), the final version of eight in the Quran, indicates the punishment and hints at the sin of Lot's city. Yet this version mentions neither Lot's wife nor "an old woman" as among those who remained behind when Lot and his family fled. The other Lot stories are at 7.80–84; 11.77–83; 15.61–74; 26.160–73; 27.54–58; 29.28–34; and 37.133–38. On the subject of the repetition of stories in the Quran, see the discussion at 51.24 (p. 526).

THE MERCIFUL
AL-RAHMĀN

55

The distinguishing feature of Sūra 55 is a repeating refrain that questions those who deny the Lord's power and justice. The sūra first recites the wonders of creation and then describes the horrors of hell and (mostly) the delights of paradise.

This sūra does not mention the name Allah but uses "Lord" (*rabb*) and "the Merciful" (*Rahman*; v. 1), after whom the sūra is named.

In the Name of God, the Merciful, the Compassionate

¹ The Merciful ² has taught the Qur'ān. ³ He created the human. ⁴ He taught him the explanation. ⁵ The sun and the moon (move) in predictable paths, ⁶ and the star and the tree prostrate themselves. ⁷ The sky – He raised it, and He laid down the scale ⁸ – do not transgress insolently concerning the scale, ⁹ but establish the weight in justice, and do not cheat concerning the scale. ¹⁰ And the earth – He laid it down for all living creatures. ¹¹ On it (there are) fruit, and date palms with sheaths, ¹² and grain with its husk, and fragrant herbs. ¹³ Which of the blessings of your Lord will you two call a lie?

¹⁴ He created the human from clay like pottery, ¹⁵ and He created the jinn from a mixture of fire. ¹⁶ Which of the blessings of your Lord will you two call a lie?

¹⁷ Lord of the two Easts, Lord of the two Wests. ¹⁸ Which of the blessings of your Lord will you two call a lie?

¹⁹ He let loose the two seas (which) meet. ²⁰ Between them (there is) a barrier

---

55.3 – *He created the human*

These words start a passage full of lovely expressions about the Creator's power and provision (vv. 3–29). See "Creation in the Quran" (p. 224).

55.13 – *Which of the blessings of your Lord will you two call a lie?*

The positive angle of this question makes it an effective appeal to the deniers. The refrain appears thirty-one times and forms the structure of the sūra.

55.19 – *He let loose the two seas (which) meet*

Shi'ite Muslims interpret the "two seas" to represent Ali and Fatima, while the "pearl and coral" (v. 22) are taken to symbolize their sons Hasan and Husayn.

(which) they do not seek (to cross). [21] Which of the blessings of your Lord will you two call a lie?

Shi'ite Interpretation of the Quran
Linda Darwish

The approach to the Quran of Shi'ite (known as "Twelver") Muslims differs from the Sunni approach in two main areas: in the Shi'ite doctrine of the Imamate and in their questions regarding the authenticity of the text of the Quran as accepted by Sunnis.

First, the word *Imam* is typically rendered "leader" in English, but Shi'ite usage refers specifically to Muhammad's descendants through his daughter Fatima and her husband Ali, Muhammad's cousin and son-in-law. Though not a direct descendant of Muhammad, Ali is taken by Shi'a Muslims to be the first Imam. Shi'a Muslims cite traditions in which Muhammad appoints Ali to this office, for an Imam, who is considered infallible, cannot be designated by a fallible human but only by God or a prophet.

Second, the debate about the authenticity of the quranic text, common in the first centuries of Islam, was premised on the absence of any mention of the Imams in the Quran, and particularly of Ali's right to succession. The Shi'a argued that such mention was excised from the text and that the true Quran – rather than the text that Muslims believe the caliph 'Uthmān produced – was with Ali. They believe that Ali's text later came to reside with the now hidden twelfth Imam, upon whose appearing in the Last Day it will be revealed. Later generations of Shi'a Muslims, accepting the text of the 'Uthmānic Quran, charged the Sunnis with alteration (*taḥrīf*) in the interpretation (*ta'wīl*) of certain verses.

According to Shi'ite interpretation, the Imams' office of leadership is seen in quranic verses such as 4.59: "You who believe! Obey God, and obey the messenger and those (who have) the command among you," with the latter phrase being interpreted as referring to the Imams. Shi'a Muslims believe the Imams are the spiritual descendants of Abraham (2.124), who, along with the prophets, are appointed leaders and guides of humanity (21.73). Allah has purified them completely (33.33) and blessed them (11.73), their purified state authenticating their unique relationship to the Quran (56.77–79). No one knows the true meaning of the Quran except for Allah and "those firmly rooted in knowledge" (3.7), whom Shi'a Muslims interpret to mean the Imams.

Thus they are "the firmest bond" (*al-urwa al-wuthqa*) linking heaven and earth. The two seas mentioned in 55.19–23 are said to symbolize Ali and Fatima, while the pearl and coral that they produce are interpreted to refer to their sons, Hasan and Husayn, the second and third Imams, respectively.

The Imams' unique relationship to the Quran is also expressed in early Imami traditions – notably, that of "the two weighty matters," which speaks of a permanent link between the Imams and the Quran. It is said that nearing his death, Muhammad said: "I have left among you two weighty matters which if you cling to them you shall not be led into error after me. One of them is greater than the other: The Book of God which is a rope stretched from Heaven to Earth and my progeny, the people of my house. These two shall not be parted until they return to the pool [of Paradise]." The Quran, in other words, cannot be correctly understood without an infallible interpreter, and no one, says another tradition, knows it fully except Ali, by which he (and, by implication, his descendants) become the "proof of God."

As recipients of divine knowledge, the Imams have infallible and comprehensive understanding of the meaning of the Quran in both its outer (*ẓāhir*) and inner (*bāṭin*) aspects, the latter containing seven dimensions. The two aspects are associated with *tanzīl* (coming down [of the text]) and *ta'wīl* (esoteric interpretation), respectively. The Imams' knowledge of the hidden meanings of the Quran is expressed in a tradition attributed to the sixth Imam: "The Book of God has four levels of meaning: literal expression, allusion, subtleties, and deepest realities. The literal expression is for the common folk, the allusion is for the elite, the subtleties are for the friends of God [the Imams], and the deepest realities are for the prophets."

In practice, Shi'ite exegesis gradually moved from reliance on the sayings of the Imams, transmitted for centuries, to the theological and philosophical approaches of modern and contemporary exegetes, such as Ṭabāṭabā'ī, Faḍlallāh, and others, whose commentaries seek, without abandoning the past, to relate the Quran to contemporary concerns. We take as an example 9.28, which bars from the sacred precincts "impure" ones who associate others with God (*mushrikūn*). Commentators differ on whether this includes Christians and Jews. Despite Ṭabāṭabā'ī's interest in comparative religion, his heavy reliance on medieval Muslim sources results in the perpetuation of false polemical assertions about the beliefs of Jews and Christians and the resulting impurity of their bodies. In contrast, Faḍlallāh uses logic to argue that the beliefs of Jews and Christians as portrayed in the Quran, though wrong, might not be normative and that the prohibition against impurity concerns the metaphysical realm of ideas, not persons in their physical state. These differences have practical implications for relations between Shi'a Muslims and those of other religions.

²² Pearl and coral come forth from both of them. ²³ Which of the blessings of your Lord will you two call a lie?

²⁴ His are the (ships) running, raised up on the sea like landmarks. ²⁵ Which of the blessings of your Lord will you two call a lie?

²⁶ All who are on it pass away, ²⁷ but the face of your Lord remains, full of splendor and honor. ²⁸ Which of the blessings of your Lord will you two call a lie?

²⁹ (All) who are in the heavens and the earth make requests of Him. Every day He (is engaged) in some task. ³⁰ Which of the blessings of your Lord will you two call a lie?

³¹ Soon We shall be free (to attend) to you, you two burdens! ³² Which of the blessings of your Lord will you two call a lie?

³³ Assembly of jinn and humankind! If you are able to pass beyond the confines of the heavens and the earth, pass! You will not pass beyond (them) except by authority. ³⁴ Which of the blessings of your Lord will you two call a lie?

³⁵ A flame of fire and a furious wind will be sent against you, and you will not (be able to) defend yourselves. ³⁶ Which of the blessings of your Lord will you two call a lie?

³⁷ When the sky is split open and turns red like oil – ³⁸ Which of the blessings of your Lord will you two call a lie?

³⁹ – on that Day neither human nor jinn will be questioned about his sin. ⁴⁰ Which of the blessings of your Lord will you two call a lie?

⁴¹ The sinners will be known by their mark, and they will be seized by the hair and the feet. ⁴² Which of the blessings of your Lord will you two call a lie?

⁴³ This is Gehenna which the sinners called a lie. ⁴⁴ They will go around between it and hot, boiling (water). ⁴⁵ Which of the blessings of your Lord will you two call a lie?

55.31 – *Soon We shall be free (to attend) to you, you two burdens!*
Guilty humans and jinn "will be known by their mark" (v. 41) and punished accordingly (vv. 31–44). See the analysis of verses about *jinn* at 72.1 (p. 593).

⁴⁶ But for the one who fears the position of his Lord, (there are) two gardens – ⁴⁷ Which of the blessings of your Lord will you two call a lie?

⁴⁸ – with branches – ⁴⁹ Which of the blessings of your Lord will you two call a lie?

⁵⁰ – in both (there are) two flowing springs – ⁵¹ Which of the blessings of your Lord will you two call a lie?

⁵² – in both (there are) two of every (kind of) fruit – ⁵³ Which of the blessings of your Lord will you two call a lie?

⁵⁴ – (they are) reclining on couches lined with brocade, and fresh fruit of both gardens is near (at hand) – ⁵⁵ Which of the blessings of your Lord will you two call a lie?

⁵⁶ – in them (there are maidens) restraining (their) glances – no man or jinn has had sex with them before them – ⁵⁷ Which of the blessings of your Lord will you two call a lie?

⁵⁸ – as if they were rubies and coral – ⁵⁹ Which of the blessings of your Lord will you two call a lie?

⁶⁰ Is the payment for good anything but the good? ⁶¹ Which of the blessings of your Lord will you two call a lie?

⁶² And besides these two (there are another) two gardens – ⁶³ Which of the blessings of your Lord will you two call a lie?

⁶⁴ – deep green – ⁶⁵ Which of the blessings of your Lord will you two call a lie?

⁶⁶ – in both (there are) two springs gushing forth – ⁶⁷ Which of the blessings of your Lord will you two call a lie?

⁶⁸ – in both (there are) fruit, and date palms, and pomegranates – ⁶⁹ Which of the blessings of your Lord will you two call a lie?

⁷⁰ – in them (there are) good and beautiful (maidens) – ⁷¹ Which of the blessings of your Lord will you two call a lie?

⁷² – dark-eyed (maidens), confined in tents – ⁷³ Which of the blessings of your Lord will you two call a lie?

55.46 – *But for the one who fears the position of his Lord*

This sūra's end time vision is weighted toward reward (vv. 46–76). The vision seems typically Middle Eastern with fruit of the "date palms and pomegranates" (v. 68). See "Eschatology in the Quran" (p. 604).

55.56 – *in them (there are maidens) restraining (their) glances – no man or jinn has had sex with them before them*

Such descriptions (also in vv. 70–74) have attracted the attention of non-Muslims. What do they mean to say about the characteristics of the "Gardens"? See the comment at 44.54 on "(maidens) with dark, wide eyes" (p. 497).

⁷⁴ – no man or jinn has had sex with them before them – ⁷⁵ Which of the blessings of your Lord will you two call a lie?

⁷⁶ – (they are) reclining on green cushions and beautiful carpets – ⁷⁷ Which of the blessings of your Lord will you two call a lie?

⁷⁸ Blessed (be) the name of your Lord, full of splendor and honor.

THE FALLING
AL-WĀQIʿA

56

A detailed picture of the "Gardens of Bliss" in the hereafter dominates this sūra, painted deftly by short verses often of only two or three words. Punishments are also graphically portrayed but not as extensively. A later part of the sūra poses a series of questions that may remind the reader of God's questions to Job in Job 38–41.

In the Name of God, the Merciful, the Compassionate.

[1] When the falling falls [2] – at its falling there will be no calling (it) a lie – [3] bringing low, raising high, [4] when the earth is violently shaken, [5] and the mountains utterly crumble, [6] and become scattered dust, [7] and you become three classes: [8] the companions on the right – what are the companions on the right? [9] And the companions on the left – what are the companions on the left? [10] And the foremost.

The foremost [11] – those are the ones brought near, [12] in Gardens of Bliss – [13] a host from the ones of old, [14] but few from the later (generations) – [15] on well-woven couches, [16] reclining on them, facing each other. [17] Boys of eternal youth will circulate among them, [18] with cups and pitchers, and a cup from a flowing spring [19] – they do not suffer any headache from it, nor do they become drunk – [20] and with fruit of their own choosing, [21] and the meat of birds of their own desiring, [22] and (maidens) with dark, wide eyes [23] like hidden pearls [24] – a reward

---

56.1 – *When the falling falls*

The event that signals the end of the world will shake the earth.

56.7 – *and you become three classes*

At the end, humanity will be divided into those on the right hand, those on the left hand, and "the foremost" (v. 10).

These "foremost" will be rewarded with "Gardens of Bliss" (vv. 10–26).

56.22–23 – *and (maidens) with dark, wide eyes like hidden pearls*

Such descriptions (also in vv. 35–38) have attracted the attention of non-Muslims. What do they mean to say about the characteristics of the heavenly "Gardens"? See the comment at 44.54 on "(maidens) with dark, wide eyes" (p. 497).

for what they have done. [25] There they will not hear any frivolous or sinful talk, [26] only the saying, 'Peace! Peace!'

[27] The companions on the right – what are the companions of the right? [28] (They will be) in (the midst of) thornless lote trees, [29] and acacia trees one after another, [30] and extensive shade, [31] and flowing water, [32] and many fruits [33] – unlimited, unforbidden – [34] and raised couches. [35] Surely We produced them specially, [36] and made them virgins, [37] amorous, (all) of the same age, [38] for the companions on the right. [39] A host from the ones of old, [40] and a host from the later (generations).

[41] The companions on the left – what are the companions on the left? [42] (They will be) in (the midst of) scorching (fire) and boiling (water), [43] and a shadow of black smoke, [44] neither cool nor kind. [45] Surely before (this) they were affluent, [46] and persisted in the great refusal, [47] and used to say, 'When we are dead, and turned to dust and bones, shall we indeed be raised up? [48] And our fathers of old (too)?' [49] Say: 'Surely those of old and the later (generations) [50] will indeed be gathered to the meeting of a known Day. [51] Then surely you – you who have gone astray and called (it) a lie! – [52] will indeed eat from the tree of Zaqqūm, [53] and fill your bellies from it, [54] and drink on (top of) it from boiling water, [55] drinking like the thirsty (camel) drinks.' [56] This will be their reception on the Day of Judgment.

[57] We created you. Why will you not affirm (it)? [58] Do you see what you emit? [59] Do you create it, or are We the Creators? [60] We have decreed death (to be)

56.27 – *The companions on the right*

This second group will be similarly rewarded (vv. 28–40).

56.35–38 – *Surely We produced them specially, and made them virgins, amorous*

Verse 36 says that Allah has "made them virgins" for the "companions on the right." On this description, see the comment at verse 22.

56.41 – *The companions on the left*

These sinners (v. 46) and disbelievers (v. 47) will experience the most excruciating punishment (vv. 42–56). For further discussion of the Quran's visions of life after death, See "Eschatology in the Quran" (p. 604).

56.57 – *We created you. Why will you not affirm (it)?*

Allah asks a long series of questions of the reader or listener (vv. 57–87) that brings to mind Yahweh's questioning in Job 38–41. The central question seems to be in verse 70: "Why are you not thankful?"

56.59 – *or are We the Creators?*

Not only is this expression in the first-person plural *we*, but the noun *Creators* is also plural (*khāliqūn*), raising a question about the concept of deity represented in

among you – We are not (to be) outrun – ⁶¹ so that We may exchange the likes of you, and (re)produce you in what you do not know. ⁶² Certainly you have known the first growth. Why will you not take heed? ⁶³ Do you see what you cultivate? ⁶⁴ Do you (yourselves) sow it, or are We the Sowers? ⁶⁵ If We (so) pleased, We could indeed make it broken debris, and you would be left rejoicing, ⁶⁶ 'Surely we have incurred debt indeed! ⁶⁷ No! We have been robbed!' ⁶⁸ Do you see the water which you drink? ⁶⁹ Do you send it down from the clouds, or are We the Ones who send (it) down? ⁷⁰ If We (so) pleased, We could make it bitter. Why are you not thankful? ⁷¹ Do you see the fire which you ignite? ⁷² Do you produce the timber for it, or are We the Ones who produce (it)? ⁷³ We have made it a reminder and a provision for the desert dwellers. ⁷⁴ So glorify the name of your Lord, the Almighty.

⁷⁵ I swear by the fallings of the stars ⁷⁶ – surely it is a great oath indeed, if (only) you knew – ⁷⁷ surely it is an honorable Qur'ān indeed, ⁷⁸ in a hidden Book! ⁷⁹ No one touches it but the purified. ⁸⁰ (It is) a sending down from the Lord of the worlds.

⁸¹ Do you hold this proclamation in disdain, ⁸² and do you make it your living to call (it) a lie? ⁸³ Why not, when the life of the dying man leaps into his throat, ⁸⁴ and you are looking on ⁸⁵ – though We are nearer to him than you, only you do not see (Us) – ⁸⁶ why, if you are not (to be) judged, ⁸⁷ do you not return it, if you are truthful? ⁸⁸ If he is one of those brought near, ⁸⁹ (there will be) comfort, and fragrance, and a Garden of Bliss. ⁹⁰ And if he is one of the companions on the right: ⁹¹ 'Peace (be) to you, from the companions on the right!' ⁹² But if he is one of those who called (it) a lie (and) went astray, ⁹³ (there will be) a reception of boiling (water) ⁹⁴ and burning in a Furnace. ⁹⁵ Surely this – it indeed is the certain truth. ⁹⁶ So glorify the name of your Lord, the Almighty.

---

this passage. Here the translator A. J. Droge has provided a direct translation of the verse where a number of Muslim translators have rendered the noun singular.

56.77–78 – *surely it is an honorable Qur'ān indeed, in a hidden Book!*

The self-referential claims in verses 77–80 became an important passage for the Islamic doctrine of scripture. At the center is the assertion that the recitation is a "sending down" (*tanzīl*) from the "Lord of the worlds." On the word *qur'ān*, see the comment at 2.185 (p. 61).

The expression in verse 78, "a hidden Book," has often been put together with another expression in 85.22 ("a guarded Tablet") to support a belief in a preexisting archetype of the Quran kept safe in heaven. Another belief from verse 79 is that no one should touch the pages of the book except Muslims who have performed ablutions. See the discussion of the Quran's "doctrine of scripture" at 85.21–22 (p. 624).

57

The central part of Sūra 57 is an appeal to the listener or reader to contribute or "spend" in the way of Allah as well as a promise of rewards for those who believe in Allah and his messengers. Rewards and punishments on the Day of Resurrection are further envisioned in a substantial judgment scene.

Near the end of the sūra, mention of ʿĪsā and his followers introduces some interesting expressions and provides an opportunity to consider the identity of ʿĪsā in the Quran.

In the Name of God, the Merciful, the Compassionate

¹ Whatever is in the heavens and the earth glorifies God. He is the Mighty, the Wise. ² To Him (belongs) the kingdom of the heavens and the earth. He gives life and causes death. He is powerful over everything. ³ He is the First and the Last, the Outer and the Inner. He has knowledge of everything. ⁴ He (it is) who created the heavens and the earth in six days. Then He mounted the throne. He knows what penetrates into the earth, and what comes forth from it, and what comes down from the sky, and what goes up into it. He is with you wherever you are. God sees what you do. ⁵ To Him (belongs) the kingdom of the heavens and the earth, and to God (all) matters are returned. ⁶ He causes the night to pass into the day, and causes the day to pass into the night. He knows what is in the hearts.

⁷ Believe in God and His messenger, and contribute from what He has made

---

57.1 – *Whatever is in the heavens and the earth glorifies God*

This lovely opening passage (vv. 1–6) offers a number of valuable materials for a description of the theology of the Quran. Verse 1 repeats at the beginnings of Sūras 59; 61; 62; and 64.

57.7 – *Believe in God and His messenger, and contribute*

This verse begins a short passage (vv. 7–11) that exhorts the believers to contribute – or "spend" – "in the way of Allah." The contributing envisioned accompanies fighting (*qātala*, v. 10) and seems to suggest a battle scene.

This verse associates the messenger with Allah as deserving of belief. The mes-

you inheritors in. Those of you who believe and contribute – for them (there will be) a great reward. [8] What is (the matter) with you that you do not believe in God, when the messenger calls you to believe in your Lord, and He has already taken a covenant with you, if you are believers? [9] He (it is) who sends down on His servant clear signs, so that He may bring you forth from the darkness to the light. Surely God is indeed kind (and) compassionate with you.

[10] What is (the matter) with you that you do not contribute in the way of God, when the inheritance of the heavens and the earth (belongs) to God? The one among you who contributed and fought before the victory is not equal. They are higher in rank than those who contributed and fought after that. Yet to each God has promised the good (reward). God is aware of what you do. [11] Who is the one who will lend to God a good loan, and He will double it for him? For him (there will be) a generous reward.

[12] On the Day when you see the believing men and the believing women: their light will run before them, and at their right (hands): 'Good news for you today! Gardens through which rivers flow, there to remain. That is the great triumph!'

[13] On the Day when the hypocrite men and the hypocrite women will say to those who believed: 'Wait for us! Let us borrow your light!' It will be said, 'Turn back and search for a light!' And a wall with a door will be set up between them: on the inside of it (there is) mercy, and on the outside of it – facing (it) – (there is) the punishment. [14] They will call out to them: 'Were we not with you?' They will say, 'Yes, indeed! But you tempted yourselves, and you waited and doubted, and wishful thinking deceived you, until the command of God came, and the Deceiver deceived you about God. [15] So today no ransom will be accepted from you, nor from those who have disbelieved. Your refuge is the Fire – it is your protector – and it is an evil destination!'

[16] Is it not time for those who believe that their hearts become humble before the Reminder of God, and (before) what has come down of the truth, and (that) they not be like those to whom the Book was given before, and for whom the time lasted too long, so that their hearts became hard, and many of them were wicked? [17] Know that God gives the earth life after its death. We have made clear to you the signs, so that you may understand.

---

senger exhorts the listeners to believe in Allah (v. 8), and a later verse commands the "believers" to believe in the messenger (v. 28).

57.12 – *On the Day when you see the believing men and the believing women*

This verse begins a judgment scene in which the believers are given their reward but the hypocrites are punished with "the Fire" (vv. 13–15).

[18] Surely the charitable men and the charitable women, and (those who) have lent to God a good loan – it will be doubled for them, and for them (there will be) a generous reward. [19] Those who believe in God and His messengers, those – they are the truthful and the martyrs in the sight of their Lord – they have their reward and their light. But those who disbelieve and call Our signs a lie – those are the companions of the Furnace.

[20] Know that this present life is nothing but jest and diversion, and a (passing) splendor, and a (cause for) boasting among you, and a rivalry in wealth and children. (It is) like rain: the vegetation it produces pleases the disbelievers, (but) then it withers and you see it turning yellow, (and) then it becomes broken debris. In the Hereafter (there is) a harsh punishment, [21] and forgiveness from God and approval. But this present life is nothing but the enjoyment of deception.

Race toward forgiveness from your Lord, and a Garden – its width is like the width of the sky and the earth – prepared for those who believe in God and His messengers. That is the favor of God. He gives it to whomever He pleases. God is full of great favor. [22] No smiting smites in the earth or among yourselves, except that it was in a Book before We brought it about – surely that is easy for God – [23] so that you may not grieve over what eludes you, nor gloat about what has come to you. God does not love anyone who is arrogant (and) boastful, [24] (nor) those who are stingy and command the people to be stingy. Whoever turns away – surely God – He is the wealthy One, the Praiseworthy.

[25] Certainly We sent Our messengers with the clear signs, and We sent down with them the Book and the scale, so that the people might uphold justice. And We sent down iron – in which (there is) harsh violence, but (also) benefits for the people – and (We did so) in order that God might know who would help Him and His messengers in the unseen. Surely God is strong, mighty.

[26] Certainly We sent Noah and Abraham, and We placed among his descendants the prophetic office and the Book. Yet (there was only the occasional) one of them who was (rightly) guided, but many of them were wicked. [27] Then in their footsteps We followed up with Our messengers, and We followed up with

---

57.27 – *We followed up with Jesus, son of Mary*

The Quran pictures ʿĪsā following in the line of earlier messengers (see also 5.46; cf. 61.5–6). The three longest passages about ʿĪsā are in the third, fifth, and nineteenth sūras, and the fourth and fifth sūras contain several very important short passages. After 57.27 in the canonical progression, the name ʿĪsā only appears twice (at 61.6, 14).

The portrayal of ʿĪsā in the Quran is of great interest to Christians. The Quran devotes some ninety verses to ʿĪsā, sixty-four of these about the birth of ʿĪsā in Sūras 3 and 19. The remaining twenty-six verses contain significant repetition, reducing the

Jesus, son of Mary, and gave him the Gospel, and placed in the hearts of those who followed him kindness and mercy. But monasticism, they originated it. We did not prescribe it for them. (It) only (arose out of their) seeking the approval

---

basic material on 'Īsā's adult life and ministry. For example, two verses contain similar content about 'Īsā's miracles (3.49; 5.110). For an analysis of these miracle verses, see 5.110 (p. 153).

For an explanation of the name 'Īsā, see the comment at 2.87 (p. 48). Like the Quran's alteration of the name of Jesus, much of the most important content on 'Īsā is a matter of confusion or denial of the identity of Jesus in the New Testament. See "The Death of Jesus in the Quran" (p. 314). For analyses and responses to verses denying the deity of 'Īsā, see 43.59 and 64 (p. 491–92). For the verses denying "Son of God," see "Son of God in the Quran" (p. 352).

The controversy sparked by quranic denials may cause readers to lose sight of the many serious gaps in the Quran's description of 'Īsā. The Quran tells nothing about the suffering of Jesus, a major theme in the Gospel accounts. There is nothing about the teachings of Jesus – including material on response to conflict that could profitably interact with the Quran's commands to fight and kill. No narrative context is provided for the miracle verses that could show the compassionate behavior of Jesus with the individuals involved. No hint is given of Jesus' polemical encounters with religious authorities, the hatred and enmity that his personal claims provoked, or the trial before the "chief priests and teachers of the law" that declared Jesus worthy of death. The Quran calls 'Īsā "Messiah," but never explains the meaning of this crucial name (see the comment at 3.45, p. 85).

57.27 – *and gave him the Gospel*

This verse says that Allah gives 'Īsā the Gospel (*injīl*), repeating the statement at 5.46 (cf. 19.30). The Quran also says that Allah teaches 'Īsā the Gospel (3.48; 5.110) or "sends down" the Gospel (3.3, 65).

The Quran's twelve references to the Gospel certainly show an awareness of the existence of the Christian scripture. The references also include exhortations to the People of the Book to observe the Torah and Gospel (5.66, 68) and claims for what the Gospel contains (7.157; 9.111; 48.29).

All the passages in which the Quran names the Gospel are uniformly positive and respectful. However, much of what the Quran says about the Gospel is false. The Gospel was not given to Jesus (or taught or revealed), but rather the Gospel is the good news *about* Jesus. As David Shenk writes, Jesus left not a book but a community (see his *Journeys of the Muslim Nation and the Christian Church* in the bibliography). The Gospel does not contain a mention of Islam's messenger, as claimed in 7.157.

of God. Yet they did not observe it as it should have been observed. So We gave those of them who believed their reward, but many of them were wicked.

²⁸ You who believe! Guard (yourselves) against God and believe in His messenger! He will give you a double portion of His mercy, and will make a light for you by means of which you will walk, and He will forgive you – God is forgiving, compassionate – ²⁹ so that the People of the Book may know that they have no power over any of the favor of God, and that favor is in the hand of God. He gives it to whomever He pleases. God is full of great favor.

The Gospel contains neither a promise that "believers" shall "fight in the way of Allah and they kill and are killed" (9.111), nor a suggestion that Jesus and his disciples fight against their enemies (61.14; cf. 3.52). Quite the opposite. These falsehoods contribute toward a very different portrayal of the New Testament Jesus by the quranic ʿĪsā.

57.27 – *and placed in the hearts of those who followed him kindness and mercy*

This verse describes the followers of ʿĪsā in a positive and generous way, as having "compassion (*raʾfa*) and mercy (*raḥma*)" in their hearts. The expression brings to mind another verse that describes Christians as closest in affection (*mawadda*) to the "believers" and not proud (5.82). May Christians today act toward Muslims (and all others) with kindness, humility, and affection!

The Quran is not against monks (*ruhbān*, 5.82), but it opposes taking them as lords (9.31) and here in 57.27 criticizes monasticism (*rahbāniyya*) as an invention that Christians in any case do not observe properly.

The Disputer
Al-Mujādila

58

At this point in the canonical progression, fifty-seven sūras remain – the same number as have already been read. However, the final fifty-seven sūras make up only one tenth of the total volume of the Quran.

The sūras in this final 10 percent become increasingly shorter, some as short as three verses. Many contain explosive descriptions of the end times. Muslim scholars believe that most of these sūras were first recited in Mecca – reflecting a kind of preaching that does not invoke political power and violence. Exceptions to this trend include the first six sūras, labelled by Muslim scholars as recited in Medina.

In the Name of God, the Merciful, the Compassionate

[1] God has heard the words of the woman who disputes with you about her husband, and (who) complains to God, and God hears the discussion of the two of you. Surely God is hearing, seeing. [2] Those of you who declare their wives to be as their mothers' backs – they are not their mothers. Their mothers are only those who gave them birth. Surely they indeed say a wrong word and a falsehood. Yet surely God is indeed pardoning (and) forgiving. [3] Those who declare their wives to be as their mothers' backs, (and) then return to what they have said, (the penalty is) the setting free of a slave before the two of them touch each other. That is what you are admonished. God is aware of what you do. [4] Whoever does not find (the means to do that), (the penalty is) a fast for two months consecutively, before the two of them touch each other. And whoever

---

58.1 – *God has heard the words of the woman who disputes with you about her husband*

Muslim tradition suggests a name for this "woman who disputes," *Khawlah bint Thaʿlaba*, along with a story about her dispute about her husband. The Quran passage itself (vv. 1–4), however, is a good example of how the Quran declines to give the names of almost all of the contemporary actors within its pages. The important point is that these verses deal with an extremely particular and occasional concern.

is not able (to do that), (the penalty is) the feeding of sixty poor persons. That is so that you may believe in God and His messenger. Those are the limits (set by) God – and for the disbelievers (there will be) a painful punishment.

⁵ Surely those who oppose God and His messenger have been disgraced, as those before them were disgraced. We have already sent down clear signs – and for the disbelievers (there will be) a humiliating punishment, ⁶ on the Day when God will raise them up – all (of them) – and inform them about what they have done. God has counted it up, though they have forgotten it. God is a witness over everything.

⁷ Do you not see that God knows whatever is in the heavens and whatever is on the earth? There is no secret talk of three men but He is the fourth of them, nor of five men but He is the sixth of them, nor less than that, nor more, but He is with them wherever they may be. Then on the Day of Resurrection He will inform them about what they have done. Surely God has knowledge of everything.

⁸ Do you not see those who were forbidden from secret talk, (and) then return to what they were forbidden, and converse secretly in sin and enmity and disobedience to the messenger? And when they come to you, they greet you with what God does not greet you with, and they say within themselves, 'If only God would punish us for what we say.' Gehenna will be enough for them, where they will burn – and it is an evil destination!

⁹ You who believe! When you converse secretly, do not converse in sin and enmity and disobedience to the messenger, but converse in piety and the guarding (of yourselves). Guard (yourselves) against God, to whom you will be gathered. ¹⁰ Secret talk is only from Satan, so that he may cause those who believe to grieve. But he will not harm them at all, except by the permission of God. In God let the believers put their trust.

¹¹ You who believe! When it is said to you 'Make room in the assemblies,' make room! God will make room for you. And when it is said, 'Rise up,' rise up! God will raise in rank those of you who have believed and those who have been given knowledge. God is aware of what you do.

58.5 – *Surely those who oppose God and His messenger have been disgraced*

Muslims believe that Sūra 58 was first recited in Medina, and like others in this category it frequently associates Allah with his messenger. This sūra holds the two together for trust (v. 4) and obedience (v. 13). It repeatedly exhorts the audience not to oppose them (vv. 5, 20, 22). Here the two also conquer together (v. 21).

58.8 – *Do you not see those who were forbidden from secret talk . . . ?*

Another example of a very particular, personal matter involving the messenger.

¹² You who believe! When you converse privately with the messenger, send forward a freewill offering before your private talk. That is better for you and purer. If you do not find (the means to do so) – God is forgiving, compassionate. ¹³ Are you afraid to send forward freewill offerings before your private talk? When you do not (do so), and God has turned to you (in forgiveness), observe the prayer and give the alms, and obey God and His messenger. God is aware of what you do.

¹⁴ Do you not see those who have taken as allies a people with whom God is angry? They are neither of you nor of them. They swear upon lies – and they know (it). ¹⁵ God has prepared a harsh punishment for them. Surely they – evil indeed is what they have done! ¹⁶ They have taken their oaths as a cover, and kept (people) from the way of God. For them (there will be) a humiliating punishment. ¹⁷ Neither their wealth nor their children will be of any use against God. Those are the companions of the Fire. There they will remain. ¹⁸ On the Day when God will raise them up – all (of them) – they will swear to Him as they swear to you, and think they (are standing) on something. Is it not a fact that they – they are the liars? ¹⁹ Satan has prevailed over them, and made them forget the Reminder of God. Those are the faction of Satan. Is it not a fact that the faction of Satan – they are the losers? ²⁰ Surely those who oppose God and His messenger – they will be among the most humiliated. ²¹ God has written, 'I shall indeed conquer – I and My messengers!' Surely God is strong, mighty.

²² You will not find a people who believe in God and the Last Day loving anyone who opposes God and His messenger, even if they were their fathers, or their sons, or their brothers, or their clan. Those – He has written belief on their hearts, and supported them with a spirit from Him, and will cause them to enter Gardens through which rivers flow, there to remain. God is pleased with them, and they are pleased with Him. Those are the faction of God. Is it not a fact that the faction of God – they are the ones who prosper?

58.22 – *You will not find a people who believe in God and the Last Day loving anyone who opposes God and His messenger*

This verse says that no love should be spared for those who oppose Allah and his messenger, even if they are close members of the same family. This theme reappears at 60.1. However, this verse also seems to say that "a spirit from Him" would affirm this lack of love for enemies. On "the spirit" (*rūḥ*) in the Quran, see the analysis at 97.4 (p. 639).

THE GATHERING
AL-ḤASHR

59

> Sūra 59 includes another example of a quranic passage that has been closely connected with a particular event in the Muslim story of Islamic origins.
>
> The sūra itself gives no details of time, place, or people; "People of the Book" is the closest it comes to identifying the actors. In Muslim narratives, this sūra is intertwined with the story of the expulsion of the Banū Naḍīr, a Jewish tribe in Medina (*Raids*, 186–88; *Sīra*, 437–39; cf. *History*, 7:156–61).

In the Name of God, the Merciful, the Compassionate

[1] Whatever is in the heavens and whatever is on the earth glorifies God. He is the Mighty, the Wise.

[2] He (it is) who expelled those of the People of the Book who disbelieved from their homes for the first gathering. You did not think that they would go forth, and they thought that their strongholds would defend them against God. But God came upon them from where they were not expecting, and cast dread into their hearts. They destroyed their houses with their (own) hands and

---

59.2 – *He (it is) who expelled those of the People of the Book who disbelieved*

This and the following verses make Allah the one who expels a group from the People of the Book. The reason for their expulsion is that they "opposed Allah and His messenger" (v. 4). Allah casts terror into their hearts (v. 2) and prescribes exile for them. According to verse 3, if this group had not been expelled, Allah would have punished them in this world. Muslim commentaries have connected these verses with the story of the expulsion from Medina of a Jewish tribe called the Banū Naḍīr.

The expression "casting terror (or 'dread,' *ruʿb*) into hearts" repeats at 3.151; 8.12; and 33.26. A related term, *rahba* ("terror," "fear"), appears in verse 13 and again in its verbal form at 8.60 (*arhaba*, "terrorize"). All of these terms appear in contexts of apparent armed conflict, and in two cases they relate to the believers' treatment of groups from the People of the Book (33.26; 59.2). This language in the Quran is relevant to the questions in the modern world about religion-based "terrorism" and "terrorists."

the hands of the believers. Learn a lesson, you who have sight! ³ If God had not prescribed exile for them, He would indeed have punished them in this world – and for them (there is) the punishment of the Fire in the Hereafter. ⁴ That is because they opposed God and His messenger. Whoever opposes God – surely God is harsh in retribution.

⁵ Whatever palm trees you cut down, or left standing on their roots – (it was) was by the permission of God, and (it was) so that He might disgrace the wicked. ⁶ What God has given to His messenger (as spoils) from them – you did not spur on any horse or camel for it, but God gives authority to His messengers over whomever He pleases. God is powerful over everything. ⁷ What God has given to His messenger (as spoils) from the people of the towns (belongs) to God and to the messenger, and to family, and the orphans, and the poor, and the traveler, so that it does not (just) circulate among the wealthy of you. Whatever (spoils) the messenger gives you, take it, and whatever he forbids you, stop (asking for it). Guard (yourselves) against God! Surely God is harsh in retribution.

⁸ (Spoils belong) to the poor emigrants, who were expelled from their homes and their wealth, seeking favor from God and approval, and helping God and His messenger. Those – they are the truthful. ⁹ And those who settled in 'the home' and in belief before them, they love whoever emigrates to them, and do not find in their hearts any need for what they have been given, but prefer (emigrants) above themselves, even though there is poverty among them. Whoever is guarded against his own greed, those – they are the ones who prosper. ¹⁰ Those who came after them say, 'Our Lord, forgive us and our brothers, who preceded us in belief, and do not place any rancor in our hearts toward those who believe. Our Lord, surely You are kind (and) compassionate.'

¹¹ Do you not see those who have played the hypocrite? They say to their brothers who disbelieve among the People of the Book, 'If indeed you are

---

59.6 – *God gives authority to His messengers over whomever He pleases*

In the midst of a passage (vv. 5–10) that seems to be about the spoils flowing to the messenger from the expelled People of the Book, the Quran says that Allah gives messengers power or "authority" over others. This verse is similar to 3.26, the wording of which is also found on a plaque that was posted above the eastern door of the Dome of the Rock in Jerusalem.

Needy people benefit from the spoils as well (vv. 7–8).

59.11 – *Do you not see those who have played the hypocrite?*

From this passage (vv. 11–17), it seems that certain "hypocrites" have promised help to the affected group from the People of the Book. But when the attack on the group starts, the hypocrites are struck with fear (v. 13) and prove false.

expelled, we shall indeed go forth with you, and we shall never obey anyone concerning you. And if you are fought against, we shall indeed help you.' God bears witness: 'Surely they are liars indeed!' ¹² If indeed they are expelled, they will not go forth with them, and if indeed they are fought against, they will not help them. And if indeed they do help them, they will indeed turn their backs. Then they will not be helped. ¹³ Indeed you (strike) greater fear in their hearts than God. That is because they are a people who do not understand. ¹⁴ They will not fight against you all together, except in fortified towns or from behind walls. Their violence among themselves is (so) harsh, you (might) think them all (united) together, but their hearts are divided. That is because they are a people who have no sense. ¹⁵ (They are) like those who shortly before them tasted the consequence of their action – for them (there is) a painful punishment. ¹⁶ (They are) like Satan, when he said to the human, 'Disbelieve!,' and when he disbelieved, he said, 'Surely I am free of you. Surely I fear God, Lord of the worlds.' ¹⁷ So the end of both of them is: they will both be in the Fire, (and) there they both will remain. That is the payment of the evildoers.

¹⁸ You who believe! Guard (yourselves) against God, and let each person look to what he sends forward for tomorrow. Guard (yourselves) against God! Surely God is aware of what you do. ¹⁹ Do not be like those who forgot God, and He caused them to forget their own selves. Those – they are the wicked. ²⁰ The companions of the Fire and the companions of the Garden are not equal. The companions of the Garden – they are the triumphant. ²¹ If We had sent down this Qur'ān on a mountain, you would indeed have seen it humbled (and) split apart out of the fear of God. These parables – We strike them for the people so that they will reflect.

²² He is God, the One who – (there is) no god but Him – is the Knower of the unseen and the seen. He is the Merciful, the Compassionate.

59.13 – *you (strike) greater fear in their hearts than God*

The opening of this sūra says that Allah cast dread into the hearts of the People of the Book. This verse says that that "believers" bring more terror or "fear" (*rahba*) to the "disbelievers" than Allah. On terror and terrorizing see the comment at verse 2.

59.22 – *He is God, the One who*

The sūra ends with a striking statement about Allah (vv. 22–24) that proclaims him to be "the Peace" (*al-salām*, v. 23).

The placement of "Peace" to describe Allah, following verses in which Allah expels people, casts terror into hearts (v. 2), and is "harsh in retribution" (v. 7), alongside being a compeller or "Sole Ruler" (*jabbār*, lit. "tyrant," v. 23), makes for an interesting theological reflection.

[23] He is God, the One who – (there is) no god but Him – is the King, the Holy One, the Peace, the Faithful, the Preserver, the Mighty, the Sole Ruler, the Magnificent. Glory to God above what they associate!

[24] He is God – the Creator, the Maker, the Fashioner. To Him (belong) the best names. Whatever is in the heavens and the earth glorifies Him. He is the Mighty, the Wise.

THE EXAMINED
WOMAN
AL-MUMTAHANA

60

This sūra begins with a command not to show friendship or love to enemies. Later in the sūra, however, several verses qualify what kind of enemy is beyond the possibility of friendship.

In order to illustrate – or justify – this attitude toward enemies, the sūra states that this was the pattern of Abraham. Here Abraham is presented as saying to those who worship a god other than Allah that enmity and hatred between him and them would be eternal.

In the Name of God, the Merciful, the Compassionate

[1] You who believe! Do not take My enemy and your enemy as allies. Do you offer them friendship when they have disbelieved in the truth which has come to you, expelling the messenger and you because you believe in God your Lord? If you have gone forth to struggle in My way and to seek My approval, do you keep secret (your) friendship for them? I know what you hide and what you speak

---

60.1 – *Do you offer them friendship when they have disbelieved . . . ?*

Sūra 60 is another of the sūras that seem to come out of a battle situation. The opening verse commands "believers" not to take their enemies as friends. Why offer enemies love (*mawadda*) if they oppose the messenger and disbelieve in his preaching? The answer appears in 58.22: "believers" will not love those who oppose Allah and his messenger.

Later in the sūra, the Quran allows love to enemies "who have not fought you in the (matter of) religion" (60.7–9).

60.1 – *If you have gone forth to struggle in My way*

"Struggle" here translates the Arabic word *jihād*. This particular noun appears only four times in the Quran (also 9.24; 22.78; 25.52). The sense of *jihad* that the Quran intends in each of these occurrences may be partly determined by context. If the context is a battle scene, or if *jihad* appears close to vocabulary of fighting (*qātala*, vv. 8, 9), *jihad* tends to pick up the sense of fighting. See "Jihad in the Quran" (p. 368).

558

aloud. Whoever of you does that has gone astray from the right way. [2] If they come upon you, they will be enemies to you, and will stretch out their hands and their tongues with evil against you, and want you to disbelieve. [3] Neither your family ties nor your children will benefit you on the Day of Resurrection. He will distinguish between you. God sees what you do.

[4] There was a good example for you in Abraham, and those who were with him, when they said to their people, 'Surely we are free of you and what you serve instead of God. We repudiate you, and between us and you enmity has shown itself, and hatred forever, until you believe in God alone' – except for Abraham's saying to his father: 'I shall indeed ask forgiveness for you, but I have no power from God to (benefit) you at all' – 'Our Lord, in You we put our trust, to You we turn (in repentance), and to You is the (final) destination. [5] Our Lord, do not make us an (object of) persecution for those who disbelieve, but forgive us, Our Lord. Surely You – You are the Mighty, the Wise.' [6] Certainly there was a good example for you in them – for whoever hopes in God and the Last Day. But whoever turns away – surely God – He is the wealthy One, the Praiseworthy.

[7] It may be that God will (yet) establish friendship between you and those of them with whom you are on hostile terms. God is powerful, and God is forgiving, compassionate. [8] God does not forbid you from those who have not fought you in the (matter of) religion, and have not expelled you from your homes, that you should do good and act fairly toward them. Surely God loves the ones who act fairly. [9] God only forbids you from those who have fought you in the (matter of) religion, and have expelled you from your homes, and have supported your expulsion, that you should take them as allies. Whoever takes them as allies, those – they are the evildoers.

60.4 – *between us and you enmity has shown itself, and hatred forever*

On the basis of his people's worship of a god other than Allah, Abraham repudiates them and declares eternal enmity (*'adāwa*) and hatred (*baghḍā'*) toward them. The Quran presents this as a "good example" for the "believers." The tone of this eighth version of Abraham's disputation with idolaters is significantly different from other versions (e.g., 26.69–102). See "Abraham in the Quran" (p. 90).

60.7 – *It may be that God will (yet) establish friendship between you*

The Quran allows friendship with enemies that do not fight against the Muslims, but it repeats the prohibition of love for those who oppose them in battle.

60.8 – *Surely God loves the ones who act fairly*

The Quran contains twenty-two statements about the kinds of people whom Allah loves. Those who act fairly (*muqsiṭīn*) are among the most frequent objects of Allah's love (also 5.42; 49.9).

The Language of Love in the Quran

Gordon Nickel

The question of whether God loves is one that people often ask when they want to understand a religion's concept of God.

The Quran certainly contains many statements about the love of Allah for humans. In the Quran, Allah loves people who do good and are just, but does not love people who do evil or are proud and boastful.

Only a few verses discuss human love for Allah or the love of humans for each other. The Quran contains no commandment to love either Allah or other humans.

The two Arabic verbs that the Quran uses to express love are *ahabba* and *wadda*. The most common of these verbs, *ahabba*, appears sixty-four times in the Quran. In forty-six instances, the subject of the verb is Allah and the objects are various people. Some twenty-two statements specify people whom Allah loves, and twenty-four statements indicate people whom Allah does not love.

Allah loves the "doers of good" (*muhsinūn*; 2.195; 3.134, 148; 5.93), the "ones who act fairly" (*muqsitūn*, 5.42; 49.9; 60.8), and the "ones who guard (themselves)" (*muttaqūn*; 9.4, 7). These three objects of Allah's love appear most frequently among a total of fourteen different objects. On the other hand, Allah does not love the "evildoers" (*zālimūn*; 3.57, 140; 42.40), the "arrogant and boastful" (*mukhtālan fakhūran*; 4.36; 31.18; 57.23), and the "workers of corruption" (*mufsidūn*; 5.64; 28.77). There are fourteen kinds of people whom Allah does not love. The Quran says that Allah does not love the "prodigal" (*musrifūn*; 6.141; 7.31). This sets up a striking contrast to Jesus' parable of the "prodigal son" in the Gospel according to Luke 15:11–32. Other noteworthy statements are that Allah loves those who are "mighty toward the disbelievers" and "struggle in the way of Allah" (5.54), and those who fight in his way (61.4).

The noun for love related to the verb *ahabba*, *mahabba*, occurs only once in the Quran, in a story about the baby Moses. There Allah says, "I cast love on you [Moses] from me" (20.39). The noun *hubb* appears several times but never in relation to Allah's love.

The second verb for love in the Quran is *wadda*. The sixteen occurrences of this verb in Muslim scripture seem to relate to what humans "wish for." However, two words derived from this verb occur in relation to Allah. On the Day of Resurrection, Allah will assign love (*wudd*) to "those who believe and do righteous deeds" (19.96). The quranic prophet Shu'ayb describes his Lord as "loving" (*wadūd*) in 11.90, and the same term is used for Allah in 85.14.

Beyond the statements about Allah using these two verbs, the Quran contains a few verses that mention human love for Allah or human love for humans.

Human love for Allah seems to be mentioned in an incidental way, such as in 5.54: "Whoever of you turns back from his religion, Allah will bring (another) people whom He loves, and who love Him." Other verses mentioning human love for Allah are 2.165 and 3.31, and possibly 2.177 and 76.8.

Descriptions of human love for other humans seem similarly incidental: 3.119, 9.24, and 59.9 (using *aḥabba*); 5.82, 30.21, and 42.23 (using *wadda*). Among these verses is the statement that Christians are closer in affection to the Muslims (5.82) and the lovely verse, "He created spouses for you from yourselves, so that you may live with them, and he has established love and mercy between you" (30.21).

The Quran forbids love (*mawadda*) for enemies in 60.1 and then says that love may be possible for enemies who have not fought against the Muslims (60.7–8). Less compromising is the statement at 58.22 that "believers" will not love those who oppose Allah and his messenger.

The difference between the Quran's material on love and biblical teaching is more than simply the New Testament affirmation that the love of God is unconditional. The God who loved humanity "while we were still sinners" (Romans 5:8) is certainly quite different from the quranic portrait of Allah. But the biblical affirmation goes further: God demonstrated his love in history by sending his Son to die for humanity (1 John 4:9–10).

That divine demonstration of love becomes an example for human behavior: "Dear friends, since God so loved us, we also ought to love one another" (1 John 4:11).

Pakistani scholar Daud Rahbar discussed the love of the Quran's Allah in a Cambridge dissertation published as *God of Justice* (see bibliography). He later wrote that he saw the love of a "worshipable" God shown by the one who forgave his killers from the cross.

[10] You who believe! When believing women come to you as emigrants, examine them – God knows their belief – and if you know them to be believers, do not return them to the disbelievers. They are not permitted to them, nor are they

---

60.10 – *You who believe! When believing women come to you as emigrants*
The lack of names and places in this sūra makes it impossible to make sense of

are permitted to them. Give them what they have spent. (There is) no blame on you if marry them, when you have given them their marriage gifts. Do not hold to ties with disbelieving women, but ask (back) what you have spent, and let them ask (back) what they have spent. That is the judgment of God. He judges between you, and God is knowing, wise. [11] If any of your wives escape from you to the disbelievers, and you take retribution, give those whose wives have gone off the equivalent of what they have spent. Guard (yourselves) against God, in whom you believe.

[12] Prophet! When believing women come to you, swearing allegiance to you on (the condition) that they will not associate anything with God, and will not steal, and will not commit adultery, and will not kill their children, and will not bring a slander they have forged between their hands and their feet, and will not disobey you in anything right, accept their oath of allegiance, and ask forgiveness for them from God. Surely God is forgiving, compassionate.

[13] You who believe! Do not take as allies a people with whom God is angry. They have despaired of the Hereafter, even as the disbelievers have despaired of the companions of the graves.

---

verses 10–12. In Muslim tradition, however, these verses are linked with women who came from Mecca to join the Muslims in Medina during the treaty of Ḥudaybiyya (*Raids*, 311).

The Lines
Al-Ṣaff

61

Sūra 61 is well-known by many because it makes a number of striking claims about 'Īsā, the quranic Jesus. This sūra also presents the belief that Allah not only allows fighting but approves those who "fight in his way." Here "the messenger" is a "conqueror of all religion."

In the Name of God, the Merciful, the Compassionate

[1] Whatever is in the heavens and whatever is on the earth glorifies God. He is the Mighty, the Wise.

[2] You who believe! Why do you say what you do not do? [3] It is very hateful in the sight of God that you say what you do not do. [4] God loves those who fight in His way, (drawn up) in lines (for battle) as if they were a solid building.

[5] (Remember) when Moses said to his people, 'My people! Why do you hurt me, when you already know that I am the messenger of God to you?' Then, when they turned aside, God caused their hearts to turn aside, (for) God does not guide the people who are wicked. [6] And (remember) when Jesus, son of Mary, said, 'Sons of Israel! Surely I am the messenger of God to you, confirming

---

61.4 – *God loves those who fight in His way*

The Quran contains twenty-two statements about the kinds of people whom Allah loves. See "The Language of Love in the Quran" (p. 560).

When the Quran describes Allah's beloved as fighting "in his way (*sabīl*)," it makes a theological claim by associating Allah with human fighting – especially in this verse. This is a good example of a verse for which the generic "God" seems quite inadequate as an English translation for the quranic "Allah." The New Testament strongly opposes the idea that human fighting is God's way. See the analysis of the expression "to fight in Allah's way" at 73.20 (p. 597), and see "Allah in the Quran" (p. 572).

61.6 – *I am the messenger of God to you, confirming what was before me of the Torah*

The idea that 'Īsā "confirms" the Torah (also 3.50; 5.46) raises the interesting question of Jesus' relationship to the Old Testament.

According to the Gospel accounts, Jesus said that he had come not to abrogate

563

what was before me of the Torah, and bringing good news of a messenger who will come after me, whose name will be Aḥmad.' Then, when he brought them the clear signs, they said, 'This is clear magic.' [7] Who is more evil than the one

---

"the Law or the Prophets" but to fulfill them (Matthew 5:17). He then commanded his disciples to turn the other cheek and love their enemies (Matthew 5:39, 44). Jesus also explained to his disciples the passages in "the Law of Moses, the Prophets and the Psalms" that were written about him (Luke 24:44; also 24:27). He highlighted especially the fulfillment of prophecies in the Hebrew Bible that "the Messiah will suffer and rise from the dead on the third day, and repentance and forgiveness of sins will be preached in his name to all nations, beginning at Jerusalem" (Luke 24:46–47).

The apostle Paul also wrote about a new way that God makes people righteous, "to which the Law and Prophets testify" (Romans 3:21). No one will be declared righteous in God's sight by observing the law, Paul wrote. Rather, God's righteousness comes through faith in Jesus the Messiah. God presented Jesus as a "sacrifice of atonement" in fulfillment of many indications in the Old Testament. By justifying people freely by his grace through the redemption that came through Jesus, God demonstrated his justice (Romans 3:22–27).

In New Testament terms, Jesus did confirm the Torah in the sense of fulfilling its intentions and prophecies. Whether the portrait of ʿĪsā in the Quran matches the identity and teaching of the Messiah prophesied in the Torah is questionable.

61.6 – *bringing good news of a messenger who will come after me, whose name will be Aḥmad*

The Quran asserts that ʿĪsā speaks of "a messenger who will come after me." The name of this messenger would be *aḥmad*, a word that literally means "more praised." Muslims have interpreted *aḥmad* to be another name for Muhammad, and many have cited this verse to claim that the coming of Islam's messenger was prophesied.

In the Gospel accounts, Jesus spoke not of a messenger but of a "Counselor" (Gk. *paraklētos*) to come, whom Jesus clearly identified as the "Holy Spirit" and the "Spirit of truth" (John 14:17, 26; 15:26; 16:15). Jesus further specified that this Counselor would be sent by the Father in Jesus' name (John 14:26), would testify about Jesus (John 15:26), would remind believers of everything that Jesus said (John 14:26), and would bring glory to Jesus by taking what belongs to Jesus and making it known (John 16:14).

Neither Quran nor hadith fulfill these prophecies about the "Counselor" found in the New Testament, and it is fair to question whether the tasks of the Holy Spirit as described by Jesus in John 14–16 are within the capabilities of any human.

The New Testament documents the fulfillment of Jesus' words in the coming of the Holy Spirit in Acts 2.

who forges lies against God, when he is called to Islam? God does not guide the people who are evildoers. [8] They want to extinguish the light of God with their mouths, but God will perfect His light, even though the disbelievers dislike (it). [9] He (it is) who has sent His messenger with the guidance and the religion of truth, so that He may cause it to prevail over religion – all of it – even though the idolaters dislike (it).

[10] You who believe! Shall I direct you to a transaction that will rescue you

---

61.9 – *so that He may cause it to prevail over religion – all of it – even though the idolaters dislike (it)*

The assignment of "His messenger" in this verse is to make Islam (see v. 7) prevail over (*aẓhara ʿalā*) all religion. The verse also claims that Islam is the "religion of truth." The same wording appears at 9.33 – and at 48.28 with slight differences – and was inscribed above the north door of the Dome of the Rock in AD 691.

The portrait of "the messenger" here is very different from that of many other parts of the Quran. For example, at 6.108 the Quran instructs the messenger not to revile objects of worship other than Allah. In that sūra, the messenger is not a "watcher" or "guardian" over the associators (6.106–7). In Sūra 61, there seems to be little concern that the associators may hate (*kariha*) the dominance of Islam.

The Quran uses the word "associators" (*mushrikūn*) in many verses and contexts that seem to apply it to the People of the Book. This is confusing, because A. J. Droge consistently translates the Arabic word as "idolaters." But the Quran clearly applies this term to Christians at 3.64; 5.72; and 9.31. In three verses the Quran puts the term together with belief in a "son of Allah" (17.111; 23.91–92; 25.2). And the accusation of associating brings with it some dangerous treatment (4.48; 9.5, 33, 36, 113; cf. 48.28). At the same time that it prohibits associating ʿĪsā with Allah (5.72; 9.31), the Quran associates its "messenger" with Allah as deserving of belief, obedience, and much more. See the discussion of verses that associate the messenger with Allah at 64.12 (p. 574).

61.10 – *Shall I direct you to a transaction that will rescue you from a painful punishment?*

This verse brings in the language of salvation (*najjā*) to describe a bargain between Allah and the "believers." The part of the "believers" is to believe in Allah and his messenger and to "struggle (*jāhada*) in the way of Allah" (v. 11). For his part, Allah will forgive their sins and admit them to the "Gardens of Eden" (v. 12). Also, Allah will help the believers to achieve a victory (v. 13).

The expression "struggle in the way of Allah" often appears in battle scenes in the Quran, and other verses in this sūra seem to picture a military situation (e.g., vv. 4, 9, 14). If this is so, the salvation offered in this passage seems to depend on the believer's participation in the battle. See "Jihad in the Quran" (p. 368).

from a painful punishment? [11] You (should) believe in God and His messenger, and struggle in the way of God with your wealth and your lives – that is better for you, if (only) you knew. [12] He will forgive you your sins, and cause you to enter Gardens through which rivers flow, and good dwelling places in Gardens of Eden – that is the great triumph! – [13] and another thing which you love: help from God and a victory near (at hand). Give good news to the believers!

[14] You who believe! Be the helpers of God, as Jesus, son of Mary, said to the disciples, 'Who will be my helpers to God?' The disciples said, 'We will be the helpers of God.' One contingent of the Sons of Israel believed, and (another) contingent disbelieved. So We supported those who believed against their enemy, and they were the ones who prevailed.

61.14 – *So We supported those who believed against their enemy, and they were the ones who prevailed*

This verse seems to say that 'Īsā and his disciples fight against their enemies with the support of Allah (cf. 3.52). If this is its meaning, the character of the quranic 'Īsā here is significantly different from that of Jesus in the New Testament. The confusion in this verse seems similar to that in 9.111, where the "Gospel" (*injīl*) is grouped together with the Torah and the Quran as promising that believers "fight in the way of Allah, and they kill and are killed."

In the insightful book *God, Muhammad and the Unbelievers*, David Marshall analyzes the suggestions of 61.14 and 3.52 and speculates that this portrayal of 'Īsā was created to support the story of Muhammad in Medina. See Marshall's focus article on "Divine Punishment of Unbelievers in This World" (p. 507).

This misunderstanding of the teaching and example of Jesus found in the Gospel accounts raises questions about the accuracy of the Quran and its origin. From a Christian perspective, it is unfortunate that the peaceable way of Jesus in the New Testament did not find a place in the Quran's portrait of 'Īsā. It could have provided a valuable contrast to the picture of a warrior who prevails over his enemies and could have offered an alternative to fighting, killing, and dying while fighting.

Christian readers may be disappointed that the last verse in the Quran that mentions the name 'Īsā is a verse that seems to portray him as a fighter.

THE ASSEMBLY
AL-JUMU'A

62

The Quran's approach to the Jews is important not only for the larger question of relationships among monotheistic faiths but also for present-day politics in the Middle East and the treatment of Jewish communities in the West. This sūra addresses Jews directly and uses a rather negative simile to describe them.

In the Name of God, the Merciful, the Compassionate

¹ Whatever is in the heavens and whatever is on the earth glorifies God, the King, the Holy One, the Mighty, the Wise.

² He (it is) who has raised up among the common people a messenger from among them, to recite His signs to them, and to purify them, and to teach them the Book and the wisdom, though before (this) they were indeed clearly astray ³ – and others of them who have not (yet) joined them. He is the Mighty, the Wise. ⁴ That is the favor of God. He gives (it) to whomever He pleases. God is full of great favor.

⁵ Those who have been loaded down with the Torah, (and) then have not carried it, are like a donkey carrying books. Evil is the parable of the people

---

62.2 – *He (it is) who has raised up among the common people a messenger from among them*

The Quran claims in this self-referential verse that Allah sends the messenger and his recitations. See "Different Kinds of Literature" (p. 14). Whose voice is speaking in verses where both Allah and messenger are described in third person, and there is no command to the messenger to "say" what Allah dictates?

This expression, to "raise up among them a messenger from among them," first appears to the reader in the prayer of Abraham at 2.129, and another verse very similar to 62.2 is found at 3.164.

62.5 – *Those who have been loaded down with the Torah*

The possessors of divine revelation do not benefit from it unless they learn and practice what is written. The following verses then directly address the Jews to assert that they will face judgment (vv. 6–8).

who have called the signs of God a lie. God does not guide the people who are evildoers. ⁶ Say: 'You who are Jews! If you claim that you are the allies of God to the exclusion of the people, wish for death, if you are truthful.' ⁷ But they will never wish for it because of what their (own) hands have sent forward. God knows the evildoers. ⁸ Say: 'Surely the death from which you flee – surely it will meet you. Then you will be returned to the Knower of the unseen and the seen, and He will inform you about what you have done.'

⁹ You who believe! When the call to prayer is made on the day of assembly, hurry to the remembrance of God, and leave business aside. That is better for you, if (only) you knew. ¹⁰ Then, when the prayer is finished, disperse on the earth and seek some favor from God, and remember God often, so that you may prosper. ¹¹ But when they see (the chance of) some (business) transaction or diversion, they rush off to it, and leave you standing. Say: 'What is with God is better than any diversion or transaction. God is the best of providers.'

62.9 – *When the call to prayer is made on the day of assembly*
Even today, Muslim businessmen leave their work aside to attend Friday prayers.

THE HYPOCRITES
AL-MUNĀFIQŪN

The "hypocrites" – after whom this sūra is named – once "believed" but lost faith. By all appearances, and by their words, they are authentic Muslims. However, according to this sūra, their words are false, and they lead many astray. Their behavior is beyond the pale, and Allah will never forgive them.

In the Name of God, the Merciful, the Compassionate

[1] When the hypocrites come to you, they say, 'We bear witness that you are indeed the messenger of God.' God knows that you are indeed His messenger, and God bears witness: 'Surely the hypocrites are liars indeed!' [2] They have taken their oaths as a cover, and have kept (people) from the way of God. Surely they – evil is what they have done. [3] That is because they believed, (and) then they disbelieved. So a seal was set on their hearts, and they do not understand. [4] When you see them, their bodies please you, but when they speak, you hear their speech as if they were planks of wood propped up. They think every cry is against them. They are the enemy, so beware of them. God fight them! How deluded they are! [5] When it is said to them, 'Come, the messenger of God will ask forgiveness for you,' they shake their heads, and you see them turning aside, and they become arrogant. [6] (It is) the same for to them whether you ask forgiveness for them or you do not ask forgiveness for them: God will not forgive them. Surely God does not guide the people who are wicked. [7] They are

---

63.3 – *That is because they believed, (and) then they disbelieved*

Hypocrisy is hard to spot because everything appears and sounds normal (vv. 1–4). Meanwhile, the hypocrites lead others astray (v. 2). At the heart of their problem is a loss of faith in the messenger.

63.4 – *God fight them! How deluded they are!*

This expression at the end of the verse is the same as that used against Jews and Christians at 9.30.

63.6 – *whether you ask forgiveness for them or you do not ask forgiveness*

Here the messenger seems to have the role of intercessor or mediator. There is

those who say, 'Do not contribute to those who are with the messenger of God until they disperse,' when the storehouses of the heavens and the earth (belong) to God. But the hypocrites do not understand (this). ⁸ They say, 'If indeed we return to the city, the mightier in it will indeed expel the lowlier,' when all honor (belongs) to God, and to His messenger, and to the believers. But the hypocrites do not know (this).

⁹ You who believe! Do not let your wealth or your children divert you from the remembrance of God. Whoever does that, those – they are the losers. ¹⁰ Contribute from what We have provided you, before death comes upon one of you, and he says, 'My Lord, if only You would spare me for a time near (at hand), so that I might make a freewill offering, and become one of the righteous.' ¹¹ But God will not spare anyone when his time comes. God is aware of what you do.

no point in asking forgiveness for the hypocrites, however, because Allah will not forgive them.

63.8 – *all honor (belongs) to God, and to His messenger, and to the believers*

Here the Quran associates not only the messenger but also the "believers" with Allah for power or "honor" ('izza). The Arabic word for "city" in this verse is *madīna*. In time, *Medina* came to mean "city of the prophet."

MUTUAL DEFRAUDING

AL-TAGHĀBUN

64

> The content of "faith" is often left unspecified in the Quran, while "believers" and "disbelievers" populate practically every sūra. Sūra 64 makes explicit what must be implicit and assumed in many other passages. The faith that is required is to "believe in Allah and His messenger" and in what Allah has "sent down" to the Quran's messenger (v. 8).

In the Name of God, the Merciful, the Compassionate

[1] Whatever is in the heavens and whatever is on the earth glorifies God. To Him (belongs) the kingdom, and to Him (belongs) the praise. He is powerful over everything. [2] He (it is) who created you. One of you is a disbeliever, and one of you a believer. God sees what you do. [3] He created the heavens and the earth in truth. He fashioned you, and made your forms well. To Him is the (final) destination. [4] He knows whatever is in the heavens and the earth. He knows what you keep secret and what you speak aloud. God knows what is in the hearts.

[5] Has the story not come to you of those who disbelieved before, and tasted the consequence of their action, and for whom (there was) a painful punishment? [6] That was because their messengers brought them the clear signs, and they said, 'Will a human being guide us?' So they disbelieved and turned away, but God had no need (of them). God is wealthy, praiseworthy.

[7] Those who disbelieve claim that they will not be raised up. Say: 'Yes indeed! By my Lord! You will indeed be raised up, (and) then you will indeed be informed about what you have done. That is easy for God.' [8] So believe in

---

64.8 – *So believe in God and His messenger, and the light which We have sent down*

This verse makes explicit what often seems implicit in verses about "believing" in the Quran: this is not some kind of generic "religious faith" about a higher power of some kind. Rather, the requirement is belief in Allah as the Quran portrays him, in a particular messenger, and in the recitations of that messenger.

God and His messenger, and the light which We have sent down. God is aware of what you do. [9] On the Day when He will gather you for the Day of Gathering – that will be the Day of Mutual Defrauding. Whoever believes in God and does righteousness – He will absolve him of his evil deeds, and cause him to enter Gardens through which rivers flow, there to remain forever. That is the great triumph! [10] But those who disbelieved and called Our signs a lie – those are the companions of the Fire, there to remain – and it is an evil destination!

Allah in the Quran

Mark Anderson

Is the Allah of the Quran the same as the God of the Bible? Yes, in the sense that *Allah* is the word Arabic-speaking Jews and Christians use for God in their Bible translations. And the Quran's choice of *Allah* specifically identified him with the God of the Bible. Much of the Quran's theological content, however, calls that answer into question. For while the God of the Quran is like the God of the Bible in many respects, he is also profoundly different, and the resulting tension has produced significant controversy among evangelical Christians.

Since Allah is the Quran's implied speaker throughout, its most obvious theological point is that God communicates in human words. It also calls such divine actions as providing sunshine and rain his "signs" (*āyāt*) because they reveal truths about him. Allah is said to be the "most just of judges" and "most compassionate of the compassionate" (e.g., 95.8; 7.151), requiring us to give quranic descriptions of God their typical meanings. Though language is here stretched to its limits, analogy is qualified only in that God's is the "loftiest of likenesses" (or "the Mighty, the Wise"; 16.60; 30.27).

Like the Bible, the Quran shows the Creator to be exalted and distinct from his creation. But it further stresses that he is unlike anything created (e.g., 112.4) and makes associating with him anything created (*shirk*) as the unforgiveable sin (4.48). Besides precluding his incarnation, this discourages us from taking the Quran's anthropomorphic descriptions of him too literally (e.g., his speaking, knowing; 15.32; 49.16). Yet these passages do imply divine-human analogy.

The Quran uses six nonintimate biblical images of God: creator, king, master, judge, guide, and deliverer, although the Quran dramatically marginalizes the role of deliverer compared to its biblical significance. It also alludes to God's being a friend in its single unexplained reference to Abraham as his friend (*khalīl*; 4.125). However, it entirely omits the central New Testament images of

God as father and lover/husband. As supreme master, the quranic God seeks no intimacy with humankind. Though he makes covenants, he answers to no one and has no interest in friendship with his servants, disclosing only what they need in order to obey him. That is, he freely reveals his will but not himself.

This is radically different from biblical theology, with its full embrace of divine-human analogy. In the Bible, God makes himself answerable to keep his word. Taking on our humanity, he comes to live among us in Christ, who sacrifices his life as the perfect servant and later indwells us by his Holy Spirit. And this fuller revelation of God points to his triunity, which the Quran explicitly denies. Neither does the Muslim scripture identify love as a primary divine attribute, nor our primary act of worship, as is the case biblically. Rather, as Iain Provan says, aside from his singularity, the quranic presentation of God is more reminiscent of the haughty and threateningly inaccessible gods of ancient Middle Eastern religions than of the Bible's self-revealing, loving, and voluntarily condescending God. (See his *Seriously Dangerous Religion* in the bibliography.) All this renders humankind's relationship to God in the Quran markedly nonintimate, in sharp contrast to biblical teaching.

The Quran broadly agrees with the Bible's ethical descriptions of God as both just and merciful. Yet God's justice in the Quran relates to a paradigm of reciprocity by which human actions (e.g., loving, forgetting) evoke corresponding actions from him. The fact that our actions seldom receive God's immediate response implies his superimposition of another paradigm – one of reversal – on that of reciprocity. Flowing from his mercy, this reversal enables him to delay the fulfillment of his promises, both to punish and to bless, till the final judgment. These paradigms operate in much the same tension that holds them together in the Bible, except that God's mercy is always conditional in the Quran. While disobedience incurs his anger, his ethical attributes are not clearly rooted in essential holiness. This explains the absence of a call to moral likeness and any concept of divine atonement. Rather, God in the Quran lacks a clear ethical core, appearing dualistic – first just, then merciful – leaving Muslims to plead his unknowability, as they have historically done.

Toshihiko Izutsu contends that the quranic concept of nobility reflects that found in early Arabic poetry. Its primary attributes are haughtiness and the refusal to submit. This notion lies at the heart of quranic theology, with its absolute Master-servant distinction. And this is what most basically excludes the New Testament's core theological concepts: what binds God's mercy and justice together biblically is his humility, so spectacularly demonstrated in Christ's incarnation and crucifixion.

[11] No smiting smites, except by the permission of God. Whoever believes in God – He will guide his heart. God has knowledge of everything. [12] Obey God and obey the messenger! If you turn away – only (dependent) on Our messenger is the clear delivery (of the message). [13] God – (there is) no god but Him. In God let the believers put their trust.

[14] You who believe! Surely among your wives and your children (there is) an enemy to you. So beware of them. If you pardon and excuse and forgive – surely God is forgiving, compassionate. [15] Surely your wealth and your children are a trial, but God – with Him (there is) a great reward. [16] Guard (yourselves) against God as much as you are able, and hear and obey, and contribute! (That is) better for yourselves. Whoever is guarded against his own greed, those – they are the ones who prosper. [17] If you lend to God a good loan, He will double it for you, and will forgive you. God is thankful, forbearing, [18] Knower of the unseen and the seen, the Mighty, the Wise.

64.12 – *Obey God and obey the messenger!*

The Quran associates "the messenger" with Allah at least eighty-five times and links the messenger with Allah for obedience and disobedience twenty-eight times (including this verse and 3.32, 132; 4.59; 5.92; 8.1, 20, 46; 24.54; 33.36; 47.33; 58.13). These several commands to obey both Allah and his messenger, as well as the many associations of the messenger with Allah (including for belief in 64.8), raise a question about one of the Quran's prohibitions. The Quran speaks strongly against "associating" (*ashraka*) with Allah any person or created thing (e.g., 4.48, 116). The Quran seems to be especially critical of the *shirk* that it claims to be involved in the Christian confession of the deity of Jesus (e.g., 9.30–33). But how should one describe the extensive pairing of "the messenger" with Allah?

The Quran's commands to obey the messenger became very important in the writings of the influential Muslim jurist al-Shāfiʿī (d. 820), who insisted they gave divine authority to the words traditionally attributed to Muhammad in the hadith. Through this argument, made in his famous works *Risāla* and *Umm*, al-Shāfiʿī cleared the way for Islamic Law to be based largely on what Muslims believe to be the words and life example of Muhammad – the *sunna*. This raises another important question: Does the Almighty Creator God intend for humanity to follow the *sunna* of Muhammad as it is portrayed in the *Sīra*, *Maghāzī*, Muslim histories, and hadith?

For readers who would like a taste of the reasoning that raised the authority of Muhammad, a translation of al-Shāfiʿī's treatise on Islamic Law by Majid Khadduri titled *al-Shāfiʿī's Risāla* is available. Also very helpful are books by Joseph Schacht and John Burton (see bibliography).

DIVORCE
AL-ṬALĀQ

The Quran addresses the prophet directly with a commandment (*amr*) for how men in his community should divorce their wives. This is described as one of the limits (*ḥudūd*) of Allah. The sūra then follows this up with a threat about the punishments that came in the past to communities that resisted the commandment of their Lord and his messengers.

In the Name of God, the Merciful, the Compassionate

¹ Prophet! When you divorce women, divorce them when they have reached (the end of) their waiting period. Count the waiting period, and guard (yourselves) against God your Lord. Do not expel them from their houses, nor let them leave, unless they commit clear immorality. Those are the limits (set by) God. Whoever transgresses the limits (set by) God has done himself evil. You do not know, perhaps after that God may bring about a new situation. ² When they reach their term, either retain them rightfully, or part from them rightfully. Call in two of your just men as witnesses, and conduct the witnessing (as if) before God. That is what anyone who believes in God and the Last Day is admonished. Whoever guards (himself) against God – He will make a way out for him, ³ and will provide for him from where he was not expecting. Whoever puts his trust in God – He will be enough for him. Surely God attains his purpose. God has appointed a measure for everything.

⁴ (As for) those of your women who have no hope of (further) menstruation: if you are in doubt, their waiting period is three months, and (also for) those who

---

65.1 – *Prophet! When you divorce women*

The Quran addresses the prophet directly with a rule for how men in his community should divorce their wives. The Arabic verb translated here "to divorce" is *ṭallaqa*, and the common Arabic noun for "divorce" is *ṭalāq*.

Verses 1–7 give further details of the divorce process, here called the "limits (*ḥudūd*) of Allah." Allah "sends down" this commandment to the community, verse 5 claims.

have not (yet) menstruated. (As for) those who are pregnant, their term (is) when they deliver what they bear. Whoever guards (himself) against God – He will bring about some relief for him from His command. ⁵ That is the command of God, which He has sent down to you. Whoever guards (himself) against God – He will absolve him of his evil deeds, and make his reward great.

⁶ Let them reside where you are residing, according to your means, and do not treat them harshly, so that you cause distress for them. If they are pregnant, support them until they deliver what they bear. If they nurse (the child) for you, give them their payment, and consult together rightfully. But if you encounter difficulties, another woman will nurse (the child) for him. ⁷ Let a man of means spend out of his means, and whoever is limited in provision, let him spend out of what God has given him. God does not burden anyone except (according to) what He has given him. God will bring about some ease after hardship.

⁸ How many a town disdained the command of its Lord and His messengers, and We made a harsh reckoning with it, and punished it with a terrible punishment. ⁹ So it tasted the consequence of its action, and the result of its action was loss. ¹⁰ God prepared a harsh punishment for them. Guard (yourselves) against God, those (of you) with understanding!

(You) who believe! God has sent down to you a reminder ¹¹ – a messenger reciting over you the clear signs of God, so that He may bring those who believe and do righteous deeds out of the darkness to the light. Whoever believes in God and does righteousness – He will cause him to enter Gardens through which rivers flow, there to remain forever. God has made good provision for him.

¹² (It is) God who created seven heavens, and of the earth a similar (number) to them. The command descends between them, so that you may know that God is powerful over everything, and that God encompasses everything in knowledge.

65.8 – *How many a town disdained the command of its Lord and His messengers*
This verse seems to back up the commandments about divorce with a threat of "harsh reckoning" for those who resist, like the punishments that came to communities in the past.

65.10 – *(You) who believe! Allah has sent down to you a reminder*
The Quran vouches for the messenger (vv. 10–11), claiming that what he recites brings believers from darkness to light, and promising a reward for obedience.

THE FORBIDDING
AL-TAHRĪM

66

A personal situation in the life of "the prophet" seems to be the occasion for the first five verses of this sūra. Though no names are given, and the actions are obscure, Muslim tradition has supplied a story about wives in conflict over their time allowances with the prophet, including the particular names of all concerned.

In the Name of God, the Merciful, the Compassionate

[1] Prophet! Why do you forbid what God has permitted to you, seeking the approval of your wives? God is forgiving, compassionate. [2] God has already specified (what is) obligatory for you in the absolution of your oaths. God is your Protector. He is the Knowing, the Wise.

66.1 – *Prophet! Why do you forbid what God has permitted to you, seeking the approval of your wives?*

The opening verses of this sūra provide a perfect example of a type of literature forecast in the general introduction (p. 14): "personal situation" passages that address the domestic details of the messenger. These verses focus a particular, private, and contingent concern.

Known as the "vocative," direct addresses to "the prophet" are not very frequent in the Quran, and most of the occurrences appear in this sūra (vv. 1, 9) and Sūras 8 and 33. This particular direct address instructs the prophet in the conduct of his marriages (vv. 1–3) and in his relationships with non-Muslims (v. 9).

The Quran directly addresses "the prophet" in this way a total of thirteen times. Since the vocative is so infrequent, it is interesting to observe the contexts in which "Prophet!" is used. The vocative precedes instructions about fighting non-Muslims six times (8.64, 65, 70; 9.73; 33.1; 66.9; cf. 33.48), instructions about relationships with wives five times (33.28, 50, 59; 65.1; 66.1), instructions about response to believing women once (60.12), and once declares the prophet to be witness, warner, and bringer of good news to the believers (33.45).

³ When the prophet confided a (certain) story to one of his wives, and when she informed (another) about it and God disclosed it to him, he made known part of it, and avoided a part. And when he informed her about it, she said, 'Who informed you of this?' He said, 'The Knowing (and) the Aware informed me.' ⁴ If both of you turn to God (in repentance), both your hearts are (well) inclined, but if both of you support each other against him, surely God – He is his Protector, and Gabriel (too), and the righteous among the believers, and beyond that the angels are (his) supporters. ⁵ It may be that, if he divorces you, his Lord will give him in exchange better wives than you – women who have submitted, believing, obedient, repentant, worshipping, fasting – (both) previously married and virgins.

⁶ You who believe! Guard yourselves and your families against a Fire – its fuel is people and stones – over which are angels, stern (and) harsh. They do not disobey God in what He commands them, but they do what they are commanded. ⁷ 'You who disbelieve! Do not make excuses today, you are only being repaid for what you have done.'

⁸ You who believe! Turn to God in sincere repentance. It may be that your Lord will absolve you of your evil deeds, and cause you to enter Gardens through which rivers flow. On the Day when God will not disgrace the prophet or those who believe with him: their light will run before them, and at their right (hands) [. . .], and they will say, 'Our Lord, perfect our light for us, and forgive us. Surely You are powerful over everything.'

66.3 – *When the prophet confided a (certain) story to one of his wives*

Like the vocative "Prophet!" (vv. 1, 9), the expression "the prophet" appears in this sūra for the last time (also v. 8). Here the context is the situation with his wives, and in verse 8 Allah will not dishonor the prophet on the Day of Resurrection.

Of its twenty occurrences in the Quran, "the prophet" appears ten times in Sūra 33 and ten times elsewhere. Several occurrences relate to battle (9.61, 113, 117; 33.13), some relate to wives (33.30, 32, 50; 66.3), a few dictate behavior in the prophet's presence (33.53; 49.2; cf. 9.61), and many accompany special claims for the messenger, such as permission to marry the former wife of Zayd (33.38; also 3.38; 7.157–58; 33.6, 56; 66.8).

66.4 – *He is his Protector, and Gabriel (too)*

The name of Gabriel (*jibrīl*) appears only three times in the Quran: 2.97, 98; and 66.4. Here Gabriel seems to be on the side of the prophet as part of a threat against two of his wives.

⁹ Prophet! Struggle against the disbelievers and the hypocrites, and be stern with them. Their refuge is Gehenna – and it is an evil destination!

¹⁰ God has struck a parable for those who disbelieve: the wife of Noah and the wife of Lot. They were under two of Our righteous servants, but they both betrayed them. Neither of them was of any use at all to either of them against God, when it was said, 'Enter the Fire, both of you, with the ones who enter!'

¹¹ And God has struck a parable for those who believe: the wife of Pharaoh,

---

66.9 – *Prophet! Struggle against the disbelievers and the hypocrites, and be stern with them*

"Struggle" translates the Arabic verb *jāhada*, from which the word *jihad* comes, and in this verse it appears in the form of a command to "the prophet" in particular. This is the final occurrence of seven commands to struggle in the Quran. In this verse (like 9.73) the surrounding words themselves seem to suggest that the meaning of *jihad* is physical fighting, and this is indeed how many Muslim commentators have understood it.

The meaning of *jihad* and its various verb forms has become a point of contention in the modern West, but the word was not so vigorously disputed among Muslims during the first centuries of Islam. The early Muslim commentator Muqātil ibn Sulaymān (d. 767), for example, finished the command "struggle against the disbelievers" in both 66.9 and 9.73 by adding the phrase "with the sword." Many Muslim commentators, including al-Ṭabarī (d. 923), insisted that *jihad* refers to participation in warfare even where the context does not clearly point the word in that direction, as in 22.78. See "Jihad in the Quran" (p. 368).

66.10 – *the wife of Noah and the wife of Lot*

Here the Quran pairs the wife of Noah with the wife of Lot, saying that they both betrayed their husbands. For doing so, they are commanded to enter hell. Though their husbands are "righteous servants," they cannot prevent God's judgment. The "parable" (*mathal*) seems to be that the relatives of God's messengers will be judged on the basis of what they do, and that blood relations will not help them.

The idea that the wife of Noah betrays her husband does not appear in any of the Quran's seven versions of the Noah story (see note at 71.1), nor in the Torah account (Genesis 6:8–9:29). Muslim commentators debated the idea that the wife of a prophet could betray her husband, showing a concern for the infallibility (*'iṣma*) of prophets.

66.11 – *And God has struck a parable for those who believe: the wife of Pharaoh*

The wife of Pharaoh asks her Lord for a place in heaven and rescue from her husband. She is also portrayed positively when she asks that the baby Moses not be killed (28.9).

when she said, 'My Lord, build a house in the Garden for me in Your presence, and rescue me from Pharaoh and his deed(s), and rescue me from the people who are evildoers.' ¹² And Mary, daughter of 'Imrān, who guarded her private part: We breathed into it some of Our spirit, and she affirmed the words of her Lord and His Books, and became one of the obedient.

66.12 – *We breathed into it some of Our spirit*

The way that God made Mary pregnant with 'Īsā (not named here) is described most explicitly in this verse and 21.91. In 19.17 the Quran says God sent his spirit to Mary in the form of a human being, but the way in which she conceived is not mentioned (similarly with the angels in 3.42–47). This is the final verse about Mary in the canonical progression.

The Gospel accounts are also guarded, and they focus on the Holy Spirit. In Luke, Gabriel says to Mary, "The Holy Spirit will come upon you, and the power of the Most High will overshadow you" (Luke 1:35), while in Matthew the angel tells Joseph something similar (Matthew 1:20). The big difference between the New Testament and the Quran is in the names that the heavenly messengers specify for the child (Matthew 1:21; cf. 1:23; Luke 1:32, 35).

THE KINGDOM
AL-MULK

67

In striking contrast to the profile of "the prophet" and "the messenger" in several of the sūras since Sūra 57, the messenger of Sūra 67 is only "a plain warner." The sūra draws attention to the Creator's power and provision and warns of punishment for the ungrateful on the Day of Judgment, but it makes no special claims for the messenger.

In the Name of God, the Merciful, the Compassionate

[1] Blessed (be) He in whose hand is the kingdom – He is powerful over everything – [2] who created death and life to test which of you is best in deed – He is the Mighty, the Forgiving – [3] who created seven heavens in stories (one upon another). You do not see any mistake in the creation of the Merciful. Cast your sight again! Do you see any fissure? [4] Then cast your sight again and again! Your sight will come crawling back to you, worn out.

[5] Certainly We adorned the lower heaven with lamps, and made them missiles for the satans – and We have prepared for them the punishment of the blazing (Fire). [6] For those who disbelieve in their Lord (there is) the punishment of Gehenna – and it is an evil homecoming! [7] When they are cast into it, they will hear its panting, as it boils up [8] (and) nearly bursts apart from rage. Whenever a crowd is cast into it, its keepers will ask them, 'Did a warner not come to you?' [9] They will say, 'Yes indeed! A warner did come to us, but we called (him) a liar, and said, "God has not sent down anything. You are simply terribly astray."' [10] And they will say, 'If (only) we had heard or understood, we would not have been among the companions of the blazing (Fire).' [11] And so they confess their sin. Away with the companions of the blazing (Fire)! [12] Surely those who fear

---

67.2 – *who created death and life to test which of you is best in deed*

The sūra opens with a declaration of the Creator's power and sovereignty.

67.7 – *When they are cast into it, they will hear its panting*

In this judgment scene (vv. 7–12), the wardens of hell question the "disbelievers" as they enter the fire.

their Lord in the unseen – for them (there is) forgiveness and a great reward.

¹³ Keep your word secret or speak it publicly – surely He knows what is in (your) hearts. ¹⁴ Does the One who created not know, when He is the Astute, the Aware? ¹⁵ He (it is) who made the earth subservient to you. So walk about in its regions, and eat from His provision, but to Him is the raising up.

¹⁶ Do you feel secure that the One who is in the sky will not cause the earth to swallow you, and then suddenly it shakes? ¹⁷ Or do you feel secure that the One who is in the sky will not send a sandstorm against you, and then you will know how My warning is? ¹⁸ Certainly those who were before them called (it) a lie, and how was My loathing (of them)?

¹⁹ Do they not see the birds above them, spreading (their wings), and they fold (them)? No one holds them (up) but the Merciful. Surely He sees everything. ²⁰ Or who is this who will be a (fighting) force for you to help you, other than the Merciful? The disbelievers are only in delusion. ²¹ Or who is this who will provide for you, if He withholds His provision? No! But they persist in (their) disdain and aversion. ²² Is the one who walks bent over on his face better guided, or the one who walks upright on a straight path?

²³ Say: 'He (it is) who produced you, and made for you hearing and sight and hearts – little thanks you show!'

²⁴ Say: 'He (it is) who scattered you on the earth, and to Him you will be gathered.'

²⁵ They say, 'When (will) this promise (come to pass), if you are truthful?' ²⁶ Say: 'The knowledge (of it) is only with God. I am only a clear warner.'

²⁷ When they see it near at hand, the faces of those who disbelieve will become sad, and it will be said, 'This is what you have been calling for.'

²⁸ Say: 'Have you considered? If God destroys me and whoever is with me, or has compassion on us, who will protect the disbelievers from a painful punishment?'

²⁹ Say: 'He is the Merciful. We believe in Him, and in Him we put our trust. Soon you will know who it is (who is) clearly astray.'

³⁰ Say: 'Have you considered? If one morning your water should sink (into the ground), who would bring you flowing water?'

67.14 – *Does the One who created not know . . . ?*

This verse begins a series of challenging questions for the "disbelievers" (vv. 14–22).

67.26 – *The knowledge (of it) is only with God. I am only a clear warner*

The messenger in this sūra is an unassuming "warner" who tolerates tough questions from his listeners, trusts and defers to Allah, and has no assurance that he and his followers will succeed (vv. 25–29). Beyond this, the sūra makes no special claims for the messenger or his preaching.

THE PEN
AL-QALAM

68

> This sūra is mainly about punishment on the Day of Judgment, and it approaches the theme through a kind of parable about the owners of a garden who are about to harvest its fruit. They neglect to glorify the Lord, and the next morning the fruit is all gone. According to this sūra, the punishment in the hereafter will be much worse.

In the Name of God, the Merciful, the Compassionate

¹ Nūn.

By the pen and what they write! ² You are not, by the blessing of your Lord, possessed. ³ Surely for you (there is) indeed a reward without end, ⁴ (for) surely you (are) indeed on a great undertaking. ⁵ So you will see, and they will see, ⁶ which of you is the troubled one. ⁷ Surely your Lord – He knows who goes astray from His way, and He knows the ones who are (rightly) guided. ⁸ So do not obey the ones who call (it) a lie. ⁹ They wish that you would compromise, and then they would compromise.

¹⁰ And do not obey any despicable swearer, ¹¹ a slanderer (who) trades in gossip, ¹² a hinderer of the good, a transgressor (and) sinner, ¹³ crude, and besides all that, a bastard, ¹⁴ (just) because he has wealth and sons. ¹⁵ When Our signs are recited to him, he says, 'Old tales!' ¹⁶ We shall brand him on the snout!

¹⁷ Surely We have tested them as We tested the owners of the garden, when

---

68.2 – *You are not, by the blessing of your Lord, possessed*

The opening verses of the sūra encourage the messenger and instruct him in how to handle those who reject his preaching (vv. 2–16). "Possessed" translates the Arabic *majnūn*, which implies possession by *jinn* (also v. 51).

68.17 – *Surely We have tested them as We tested the owners of the garden*

To emphasize that punishment will come to those who reject it, the Quran presents a parable about gardeners who anticipate harvesting their garden's fruit but neglect to glorify their Lord (vv. 17–32).

they swore they would indeed harvest it in the morning, [18] but did not make exception. [19] And so a circler from your Lord went around it while they were sleeping, [20] and in the morning it was as if it had been harvested. [21] They called to each other in the morning: [22] 'Go out early to your field, if you are going to harvest (it).' [23] So they set out, murmuring among themselves: [24] 'No poor person will enter it today in your presence.' [25] They went out early, able to (their) task. [26] But when they saw it, they said, 'Surely we have gone astray indeed! [27] No! We have been robbed!' [28] The most moderate one of them said, 'Did I not say to you, "Why do you not glorify (God)?"' [29] They said, 'Glory to our Lord! Surely we have been evildoers!' [30] So some of them approached others blaming each other. [31] They said, 'Woe to us! Surely we have been insolent transgressors! [32] It may be that our Lord will give us a better one in exchange for it. Surely we turn in hope to our Lord.' [33] Such was the punishment. Yet the punishment of the Hereafter is indeed greater, if (only) they knew.

[34] Surely for the ones who guard (themselves) (there will be) Gardens of Bliss with their Lord. [35] Shall We treat those who submit like the sinners? [36] What is (the matter) with you? How do you judge? [37] Or do you have a Book which you study? [38] Surely you (would) have in it whatever indeed you choose! [39] Or do you have guarantees from Us, reaching to the Day of Resurrection? Surely you (would) have whatever indeed you judge! [40] Ask them which of them will guarantee that. [41] Or do they have associates? Let them bring their associates, if they are truthful. [42] On the Day when the leg will be bared, and they will be called to (make) prostration, but are unable: [43] their sight will be downcast, and humiliation will cover them, because they had been called to (make) prostration when they were able.

[44] So leave Me (to deal with) anyone who calls this proclamation a lie. We shall lead them on step by step without their realizing it. [45] And I shall spare them – surely My plan is strong.

[46] Or do you ask them for a reward, so that they are burdened with debt? [47] Or is the unseen in their keeping, and so they are writing (it) down?

[48] Be patient for the judgment of your Lord, and do not be like the com-

---

68.35 – *Shall We treat those who submit like the sinners?*

This verse begins a series of challenging questions to the audience (vv. 35–41) and to the messenger (vv. 46–47).

68.48 – *do not be like the companion of the fish*

In the Quran, the "companion of the fish" seems to be a nickname for Jonah (also at 21.87).

panion of the fish, when he called out, choked with distress. ⁴⁹ If a blessing from his Lord had not reached him, he would indeed have been tossed on the desert (shore), condemned. ⁵⁰ But his Lord chose him, and made him one of the righteous.

⁵¹ Surely those who disbelieve almost indeed make you stumble with their look, when they hear the Reminder. They say, 'Surely he is possessed indeed!' ⁵² Yet it is nothing but a reminder to the worlds.

THE PAYMENT DUE

AL-ḤĀQQA

69

Many sūras include "judgment scenes" in which the Quran pictures the Day of Resurrection and the actions and words of people gathered for judgment. In this sūra's scene, one individual is happy for his book of reckoning to be read aloud, while another does not even want his book to be opened.

In the Name of God, the Merciful, the Compassionate

¹ The payment due! ² What is the payment due? ³ And what will make you know what the payment due is? ⁴ Thamūd and ʿĀd called the striking a lie. ⁵ As for Thamūd, they were destroyed by the outbreak. ⁶ And as for ʿĀd, they were destroyed by a furious, violent wind, ⁷ which He forced on them for seven nights and eight days consecutively, and during which you (could) see the people lying flat, as if they were the trunks of collapsed date palms. ⁸ Do you see any remnant of them (now)? ⁹ And Pharaoh (too) – and those who were before him, and the overturned (cities) – committed sin, ¹⁰ and they disobeyed the messenger of their Lord, so He seized them with a surpassing seizing. ¹¹ Surely We – when the waters overflowed – We carried you in the running (ship), ¹² so that We might make it a reminder to you, and (that) an attentive ear might attend to it.

¹³ When a single blast is blown on the trumpet, ¹⁴ and the earth and the mountains are lifted up and shattered with a single shattering, ¹⁵ on that Day

---

69.4 – *Thamūd and ʿĀd called the striking a lie*

The sūra opens with references to peoples who were destroyed for unbelief and disobedience (vv. 4–12). On Thamūd and ʿĀd, see the comments on these names at their first appearances, 7.65, 73 (p. 182–83).

69.13 – *When a single blast is blown on the trumpet*

After describing punishments in this world, the sūra pictures rewards and punishments on the Day of Resurrection (vv. 13–37). In this scene, every person's past actions are found recorded in a book of "reckoning."

586

the falling will fall, [16] and the sky will be split open, (for) on that Day it will be frail, [17] and the angels (will stand) on its borders, and they will bear the throne of your Lord above them on that Day – eight (of them). [18] On that Day you will (all) be presented – not a secret of yours will be hidden.

[19] As for the one who is given his book in his right (hand), he will say, 'Take (and) read my book. [20] Surely I thought that I would meet my reckoning.' [21] And he will be in a pleasing life, [22] in a Garden on high, [23] its clusters (of fruit) near (at hand). [24] 'Eat and drink with satisfaction, (in return) for what you did in days past.' [25] But as for the one who is given his book in his left (hand), he will say, 'Would that I had not been given my book, [26] and not known what my reckoning is! [27] Would that it had been the end! [28] My wealth is of no use to me. [29] My authority has perished from me.' [30] 'Seize him and bind him! [31] Then burn him in the Furnace, [32] (and) then put him in a chain of seventy cubits. [33] Surely he never believed in God, the Almighty, [34] nor did he ever urge the feeding of the poor. [35] So today he has no friend here, [36] nor any food except refuse, [37] which only the sinners eat.'

[38] I swear by what you see [39] and what you do not see! [40] Surely it is indeed the word of an honorable messenger. [41] It is not the word of a poet – little do you believe! [42] Nor (is it) the word of an oracle-giver – little do you take heed! [43] (It is) a sending down from the Lord of the worlds. [44] If he had forged any (false) words

---

69.40 – *Surely it is indeed the word of an honorable messenger*

The third part of the sūra is an extended self-affirming passage that claims revelation for the recitation and vouches for the messenger (vv. 38–51).

69.41 – *It is not the word of a poet*

On the negative sense of "poet," see the comment at 21.5 (p. 331).

69.44 – *If he had forged any (false) words against Us*

This passage seems to anticipate that the listeners would call the recitation "forged." Verse 43 claims rather that the speech of the messenger is "a sending down from the Lord of the worlds," and verses 45–47 add an interesting argument: if the messenger had invented his speech, Allah would have killed him (vv. 45–47)!

The concern that the message is invented or "forged" is one of the central questions of the Quran. Are these recitations sent down by God, or are they the compositions of one or more human "messengers"? The listeners ask this question or accuse at 10.38; 11.13; 16.101; 21.5; 25.4; 32.3; 34.8, 43; 46.8; and 52.33. The Quran generally answers the charge with strong denials (e.g., 10.37; 25.4–6; 32.3; 46.8) or with challenges to produce a similar text (e.g., 10.38; 11.13; 52.33–34). At 16.102 the Quran claims that "the holy spirit has brought it down." Is it so? Believing or disbelieving this claim makes one a Muslim or a non-Muslim.

against Us, [45] We would indeed have seized him by the right (hand). [46] Then We would indeed have cut his (main) artery, [47] and not one of you could have defended him from it. [48] Surely it is a reminder indeed to the ones who guard (themselves). [49] Yet surely We indeed know that some of you are calling (it) a lie. [50] Surely it will be a (cause of) regret indeed to the disbelievers. [51] Yet surely it is the certain truth indeed. [52] So glorify the name of your Lord, the Almighty.

THE STAIRWAYS
AL-MA'ĀRIJ

70

Readers who have been reading steadily through the Quran to this point will certainly understand its message of punishment for "disbelievers." Muhammad Daud Rahbar, who completed a Cambridge PhD on the theology of the Quran, estimated that every third verse of the Quran is about judgment (see his *God of Justice* in the bibliography). Sūra 70 offers further detail on hell, heaven, and the criteria of the Judge.

In the Name of God, the Merciful, the Compassionate

[1] A questioner questioned about the punishment going to fall [2] – the disbelievers have no one to repel it! – [3] from God, controller of the stairways. [4] The angels and the spirit ascend to Him in a day, the measure of which is fifty thousand years. [5] So be patient with a patience that becomes (you). [6] Surely they see it as far off, [7] but We see it is near [8] – the Day when the sky will be like molten metal, [9] and the mountains will be like (tufts of) wool, [10] and friend will not question friend. [11] (As) they come into sight of each other, the sinner will wish that he (could) ransom (himself) from the punishment of that Day with his sons, [12] and his consort, and his brother, [13] and his family who gave him refuge, [14] and whoever is on the earth – all (of them) – (wishing that) then it might

---

70.1 – *A questioner questioned about the punishment going to fall*

The first verse indicates the theme of the sūra – the punishment in store for disbelievers. The sūra answers the questioner's query with vivid scenes of judgment in verses 8–18 and 42–44.

70.8 – *the Day when the sky will be like molten metal*

The first judgment scene (vv. 8–18) includes apocalyptic changes in the universe and the desperation of sinners who have lost their last chance to repent.

70.11 – *the sinner will wish that he (could) ransom (himself)*

On the Day of Judgment, the sinner wants to redeem himself in return for all his relatives in the hope that this may save him (v. 14). But there is no escape (v. 15). See "Salvation in the Quran" (p. 180).

rescue him. [15] By no means! Surely (there is) a flame, [16] a scalp remover! [17] It will call the one who turned and went away, [18] and (who) accumulated and hoarded.

[19] Surely the human was created anxious (for gain). [20] When misfortune touches him, (he is) complaining, [21] but when good touches him, refusing (to give), [22] except for the ones who pray [23] (and) who continue at their prayers, [24] and in whose wealth (there is) an acknowledged (portion) due [25] for the beggar and the outcast, [26] and who affirm the Day of Judgment, [27] and who are apprehensive of the punishment of their Lord [28] – surely no one feels secure (against) the punishment of their Lord – [29] and who guard their private parts, [30] except concerning their wives or what their right (hands) own – surely then they are not (to be) blamed, [31] but whoever seeks beyond that, those – they are the transgressors – [32] and those who keep their pledges and their promise(s), [33] and who stand by their testimonies, [34] and who guard their prayers. [35] Those will be honored in Gardens.

[36] What is (the matter) with those who disbelieve, rushing toward you, [37] from the right (hand) and from the left in groups? [38] Is every person among them eager to enter a Garden of Bliss? [39] By no means! Surely We have created them from what they know. [40] I swear by the Lord of the Easts and the Wests! Surely We are able indeed [41] to exchange (others who are) better than them – We are not (to be) outrun! [42] So leave them! Let them banter and jest, until they meet their Day which they are promised, [43] the Day when they will come forth from the graves rushing – as if they were running to some goal – [44] their sight downcast, humiliation covering them. That is the Day which they were promised.

70.19 – *Surely the human was created anxious*

The Quran contains several statements about the condition in which humans were created (also 4.28; 21.37). Here humans were created "anxious," "complaining," and "refusing" (vv. 19–21). See the analysis of verses about human nature at 79.40 (p. 612).

70.24–25 – *and in whose wealth (there is) an acknowledged (portion) due for the beggar and the outcast*

The Quran's meaningful warning to the rich to care for the poor and orphans, among others, will be familiar to readers of the Bible (e.g., Isaiah 1; James 2).

70.42 – *So leave them! Let them banter and jest, until they meet their Day*

The sūra directly addresses the messenger encouraging him to leave it to Allah to deal with the disbelievers and to be patient (see v. 5). The reckoning will come on the Day of Resurrection (v. 43).

NOAH

NŪḤ

71

> Much like Sūra 12 ("Yūsuf"), Sūra 71 is completely taken up with the story of one biblical character – in this case Noah. The story of Noah appears seven times in the Quran, and a comparison of the different versions raises interesting questions about their similarities and differences. Why do so many versions of the story appear? What should account for their differences?

In the Name of God, the Merciful, the Compassionate

¹ Surely We sent Noah to his people: 'Warn your people before a painful punishment comes upon them.' ² He said, 'My people! I am a clear warner for you. ³ Serve God, and guard (yourselves) against Him, and obey me! ⁴ He will forgive you your sins, and spare you until an appointed time. Surely the time of God, when it comes, cannot be postponed. If (only) you knew!'

71.1 – *Surely We sent Noah to his people*

Sūra 71 is the second of only two sūras that contain a single story (the other is Sūra 12, "Yūsuf"). This indicates the importance of the figure of Noah and his story in the Quran.

In this sūra Allah sends Noah to his people with a message of warning. Noah proclaims the message (vv. 2–4) but then complains to Allah that, despite his efforts, the people disobey him (vv. 5–24). Noah's preaching to his people includes appeals to Allah's willingness to forgive (v. 10) and to the blessings of creation (vv. 14–20).

This is the final of seven Noah stories in the Quran. Other versions appear at 7.59–64; 10.71–73; 11.25–48; 23.23–30; 26.105–20; and 54.7–17. In addition to this, nineteen other sūras mention the name of Noah (*Nūḥ*). On the subject of the repetition of stories in the Quran, see the discussion at 51.24 (p. 526).

Bible readers may notice that Noah says nothing before the flood in the biblical account (Genesis 6:8–7:24), while the quranic versions feature extensive conversations between Noah and his people and between Noah and Allah prior to the flood. Later extrabiblical Jewish and Christian writings include speculations on what their authors imagined Noah might have said to his countrymen with the flood approaching.

⁵ He said, 'My Lord, surely I have called my people night and day, ⁶ but my calling has only increased them in flight. ⁷ Surely I – whenever I called them, so that You might forgive them, they put their fingers in their ears, and covered themselves with their clothes, and persisted (in disbelief), and became very arrogant. ⁸ Then surely I called them publicly, ⁹ then surely I spoke openly to them, and I confided to them in secret, ¹⁰ and I said, "Ask forgiveness from your Lord, surely He is forgiving, ¹¹ and He will send the sky (down) on you in abundance, ¹² and increase you with wealth and sons, and make gardens for you, and make rivers for you. ¹³ What is (the matter) with you that do not expect seriousness (of purpose) on the part of God, ¹⁴ when He created you in stages? ¹⁵ Do you not see how God created seven heavens in stories, ¹⁶ and placed the moon in them as a light, and placed the sun (in them) as a lamp? ¹⁷ And God caused you to grow from of the earth, ¹⁸ (and) then He will return you into it, and bring you forth again. ¹⁹ God has made the earth an expanse for you, ²⁰ so that you may traverse its open (path)ways."'

²¹ Noah said, 'My Lord, surely they have disobeyed me, and followed one whose wealth and children increase him only in loss, ²² and they have schemed a great scheme, ²³ and said, "Do not forsake your gods, and do not forsake Wadd, nor Suwā', nor Yaghūth, and Ya'ūq, and Nasr." ²⁴ And they have led many astray. Increase the evildoers only in going astray!'

²⁵ They were drowned on account of their sins, and forced to enter a fire, and they found they had no helpers other than God. ²⁶ Noah said, 'My Lord, do not leave any of the disbelievers as an inhabitant on the earth. ²⁷ Surely You – if You leave them, they will lead Your servants astray, and will give birth only to depraved disbeliever(s). ²⁸ My Lord, forgive me and my parents, and whoever enters my house believing, and the believing men and the believing women, and increase the evildoers only in destruction!'

71.23 – *do not forsake Wadd, nor Suwā', nor Yaghūth, and Ya'ūq, and Nasr*

Noah reports to his Lord the names of the gods worshiped by his people. These names are unknown and appear only here in the Quran.

71.25 – *They were drowned on account of their sins, and forced to enter a fire*

The other quranic versions of the Noah story mention that the opponents of Noah were drowned, but this version states that they were also punished with fire.

71.28 – *My Lord, forgive me and my parents*

In the Quran, biblical characters often ask God for forgiveness. Noah's request in this verse matches his prayer in 11.47, where he asks forgiveness for complaining about the fate of his son. At the same time, the Quran contains no reference to the rather embarrassing scene in Genesis 9:20–25. See the analysis of the requests of quranic prophets for forgiveness at 48.2 (p. 513).

The Jinn
Al-Jinn

72

> The existence and activities of *jinn* are a curious element in the Quran. Mentioned sporadically throughout the Quran, here the *jinn* are featured in their own sūra. The second half of the sūra deals largely with the tasks and profile of an unassuming messenger.

In the Name of God, the Merciful, the Compassionate

[1] Say: 'I am inspired that a band of the jinn listened, and they said, "Surely we have heard an amazing Qur'ān! [2] It guides to the right (course). We believe in it, and we shall not associate anyone with our Lord. [3] And (we believe) that He – exalted (be) the majesty of our Lord! – He has not taken a consort or son. [4] And that the foolish among us used to say an outrageous thing against God. [5] And that we had thought that humans and jinn would never say any lie against God. [6] And that individuals of humankind used to take refuge with individuals of the jinn, and they increased them in depravity. [7] And that they thought as you (also) thought, that God will not raise up anyone. [8] And that we touched the sky

---

72.1 – *I am inspired that a band of the jinn listened*

Much of the first half of the sūra is presented as the speech of *jinn* (vv. 1–5, 8–14), recited by the messenger with a claim of inspiration.

The Quran presents the *jinn* as a species of created being (6.100) alongside humankind and angels. They are created from fire (55.15). The Quran pairs jinn with humans twenty times, including in the very last verse of the book, "of the jinn and of humankind" (114.6). Iblīs is described as one of the jinn (18.50; cf. 7.12), though elsewhere he seems to be one of the angels (e.g., 2.34). The jinn seduce humans (6.128). Allah sends messengers to jinn (6.130) and will judge them (37.158). Solomon commands jinn (27.17, 39; 34.12, 14), though elsewhere his helpers are called "satans" (*shayāṭīn*, 21.82; 38.37) – leading to the idea that these invisible beings are equivalent in the Quran.

In the following verses, the jinn say that there are both good and bad among them (vv. 11, 14).

and found it filled with harsh guards and piercing flames. ⁹ And that we used to sit there on seats to listen (in), but whoever listens now finds a piercing flame lying in wait for him. ¹⁰ And that we do not know whether evil is intended for those who are on the earth, or whether their Lord intends right (guidance) for them. ¹¹ And that some of us are righteous, and some of us are other than that – we are on different roads. ¹² And that we (now) think that we shall not be able to escape God on the earth, and shall not escape Him by flight. ¹³ And that when we heard the guidance, we believed in it, and whoever believes in his Lord will not fear any deprivation or depravity. ¹⁴ And that some of us have submitted, and some of us are the ones who have deviated. Whoever submits, those have sought out right (guidance), ¹⁵ but as for the ones who have deviated, they have become firewood for Gehenna!"'

¹⁶ And (We say) that if they had gone straight on the road, We would indeed have given them water to drink in abundance, ¹⁷ so that We might test them concerning it. Whoever turns away from the remembrance of his Lord – He will place him in hard punishment. ¹⁸ And that the mosques (belong) to God, so do not call on anyone (along) with God. ¹⁹ And that when the servant of God stood calling on Him, they were almost upon him in hordes.

²⁰ Say: 'I call only on my Lord, and I do not associate anyone with Him.'

²¹ Say: 'Surely I possess no power over you, either for harm or for right (guidance).'

²² Say: 'No one will protect me from God, and I shall not find any refuge other than Him. ²³ (I bring) only a delivery from God and His messages.' Whoever disobeys God and His messenger, surely for him (there is) the Fire of Gehenna, there to remain forever. ²⁴ – Until, when they see what they are promised, they will know who is weaker in helper(s) and fewer in number.

72.15 – *as for the ones who have deviated, they have become firewood for Gehenna!*

The second half of the sūra begins with this striking description of the ones who have "deviated."

72.21 – *Surely I possess no power over you, either for harm or for right (guidance)*

The tasks of the messenger in this sūra are prayer (v. 20) and proclamation (v. 23). This verse specifies that his role does not include exercising power over others. The sūra even says that Allah assigns two watchers to the messenger to make sure he proclaims the message (vv. 27–28).

72.23 – *whoever disobeys Allah and His messenger*

Associating the messenger with Allah for obedience is unusual for a sūra of this type and seems out of tune with verse 21 and the first part of verse 23. In any case, the punishment for disobedience comes not in this world but in the hereafter.

²⁵ Say: 'I do not know whether what you are promised is near, or whether my Lord will appoint a (distant) time for it. ²⁶ (He is) the Knower of the unseen, and He does not disclose His unseen to anyone, ²⁷ except to a messenger whom He has approved, and then He dispatches before him and behind him (watchers) lying in wait, ²⁸ so that He may know that they have delivered the messages of their Lord. He encompasses all that is with them, and He counts everything by number.'

The Enwrapped One
Al-Muzzammil

73

> This sūra takes its name from an expression in the first verse, meaning "enwrapped one." This way of addressing the messenger, as it is understood in Muslim tradition, also begins the following sūra. The trend in sūras at this point is toward increasingly short sūras with shorter verses. Sūra 73, however, ends with a verse much longer than all the others.

In the Name of God, the Merciful, the Compassionate

¹ You, enwrapped one! ² Stay up through the night, except a little ³ – half of it or a little less, ⁴ or a little more – and arrange the Qur'ān very carefully. ⁵ Surely We shall cast upon you a heavy word. ⁶ Surely the first part of the night – it is more efficacious and more suitable for speaking. ⁷ Surely during the day you have protracted business, ⁸ but remember the name of your Lord and devote yourself to Him completely.

⁹ Lord of the East and the West – (there is) no god but Him, so take Him as a guardian, ¹⁰ and be patient with what they say, and forsake them gracefully. ¹¹ Leave Me (to deal with) the ones who call (it) a lie – (those) possessors of prosperity – and let them be for a little (while). ¹² Surely We have chains and a Furnace, ¹³ and food that chokes, and a painful punishment, ¹⁴ on the Day when the earth and the mountains will quake, and the mountains will become a heap of shifting sand.

73.1–2 – *You, enwrapped one! Stay up through the night, except a little*

The first fourteen verses of the sūra are addressed to "you" (supposedly the messenger), first prescribing a seemingly rigorous nighttime worship regimen.

73.10 – *be patient with what they say, and forsake them gracefully*

The Quran frequently encourages the messenger to be patient and to leave to Allah the recompense of those who resist the message (vv. 11–14).

[15] Surely We have sent to you a messenger as a witness over you, as We sent to Pharaoh a messenger. [16] But Pharaoh disobeyed the messenger, and We seized him harshly. [17] If you disbelieve, how will you guard (yourselves) against a Day which will turn the children grey, [18] on which the sky will be split open and His promise comes to pass? [19] Surely this is a Reminder, and whoever pleases takes a way to his Lord.

[20] Surely your Lord knows that you stay up nearly two-thirds of the night – or a half of it or a third of it – and (so do) a contingent of those with you. God determines the night and the day. He knows that you do not count it up, and He has turned to you (in forgiveness). So recite what is easy (for you) of the Qur'ān. He knows that some of you are sick, and others are striking forth on the earth, seeking some of the favor of God, and (still) others are fighting in the

---

73.15 – *Surely We have sent to you a messenger … as We sent to Pharaoh a messenger*

The Quran compares the messenger to the messenger that God sent to Pharaoh. Just as God dealt harshly with Pharaoh, so too he will he judge those who disbelieve in the warnings of the messenger. Notice that the Quran refers to Moses without giving his name (also 44.17–33).

73.20 – *So recite what is easy (for you) of the Qur'ān*

The first part of this very long verse seems to abrogate the rigorous commands of the first eight verses of the Sūra, replacing it with a much more manageable night-time ritual.

73.20 – *others are fighting in the way of God*

When the Quran describes "believers" as "fighting in the way of Allah," it makes a theological claim by associating Allah with human fighting (*qātala*). This verse provides the final occurrence of thirteen such associations in the Quran. The claim that human fighting is "God's way" is problematic, not only in its conception of God but also because it makes it possible for warriors – from the Arab Conquests to modern conflicts – to justify their violence by saying they are fighting in the name and cause of Allah.

Interestingly, the Quran draws the Bible into this theological discussion in two striking passages. One passage seems to refer to an event in the history of the Children of Israel when the people tell a prophet that they want a king and promise to "fight in the way of Allah" (2.246). The name of the prophet is not given, and the king is called here *Ṭālūt*, but the story is recognizable from the account of Israel's request to Samuel in 1 Samuel 8.

The second passage is explicit. It claims the Torah, Gospel, and Quran agree that believers "fight in the way of Allah, and they kill and are killed" (9.111). But can this be

way of God. So recite what is easy (for you) of it, and observe the prayer and give the alms, and lend to God a good loan. Whatever good you send forward for yourselves, you will find it with God – it will be better and greater as a reward. Ask forgiveness from God. Surely God is forgiving, compassionate.

---

said to be a true description of the Gospel? In the Gospel accounts, Jesus forbids violence, and the only place in the New Testament where the verb "fight" appears in the imperative is in a figurative usage: "Fight the good fight of the faith" (1 Timothy 6:12).

As for fighting in the Hebrew Bible (Old Testament), the subject deserves more nuance than it is generally given in comparisons to the Quran. While the Quran seems to know of fighting in the time of Saul and David and vaguely hints at the conquest of Canaan under Moses (5.20–26), it is silent on major prophetic books like Isaiah, which paints a different portrait for Israel in the suffering servant of Yahweh.

The 1 Samuel 8 passage itself is full of ambiguity. Though the people clamor for a king (vv. 5, 19), Samuel is displeased with the request (v. 6), and Yahweh says that Israel has rejected him (v. 7). Here it is not "the way of God" that kings lead Israel in battle "like all the other nations" (v. 20). Also noteworthy is the reason why God did not allow David to build the temple: "because you are a warrior and have shed blood" (1 Chronicles 28:3).

According to the Gospel accounts, Jesus said he had come not to abolish the Law (Torah) and the Prophets but to fulfill them (Matthew 5:17). Jesus then gives a series of commandments that have much to do with human violence (Matthew 5:21–48). The final two commandments in the group are to "turn the other cheek" (v. 39) and to love one's enemies (v. 44). There is good reason to see in Jesus' preaching and behavior the restoration of an original divine intention, scuttled by humans in such events as Israel's 1 Samuel 8 request for a king. Perhaps for this reason, many Christians choose to view Old Testament violence through the prism of the life and teaching of Jesus.

In any case, Matthew 5 and other Gospel passages do not match the claim in 9.111 that the Gospel agrees with the Quran on the subject of fighting. On this important issue, the Quran does not "confirm" the Gospel as it so claims.

THE CLOAKED ONE
AL-MUDDATHTHIR

74

The central part of this sūra illustrates a difficult literary phenomenon that occurs frequently in the Quran. The sūra mentions the number nineteen and then seems to attempt to explain what this means. By itself, the explanation fails to clarify the meaning, and there is nothing in the context of the sūra or elsewhere in the Quran to shed light on the mystery.

In the Name of God, the Merciful, the Compassionate

¹ You, cloaked one! ² Arise and warn! ³ Magnify your Lord, ⁴ and purify your clothes, ⁵ and flee from the defilement! ⁶ Do not confer a favor to gain more, ⁷ and be patient before your Lord. ⁸ When there is a blast on the trumpet, ⁹ that Day will be a hard Day ¹⁰ – far from easy on the disbelievers.

¹¹ Leave Me (to deal with) him whom I created alone, ¹² and for whom I supplied extensive wealth, ¹³ and sons as witnesses, ¹⁴ and made everything smooth for him. ¹⁵ Then he is eager that I should do more. ¹⁶ By no means! He is stubborn to Our signs. ¹⁷ I shall burden him with a hard climb. ¹⁸ Surely he thought and decided – ¹⁹ so may he perish (for) how he decided! ²⁰ Once again, may he perish (for) how he decided! ²¹ Then he looked, ²² then he frowned and scowled, ²³ then he turned back and became arrogant, ²⁴ and said, 'This is nothing but ordinary magic. ²⁵ This is nothing but the word of a human being.' ²⁶ I shall burn him in Saqar!

²⁷ And what will make you know what Saqar is? ²⁸ It spares nothing, and

---

74.1–2 – *You, cloaked one! Arise and warn!*

The sūra begins with a series of short commands to the "cloaked one," supposedly the messenger, in a manner similar to the previous sūra.

74.11 – *Leave Me (to deal with) him whom I created alone*

Like the previous sūra (73.11), the Quran recounts how Allah creates and provides for humans and how humans fail to respond appropriately (74.11–29).

leaves nothing, [29] scorching all flesh. [30] Over it are nineteen. [31] We have made only angels as keepers of the Fire, and We have made their number only as a test for the disbelievers, so that those who have been given the Book may be certain, and that those who believe may increase in belief, and that those who have been given the Book and those who believe may not be in doubt, and that those in whose hearts is a sickness and the disbelievers may say, 'What did God intend by this as a parable?' In this way God leads astray whomever He pleases and guides whomever He pleases. No one knows the (angelic) forces of your Lord but Him. It is nothing but a reminder to humankind.

[32] By no means! By the moon, [33] and the night when it retreats, [34] and the morning when it brightens! [35] Surely it is indeed one of the greatest things [36] – a warning to humankind – [37] to whoever of you pleases to go forward or lag behind.

[38] Each person (is held) in pledge for what he has earned, [39] except for the companions on the right. [40] In Gardens they will ask each other questions [41] about the sinners: [42] 'What put you into Saqar?' [43] They will say, 'We were not among the ones who prayed, [44] and we did not feed the poor, [45] and we bantered with the banterers, [46] and we called the Day of Judgment a lie, [47] until the certainty came to us.' [48] The intercession of the intercessors will not benefit them.

[49] What is (the matter) with them, turning away from the Reminder, [50] as if they were frightened donkeys [51] fleeing from a lion? [52] No! Each one of them wants to be given scrolls unrolled. [53] By no means! No! They do not fear the Hereafter. [54] By no means! Surely it is a reminder, [55] and whoever pleases takes heed of it. [56] But they will not take heed unless God pleases. He is worthy of guarding (oneself) against, and worthy of (dispensing) forgiveness.

74.31 – *We have made only angels as keepers of the Fire*

This long verse, visibly out of sync with the rest of the sūra, seems designed to explain the mysterious number "nineteen" in verse 30. However, the verse also seems to say that no one understands the matter except the Lord.

74.40 – *In Gardens they will ask each other questions*

Most of the last part of the sūra concerns punishment in the hereafter. Verses 40–47 picture a conversation between the inhabitants of heaven and hell.

THE RESURRECTION
AL-QIYĀMA

75

The title of this sūra, "The Resurrection," suits its theme. Its style of short – and often explosive – verses on judgment and the shape of the hereafter will become the dominant style in the remainder of the Quran.

In the Name of God, the Merciful, the Compassionate

[1] I swear by the Day of Resurrection! [2] And I swear by the accusing self! [3] Does the human think that We shall not gather his bones? [4] Yes indeed! We are (even) able to fashion his fingers (again). [5] Yet the human (still) wants to know what is in store for him. [6] He asks, 'When is the Day of Resurrection?' [7] When the sight is dazed, [8] and the moon is eclipsed, [9] and the sun and moon are brought together, [10] on that Day the human will say, 'Where is the escape?' [11] By no means! (There is) no refuge! [12] The (only) dwelling place on that Day will be to your Lord. [13] On that Day the human will be informed about what has he sent forward and kept back. [14] No! The human will be a clear proof against himself, [15] even though he offers his excuses.

[16] Do not move your tongue with it to hurry it. [17] Surely on Us (depends) its collection and its recitation. [18] When We recite it, follow its recitation. [19] Then surely on Us (depends) its explanation.

75.3 – *Does the human think that We shall not gather his bones?*

After an opening oath, the sūra emphasizes that Allah is able to resurrect every person for judgment. The Quran argues that since Allah creates humans from "a drop of semen" (v. 37), he can certainly reassemble their bones from the grave.

75.7–8 – *When the sight is dazed, and the moon is eclipsed*

Apocalyptic signs in the heavens will bring in the Day of Resurrection.

75.13 – *On that Day the human will be informed*

Every person will need to account for what he or she has done.

75.16 – *Do not move your tongue with it to hurry it*

This and the following three verses break the flow of the resurrection theme in order to instruct the messenger in how to recite.

²⁰ By no means! No! You love this fleeting (world), ²¹ and neglect the Hereafter. ²² (Some) faces that Day will be radiant, ²³ looking to their Lord, ²⁴ and (other) faces that Day will be scowling, ²⁵ thinking that a calamity will be visited on them. ²⁶ By no means! When it reaches the collarbones, ²⁷ and it is said, 'Who will carry (him) off?,' ²⁸ and he thinks that the parting has come, ²⁹ when leg is tangled with leg, ³⁰ the (only) drive on that Day will be to your Lord.

³¹ (For) he did not affirm (it), nor did he pray, ³² but he called (it) a lie and turned away. ³³ Then he went to his household with an arrogant swagger. ³⁴ Nearer to you and nearer! ³⁵ Once again, nearer to you and nearer! ³⁶ Does the human think that he will be left to go about at will? ³⁷ Was he not a drop of semen emitted? ³⁸ Then he was a clot, and He created and fashioned (him), ³⁹ and made from it the two sexes, the male and the female. ⁴⁰ Is that One not able to give the dead life?

75.34 – *Nearer to you and nearer!*

This sūra seems to conceive of the Day of Resurrection as rapidly approaching. See "Eschatology in the Quran" (p. 604).

The Human
Al-Insān

76

> This sūra briefly refers to disbelievers and the punishments coming to them, but its main theme is the efforts of the "righteous" and the rewards they deserve in the hereafter.

In the Name of God, the Merciful, the Compassionate

¹ Has (there) come upon the human a period of time when he was a thing not mentioned? ² Surely We created the human from a drop, a mixture – We test him – and We made him hearing (and) seeing. ³ Surely We guided him to the way, (to see) whether (he would be) thankful or whether (he would be) ungrateful.

⁴ Surely We have prepared for the disbelievers chains and fetters and a blazing (Fire). ⁵ Surely the pious will drink from a cup containing a mixture of camphor, ⁶ (from) a spring at which the servants of God drink, making it gush forth abundantly. ⁷ They fulfill (their) vows, and fear a Day – its evil is (already) in the air – ⁸ and they give food, despite their love for it, to the poor, and the orphan,

---

76.3 – *Surely We guided him to the way, (to see) whether (he would be) thankful or whether (he would be) ungrateful*

Humans respond to the Creator by showing themselves either grateful or not.

76.5 – *Surely the pious will drink from a cup*

In this verse "pious" translates the Arabic *abrār* (sing. *barr*). Other definitions of this word are "righteous," "reverent," and "upright." In the verses that follow, the Quran lists what makes these people pious (vv. 7–10) and thus why Allah rewards them (vv. 11–21).

This passage is noteworthy because it declares that people can be righteous by their own deeds and attitudes and that Allah will reward them in the hereafter for their effort, or "striving."

76.8 – *they give food, despite their love for it, to the poor, and the orphan, and the captive*

The phrase "despite their love for it" could also be translated "for love of him" (meaning Allah), and several translations render it this way. The following verse

603

and the captive: [9] 'We feed you only for the face of God. We do not desire any payment or thanks from you. [10] Surely we fear a grim (and) ominous Day from our Lord.' [11] So God has guarded them against the evil of that Day, and made them encounter radiance and happiness, [12] and repaid them for their patience with a Garden and silk. [13] Reclining there on couches, [14] they do not see there any (hot) sun or bitter cold, and its shades are close upon them, and its clusters (of fruit) near (at hand). [15] Vessels of silver and cups made of crystal are passed around among them [16] – crystal of silver which they have measured very exactly. [17] There they are given a cup to drink, containing a mixture of ginger, [18] (from) a spring there named Salsabīl. [19] And boys of eternal youth circulate among them. When you see them, you (would) think them scattered pearls. [20] When you see (it all), then you will see bliss and a great kingdom. [21] On them are green clothes of silk and brocade, and they are adorned with bracelets of silver, and their Lord gives them a pure drink to drink. [22] 'Surely this is a payment for you, and your striving is appreciated.'

Eschatology in the Quran
David Cook

Inside the Quran, eschatology – beliefs about the end of the world and life in the hereafter – is a major theme. The first part of eschatology is concerned with the end of the world as an event that will happen by necessity to the world, with specific signs leading up to this end. The second part describes the Day of Judgment, when Allah will judge humanity, as well as the shape of the hereafter.

Most of the quranic apocalyptic material is localized with the word *al-sāʿa* (the Hour [of Judgment], closely related to the Hebrew and Aramaic terms), which appears in the text about forty-five times. Because the seventh century began with a lengthy war between the Byzantines and the Sasanian Persians (602–28), it is not surprising that people were asking about the end of the world.

In the Quran there is no doubt that the Hour will come (18.21; 22.7; 40.59; 45.32). It is said to be very close (16.77), and it will come suddenly (6.31; 12.107;

---

seems to suggest that the "pious" feed the poor for love of Allah. See the comment at 5.54 (p. 146) and "The Language of Love in the Quran" (p. 560).

76.13 – *Reclining there on couches*

This passage (vv. 12–21) pictures further details of life in the heavenly "Garden."

22.55; 47.18). Only Allah knows its exact time (7.187; 31.34; 43.85), though he has promised that it will indeed come (18.21; 45.32). Unbelievers, who are the majority of the people (40.59), say that it will not come (22.55; 25.11; 34.3) and are said to be making a grave error by making this assumption (42.18). They will see the punishment and the Hour which God has promised with their own eyes (19.75).

As with other unfamiliar quranic concepts, people are uncertain about the exact meaning of "the Hour" (45.32), while others are said to be ignorant of its portents (12.107), so they are encouraged to watch carefully (43.66; 47.18) and to ask the Prophet: "When is it, and what are its signs?" (7.187; 79.42). Its coming was heralded by the splitting of the moon (54.1), and its arrival is likened to an earthquake (22.1). That the audience was intensely interested in the coming of the Hour is obvious from the quranic text, as people continually ask about it (33.63; 42.17).

What happens after the end of the world is of even greater concern in the Quran. There are many different terms for the bridge event between the end of the world and the beginning of the hereafter: the Last Day (*al-yawm al-ākhir*), the Day of Resurrection (*yawm al-qiyāma*), the Day of Judgment (*yawm al-dīn*), some of which are related to analogous biblical terms. During this event every human will be raised from the dead, or brought forth, and separated into two groups (3.106; 88.2, 8), the blessed and the damned, on the basis of their deeds and belief. Unlike in later Islam, in the Quran there is not much room for any third category.

In general, the Quran gives more details about heaven than hell. There are seven heavens (17.44), which are described in terms of verdancy and luxury: "Reclining there on couches, they do not see there any (hot) sun or bitter cold ... and its clusters (of fruit) near (at hand). Vessels of silver and cups made of crystal are passed around among them. . . . There they are given a cup to drink, containing a mixture of ginger" (76.13–17). There are numerous other descriptions along these lines.

Hell in the Quran is described in terms of psychological terror, burning heat, and being compelled to consume loathsome or disgusting things. "On the day when they are dragged on their faces into the Fire" (54.48). And again: "They will burn in a scorching Fire, and will be made to drink from a boiling spring. They will have no food except dry thorns" (88.4–6). But while one can get a sense of the topography of heaven from the Quran, it is not easy to see what hell looks like other than being a furnace and a torture chamber.

Quranic eschatology is immediate in the sense that it is assumed to be happening in the near future and completely transformative in the sense that after its occurrence the world will be entirely different or destroyed. Most likely as a preaching theme, the dramatic quranic eschatology was designed to cause people to change their lives. In this sense eschatology was undoubtedly one of the foundations of the early Muslim community.

²³ Surely We – We have sent down on you the Qur'ān once and for all. ²⁴ So be patient for the Judgment of your Lord, and do not obey any sinner (or) ungrateful one among them. ²⁵ But remember the name of your Lord morning and evening, ²⁶ and part of the night, and prostrate yourself before Him, and glorify Him all night long.

²⁷ Surely these (people) love the fleeting (world), and leave behind them a heavy Day. ²⁸ We created them and strengthened their constitution, and when We please, We shall exchange the likes of them. ²⁹ Surely this is a Reminder, and whoever pleases takes a way to his Lord. ³⁰ But you will not (so) please unless God pleases. Surely God is knowing, wise. ³¹ He causes whomever He pleases to enter into His mercy, but the evildoers – He has prepared a painful punishment for them.

76.23 – *Surely We – We have sent down on you the Qur'ān once and for all*

Once more the Quran breaks the flow of the resurrection theme to address several verses directly to the messenger (see 75.16), including this self-affirming claim to be "sent down." On the word *qur'ān*, see the comment at 2.185 (p. 61).

THE ONES
SENT FORTH
AL-MURSALĀT

This sūra seems to stitch together by now very familiar themes with the help of a repeating refrain. On the positive side are the signs of the Creator and a vision of rewards in heaven. On the warning side are frightening signs in the universe, the destruction of former peoples, and the sights and suffering of hell.

In the Name of God, the Merciful, the Compassionate

¹ By the ones sent forth in succession, and the ones blasting (with their) blast! ² By the scatterers ³ (with their) scattering, ⁴ and the ones splitting asunder, ⁵ and the ones casting a reminder, ⁶ as an excuse or warning! ⁷ Surely what you are promised is indeed going to fall!

⁸ When the stars are obliterated, ⁹ and when the sky is split open, ¹⁰ and when the mountains are scattered (as dust), ¹¹ and when the messengers' time is given – ¹² for what Day are these things appointed? ¹³ For the Day of Decision!

¹⁴ And what will make you know what the Day of Decision is? ¹⁵ Woe that Day to the ones who call (it) a lie!

¹⁶ Did We not destroy those of old? ¹⁷ Then We caused later (generations) to follow them. ¹⁸ In this way We deal with the sinners. ¹⁹ Woe that Day to the ones who call (it) a lie!

77.1 – *By the ones sent forth in succession*

A series of oaths (vv. 1–6) leads up to a promise that the "Day of Decision" (*faṣl*) will surely come (v. 13).

77.15 – *Woe that Day to the ones who call (it) a lie!*

This striking refrain repeats throughout the sūra.

77.16 – *Did We not destroy those of old?*

The first of familiar themes signaled in this sūra is the way Allah dealt with peoples in the past (vv. 16–18).

²⁰ Did We not create you from despicable water, ²¹ and put it in a secure dwelling place ²² for a known term? ²³ We determined (it) – excellent were the Ones able (to do that)! ²⁴ Woe that Day to the ones who call (it) a lie!

²⁵ Did We not make the earth as a container ²⁶ of the living and dead? ²⁷ And did We not place on it lofty mountains, and give you fresh water to drink? ²⁸ Woe that Day to the ones who call (it) a lie!

²⁹ Depart to what you called a lie! ³⁰ Depart to a three-branched shadow ³¹ – (it affords) no sheltering (shade) and (it is of) no use against the flame. ³² Surely it shoots out sparks, (each one) the size of a castle, ³³ as if it were (the color) of yellow camels. ³⁴ Woe that Day to the ones who call (it) a lie!

³⁵ This is a Day when they will not speak, ³⁶ nor will it be permitted to them to make excuses. ³⁷ Woe that Day to the ones who call (it) a lie!

³⁸ 'This is the Day of Decision. We have gathered you and those of old together. ³⁹ If you have a plot, plot against Me!' ⁴⁰ Woe that Day to the ones who call (it) a lie!

⁴¹ Surely the ones who guard (themselves) will be in (the midst of) shades and springs, ⁴² and fruits of whatever (kind) they desire: ⁴³ 'Eat and drink with satisfaction (in return) for what you have done.' ⁴⁴ Surely in this way We repay the doers of good. ⁴⁵ Woe that Day to the ones who call (it) a lie!

⁴⁶ 'Eat and enjoy (life) a little. Surely you are sinners!' ⁴⁷ Woe that Day to the ones who call (it) a lie!

⁴⁸ When it is said to them, 'Bow down,' they do not bow down. ⁴⁹ Woe that Day to the ones who call (it) a lie!

⁵⁰ In what proclamation will they believe after this?

77.20 – *Did We not create you from despicable water . . . ?*

The second familiar theme is the signs of the Creator's power and provision (vv. 20–27).

77.29 – *Depart to what you called a lie!*

The third familiar theme is descriptions of hell (vv. 30–36) and heaven (vv. 41–43).

77.44 – *Surely in this way We repay the doers of good*

Similar to verses in the previous sūra, Allah rewards the "doers of good" with heaven because they are pious, or righteous, or "the ones who guard (themselves)" (v. 41).

THE NEWS
AL-NABA'

78

Sūra 78 repeats themes that have appeared frequently: the power of the Creator, the Day of Decision, the punishment of the rebellious, and the delights of heaven. This and the previous two sūras highlight the Quran's concept of how people reach the "Gardens": by achievement and reward.

In the Name of God, the Merciful, the Compassionate

[1] What are they asking each other questions about? [2] About the awesome news, [3] concerning which they differ. [4] By no means! Soon they will know! [5] Once again, by no means! Soon they will know!

[6] Have We not made the earth as a bed, [7] and the mountains as stakes? [8] We created you in pairs, [9] and made your sleep as a rest, [10] and made the night as a covering, [11] and made the day for (your) livelihood. [12] We have built above you seven firm (heavens), [13] and made a blazing lamp. [14] We have sent down water from the rainclouds, pouring forth, [15] so that by means of it We may bring forth grain and vegetation, [16] and luxuriant gardens.

[17] Surely the Day of Decision is an appointed time: [18] the Day when there will be a blast on the trumpet, and you will come in crowds, [19] and the sky will be opened and become gates, [20] and the mountains will be moved and become a mirage. [21] Surely Gehenna lies in wait [22] as a (place of) return for the insolent transgressors, [23] there to remain for ages. [24] They will not taste there any coolness

---

78.4 – *By no means! Soon they will know!*

The repetition of this phrase in verses 4–5 is an element of style that has not occurred frequently in the Quran up to this point.

78.6 – *Have We not made the earth as a bed … ?*

This verse starts a creation passage that features some lovely expressions (vv. 6–16).

78.17 – *the Day of Decision is an appointed time*

The sūra then turns toward the Judgment Day and the punishments that will come to those who "were not expecting a reckoning" (vv. 17–30).

or drink, ²⁵ except for boiling (water) and rotten (food) ²⁶ – a fitting payment! ²⁷ Surely they were not expecting a reckoning ²⁸ when they called Our signs an utter lie. ²⁹ But We have counted up everything in a Book. ³⁰ So: 'Taste (it)! We shall only increase you in punishment.'

³¹ Surely for the ones who guard (themselves) (there is) a (place of) safety: ³² orchards and grapes, ³³ and full-breasted (maidens), (all) of the same age, ³⁴ and a cup full (of wine) ³⁵ – in which they will not hear any frivolous talk, nor any lying ³⁶ – a payment from your Lord, a gift, a reckoning!

³⁷ Lord of the heavens and the earth, and whatever is between them, the Merciful, of whom they have no power to speak. ³⁸ On the Day when the spirit and the angels stand in lines, they will not speak, except the one to whom the Merciful has given permission, and he will say what is correct. ³⁹ That is the true Day. Whoever pleases takes a (way of) return to his Lord. ⁴⁰ Surely We have warned you of a punishment near (at hand), on the Day when a person will see what his hands have sent forward, and the disbeliever will say, 'Would that I were dust!'

78.33 – *and full-breasted (maidens), (all) of the same age*

Such descriptions have attracted the attention of non-Muslims. What do they intend to portray about the characteristics of the heavenly "Gardens"? Elsewhere the Quran mentions "(maidens) with dark, wide eyes" (44.54; 52.20; 56.22; cf. 55.72), "(maidens) restraining (their) glances" (38.52; 55.56), and "virgins" (56.36). See the comment at 44.54 (p. 497).

THE SNATCHERS
AL-NĀZIʿĀT

79

Few sūras since Sūra 54 have included stories of biblical characters, but in this sūra Moses reappears. "Has the story of Moses come to you?" The referential style of the episode raises questions: Is this an Arabic retelling of something overheard? Is it a new spin on a well-known story?

In the Name of God, the Merciful, the Compassionate

¹ By the ones who snatch violently! ² By the ones who draw out completely! ³ By the ones who glide smoothly, ⁴ and race swiftly, ⁵ and direct the affair! ⁶ On the Day when the (earth)quake quakes, ⁷ and that which ensues follows it, ⁸ hearts on that Day will pound, ⁹ their sight downcast. ¹⁰ They will say, 'Are we indeed being turned back into (our) former state? ¹¹ When we were rotten bones?' ¹² They will say, 'That would then be a losing turn!' ¹³ Yet it will only be a single shout, ¹⁴ and suddenly they will be awakened.

¹⁵ Has the story of Moses come to you? ¹⁶ When his Lord called to him in the holy wādī of Ṭuwā: ¹⁷ 'Go to Pharaoh! Surely he has transgressed insolently. ¹⁸ And say: "Do you have (any desire) to purify yourself?" ¹⁹ And: "I would guide you to your Lord, and then perhaps you will fear (Him)."' ²⁰ So he showed him the great sign, ²¹ but he called (it) a lie and disobeyed. ²² Then he turned away in haste, ²³ and he gathered (his people) and called out, ²⁴ and said, 'I am your Lord,

---

79.1 – *By the ones who snatch violently!*

A series of oaths leads once more to announcement of the Judgment Day. The audience asks whether it is really possible that they would be resurrected (vv. 10–11). The Creator's power to do so is described later in the sūra (vv. 27–33).

79.15 – *Has the story of Moses come to you?*

The question itself seems to imply that the story has indeed previously come to the messenger, and the referential style of the story suggests that the audience knows the larger narrative framework of which this episode (vv. 15–25) is one part. This raises questions about the identity and context of both messenger and audience.

the Most High!' [25] So God seized him with the punishment of the last and the first. [26] Surely in that is a lesson indeed for whoever fears.

[27] Are you a stronger creation or the sky? He built it. [28] He raised its roof and fashioned it. [29] He darkened its night and brought forth its morning light. [30] And the earth, after that, He spread it out. [31] He brought forth from it its water and its pasture [32] – and the mountains, He anchored it (to them) – [33] a provision for you and for your livestock.

[34] When the great overwhelming comes, [35] on the Day when a person will remember what he strove for, [36] and the Furnace will come forth for all to see: [37] as for the one who transgressed insolently, [38] and preferred this present life, [39] surely the Furnace – it will be the refuge. [40] But as for the one who feared

---

79.40 – *But as for the one who . . . restrained himself from (vain) desire*

In this verse the soul, or "self" (*nafs*), needs to be restrained from "desire." Here desire, or lust (*hawā*), is something outside of the self that attracts it. Also, in 114.4–5 a "slinking one" whispers to the human heart. In other verses, the soul itself seems to be the problem: Cain's soul, or "self," compels him to kill his brother (5.30); "the self is an instigator of evil," says Joseph (12.53); and Allah knows what the soul "whispers" to a person (50.16). In 25.43 a man chooses "his own desire" as his god.

Some scholars and polemicists declare that Islam has no concept of "original sin." However, this claim may cause the reader to miss what the Quran actually says about the soul and human nature. It is true that Islamic doctrine does not clearly connect the sin of Adam with a predisposition to sin in Adam's descendants. But in the Quran, at the time of Adam's creation the angels say that the human "will foment corruption" on the earth "and shed blood" (2.30). The Quran also says that humans were created weak (4.28) and anxious (70.19), fretful (70.20) and grudging (70.21), alone (74.11) and "out of haste" (21.37). They are despairing (11.9), unjust (14.34), rebellious (96.6), ungrateful (80.17; 100.6), "in loss" (103.2), and ignorant (33.72).

More than anything, according to the Quran, humans are "contentious" (18.54; 16.4). This reminds the reader that in almost all of the Quran's many punishment stories, the audiences of past messengers resist the message (e.g., 6.4–6; 35.42; 36.46). This is also the case in most of the disputation scenes involving the Quran's messenger. In all of these passages, most humans show themselves impervious to preaching. "Most of the people refuse (everything) but disbelief" (25.50). Those who "believe and do good works" seem to be an exception – sometimes almost an afterthought. And yet nowhere does the Quran propose a solution for human incorrigibility other than Allah's destruction of sinful peoples (e.g., 17.58; 20.128–29).

Another dimension to this theme is the Quran's assertion that Allah, at the beginning of human history, forecasts that he will fill hell with all those whom Satan

the position of his Lord, and restrained himself from (vain) desire, [41] surely the Garden – it will be the refuge.

[42] They ask you about the Hour: 'When is its arrival?' [43] What do you have to do with the mention of it? [44] To your Lord is its (ultimate) goal. [45] You are only a warner for whoever fears it. [46] On the Day when they see it, (it will seem) as if they had remained (in the grave) for only an evening or its morning light.

---

will beguile (7.18; 38.85). Twice Allah promises to "fill Gehenna with jinn and people – all (of them)!" (11.119; 32.13), and at 50.30 Allah asks hell, "Are you filled?" The Quran even seems to say that everyone will initially go to hell (19.71). Why would hell be filled with humanity if human nature is basically good?

For a Bible reader, this analysis might bring to mind verses like 2 Peter 3:9, "The Lord is not slow in keeping his promise, as some understand slowness. He is patient with you, not wanting anyone to perish, but everyone to come to repentance," and 1 Timothy 2.4: "[God our Savior] wants all people to be saved and to come to a knowledge of the truth."

In two verses the Quran says, "If Allah were to take the people to task for what they have earned, He would not leave on it [earth] any living creature" (35.45; 16.61: "for their evildoing"). This seems to suggest a concept of a holy God and the seriousness of human sin that is deeply biblical. In these verses Allah reprieves humanity "until an appointed time," which is a sign of his mercy. But if this reprieve lasts until the Day of Judgment, the Quran offers no treatment of human sin before then. A reader could reasonably conclude from many quranic passages that the symptoms of human sinfulness are visible, but that there is no deeper diagnosis or proposed cure.

The theological points here are significant. Does God create humanity, give his law, and then on the Day of Resurrection judge a "weak" and "contentious" humanity strictly on the basis of human deeds, as the Quran suggests? Or does God in grace and love arrange for a way of salvation that takes human sinfulness in its full measure and conquers it, as the Bible presents?

An excellent resource that takes this analysis and response much further is "Different Diagnoses of the Human Condition" by Dudley Woodberry in *Muslims and Christians on the Emmaus Road* (see bibliography).

HE FROWNED
ʿABASA

80

By this point in the Quran, the reader is familiar with its main themes and the kinds of literature it includes. These themes and text types repeat in the remaining sūras and need no further explanation. Comments and sūra introductions will mainly focus on new material or striking expressions.

In the Name of God, the Merciful, the Compassionate

[1] He frowned and turned away, [2] because the blind man came to him. [3] What will make you know? Perhaps he will (yet) purify himself, [4] or take heed, and the Reminder will benefit him. [5] As for the one who considers himself independent, [6] you give your attention to him. [7] Yet it is not (dependent) on you if he does not purify himself. [8] But as for the one who comes running to you, [9] and (who) fears (God), [10] from him you are distracted.

[11] By no means! Surely it is a Reminder [12] – and whoever pleases (may) take heed of it – [13] (written) in honored pages, [14] exalted (and) purified, [15] by the hands of scribes, [16] (who are) honorable (and) dutiful.

[17] May the human perish! How ungrateful he is! [18] From what did He create him? [19] From a drop! He created him, and determined him, [20] then He made the way easy for him, [21] then He caused him to die and buried him, [22] then, when

---

80.1–2 – *He frowned and turned away, because the blind man came to him*

The sūra opens with a story of interaction with a blind man. However, because this passage (vv. 1–10) gives no names but only pronouns ("he," "you"), it is difficult to make out what the story might be about.

Muslim commentators on this passage told a story about Muhammad and his behavior with a blind man who asked to be taught.

80.17 – *May the human perish! How ungrateful he is!*

The picture of humanity in this passage (vv. 17–23) is rather negative. Though Allah creates and makes the way easy for people, they do not fulfill Allah's commandments but instead are ungrateful. On the Quran's concept of human nature, see the analysis at 79.40 (p. 612).

He pleases, He will raise him (again). ²³ By no means! He has not accomplished what He commanded him.

²⁴ Let the human consider his food: ²⁵ We pour out water in abundance, ²⁶ then We split open the earth in cracks, ²⁷ and We cause grain to grow in it, ²⁸ and grapes and green plants, ²⁹ and olives and date palms, ³⁰ and lush orchards, ³¹ and fruits and herbs ³² – a provision for you and your livestock.

³³ When the blast comes, ³⁴ on the Day when a person will flee from his brother, ³⁵ and his mother and his father, ³⁶ and his consort and his sons, ³⁷ each of them that Day will have some matter to keep him busy. ³⁸ (Some) faces that Day will be shining, ³⁹ laughing, rejoicing at the good news. ⁴⁰ But (other) faces that Day – dust will be upon them, ⁴¹ (and) darkness will cover them. ⁴² Those – they are the disbelievers, the depraved.

80.24 – *Let the human consider his food*

The way Allah provides fruits and vegetables (vv. 24–32) is a sign of his presence and power.

80.33–34 – *When the blast comes, on the Day when a person will flee from his brother*

Believers and unbelievers will have very different responses when the Day of Resurrection breaks.

THE SHROUDING
AL-TAKWĪR

81

The series of short "when" statements about the Day of Resurrection in the first half of this sūra follows a style of expression not yet seen in the Quran.

In the Name of God, the Merciful, the Compassionate

[1] When the sun is shrouded, [2] and when the stars become dim, [3] and when the mountains are moved, [4] and when the pregnant camels are abandoned, [5] and when the wild beasts are herded together, [6] and when the seas are made to surge, [7] and when selves are paired, [8] and when the buried baby girl is asked [9] for what sin she was killed, [10] and when the pages are spread open, [11] and when the sky is stripped off, [12] and when the Furnace is set ablaze, [13] and when the Garden is brought near, [14] (then each) person will know what he has presented.

[15] I swear by the slinking (stars), [16] the runners, the hiders, [17] by the night when it departs, [18] by the dawn when it breathes! [19] Surely it is indeed the word of an honorable messenger [20] – one full of power, secure with the Holder of the throne, [21] one (to be) obeyed, (and) furthermore trustworthy. [22] Your companion

---

81.1–2 – *When the sun is shrouded, and when the stars become dim*

This sūra opens with a picture of the apocalyptic changes that will appear on the Day of Resurrection, when every person will be called to account (v. 14).

81.19 – *Surely it is indeed the word of an honorable messenger*

A series of oaths (vv. 15–18) introduces the claim that the recitation is the word of an honorable messenger, one full of power and to be obeyed (vv. 19–21) – and not the word of an accursed satan (v. 25). If a human messenger is intended here, this would correspond to how many non-Muslims view the Quran. In Muslim tradition, however, the messenger is understood to be Gabriel.

81.22 – *Your companion is not possessed*

One of the frequent accusations against the messenger is that he is possessed by *jinn* (*majnūn*). In Muslim tradition, what "your companion" sees "on the clear horizon" (v. 23) is Gabriel.

is not possessed. [23] Certainly he did see Him on the clear horizon. [24] He is not grudging of the unseen. [25] It is not the word of an accursed satan. [26] So where will you go? [27] It is nothing but a reminder to the worlds [28] – to whoever of you pleases to go straight. [29] But you will not (so) please unless God pleases, the Lord of the worlds.

THE RENDING
AL-INFIṬĀR

82

This sūra directly addresses the "human" in a powerful appeal that reaches out to all of humanity (vv. 6–8).

In the Name of God, the Merciful, the Compassionate

¹ When the sky is rent, ² and when the stars are scattered, ³ and when the seas are made to gush forth, ⁴ and when the graves are ransacked, ⁵ (then each) person will know what he has sent forward and kept back.

⁶ Human! What has deceived you about your generous Lord, ⁷ who created you and fashioned you and balanced you? ⁸ He constructed you in whatever form He pleased. ⁹ By no means! No! You (still) call the Judgment a lie. ¹⁰ Surely (there are) indeed watchers over you, ¹¹ honorable, writing. ¹² They know whatever you do. ¹³ Surely the pious will indeed be in (a place of) bliss, ¹⁴ and surely the depraved will indeed be in a Furnace. ¹⁵ They will burn in it on the Day of Judgment, ¹⁶ and from it they will not be absent.

¹⁷ What will make you know what the Day of Judgment is? ¹⁸ Once again, what will make you know what the Day of Judgment is? ¹⁹ The Day when no one will have any power to (help) another. The command on that Day (will belong) to God.

82.1–2 – *When the sky is rent, and when the stars are scattered*

A series of "when" statements leads into an appeal to the "human" to take the Day of Judgment seriously.

82.6–7 – *Human! What has deceived you about your generous Lord, who created you*

One of the most powerful appeals of the Quran is the challenge to humankind to respond appropriately to the One who created them.

82.10–11 – *Surely (there are) indeed watchers over you, honorable, writing*

Recording angels keep track of each person's deeds. Each will receive either a reward or a punishment on the Day of Judgment (v. 15). Verse 14 gives the name *jahīm*, here translated "Furnace," for hell.

THE DEFRAUDERS
AL-MUṬAFFIFĪN

83

The Quran's emphasis on justice in the marketplace (see 83.1–6) has been a benefit to shoppers in souk and bazaar throughout Islamic history.

In the Name of God, the Merciful, the Compassionate

¹ Woe to the defrauders, ² who take full measure when they measure against the people, ³ but give less when they measure for themselves or weigh for themselves. ⁴ Do those (people) not think that they will be raised up ⁵ for a great Day, ⁶ a Day when the people will stand before the Lord of the worlds? ⁷ By no means! Surely the book of the depraved is indeed in Sijjīn. ⁸ And what will make you know what Sijjīn is? ⁹ A written book. ¹⁰ Woe that Day to the ones who call (it) a lie, ¹¹ who call the Day of Judgment a lie! ¹² No one calls it a lie except every transgressor (and) sinner. ¹³ When Our signs are recited to him, he says, 'Old tales!' ¹⁴ By no means! No! What they have earned has rusted on their hearts. ¹⁵ By no means! Surely on that Day they will indeed be veiled from their Lord. ¹⁶ Then surely they will indeed burn in the Furnace. ¹⁷ Then it will be said to them, 'This is what you called a lie.'

¹⁸ By no means! Surely the book of the pious is indeed in 'Illiyyīn. ¹⁹ And what will make you know what 'Illiyyīn is? ²⁰ A written book. ²¹ The ones brought near bear witness to it. ²² Surely the pious will indeed be in (a place of)

83.1 – Woe to the defrauders

Those who cheat others instead of giving the full measure will one day "stand before the Lord of the worlds" (v. 6). Their deeds are recorded, they will be judged on this basis, and they will burn (v. 16).

83.7 – By no means! Surely the book of the depraved is indeed in Sijjīn

This verse begins with the exclamation *kallā*, which means "certainly not!" The expression also appears at the beginning of verses 14, 15, and 18.

The meanings of several words in this sūra are not known. *Sijjīn* and *'Illiyyīn* (v. 18) are described as written books of the depraved and the pious, respectively. *Tasnīm* (v. 27) seems to be a name for a spring.

bliss, [23] (lying) on couches gazing about. [24] You will recognize in their faces the radiance of bliss. [25] They are given a pure, sealed wine to drink, [26] its seal is musk – for that let the seekers seek! – [27] and its mixture contains Tasnīm, [28] (from) a spring at which the ones brought near drink.

[29] Surely those who sinned used to laugh on account of those who believed, [30] and when they passed them by used to wink at each other. [31] And when they turned back to their people, they turned back amused, [32] and when they saw them, they said, 'Surely these (people) have gone astray indeed!' [33] Yet they had not been sent as watchers over them. [34] So today those who believed are laughing on account of the disbelievers, [35] (as) they gaze about (lying) on couches. [36] Have the disbelievers been rewarded for what they have done?

83.25 – *They are given a pure, sealed wine to drink*

The Quran shows an inconsistent attitude toward wine. In this verse wine is one of the rewards in heaven, similar to 47.15. Wine is a benefit in 16.67. Elsewhere, wine is said to cause more sin than benefit for humankind (2.219; 5.90).

83.34 – *So today those who believed are laughing on account of the disbelievers*

The sinners used to laugh at the believers and say the believers have gone astray. But on the Day of Judgment it will be the comfortable believers who laugh at the unbelievers.

THE SPLITTING
AL-INSHIQĀQ

84

> When people deny Allah's message, has Allah run out of options? This sūra ends with the instruction that if people will not respond to the recitations, the messenger is to announce to them "news of a painful punishment."

In the Name of God, the Merciful, the Compassionate

¹ When the sky is split open, ² and listens to its Lord and is made fit, ³ and when earth is stretched out, ⁴ and casts forth what is in it and becomes empty, ⁵ and listens to its Lord and is made fit, ⁶ you human – surely you are laboring to your Lord laboriously and are about to meet Him.

⁷ As for the one who is given his book in his right (hand), ⁸ he will receive an easy reckoning, ⁹ and turn back to his family, rejoicing. ¹⁰ But as for the one who is given his book behind his back, ¹¹ he will call out for destruction, ¹² and burn in a blazing (Fire). ¹³ Surely he used to be among his family, rejoicing. ¹⁴ Surely he thought that he would not return. ¹⁵ Yes indeed! Surely his Lord was watching him.

¹⁶ I swear by the twilight, ¹⁷ by the night and what it envelops, ¹⁸ by the moon when it becomes full! ¹⁹ You will indeed ride story upon story.

²⁰ What is (the matter) with them that they do not believe, ²¹ and when

---

84.1 – *When the sky is split open*

The sūra begins by projecting an apocalyptic scene at the end of time (vv. 1–5), leading to the message that the people are about to meet their Lord (v. 6)

84.7 – *As for the one who is given his book in his right (hand)*

The "book" here is the record of one's deeds; and the way in which humans will be given their books will make a serious difference.

84.16 – *I swear by the twilight*

A series of oaths leads to an obscure prophecy (v. 19).

84.20 – *What is (the matter) with them that they do not believe . . . ?*

The Quran asks why people do not believe the recitations and then commands

the Qur'ān is recited to them, do not prostrate themselves? [22] No! Those who disbelieve call (it) a lie. [23] Yet God knows what they hide away. [24] So give them news of a painful punishment [25] – except for those who believe and do righteous deeds. For them (there is) a reward without end.

the messenger to deliver a message of doom (v. 24). "Those who believe and do righteous deeds" (v. 25) seems to be an exception – perhaps even an afterthought?

THE CONSTELLATIONS
AL-BURŪJ

85

The quranic "doctrine of scripture" is not given in a systematic way anywhere in the Quran, so scholars have worked it out from scattered verses. This sūra's mention of a "guarded Tablet" provides an opportunity for a consideration of that doctrine.

In the Name of God, the Merciful, the Compassionate

[1] By the sky full of constellations, [2] by the promised Day, [3] by a witness and what is witnessed! [4] May the companions of the Pit perish [5] – the Fire full of fuel – [6] when they are sitting over it, [7] and they (themselves) are witnesses of what they have done to the believers. [8] They took vengeance on them only because they believed in God, the Mighty, the Praiseworthy, [9] the One who – to Him (belongs) the kingdom of the heavens and the earth. God is a witness over everything.

[10] Surely those who persecute the believing men and the believing women, (and) then have not turned (in repentance) – for them (there is) the punishment of Gehenna, and for them (there is) the punishment of the burning (Fire). [11] Surely those who believe and do righteous deeds – for them (there are) Gardens through which rivers flow. That is the great triumph!

[12] Surely your Lord's attack is harsh indeed. [13] Surely He – He brings about (the creation) and restores (it). [14] He is the Forgiving, the Loving, [15] Holder of the throne, the Glorious, [16] Doer of what He intends.

85.1 – *By the sky full of constellations*

A series of oaths leads to the wish that the "companions of the Pit" be punished in hell (v. 4). The people in view took vengeance on the believers simply because they believed (v. 8). Those who persecute believing men and women will be punished in Gehenna (v. 10).

85.14 – *He is the Forgiving, the Loving*

Here Allah is described as affectionate or "loving" (*wadūd*) as part of an interesting

[17] Has the story of the forces come to you, [18] of Pharaoh and Thamūd? [19] No! But those who disbelieve persist in calling (it) a lie. [20] Yet God surrounds them from behind.

[21] Yes! It is a glorious Qur'ān, [22] in a guarded Tablet.

---

short description of Allah. This term appears in one other verse in the Quran, 11.90. See "The Language of Love in the Quran" (p. 560).

85.21–22 – *Yes! It is a glorious Qur'ān, in a guarded Tablet*

The word *tablet* appears elsewhere in relation to the tablets of Moses (7.145, 150, 154). Muslim commentators have interpreted verses 21–22 to mean that the Quran has been kept safe on a heavenly tablet from eternity.

Other quranic passages that seem to support this idea are 80.11–16, which says that the "reminder" is written in "honored pages, exalted (and) purified," and 56.77–80, where the "honorable *qur'ān*" is in "a hidden book" that only the "purified" may touch. Three verses also refer to "the mother of the Book" (3.7; 13.39; 43.4), which may indicate a concept of a heavenly source of revelation.

These verses contribute to a quranic "doctrine of scripture" that is never fully explained but rather comes from scattered hints. The claims that Allah reveals (*anzala, nazzala, tanzīl*) his word and inspires (*awḥā, waḥy*) the messenger are clear. But is the Quran revealed in a night (44.3) or a month (2.185), or is it sent down in parts for gradual recitation (17.106)? Another intriguing verse says that Allah speaks to a human by inspiration, from behind a veil, or by sending a messenger (42.51).

A thorough study of this theme is available in a series of articles by Arthur Jeffery titled "The Qur'ān as Scripture" (see bibliography).

THE NIGHT VISITOR

AL-ṬĀRIQ

86

The title of this sūra, *al-Ṭāriq*, is the name of the "morning star" and means literally "night visitor." The oaths in many sūras in this part of the Quran appeal to sights in the heavens.

In the Name of God, the Merciful, the Compassionate

¹ By the sky and the night visitor! ² And what will make you know what the night visitor is? ³ The piercing star! ⁴ Over every person (there is) a watcher. ⁵ So let the human consider: what was he created from? ⁶ He was created from spurting water. ⁷ It comes forth from (a place) between the spine and the ribs. ⁸ Surely He is able indeed to bring him back, ⁹ on the Day when (all) secrets will be examined, ¹⁰ and he will have no power (and) no helper.

¹¹ By the sky full of returning (rain), ¹² by the earth full of cracks! ¹³ Surely it is a decisive word indeed! ¹⁴ It is no joke.

¹⁵ Surely they are hatching a plot, ¹⁶ but I (too) am hatching a plot. ¹⁷ So let the disbelievers be, let them be for a little (while).

86.1 – *By the sky and the night visitor!*

Oaths introduce the messages of this sūra at verses 1 and 11–12.

86.5 – *So let the human consider: what was he created from?*

A concept of how humans develop in the womb (vv. 6–7) supports the message that the Creator is able to bring humans back from the dead for judgment (v. 8).

86.14 – *It is no joke*

The recitations of the messenger are serious (v. 13) and not just for fun.

THE MOST HIGH
AL-A'LĀ

87

A verse in this sūra raises the possibility that the messenger may forget some of his recitations – if Allah so wills. The thought seems to correspond to 2.106, which says that Allah may cause some of his verses to be forgotten.

In the Name of God, the Merciful, the Compassionate

¹ Glorify the name of your Lord, the Most High, ² who creates and fashions, ³ who determines and guides, ⁴ who brings forth the pasture, ⁵ and then turns it into darkened ruins. ⁶ We shall make you recite, and you will not forget – except whatever God pleases. ⁷ Surely He knows what is spoken publicly and what is hidden. ⁸ We shall make it very easy for you. ⁹ So remind (them), if the reminder benefits. ¹⁰ He who fears will take heed, ¹¹ but the most miserable will turn away from it ¹² – who will burn in the great Fire. ¹³ Then he will neither die there nor live.

¹⁴ Prosperous is he who purifies himself, ¹⁵ and remembers the name of his

---

87.1 – *Glorify the name of your Lord, the Most High*

The Quran exhorts the messenger directly to exalt the name of his Lord. "The Most High" (*al-A'lā*) is the title of the sūra. This sūra claims that the same God who creates (v. 2) makes the messenger read or "recite" (v. 6).

87.6 – *you will not forget – except whatever God pleases*

The idea that the messenger would forget some of his recitations – according to the will of Allah – plays into some Muslim theories of abrogation. See the discussion of verses related to abrogation at 16.101 (p. 282).

87.9 – *So remind (them), if the reminder benefits*

The task of the messenger is to remind people of the signs of Allah and the judgment to come. People are free to take heed or not, and Allah will judge those who turn away on the Judgment Day (vv. 10–13). The audience prefers the present life to the hereafter (vv. 16–17).

Lord, and prays. [16] No! But you prefer this present life, [17] when the Hereafter is better and more lasting. [18] Surely this is indeed in the former pages, [19] the pages of Abraham and Moses.

87.18–19 – *Surely this is in the former pages, the pages of Abraham and Moses*

These verses seem to indicate a belief that scriptures were given to both Abraham and Moses. The "pages" are literally "leaves" or "sheets," and this expression appears also at 53.36–37 with the names switched.

THE COVERING
AL-GHĀSHIYA

88

This sūra envisions the fate of two different groups on the Day of Judgment, distinguished by their faces. The two groups experience either reward or painful punishment.

In the Name of God, the Merciful, the Compassionate

[1] Has the story of the Covering come to you? [2] (Some) faces that Day will be downcast, [3] laboring, weary. [4] They will burn in a scorching Fire. [5] They will be made to drink from a boiling spring. [6] They will have no food except dry thorns, [7] (which) neither nourishes nor satisfies hunger. [8] (Other) faces that Day will be blessed, [9] content with their striving, [10] in a Garden on high [11] – where they will hear no frivolous talk, [12] where (there is) a flowing spring, [13] where (there are) raised couches, [14] and cups laid down, [15] and cushions lined up, [16] and carpets spread out.

[17] Will they not look at the camels, how they were created, [18] and at the sky, how it was raised up, [19] and at the mountains, how they were constructed, [20] and at the earth, how it was spread flat?

[21] So remind (them)! You are only a reminder. [22] You are not a record-keeper

---

88.1 – *Has the story of the Covering come to you?*

The Quran poses the question and then proceeds to tell the story. The word *covering* is associated with punishment on the Day of Judgment in 12.106. The story here is about the downcast faces of those who will face punishment on "that Day" (v. 2), and about the faces that will be blessed (v. 8). The sūra portrays the punishments of hell rather graphically (vv. 4–7) and describes the pleasant rewards of the Garden (vv. 11–16).

88.17 – *Will they not look at the camels, how they were created . . . ?*

The Creator has given signs of his presence and power in the natural world (vv. 17–20) – signs that the messenger must feature in his preaching.

88.21 – *So remind (them)! You are only a reminder*

As in many sūras, the profile of the messenger is rather limited. He is "only a

over them [23] – except for the one who turns away and disbelieves. [24] God will punish him with the greatest punishment. [25] Surely to Us is their return. [26] Then surely on Us (depends) their reckoning.

---

reminder," and verse 22 specifies that he is not a record-keeper over the people. Allah – not the messenger – will reckon with the one who "turns away and disbelieves."

THE DAWN
AL-FAJR

The phrase "as for the human" begins a verse in the middle of this sūra, which then portrays humanity in a negative light. See an analysis of the Quran's view of human nature at 79.40 (p. 612).

In the Name of God, the Merciful, the Compassionate

¹ By the dawn ² and ten nights! ³ By the even and the odd! ⁴ By the night when it journeys on! ⁵ (Is there) in that an oath for a person of understanding?

⁶ Do you not see how your Lord dealt with 'Ād, ⁷ Iram of the pillars, ⁸ the like of which was never created in (all) the lands, ⁹ and Thamūd, who carved out the rock in the wādī, ¹⁰ and Pharaoh, he of the stakes, ¹¹ who (all) transgressed insolently in (their) lands, ¹² and spread (too) much corruption there? ¹³ So your Lord poured on them a scourge of punishment. ¹⁴ Surely your Lord indeed lies in wait.

¹⁵ As for the human, whenever his Lord tests him, and honors him and blesses him, he says, 'My Lord has honored me.' ¹⁶ But whenever he tests him,

---

89.1 – *By the dawn and ten nights!*

The sūra begins with a series of oaths (vv. 1–5), though in this case the reason for the oaths is missing.

89.6 – *Do you not see how your Lord dealt with 'Ād . . . ?*

In a kind of shorthand, the Quran refers to a series of punishment stories that have already appeared a number of times. For the 'Ād and Thamūd stories, see 7.65 and 7.73, respectively. "Iram" (v. 7) and the "stakes" of Pharaoh (v. 10) are obscure, but what these stories are to illustrate is clear: peoples who "transgressed insolently" (v. 11) were punished.

89.15 – *As for the human, whenever his Lord tests him*

When the Lord tests humans by restricting their provisions, they fail the test because they say that the Lord despises them. They love wealth (v. 14), neglect the orphan and the poor, and apparently themselves devour the inheritance of the poor (v. 19).

and restricts his provision for him, he says, 'My Lord has humiliated me.' ¹⁷ By no means! No! You do not honor the orphan, ¹⁸ nor do you urge the feeding of the poor, ¹⁹ yet you devour the inheritance greedily, ²⁰ and love wealth passionately.

²¹ By no means! When the earth is shattered with a double shattering, ²² and your Lord comes, and the angels, line after line, ²³ and Gehenna is brought (forth) on that Day – on that Day the human will (finally) take heed, but how will the reminder be for him? ²⁴ He will say, 'Would that I had sent forward (righteous deeds) for my life!' ²⁵ On that Day no one will punish as He punishes, ²⁶ and no one will bind as He binds. ²⁷ 'You, secure one! ²⁸ Return to your Lord, approving (and) approved! ²⁹ Enter among My servants! ³⁰ Enter My Garden!'

89.21 – *When the earth is shattered with a double shattering*

In this judgment scene (vv. 21–30) the Lord comes with the angels, bringing the punishment of Gehenna for many (v. 23), and addressing the righteous with welcoming words (vv. 27–30).

THE LAND
AL-BALAD

90

As the sūras of the Quran become increasingly short, the opening oaths continue and scenes of punishment on the Day of Judgment seem to dominate. These short sūras do offer some unique expressions, however – for example "the setting free of a slave" in Sūra 90.

In the Name of God, the Merciful, the Compassionate

[1] I swear by this land [2] – and you are a lawful (resident) in this land – [3] by a begetter and what he begot! [4] Certainly We created the human in trouble. [5] Does he think that no one has power over him? [6] He says, 'I have squandered vast wealth!' [7] Does he think that no one has seen him? [8] Have We not made two eyes for him, [9] and a tongue, and two lips? [10] And have We not guided him to the two ways? [11] Yet he has not attempted the (steep) ascent.

[12] And what will make you know what the (steep) ascent is? [13] The setting free of a slave, [14] or feeding on a day of hunger [15] an orphan who is related, [16] or a poor person (lying) in the dust. [17] Then he has become one of those who believe, and (who) exhort (each other) to patience, and (who) exhort (each other) to mercy.

[18] Those are the companions on the right. [19] But those who disbelieve in Our signs, they are the companions on the left. [20] A fire (will be) closed over them.

90.12 – *And what will make you know what the (steep) ascent is?*

This sūra highlights social justice as the "ascent": care for the poor and orphan (vv. 14–16) and – notably – to free a slave (v. 13).

THE SUN
AL-SHAMS

91

The opening oaths make up more than half of this sūra. Many sūras since Sūra 75 begin with oaths, and a similar number follow Sūra 91.

In the Name of God, the Merciful, the Compassionate

[1] By the sun and her morning light! [2] By the moon when he follows her! [3] By the day when it reveals her! [4] By the night when it covers her! [5] By the sky and what built it! [6] By the earth and what spread it! [7] By the self and what fashioned it, [8] and instilled it with its (tendency to) depravity and its (sense of) guarding (itself)! [9] He has prospered who purifies it, [10] and he has failed who corrupts it.

[11] Thamūd called (it) a lie by their insolent transgression, [12] when the most miserable (one) of them was raised up, [13] and the messenger of God said to them, 'The she-camel of God and her drink!' [14] But they called (him) a liar and wounded her. So their Lord covered them over for their sin and leveled it. [15] He was not afraid of its outcome.

91.1 – *By the sun and her morning light!*

The opening oaths highlight many wonders of the heavens and leads to an affirmation of one "who purifies it" (v. 9).

91.8 – *and instilled it with its (tendency to) depravity and its (sense of) guarding*

This wording is a good example of how translator A. J. Droge provides a straightforward translation while most Muslim translators interpret the words to bring them in line with Islamic teaching. For example, Yusuf Ali interpreted the words to mean, "and enlightenment as to its wrong and its right." In fact, the Arabic of the expression in view is *alhamahā* ("inspired it") *fujūrahā* ("its immorality"). On human nature in the Quran, see the analysis at 79.40 (p. 612).

91.11 – *Thamūd called (it) a lie by their insolent transgression*

On Thamūd, Ṣāliḥ, and the "she-camel of Allah" (vv. 11–15), see the explanation at 7.73 (p. 183).

THE NIGHT
AL-LAYL

> "You can't take it with you" notes this short sūra. Wealth loses its usefulness at the moment of death.

In the Name of God, the Merciful, the Compassionate

¹ By the night when it covers! ² By the day when it reveals its splendor! ³ By what created the male and the female! ⁴ Surely your striving is indeed (to) divided (ends). ⁵ As for the one who gives and guards (himself), ⁶ and affirms the best (reward), ⁷ We shall ease him to ease. ⁸ But as for the one who is stingy, and considers himself independent, ⁹ and calls the best (reward) a lie, ¹⁰ We shall ease him to hardship. ¹¹ His wealth will be of no use to him when he perishes. ¹² Surely on Us (depends) the guidance indeed. ¹³ Surely to Us indeed (belong) the last and the first.

¹⁴ I have warned you of a flaming Fire. ¹⁵ Only the most miserable will burn in it: ¹⁶ the one who called (it) a lie and turned away. ¹⁷ But the one who guards (himself) will avoid it: ¹⁸ the one who gives his wealth to purify himself, ¹⁹ and (confers) no blessing on anyone (expecting) to be repaid, ²⁰ but only seeks the face of his Lord, the Most High. ²¹ Soon indeed he will be pleased.

92.8 – *But as for the one who is stingy*

The contrast in this sūra is between people who give (vv. 5, 18) and people who hold tight to their wealth (v. 11). Those who hoard are destined for the fire (v. 14).

THE MORNING LIGHT
AL-ḌUḤĀ

When the Quran addresses a singular "you" without naming who this might be, Muslims have interpreted this to be Muhammad. This sūra addresses an "orphan," and sure enough, in the Islamic story of Muslim origins, Muhammad is an orphan (*Sīra*, 69–79).

In the Name of God, the Merciful, the Compassionate

¹ By the morning light! ² By the night when it darkens! ³ Your Lord has not forsaken you, nor does He despise you. ⁴ The last will indeed be better for you than the first. ⁵ Soon indeed your Lord will give to you, and you will be pleased.

⁶ Did He not find you an orphan and give (you) refuge? ⁷ Did He not find you astray and guide (you)? ⁸ Did He not find you poor and enrich (you)?

⁹ As for the orphan, do not oppress (him), ¹⁰ and as for the beggar, do not repulse (him), ¹¹ and as for the blessing of your Lord, proclaim (it).

93.3 – *Your Lord has not forsaken you, nor does He despise you*

The Quran reassures the messenger – possibly in response to the heckling of his audience.

93.6 – *Did He not find you an orphan and give (you) refuge?*

Because the Quran addresses these words directly to a singular "you," Muslims have interpreted it to mean that Muhammad was this orphan.

With the same understanding, verse 7 has raised the question of how the messenger could have been found misguided or "astray."

THE EXPANDING
AL-SHARḤ

94

This sūra continues the Quran's second-person-singular address from the previous sūra. Andrew Rippin claims that while many readers – including non-Muslims – commonly read such direct address as if it refers to Muhammad, "there is nothing absolutely compelling" about interpreting it in this way. The reference in Sūra 93 to an orphan and in Sūra 94 to a "burden," he suggested, could simply be the typical material of monotheistic preaching. (See Dr. Rippin's article "Muḥammad in the Qur'ān" in the bibliography.)

In the Name of God, the Merciful, the Compassionate

[1] Did We not expand your heart for you, [2] and deliver you of your burden, [3] which had broken your back? [4] Did We not raise your reputation for you? [5] Surely with hardship (there is) ease. [6] Surely with hardship (there is) ease. [7] So when you are free, work on. [8] And to your Lord set (your) desire.

94.2–3 – *and deliver you of your burden, which had broken your back?*

The expression translated here "burden" can also mean "sin" or "crime" and is the same word found in the repeating verse, "No one bearing a burden bears the burden of another" (e.g., 6.164; 17.15). If this sūra is understood to be addressing the messenger, it raises a question about the sin weighing on him.

See an analysis of prophetic requests for forgiveness at 48.2 (p. 513) and the discussion of human "burdens" at 53.38 (p. 533).

THE FIG
AL-TĪN

95

> The idea that Allah created the human in a fine state but then returned him
> "to the lowest of the low" (v. 5) brings to mind Psalm 8:5: "You made him a
> little lower than the heavenly beings and crowned him with glory and honor."

In the Name of God, the Merciful, the Compassionate

[1] By the fig and the olive! [2] By Mount Sinai! [3] By this secure land! [4] Certainly We created the human in the finest state. [5] Then We return him to the lowest of the low [6] – except for those who believe and do righteous deeds. For them (there is) a reward without end. [7] What will call you a liar after (that) in (regard to) the Judgment? [8] Is God not the most just of judges?

95.2 – *By Mount Sinai!*

This expression appears only once elsewhere in the Quran, and in a slightly different form, at 23.20. Curiously, neither verse connects to Moses and his receiving of the law, nor does the shorter expression "mountain" at 52.1.

95.4–5 – *Certainly We created the human in the finest state. Then We return him to the lowest of the low*

This seems to indicate a reduction of the greatest part of humanity, with "those who believe and do righteous deeds" (v. 6) being an exception.

95.8 – *Is God not the most just of judges?*

This verse makes explicit what is implicit in the vast amount of material related to judgment in the Quran: Allah is the judge over creation.

637

THE CLOT
AL-'ALAQ

96

> Muslims believe that this sūra was the first recitation of their messenger, Muhammad. The assertion that Allah "sent down" his word to the messenger is the fundamental truth claim of Islam.

In the Name of God, the Merciful, the Compassionate

[1] Recite in the name of your Lord who creates, [2] creates the human from a clot. [3] Recite, for your Lord is the Most Generous, [4] who teaches by the pen, [5] teaches the human what he does not know.

[6] By no means! Surely the human transgresses insolently indeed, [7] for he considers himself independent. [8] Surely to your Lord is the return.

[9] Have you seen the one who forbids [10] a servant when he prays? [11] Have you seen whether he (relies) on the guidance, [12] or commands the guarding (of oneself)? [13] Have you seen whether he calls (it) a lie, and turns away? [14] Does he not know that God sees? [15] By no means! If indeed he does not stop, We shall indeed seize (him) by the hair – [16] (his) lying, sinful hair. [17] So let him call his cohorts! [18] We shall call the guards of Hell. [19] By no means! Do not obey him, but prostrate yourself and draw near.

96.1–2 – *Recite in the name of your Lord who creates, creates the human from a clot*

The command to read or "recite" (*iqrā*) comes from the same verb as *qur'ān* ("recitation") and supplies the vocabulary for the task of the messenger. Muslim tradition asserts that verses 1–5 make up the first revelation to Muhammad – a fundamental claim that invites a process of discernment in readers of the Quran today.

96.6 – *Surely the human transgresses insolently indeed*

The statement that humans rebel, or "transgress" (*ṭaghā*), raises interesting questions about human nature, especially being mentioned so soon after their creation (vv. 1–2). See the discussion of this theme at 79.40 (p. 612).

96.9–10 – *Have you seen the one who forbids a servant when he prays?*

The Quran asks a series of questions about an unidentified individual who seems to discourage the messenger addressed in the first verses of the sūra.

THE DECREE
AL-QADR

97

Along with Sūra 96, Muslims believe that Sūra 97 refers to the first recitations by the messenger. In fact, Ibn Isḥāq quotes the entire sūra at the very beginning of his account of "the beginning of the sending down of the Qurān" (*Sīra*, 111).

In the Name of God, the Merciful, the Compassionate

[1] Surely We sent it down on the Night of the Decree. [2] And what will make you know what the Night of the Decree is? [3] The Night of the Decree is better than a thousand months. [4] The angels and the spirit come down during it, by the

---

97.1 – *Surely We sent it down on the Night of the Decree*

It is not clear what "it" refers to in this verse, because no antecedent is given to which it could refer. Muslim tradition has identified "it" with the Quran and has explained the "night of the decree" (or "power") as a night during the month of Ramadan (see 2.185).

97.4 – *The angels and the spirit come down during it*

Throughout the Quran the meaning of the spirit (*rūḥ*) is uncertain. At 17.85 the Quran says, "They will ask you concerning the spirit." But little information is given in response, and the subject of "the spirit" remains mysterious from its first appearance at 2.87 up to this final appearance in the canonical progression.

This verse says that "the spirit" comes together with the angels, implying that they are separate entities. On the four occurrences of "the holy spirit," see the comment at 16.102 (p. 283). On the three occurrences of "the spirit of our command," see the comment at 42.52 (p. 486). Among the remaining appearances of this word, 4.171 seems to say that 'Īsā is "a spirit" from Allah. The spirit comes to Mary in a human form at 19.17, while at 21.91 and 66.12 Allah breathes into Mary "from our spirit." The spirit is trustworthy or "true" at 26.193, and at 58.22 "a spirit from Allah" seems to affirm the denial of love to those who oppose Allah and his messenger.

The lack of a clear explanation of the spirit in the Quran – and its inconsistent use

permission of their Lord, on account of every command. ⁵ It is (a night of) peace, until the rising of the dawn.

---

whenever it appears – contrasts with the Bible, which offers a wealth of information about the Holy Spirit of God. Islam's eventual limiting of the spirit of God to an angel, namely Gabriel (see comment at 16.102), closes off a dimension of the human experience of God's presence and power that both encourages people and helps them to do what pleases God.

THE CLEAR SIGN
AL-BAYYINA

98

This important sūra returns to the "People of the Book" to make a rather revealing statement about the value of their faith. All who do not believe in the "clear sign" – here identified as the messenger – are destined for hell and are the worst of created beings.

In the Name of God, the Merciful, the Compassionate

¹ Those who disbelieve among the People of the Book, and the idolaters, were not (to be) set free until the clear sign had come to them ² – a messenger from God,

---

98.1 – *Those who disbelieve among the People of the Book*

With such a beginning, the sūra signals that "belief" in its verses is not simply "religious faith" in general (also v. 6) but specifically belief in "the clear sign." This sūra also returns to polemic against the People of the Book (vv. 1, 4, 6) – a target who have not appeared since Sūra 62.

The expression "People of the Book" has been understood by many non-Muslims to mean a positive and respectful name for communities who possess a scripture. There are a few verses in the Quran that give this sense, but in fact most of the verses about the People of the Book are negative toward Jews and Christians, their beliefs, and their practices.

There are 31 verses that contain this expression, in addition to many others that mention "those to whom the book was given" or "a portion of the book was given." Most of the occurrences appear in Sūras 3–5 in passages that some scholars describe as "diatribes" (e.g., translator A. J. Droge). The Quran describes the People of the Book as jealous of the Muslims (2.105, 109; cf. 57.29), disbelieving (3.70, 98, 110; 5.65), deceptive (3.72, 75), and wicked (3.110; 5.59; cf. 4.123).

The Quran claims that the People of the Book believe in "al-Jibt and al-Ṭaghūt" (4.51; cf. 5.60), lead believers astray (2.109; 3.69, 99–100; 4.44), and tamper with scripture (3.71, 78, 187). They are enemies of Allah and the Muslims because they do not accept that the recitations of the messenger are revealed by God (see 2.98; 4.44–45; 5.82 [Jews]). Three verses seem to indicate violence toward the People of the Book:

reciting purified pages, [3] in which (there are) true books. [4] Those who were given the Book did not become divided until after the clear sign had come to them. [5] They

---

in 33.26 they are "brought down from their fortifications," some killed and some taken captive; in 59.2 they are expelled from their homes (cf. 59.11); and 9.29 contains the famous command to fight "those who have been given the Book."

A remarkable series of direct appeals to the People of the Book appears in Sūras 3–5. It begins with the verse that has come to be linked with the Muslim "Common Word" statement of 2007, 3.64, which calls the People of the Book to worship Allah alone. The following verses declare that Abraham was neither a Jew nor a Christian but rather a Muslim (3.67). Other verses appeal to the People of the Book to believe in what they claim Allah has "sent down" to the messenger (4.47; 5.15, 19) and to stop expressing beliefs about God that the Quran considers false (4.171; 5.77).

The Quran approves the People of the Book who believe in Muslim truth claims (3.110, 199; 29.47; cf. 5.68), are honest with money (3.75), and practice piety (3.113–14). Positive verses also include the peaceable 29.46: "Do not dispute with the People of the Book except with what is better."

98.2 – *a messenger from God, reciting purified pages*

The construction of verses 1–2 in Arabic has "the clear sign" right up against "a messenger," implying that the clear sign is the messenger himself. Certainly this is how the classical Muslim commentators understood this passage. Muqātil ibn Sulaymān (d. 767), for example, author of the earliest extant complete commentary, wrote on verse 4: "Those who disbelieve never ceased agreeing on the truth of Muhammad until he was sent, because they had his description in their books. When Allah designated him from the offspring of someone other than Isaac, they disagreed about him. Some of them believed." Translations of seven important Muslim commentaries on this sūra are provided in *Classical Islam: A Sourcebook of Religious Literature* (see bibliography).

Verses 2–3 also assert that the messenger recites from "purified pages," making this passage a claim for both the messenger and his recitation.

98.4 – *Those who were given the Book did not become divided until after the clear sign had come to them*

By repeating the expression "clear sign," this verse seems to say that "those who were given the book" divided over the messenger at the time of his appearance. Would they accept the Muslim truth claims that the messenger is a true prophet of Allah, that his recitations are from Allah, and that Islam is Allah's true religion?

This is the final statement that "those who were given the book" divide (*farraqa*), differ and disagree (*ikhtalafa*), or are in doubt (*shakk*). Such statements begin at 2.213, where the basic charge is that those who were given the book differ concerning it.

were commanded only to serve God, devoting (their) religion to Him, (being) Ḥanīfs, and to observe the prayer and give the alms. That is the right religion.

⁶ Surely those who disbelieve among the People of the Book, and the idolaters, will be in the Fire of Gehenna, there to remain. Those – they are the worst

---

They differ after "clear signs" come to them because of "envy" among them. By context, some of these statements refer to the Children of Israel and the book of Moses (2.213; 11:110; 32.25; 45.17), but the Quran seems even more interested in the divisions of Christians (2.253; 5.14; 19.34; 23.53; 43.65). In several of the statements, disagreement with the "clear signs" (2.213; 2.253; 3.105) and "knowledge" (3.19; 42.14; 45.17) that came to the People of the Book seems to concern the Quran's messenger and his recitations.

Disagreement over the meaning of scripture, or over the identity of Jesus, is common. The same verb, *ikhtalafa*, is used repeatedly by commentators like al-Ṭabarī (d. 923) to say that Muslim interpreters do not agree about the meaning of most verses in the Quran. However, many Christians would join the Quran in lamenting the envy (2.213; 3.19; 42.14; 45.17), "suspicious doubt" (42.14), enmity and hatred (5.14), and especially the in-fighting (*iqtatala*, 2.253) among Christian groups prior to the rise of Islam – and continuing to the present day.

In response to this well-taken criticism, a few comments are called for: Disagreement over the Torah or the Gospel accounts does not form an argument for invalidating their contents. There seems to be a sense in many of the Quran's statements that attributing failure to the custodians of the Bible justifies dismissal and ignorance of the Bible. For example, the Quran uses disagreements among Christian groups in the seventh century regarding how to describe the humanity of Jesus in order to negate his deity and death as portrayed in the Gospel accounts.

Second, disagreement with Islamic truth claims does not place people "in the fire of Gehenna" or make people "the worst of creation" (98.6). People of faith make their decisions about Muslim claims according to their own criteria – often according to scriptures the Quran itself acknowledges. After reading the Quran carefully and respectfully, many "People of the Book" will conclude that the Quran does not amount to a "clear proof" of its extravagant claims.

98.6 – *Those – they are the worst of creation*

Epithets like "the worst of creation" invite poor relationships and can be used to rationalize mistreatment and violence. By contrast, the Bible's upholding of humanity's common creation "in the image of God" (Genesis 1:26–27) can lay a foundation for mutual respect. In today's global multifaith community, people will disagree about religious claims, but according to the Bible they can and should respect each other as creatures for whom God cares.

of creation. [7] Surely those who believe and do righteous deeds, those – they are the best of creation. [8] Their payment is with their Lord – Gardens of Eden through which rivers flow, there to remain forever. God is pleased with them, and they are pleased with Him. That is for whoever fears his Lord.

THE EARTHQUAKE
AL-ZALZALA

99

This sūra states the Quran's concept of judgment with stark simplicity: each human will be judged with mathematical precision according to his or her deeds.

In the Name of God, the Merciful, the Compassionate

[1] When the earth is shaken with her shaking, [2] and the earth brings forth her burdens, [3] and a person says, 'What is (the matter) with her?'[4] On that Day she will proclaim her news, [5] because your Lord has inspired her (with it). [6] On that Day the people will come forth separately to be shown their deeds. [7] Whoever has done a speck's weight of good will see it, [8] and whoever has done a speck's weight of evil will see it.

99.6 – *On that Day the people will come forth separately to be shown their deeds*

On the Day of Resurrection, the deeds of people will be judged down to an atom's or "speck's weight" (vv. 7–8). The reference to "weight" in turn brings to mind the judgment weigh scale. See "The Place of the Scale(s) in the Reckoning" (p. 481).

THE RUNNERS
AL-'ĀDIYĀT

100

The view of the human in many parts of the Quran is rather negative. In Sūra 100, the human is ungrateful and greedy, and "those who believe and do good deeds" are not to be found.

In the Name of God, the Merciful, the Compassionate

[1] By the runners panting, [2] and the strikers of fire, [3] and the chargers at dawn, [4] when they kick up a (cloud of) dust, [5] and pierce through the midst of it all together! [6] Surely the human is indeed an ingrate to his Lord, [7] and surely he is indeed a witness to that, [8] and surely he is indeed harsh in (his) love for (worldly) goods. [9] Does he not know? When what is in the graves is ransacked, [10] and what is in the hearts is extracted [11] – surely on that Day their Lord will indeed be aware of them.

100.6 – *Surely the human is indeed an ingrate to his Lord*

A striking oath (vv. 1–5) leads up to the sūra's central statement, that the human is ungrateful. On the Judgment Day, the Lord will know fully what each human has done and thought (v. 10). On the Quran's concept of human nature, see the discussion at 79.40 (p. 612).

THE STRIKING
AL-QĀRIʿA

101

Sūra 101 returns to the concept of a "weighing" of humanity on the Day of Judgment, specifying that weigh scales will separate the "heavy" from the "light."

In the Name of God, the Merciful, the Compassionate

[1] The striking! [2] What is the striking? [3] And what will make you know what the striking is? [4] The Day when the people will be like scattered moths, [5] and the mountains will be like (tufts of) wool. [6] As for the one whose scales are heavy, [7] he will be in a pleasing life, [8] but as for the one whose scales are light, [9] his mother will be Hāwiya. [10] And what will make you know what she is? [11] A scorching Fire!

101.6 – *As for the one whose scales are heavy*

The gathering of humankind on the Day of Judgment may seem like chaos, but the weigh scales will be well organized. See "The Place of the Scale(s) in the Reckoning" (p. 481).

RIVALRY
AL-TAKĀTHUR

102

The style of many of the Quran's final sūras is different from most of the Quran to this point. The eight short Arabic lines of Sūra 102 rhyme in couplets.

In the Name of God, the Merciful, the Compassionate

[1] Rivalry diverts you, [2] until you visit the graves. [3] By no means! Soon you will know! [4] Once again, by no means! Soon you will know! [5] By no means! If (only) you knew (now) with the knowledge of certainty: [6] you will indeed see the Furnace. [7] Once again, you will indeed see it with the eye of certainty. [8] Then, on that Day, you will indeed be asked about (what) bliss (is).

102.1–2 – *Rivalry diverts you, until you visit the graves*

The emphasis on jostling for such things as wealth as a key human problem matches the violent "love for (worldly) goods" in 100.8. As with many of these shortest sūras, the outlook for humanity is bleak. "Furnace" in verse 6 translates the Arabic *jaḥīm* (also 82.14).

THE AFTERNOON
AL-'AṢR

Sūra 103 focuses on the exception to the "rule" of human behavior: those who "believe and do righteous deeds."

In the Name of God, the Merciful, the Compassionate

¹ By the afternoon! ² Surely the human is indeed in (a state of) loss ³ – except for those who believe and do righteous deeds, and exhort (each other) in truth, and exhort (each other) in patience.

103.2 – *Surely the human is indeed in (a state of) loss*

Many statements in the Quran characterize the human in negative ways. Here the human is "in loss." See the analysis of verses on human nature at 79.40 (p. 612).

103.3 – *except for those who believe and do righteous deeds*

Those who do not go the way of all flesh often appear as exceptions in the Quran. Their escape from "loss" is described as their own achievement.

THE SLANDERER
AL-HUMAZA

104

The focus on temptations to wealth-seekers in Sūra 104 and two other nearby sūras may remind many readers of the statement in 1 Timothy 6:10, "For the love of money is a root of all kinds of evil."

In the Name of God, the Merciful, the Compassionate

[1] Woe to every slanderer, fault finder, [2] who accumulates wealth and counts it over and over! [3] He thinks that his wealth will make him last. [4] By no means! Indeed He will be tossed into al-Ḥuṭama. [5] And what will make you know what al-Ḥuṭama is? [6] The Fire of God ignited, [7] which rises up to the hearts. [8] Surely it (will be) closed over them [9] in extended columns (of flame).

104.3 – *He thinks that his wealth will make him last*

For the third time in this series of short sūras, the wealthy are in the spotlight (also 100.8; 102.1). This verse seems to imply that they take pride in their wealth and therefore perhaps see no need for God. Their destiny is the "Fire of Allah" (v. 6), here also called *al-Ḥuṭama* (vv. 4-5).

The Elephant
Al-Fīl

Muslim tradition connects this sūra with a story that a Christian ("Abyssinian") ruler of Yemen attacked Mecca with the help of an elephant in the year of Muhammad's birth, which Muslims believe to be AD 570.

In the Name of God, the Merciful, the Compassionate

[1] Have you not seen how your Lord did with the companions of the elephant? [2] Did He not make their plot go astray? [3] He sent against them birds in flocks [4] – (which) were pelting them with stones of baked clay – [5] and He made them like chewed-up husks (of straw).

105.1 – *Have you not seen how your Lord did with the companions of the elephant?*

This sūra is a good example of a short sūra that has little meaning apart from Muslim tradition. Muslim narratives present the back story not as a parable but as an event in history (*Sīra*, 21–28). Scholars are divided on the historicity of the event, and some have suggested that the story in Muslim tradition is actually an echo of a tale from early Jewish or Christian writings.

QURAYSH
QURAYSH

106

The Quran contains remarkably few references to individuals and groups who lived at the time of its writing. This sūra refers to the Quraysh, an Arab tribe who, according to Muslim tradition, controlled commerce in Mecca during the life of the messenger.

In the Name of God, the Merciful, the Compassionate

[1] For the uniting of Quraysh, [2] for their uniting for the caravan of the winter and the summer: [3] Let them serve the Lord of this House, [4] who has fed them on account of (their) hunger, [5] and secured them on account of (their) fear.

106.1 – *For the uniting of Quraysh*

This verse gives the only quranic mention of the Quraysh – the dominant tribe in Mecca during the life of the messenger according to Muslim tradition.

106.3 – *Let them serve the Lord of this House*

This is also the only occurrence of the expression "Lord of this House." At 5.97 the Quran associates "the House" (*al-bayt*) with the Ka'ba, believed to be the cube-shaped structure at the center of Muslim worship in Mecca.

ASSISTANCE
AL-MĀ'ŪN

107

The themes of caring for the poor and practicing authentic religion will be familiar to readers of the Bible. James wrote about "pure and faultless" religion in James 1:27, and Jesus warned against those who give to the poor in order to be seen by others (Matthew 6:1–4).

In the Name of God, the Merciful, the Compassionate

[1] Have you seen the one who calls the Judgment a lie? [2] That is the one who shoves away the orphan, [3] and does not urge (people) to the feeding of the poor.

[4] Woe to the ones who pray, [5] who – they are heedless of their prayers, [6] who – they (only) make a show, [7] and withhold assistance!

107.2–3 – *That is the one who shoves away the orphan, and does not urge (people) to the feeding of the poor*

These verses helpfully emphasize care for the poor as an essential part of true religion. The purpose of worship is not only to be seen (v. 6) but to inspire kind actions to others (v. 7).

ABUNDANCE
AL-KAWTHAR

108

Studying the shortest sūras of the Quran, scholars have noted the relative frequency of Arabic words that appear nowhere else – known as *hapax legomena*. Sūra 108, the shortest sūra of all, includes two *hapax* words in important positions.

In the Name of God, the Merciful, the Compassionate

¹ Surely We have given you the abundance. ² So pray to your Lord and sacrifice. ³ Surely your hater – he is the one cut off!

108.1 – *Surely We have given you the abundance*

The word translated here as "abundance," *kawthar*, gives the sūra its name. However, the meaning of the word is uncertain because it appears only here in the Quran. As such, it has challenged centuries of Muslim commentators and scholars.

A second *hapax legomenon* in this sūra is the word *abtar*, translated "one cut off" (v. 3). If these short sūras were first recited early in the preaching of the messenger, as Muslim tradition holds, it seems strange that two important words were never repeated in the many long sūras recited later.

THE DISBELIEVERS
AL-KĀFIRŪN

109

Is this short sūra an expression of freedom of religion – a willingness to live in peace with people who hold different religious beliefs and practices? Or is it an expression of a clean break with the "disbelievers" – a refusal to compromise with others in matters of worship?

In the Name of God, the Merciful, the Compassionate

¹ Say: 'You disbelievers! ² I do not serve what you serve, ³ and you are not serving what I serve. ⁴ I am not serving what you have served, ⁵ and you are not serving what I serve. ⁶ To you your religion and to me my religion.'

109.2 – *I do not serve what you serve*

The Arabic lines of this sūra have a unique rhythm. In each of verses 2–5, the verb for worship – *'abada* – appears twice. In verse 6 the word "religion" (*dīn*) repeats.

HELP

AL-NAṢR

110

Many Muslims believe Sūra 110 to be the final sūra recited by the messenger. In just a few words the sūra portrays a scene of political and religious victory.

In the Name of God, the Merciful, the Compassionate

[1] When the help of God comes, and the victory, [2] and you see the people entering into the religion of God in crowds, [3] glorify your Lord with praise, and ask forgiveness from Him. Surely He turns (in forgiveness).

110.1 – *When the help of God comes, and the victory*

The word *victory* brings to mind another verse that features the same word: "We have given you a clear victory" (48.1). The link suggests a political victory simultaneous with the religious triumph in verse 2: "people entering into the religion of Allah in crowds."

110.3 – *and ask forgiveness from Him*

If the link between verse 1 and 48.1 is feasible, it is interesting to note that 48.2 continues, saying, "that Allah may forgive you what is past of your sin and what is (still) to come." Both 48.2 and 110.3 address a single person, understood to be the messenger. If so, why is the messenger to ask forgiveness of his Lord immediately after the triumph? See a discussion of the requests of prophets and messengers for forgiveness at 48.2 (p. 513).

THE FIBER
AL-MASAD

111

Sūra 111 is thought to be the only place in the Quran where an opponent of the messenger is named. If so, this draws attention to the Quran's general lack of historical context. Furthermore, *Abū Lahab* translates to "father of flame," so the name may be only a nickname.

In the Name of God, the Merciful, the Compassionate

¹ The hands of Abū Lahab have perished, and he has perished. ² His wealth and what he has earned were of no use to him. ³ He will burn in a flaming Fire, ⁴ and his wife (will be) the carrier of the firewood, ⁵ with a rope of fiber around her neck.

111.1 – *The hands of Abū Lahab have perished, and he has perished*

The sūra seems to be a condemnation of Abū Lahab and his wife. The verses consign both of them to hell.

In Muslim tradition, Abū Lahab is an uncle of Muhammad who opposes him.

DEVOTION
AL-IKHLĀṢ

112

> This very short sūra has exerted an influence out of proportion to its length. Christians living in the Muslim world have experienced the double negation of verse 3 as a source of vigorous Muslim polemic against the divine Sonship of Jesus.

In the Name of God, the Merciful, the Compassionate

¹ Say: 'He is God. One! ² God the Eternal! ³ He has not begotten and was not begotten, ⁴ and He has no equal. None!'

112.1 – *Say: "He is God. One!"*

Scholars have pointed out that the word translated here "One," *aḥad*, is not the standard Arabic word, which is *wāḥid*. They have also noted that *aḥad* appears nowhere else in the Quran. Some have suggested influence from the Jewish Shema (Deuteronomy 6:4), which uses the Hebrew *'eḥād*.

112.3 – *He has not begotten and was not begotten*

Muslim commentators have disagreed about the context for the recitation of this verse. Some contended that the audience was pagan or even Jewish. However, it is interesting to note the number of times that this verse is inscribed in the Dome of the Rock in Jerusalem, built in AD 691. Jerusalem at that time was a city full of Christians.

Some scholars have suggested that this verse is a deliberate denial of the Nicene Creed, which affirms that Jesus is the "only begotten Son of God, begotten of the Father" and "begotten, not made." The Quran's claim is rather that 'Īsa is "created not begotten" (3.59; 19.35). See "Son of God in the Quran" (p. 352).

Muslims know Sūra 112 as well as any passage in the Quran, because many recite it daily in their ritual prayers.

THE DAYBREAK
AL-FALAQ

113

The final two sūras of the Quran are described by some as prayers for protection, but they are not in fact prayers. The Quran begins with a prayer: al-Fātiḥa ("The Opening") is addressed to Allah and uses the language of praise and worship. These "closing" sūras do not address Allah and are both presented as text that the messenger is commanded to "say." These sūras also use the language of seeking refuge, which may take them in the direction of incantation and charm.

In the Name of God, the Merciful, the Compassionate

¹ Say: 'I take refuge with the Lord of the daybreak, ² from the evil of what He has created, ³ and from the evil of darkness when it looms, ⁴ and from the evil of the women who blow on knots, ⁵ and from the evil of an envier when he envies.'

113.1 – *I take refuge with the Lord of the daybreak*

The reciter is commanded to "say" that he seeks refuge from four kinds of evil. Elsewhere, the Quran says, "When you recite the Qur'ān, take refuge with Allah from the accursed Satan" (16.98; cf. 42.62). The reason for taking refuge is not clear. The following verse in Sūra 16 says that Satan "has no authority over those who believe and put their trust in their Lord" (16.99).

THE PEOPLE
AL-NĀS

114

In the Name of God, the Merciful, the Compassionate

¹ Say: 'I take refuge with the Lord of the people, ² King of the people, ³ God of the people, ⁴ from the evil of the whispering one, the slinking one, ⁵ who whispers in the hearts of the people, ⁶ of the jinn and the people.'

114.4 – *from the evil of the whispering one, the slinking one*

The idea of ending the Quran with an unnamed "slinking one" who whispers in the hearts of people, and yet another mention of the frivolous *jinn*, is difficult to account for.

On the *jinn*, see the comments at 72.1 (p. 593). On human nature and whispers to the soul, see the analysis and response at 79.40 (p. 612).

There is a strong tradition in early Muslim sources that Sūras 113–114 were not included in the Quran recension of Ibn Mas'ūd, who is believed to be a companion of the messenger. After the Quran's many ringing attacks on idolatry and powerful affirmations of Allah's supremacy, these final two sūras do indeed seem to close the book with a whimper of incantation about evil whispering and blowing on knots.

ANALYSIS INDEX

The Quran repeatedly refers to a large number of important themes. This commentary notes the occurrences of many of these themes and briefly explains them as they appear and at one point offers a summary and/or analysis – and often a response – to each theme. In this index, the first reference for each theme is the verse number where the analysis appears. Verse references for individual occurrences of each theme follow.

* * *

Subject Index

Aaron, 164, 186
  children of Israel rebel against, 326
  house of, 71
  Mary his descendant, 313
  messengership of, 187, 232, 323, 324, 325,
    334, 349, 367, 394
  received scripture, 127, 317, 451. *See also*
    Moses
Abel, 138–139, 300. *See also* Cain
ablution, 545
Abraham, 89–92, 219, 266, 271, 316–317, 335,
  341, 400, 421, 449, 526, 533, 559, 627
  builds Ka'ba, 54–55, 95, 341
  chosen by God, 83, 90–92, 163–164, 249,
    285, 334
  covenant, 54, 421
  descendants and followers of, 55, 90, 173,
    243, 457
  destroyed idols, 334
  discovers God, 163–164
  stood in first temple at Becca, 95
abrogation, 51, 206, 262, 282, 283, 344, 626
Adam, 39–40, 293, 318, 327
  angels prostrate before, 40, 175, 271, 305,
    327
  banishment from garden, 40, 176
  sons, 138, 293
  taught names, 39–40
  tree of knowledge, 40
adultery, 109, 141, 290, 291, 355–356, 562
adversity
  not burdened beyond capability to
    withstand, 77, 576
  not burdened with another's burden, 173,
    290, 438, 461, 481, 533, 636
aggression, 62–63, 64, 134
Aḥmad, 564
al-ḥajj, 339

al-Rass, 367, 523
alcohol. *See* intoxicants
Allah. *See* God
allies
  to believers, 113, 146, 202, 231, 499, 559, 578
  not to believers, 78, 119, 145, 202, 207,
    247, 396, 499, 553, 561. *See also* battles
angels
  belief in, 61–62, 124
  creation of man, 39, 175, 270, 293, 327, 458
  disbelievers demand to see, 66, 168, 269,
    195, 348, 475, 490
  enemies of, 49–50, 94
  guards, 162, 618
  in hereafter, 103, 365, 436, 447, 466, 578,
    600
  idolization of, 93, 291, 436, 452, 488
  messengers, 71, 84, 162, 177, 245, 271,
    275, 345, 437, 493, 607, 611
  pray for believers, 467
  worship God, 80, 129, 193, 479
animals, forbidden, 60, 134, 161, 285
Arabs, 216, 514, 520
Arafat, 65
ark. *See Noah*
atonement, 144, 151, 315, 439, 481, 533, 564,
  573
authority
  God's, 179, 224, 257, 468
  humans given, 39–40, 246, 291, 394, 469,
    527
  Satan's, 282, 445
astronomy
  moon and sun, 179, 226, 275, 333, 370,
    415, 444, 461, 592, 600, 633
  constellations, 270, 370, 623
  stars, 166, 179, 249, 275, 276, 341, 447,
    530, 545, 607